WALTER B. CANNON

Walter Bradford Cannon seated in front of a kymograph in the physiology laboratory, Harvard Medical School, 1902.

Walter B. Cannon

The Life and Times of a Young Scientist

SAUL BENISON
A. CLIFFORD BARGER
ELIN L. WOLFE

THE BELKNAP PRESS OF
HARVARD UNIVERSITY PRESS
CAMBRIDGE, MASSACHUSETTS
AND LONDON, ENGLAND
1987

Text design by Joyce C. Weston

Library of Congress Cataloging-in-Publication Data

Benison, Saul.
  Walter B. Cannon : the life and times of a young scientist.

  Bibliography: p.
  Includes index.
    1. Cannon, Walter B. (Walter Bradford), 1871–1945. 2. Physiologists—United States—Biography. 3. Medical teaching personnel—United States—Biography. 4. Harvard Medical School—History—20th century. I. Barger, A. Clifford, 1917– II. Wolfe, Elin L. III. Title.
[DNLM: 1. Cannon, Walter B. (Walter Bradford), 1871–1945. 2. Education, Medical—biography. 3. Education, Medical—history—Massachusetts. 4. Physiology—biology.
  WZ 100 C226B]
  QP26.C3B46   1987   612'.0092'4 [B]
86-25951
ISBN 0-674-94580-8 (alk. paper)

Foreword

by Howard E. Morgan, M.D.

The scientific and professional values of this book stem from the importance of Walter B. Cannon in American biomedical science, the impact of the Harvard Medical School on American medicine, and the discussion that will be found here of pivotal events that occurred at the beginning of the twentieth century and relate to topics of current interest in the fields of medicine and science. The book is far more than a biography limited to painting a portrait of the young Walter Cannon. Persons with interests in the history of medicine, in the conflict between scientists and those opposed to scientific inquiry, and in higher education will be attracted to this remarkable volume. I have been fortunate to be able to follow the preparation of the final manuscript because of my roles as chairman of the publication committee of the American Physiological Society, president of the society, and reviewer for Harvard University Press. I found all of my experiences with the manuscript to be extremely pleasurable and scientifically rewarding.

Without question, Walter B. Cannon was one of the great figures in physiology, and he headed a department that had a major impact on the discipline as it developed in the United States. His early contributions to gastrointestinal physiology are already legendary, but the account here has added interest because it relates the very early use of x-rays and the subsequent dawning of an awareness of the dangers associated with them. The book presents a clear description of Cannon's conception of the "fight or flight" response as it evolved through his work on the physiology of the adrenal medulla and enables the reader to appreciate the flow of ideas that led to Cannon's discoveries. Finally, the book gives a superb description of a way of life, especially of academic life, that has now vanished.

The period of time that is covered by Cannon's early years (1871–1917) represents the transition to a scientifically based medical education at Harvard. The factors involved in this transition—the competitive (and sometimes conflicting) claims of laboratory scientists and clinicians, the problem of gaining academic control of the teaching hospitals, and, not the least, the development of a full-time system of faculty appointments in clinical departments— are all of interest and provide insights into similar problems that exist today. At times it almost seems as though we lose sight of Cannon in these struggles at the Harvard Medical School, but later when he emerges as an arbitrator and peacemaker, we see clearly that he has been there all along, providing a stabilizing force through his very presence.

In light of present events the activities of antivivisectionists and their opposition to medical research as they are discussed here are of particular interest. At the turn of the century the issue of the use of animals for laboratory experiments was contested at both the local and national levels. Those contests are still going on. But there are many differences between what happened then and what is happening now. In the early 1900s, for example, those who attempted to restrict or abolish animal use in biomedical research were also opposed to human experimentation; today the attention of animal rights groups focuses less and less on the use of the human animal.

It is fitting that the publication of *Walter B. Cannon: The Life and Times of a Young Scientist* coincides with the celebration of the centennial of the American Physiological Society (1887–1987). Cannon was elected a member of the APS in 1900, the year he received his medical degree. Earlier, when he was a student of Henry P. Bowditch (the first president of the society), he gave a public demonstration to show visitors attending an APS meeting in Boston the movements of the alimentary canal by means of x-ray; and he published his first paper on deglutition in the goose in the first issue of the *American Journal of Physiology*. Cannon took an active role in the society and served as its treasurer from 1905 to 1912. He was a member of the conference committee that established the Federation of American Societies for Experimental Biology in 1912. During his term as president of the American Physiological Society in 1914–1916, he was instrumental in arranging for the society to assume full ownership and management of the *American Journal of Physiology*. After completing the presidency, Cannon continued to remain active in the society. He was in charge of local arrangements for the Thirteenth International Physiological Congress, which met in Boston in 1929, and he participated in the fiftieth anniversary of the APS in 1938, not only delivering a speech on Bowditch, his mentor, but also joining in the tribute honoring William T. Porter, his long-time colleague at Harvard. Today the society continues to express its appreciation for Cannon's contributions via the Walter B. Cannon Memorial Lecture delivered at its annual meetings.

Some years ago Philip Bard, one of Cannon's prize pupils who became professor of physiology at Johns Hopkins and was himself a president of the American Physiological Society, expressed to a meeting of physiologists the love and admiration of Cannon's friends and colleagues, who viewed him as a great international humanitarian and as a great teacher and scientist. Through his wit and sincerity, his commitment to excellence in all he said and did, and his willingness to serve the interests of both science and society, Cannon had a pervasive influence on the teaching of medicine, on American physiology, and on the development of biomedical science. I feel confident that he will continue to be a splendid source of inspiration to present and future generations of physiologists and biomedical scientists.

Acknowledgments

This book could not have been completed without help from many people. We owe a profound debt to members of the Cannon family—especially to Bradford Cannon and his wife Ellen and to his sisters Wilma Fairbank, Linda Burgess, Marian Schlesinger, and Helen Bond—who placed at our disposal their father's and mother's diaries, letters, and photographs and added their own recollections of Cannon family life.

Former colleagues and students of Walter B. Cannon helped as well. Both Philip Bard, late professor of physiology at the Johns Hopkins Medical School, and Walter C. Alvarez, late member of the Mayo Clinic, not only shared their memories with us about their special relations with Cannon but also deposited materials in the Cannon Archive. In addition, we owe a debt to Herbert L. Abrams, former chairman of the department of radiology at the Harvard Medical School, who at an important juncture in our work invited Cliff Barger to give the prestigious Sosman Lecture—a circumstance that ultimately gave impetus to our reconstruction of Cannon's early use of x-ray in his research.

There is no history without primary materials and we were greatly helped in our search for such documents relevant to Cannon's life by the staff members of a large number of libraries and archives, chief among them those at the Francis A. Countway Library of the Harvard Medical School, where both the Cannon Papers and the Cannon Research Project are located. The staff of the Rare Books and Manuscripts Department under the direction of Richard J. Wolfe deserves our special gratitude for an unfailing effort in our behalf over a period of years. We are also obliged to others throughout the Harvard library system, in particular the staffs at the Harvard University Archives under the direction of Harley P. Holden, and at the Baker, Houghton, Schlesinger, and Widener libraries. These and a great many other libraries and archives allowed us access to their collections (listed on pages 397–400), promptly and courteously met our various requests, supplied us with photocopies, and granted us permission to publish photographs and excerpts from materials in their charge. It is seemly that we note here our thanks to Nancy McCall of the Alan M. Chesney Archives at the Johns Hopkins Medical School, Thomas Rosenbaum at the Rockefeller Archive Center, and Carolyn Kopp at the Rockefeller University Archives, for their various efforts in our behalf. We also wish to express our appreciation to L. J. Henderson, Jr., who authorized us to consult his father's memoir; Richard Hocking, who allowed us access to the Richard C. Cabot Papers; and Lady Alison Todd, who generously supplied us with a copy of the unpublished autobiography of her father, Sir Henry H. Dale.

Throughout, we were aided by a host of friends and colleagues who read and criticized various drafts of the manuscript, exchanged ideas with us, brought materials to our attention that they thought would be useful, and above all, guided and encouraged us: at Harvard, Thomas E. Cone, Jr., Donald Fleming, Judith H. Goetzl, Raj K. Goyal, Laurie Rae Greene, Lloyd E. Hawes, Samuel Hellmann, Evelyn Stone, Eugene Taylor, and Paul M. Zoll; Whitfield Bell and Murphy Smith at the American Philosophical Society; Leonard Wilson and his wife Adelia at the University of Minnesota Medical School; Horace W. Davenport at the University of Michigan Medical School; Arthur Viseltear at the Yale University Medical School; Maurice Fox, Jerome Y. Lettvin, and Charles Weiner at the Massachusetts Institute of Technology; John and June G. Alexander, Roger Daniels, William Dember, Raymond Suskind, and Stanley Troup at the University of Cincinnati; Nathan Reingold at the Smithsonian Institution; George Dalton at Northwestern University; Leonard Levy at Claremont College.

Others helped as well. Anita Swanson rendered great service by transcribing Cannon's diaries and manuscript materials at the beginning of our work. Birthe Creutz performed outstanding feats putting our manuscript onto the word processor and seeing it through countless revisions, always with good cheer. Steve Borak's artistic and technical expertise as a photographer yielded high-quality results that enabled us to use a good number of the photographs we had at our disposal. Angela von der Lippe, Patricia Flaherty, Jodi Simpson, and the staff of Harvard University Press used their professional skills to guide us through the editorial, design, and production phases of publication.

We might never have begun, much less finished, this book without financial support in the form of grants from the U.S. Department of Health, Education and Welfare, Public Health Service; from the Josiah Macy, Jr., Foundation, courtesy of John Z. Bowers; from the Commonwealth Fund, courtesy of Reginald Fitz; from the Eleanor Naylor Dana Charitable Trust, courtesy of Mark D. Altschule; and from the Rockefeller Archive Center of the Rockefeller University. We owe special thanks to Edward D. Miller, Jr., at the Columbia University College of Physicians and Surgeons, for his generosity. At a critical time the University of Cincinnati made it possible for Saul Benison to take a leave of absence to continue his work on the book.

We would be remiss if we did not give a special accolade to three very dear friends for the extraordinary support and assistance they provided at all times: Mark Altschule, Claire Barger, and Dick Wolfe. To them and to members of the Benison, Barger, and Wolfe families we owe a debt that can never be repaid.

Contents

Illustrations

Credits

All portraits and photographs are from the Cannon Papers and the Harvard Medical Archives, both in the Countway Library of Medicine, Boston, except as noted below. Portraits of Otto Folin, W. N. Bullard, and Thomas Dwight in Figure 7 come from the iconographic files of the Boston Medical Library. In Figure 8, the portraits of G. W. Pierce, R. B. Perry, and Hugo Münsterberg are by courtesy of the Harvard University Archives; the portrait of William James by courtesy of the Houghton Library. The portrait of T. R. Elliott in Figure 13 is by courtesy of the Wellcome Institute Library, London; the photograph of the General Education Board in Figure 15 by courtesy of the Rockefeller Archive Center, North Tarrytown, New York.

WALTER B. CANNON

1   *A Family History*

L ATE IN THE afternoon of October 7, 1909, some hours after a luncheon given in honor of the inauguration of Abbott Lawrence Lowell as the twenty-fourth president of Harvard University, Walter Bradford Cannon was seen entering his office in the physiology department at the Harvard Medical School. The day had been a hectic one for Cannon: following a morning spent preparing a statement on animal experimentation for former president Charles W. Eliot, mingling with crowds of delegates from various universities who had been invited to participate in the festivities, and later welcoming guests who came to tea and toured the medical campus, he had become tired and sought some time to himself before setting out for the evening dinner and yet another round of celebration.[1] Cannon, although pleasant looking, was not an imposing figure. Stocky, of medium height, with neatly combed dark hair parted just off-center that framed a round, open face, he had none of the stateliness of some of his bearded and impeccably dressed medical colleagues. Indeed, save for the small steel-rimmed glasses, which gave him a serious purposive look, there was nothing special in his bearing to set him apart from others, and few who lingered on the medical campus gave him a second glance. He hardly appeared the remarkable figure whom many in the administration and faculty regarded as one of the bright hopes of the Medical School.

Cannon's office was spacious and contained several pieces of furniture. In one corner near two windows looking out over the Longwood Avenue quadrangle was a swivel chair in front of an open rolltop desk with a long-necked telephone to one side. Against an adjacent wall was a row of waist-high wooden cabinets topped by bookcases that reached to the ceiling, their shelves brimming with books. In the center of the room was a long, large table with papers stacked in neat piles, two of them held down by a pair of ceramic cats. At the end of the room was a wood-burning fireplace with a mahogany mantel holding a number of photographs of teachers and colleagues. On the wall above was a framed print of Claude Bernard instructing a group of his students and a portrait of Charles Darwin as an elderly man.

The office was Cannon's retreat, a place where he could go to sort out problems and to think. This day, in addition to being tired, he had several things on his mind. Not only did he reflect on the changes he felt were sure to come to the Medical School with the new administration; he was also planning a lecture on the effects of the emotions on the digestive process. Most of all he was worried about his stepmother, who was gravely ill. To calm himself, he decided to complete a questionnaire that the zoologist Charles B. Davenport had sent him some time before.[2] Part of a survey of family traits, the questionnaire fit in well with one of Cannon's long-time interests—family history. This interest, he later explained to one of his uncles during a search for family information, had a specific scientific purpose. "I am not interested in my ancestors," he wrote with candor, "merely for reasons of curiosity and a sense of family pride, but chiefly to obtain information regarding the characteristics of forebears which may be appearing in my own children."[3] Cannon's concern with hereditary characteristics was by no means unique. Actually it was widespread, particularly among biological and medical investigators.

Following the rediscovery in 1900 of Gregor Mendel's pioneer work in genetics, several members of the zoology department at Harvard—among them some of Cannon's teachers—began to devote themselves to the study of heredity. A few, like William E. Castle, applied themselves to experiments in an attempt to discover whether the fundamental nature of the gene could be modified by the process of selection. Others, like Charles B. Davenport, began to examine the nature of inheritance of human traits that appeared to be involved in crime, insanity, and pauperism. Such studies were popular; they carried the cachet of science and, at the same time, seemed to hold out the promise of controlling some of the major intractable social problems of the day.[4]

To aid these studies and as a preliminary step in the establishment of a eugenics record office, Davenport, supported by the Carnegie Institution of Washington, began to gather information that would help to develop "a good index of the natural traits of better American families." The key to this proposed index was the development of a questionnaire entitled "Record of Family Traits," which would be sent out to a select group of middle- and upper-class American families. Cannon's answers to questions about his mother and father were detached and almost clinically impersonal in tone. He described his father, for example, as "ingenious—devised graphic record of car movements on railroad. Careful worker with tools. Careless of personal appearance. Very industrious. Not dependent on social relations in later years." His mother was depicted in equally terse terms: "Quiet, refined, modest. Very neat and orderly. Nervous, inclined to worry. Mentally active with quick perception. Unselfish."[5] Although these characterizations furnish an important insight into Cannon's perceptions in early middle age of his parents, they are hardly by themselves an adequate guide to family history. The mundane entries of dates and places of births and deaths that Cannon assiduously collected through the years offer an additional and fuller frame of reference—that of families moving over land and sea, buffeted by forces they often scarcely understood and over which they had no control.

⚜ ⚜ ⚜

The Cannon family name first appears in a historical record as Carnahan or Carnachan during the early eighteenth century.[6] It occupies a line in a ship's manifest, part of a record of migration of that host of men, women, and children who were uprooted from their native soil through forces set in motion by economic circumstances and especially by England's efforts throughout the seventeenth century to conquer Ireland.

Each English military success in Ireland brought in its wake a multitude of English and lowland Scots farmers who eagerly occupied the lands evacuated by the defeated Irish lords and peasants. Within a relatively brief period of time these migrants created a prosperous cattle and sheep industry so successful that by the end of the century Parliament passed a series of laws designed to protect landholders in England against what they perceived to be a growing and menacing competition from Northern Ireland. There were other hardships. Hard-working migrants, who on their arrival in Ulster leased their farms from absentee English landlords, discovered that when their leases ran out early in the eighteenth century the new rents for farms they had improved over the years were twice and often three times as high as the original rents. To add to their distress, they found themselves excluded from meaningful political participation in their affairs by new parliamentary laws that prevented Presbyterian Scotch-Irish from holding public office unless they took an oath to support the Anglican Church.[7]

In 1718 Samuel Carnahan, a Scottish farmer living in the valley of the River Bann in Ulster, unhappy with the increasingly difficult economic and political conditions there, decided to seek a new life for his family in the Massachusetts Bay Colony in America. At first, he settled in Hopkinton, a small village just south of Worcester. A number of years later, however, eager to acquire more land for his growing family, he moved with a group of sixty other church members to Blandford, a newly founded village in the Berkshire Mountains, then the forward edge of the western frontier. The migration of the Carnahan family was not unusual; it was part of a larger migration of Scotch-Irish farmers—a migration that was to populate the American frontier from Massachusetts to the Carolinas during the eighteenth century. In the years that followed, the Carnahan family—now called Cannon with the name spelled as it was pronounced—prospered in Blandford. Samuel Cannon continued to acquire land, and he and his three sons took an increasingly active role in town affairs, ranging from such humble local duties as hog reeve and surveyor to more important civic functions as town councillor and representative to the general court.[8] The Cannons remained in Blandford working their land for eighty-six years.

In the winter of 1804–05 Stephen Cannon, one of Samuel Cannon's grandsons eager to make his own way, left Blandford with several other young men to look over the well-advertised lands of the Western Reserve in Ohio. The next year, following the death of his father, Stephen, now the family breadwinner, returned to Massachusetts and moved his mother and the rest of the children to land he had taken up in Aurora, Ohio. Once again, the Cannons had become part of a larger migration—this time of New Englanders who, in search of promised fortune, began to settle the rich farmlands within the borders of the new states organized by the Northwest Ordinance.[9] In later years his great-grandson Walter would take particular pride in the courage and fortitude of his pioneer ancestors and especially of Stephen's wife, Laura Cochran Cannon, for her devotion to her family, as well as her tending of the sick and the infirm in Aurora and the surrounding countryside. "It is reported," he wrote, "that the extra work done by her in one year included weaving six hundred yards of woolen cloth, one hundred yards of yarn carpet, five blankets and five plaid shawls. She bore eight children and lived to be nearly ninety years old. It is at least pleasant to think that bodily energy is heritable, as has been claimed, and that the group of genes responsible for it have had their way in some of Laura Cochran's descendants."[10]

Initially Stephen enjoyed a modest success. Later, however, through a series of financial reverses, he lost his farm, and in 1855 he and his wife left Aurora with one of their children's families to pursue the will-o'-the-wisp promise of prosperity in the farmlands of Iowa. Two years later, during the depression of 1857, he died.[11] Stephen Cannon's move to Ohio ultimately proved to be more than a change in geography for his family. Although he remained a farmer all of his life, his fifth child, Lucius, became a merchant in the nearby village of Gustavus. Unfortunately, Lucius did not prosper, and he, too, turned west in search of greater economic opportunity.

In 1848 Lucius Cannon moved to Madison, Wisconsin, then an unincorporated village, and set up a store. Although he was well thought of and even looked up to by his neighbors, his store did not flourish. Seven years later he moved to Pepin, Wisconsin, and established yet another store; but again he was unsuccessful. While living in Pepin, he was obliged to supplement his income for a time by serving as recorder of deeds and later as a state senator.[12] In 1861 Lucius moved his family once more, this time to Milwaukee, where through the good offices of friends he obtained a position as a route agent for the Chicago, Milwaukee and St. Paul Railroad. He remained with the railroad until his death in 1873. There was little to distinguish Lucius Cannon from many of his contemporaries. He lived in genteel poverty, and family memories depict him as inept, a man who could hardly drive a nail. All, however, note his rectitude and honesty. In an era when the votes of state legislators were often bought with ease and scarcely a backward glance, Lucius Cannon during his tenure in the Wisconsin legislature maintained his honesty and truly served the public interest. That service was his greatest achievement and that honesty, his proudest possession.[13]

Lucius left one other legacy: three sons. While all of them shared some of his characteristics, each possessed distinctive and even exceptional qualities of mind. The youngest son, named Lucius after his father, became a librarian at St. Louis. Although his nephew Walter would later characterize him as "queer, cranky and a Theosophist," it is clear that he had an independence of mind that expressed itself no matter what others thought or said. The middle son, Edward, was equally strong-minded. When a local minister publicly reproved his mother because she left the decision of church membership to her young sons, Edward, then barely in his teens, in support of his mother and despite local opinion immediately resigned from the church. Later, he became an inventor who demonstrated marked mechanical abilities. Unfortunately, he also shared his father's ineptitude for business affairs so that others profited from the fruits of his labors. The oldest son, Colbert, perhaps best reflected the characteristics of his mother, especially her drive and pride.

Lucius' wife, Helen Minerva Hanchett, a descendant of an old distinguished family from Windsor Locks, Connecticut, traced her forebears back to Oliver Cromwell and did everything in her power to celebrate that heritage. She gloried in the fact that, soon after settling in Madison, she was appointed official reporter to the Supreme Court of Wisconsin. In an effort to live up to what she believed to be her station in life, she hobnobbed with the wealthy in Madison and frequently arranged sumptuous dinners for the movers and shakers in the state legislature—although such feasts were invariably followed by days of meager meals in order to balance the family budget. Such was her pride that once when her granddaughter Bernice Cannon entered the house through the rear door, her grandmother sharply rebuked her: "No granddaughter of mine," she scolded, "will ever come in through the back door."[14] Hanchett family pride was to become an important ingredient in her son Colbert's efforts to make his way in the world.

Colbert Cannon early in life tied his fortune to the same railroad that his father was serving, the Chicago, Milwaukee and St.

Paul. During the first days of the Civil War, although barely in his teens, Colbert became a newsboy on the railroad. Several years later he took a post in the ticket office of another local railroad. In 1867, at the age of nineteen, he rejoined the Chicago, Milwaukee and St. Paul. His new job, that of managing newsboys, offered him little in the way of prospects, and under the influence of a local physician whom he admired, he began to dream of becoming a doctor. In 1870, while working for the railroad in Prairie du Chien, Wisconsin, he met and fell in love with a young school-teacher, Wilma Denio, and for a time put his dream aside.[15]

The early lives of the Denios, like those of the Cannons, were rooted in the Massachusetts soil—beginning with the birth of Wilma Denio's great-great-grandmother, Abigail Stebbins, in Deerfield in 1684.[16] At that time Deerfield was little more than a frontier outpost that attracted French *coureurs de bois* who regularly navigated the rivers and lakes from Montreal and Quebec to hunt and trade for furs in western Massachusetts. Early in 1704 a young *coureur de bois* from Quebec named Jacques de Noyon, who had previously visited Deerfield several times before to trade for furs, courted and married Abigail Stebbins. The marriage proved to be a godsend to the Stebbins family: several months later, when the French and their Indian allies during Queen Anne's war attacked and deci-mated Deerfield, Jacques de Noyon, who knew the raiders, was able to intercede in behalf of the Stebbins family and save their lives. He was, however, unable to prevent them from being taken as captives to Montreal. Here they remained for a number of years before being allowed to return to Deerfield. Nevertheless, Jacques de Noyon and his young wife chose to remain in Canada and later settled in Boucherville, a small village not far from Montreal. Little more than a decade later, the oldest son, René, went to Deerfield to visit his grandfather and stayed on in the Stebbins' house. Before long, the boy's name was anglicized to Aaron Denio (pronounced *Dē-nī'-oh*), and in time he inherited his mother's share of his grand-father's estate. Aaron Denio prospered in Deerfield, and he and his family remained there until after the American Revolution.[17]

In the unsettled economy of Massachusetts following the Rev-olution, members of the Denio family decided to move west. In-itially the family migrated to western New York. In the 1840s one branch of the family, that led by Hardin Fitzgerald Denio (the grandson of Aaron), established a farm in Helena, New York. In

1848 Sarah Wilma, the second of seven children, was born. Little is known of the fortunes of the Denios in Helena save that following the Civil War the family moved once more, this time to a farm in Elba, Minnesota, some fifty miles from St. Paul.[18] In 1870 Wilma (as she was known), who was then teaching school and living with one of her uncles in Prairie du Chien, Wisconsin, married Colbert Hanchett Cannon.

&» &» &»

Colbert's marriage began with high hopes but undefined prospects. He was handsome, young, and strong and had a good deal of physical courage. Initially his post with the railroad kept the young couple in Prairie du Chien. There, on October 19, 1871, their first child, Walter Bradford, was born.[19] Thus W. B. Cannon, a physiologist who early in life was to distinguish himself through his studies on the process of gastrointestinal motility, was born in the village, formerly the site of Fort Crawford, where William Beaumont forty years earlier had conducted some of his classic observations on gastric function.[20]

Shortly after the birth of his son, Colbert was kicked by a horse and suffered a fractured skull. Little is known of the extent of the injury, but those who knew him best later maintained that after the accident Colbert became markedly difficult to get along with and was often quick-tempered and moody. Following the incident, for example, he inexplicably left his post with the railroad, moved near his wife's family in Elba, and began a new career as a farmer. Three years later, after the birth of a daughter, Bernice May, he gave up farming and moved once more, this time to Milwaukee where he obtained a position as an office clerk. In 1877, another daughter, Ida Maude, was born. Two years later, perhaps in deference to the needs of his rapidly growing family, Colbert moved again—this time to St. Paul, where he went to work as chief clerk in the car service department of the St. Paul and Pacific Railroad, then part of James J. Hill's Great Northern Railroad system. Two months after his move to St. Paul a third daughter, Jane Laura, was born on the Denio family farm in Elba.[21]

Colbert Cannon's new position proved to be more permanent than the ones he had previously held, and the growing family settled in a large house on Dayton's Bluff in St. Paul. His work went well and although his salary was not large, the family lived comfortably, in large measure because of Wilma's expertise in running the household. The future appeared bright. In 1881, however, several weeks after the birth of another daughter, Wilma contracted pneumonia. The disease, all too often a death warrant, soon took its toll. Ida later remembered that when her mother was on her deathbed, she called the children to her side, sang a hymn, and then bade them each goodbye. At the last, she left a special instruction to her son: "Walter, be good to the world." The wish was to remain a memory that haunted him to the end of his days. Several weeks later, the baby followed her mother to the grave.[22]

The death of his young wife shattered Colbert. Not only had he loved her but he was utterly dependent on her, and the thought of running the house and raising the family alone overwhelmed and depressed him. Despite the help of his wife's sister Emma, who came to live with the family, the mood in the house quickly became grim. Colbert's depression ruled the household—the children were forbidden to speak their mother's name in his presence. At times he even took Walter to bed with him while he sobbed and cried out his grief uncontrollably.[23] A year and a half after Wilma's death, Colbert married again—choosing Caroline Mower of Cedar Rapids, Iowa, a friend from his boyhood. He had little love for his new wife, and it is evident that his primary motive in this marriage was to find a housekeeper and a caretaker for his children. Throughout his life many of Colbert's schemes misfired; on this occasion, however, he planned well. Carrie Mower Cannon, despite her husband's manifest lack of interest in her, remained completely loyal to him and to the children. Indeed, she grew to love them, and they in turn became devoted to her.[24]

Following his marriage, Colbert's fortunes changed for the better. His energy and ingenuity began to attract James J. Hill's attention, and in 1885 he was appointed car accountant to the railroad. In this new post he devised an ingenious graphic method of recording railroad car movements, which allowed railroad officials to ascertain at a moment's notice on what tracks their various freight cars and the cars of other railroads were located. Colbert's innovation brought new recognition, and only a short time later he was made superintendent of the railroad car service department[25]—a promotion that enabled him to move the family to a more attractive neighborhood in St. Anthony Park.

There can be little doubt that Colbert's success stirred his ambition. But instead of trying to obtain further advancement with the railroad, which was then flourishing, he began to dream once more of becoming a doctor. He fitted out an office in his house and practiced medicine whenever time allowed, treating his friends and neighbors without charge. Colbert had no formal medical training; he knew little of physiology and anatomy and nothing of therapeutics. His knowledge was essentially based on a random reading of some medical books and an abiding faith in the efficacy of folk remedies and nostrums. He was, in fact, willing to try anything that came to mind. When he heard, for instance, that some doctors employed electricity therapeutically, he rigged up a huge battery and produced enough electricity to shock patients who flocked to him for the new medical treatment he had praised. To cure tuberculosis, he first cupped his patients and then prescribed a vigorous exercise program. In 1886 when Reginald Heber Fitz established early diagnosis and treatment for appendicitis, Colbert, who believed that an inflamed appendix was in large part the result of eating too many currant seeds, injected an herbal substance into his patients' buttocks and then raised their feet on an incline so "the poison that caused the mischief" would flow up and out of the body.[26]

The children were perhaps his longest-suffering patients. Colbert, who firmly believed that the best way of coping with disease was to prevent it, rubbed them with coconut oil and then made them wear chest protectors of red flannel and chamois skin pinked at the edges. Some of his other medical ideas were more rational: he believed, for example, that feet were deformed by the pointed shoes then in fashion, and when getting shoes for the children, he would trace the shape of their feet and have their shoes made to fit that outline. The children hated such shoes because they were extraordinarily wide and clumsy-looking and very different from the shoes their friends wore. Jenny expressed her displeasure by kicking rocks and stones until the toes of her shoes wore out; Colbert's cure, to her great distress, was to make her wear boys' shoes with copper-reinforced toes.[27] Perhaps the health measures that disturbed the children most were the various diets their father planned. A food faddist, Colbert did not believe in eating meat and often provided meals of nuts, distilled water, Graham bread, and Postum. The Saturday evening supper was particularly despised because Colbert, in an effort to provide the children with the minerals he thought their bodies needed and to alleviate abdominal distress, gave them nothing but charcoal and milk.[28]

There were happier results when Colbert put his mechanical skills to work at home. An expert carpenter, he delighted in making toys—building a doll house for the girls and fashioning skis and a huge bobsled complete with steering wheel for Walter.[29] For all of his effort, however, Colbert demonstrated a curious ambivalence toward the children. Although he never physically punished them or criticized them overtly, he often made them feel that they were a basic problem. When they would ask him what he wanted, he would reply in a heavy, revealing humor, "I want to go to Oregon and be a doctor." At other times he would make the children share his difficulties. Bernice later remembered that when he fell behind in paying the interest on the mortgage of their house, he would invariably take her to the bank, to her great embarrassment, to act as a buffer between him and the bank agent, whom he tried to put off with excuses.[30]

Essentially, Colbert wanted the children to be self-sufficient early, and he devised all sorts of educational schemes to encourage them to be independent and stand on their own feet. At no time, however, did he consider their fundamental needs, and as a result they often felt enslaved and embarrassed by his plans for them. Once, for example, Colbert decided that it would be useful for the children to learn how to raise chickens and placed a brooder and incubator in the family dining room. Family meals were disrupted by the constant chirping of the chicks, and the children were mortified when their friends visited and saw this equipment in the dining room. Nevertheless, one of Bernice's friends, Cornelia James, later reminisced, "I remember my own envy of such delightful ornaments. Our own dining room had nothing beyond the conventional fittings except the bookcase with an encyclopedia which was there as ready reference to settle family disputes at meals."[31]

Books were certainly not lacking in the Cannon home. Convinced that education was the road to success, Colbert kept his home well stocked with books and magazines. Indeed, he proved an easy mark for every book salesman in the city. The purchase of books was symptomatic of Colbert's financial improvidence: although he was well paid by the railroad, he was almost continually in debt because he bought books as well as everything else in the house "on time." Often while new items came into the house through the front door, the children were shamed to hear Colbert or their stepmother make excuses to creditors at the rear door.[32]

When Walter reached his fourteenth birthday, Colbert despite his belief in education took him out of school and put him to work in a railroad office. The boy went willingly because he thought his wages were needed to help support the household. Years later he learned from a great-aunt that his father put him to work not because of family need but because he believed that a job was more useful "than loafing in school."[33] Whatever Colbert's motivation, in the long run the experience proved extraordinarily useful.

2 St. Paul High School and Harvard College

A FTER TWO YEARS of dull work for the railroad, Cannon convinced his father that he ought to return to school. The years spent in the railroad office, nevertheless, left an indelible mark on his character. From that time forward he became compulsive about time and, to his sisters' distress, continually harped on the necessity of being punctual. He also became concerned about family finances and sought to earn money by taking odd jobs after school, even serving for a while as janitor in the local Congregational Church. Still, for all of these virtues, he appeared to be like other boys his age in St. Paul—whether indulging his fondness for winter sports, raiding local neighborhood gardens for watermelons, showing off his ability to do difficult arithmetic sums in his head, or teasing and playing practical jokes on his sisters.[1] When many years later his wife wrote him about their son's angelic behavior while on a visit to Cape Cod, Cannon replied, "It was so reminiscent of my own boyhood. Among people that I visited, I had the reputation of being a holy saint in miniature—liable to die young because of excessive goodness. Fortunately, my behavior at home and especially my treatment of my sisters saved me from an early grave."[2]

When Cannon entered the St. Paul High School in 1888, it contained 750 students and was housed in a large rococo turreted building, which stood on the corner of Olive and 15th Streets; he was sixteen years old, the school itself but one year older.[3] From its inception the St. Paul High School had an excellent reputation, offering three separate programs—one in general studies, another in classics, and a third in commerce. Its faculty of men and women, although not all equally well trained, were excellent teachers. The student body was also of high quality, and upon graduation its members often went on to the state university of Minnesota or, in special circumstances, to well-known private colleges in the East such as Swarthmore, Columbia, Harvard, and Yale. The cultural diversity of the city and its increasing social and economic problems made politics the order of the day. St. Paul was one of the centers of Populist thought in the United States, and there were few teachers or students in the high school who did not argue or examine the issues raised by this movement.[4] In this heady environment Cannon began to assert himself intellectually. It was a development that initially made his father very unhappy.

While in high school Cannon became interested in the ongoing debate between Thomas Huxley and William Wilberforce, Bishop of Oxford, on the relations between science and religion.[5] That great Victorian controversy about the implications of Darwinian thought shook Cannon's belief in the strict Calvinist faith in which he had been brought up, and he began to read omnivorously in the family library about the sources of Christian doctrine. The more he read the more his doubts grew, until he openly admitted that he no longer believed in the tenets of the Congregational Church and was sent to discuss his uncertainties with a local minister. "The clergyman in the church, to whom I was sent for counsel," Cannon later recalled, "took precisely the wrong course in dealing with my difficulties; he wanted to know what right I had, as a mere youth, to set up my opinion against the opinion of great scholars who supported the church's doctrines. This appeal to authority did not impress me at all, because I knew that there were great scholars in the opposition. Furthermore, I had the feeling that I was entitled to my independent judgment."[6] Finally, to the astonishment of the minister, the young man resigned from the church. Colbert Cannon, who was a Sunday School teacher and a deacon in the church, was so angered by his son's action that for a time he would not speak to him. Worse, the precipitous act of the young heretic became a subject of local discussion and gossip.[7]

However traumatic the incident, Walter's show of independence brought its own reward—it resulted in his making new friends and developing new interests. One of those new friends was a young Unitarian minister, Samuel McChord Crothers, who had recently come to St. Paul. Crothers, a graduate of the Harvard Divinity School, had gone through a similar experience in his own youth and had a special understanding of Cannon's problem. Moreover, his preaching "of the freedom of the human soul to think for itself so long as such action did not interfere with the freedom of others" helped to sustain Cannon's idealism and gave him strength to meet the pressures at home and in the community caused by his decision.[8] Cannon and Crothers remained friends for the rest of their lives. In addition, Cannon's reading of Huxley awakened a curiosity in areas he had never seriously thought of before, and he began to steep himself in the works of Darwin, Spencer, Tyndall, Yeomans, and White. In the process his interest in science continued to grow.

Cannon completed the four-year general course at the St. Paul High School in three years. By his senior year he had easily taken his place among the top students in his class. Indeed, in the estimation of the principal and many of the faculty he was probably the best student in the school. It was no small judgment; the school contained a number of bright and talented students, many of whom would later go on to distinguished careers in law, government, education, and science. Most of the honors the school and his class could bestow came to Cannon. He was elected class president and named by the faculty to be a speaker on the commencement program. His classmates also voted him the most popular boy in the class and in a teasing mood prophesied that he would become the director of an institution for homeless cats and dogs. Perhaps the honor that pleased him most was his appointment as editor of the class yearbook, *Negatives of '91*, because it gave him a unique opportunity to express his ideas. In addition to reporting class and faculty activities, the yearbook included essays written by Cannon and his friends on a variety of issues. Fred Marvin, one of his closest friends, wrote about the rights of women and urged that they be given the vote as a matter of justice as well as right. Nellie Griswold, another friend, examined the race question and with remarkable perception argued that the solution to that knotty problem was to be found not in increased philanthropy but rather in equal economic and political opportunity. Cannon's contribution, "Don't Be a Clam," was his commencement address, a commentary on his previous attempt to examine the relations of science and religion, in which he advocated the necessity of tolerance for the development of thought. His avowal of the need for such freedom to escape from the errors of the past as well as his optimistic view of the future captivated the graduation audience, and a group of teachers and alumni judging various student essays awarded him the school's prestigious Benz Prize.[9]

✌️ ✌️ ✌️

The idealism expressed by Cannon and his friends, characteristic of young minds coming of age, reflected the teaching of the faculty at the St. Paul High School and in particular that of Mary Jeannette Newson. In 1891 "Miss May" Newson had been an English teacher in the high school for fourteen years. She had not been particularly well prepared for the post; as a matter of fact, she began to teach the year after she graduated from high school in 1877. Her father, one of the pioneer newspaper editors in St. Paul, was active in local politics, and one might reasonably suspect that her initial appointment had less to do with what she knew than who she was. If so, in this particular instance nepotism and politics served St. Paul well.[10] May Newson possessed three important qualities: an inquiring mind, a sense of history, and a genuine concern for her students. For them, her classes became an introduction to the world of ideas. Not only did she teach them language and literature, she entered their private lives as well, encouraging their promise and acting as both critic and confidante. She also directed many of her finest students toward eastern colleges; on more than one occasion the local school board attempted to censure her, arguing that her advice was depriving the University of Minnesota of good students.[11]

From the moment Cannon entered her classes, May Newson, attracted by his independence, stirred his ambition. She frequently invited him to her home not only to talk about new books and ideas but to discuss his hopes and dreams as well. Cannon was so absorbed in these visits that sometimes he did not know when to say good night. If Miss Newson noticed his awkwardness, she said nothing and continued to encourage Cannon to go to college, preferably Harvard. For May Newson, no other college would serve to develop Cannon's budding abilities. To be sure, many in St. Paul spoke well of the University of Minnesota. But Minneapolis was not Cambridge, and the University of Minnesota despite its excellence and promise was barely forty years old in 1891;

five years earlier Harvard had celebrated its two-hundred-and-fiftieth anniversary.[12] Still, for all of Miss Newson's adulation of New England and Harvard, she knew nothing of either first hand. In 1891, after the high school's graduation exercises, she traveled to Massachusetts and used the occasion to whet Cannon's appetite for the opportunities he would have by living in Cambridge and attending Harvard.

Writing to him about her visit to the college she had so often praised but until then had never seen, she described in detail Harvard Yard, Memorial Hall, the dormitories, classrooms, laboratories, and museums, but saved her superlatives, as befit an English teacher, for the library: "O, Walter, nothing but exclamation points will answer. Into the Holy of Holies we were ushered where *only students* are allowed to use the valuable books—original editions . . . Everywhere beautiful pictures, busts in white marble of the illustrious dead, poets, artists, musicians, scientists, patriots—you will be wild in a perfectly calm and dignified way. On the same shelf in the Library (with a capital L.) I saw 'Cardinal Newman's Life,' 'The History of the Baptists,' 'Darwin's Voyage around the World,' 'The Hist. of the Tractarian Movement of '45,' &c. &c. Culture and liberality combined."[13] The library was by no means the only high point of Miss Newson's visit to Harvard; equally important was her interview with Montague Chamberlain, the recorder of the college, about the prospects of support for serious students. "Mr. Chamberlain," she reassuringly wrote Cannon, "says they want earnest boys and 'digs' and that such have the aid and respect and esteem from the Professors beside the very material aid of the numerous scholarships and fellowships."[14]

The policy Chamberlain described was not one of Harvard's old traditions; it was in fact relatively new and as strongly opposed as were the other innovations that Charles W. Eliot attempted to introduce at Harvard. When Eliot became the president of Harvard in 1869, he vowed that not only would he change it from a regional college to a national university but that it would also become a university of an elite based on merit rather than one that was sustained by privilege and class.[15] Although he was able to effect significant changes in entrance standards, curriculum, religious requirements, and faculty, Harvard for the most part continued to enroll its students from the economically privileged whose sons attended private New England schools. By the mid-1880s, however, when Eliot recognized that continuation of this practice endangered his goal of making Harvard a truly national institution, he moved to recruit qualified students from public high schools throughout the country. Such recruiting bore a rich harvest, and in the following years a larger number of students came to Harvard from public high schools than ever before, particularly from schools outside Massachusetts and New England. By 1892, the year Cannon entered Harvard, nearly 30 percent of the freshman class were graduates of public high schools.[16] Inevitably, the newcomers began to work changes in the attitude and behavior of the student body. The class of 1891, to take but one example, drew national attention when its members staged an unexpected revolt and elected Clement Morgan, a black, to be class orator.[17] Previously that honor had always been bestowed on proper Back Bay Bostonians. Other traditions and usages by which the socially elect lived at Harvard proved more difficult to change.

Eliot's policies were not designed to make entrance to Harvard easy. In addition to having an excellent academic record and letters of recommendation, each student had to pass a series of rigorous entrance examinations in both elementary and advanced subjects. Whereas private schools prepared their students for the exams as part of their regular course offerings, public schools had no such tradition. To compensate for these differences, Harvard allowed all students the option of taking their examinations in stages over a period of a year following graduation.[18] Initially, Cannon took and passed his exams in elementary subjects after graduation in June of 1891. Like most public high school students, however, he postponed taking those in advanced subjects and devoted the next year to preparing for the second stage, continuing his studies at the St. Paul High School in trigonometry, Greek, French, and German. The only obstacle that remained was getting enough money to pay for his tuition, room, and board.

Colbert Cannon, for all his pride in his son's academic achievement, could not finance a Harvard education. It was a problem that May Newson recognized and quickly moved to overcome by soliciting letters on Cannon's behalf for financial aid from his teachers and from Harvard alumni living in St. Paul. In December 1891 a number of strong letters describing Cannon's worth were sent to Harvard from the high school principal and faculty. Typical was the summation offered by Frederick W. Fiske, Cannon's teacher of Latin and Greek. "He is in my opinion," Fiske wrote Eliot, "one of those young men who would make the most of the superior advantages that I, graduate of another college—Williams—, recognize as offered by Harvard; and for that reason I advise him to study there rather than at our State University, or my own College, or Yale where a number of boys go from our High School. I easily see in him qualities of native ability and earnestness and perseverance that will make him succeed in his college course and in the profession that he chooses."[19] Impressed by his academic record, preliminary examination results, and letters of support, Harvard officials awarded Cannon $250 in aid from the Ezekiel Price Greenleaf Fund for needy students even though he had not yet taken his final exams. Cannon was fortunate in the time he applied for entrance to Harvard: three years earlier no scholarship funds were available to aid applicants who lacked the necessary financial means.[20]

At the end of June 1892, after a pleasant week of attending commencement exercises at the high school as well as an alumni reunion and banquet, Cannon began the first of his advanced entrance exams. "Took Harvard examination in elementary Greek," he wrote in his diary on June 30. "Professor Royce, assistant in philosophy, conducted the examination." The next day he took an exam in English and the following day exams in trigonometry, elementary German, and French. "Think that I passed everything," he noted, and then added with some trepidation, "Not sure of German."[21] Later Colbert arranged a summer job for him as an assistant to the paymaster of the Great Northern Railroad (which was then expanding the line to Spokane Falls, Washington) so that he might earn enough to cover some of his sundry college expenses. The job was not demanding; moreover, it gave Cannon, who enjoyed the outdoors, a splendid opportunity to view for the first time the mountains and valleys of the northern Great Plains. Over and over he exulted about the sights he saw—whether pieces of petrified wood found by digging through fifty feet of blue clay in Montana, or Indians paddling their birchbark canoes in Idaho. Nothing, however, impressed him as much as the scenes that greeted him in Spokane Falls in Washington:

Went out to the end of track on a supply train carrying rails, ties, spikes, etc. Beheld strange sight of a railroad pushing its way across the continent. First encountered men putting up the telegraph poles. Then came upon construction and boarding trains. A continuous stream of wagons surrounded with heavy clouds of dust came and went carrying the ties to the front and returning empty. Rails, bolts and joiners were thrown from the construction train upon the grade— the train backed up—small cars came running back—were loaded with the rails, bolts, spikes etc. Horses lashed into a run hurried the car to the end of track. There were two gangs of men—each gang seized a rail and laid it in contact with the last rail—the nails were placed at a uniform distance apart, the car was jerked forward—two more rails were laid—and so the work went on . . . Men worked as if their lives depended upon accomplishing as much as possible each second. The great clouds of choking dust blackened their eyelids and covered their lips and made their voices hoarse. The laborers were great hard men with their hair and face-lines and clothing filled thick with dirt.[22]

The experience was graven in his mind, and he later used it to evoke for his teachers at Harvard his image of the role of railroads and western pioneers in the expansion of the nation.

The conclusion of Cannon's work for the Great Northern Railroad in midsummer brought welcome news—a telegram that announced he had passed his entrance examinations.[23] Several weeks later, his joy was tempered by the sadness of leaving home. Colbert, whether through poor planning or to avoid the difficulties of saying goodbye with others present, abruptly informed his son a week before he was to start for Harvard that he was going on vacation to the West Coast and would probably not see him again before the following summer. Cannon had hardly swallowed his disappointment when, to his astonishment, his father gave him $100 as a going-away present.[24] Saying goodbye to his stepmother and sisters and especially to Miss Newson a week later proved even more trying. "Saw Miss May Newson and her mother for last time," he wrote in his diary, "Everything was pleasantly arranged, but for me there was a shadow of sadness over all. I was leaving my best friend, who had helped me and urged me on when I felt weak and had brought out the good in my character when the evil seemed about to conquer. I shall never be able to repay her. She told me as I left that if ever I felt that my life was a failure, I should remember some back in St. Paul who would never think so."[25]

In the days that followed Cannon made a slow pilgrimage to

bid other farewells, stopping first to visit his grandmother and grandfather Denio at the family farm in Elba. "Worked in the fields all day," he noted, "—raise several blisters and stretch many muscles—go to bed tired and sleepy. Leaving home is more painful than I anticipated." The next day he continued, "Was repacking my valise when I found a copy of Marcus Aurelius slipped in by Miss Newson. It was very kind of her to think of my wants and very thoughtful of her to think of my wants in just the way she did. It makes me feel good to think that there are those who care for me. Went out into the fields again."[26] Leaving Elba, he went on but stopped again to see his grandmother, Helen Hanchett Cannon, in Milwaukee. Although he was then almost twenty-one years of age, except for his summer job Cannon had never been away from home before. Leaving for college was an uprooting that was as traumatic for him as that faced by his ancestors who left their Massachusetts farms for the Western Reserve at the beginning of the nineteenth century. He, too, was seeking a new life and future and in a place that was as much a *terra incognita* for him as Ohio had been for them.

✑ ✑ ✑

From the time his train left Chicago for the East, Cannon recorded his impressions of the countryside and the people he saw along the way. Some of the exigencies involved in traveling annoyed him; others he found exciting and new. "Went through Washington," he noted at one point, "G.A.R. encampment just over—great crowds of G.A.R. men. Passed through Harper's Ferry. Strange exultant feeling at being for the first time on historic ground. Saw canal for first time." When he arrived in New York, instead of stopping to explore the great city he had read about, he immediately took a train to Windsor Locks, Connecticut, to visit his Hanchett family cousins. The next day brought its own reward: "Saw a genuine Yankee type today," he noted with glee, "nasal twang, bones and all!"[27] At last he reached Harvard. Almost a decade later he described to his bride-to-be his thoughts upon his arrival: "What impressed me most, I think, was the thought that I, a poor untrained outlander, could come here and find myself the heir of all the gifts and sacrifices and hopes and strivings of the fathers for generations and generations of Harvard sons."[28] Cannon did not spend many moments in such reverie and immediately set about dealing with the money problems he faced. His scholarship, his summer earnings, and his father's gift gave him the wherewithal, if he watched every penny, to stay within the low budget of $372 that the Harvard College catalogue promised its poorer students was sufficient to pay the yearly costs of tuition, room, board, plus expenses.[29] After staying overnight in a local hotel, he rented a room at 5 Avon Street for $57 a year and then joined the Foxcroft Club—a boarding plan managed by its student membership in quarters furnished by the college—for an additional $6 per year. Here meals were served a la carte, the items on the bill of fare bearing a nominal cost of as little as one cent for butter or ten cents for two eggs on toast. In addition, the club provided its members with reading rooms and a reference library. Again, Cannon was fortunate in the time he arrived at Harvard— the Foxcroft Club was a relatively new venture. Several months after Cannon joined the club, an alumnus writing on the student diet for the *Harvard Graduates' Magazine* praised the club as an interesting experiment, "serving as a useful means of aiding the needy student without loss of self-respect or the harm incident to high pressure scholarship competition as exists today in Cambridge."[30]

Cannon had little difficulty with his program; that, in fact, had been organized for him by Mr. Fiske, his Latin teacher at the Central High School, before he left St. Paul. Fiske, taking into account that Cannon wished to prepare for a career in medicine and having a high regard for his abilities, arranged a challenging program in English rhetoric and composition, French, German, chemistry, botany, and zoology.[31] The course load, while heavy, did not prove difficult. In the beginning, however, Cannon had some trouble in adjusting to taking notes during lectures. At the first lecture he attended, he later reminisced, "I happened to sit beside a rather badly battered and very ponderous member of the football team. In my ignorance I turned to him for advice, asking him what to put down in my notebook. He growled back *sotto voce*, 'Wait till he says something loud, put that down'." "It was not long," Cannon continued, "before I learned that, in spite of such expert testimony, there was a great difference between sound and sense."[32]

Other matters, however, weighed on him. When Cannon came to Cambridge, the first person he sought out following May Newson's advice was Montague Chamberlain, the recorder of the College. Chamberlain, an adept administrator, helped Cannon get a job as a monitor to tide him over and conscientiously instructed him in what he would have to do to renew his scholarship.[33] The need to perform well at all times became the sine qua non of Cannon's existence. "This one of my blue days," he lamented after one of his first midterm exams. "Had examination in German—had failed to arrange exam books in alphabetical order. A poor fool whose removal from the anthropoid apes was not noticeable taunted me with being a freshman. My *feelings* are too easily influenced by sayings of others."[34] The next day he learned that he had worried needlessly; his grade in the examination was an A minus.

Several days later there were new worries and even complaints: "Had exam in chemistry today. Felt not well when I entered the room. Am afraid that I made a very poor showing. Feel tired and discouraged with my work already. I have no society but study books which I do not especially care for. The only thing that keeps me going is the thought that they are foundations for something higher. Never supposed that the absence of sympathy and what little social life I used to have would be missed so much." The next day the litany continued: "Heard a woman's voice in the recorder's office today. The first one I have heard for about two weeks it seems. Begin to realize how one-sided my life here is."[35]

Cannon said little of his despair and loneliness when he wrote home. Instead, as he had in high school, he confided his troubles to May Newson. She, in return, guided him to people she knew living in and around Cambridge who could befriend him; then through a series of long letters sent regularly, she once again became his guide and mentor. "I am delighted that your work is so arranged that you will have free evenings. I have worried somewhat over your driving so," she wrote in answer to one complaint. More especially, she encouraged him to put his shyness aside and aggressively seek other ways of looking at things. "You need to grow taller in other views," she advised him. "Go to the professors. You are not wasting their time if they are true teachers of men . . . In the future when the young shall be looking for help and strength will you feel that they 'waste your time' if they come to you?" Above all, she urged him to take steps to meet needs he had hinted at but did not fully express: "You must not go through your college course without woman's companionship and influence," she bluntly told him. "Men and women are not alike, whatever equality may exist, as there is one glory of the sun [and] another of the stars, so their glories—and they help each other. Now that your evenings are somewhat freer consider it part of your education to seek when you can homes and woman's society. I wish I knew some young ladies in your vicinity but they are there and you must meet them."[36]

May Newson's display of friendly concern came at a time when Cannon needed it and gave him the courage to face his new situation. Although he did not immediately seek the companionship of women, he did get in touch with the families and friends she had recommended to him and even accepted an invitation to spend Thanksgiving with the Jaynes family—relatives of Henry Clay James, one of St. Paul's Harvard alumni who had written in his behalf for scholarship aid. "It was the Thanksgiving," he wrote, "that one might dream of in New England. It was true thankfulness."[37] Although Cannon subsequently went to a number of other holiday festivities, including one before Christmas in Charles Eliot Norton's home, his loneliness increased.[38] Spending Christmas at the Foxcroft Club instead of at home was difficult for him, and he felt keenly the lack of friends and his continuing sense of being an outsider at Harvard.

Brahmin undergraduates did not extend a welcome hand to newcomers from the West and South or to Jews and blacks. Their relations with such students were polite and proper on the surface, but those who did not belong to Harvard by class and descent were made to know they did not belong. Although Cannon said little when in the company of his classmates or other undergraduates, he used the daily themes he wrote for his rhetoric and composition classes to voice his true feelings. Time and again he celebrated in these essays the individualism found on the western frontier or the heroism of those who built and worked for the railroad, as if to assert his identity and the importance of his own family origins.[39] Some of the essays bluntly criticized the values of proper Bostonians. In one, for instance, Cannon, as befit a Minnesotan brought up on tales of the massacres of the harsh Sioux wars of 1862, attacked Bostonians for romanticizing the names and appearance of Indians. "Bah!" he wrote, "such women and

Indians—fools and devils. This is what is called a social fad, is it? This is the way, is it, that cultured Boston stands at an enchanting distance and idealizes the dirtiest, laziest, most undeserving beings in America. Let the degenerate Hub have its baubles."[40] When his English instructor found fault with the essay, Miss Newson sought to mitigate the criticism. "You need not feel humiliated," she wrote Cannon. "Tell the Professor that in the West, Indians are not the *capital* objects of sentiment that they are at present to the benevolent Yankees and that Longfellow would have changed those lines 'In the land of the Dacotahs / In the land of handsome women' if he had ever been introduced to the sisterhood of old Betz. Tell Mrs. Jaynes that story of Indians and she will laugh heartily; she has little patience with Eastern idealization of Poor Lo."[41]

In other essays Cannon vented his anger and sometimes his envy of Brahmin classmates, bitterly attacking their dress, manners, and social clubs. His meticulous description and graphic language left no doubt of his targets or his feelings. "The two came swinging down Brattle Street," he began one such essay, "with their brilliant black shoes, prominently creased trousers, long overcoats flaring from the waist downwards, new yellow gloves and heavy canes, all of the newest and most approved style. Their faces smooth and clearcut looked striking under their shiny silk hats. As the two glided lithely along they met a little mucker who stopped short on seeing them. He stared at them with wide-open eyes and mouth as they approached and when they had passed he turned and watched them swagger on. Then continuing his walk, he muttered, 'Dey oughter git off de eart'.' "[42]

Cannon's perception of social barriers was not the result of imaginary slights. Class distinctions not only existed at Harvard, they were sharply defended as well—especially when Brahmin students and alumni felt that newcomers were making inroads on their privileges and preserves. A few years later when the University planned to move the Foxcroft Club to the aristocratic vicinity known as the Gold Coast, the trustees of the Hasty Pudding Club vigorously protested to the president that the projected building might adversely affect the value of their property. "The neighborhood," they wrote him, "is hardly the most suitable to the class of men who will use the new Club, situated as it would be in the middle of the ground now occupied by the richer class of men. It has been suggested to us that a more suitable site would be on the other side of Cambridge, say to the North of the yard."[43]

∾ ∾ ∾

Despite his alienation Cannon met the academic requirements of his first year with ease. Except for a B in intermediate German, he earned A's in all of his courses. His scholarship was renewed for the following year, and in September 1893 he moved to new lodgings at College House, a dormitory on Massachusetts Avenue across from the Yard near the present site of the Harvard Coop, where his room rent was $60 for the year.[44] Keeping a wary eye on his expenses, he continued to board at the Foxcroft Club. In later years his wife remembered that whenever Cannon passed Randall Hall (the successor to the Foxcroft Club), he would have fits of nostalgia, thinking of the meals he had once calculated to the penny to get the most food for the least money.[45] Lack of funds, however, remained a persistent problem, and to add to his income, Cannon, in addition to monitoring, began to tutor some of his fellow students.

Although the need to take on extracurricular jobs made inroads on his time, Cannon arranged an even more strenuous program of study for his sophomore year. In addition to continuing his course in English composition, he took two more courses in botany and one each in European history, geology, physics, and zoology. Notwithstanding the heavy workload, the quality of Cannon's social life improved as he found and made friends with a number of kindred souls who like himself were outlanders or in some way different from others on campus. None, however, shared his interest in medicine. One of his friends, T. Wayland Vaughan, was a graduate student in geology from Texas; another, a senior, George Grant McCurdy, was from Missouri and interested in paleontology; a third, Louis Gerteis, was a special student in education from Kansas. Except for Harry Bigelow and "Billy" Gray, two pre-law students, none of his friends were members of his class or from New England—although it should be noted that the class of 1896 had a number of very talented and unusual students.[46]

Perhaps the most important reason for the improvement of Cannon's social life was the arrival of his friend Samuel McChord Crothers, who came as a minister to the Cambridge Unitarian Church and preacher to Harvard in 1893. Almost at once the Croth-

Colbert Cannon's family soon after his marriage to Caroline Mower; the children, from left to right, are Ida, Walter, Jennie, and Bernice.

Wilma Denio Cannon, Walter's mother.

Walter's high school graduation picture, 1891.

Cannon with Harvard College friends in Norton's Woods, Cambridge, 1893: from left to right, Louis Gerteis, Cannon, Robert Olds, and T. Wayland Vaughan.

Cornelia James and Walter Cannon at the time of their engagement, 1900.

ers family made their home a refuge for him. Under their influence Cannon began to take advantage of other opportunities that Harvard and Cambridge offered. He increasingly attended the concerts given by the Boston Symphony Orchestra at Sanders Theatre or went to the debates on public issues at the Harvard Union or sampled the rich fare of free evening lectures offered by such Harvard notables as Josiah Royce in philosophy, Edward Channing in American history, Frank Taussig in economics, and Francis G. Peabody in social ethics.[47] Imperceptibly a good deal of the subject matter of the debates and lectures found their way into his English themes, and instead of focusing, as he had the year before, on the inequities he found in campus life, he began to explore a variety of social and political questions ranging from the sanitary problems involved in the burial of the dead to control of crime or the forbearance of Americans. In one long expository paper he even indulged his interest in medicine by exploring some of the contributions of Oliver Wendell Holmes to the development of American thought.[48]

Throughout Cannon's early years at Harvard May Newson continued to send him letters filled with strong support and apt advice. But as time passed, she increasingly dwelt on her own problems—the downward course of her sister's mental illness, the death of her father while serving as United States counsel in Malaga, and the persistent sniping of her colleagues at the high school.[49] At one point during his sophomore year when Cannon thought she was losing interest in him, she wrote, "Just this word to let you know that I do not forget my boy and that you are 'my boy' no matter what other claims may come into your life until the end of time."[50] Miss Newson was as good as her word. Her interest in Cannon never flagged. Near the end of his junior year when she learned that he thought of interrupting his studies to help his sister Bernice, who was having some difficulty at school, she did her best to deflect him. "I heard of your decision," she wrote,

—never mind how— and I first had a talk with your Father to assure myself that I would not be intermeddling too far if I wrote you to refrain from such a step.

My dear boy—if you stop now in your college career you will practically lose what you have set yourself to acquiring in the last three years—the needful *velocity* in your chosen profession. It will be a loss of time for you, particularly at your age. Then, too, the amount of college training acquired so necessary for your chosen work will really be of no benefit in a financial way should you apply for a situation.

. . . If you pardon this on my part, will you write me a short note telling me just how much it is costing you to live and if you find it necessary to call upon your Father for anything? If this question is presumptuous just forget to answer it and remember that though seeming to forget you, you are daily in my thoughts and that I would gladly do anything to help you and yours.[51]

In the end, Miss Newson's letter convinced Cannon to change his mind.

There was no limit to the number of courses a student could take under Eliot's elective system, and after a second very successful year Cannon decided to expand his studies once again. As a junior, in addition to a writing course in English and three advanced courses in zoology, he elected work in Italian, government and law, philosophy, and psychology. During his undergraduate days the philosophy department headed by William James and with the cooperation of George Santayana, G. H. Palmer, and Josiah Royce challenged and enthralled class after class of Harvard men with the importance of the study of thought and mind. During Cannon's first year at Harvard, James in an effort to enhance offerings in psychology invited Hugo Münsterburg, one of the capable young graduates of Wilhelm Wundt's laboratory in Germany, to establish an experimental psychology laboratory in Cambridge. The courses that Cannon took with James and Münsterburg during his junior year so stimulated his interest in philosophy and psychology that at one point he was tempted to drop his plans to study medicine and go on to graduate study with them. When he told James of his inclination, the noted philosopher advised him, "Don't do it, you will be filling your belly with the East wind."[52]

Throughout the year Cannon particularly excelled in his zoology courses. Many of the zoology faculty looked on him as one of their most promising students, and some also began to extend their friendship. Students in the department looked up to him as well. Some time later when Herbert S. Jennings, then a young doctoral candidate, wrote to a friend about his experiences at Harvard, he noted, "I have made a number of very pleasant acquaintances this year—a Mr. Cannon, from Minnesota, and a Mr. Linville from Kansas, especially. Cannon is going into Medicine, with the nervous system as a specialty, and a decided leaning toward sociological matters . . . He is a very fine fellow, whole-souled and genuine—no veneer or falsity, like the easterners, many of them."[53]

Both Jennings and Cannon held each other in high regard for the rest of their lives. When Samuel W. Geiser, a professor of biology at Southern Methodist University, wrote Cannon many years later for some biographical material about Jennings, Cannon nostalgically told him of their relationship as students. It was their custom, he wrote, "to take rather long walks about Cambridge in the late afternoon before dinner. On these walks we would discuss all sorts of questions relating to our studies, the general concept of biology, ideals as motivating agents, personal plans for future work, and such questions in amateur philosophy as young men concern themselves with. These conversations would be broken up with reminiscences of our past lives, humorous stories and incidental remarks on passing events. I do not suppose that Jennings got very much from me, but certainly I had much stimulation from my companionship with him."[54] Cannon in all probability gave as good as he got. At the end of his junior year he received three A pluses in zoology and was offered an invitation to spend the summer in Alexander Agassiz's laboratory in Newport, Rhode Island, as well as a teaching assistantship for the following year. There was other recognition of his talent: earlier that spring, he was one of eight members in the junior class elected to Phi Beta Kappa.[55]

At the beginning of his senior year in September 1895 Cannon moved from his lodgings in College House to Divinity Hall. Although the latter dormitory was originally constructed for theology students, when Cannon entered such students were a minority who often as not kept to themselves in order to avoid contamination from the coarse secularism of law students and other strange types who had invaded their domain.[56] Cannon's move, however, was less an invasion than an attempt to find more time for himself and to concentrate on his studies. His courses were no more numerous or difficult than those he had taken the year before, but he had the added burden of teaching an introductory course in zoology to Radcliffe undergraduates as well as meeting an obligation he had previously undertaken to assist Charles B. Davenport in his research.[57] Despite the pressure, his work went well.

Best of all he began to enjoy a new status: professors who only a year or two before were his teachers began to ask him to their homes or to go out together. "Invited to Professor Royce's," he noted in his diary early in 1896. "Meet there Lloyd Morgan. Spend pleasant evening talking and listening. Prof. Shaler & Morgan swap stories of animals. Profs. James, Thaxter, Mark, Cummings, Ashley & Ladd (Yale) present. Several students invited in after the dinner."[58] Several weeks later there was another indication that some of his professors were beginning to look on him as an equal: "Heard the Symphony tonight with Dr. Parker. We walked back to Cambridge together and had a glorious talk . . . discussing the inadequacy of a mechanical theory of mental life in explaining the most precious experiences of life."[59] Still later, he learned that he had even come to Eliot's attention when the president appointed him an auditor of the Foxcroft Club.[60]

Cannon's major problem that final spring as an undergraduate related to his future education in medicine. Coming to a decision was not easy, and he turned once again as he had so often in the past to May Newson for advice. "As for your work next year," she replied, "I find it extremely difficult to advise you but from all that I can see of the situation I should say remain at Harvard. You avoid debt, your friends are there. There will be opportunity for money-making. You need now the plain facts of your profession, the finer shadings and finishing will come later and may even be done by yourself."[61] Cannon, however, had become used to a climate of excellence and was interested in attending what many considered to be the best school then available. In April of 1896 he wrote to William H. Welch at the Johns Hopkins Medical School about the possibility of obtaining part-time employment in order to support his medical studies there. Unfortunately Welch either could not or would not assure him of such financial assistance, and in the end Cannon took May Newson's advice and enrolled at the Harvard Medical School.[62] If this was a disappointment, it was tempered by a final triumph: on June 12, 1896, Cannon learned that he had graduated summa cum laude. The distinction required fifteen courses with A's; Cannon's final tally was twenty-four.[63]

3 *Reforming Medical Education*

W|HEN CANNON began to think about applying to medical school, contemporary American medical schools, with few exceptions, were distinguished more by the quantity of students who were awarded diplomas than by the quality of the training they received.[1] Of all American medical schools, even those affiliated with universities, only Johns Hopkins demanded that its entering students be "graduates of approved colleges or scientific schools, and have fulfilled the requirements as to a knowledge of French and German, and of Physics, Chemistry and Biology."[2] The entrance requirements represented a new ideal for medical education, but it must be remembered that the school actually began its existence in 1893 with these high standards. The introduction of reforms at Harvard Medical School was a far more difficult matter because a well-entrenched system of proprietary instruction had to be dislodged before it could be replaced. The process, which had begun well before Johns Hopkins was even thought of, was to take half a century.[3]

Dissatisfaction with the quality of instruction offered by the Harvard Medical School began before the Civil War. In 1847, for example, the Boylston Medical School was organized by several Harvard medical graduates and offered aspiring medical students a three-year graded course of instruction in place of the repetitious two-year course then given at Harvard.[4] Despite a first-rate faculty, the School failed several years later because the state legislature declined to empower it to give regular courses and to grant medical degrees. In 1860 William Johnson Walker, anxious to replace the deadening lecture system of medical instruction at Harvard with more laboratory and clinical work, offered the University a sum of $135,000 if it would reform the Medical School. Although the offer was attractive, the Harvard Corporation ultimately refused it because Walker demanded as a condition of the gift an entirely new faculty acceptable to himself.[5] Immediately after the Civil War George Cheyne Shattuck, following a tradition begun by his father, opened a private dispensary adjoining his office on Staniford Street to provide both medical care to the poor and clinical teaching facilities for his students. In due course Shattuck was joined by a group of other young Harvard physicians and organized a formal schedule of clinical conferences and instruction at the dispensary. Notwithstanding the practical value of this development, the University viewed it as a threat to the well-being of the Medical School and, to thwart its growth, forbade members of the medical faculty, especially those collaborating with Shattuck, to engage in formal outside teaching.[6]

Others in the Boston medical community saw the problems and needs of the Medical School in a different light. James Clarke White, a young German-trained adjunct professor of chemistry at the School who sought to establish "standards of scientific medical education comparable to those existing in Germany and Austria," argued in the *Boston Medical and Surgical Journal* just after the Civil War that the time had come for a complete overhaul of the system for training physicians at Harvard.[7] Despite these increasing calls for reform, the University did nothing. Its medical department had a flourishing enrollment and income and by these criteria was deemed a success. Nothing changed until Charles W. Eliot became president of Harvard in 1869. In Eliot, the reformers found a kindred spirit. White, a former classmate, was well aware that Eliot not only shared his views of the inadequacy of the educational program at the Medical School but, equally important, agreed with him as to the growing significance of science in medical education. As a young man Eliot had been appalled by the quality of the students and the poor standard of instruction at the School when he taught chemistry there in 1856. It is not surprising, therefore, that more than a dozen years later Eliot set out to transform Harvard's medical program soon after taking office.[8] It was his first effort to institute reforms at the University.

One of Eliot's initial proposals was to replace the basically repetitious two-year course of lectures and lax examination system with a progressive and graded three-year course of instruction leading to the M.D. degree. Recognizing that the system at the Medical School was essentially buttressed by the fees professors collected from students attending the lectures, Eliot also urged the Harvard Corporation and Board of Overseers to empower the University to collect tuition directly from the students and put their teachers on a regular salary. The president's call for reform immediately placed him at odds with Henry Jacob Bigelow, professor of surgery and one of the powers at the Medical School.[9] Almost simultaneously, the faculty split into two factions, one dedicated to preserving the old ways, the other eager for change. Bigelow and the conservatives who sided with him opposed the reforms for a variety of reasons—some because they perceived the proposed changes as a threat to their power as well as to the lucrative proprietary nature of the School; others because the cry for increased instruction in science challenged their deepest convictions of the ultimate purpose of medical education.[10]

In the months that followed Eliot's appointment, White, on behalf of the reformers, began to lecture the faculty and student body whenever an occasion presented itself on the importance of introducing the scientific method into the curriculum. White's lectures punctuated a period of nearly two years of sharp academic infighting. In January 1871 Dean Calvin Ellis, who had withheld judgment during the previous faculty debates, suddenly voiced his support for one of White's continuing resolutions calling for change, to the amazement of Bigelow who had regarded him as one of his men. The medical dean's calm, measured avowal that the time had come to adopt the president's proposed changes led to resolution of the dispute. After several special meetings held to discuss the proposals, a majority of the medical faculty, including such former Bigelow supporters as Oliver Wendell Holmes, approved Eliot's program.[11]

Although the victory was sweet, the young president recognized that his ultimate goals for the School depended largely on the quality of the teachers he could attract. One of the first new faculty members he tried to recruit was Henry Pickering Bowditch.[12] There were good reasons for Eliot's choice.

✎§ ✎§ ✎§

Bowditch, a scion of one of the most distinguished scientific families in New England,[13] was a graduate of both Harvard College and the Harvard Medical School. From the beginning of his academic career, he had given evidence of a keen interest in science by adding to his collegiate courses a term of special study in chemistry, natural history, and comparative anatomy at the Lawrence Scientific School. In the summer of 1868 soon after he received his M.D. degree, Bowditch, stimulated by Jeffries Wyman with whom he had previously studied comparative anatomy, sailed for Paris to continue his studies in the clinics of Paul Broca, Pierre Louis, and Jean Charcot. He especially hoped to work under the direction of C. E. Brown-Séquard, who had taught for a time at Harvard and who had stirred his imagination with his enthusiastic lectures on the glories of experimental science.[14] When Brown-Séquard failed to establish a laboratory where he could work in Paris, Bowditch turned to study with Claude Bernard and Louis Ranvier, dividing his time equally between training in physiology and microscopy.

Despite the eminence of his teachers, Bowditch was dissatisfied because neither laboratory provided adequate accommodations for visiting students, and he began to think of continuing his studies elsewhere. He was still unsure in his own mind whether it was possible for him to pursue a career exclusively devoted to scientific research. In 1832, when James Jackson, Jr., then studying medicine in Paris, had told his father that he would like to become a medical investigator, the senior Jackson regretfully informed his son that he could not earn a living from medicine in the United States unless he set up practice. Little more than thirty-five years later when Bowditch in similar fashion shared his dreams with his father (a wealthy Boston merchant), he was assured that he would be financially independent and was in fact urged to pursue a career in science.[15] Encouraged by his father's support, Bowditch, at the suggestion of a visiting German physiologist Willy Kühne, decided to leave Paris to work for a term with Max Schulze, a histologist in Bonn, and for an even longer period with the physiologist Carl Ludwig in Leipzig.

Kühne's advice could not have been better. Schulze, through his histologic studies, had already made important contributions to the development of cell theory, while Ludwig directed one of the most stimulating and productive centers of research on the heart, circulation, and kidney in Europe.[16] Bowditch was fortunate in the time he chose to study in Germany. When he arrived in Leipzig he immediately became part of an extraordinary fellowship of young medical scientists who were then working in Ludwig's laboratory. These men, who later became the physiological leaders of their generation, included, among others, Thomas Lauder Brunton, Elie von Cyon, Edward Ray Lankester, Hugo Kronecker, Angelo Mosso, and K. N. Ustimovitch. Bowditch had one other piece of good fortune: he was able to capture Ludwig's attention soon after his arrival by his skill and inventiveness in designing new physiological apparatus—in this instance making an improvement of the kymograph Ludwig had recently invented that allowed for the timing of physiological processes on a moving surface. "It was real fun," he later wrote his family, "to see how delighted the professor was with it." Ludwig promptly inducted Bowditch into the work of the laboratory and gave him a problem in cardiac muscle physiology to investigate. Some months later, with Ludwig's help and encouragement, Bowditch developed two new major physiological concepts. The first demonstrated the *Treppe* effect, stepwise increase in force of contraction of cardiac muscle during successive uniform stimuli; the second, the "all-or-none" law, showed that the strength of contraction was independent of the strength of the stimulus—that is, cardiac muscle will either contract to a maximal limit or not contract at all. These classic studies were later described in the publications of the Leipzig Institute where they received wide attention.[17] For a number of years afterward, the action of the nerves and muscles of the heart continued to be a favorite subject of study for Bowditch.

In December 1869 Eliot wrote to Bowditch in Leipzig and invited him to give a university course of lectures in physiology at Harvard in the second term of the ensuing year. The invitation, although flattering, was not strong enough to tempt the young investigator to give up his research in Ludwig's laboratory and he politely declined. Little more than a year later, Eliot returned with a new offer: this time he invited Bowditch to come back to the Medical School as an assistant professor of physiology—and "to take part in the good work of reforming medical education." The new invitation implied a more promising future and Bowditch accepted.[18] In the autumn of 1871 he returned to Boston, bringing with him physiological apparatus and other materials purchased at his own expense for setting up a new laboratory. He also brought back a young German wife, Selma Knauth, whom he had married five days before sailing. Through marriage and postgraduate training he had forged indissoluble links with Leipzig and German medical science, a circumstance that was to help shape the environment of the physiology laboratories at Harvard Medical School.

Bowditch was not the only one with scientific interest to be added to the medical faculty at this time.[19] In 1871, upon the resignation of John Bacon from the professorship of chemistry, Eliot appointed a recent medical graduate, Edward Stickney Wood, as assistant professor, and then promptly sent him off to Europe for additional training. Three other young instructors were also named to positions. Bowditch's lifelong friend, John Collins Warren, received an appointment as instructor in surgery and was assigned a course in surgical pathology. Earlier, Reginald Heber Fitz, who was to demonstrate the practical value of a pathological approach to clinical problems with his work on appendicitis, was appointed instructor in "morbid" or pathological anatomy. The following year, Warren's cousin, Thomas Dwight, who had studied abroad with him, became instructor in comparative anatomy. To accommodate the new medical scientists, the faculty voted to divide the so-called commodious attic at the North Grove Street building into three rooms.[20]

Despite his junior title, Bowditch, armed with Eliot's mandate and imbued by the spirit of scientific research he had absorbed in Ludwig's laboratory, took full charge of instruction in physiology.[21] The teaching method he developed was characteristic of the Leipzig fashion, with elaborate finished lectures and careful detailed demonstrations. Putting all of his enthusiasm, vigor, and interest into his exposition, Bowditch stimulated some medical students to search out the original literature mentioned in their textbooks and, on occasion, even persuaded a few to undertake research projects in the small laboratory he had set up in the two attic rooms assigned for his use. Frederick Ellis, who was one of Bowditch's students in 1877, in speaking of his laboratory experiences later recalled that the class was divided into squads "which were summoned to the laboratory twice during the first year. I remember that on the first occasion that I enjoyed this privilege Garland showed us how to make the classic nerve-muscle preparation from the frog's leg, and that on my second visit Bowditch was on hand to initiate us into the mysteries of graphic registration on the smoked drum."[22]

Others who visited the North Grove Street building at the

time were not impressed by the physiology students, the quality of their work, or the laboratories that Bowditch had organized. A. B. Palmer, who taught at both Bowdoin and Michigan medical schools (and was a spokesman for the "old" rather than the "new" medicine), was particularly critical: "The interest taken in the Physiology Laboratory there, and the number of students at work in it—the condition and working order of the apparatus, &c. disappointed me decidedly . . . I observed particularly the appearance of the students—their general 'Style' and interest in their work, and if there is anything in the physiognomy and appearances the Students here at Bowdoin in our Med School are of a higher type and much more mature class of men, and both here and at the U. of Mich. there are more interest, zeal and sharp work than at the Harvard School."[23]

Although it is true that Harvard students did little physiological experimentation and were essentially taught by didactic lecture and demonstration, the laboratory enterprise begun by Bowditch was considerably more than Palmer had observed or Ellis remembered. By the mid-1870s, although still modest in size, Bowditch's attic domain had become a center of experimental research for a small but dedicated group of advanced workers in a variety of medical disciplines.[24] Thomas Morgan Rotch, as a postdoctoral project, engaged in an investigation of the absence of resonance on percussion as diagnostic of pericardial effusion. Two young instructors, James Jackson Putnam in the department of nervous diseases and William James in the anatomy department, explored the effects of electrical stimulation of the cerebral cortex. George M. Garland, first as a student and then as one of Bowditch's earliest laboratory assistants, worked on several physiological problems ranging from the nature of digestion to pharyngeal respiration in lower animals.[25]

Bowditch himself continued to design and produce a number of instruments useful in physiological research including, among others, a new apparatus for artificial respiration and a significant modification of the plethysmograph invented by his friend Angelo Mosso to measure the changes of the volume of various organs during the course of laboratory experiments. In addition, Bowditch, sometimes alone and sometimes in collaboration with advanced workers such as Charles Sedgwick Minot, continued the investigations of cardiac and circulatory physiology he had begun in Ludwig's laboratory by examining such problems as the spontaneous rhythmicity of the apex of the heart and the influence of anesthetics on vasomotor centers. At other times he departed from strictly physiological investigations and instituted studies of a medical-social nature. One of these was begun in 1875 when, perturbed like others of his generation by assertions from social commentators of the increasing physical inferiority of American-born children (especially girls), he initiated a systematic study of the growth of Boston school children.[26]

At no time, however, did Bowditch direct the laboratory to concentrate on any specific physiological problem, unlike Michael Foster in England, for instance, who organized his laboratory at Cambridge University around the central theme of the heart beat. Beginning students as well as advanced workers were encouraged to pursue their own interests and problems. The purpose of such a policy was perhaps best expressed in Bowditch's foreword to a volume of the first group of research papers published by various investigators who had worked in the laboratory. The papers, Bowditch wrote, were presented "not from any exaggerated idea of their value and importance, but with the hope that by calling attention to the facilities offered in the laboratory for original research, a greater number of workers may be encouraged to attempt the investigation of the many physiological problems now pressing for solution."[27]

Although the physiology department under Bowditch strengthened the trend toward experimental medicine at Harvard, it was only one of several activities in the direction of research at the School. In the third partitioned attic room, for instance, Dwight initiated a series of notable frozen cross-sections of a child and gave special attention to the anatomy of the skeleton of the joints. Under Wood's direction the chemistry department began work on the nature of drinking water supplied to some of the towns surrounding Boston. Together, these investigations had an impact that transcended their value as contributions to medical knowledge. In time they became potent factors in the effort to dislodge the Medical School from its inadequate quarters at North Grove Street.[28]

› › ›

When Eliot proposed his innovations in medical education, the opposing faction predicted that student enrollment, then the chief measure of a medical school's success, would decline at Harvard. At least, this is what Bigelow and his allies expected. To their surprise, however, enrollment increased after the first few years. It soon became apparent that the facilities on North Grove Street were rapidly becoming obsolete and that the overcrowded, antiquated premises would no longer serve the School's needs. In 1874, only three years after Eliot's reforms had been adopted, a large civic meeting was held to apprise public-spirited citizens and influential physicians of the Medical School's need for a new physical plant.[29] Following the meeting, Eliot, ever the superb organizer, appointed a steering committee to develop the project. The so-called Committee of Seven included, in addition to Eliot, two Bostonian philanthropists, George Higginson and Martin Brimmer, as well as four staunch supporters on the medical faculty— J. Collins Warren, James C. White, William L. Richardson, and Henry P. Bowditch.[30]

In December 1883, after nine years of fund-raising and planning, the Medical School opened the doors of its new building on the corner of Boylston and Exeter Streets in Boston's Back Bay.[31] The structure at first sight appeared to provide a firm and long-lasting architectural base for the improvements Eliot had introduced. The space allotted to laboratories awed visitors. The physiology department, for example, which had occupied two small attic rooms in the old building, was allocated more than a quarter of the space of the entire second floor in the new one. The neat rows of work tables and benches, the huge glass-enclosed double cases containing intricate physiological apparatus, and even the gallery that ringed the spacious general room lent a special aura to the scientific enterprise and gave promise of meeting the needs of physiological investigation far into the future.[32] As if to emphasize the increasing role of science in medical education, the president named Bowditch to succeed the ailing Calvin Ellis as dean and to supervise the move of the Medical School to Boylston Street.

By 1883 Bowditch had become a major force in the Boston medical and scientific community. Everyone who came in close contact with him was impressed by his stately appearance, sure judgment, and earnest devotion to his profession. In the faculty room of the Medical School, his counsel had become recognized as indispensable, and from first to last, when he rose to speak, he was listened to with respectful attention. Still, Bowditch did not accept his appointment as dean without some reservations. Little more than a decade earlier he had joined the faculty to teach medical students and do physiological research; now, at the height of his career, he was asked by the president to take on new responsibilities as an administrator as well. There is no evidence that Bowditch anguished about making a decision; the same sense of public obligation that had sent him as a youth to serve in the Union Army during the Civil War led him to accept the appointment as dean. Throughout the next decade he helped to direct the progress of the Medical School through a period of ever-increasing growth.[33]

Although the anticipated conflict between scientific study and administrative activities troubled Bowditch, it actually interfered little at first with his conduct of the department, the level of his research, or the work of the physiology laboratory. The policies that guided the laboratory from its inception continued; indeed, the expanded facilities in the new building attracted a larger and even more diverse group of young investigators. One was Harold C. Ernst, then taking graduate courses and doing hospital service, whose interest in the new field of bacteriology prompted Bowditch to give him a place to conduct some of his early experiments. Another newcomer, G. Stanley Hall, a university lecturer in English, was encouraged to pursue his psychological experiments on the optical illusions of motion as well as his investigations of the reaction time and attention of subjects in a hypnotic state. Robert L. Lovett, a young surgeon, was put to work on problems in experimental pharmacology. In sum, the physiology laboratory carried on as the prime center for medical research in the School.[34]

As was his custom, Bowditch continued to work in collaboration with both students and younger colleagues. The only manifest change was in his interests. Although he pursued his studies on the growth of children and kept on inventing and modifying physiological apparatus, the problems that now absorbed him were those dealing with the physiology of the senses and the nervous system.[35] Nevertheless, his greatest achievements were not singular physiological discoveries but rather the establishment of standards and his stimulation of several generations of students and advanced workers to engage in scientific research. From 1883 to 1889 investigators in the physiological laboratories published twenty-three papers.

Bowditch's success as dean of the Medical School and director of the physiological laboratories in time exacted a price. By the end of the 1880s he had become less a working physiologist and more a statesman of science. Not only did his old friend Michael Foster enlist him to serve as American editor of the newly founded English *Journal of Physiology*, but also the *Boston Medical and Surgical Journal* depended on him to report regularly on the progress of physiology on both sides of the Atlantic. With the rise of physiology as a distinct new discipline, he joined with H. Newell Martin and S. Weir Mitchell in 1887 to help found the American Physiological Society. The following year, he collaborated with numerous friends in England, America, and Europe to organize the first International Physiological Congress.[36] By the early 1890s it had become plain that Bowditch needed the help of a vigorous full-time associate if the physiology department and the laboratories at Harvard were to develop further as a productive unit of its Medical School.[37]

When Bowditch stepped down as dean in 1893, the Medical School was preparing to introduce even more vital innovations than those that prompted the move to Boylston Street. Some of the changes appeared in the early years of the decade and signaled the increasing thrust of scientific training in the curriculum. In the 1892–93 academic year—Bowditch's last year in the deanship— the medical course was lengthened to four years, a policy that had been under consideration for some time.[38] As if to ensure the widening of the base of scientific instruction, it was proposed that salaries for full-time preclinical teachers be raised to correspond with those prevailing in the Faculty of Arts and Sciences.[39] In another effort to further strengthen the School the medical faculty brought in William T. Councilman from Johns Hopkins as professor of pathological anatomy and William H. Howell from Michigan as associate professor of physiology. Still, when the Johns Hopkins Medical School opened its doors in the fall of 1893, Harvard, despite its changes and promise, stood second to the new school.

In large part, the success of the Johns Hopkins Medical School was the result of the prescience of John Shaw Billings, the remarkable planner of both the medical school and the hospital, which had opened four-and-a-half years earlier. Unlike most medical administrators of the time, Billings saw the medical school and the hospital as a single unit with a double function—to advance science and increase knowledge, as well as to teach the best methods of curing and caring for the sick.[40] Perhaps Billings's most important contribution was the faculty that he helped to select and recruit. At the time of its opening the medical faculty at Hopkins included not only a large number of notable practitioners led by the eminent William Osler but a host of able investigators as well. Some of them, like William Welch in pathology and William Halsted in surgery, were already on the scene; others were called from positions elsewhere, such as Franklin P. Mall, who relinquished his post at Chicago to direct the department of anatomy, and William H. Howell, who left his associate professorship at Harvard to head the physiology department.[41] The character of this extraordinary faculty in turn determined the nature of the student body. When Welch proposed stringent requirements for admission to the school, they were almost immediately approved by the faculty, leading Osler to remark: "Welch, it is lucky that we get in as professors; we never could enter as students." The new requirements led to the selection of a small but elect student body that was national rather than local in make-up and, equally important, stood in an almost one-to-one ratio with the faculty.[42]

The differences between Hopkins and even the top rank of other medical schools were almost immediately apparent. In Harvard's case, for example, there was no university hospital and therefore no control over clinical material; as a result its students were dependent on clinical facilities supplied in large part by the Massachusetts General Hospital and by the Boston City Hospital— a circumstance that made it necessary for Harvard to limit its calls to men with appointments at these hospitals for its clinical faculty.[43] In 1893 Harvard still had no stringent rules for admission and, unlike Hopkins, did not yet require a bachelor's degree. It is true that Harvard had its share of able investigators, but overall the School lacked an élan of scientific research. Certainly, its scientific vigor and productivity were not comparable to what was taking place at Hopkins—even in the case of the physiological laboratory, which had provided research opportunities only for a relative handful of advanced workers and, at best, had introduced medical students to the prospects of scientific research.

৵৶ ৵৶ ৵৶

In the spring of 1893 the physiology department at Harvard received the startling news that Howell was resigning his post to become professor of physiology at Johns Hopkins. Without doubt Howell's resignation (after only a year) created a dilemma. There were simply few men in the United States at that time who had both the medical and scientific training to meet Harvard's growing needs in physiological instruction and investigation. After casting about for several months, Bowditch by good fortune settled on William Townsend Porter, a young and energetic physiological investigator at the St. Louis Medical College (later the Washington University Medical School) as a replacement.[44]

In many ways Porter's curriculum vitae appeared to mirror certain aspects of Bowditch's training and research interests. Like Bowditch, Porter, after graduation from medical school, had sought special training in a number of German laboratories and institutes in histology as well as in respiration and cardiovascular physiology.[45] Porter's investigations in cardiovascular physiology were especially noteworthy. A year earlier he had created a stir in German physiological circles with a small but elegant series of cardiovascular investigations ranging from research on the filling of the heart—a study of the results of differences of pressure between the great veins, atria, and ventricles—to an examination of the results of ligation of the coronary arteries. The latter study was especially impressive. Prior to Porter's investigation only a handful of studies had been published on the effects of coronary occlusion on ventricular function, and most were at variance with one another. Ultimately, from a masterful survey of the existing literature on the subject as well as his own exhaustive research, Porter was able to conclude that the ligation of a small coronary artery did not lead to standstill of the heart but that tying off of large arteries, particularly on the left side of the heart, led to a decrease in ventricular pressure and then standstill of both ventricles followed by ventricular fibrillation. Porter's paper ended a century and a half of controversy on the effects of coronary ligation on ventricular function; it also suggested that the coronary arteries were end arteries.[46]

Apart from Porter's cardiovascular research, perhaps the most attractive aspect of his curriculum vitae was the broad range of his interests.[47] Bowditch once again found an unusual congruence between Porter's concerns and his own. Like Bowditch, Porter was intrigued by problems of growth and as early as 1891 had instituted a study of children in St. Louis public schools to ascertain whether there was a relationship between body size and apparent ability in school work.[48] Equally important was Porter's expertise with the newer techniques and apparatus of physiologic research and his conviction that laboratory instruction was the key to introducing science into the medical curriculum. Actually, one of the prospects that persuaded Porter to leave St. Louis for Boston was Bowditch's promise that he would be given the opportunity to establish more extensive and modern laboratory instruction than had previously existed.

When Porter arrived at Harvard in the fall of 1893, he was met by a series of educational challenges. Athough he found the dissecting room and the chemical laboratory in the Medical School to be first-rate, other matters were not as he had anticipated. He discovered to his chagrin that all first-year subjects were taught in parallel fashion and, worse, that the course in physiology was altogether textbook and talk. In place of regular laboratory instruction, there was a single exercise on the frog and, from time to time, a demonstration, the details of which not many students could see. The net result was student boredom. Most of the men postponed devoting any time to the course until six weeks before the final examination at which time they bought stenographic notes of Bowditch's lectures, crammed for the exam, and, with a few exceptions, passed.[49]

Porter wanted to take charge of the course but realized that, in deference to Bowditch who had signaled his retirement by 1900, he would have to proceed slowly. Thus the centerpiece in physiological instruction continued to be Bowditch's didactic lectures, but Porter gradually increased the number of demonstrations accompanying each lecture. Furthermore, he suggested to Bowditch that students be permitted to perform a series of experiments themselves. Despite the attractiveness of this scheme, it appeared to be impractical because of the time and cost involved in securing the apparatus necessary for such instruction. For example, one of the major instruments needed for physiological experiments was the kymograph. At this time kymographs, which were made by hand in Leipzig, cost more than $200; shipment to America took approximately six months. Even if first-year students were to work in pairs, the laboratory would still need at least one hundred kymographs—an expense well beyond what the department or the School could afford. To circumvent this problem, Porter, who like Bowditch had a mechanical bent, simplified the design of an older kymograph model in his possession so that it could be inexpensively produced by rapid assembly-line techniques. Initially, he tried to have the kymographs and other needed physiological equipment manufactured by commercial firms. When that effort did not meet with success, Porter, with Bowditch's encouragement, arranged to have the apparatus produced by the various mechanics working in the physiology department.[50] The Harvard apparatus proved to be not only inexpensive but of excellent quality as well, and in a brief period of time it paved the way for Porter to put his various educational plans into operation.

Although Bowditch continued to lecture medical students in his usual manner, Porter introduced them to the experimental method in an optional one-day laboratory exercise. By 1896 Porter was able to offer participating students a laboratory exercise in which they could perform fifteen different experiments on a single pithed frog. The experiments, admirably described in a brief instruction manual which Porter published, were so cleverly arranged that they allowed students to examine a variety of basic problems in muscle physiology as well as a number of questions relating to the organization of the cardiovascular and central nervous systems. For those who wished to continue their work in experimental physiology, an elective course met three afternoons a week in the second semester.[51] By 1898 student laboratory work, although still largely voluntary, had become a regular feature of physiological instruction at Harvard. Encouraged by this success, Porter took his cause before the public in an address to the Society of American Naturalists later that year and urged the necessity of experimentation for all medical students: "The mass of knowledge in every department of medicine is grown so huge as to overwhelm both professors and students," he claimed. "The only refuge lies in the thorough mastery of the scientific method. The medical student must acquire power rather than information. Only thus will he be able to hold a steady course through the baffling winds and cross-currents of the veritable sea of knowledge."[52]

The next year laboratory experiments in physiology, accompanied by a series of stringent practical examinations, became a required course for first-year medical students at Harvard. The new requirement in place, Porter presented the medical faculty with still another pedagogical proposal, which he called "a concentration system." Under this system—already in operation to some extent at Johns Hopkins where it had been introduced by Porter's friend Franklin Mall—students were required to study intensively, for a relatively brief period, each preclinical subject in turn, in the interests of thoroughness and economy of time. Such a system, Porter told the faculty, benefited both the students— who would have some knowledge of the structures of the body before being called on to examine its functions—and preclinical faculty who, under the old system of giving instruction in a series of parallel courses, frequently presented work which the students were unprepared to understand or utilize effectively.[53] By the end of the decade, despite some faculty opposition, all of Porter's pedagogical innovations were accepted by the medical faculty. In a small way, over a period of barely half a dozen years he had worked his own revolution in medical education.

Throughout this time Porter continued to be a very productive investigator, both working alone and directing the many promising advanced students who were attracted to his laboratory.[54] His papers on cardiovascular physiology were especially prized by editors of medical journals. For instance, when W. H. Welch, then preparing the first number of the *Journal of Experimental Medicine*, learned that Porter had a paper containing the results of a new investigation on the effects of ligation of the coronary arteries, he wrote to Bowditch and solicited the paper for his new journal. When Porter later sent the article, accompanied by a second one describing a new method for the study of the intracardiac pressure curves, Welch enthusiastically replied, "Your articles will be a chief ornament of our first number and I am greatly obliged to you for them."[55] Porter, however, turned out to be a demanding contributor. When he discovered that the printers had not reproduced the curves in the illustrations for his second article according to his satisfaction, he withdrew the article until Welch agreed to give him control over the reproduction of his illustrations. For Welch, it was worth relinquishing some editorial control in order to have Porter's papers for his journal. "Your articles in my opinion," he declared some time later, "have been the best of the physiological ones which have appeared in the Journal. They have interested me as they will all pathologists, for their bearing on disturbances of the heart in disease, especially on so-called 'heart failure,' is most important."[56]

In Porter's view the incident with Welch was but another

example of a basic problem that he felt had long plagued American physiologists, namely, their dependence on foreign physiological journals or general American medical journals for publication of their research. When Porter first came to Harvard, he approached Bowditch, who was then president of the American Physiological Society, with the idea that the Society publish its own journal. When the Council of the Society rejected the proposal, Porter was not deflected. At ensuing annual meetings he reintroduced the issue time and again without results. In 1897, after four years of debate, Porter finally resolved the question by volunteering to undertake not only the editorship of such a journal but full financial responsibility as well.[57] Porter's offer, which was promptly accepted by the Society, had far-reaching effects, including the unexpected result of establishing Harvard Medical School as the forum for physiological research throughout the United States.[58] When the first volume of the *American Journal of Physiology* appeared in 1898, it contained papers not only by such established investigators as W. H. Howell, L. B. Mendel, Graham Lusk, and R. H. Chittenden but also by some of Porter's advanced co-workers, such as Ida H. Hyde, Frederick H. Pratt, and Frank Watts Bancroft.[59] In addition, it contained two remarkable papers by a second-year medical student, Walter B. Cannon.

4   *Harvard Medical Student*

W|HEN CANNON entered Harvard Medical School in the fall of 1896 the School was in the midst of another wave of new and far-reaching changes as well as difficulties.[1] The Boylston Street building, although recently renovated and wired for electricity, was found to be inadequate to meet a new and unprecedented need for additional space.[2] When the medical course had been lengthened to four years in 1892, many cautious faculty members thought that reform would bring about smaller classes. Two years later those fears proved to be unjustified; instead of a decline, there was a deluge of new matriculants. All too soon, the increases exacerbated an already perceived trend toward larger numbers of men entering without college degrees. In 1895 Harvard gave notice that beginning in 1901 all candidates for admission to its Medical School would be required to have a bachelor's degree.[3] The announcement, another indication of Eliot's mandate to raise the professional schools within the University to graduate status, brought a new flood of students in its wake— many hoping to gain admission before the degree requirement took effect. The increase in enrollment continued throughout Cannon's student days[4] and exacerbated many of the difficulties associated with the crowded conditions of the Boylston Street School.

When Cannon began his first year, there were only three members on the staff of the physiology department: Bowditch, Porter, and F. S. Locke, who served as an instructor.[5] Cannon later recalled that he did not receive a warm welcome when he entered the physiology laboratory in the Boylston Street building. "There," he remembered, "I was met by Frank Foley, the laboratory boy who informed me that students were not allowed in the laboratory and that I had better get out."[6] Cannon had little time to be bothered by the affront, however, because a full schedule of courses kept him occupied between the hours of nine and six every day. What other time he had at his disposal was spent in bicycling back and forth from his room at the Foxcroft Club in Cambridge to Boston's Back Bay and in studying. Now and then the routine was broken by a special occasion. "Attended celebration of 50th anniversary of discovery of ether," he noted in his dairy on October 16, 1896:

> Heard Drs. McBurney (Chas), Tiffany (Johns Hopkins), S. Weir Mitchell, Warren, Davis, a witness of 1st operation, Cheever and others. A most inspiring meeting, every speaker gave the impression of there being much in medical practice besides the practice alone.
> Tiffany gave a beautiful talk—likening medical work to Jacob's struggle with the angel. Don't let it go and in the end it will bless you.
> Dr. McBurney said two things in world most beautiful to watch, youth and convalescence. You are youth—may you see convalescence.
> Students loudly applauded Cheever & Mitchell.[7]

The occasion was indeed a momentous one, because it was the first of what were later to become annual celebrations of Ether Day at the Massachusetts General Hospital.[8] Cannon's diary entry, however, is also remarkable for its omissions. Curiously, he made no note of the keynote address by William H. Welch to whom he had written earlier that year about the possibility of entering Johns Hopkins. Nor did he mention witnessing the public demonstration after the speeches, given by Walter Dodd, the chief apothecary and photographer at the hospital, of the new roentgen-ray apparatus that had been recently acquired—a technology that Cannon was soon to use in his physiological research.[9]

Like other first-year students, Cannon soon found that although the lectures for some of the preclinical courses (anatomy, histology, physiology, hygiene, and bacteriology) were often long and boring, the time alloted for work in the dissection room and in the physiology laboratory was all too short. Further, he discovered that the curriculum was so poorly organized that often material in one course was given before he was adequately prepared in another to appreciate the presentation. Thus Porter, who gave well-conceived and profusely illustrated lectures on the physiology of the brain, presented his material before Dwight, the professor of anatomy, had instructed the class on the structure of the brain, leaving Cannon and the rest of the students totally bewildered.[10]

Certain that he could master some of the courses without attending the lectures, Cannon began to seek a more productive way to spend his time.[11] Early in the first semester he and Albert Moser, a second-year student, convinced that it would be more fruitful to do independent research, asked Bowditch for advice regarding a possible project they might engage in together.[12] They could not have come at a better time. Bowditch, impressed by the opportunities presented by the recently discovered roentgen rays, suggested that they use the rays and an opaque contrast medium to test a concept of deglutition that his friends Hugo Kronecker and Samuel Meltzer had developed sixteen years before—namely, that the pressure developed by the muscles of the mouth during the act of swallowing was sufficient to force liquids and semisolids into the stomach without the aid of peristaltic action.

As a first step, Bowditch asked another friend, Ernest Amory Codman, who was already using x-rays in his clinical work, to conduct a preliminary experiment with the students in order to introduce them to the x-ray tube and to alert them to techniques that might be useful in their research.[13] Moser could not attend Codman's demonstration on the date arranged, and as a result the first experiment on deglutition by x-ray was performed by Codman and Cannon. Almost forty years later Cannon described the equipment and the course of the experiment to John F. Fulton, the noted physiologist and medical historian at Yale:

> The early apparatus used in Boston came altogether from Swett and Lewis of Bromfield Street. It was their tubes which we used in the early work by Dr. Codman and by me. They were trifling affairs compared with modern tubes and fairly soon became useless because of a hole burned through the very thin anode. I was not at any time associated with Walter Dodd. Dr. Amory Codman, however, brought a tube, a large secondary coil and an interrupter to the Medical School early in December, 1896. The apparatus was set up in the small prosector's room in the Anatomy Department of the Medical School at the corner of Boylston and Exeter Streets. It was thought best to try first a small dog as a subject, and I was

commissioned to get a card of globular pearl buttons for the dog to swallow. Dr. Dwight, Professor of Anatomy, and Dr. Bowditch, Dr. Codman and I were the only witnesses. We placed a fluorescent screen over the dog's esophagus, and with the greenish light of the tube showing below we watched the glow on the fluorescent surface. Everyone was keyed up with tense excitement. It was my function to place the pearl button as far back as possible in the dog's throat so that he would swallow it. Nothing was seen! As intensity of our interest increased someone exploded: "Button, button, who's got the button?" We all broke out in a sort of hysterical laughter.[14]

Although Codman had been warned as early as November 21, 1896, by Elihu Thomson at the General Electric Company about the dangers of x-ray irradiation, he apparently did not think it important enough to pass on the information to Bowditch or Cannon. Thomson's warnings were subsequently printed in the *Boston Medical and Surgical Journal* on December 10, 1896, and while they must have been known to Cannon, he, too, did not appear to credit them. He did not try to protect himself from the rays until the following spring when he began to surround the tube with some sort of protective metal box.[15]

On December 9, 1896, using the technique Codman had demonstrated, Cannon and Moser recorded their first experiment: "Dog. Fluoroscope lengthwise over body, pearl button clearly visible above diaphragm. Movement regular."[16] The next Monday, December 14, they repeated the experiment, this time using a rooster whose neck was kept straight by fastening the head and body in a fixed position. The pearl button descended only half-way down the esophagus—a condition they ascribed to the rooster's head being too far back. Two days later they administered radio-opaque bismuth subnitrate in a gelatin capsule to a frog. When the swallowed capsule was dissolved, Cannon noted that two dark patches were formed in the stomach. The following day when the young investigators opened the frog, they found that the stomach was full of bismuth and "that a mass stretched along the first part of the intestine." Encouraged by their findings, they gave two gelatin capsules with bismuth subnitrate to a dog. This time they observed that a dark rounded area was produced as a stomach shadow.

Cannon and Moser next procured a goose and made it a box and cover which was arranged so that the long neck was held in place to present a satisfactorily extended esophagus to the fluoroscopic screen. When the American Physiological Society held its ninth annual meeting in Boston on December 29, Bowditch, after presentation of the first day's papers, invited members of the society into his laboratory. There, in a darkened room beneath the lecture hall, Cannon used the goose that he and Moser had previously procured to show the visitors the phenomenon of deglutition by x-ray. It was the first public demonstration of movements of the alimentary canal by means of x-ray in the conscious animal. Unfortunately, there is no record of the discussion that followed; Meltzer was present and, given his sharp tongue, one can imagine what might have been said. Although Cannon's demonstration did not essentially contravene his and Kronecker's concept of deglutition, it is hard to believe that Meltzer would have let the occasion pass without some comment. Forty years later on the anniversary of the occasion, when Cannon wrote the secretary of the American Physiological Society to ask if there was an account of the experiment in the society minutes, he was disappointed to learn that there was no mention of the event. All that remained was a note that Bowditch had invited the members to visit his laboratory.[17]

On January 9, 1897, Moser and Cannon began a new series of experiments designed to extend their preliminary observations. This time they fed their experimental goose a variety of foods mixed with bismuth subnitrate, varying the consistency from a rather dry, stiff mass to a very soft, mushy mixture. Further, they became more quantitative in their observations, marking the fluorescent screen they had placed over the goose's neck into equal divisions of two centimeters to enable them to time more accurately the rate of descent of the various food mixtures. During a period of little more than two months from January 9 to March 11, in fifteen separate sessions the young investigators made more than 130 observations of the process of deglutition in the goose (and in one session, a horse) and came to a preliminary conclusion that the rate of descent depended on the consistency of the food mixture—ranging from regular movement with a slow descent toward the cardiac sphincter of the stomach when the food was solid and dry to a shooting of liquids directly into the stomach.

As the research continued, Cannon began to read the extensive French and German literature of deglutition and interleaved abstracts of what he had read with notes that he kept of the experiments. Early in April the goose they were using died, and Cannon and Moser began to use a cat in their research. From the beginning the animal appeared to be well suited for their experiments. Some weeks later they received an unexpected reward. "Cat not anesthetized," Cannon noted, on April 23, 1897:

Tied so head free to move up and down between bars for 2–3 cm. Board laid flat. Cat fed about 10:15 A.M. w. bread soaked in warm water. Cat had received no food since morning of day previous, so readily swallowed the food. With the bread was given capsule of Bi subnitrate. This broke up soon after introduction and by 11:15 was spread out in the stomach. Massage however showed that the Bi. was in lumps. Another capsule was now introduced and it soon spread so that stomach was outlined so:

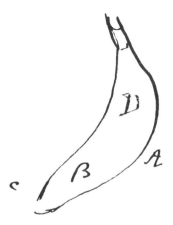

    On returning from large room and turning on rays about 11:40 I noticed that a constriction seemed to start at A making a clear line there and forcing a black round mass into the region of B. The constriction passed downward from A to C but as the pylorus did not give way the contents of the stomach at B were forced back thro' the constricted region into the larger part D. As soon as the constriction had passed from A to C it began again at A and the food was thus squirted through the narrow orifice caused by the constriction. This process continued a number of times, the food in region D apparently not involved at all in the movement.
    The animal was now left for a few moments (c10 min). On returning and turning on the rays the movement of the stomach was seen to be going on as before, only some of the food had been forced through the pylorus and could be seen in the windings of the small intestine.

The peristaltic waves that Cannon and Moser clearly saw in the stomach were the first such observations as seen by x-ray in the unanesthetized mammal. Bowditch was so impressed with the observations of the young investigators that although their research was still far from complete, he asked Porter to present an account of their results at a meeting of the American Physiological Society to be held that May in Washington, D.C. A month later a summary of Cannon and Moser's observations appeared in *Science* as well.[18] "The account of work done in the Harvard laboratory which was published June 11, 1897," Cannon wrote years later, "was the first record of the use of a heavy salt mixed with food— the method now employed—to render visible by means of roentgen rays the movements of the alimentary tract and the effect of these movements on the contents."[19]

⁝ ⁝ ⁝

During the late summer and fall of 1897 Cannon and Moser continued their investigation of deglutition in the cat, shifting on occasion to making observations on a dog and in one instance on a seven-year-old girl. Subsequently, they concluded that deglutition largely depended on the animal as well as on the consistency of the food used in their experiments. In the fowl, they observed, there was a slow peristaltic passage of food without regard to consistency, whereas in the cat such movement although peristaltic was slightly faster. In the dog they noted other variations— namely, that food was propelled rapidly in the upper esophagus but descended more slowly below that point. In man they found that solid and semisolid foods descended by peristalsis throughout the esophagus, although fluids (as Meltzer had previously observed) passed rapidly to the stomach. Indeed, there were few contradictions between the observations of Cannon and Moser and those of Kronecker and Meltzer except that the younger men used a wider variety of experimental animals in their research, emphasized different matters, and, perhaps most significantly, employed a method that allowed them to make observations that could be more easily equated with the normal process of deglutition than any method used previously.[20]

In December, a year after Cannon and Moser had begun their research, Porter presented a summary of their completed work at the annual meeting of the American Physiological Society.[21] This time there was an added bonus for the audience: in addition to presenting Cannon and Moser's work, Porter used the occasion to tell about his own research on the use of x-rays for the study of the pattern of blood flow at the root of the aorta. The techniques he described were clearly an early and crude form of contemporary aortography.[22]

Although the substance of the medical course during the first year did not prove difficult for Cannon, the extra work he had undertaken presented a major problem—he had no time left for outside employment. On January 1, 1897, he noted in his diary the extent of that burden: "The most miserable New Year's day I have spent. Learn in morning that the freshman scholarship at the Medical School is not awarded to me. The outlook of giving up my interesting researches and struggling for existence at the Medical School by means of work that kills—is my *Happy* New Year." Several days later the gloom lifted when the secretary of the Medical School informed Cannon that the faculty had granted him the David Williams Cheever scholarship.[23] Traditional Boston philanthropy had come to his rescue, and in the months that followed he was able to continue his studies and research without undue strain.

Although Cannon enjoyed the opportunity to engage in research, not all his experiences as a medical student were so felicitous. As he and his fellow students proceeded through their preclinical courses they became increasingly critical of the curriculum and its organization. Their criticism was not an isolated phenomenon; complaints about the substance of the medical course and the nature of instruction pervaded the entire student body. The level of concern grew to such an extent that in 1898 a faculty committee on education organized special student committees to make a detailed examination of the quality of the courses given at the Medical School.[24] In no instance did students spare the School, or for that matter, themselves. The second-year class, for example, was both forceful and fair. Although they had kind words and even praise for some instructors such as Vincent Y. Bowditch and George C. Sears who taught percussion and auscultation, and for William T. Councilman who directed the pathology course, most of their comments on the substance of the second-year courses were negative.[25] They complained that the methods of instruction in anatomy by didactic lectures and demonstration were barely adequate to meet their needs. The teaching in clinical chemistry, in particular that portion of the course that dealt with laboratory examination of blood and gastric contents, was deemed to be so poor that a radical reconstruction of the course was demanded. Perhaps the sharpest criticism was leveled against the various clinics that were conducted during the second year: none of these, the students charged, had any relationship to the other courses given that year.[26] Nor were the students lenient with themselves; they had discovered that many in their class were unprepared to do the required work in chemistry and materia medica and as a result asked that the School require organic chemistry as a prerequisite for admission.

Despite the success of his early research, Cannon remained determined to carry out his longstanding ambition to become a medical practitioner.[27] Whenever an opportunity presented itself to gain clinical experience, he grasped it. In December 1897, when May Newson informed him that C. Eugene Riggs, a neuropsychiatrist who was her personal physician, was willing to take him on the following summer as an assistant in his practice as well as to translate French neurological literature, Cannon immediately agreed. Although he did not subsequently take the job, it was not for lack of interest but rather because of added conditions Riggs demanded that extensively modified the original offer.[28]

If Cannon was disappointed in the outcome of his negotiations with Riggs, he did not show it. On the contrary, his interest in becoming a medical practitioner continued to grow, nurtured in large measure by the clinical courses he took during his third year and by his work as an externe in obstetrics. The Medical School required all third-year students to receive instruction in at least one obstetrical case and then to take charge of six patients in labor from the delivery of the baby through the convalescence of the mother. That requirement brought Cannon into the homes of the poor of South and West Boston and exposed him to immigrant nationalities and living conditions he had read about but never seen. Although some student externes were put off by the seemingly strange behavior and habits of the immigrant families they tended, the reverse was true for Cannon. Rather, these experiences fulfilled his expectations of what it would mean to be a practicing physician. The empathy he had for his patients and their families as well as their impact on him can be gleaned from a letter his friend Louise Crothers sent him just before he finished his service in obstetrics:

Dear Walter,

It was such a pleasure to get your letter this morning and to know that your experiences have been just as interesting as I knew they would be. It warmed our hearts to have you say you liked people. Sam and I smiled over the "unreasonably grateful."

As long as you go around among people in your warm-hearted way you will find them grateful but by & by when you see that rich & poor alike are starving for just the quick understanding & sympathy & hopefulness & the sense that life is worth while that you gave them in such full measure it won't seem "unreasonable."

It's very broadminded of you to approve of the old women & to admit that they know anything about babies. I never knew a young doctor before to admit it. The other fact of their unsanitary methods obscured the fact that they really do know something that science didn't invent & can't teach.

What you say about the jewesses made me think of what President Eliot said to me once that the most loving & solicitous parents among the students (a little mixed but you understand) were the jews, that he thought the Hebrew family life as a rule was a tenderer thing than with other nationalities.

It's rather a strange thing to begin your professional life with the deepest & most tremendous experience that comes in our ordinary human life. You get so much beside the medical experience, so much that makes one shudder.

I am afraid the hopeless side, the thought of the stupid husband and the baby launched without help into its probable world & fate of more stupidity & brutality would blind me to the wholesome, good side.

It's hard not to lay undue stress on what are to me the necessities of life, the having enough to eat & wear, the ability to pay one's debts & the knowledge that we can do it next month as well as this, not to speak of the other things that are really so much more the breath of life. The love and all the best.

Well it will be very good to have you back again . . . I am afraid when you come back you'll be tired out. It seems to me you've had your share of cases now & I hope they will continue to slow up & give you a chance to sleep.[29]

Cannon's abiding interest in practicing medicine became particularly manifest when soon after serving as an externe he accepted the chairmanship of the student committee chosen to review and evaluate the third-year clinical curriculum in the Medical School.[30]

There was a remarkable unanimity among third-year students about the courses they liked and found useful and those they believed to be a waste of time. Although Cannon's committee reported approval of the way some courses in pediatrics were taught, little enthusiasm was expressed for the rest of the clinical curriculum. By and large, there were only complaints, ranging from condemnation of the lectures in gynecology "which were word for word from the assistant professor's textbook" to the crush at ward rounds and surgical visits where few students got close to patients or could see what the surgeon was doing. Some of the criticisms were ambivalent: the students praised lectures in obstetrics for being lucid and well prepared, but they also complained that little was taught regarding the conduct of the cases for which they were responsible preparatory to parturition or the treatment of the mother and child after delivery. Over and over, students urged that they be allowed to see more of the common problems of everyday outpatient practice and that they be given the practical experience of following the entire course of a disease at the patient's bedside in the hospital. In light of these criticisms, it is not surprising that one of the recommendations made to upgrade instruction was to increase the workload for third-year students. Only in passing did Cannon's committee call for a reduction of the burden of one of the time-honored requirements of the Medical School: "The eight examinations at the end of the third year," the report complained, "make such a severe ordeal that many a student at the last feels as if he were undergoing autopsy rather than being examined in his right mind."[31] The committee on education was so pleased by the report submitted by Cannon that they accepted it without revision.

Cannon's concern about the teaching of clinical medicine did not spring solely from his desire to become a practicing physician or from his clinical experience as a third-year student. An equally important part was the result of the research he undertook while still working with Moser on deglutition. Some weeks after he and Moser had first observed peristalsis in the stomach during the spring of 1897, Cannon decided to undertake an independent investigation of the nature of the motor activity of the stomach. The problem—far more complex and difficult than deglutition—was one that had engaged the attention of physiologists and physicians in both Europe and America for well over half a century. As late as 1893 Carl A. Ewald, dean of the European gastroenterologists, still complained that no suitable method for determining the motor function of the stomach existed.[32] Three years later Bowditch voiced the same sentiment in stronger language: "Butchers," he told his students at Harvard, "know as much as physiologists about the motions of the stomach."[33]

When Cannon began his investigation of the movements of the stomach during the summer of 1897, the question was still an open one. Armed with the new x-ray technology and more especially with the techniques that he and Moser had utilized to study deglutition, he had—unlike most previous investigators—powerful tools with which to visualize the movements of the stomach under normal conditions. Cannon, however, was not alone: several months earlier two young investigators, Jean-Charles Roux and Victor Balthazard at the Hôpital St. Andral in Paris, had started to work on the same problem and, like Cannon, used x-rays and a mixed meal of solid food and bismuth subnitrate as their method. The young Frenchmen differed from Cannon only in their choice of experimental animals: Cannon initially made his observations solely on the cat, whereas Roux and Balthazard used a frog, a dog, and a human. The results of their experiments, however, were quite similar.[34]

At the start of his research early in July, Cannon discovered that he could not repeat his earlier observations of gastric peristalsis. He was well into the second week of his investigation before the quality of his observations improved and he could once again follow the movements he had seen so clearly several months earlier. In order to make a permanent record of the images, he used sheets of toilet paper to trace the outlines of the stomach that appeared on the fluorescent screen, carefully noting that the peristaltic movements began in the pyloric end and that the shape of the stomach changed dramatically during digestion. Despite his progress, in mid-July Cannon put his research aside and began once more to work with Moser on deglutition. The delay proved to be beneficial. When Cannon resumed his experiments on motions of the stomach in mid-October, he had become more adept in using x-rays and was able to chart with increasing precision the impact of peristaltic movement on food within the stomach. Further, he began to compare more critically his observations with those of other investigators, taking a certain satisfaction in detailing how the defects in the methods used by such pioneer investigators as William Beaumont and Franz Hofmeister had served to create abnormal conditions and actually led physiologists astray in their understanding of the normal motions of the stomach.[35]

From time to time during his experiments Cannon noticed that when some of the cats he was observing became enraged, the peristaltic movements in their stomach halted briefly. At first he gave little thought to the phenomenon; but during an experiment on November 28, 1897, when he saw it again, he pursued it:

> Noticed sev times very distinctly (so absol no doubt) that when cat passed fr quiet breathing into a rage w struggling, the movements stopped entirely and the stomach outlines in pyloric region widened & became smooth as shown in dotted line in A. After about ½ minute the movements started again, first 2 or 3 constrictn rings starting at 1 - then starting at 2, & finally at 3 or at regular starting place . . .
>
> Looked again—movements passing o.k. Cat breathing quietly. Placed handkerchief over cat's mouth & stopped breathing. In a moment cat began to struggle, then the hand was removed & breathing was resumed. An examination now showed the stomach with the same smooth outline as seen in rage. About ½ minute later, constriction took place (at 1) and passed off, then a very slight constriction started at reg starting place and went to end deepening at 1. Another similar one followed and within a minute and a half the waves were passing as before.

Cannon stopped the cat from breathing eight more times with the same result: "Every time . . . movements resumed after the struggle stopped."

Cannon's observations of the effects of rage on the movements of the stomach proved to be one of the high points of his investigation. After several more experiments in early December, he prepared a brief report on the outcome of his research for a meeting of the Boston Society of Medical Sciences. The report was unadorned and straightforward. After describing the nature of the movements of food in various parts of the stomach and especially the changes in the shape of the stomach during digestion, Cannon concluded that the stomach was composed of two distinct physiological parts: a fundus, which served as an active reservoir of food where some digestion of sugars and starches took place, and the pyloric region, where most of the motor activity of the stomach occurred. He saved for the last the observations he had made on

November 28 and stressed that the cessation of movement he had seen was probably due to nervous influences.[36] When he later published a fuller account of his experiments in the *American Journal of Physiology*, he expanded on these last comments: "It has long been common knowledge," he wrote, "that violent emotions interfere with the digestive process, but that the gastric motor activities should manifest such extreme sensitiveness to nervous conditions is surprising."[37]

One aspect of Cannon's investigation that he neglected to mention in his papers was to bear directly on his future research. When he began his study on the motions of the stomach, his experimental subject was the cat. In December 1897 as his research drew to a close, Cannon extended his observations in one experiment to a twelve-year-old boy named Fred Bryant.[38] Although Cannon did not subsequently see the stomach movements he expected, the experiment nonetheless proved to be important because of the assistance of Francis Williams, one of the pioneer roentgenologists in Boston. Williams, then attached to the outpatient department at the Boston City Hospital, was a forward-looking physician dedicated to applying the latest advances in science to solving difficult clinical problems. For instance, it was Williams who initiated bacterial examinations of patients at the City Hospital. Later, he was one of the first physicians in Boston to use antitoxin in the treatment of diphtheria. In 1898 some time after the discovery of x-ray, he began to investigate its use as a tool for diagnosis of various thoracic lesions and as a therapeutic agent.[39] Williams was impressed with the care that Cannon had exhibited with Fred Bryant and decided to recruit him to assist in a study requiring the use of human subjects in an x-ray examination of three separate problems relating to the stomach: the differences in the position of the stomach in the standing and prone positions; the movement of the stomach during respiration; and the changes in the shape of the stomach during digestion. The ultimate purpose of the investigation was perhaps best expressed by Williams: "After the various characteristics belonging to the stomach in health have been established, the presence of abnormal conditions of this organ, such as some cases of malignant disease, will perhaps be more readily recognized than at present. The constant presence of a darkened area in the stomach, for example, may suggest the thickening of its walls due to a malignant disease; some displacements or adhesions may be recognized, as well as hour-glass contractions, or an unusual delay of the digestive process."[40]

Williams's objectives coincided with Cannon's view of the importance of applying physiological research to the solution of clinical problems. The research, however, was not without its own special problems. To get the study underway, Williams persuaded the parents of three small children recuperating from various illnesses at the City Hospital to allow him to use them as subjects in his investigation. It is clear that he was aware of the ethical problem involved in using children in experimental research not only because he asked the parents for their consent but also because before proceeding he was careful to provide a special lead shield to protect those areas not under investigation from x-ray burns and dermatitis. However, neither Williams nor Cannon knew or even suspected the other dangers (besides burns and dermatitis) that might be involved in exposing children to x-rays for prolonged periods of time.[41]

The investigation went smoothly, not the least because Cannon succeeded in keeping the children quiet and preoccupied during the long tedious hours of observation by reading fairy tales to them. A number of the findings were of immediate use to Williams. Observations of the differences in the position of the stomach made between the standing and prone positions proved that the previous estimations of those positions obtained by percussion and sound palpation were far more accurate than estimations obtained by post mortem examination or through the use of an electric bulb introduced into the stomach. Other findings such as the changing shape of the stomach during digestion corroborated similar observations Cannon had previously made on the cat. Perhaps the most unexpected finding, and one that startled Cannon, related to the question of hunger and the presence of food in the stomach. In one experiment, only two hours after being fed one child complained of being "very hungry." When the shape and content of the child's stomach was examined and found to be similar to an observation made directly after the meal, Cannon presciently observed in his notes, "This statement brings direct testimony against the argument of those who hold hunger is a sensation due to an empty stomach and sustains rather the theory that the sensation is a diffuse sensation coming from a general bodily demand for nourishment." A little more than a decade later Cannon tested this observation in a study of the nature of hunger. Following the completion of these experiments, Cannon began to write a paper on the investigation but despite Williams's encouragement never finished it.[42] Two years later Williams himself briefly described the research in his compendious textbook *The Roentgen Rays in Medicine and Surgery.*

Generally Cannon took pride in his research and preparing the results for publication. When the detailed report of his study on the movements of the stomach in the cat was published in the *American Journal of Physiology* in 1898, he promptly sent out un-solicited reprints to well-known physiologists in Europe and America, to his teachers and fellow students, and to his family and friends. The complimentary responses he received delighted him,[43] but the letter he found most gratifying came from one of his benefactors at the Medical School. "It is with particular satis-faction that I received your essay on the movements of the stomach and the note that accompanied it," David W. Cheever wrote Can-non. "I regard the money which I gave for a first year Scholarship in the Medical School as the best investment I ever made. It bears Compound interest to me, in lightening some people's load, and in inciting the earnest student. It is also a permanent investment— and it is all the more gratifying to my pride, as I know that I earned the money.

Your note has induced me to express my personal feelings more than I usually do. And I can only add that I hope you may continue to prosper in your pursuit of Science."[44]

᷐ᷤ   ᷐ᷤ   ᷐ᷤ

Throughout his third year Cannon became increasingly frus trated with his clinical courses. The passivity of his course work contrasted sharply with his experience in the laboratory and even more with the lively and stimulating debates that took place when his friend Harry Bigelow, a third-year student at the Harvard Law School, and other law students discussed their work. The key to their excitement, he discovered, was an innovation that C. C. Langdell had introduced in his teaching at the Law School more than a quarter of a century before. Instead of presenting his stu-dents with ready-made doctrines of law, Langdell assigned actual cases and required students to identify similar cases and analyze them with him and other students until a unifying principle of law emerged. The more Cannon learned about the case method, the more enthusiastic he became about the possibility of adapting it to the study of medicine, and he began to look for an opportunity to demonstrate its feasibility.[45] In December 1899, while taking an advanced course in neurology, he persuaded G. L. Walton, his instructor, to present one of the cases from his private practice as an experiment. Walton printed a sheet with the patient's history and allowed the students a week to study it. The discussion that later ensued made Walton an immediate convert. "In the single experience which I have had with this method," he later explained, "the interest in the subject was lively, and the case was sifted more thoroughly than any other in the course."[46]

In January of his senior year Cannon, encouraged by Walton's reception of the case method, published his proposals in the *Boston Medical and Surgical Journal*, deftly arguing that the method was in no sense a replacement for lectures or section teaching but rather an adjunctive technique that allowed for the correlation of the scientific and clinical aspects of medicine. "With a good leader . . . and the habit of careful thought established among students," the young author advised his readers, "the underlying pathological condition, the disturbed physiology, the therapeutic action of the drugs employed, could constantly be brought forth to give the cases a rational explanation and to teach the students the deeper insight which vision through general principles affords."[47]

The responses to Cannon's article varied. William Osler, then regarded as the dean of clinical instruction in the United States, after thanking Cannon for sending him the article, added, "I have long held that the only possible way of teaching students the subject of medicine is by personal daily contact with cases, which they study not only once or twice, but also follow systematically." George Dock, the professor of medicine at the University of Michigan, was more forthcoming and allowed that he "would establish the method at the first opportunity."[48] Others wrote in the same vein, but none matched the enthusiasm of the faculty at Harvard. James Jackson Putnam immediately adopted the case method for his class and then asked Cannon if he would help him prepare a case book to be used in neurology. Charles Montraville Green, an assistant professor of obstetrics, invited Cannon to visit him to

The Harvard Medical School on Boylston Street, Boston.

Students in newly electrified physiology laboratory.

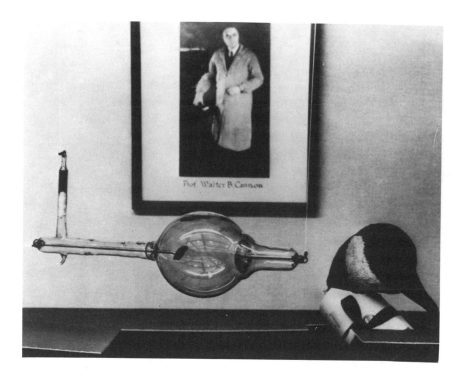

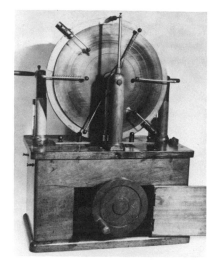

X-ray equipment used by Cannon, and his handwritten notes, including his first experiments on swallowing, December 1896.

discuss the method in detail. Others began to proselytize actively for the case method with colleagues in other medical schools. When Herbert L. Burrell in the department of surgery visited the University of Pennsylvania in February 1900, he made a special effort to discuss the method with one of his friends. "By the bye," he wrote Cannon, "I have just returned from Philadelphia where I had a talk with Dr. J. Wm. White, who is the Professor of Surgery in the University of Pennsylvania, and you I think will be interested in knowing that he put your suggested method into effect at once . . . A little later I am going to ask you to talk this subject over with me as there are certain points that I want to clear up by personal interview."[49]

Early in March Cannon was invited by the Boston Society for Medical Improvement, along with Eliot and Edward H. Bradford, William T. Councilman, Herbert L. Burrell, and Arthur H. Wentworth, to speak at a special meeting organized to consider new methods in medical education. His presentation on the case method was enthusiastically received by many of those present, especially by Richard C. Cabot, who in later years was to become even more closely identified with the case method than Cannon. "There is one point not yet emphasized as much as it should be in regard to this case system," Cabot told the audience, "and that is the *pleasure* of it. The touch with the men is delightful. They answer up in a way I never heard them in any other course, because questions are thrown at them so constantly that they must be wide awake and because they are vitally interested in the story of the case. They want to know how it is coming out. It is the easiest and pleasantest method of teaching I have known anything about."[50]

Not all of those present, however, were quite so eager with their endorsements. Wentworth, although expressing his conviction that the case method of teaching would prove to be of great value, warned that it was no substitute for section teaching, a method about which he had just addressed the meeting. Perhaps the doubts and reservations that existed were best expressed by Bowditch: "I think we have a little uphill work ahead of us," he cautioned. "I am inclined to think that teaching men to think is not an advantage exclusively of the case method or any other method of instruction. It is the object aimed at by all good teachers." "Men," he concluded, "are more important than methods."[51]

Despite the demurrers, the reception at the meeting was a

heady experience for Cannon. Some weeks later Cannon attended trial sessions of the case method that Cabot arranged for his course in clinical medicine at the Massachusetts General Hospital. "The exercises at which these cases are discussed," he later wrote, "have the largest regular attendance of all clinical exercises in this last half of the fourth year. Again and again, I have heard students say, 'Why could we not have had this way before?' "[52]

During his last year in medical school Cannon carried a full slate of clinical courses as well as elective courses in physiology and neurology. When he began the year all the auguries were that he would devote himself to a career as a practicing physician, even though he had already demonstrated talents as a scientific investigator. Those talents had caught the attention of Eliot and were soon to provide Cannon with prospects he had not dreamed were possible. In October 1899 after careful inquiry Eliot appointed Cannon an instructor in zoology in order to meet an emergency that had developed in that department. Throughout the year Cannon gave lectures on the comparative anatomy of vertebrates to both Harvard and Radcliffe undergraduates. The appointment not only helped to reestablish his contact with such exceptional investigators as E. L. Mark, G. H. Parker, and W. E. Castle but also rekindled his interest in biological research. The department was so pleased with Cannon's performance that he was invited to become a full-time instructor in zoology after graduation from medical school.[53]

There were other opportunities as well. Looking forward to changes in departmental instruction, and a sabbatical leave, Porter began to lay the groundwork to recruit Cannon for the physiology department. During the fall of 1899 he carefully broached the subject of an instructorship for Cannon to Eliot:

> Mr. Cannon is a man of unusual capacity for work. He has had already some experience in investigation, both in Prof. Mark's laboratory and here. So far as my observation goes, he is capable of setting problems and carrying them through to a definite conclusion with very little assistance or encouragement. He has, too, a considerable appreciation of workmanship, and understands that an investigation is only well-begun at the stage when most students think it is finished.
> Whether Mr. Cannon is sound on the thesis that the principal business of a scientist is research, I am not quite sure. I may be

somewhat influenced by my strong feeling against dabblers who pursue the medical sciences because they are respectable, or amusing, or are a step towards a clinical position, or something to pay office rent with while patients are slow in coming, or for any other philistine reason. Mr. Cannon has said that he does not care for investigation as a profession, but he may change his mind. It can safely be predicted that with suitable opportunities he would succeed well in clinical investigation. His success in "pure science" would depend, in my opinion, on the spirit in which he approached the work.

On the whole, he seems to me unusually promising.[54]

When Cannon was later made a private promise of such a post, it startled him. Although he was flattered and elated by the offer, he was still not sure in his own mind that he wanted a career as an investigator, or even if he had the ability to take on the work in the physiology course. Councilman, also eager to recruit Cannon to the medical faculty, sought to reassure him about the teaching responsibilities in physiology and offered his personal assistance in case of future need. Making a career choice proved difficult for Cannon. It was not simply a matter of giving up a long-felt need to serve mankind as a physician; the actual decision was complicated by an emotional turmoil that made the winter of his last year in medical school a time of abject misery.

While a senior at Harvard College, Cannon had begun to call upon Cornelia James, then a freshman at Radcliffe. It was not a new friendship; actually, they had known each other since high school days in St. Paul. And perhaps it was this prior acquaintance that helped Cannon, who was essentially shy and reserved, to call on her. Cornelia had admired Cannon ever since the days when he was a postgraduate student at the St. Paul High School. She was pleased with the attention she received and kept her mother apprised of the budding romance. "Walter Cannon had called when I was away," she wrote her family in October 1895, "and Mrs. Howard told me that a young man had called. 'Which one?' I said, as if it might be one of hundreds. 'Oh! the one who comes so often,' she answered, with a significant smile. I nearly fainted on the spot but came to in gales of laughter, so I wish you all to understand that I have a young man and his name is Mr. Cannon."[55]

In the year that followed, almost every letter Cornelia sent

home to St. Paul contained a mention of Walter Cannon as a
companion at lectures and concerts and on walks. The romance
continued during Cannon's early years at the Medical School, and
as it became more serious, Cornelia stopped mentioning his name
in her letters. At the same time, Cannon confessed to his confi-
dantes Louise Crothers and May Newson his awakening interest
in Cornelia James.[56] Despite their growing fondness for one another, the young couple did not become engaged—in part, because
they were not sure they truly loved each other, and in part, because
they had not yet made up their minds about their respective fu-
tures. It was only after a summer visit Cannon made to St. Paul
in 1899 that Cornelia finally intimated that she might love him.[57]

For Cannon, Cornelia's tentative avowal of love became a firm
promise, and he returned to his last year in Medical School convinced that she had agreed to be his bride. Early in the new year
he learned there were no firm promises in love. Cornelia had
changed her mind.[58] Her rejection plunged Cannon into a despair
that numbed his existence. Unable to write to his family, he poured
out his misery to Louise Crothers, who wisely offered solace but
little advice. Nevertheless, despite the conflict of emotions, he
successfully carried on his teaching at the College as well as his
final studies at the Medical School. In one sense Cornelia's rejection allowed him to come to a decision more easily because, in
choosing between his offers, he no longer had to consider the
wishes and needs of the woman he thought was going to be his
wife. Some time in the winter of 1900 Cannon accepted the post
as instructor of physiology for the following year.[59] Only the pain
of Cornelia's refusal remained. Late in April, however, he received
a letter from St. Paul that astonished him. In the months that had
passed, Cornelia discovered that she loved him after all and wondered whether he still loved her. In a moment of anger he wrote
a bitter letter of denial. Two days later he begged her forgiveness
and asked if she would marry him. Cornelia generously agreed.[60]

Shortly thereafter, Cannon, realizing that Cornelia was unaware that he had accepted a post in the physiology dpartment for
the coming year, disclosed that he no longer planned to be a
medical practitioner. "It means, perhaps, so different a life from
what you had thought for me," he wrote her.[61] If Cornelia had
second thoughts, she kept them to herself. A month later Cannon
reported to his bride-to-be that he had successfully completed the
medical course:

I have finished in the Medical School safely, Cornelia. Do you want to know how? My general average in percent for the four years is 88, the man who led the class has 91, so that you must be satisfied with me as seventh man in the class instead of the first man. However, I shall get the honor-degree, and not all get that. I have felt rather safe since last Saturday, for my appointment for next year came then, and I did not much care what further recognition was given me. I put the appointment, "Instructor in Physiology, Harvard University," away, thinking just for a moment that possibly this was the beginning of a career. Who can tell?[62]

5   *Beginning of a Career*

WHEN CANNON entered the physiology laboratory in July 1900, he expected that he would be allowed to spend the summer working on some of his experiments on the gastrointestinal tract. Instead Porter, who was to leave on a European sabbatical early in the fall, began to prepare him to take over various administrative duties in the department. Writing almost daily from his rooms in Cambridge to his bride-to-be then teaching school eighteen hundred miles away in St. Paul, Cannon not only poured out his love but also described in detail some of his early experiences as a member of the physiology department.[1]

Although Cannon's first days of slow and careful learning under Porter's meticulous direction proved trying, he soon discovered that there were advantages as well, not the least of which was the opportunity to help Porter edit the *American Journal of Physiology*. Not only did this work provide Cannon with some needed extra income, but more important, it put him in touch with the newest research in physiology—a circumstance that he found both stimulating and highly suggestive.[2] Instead of brooding, he looked on the bright side and began to plan ahead to the time when he would be doing his own research. He found added incentive in the promise implied by Porter's oft-repeated homily to him, "Succeed this year and your fortune is made."[3] Success came almost at once. At the end of his first month as an instructor Cannon wrote Cornelia with great pleasure of the interest shown by some of his colleagues at the Medical School in his innovative application of the case method to medical education. "Just as I was waiting for the Cambridge car," he told her, "Dr. Cabot appeared and informed me that the whole course of teaching theory and practice of medicine had been rearranged along the lines of the new method and that the young doctors who had attended his exercises for the discussion of printed cases had been appointed to regular positions and would push the system vigorously. Every word he spoke made me happy because I felt you would be glad."[4]

Each day seemed to bring small but meaningful acknowledgments of the value of his early research. The recently published edition of the *American Textbook of Physiology* contained repeated references to Cannon's work under the heading of "Mechanics of Digestion."[5] Or again, while reading proof one day for the Journal, he felt a shock when coming upon the words, "Henceforth Cannon's discoveries must be reckoned with in considering the matter."[6] At times he exulted over compliments paid him by Porter for devising new physiological apparatus or for his well-written reviews of scientific articles. About one such review of an article by Porter, Cannon revealed that Porter had turned to him upon reading it, with a curious look on his face, and remarked, "Cannon, you express me better than I express myself. I wish I had stated the problem as you have stated it here."[7] On another occasion he savored catching Porter in some mistakes: "Dr. Porter has asked me to look over the copy of his new book and twice I have caught him in inconsistencies; for some reason finding errors in the thought of a shrewd open-minded man is a satisfaction."[8]

When Porter left for Europe in mid-September of 1900, Cannon for the first time viewed his immediate future with some apprehension. "Dr. Porter sails for Naples Saturday," he told Cornelia fretfully; "thereafter, I am without counsel, left to edit a Journal, run a laboratory, and manage a class of two hundred men in the new course in physiology."[9] Although he complained that administrative work caused him to be "deviled" a good part of the time, as the days passed Cannon soon developed the necessary organizational skills and became more confident. Before long, he even wondered how he would do as an administrator of a large business. "I rather like to run the machine," he admitted, "and take satisfaction in seeing it go smoothly. It is a real catastrophe to like to do so many things, for fruitless diffusion of energy is so easily the result."[10] In an account of a conference he had with Bowditch about one of his schemes for handling the unusually large number of students in physiology, he boasted that the plan "commended itself to him so that I feel that the threatened trouble from that quarter is allayed." The next day most of his fears seemed to have disappeared: "Matters at the Medical School are settling right," he wrote. "As I learn more how to organize work and keep workers busy, I am finding more time for myself. It seems to me at times incredible that I am there dictating official letters, conferring with students on research work, answering newspaper reporters, reading, studying and writing in a professor's place."[11]

Although some of Cannon's early letters to Cornelia gave the impression that he was the sole junior member in the physiology department, in fact other instructors and assistants were serving with him.[12] One, Allen M. Cleghorn, a graduate of the University of Toronto Medical School, had been an assistant in the department for the past two years. Trained in chemical physiology, he had already given evidence of his promise with an excellent article on the physiological action of extracts of the sympathetic ganglia. Another, Albert P. Mathews, a young Ph.D. also trained in chemical physiology, had been appointed to an instructorship at the same time as Cannon. Both men were far more experienced than Cannon; indeed, Mathews had previously headed the department of physiology at Tufts.[13] Cannon, who lacked advanced training in chemistry, physics, and mathematics, recognized Cleghorn's and Mathews's abilities in these areas and clearly regarded them as rivals. As the year progressed, whenever opportunity presented he measured himself against them in departmental debates. The importance of these encounters for Cannon is revealed in his account of an exchange he had with Mathews one afternoon early in the second term: "After the strenuous work of the morning, a discussion arose between Dr. Mathews and myself—a scientific discussion on electrical changes in living tissues—so that, in spite of its seriousness, it was very good-natured in spirit. Others in the laboratory took sides, and the fight waxed hot and continued thus for nearly two hours. At the end I was nearly voiceless and thoroughly tired out, but Dr. Mathews had agreed to my points."[14] While Cannon's debate with Mathews may in part have been a youthful effort to establish his niche in the department, it was also a measure of his enthusiasm for the work he had undertaken. That enthusiasm allowed him to accept the burden of time-consuming chores without protest and helped harness his energies for the work at hand.

❧ ❧ ❧

Early in November Cannon learned that Porter had changed his plans and was returning to America before the new year. Naples, Porter discovered, did not offer the opportunities for study that he originally anticipated; worse, his daughter had become seriously ill. Bowditch, sincerely concerned for Porter's well-being, urged him to take an extended vacation before coming home; Cannon, for his part, welcomed the prospect of Porter's return. "I should be glad to have him do so," he informed Cornelia, "not because I fear responsibility, but because the routine, which he could help me to bear, is keeping from me the time I should like to have for research and reading in medical subjects."[15] For it was in the laboratory that Cannon found his greatest satisfaction. "We have such jolly times in the laboratory now," he wrote a few weeks later; "new workers are continually appearing so that the rooms have never been so busy and there has never been so much enthusiasm for research . . . Dr. Bowditch joins with the humblest of us in genial good comradeship. It is so good to do work you enjoy." The next day, he continued in the same vein: "You see, there is no boss; each man is supposed to make the best use of his time in doing his own work. It is not 'work,' it is a pleasant strenuous play for which the securing of results is our compensation, while the University provides for our simple living."[16]

Despite the lack of free time and the drudgery of administrative routine, Cannon continued his gastrointestinal studies and was able to work on two additional research projects during his first year as a full-fledged physiologist. The first of these, an effort to measure the effect of sunlight on bacteria, was in part an outgrowth of his earlier work with Davenport on the determination of the direction and rate of movement of organisms induced by light and in part the result of preliminary investigations that investigators had more recently undertaken to test the effect of sunlight on bacterial growth. Some had claimed that this light source had the capability of weakening bacteria in culture media, but other results were equivocal. Niels Finsen, a photobiologist in Copenhagen, to take an example, conducted experiments on a broad spectrum of bacteria, including cholera, diphtheria, typhoid and tubercle bacilli, and claimed sunlight was remarkably effective in either halting their growth or killing them.[17] Cannon was so enthusiastic about the prospects of this new research that he decided to enter the field. When Bowditch and Harold C. Ernst of the bacteriology department endorsed his research plan, he promptly began his investigation.

Cannon kept Cornelia informed almost daily of the progress of his work:

> I have been plunging into German, French and Italian articles, snatching out the heart of them and rushing on. All the preparatory work has been done, all but this final thing of testing the effect of light which has passed through tissues. I fear that others must be on the trail, too—others who live in parts of the country where sunlight is more abundant to try the experiments. If it only will turn out as I hope it may, what a find it will be! And do you know, Cornelia, it all goes back to my sunburn theory again. The previous work on bacteria shows that the effect of sunlight depends on moisture and oxygen; the process apparently is one in which "active oxygen" is produced by sunlight and the active oxygen kills the bacteria—just as I supposed active oxygen to attack the skin in so-called sunburn. Everything seems to be ready for just this next step—and I have the same strange intuition that it is true, that I am on the right track that I had when the case method was interesting me. Now wouldn't it be glorious to find the sunlight we love so much is the good angel we have been shutting out of our lives by smoky cities and dark streets, the roof and four walls and our clothes—letting the evil spring up in the dark corners. Can it be possible? Something tells me over and over again, it *must* be so, it *must* be so.[18]

In this instance, enthusiasm and intuition failed, and after a few months of work Cannon dropped the investigation.

The second research project, an examination of the pathophysiological effects of trauma on intracranial pressure, proved more fruitful. The origin of this latter research lay in the clinical observations of William Norton Bullard, a neurologist at the Boston City Hospital. As early as 1895 Bullard had recognized that some of the symptoms of his patients following cranial injury, particularly the depth of unconsciousness, were related to an increase in intracranial pressure.[19] The cause of such increased pressure, however, was not altogether clear. When some of his cases later came to autopsy, Bullard discovered to his surprise that there was little intracranial hemorrhage or sufficient bone depression to account for the symptoms of increased cerebral tension he had previously observed. Convinced that existing neurological theory did not adequately explain the cause of such pressure, Bullard approached Cannon, who had then just completed his third year as a medical student, and offered him funding if he would undertake an experimental analysis of the problem. Bullard's offer was not unusual for him; a generous man, he often took pleasure in encouraging and aiding promising medical students in their careers.[20]

During the summer of 1899 Cannon began his investigation but soon discovered through correspondence with neurologists engaged in similar research that the problem was far more complex than he originally thought. Throughout the fall of his senior year, whenever time allowed, he attempted to work on it, but without definitive results. The lack of success finally convinced him to put the research aside, and he did not resume work on it until the following year. The delay proved advantageous. In the interim Cannon took an elective course in neurology, which gave him access to patients with cranial injury in local hospitals and allowed him to familiarize himself with the clinical aspects of such cases firsthand. Moreover, he studied the neurological literature and in particular the work of Ernest von Leyden, one of the leading German investigators of the anatomy and physiology of the central nervous system.[21]

Previously von Leyden had reported that intracranial pressure had to rise enough to equal arterial pressure in order to produce death. Pursuing his lead, Cannon found through experiments on anesthetized cats that the rise in intracranial pressure following the moment of cranial injury was not sufficient to check blood flow into the brain or to cause the pressure symptoms he had observed in various clinical cases. It became clear to him that secondary factors, rather than the primary lesion itself, were the key to the development of increased cerebral pressure. To examine these secondary factors experimentally, Cannon took as a model one of Jacques Loeb's experiments with muscle of the frog. Some time earlier Loeb had shown that when muscle was deprived of blood, the lack of oxygen led to chemical changes that increased intracellular osmotic pressure, which in turn induced an uptake of water and a dramatic swelling of the tissue. Loeb's study provided the key necessary for the completion of Cannon's research.[22]

Using anesthetized cats, Cannon postulated that the swelling of the brain that followed a blow to the head was not the result of a filtration of fluid from the capillaries into the intercellular space of the brain, as some neurologists had claimed, but stemmed rather from an interference with the blood supply to the brain. It was such interference, he pointed out, that caused an increased osmotic pressure within the brain tissues and a consequent taking up of water from the surrounding plasma. "The mischief" following cranial injury, he concluded, "arises because the brain is surrounded by a rigid case. Swelling of a part consequently compresses the only compressible portion of the cranial contents—the blood vessels. Thereby new areas are shut out from normal blood supply, and changes now take place in these tissues as well, with the result that water passes into them; thus the swelling spreads until the flow is so greatly excluded from the brain that life is no longer possible."[23] Although these important findings by Cannon attracted the attention of a number of contemporary clinicians, after publication of the paper he did no further research in this field, and his contribution was subsequently forgotten.[24]

ॐ   ॐ   ॐ

Shortly after Porter returned to the department, Cannon revealed to Cornelia that Porter was already talking about next year, "so that my position is apparently assured."[25] Nevertheless, when the physiology course began in the second half of the academic year, some of Cannon's former fears returned. In March 1901 he described several of the problems of the course, not the least of which were the enormous size of the class and the poor quality of the students: "If I could only see the men personally and have time for a good talk with them frequently I am sure I should feel better satisfied, but the big, dead mass of them, so unwieldy and, in part, so very stupid, forbids any such hope. All of the instructors this year have simply taken the tolerant enduring attitude and done their best, with prayer for better times next year."[26]

Nor were the students themselves any better satisfied. Although his early lectures seemed to be well accepted, Cannon soon discovered a ground swell of resentment among the men. At first he thought the resentment was directed against him, and he arranged for Porter to give two or three talks on the heart because, as he told Cornelia, "some of his work on the heart is classic in physiological literature and the students should get the knowledge first hand."[27] Later, much to his relief, he discovered that student disappointment was due to the fact that Bowditch, affectionately esteemed by generations of first-year classes at the Medical School, had given up his lectures in physiology.

Although the protest came to nothing, it reawakened the doubts Cannon had about himself. These doubts were not new; from the beginning of his tenure at the Medical School he wrote Cornelia time and again of the value of research and especially the success that one could find in teaching, as if to reaffirm his faith in the path he had chosen. Typical was a note about the success a friend, Colin C. Stewart, had recently found as an academic physiologist:

> He was Assistant in Physiology at the Medical School three years ago on a salary of $400.00. Two years ago he accepted a position at the College of Physicians and Surgeons in New York City, at a salary of $1000.00. He, like me, had been in the state of chronic penury during his college days, and came to me with the announcement of this huge salary. "Cannon," he gasped, "Cannon, what can I do with it all?" I thought for a moment and then remarked, "Give it up, Stewart, I don't know *what* I could do with all that!" Well, what he did was to marry a very sweet gentle little woman who had been waiting long for him, and they went to New York with that financial outlook. Last year he had $1100.00. Next year he goes to Pennsylvania at $1800.00.[28]

At other times Cannon held out the prospect of joining his research interests with those that Cornelia had in social issues. "*That* is the very centre of life and movement and promise of great things in this day." he wrote her:

> In my time of planning for active practice it was the doctor as a social factor, as a teacher, counsellor, guide rather than as a remedial agent for past delinquencies, that appealed to me. I thought of you by my side caring for these things with me and making my life a greater force than it could ever be, were you not there. And now that it seems to me that I can make better use at the present of my talents by the work of research, I find wonderfully opened to me the possibility of satisfying through your interests the interests which lie so deeply rooted in my own life.[29]

His purpose in writing in this manner may have been calculated in part to prepare his bride for her role as the wife of an investigator, but it may also have served as a device to persuade himself of the correctness of his career course. From time to time, especially when he was worn down with fatigue, Cannon still contemplated the possibility of practicing medicine—a choice his father actively encouraged.

Whatever his doubts, it is evident that Cannon took pride not only in his work but in the department of physiology as well. "The laboratory has had a good many visitors lately," he reported to Cornelia early in April, "bringing evidence that Harvard methods in physiology were having fame abroad. A professor from Leland Stanford spent an entire morning studying our ways, today a representative from Yale was going the rounds. Next year the Harvard plans are to be introduced at the Columbia Medical School in New York."[30] A month later he boasted that the students had asked him for a special lecture on the value of suggestion in medicine, and, in addition, Porter had repeated to him Eliot's statement in a faculty meeting that "he regarded Cannon as a valuable person to hold onto! (Please do not tell this to anybody.)" "These things," he confessed, "have helped to cheer me up a little."[31] On the morning of Cannon's last lecture the men applauded him roundly as he passed from the room. He might have suspected that they were merely following a time-honored custom, but he told Cornelia that he had heard from several sources that the lectures were giving good satisfaction and arousing student interest.[32] A few days later Cannon had even more important news: at a recent faculty meeting where it was voted to reduce positions in the physiology department, he had been chosen over Mathews to stay on for the following year.[33] In assuring Cornelia that he had come through his gruelling year without serious fatigue, Cannon observed that he was in far better condition than any other person in the laboratory, with the exception of Porter.

Perhaps his growing sense of self-esteem can best be seen when, near the end of his first year as an instructor, Cannon prepared his work on brain trauma for publication. There can be little doubt that he took a great deal of pride in the research he had completed. Although the problem had originally been suggested to him and supported by Bullard, Cannon had carried the research through and written the paper detailing the results without any supervision or help. It became, in fact, his first postdoctoral research paper, and he especially relished Porter's approbation: "It will bring you a great deal of credit, perhaps more credit than you deserve," Porter told him, "because it introduces to the clinician the new trend in physiology."[34] Cannon hardly had time to savor the praise before he was faced with a situation he clearly never anticipated. While preparing the paper for preliminary presentation to the Massachusetts Medical Society, Cannon was told by Bullard that he expected to be named as co-author. The demand was not unusual; it was (and still is) common practice among some senior faculty at the Medical School. Cannon was indignant, however, and refused. Although Bullard continued to press his case, Cannon stood firm and with the strong backing of Bowditch and Porter succeeded in rejecting Bullard's claim. In the end Bullard contented himself by introducing the paper at the meeting. Although the dispute with Bullard was unpleasant, it had its rewarding aspects, not the least of which was Cannon's reassurance of the regard both Bowditch and Porter had for him.[35]

Certain of his post for the coming year, Cannon shared with Cornelia some of his new plans, including a proposed trip to Europe which he had been urged to take by both Porter and Eliot. "Apparently what I am expected to get there," he wrote, "is not so much an acquisition of new knowledge as an experience of the university spirit and a greater breadth of view."[36] With his customary zeal he began to engage in a variety of new activities ranging from attending antivivisection hearings to measuring the effect of sustained exercise on marathon runners sponsored by the Boston Athletic Association. During one marathon, he wrote Cornelia, the runners "were in a desperate state, though the winner, who ran the 26 miles in two hours and 29 minutes (149 minutes!) was as fresh as a lark when he pushed through the cheering crowd. A Mohawk Indian was second—five minutes later."[37] Near the end of the year's work Cannon began to prepare Cornelia for meeting his colleagues. About Porter he confided, "I have come to have a very great admiration for him. He is a very nervous high-strung man, and yet in most trying times he never loses control of himself. And he is an exceedingly kind-hearted considerate person, though rigidly just in his judgments. I am curious to see how you will like him."[38] As the semester drew to a close, Cannon could hardly wait to leave for St. Paul to claim his bride.

⚜ ⚜ ⚜

June 25, 1901, was one of the hottest days of the year in St. Paul. But if the 98° heat wilted most of the sixty wedding guests who gathered in the James's front parlor, it did not mar the joy of the occasion. Mrs. James, later describing the wedding ceremony to her sister in West Newton, Massachusetts, wrote: "I am sure that Walter thought all beauty, grace and divinity were contained in her little figure as they stood before Mr. Boynton in front of the window. I could see Walter's face but not Cornelia's, but I assure you his was a good face to look at. He took the wedding ceremony like the solemn sacrament it is and I love to remember the serious holy look he wore all through it. And when he held Cornelia's hand to give his promise, I knew that hand was something to shelter and shield her all his life long."[39]

After the wedding Cannon took his bride on what turned out to be a strenuous honeymoon trip of canoeing, camping, and mountain climbing. Although this was the first time Cornelia had stayed in the wilderness for very long, she soon showed her mettle. In the weeks that followed the young couple paddled their Indian birchbark canoe first down the historic St. Croix River and then between the high bluffs of the broad Mississippi. There they met with a series of trials that included sudden storms, excruciating sunburn, having their provisions raided by a herd of cattle, and even life-threatening mishaps. But always, as Cannon later remembered in his diary of the wedding journey, they were "saved for each other" and their spirit of adventure remained undaunted.[40] Browned and toughened by the outdoor life, they were soon either regarded as harvest hands looking for work or mistaken for Indians. "I am taken everywhere for a squaw," Cornelia wrote home. "Walter says it is because I do all the work, but I ascribe it to my looks."[41] Returning to St. Paul in mid-July to visit with their families and claim the railroad passes provided as a wedding gift by Colbert Cannon, Walter and Cornelia set off again on the Great Northern "Flyer" for northwestern Montana.[42] There they sought out the area now known as Glacier National Park and made a pioneer climb of the ten-thousand-foot Goat Mountain, at the northern end of Lake MacDonald. In honor of their achievement, the U.S. Geological Survey later renamed the mountain Mt. Cannon.[43]

Their honeymoon over, the young couple set up housekeeping at 76 Concord Avenue in Cambridge. Always nervous about money and terrified of debt, Cannon became so anxious about the management of the household as well as of his income that Cornelia took over the responsibility as soon as they were settled. Some time later, when asked by a group of doctors what he would do if he had all the money he wanted, Cannon replied, "Why, I *have* all the money I want. Mrs. Cannon gives me ten dollars a month and with that I pay my carfare, buy my lunches, and get my hair cut." Living with an experimental physiologist, however, did present some unusual problems. From time to time Cannon kept live laboratory frogs in the ice compartment of the icebox. The frogs on more than one occasion escaped from their frigid prison, and one day Cornelia found a large green frog comfortably ensconced in a potato salad she had just prepared for some dinner guests. "I hastily removed him and the salad in his immediate vicinity," she later recalled, "and stirred up the remainder to a normal appearance for the evening meal."[44] There were other times when efforts to join laboratory and home misfired, but instead of becoming bones of contention these incidents quickly passed into the family repertoire of stories to laugh at and savor. The keys to this felicitous beginning of married life were Cannon's adoration of Cornelia and Cornelia's undaunted spirit and optimistic outlook. In all things, she was her mother's daughter.[45]

Without doubt, there was a *joie de vivre* in the James household in St. Paul,[46] and much of the joy came from Mrs. James who had an intellectual curiosity, displayed great sensibility, and expressed her thoughts and convictions without reservation. She provided important support to Cornelia and dispensed good homely advice whenever it appeared to be needed. When Cornelia wrote her mother several months after her marriage that Walter appeared to be depressed and she was doing all she could to lift his spirits, Mrs. James responded, "I am rejoiced that you are overcoming Walter's blues. When the charm of your presence fades, don't forget *food*. There is nothing like proper nourishment to keep alive a happy disposition." At other times she forcefully reminded Cornelia of the virtues of her young husband: "Thank Walter for his letter," she wrote. "You have a rare treasure in him, Cornelia, dear, and you will realize it more as life goes on."[47]

Mrs. James's letters carried more than advice and family news. They also conveyed her liberal social, political, and cultural interests. Her lively comments on events reported in the daily newspapers quickly found their way into the Cannon household. When President McKinley was shot by the anarchist Leon F. Czolgosz, Mrs. James wrote Cornelia, "We all feel dreadfully depressed by this tragedy in Buffalo. I haven't seen Papa so sad for a long time. All business is disorganized for the time being—and Papa was hoping very earnestly if poor McKinley had to die, that it would be in the night rather than the day as there would be great danger of a panic should it occur at the noon hour. His wish is gratified so that complication is past." For her own part, she immediately began a systematic examination of anarchist thought and announced to her family that she was changing her intention to lecture on the solar system at the next Federation of Women's Clubs meeting in St. Paul and would speak instead on the subject of anarchism.[48] Several weeks later Mrs. James told Cornelia of her plans to meet with Jane Addams, who was coming to St. Paul to lecture on Tolstoy. "She, I think, knows Emma Goldman," she explained, "and I am anxious to talk with her about that young woman, and get her personal impressions. She visited the Chicago anarchists when they were arrested after the death of McKinley so [she] must know something about them."[49] Some time later Mrs. James could not resist a barbed comment on reading a news item about one of Harvard's illustrious figures: "I saw in the paper that Professor Münsterberg had declined the German offer. Is that true, and if so, why so? I thought life here was only a probation, a necessary discipline to fit one for the perfect life in the Fatherland."[50] Nothing was outside Mrs. James's ken. Few letters did not carry some information or opinion to the young couple on the literature of the day, ranging from the works of Gertrude Atherton and Maurice Maeterlinck to John Fiske and Herbert Spencer, or news of the latest development in her battles to uphold her social convictions.

Following her mother's lead, Cornelia began to lay the foundation for a similar atmosphere in her own home. When she wrote to St. Paul several months after her marriage that she was thinking of taking up her teaching career, she scandalized her younger sister Helen, who did not share her values.[51] But Mrs. James had no such qualms; for years she had supplemented her husband's undependable income by decorating household objects and painting miniatures, and instead of deflecting Cornelia, she continued to instill in her the value and joy of self-reliance. Some months later she made a point of telling Cornelia how she had helped deliver her next-door neighbor's baby when the doctor did not arrive on time. "I had never done it before," she exulted.[52] Although Cornelia did not take up her teaching career, she was far from being idle. During the winter and spring of 1902 she kept alive their previous idea of a European trip and made plans so that she and Walter could see for themselves the wonders of the old world. There were all sorts of familial objections to such a course: "Your European plans rather took away our breaths," Helen James informed her sister. "Papa thinks you are very unwise. Mama is inclined to regard it as taking rather a large risk . . . It will mean putting off your own home for several years . . . What does Walter think of the European plan? Does he approve or is he carried away by your longing to go?"[53] Cornelia listened and then followed her own judgment. Material possessions and creature comforts were not her top priorities; her notion of what was important and of lasting value clearly lay in other directions.

✠   ✠   ✠

From the beginning Cornelia with her mother's assistance endeavored to draw the Cannon and James families closer together. Even though the young couple's rented houses in Cambridge were not large or well furnished, they soon became the center for visits from St. Paul friends and family. When Cannon forgot to write his father, it was Cornelia who took up her pen and smoothed over relations between father and son.[54] When Ida Cannon appeared to be depressed by her work as a visiting nurse, Mrs. James alerted Cornelia that "the constant association with wanton misery" was "taking the heart out of her," and suggested that an invitaton to Ida to come to Cambridge for a vacation might be a good tonic.[55]

In time both families came to sustain each other in dealing with personal problems, especially about a problem that caused Cornelia and Cannon some anguish during the early years of their marriage. In brief, the young couple found it difficult to start a family. It was not a problem that was then discussed openly, but finally at the end of 1903 after seeing a physician, Cornelia confided the difficulty to her mother. Mrs. James, usually discreet, in this instance behaved in an uncharacteristic manner and shared the secret with Cannon's sister Ida. "I have a confession to make to you, my dear," she wrote to Cornelia, "of a slip about one of our private letters which I usually destroy after reading. The day your last one came, Ida dropped in, and in talking, asked in such a sympathetic way about your health that it flashed across me that she knew of your perplexities through talking with you . . . She is coming to see you in January and is looking forward to it most touchingly, so she said she is going to impress on you the need of rest and was deeply moved by your attitude."[56]

Such was the perception of the time that if a woman could not conceive, the difficulty was assumed to be with her. In this instance the assumption may have been justified[57] but the difficulty more likely was caused by Cannon's use of x-rays in his physiological research. Little more than a year after Cornelia wrote to her mother, F. Tilden Brown and Alfred T. Osgood of New York reported in the *American Journal of Surgery* that eighteen workers with x-rays who had consulted them had total azoospermia or oligonecrospermia.[58] "This sterility," they announced, "has been produced without the slightest subjective or objective sign denoting its insidious development . . . in no case has there been evidence of deterioration of sexual activity." The authors concluded their report with a strong admonition: "We want to give this warning to those who are employing or will make use of Röntgen rays: Repeated, prolonged exposure of the testes does produce sterility in the human being."[59] The discovery by Brown and Osgood of some of the subtle effects of x-rays on deep, healthy tissues of humans—one of the first such studies after nearly a decade of active use of the new technology—became the subject of long editorials in the major medical journals.[60]

In Boston E. A. Codman, following a correspondence with F. Tilden Brown, invited a group of physicians and technicians who were using x-rays in their work, Cannon among them, to a private meeting to discuss the implications of Brown and Osgood's article.[61] Codman, a plain-spoken man, told his assembled guests that their continued exposure to x-rays might result in sterility. "It is undeniable," he maintained, "that of the married men in this vicinity who have used the X-Ray but one has had children since he began the use of this apparatus. Even this one has used the X-Ray very little." "Another of us," he continued, "had two children shortly before using the X-Ray. He has had none since he began its use. Is he sterile now?" Keenly aware of the difficulties involved in collecting the necessary data to confirm the danger of sterility, Codman offered two options to the gathering—they could examine their own semen or send specimens to a special committee organized to make such an examination. Most of those present, Cannon included, chose the first method. Soon after, he reported to Codman that his own personal examination had revealed "many active sperm."[62] Relieved by these findings, he continued to use x-ray intensively in his research. In the year that followed, however, he began to worry that apart from Cornelia's evident gynecological problem, he too might bear a responsibility for the difficulty in starting a family.

At one time during the early months of their engagement Cannon had written Cornelia, "Never let me become narrowed to the little world of a laboratory, my dear, it is very important work but I need the world of men besides."[63] Cornelia needed no such admonition. After their marriage, the Cannon household became a common meeting place for young academics and their families as well as for a group of outlanders from the Midwest and a host of Cantabrigians who had banded together in a variety of projects designed to improve the lot of Irish immigrants in East Cambridge. Cornelia became the very core of Cannon's existence. Without her his world seemed to go awry—work alone was not sufficient. In the spring of 1903, shortly after Cornelia left for an extended visit with her family in St. Paul, Cannon described his sense of loss to her in a letter: "When I came down from the laboratory yesterday Frank remarked, 'My, but you looked so glum when you came back from that train. You looked as if you had lost your last friend.' I told him to wait till he was married and his wife left for the North Pole."[64] The separation underscored the importance of Cornelia to his life and work, and, as it continued, it became even harder for Cannon to bear. Two weeks later he related to Cornelia, "This morning sleep left me at 4:30 and I have not shut my eyes since. How I have [been] thinking of you and counting the days and hours till this hard part of the work is over and you are back again! . . . I want to see you so much, so very, very much. It would set me all straight again, I am sure, and I could go into this work rejoicing if you were only here. What a world of difference you make in my life!"[65]

Important as Cornelia was, she was not the only force to work changes in Cannon. Developments at the Medical School in the new century helped to transform him as well.

6   *Divergent Pathways*

W HEN CANNON began his instructorship at the Medical School, in 1900, Bowditch was sixty years old and in failing health. Although Bowditch was nominally the chairman of the physiology department, the thrust of his remaining energies did not lie in physiology but rather in planning and raising funds for the construction of new buildings for the Medical School in what later came to be known as the Longwood quadrangle.

Years before, when Bowditch had taken the deanship in 1883 and supervised the move of the Medical School from North Grove Street to Boston's Back Bay, it was believed that the new quarters would be adequate to serve the needs of the School for at least the next half century. No one, however, had anticipated the substance or number of changes in medical education and research that were to take place at Harvard under the leadership of Eliot. All too soon it became apparent that the School not only needed more space but also would benefit from a teaching hospital under its own control.[1] If Eliot's reforms had ceased in the early 1890s, it is conceivable that the Medical School might have been able to meet its needs by erecting a second building on the site at Boylston and Exeter Streets.[2] But Eliot's vision that the true function of medicine was to prevent disease and premature mortality required additional changes and expansion.

The president proposed adding a graduate department to the Medical School in which a body of experts in comparative physiology, anatomy, and pathology would be trained "for laboratory service rather than for the ordinary practice of medicine."[3] To give substance to this vision, Eliot in 1896—on his own initiative and without formal action by the medical faculty—appointed Theobald Smith, then bacteriologist to the Massachusetts State Department of Health, as Fabyan Professor of Comparative Pathology.[4] Subsequently, he consolidated the medical, dental, and veterinary schools into one Faculty of Medicine and began to channel funds from unrestricted bequests to the University into the Medical School appropriations. Eliot's idea of a graduate department of comparative medicine appealed to some members of the preclinical faculty, and soon a few, notably C. S. Minot and W. T. Porter, began to inundate him with a variety of departmental plans to carry his purpose forward.[5] These new plans, as well as a number of innovations already under way, made the need for space at the Boylston Street School even more pressing throughout the late 1890s. As if to underscore the growing crisis, Dean William L. Richardson gloomily reported in 1899 that scientific research at the Medical School was almost at a standstill, "all the available room," he complained, "being needed for the sole purpose of teaching students."[6]

Under such pressure the medical faculty reluctantly began to examine proposals for solving the School's space problems. Some of the early proposals, clearly stop-gap measures, caused extraordinary bickering. Little progress was made until Bowditch, in the role of faculty peacemaker, suggested that a portion of the considerable funds from the estate of Henry L. Pierce and from the bequests of former dean Calvin Ellis and his sister Lucy be used to secure enough land to erect "the various buildings needed by the enlarged Faculty, including hospitals." Although the plan was initially rejected, before long the medical faculty accepted it in part and, in deference to Bowditch's persuasive skills, also appointed him and his long-time friend, J. Collins Warren, Moseley Professor of Surgery, as members of a special committee to consider use of both the Ellis and Pierce bequests.[7] Within weeks the committee recommended purchase of the Francis Estate between Longwood Avenue and Francis Street in Boston as a suitable location for the new buildings and hospital.[8] It also suggested that some of the funds from the various bequests made to the Medical School be allocated for a professorship in physiology and a new physiological laboratory as well as a chemical laboratory. Most important, it inaugurated a vigorous fund-raising campaign.

Although a number of other committees were subsequently

appointed during various phases of the medical project, Bowditch and Warren continued to take the major responsibility for both the planning and fund-raising for the new school buildings.[9] Their plans, however, did not always coincide with Eliot's vision for the Medical School and at one point almost brought the project to a halt. Late in 1901 Eliot learned that Bowditch and Warren were quietly opposing the introduction of comparative medical studies at the Medical School—a plan he had carefully fostered by persuading the Harvard Corporation to assign $300,000 from the Pierce bequest for their future support. Eliot was not easily thwarted and quickly brought the issue to a head by warning Bowditch and Warren of the implications of their opposition. "On that point," he forcefully wrote Warren,

> I part company from you absolutely and for good, for I believe with Virchow that the future progress of medicine depends primarily on comparative studies. If the present Medical Faculty makes up its mind to keep Comparative Anatomy and Comparative Pathology out of the School, I for one shall be opposed to using in the Medical School either the Pierce money or the Billings money; and it seems to me very desirable that an understanding should be come to on this subject forthwith. If the Medical Faculty does not wish to take charge of these subjects, I should prefer to keep the Pierce and Billings money to promote these subjects in some other department of the University. I feel bound to say further that, as at present advised, I do not believe that the Corporation will go into the construction of five buildings for the Medical School unless they know beforehand where the money is to come from to run them. At the last meeting at which this subject was discussed, there was not a single member of the Board that was in favor of taking that risk.

Adding a carrot to his stick, Eliot continued, "What we are trying to do at this moment—and I think we ought to try all together—is to get a large sum of money from Mr. Rockefeller through Mr. Murphy. In my opinion, the only way to do that is to show him through Mr. Murphy that if we multiply our plant by five, we can do some good work in addition to what we now do."[10] The lesson once read needed no repetition.

The more Bowditch became engrossed in planning the new School, the more impatient Porter became about his status and authority in the physiology department. When Porter took up his post at Harvard in 1893, Bowditch had assured him that he would retire in 1900. For Porter, Bowditch's assurance was in effect a promise that he would succeed him as professor of physiology and chairman of the department.[11] The vigor with which Porter addressed himself to transforming the teaching of physiology in large measure was animated by the vision that he was creating a department in his own image. Nearing the turn of the century Porter directed virtually all of the research in the department[12] and assumed the bulk of its growing teaching responsibilities as well. He was in fact chairman of the department in all but name.

Early in 1900 Bowditch informed Porter that he wished to be relieved of most of his departmental responsibilities. He also informed him that he did not intend to resign his professorship and indeed hoped in future to introduce new elective didactic lectures as well as devise demonstrations for such lectures.[13] Bowditch's revised plans were a blow to Porter. They not only thwarted his anticipated hopes for complete control of the department but also implied a threat to the new teaching program based on student experimentation he had so carefully constructed over the years. Alarmed at this sudden change in his prospects, Porter complained bitterly to Eliot about Bowditch's continuing hold on the department, adding that he would even be willing to give up his long-expected sabbatical "if it shall be clearly understood that instruction in physiology is to proceed under my direction along lines which seem to me more fruitful than the largely didactic methods of the past."[14]

Porter's demands put Eliot in an awkward position. On the one hand, he sympathized with Porter's efforts to advance the laboratory method in the medical curriculum, but on the other, he found it impossible to take steps that would undermine Bowditch's authority or status. Bowditch was an honored and powerful associate who over the years had faithfully labored beside him in transforming the Medical School and who was (even as Porter wrote), through his planning and vigorous fund-raising for new buildings, still advancing the prospects of the School. Eliot's solution to the dilemma was to do nothing, save make an effort to salve Porter's thwarted expectations by asking him what ideas he might have for use of the Pierce or Ellis funds in the development of physiology. Porter saw Eliot's query as implying that the president was looking for ways to advance his interests and he quickly suggested establishing a new professorship of comparative physiology—an idea that he knew was close to Eliot's heart.[15] Again nothing happened. The Pierce and Ellis funds were shortly pressed into service for other ventures.

In June of 1901 Porter once more complained to Eliot about the administration of the physiology department. "The past year," he wrote the president, "has been unsatisfactory in many ways. Under the present conditions in the Department of Physiology the Associate Professor bears the full burden of work and criticism without proper means of administration, sufficient time for research, adequate title, or the usual compensation."[16] This time Eliot did not completely deny Porter. Instead he arranged a raise in salary and gave Porter to understand that in future he would informally share the direction of the department with Bowditch. The new arrangement solved nothing; indeed, it only exacerbated the differences between Bowditch and Porter. Late in 1902 Porter had further cause for chagrin when Bowditch was named to a new professorship of physiology endowed by the children of George Higginson.[17] Although the Higginson Professorship was created for Bowditch in recognition of his unequaled efforts in behalf of the Medical School, Porter found the new title particularly galling. He remembered that in one of his previous letters to Eliot he had suggested a chair for himself endowed by the Pierce or Ellis funds as a means of settling the administrative dilemma in the physiology department.

&ea; &ea; &ea;

Throughout Cannon's early years in the department he and Porter worked amicably and well together. Despite the tension between Porter and Bowditch about administrative matters, both were united in supporting Cannon's career. Bright young physiologists were at a premium early in the century, and the demand for them far outstripped the existing supply.[18] Porter, for example, encouraged Cannon to take a trip soon after his marriage to observe laboratory research in Europe and also urged Eliot to promote Cannon to assistant professor and increase his salary. In this he was immediately joined by Bowditch: "I would say that I heartily endorse what Dr. Porter wrote you recently about Dr. Cannon," Bowditch informed the president. "It would be a great misfortune to lose his services and I know of no one who could take his place . . . You will remember how quickly Dr. Mathews found a place in Chicago when we let him go, and Dr. Cannon, though less brilliant, is, in my opinon, a safer instructor and a more valuable man than Dr. Mathews." Bowditch was prescient: little more than a year later Western Reserve offered Cannon a professorship.[19]

The letters of commendation from Porter and Bowditch had an impact on the president, and soon he was voicing their opinions of Cannon at faculty meetings. Late in 1902 he made Cannon an assistant professor. For Cannon the promotion was yet another expression of Harvard's generosity. "Such a fostering mother calls forth the most devoted affection," he wrote Eliot. "In this new and closer relation with her I feel more deeply grateful than ever before for all that she has done; and in the years of service I shall do my best to show my loyalty and devotion to her."[20] The president, for his part, recognized Cannon as one of Harvard's own—one who would not say no to calls for service—and took him at his word in having the University's best interests at heart. Following Cannon's promotion, Eliot placed him on the Administrative Board and on a number of other important committees where his views would be of value. In a more subtle show of support he began to seek the younger man's advice on a broad number of problems ranging from raising graduate school fees to the reorganization of the Medical School. Although some of Cannon's opinions were naive and showed his lack of experience, he did not hesitate to speak his mind bluntly and forcefully—a quality Eliot well understood.[21]

As Cannon's star began to rise, Porter became increasingly embroiled in controversy. Although Eliot had previously shown some sympathy and support for Porter, a falling out gradually developed between them regarding two important and related issues. The first involved the manufacture of apparatus by the mechanics of the physiology department at the Medical School; the second was related to Porter's pedagogy.

The departmental manufacture of physiological equipment, originally established by Porter in the mid-1890s, was organized for a dual purpose: to copy or make less costly simplified models of German laboratory apparatus for student experimentation and to develop and produce new instruments for physiological research.[22] Both Bowditch and Eliot supported Porter in this venture and agreed with him that such equipment was central to introducing laboratory instruction into the physiology curriculum. Porter's innovative assembly-line production techniques enabled him not only to supply Harvard's needs but to produce a surplus as well. Soon other schools, wishing to follow Porter's pedagogic lead, applied to him for such surplus apparatus. As demand for the Harvard apparatus increased, Porter, with Bowditch's assistance, petitioned the president and fellows of the University at the end of 1903 for an expanded apparatus manufacturing facility to be included in the plans for the new Medical School buildings.[23] Eliot, basically in sympathy with the project, urged the Harvard Corporation's support of the petition on the grounds that their manufacturing venture would provide the School with an opportunity to revolutionize the teaching of physiology in the United States. Despite the president's pleas, the Corporation denied the petition on the basis that the enterprise was too commercial and could not be allowed on nontaxed property. Eliot, however, softened the blow by helping Porter to raise capital for the project elsewhere. Subsequently Porter organized the "Harvard Apparatus Company for the advancement of laboratory teaching in physiology and allied sciences." When he tried to find quarters for the company in an adjoining building, he was told that he must move the manufacture of physiologic apparatus off the premises of the Medical School.[24]

The second issue was related in part to the first. When Porter arrived at Harvard in 1893, he complained that almost all students were passed through their courses with little regard for standards of excellence. As the course in physiology increasingly became his responsibility, he not only introduced new methods of instruction but also initiated the practice of giving his students short, rigorous examinations. These daily examinations became the yardstick for Porter's judgment of students' abilities. Others at the Medical School, however, viewed his examination system, as well as his other efforts to set higher standards, in a different light.

Dean William L. Richardson, for example, a leading spokesman for the clinical faculty's opposition to the growing status of the laboratory departments, saw Porter as a continuing divisive force in the Medical School—one who by his strident calls for teaching reform was impairing the development of the School. Equally important, a number of the students themselves began to grumble about Porter's rigorous examination system and the increasing cases of failure in physiology. At the end of 1904, when approximately 40 percent of the first-year class failed their final physiology examination, student grumbling escalated into revolt, and after a meeting conducted by class officers and leaders, a formal petition protesting Porter's examinations and rigorous grading was given to Richardson for action.[25] The student protest provided an opportunity for the dean to push his own war against Porter. Instead of presenting the petition to the medical faculty for consideration, Richardson sent it directly to Eliot, buttressed by statistics designed to show that the examinations conducted by Porter were excessively demanding, especially when compared with those given by other departments in the Medical School.

Eliot, who by this time knew Porter well, quietly suggested that he could further his new methods of instruction more effectively if he were more politic. "Conference, discussion, and a reputation for fairness," he counseled him, "will do much more to further a new and desirable method of instruction than severe examinations." Porter, who thought the students' and dean's complaints outrageous, was in no mood to be politic and instead mounted a spirited rebuttal. In a specially printed eleven-page letter to Eliot he focused his attention on two issues—the origin of the student petition and the statistics and analysis of failures in physiology.[26] The petition, Porter pointed out, was the work of a small number of students who pushed it through a special meeting attended by less than a third of the first-year class, and further, at least half the class had not seen or read the petition before it was sent to the dean. No one, he claimed, had the courtesy to come to him to discuss student complaints about failures in the examinations before the petition was drawn. He reserved his scorn for the statistics supporting the petition, declaring that they were incorrectly drawn and poorly analyzed. There was no valid statistical evidence, Porter told Eliot, to show that the percentage of failures in physiology was increasing or that there was any relation of the failures to the new methods of instruction that he had instituted. The latter charges particularly upset him, and he took care to show how carefully he and others in the department prepared students for their laboratory as well as their final examinations. As to the charge that the final examinations he gave were unusually difficult, Porter noted that the questions were essentially the same as those used during the past twenty-eight years in the course.

Early in 1905, in an effort to contain the student revolt, Eliot sent a copy of Porter's letter to Frank Burnett, one of the student leaders. "May I ask you," he wrote him, "to call together the signers of the paper on which your name stood first and ask them . . . whether the considerations presented by Professor Porter constitute an adequate answer to the views which you expressed in your communication addressed to the Dean of the Faculty." In a remarkable interpretation of Porter's letter (certainly not warranted by any of its content), Eliot continued: "That communication has had the effect of making the department of physiology reconsider its methods and plans, and has produced the present exposition in defense of those plans. Perhaps you will regard this as an adequate result of your endeavors."[27] Adequate or not, student complaints stopped following receipt of the president's letter, less perhaps in deference to his arguments than in the realization that they had made their point.

Throughout the student protest Bowditch stood aloof from the conflict, in part because he, too, had some differences with Porter's approach to instruction in physiology. Bowditch saw Porter's conviction that student laboratory training was basically the only way to teach physiology as a threat to the traditional didactic lectures and demonstrations he had long favored and used. These differences, in fact, had emerged some time before the student revolt. Still, when Richardson continued to claim that Porter's teaching innovations had a deleterious effect on the development of the Medical School, Bowditch closed ranks and in a letter to Eliot mounted a fierce defense of Porter's talent as an investigator and of his method of instruction as well.[28] Although Porter escaped Eliot's censure, he did not go unscathed. The antagonism that he had aroused by his relentless drive for change was another instance in an increasing catalogue of complaints at the Medical School either about Porter or by him. In short, Porter's troubles had become a persistent administrative thorn and as such began to instill doubts in the president's mind as to his future value to the School.

❧ ❧ ❧

Throughout the period of turmoil within the department Cannon remained aloof from the battle—in part because he recognized that his advancement might well depend less on taking sides in departmental politics and pedagogical debates than on the successful completion of his research. During the second year of his instructorship Cannon turned once again to an investigation of the functions of the digestive tract. Although physiologists at this time such as Ivan Pavlov in Russia and William Bayliss and Ernest Starling in England were revolutionizing the understanding of the role of gastric and pancreatic secretions in the digestive process,[29] Cannon continued to direct his attention to the mechanical factors of digestion and began a study of the movements of the small and large intestines. Although such an investigation was seemingly removed from the mainstream of research on the physiology of alimentation, it was nevertheless a logical extension of his work on deglutition and the motions of the stomach. Equally, it was testimony of both his weakness and strength as an investigator. On the one hand, Cannon at this time had no expertise in chemical physiology, and he would have had difficulty in working effectively on the chemical factors of digestion. On the other hand, he had a remarkable mastery of the techniques necessary for observing the normal movements of the digestive organs in experimental animals—and it is these that he proceeded to explore.[30]

Using x-ray, food mixed with bismuth subnitrate, and a number of experimental animals (mostly cats), Cannon soon found that the movements in the small intestine were far more complex than those he had previously seen in the antrum of the stomach. As a mass of food accumulated in the duodenum after repeated relaxations of the pylorus, Cannon observed that irregular movements suddenly took place and were followed by regular constrictions, which separated the mass of food into a number of segments of equal size. This process, which Cannon called "rhythmic segmentation," then continued over and over in a regular fashion in the duodenum (at a rate of 28 to 30 per minute in the cat) thoroughly mixing the food with an outpouring of secretions of the liver and pancreas. Subsequently he noted that partially digested segmented food masses were brought forward by peristalsis farther along the small intestine. There a slightly different process of segmentation was repeated in which food and digestive fluids were once again churned together and then, through a pendular motion, brought into intimate contact with the absorbing mucous lining of the small intestine. Given his observations, he concluded that movement in the small intestine promoted both the digestion and absorption of food.

The motions of the large intestine proved equally complex,

but in a different manner. Here Cannon claimed that once food passed from the small intestine into the caecum and ascending and transverse colon, the early distinctive movement was a reverse peristalsis—or antiperistalsis. Instead of the food immediately being moved into the descending colon, hundreds of waves regularly carried it backward toward the caecum and ileocecal valve, again subjecting it to a thorough mixing and exposing it to another opportunity for absorption.[31] In these experiments Cannon charted for the first time the nature and functions of the movements of the intestines and once again challenged existing beliefs. For example, contrary to long-held physiological doctrine that the movements in the small intestine stopped during sleep, he was able to show that all movements in the intestines continued during sleep in the same way as in waking hours.[32]

One of the more provocative findings of Cannon's investigation was his observation of the effect of the emotions on the process of digestion—namely, that whenever his experimental animals manifested signs of anxiety, rage, or fear, their peristaltic activity was inhibited.[33] It was not a new observation; Cannon had made a similar observation in his earlier study on the movements of the stomach. Further, a number of physicians had previously maintained on clinical grounds that emotional states, such as fear, anxiety, and sorrow, brought in their train a long series of digestive disturbances. Now, however, Cannon's experimental observations put the physiological pathology of such disturbances on a more scientific basis. It was a subject he would return to again and again.

Within a short space of time the growing corpus of Cannon's research on the mechanical factors of digestion began to command attention both at the Medical School and in the wider clinical and scientific community. Leading physiologists and physicians increasingly signaled acceptance of his work by summarizing or citing it in review articles and textbooks and by integrating its substance into their lectures. Thus, when Russell Chittenden of Yale, one of the leaders in physiology of nutrition in the United States, came to Harvard in 1901 to lecture on deglutition to medical students, he abandoned the Kronecker-Meltzer theory and featured Cannon's findings in its place.[34]

Encouraged by these signs of success, Cannon decided that the time had come to fulfill the dream he and Cornelia had long shared of going abroad. In the late summer of 1902 the young couple set out on a whirlwind tour of England and several European countries, determined to see all the people, churches, castles, and paintings that time allowed. Cannon, mindful of Eliot's and Porter's earlier suggestions to him that a European trip would be useful to broaden his point of view, took time to stop at certain laboratories, such as those of Hugo Kronecker in Berne and Rudolph von Magnus in Utrecht.[35] Although these visits were too brief to be of particular use in his immediate research, this was the first chance he had to meet personally with some of the English and European physiologists whose work he had previously read and admired. Upon his return to Boston Cannon took up his teaching and research with renewed vigor and began a study of the nature of enzymatic activity in the stomach. Unconvinced by the reasons commonly advanced by physiologists that salivary digestion in the stomach was possible only for a brief period of time, Cannon, with the aid of Hilbert F. Day, a second-year medical student, began an investigation of the conditions of salivary digestion in the cardiac and pyloric regions of the stomach.[36]

Several years earlier Cannon had shown that there was relatively little motion in the cardiac region (or upper end) of the stomach and that as a result food there remained unexposed to acid gastric juice for a long period of time, which promoted salivary digestion of starches and carbohydrates. Conversely, he discovered that in the pyloric region (or lower end) of the stomach, very active peristaltic movements quickly mixed food with acid gastric secretions, which inhibited salivary digestion. The new study with Day did little more than confirm Cannon's previous observations. At best, it specifically underscored the importance of mastication to salivary digestion. Even so, a number of commentators found Cannon and Day's work to be useful. The editors of *Progressive Medicine*, in a review of the paper, informed their readers, "The practical lesson to be drawn from this is to emphasize the need of good teeth and thorough mastication of food since ptyalin must play a much greater part in starch digestion than it was thought to do previously."[37] Others were even more laudatory. Horace Fletcher, a food faddist who captured the nation's attention with a campaign featuring the importance of chewing food thoroughly as a technique for inducing weight loss as well as in promoting digestion and good health, broadcast Cannon's work on salivary digestion to his followers throughout the country. For him it was scientific proof of the validity of his theories.[38]

At no time after his return from Europe did Cannon pause in his research. The investigation of one problem appeared logically to lead to a series of even more complex questions. For instance, during the course of his research on intestinal movements Cannon had noticed that some of the foods he fed his experimental animals, notably salmon, left the stomach later than either bread or milk and, further, that the salmon was slower in reaching the large intestine than either of the latter foods.[39] It was by no means a unique observation; other investigators had made similar reports, and some, in an effort to extend their research, had even attempted to chart the rate by which certain foods left the stomach. Cannon, however, saw the question of the rate of discharge of food from the stomach and small intestine in a different light. As far as he was concerned, a solution to the problem was not merely a matter of adding new information on the mechanical movements of the alimentary canal. He saw it rather as a possible opportunity for discovering the mechanism that controlled the movements of the stomach and small intestine. Although the problem he now addressed was substantially different from those he had investigated before, the research techniques he utilized were the familiar ones of observing the process of digestion in experimental animals by means of x-ray and the mixed meal of food and bismuth subnitrate.

In this new investigation Cannon initially fed his animals a uniform amount of carefully prepared carbohydrates, proteins, and fats mixed with bismuth subnitrate in a particular sequence. Subsequently he fed his animals not only in a variety of sequences but with a number of different food combinations as well. During each series of feedings he carefully observed the passage of the various foodstuffs through the stomach and small intestine, charting at regular intervals the length of shadows cast by the radio-opaque food on tissue paper and then comparing the aggregate length of the shadows to determine the relative amounts of different foods at different times in both of these regions of the alimentary canal. Using this semiquantitative method Cannon, after approximately twelve hundred observations on one hundred and fifty cases, concluded that a carbohydrate meal left the stomach far more rapidly than a protein meal and that the gastric emptying of fats was the slowest of all.[40]

Cannon's new findings marked the end of the first phase of his research on the mechanical factors of digestion. In a period of five years he had detailed the three major mechanical functions of the alimentary canal: propelling food, mixing food with the digestive juices, and exposing the digested food to the absorbing mucous membranes of both the small and large intestines. It was an impressive accomplishment.·

The results of these experiments proved particularly important as they raised even more complex questions. Cannon had learned, for example, that at the end of digestion the stomach did not empty all at once but progressively. "Why," he began to speculate, "are the carbohydrates, which are not digested by the gastric juices, permitted to go quickly onward into the intestines, where they are digested, while the proteids, digested in the stomach, are retained here to undergo digestion?" "What fine mechanism of the digestive economy," he asked, "could see to it that the gastric part performs its function well when the food it acts on is present, and lets it waste but little time or energy with food it can not change?" Was the mechanism mechanical or chemical or both?[41]

Cannon did not dwell on these questions privately. On the contrary, he saw very clearly that they represented new opportunities for advancing the understanding of problems of human digestive function, and he moved to take advantage of the situation. As early as 1903 in an address to the American Medical Association in which he summarized the results of his research in the previous five years, he publicly laid claim to the field of the mechanics of digestion as his own and announced that his past studies were prologue to "an extensive investigation into the mechanical factors of digestion to be carried on during the next few years."[42] He need hardly have said anything at all. He was at the time almost alone in using x-ray and its attendant techniques in studying the normal movements of digestion in experimental animals.[43]

✺ ✺ ✺

In addition to preparing papers for the *American Journal of Physiology* and other scientific publications, Cannon submitted long digests and reviews of his research to various clinical societies because it afforded him an opportunity to demonstrate to practitioners the relevance of his research to the solution of problems they faced every day in dealing with digestive diseases. Nor was his interest in these clinical problems transitory; from the beginning of his career as an investigator he was concerned with the practical application of the results of his work. In 1902, for example, while observing the movements of the intestine, he noted an instance of accompanying rhythmic sounds, and it occurred to him that the sounds heard over the abdomen might indicate the mechanical activities going on in the alimentary canal. Recognizing that air mixed with food, when churned together, produced sound, Cannon, using himself as a guinea pig, ingested a variety of specially prepared "fluffy" meals and then kept a stethoscope near his bed to listen to the sounds of digestion whenever an occasion presented itself. Later he designed an apparatus to record the alternate intensity and frequency of such sounds in experimental cats. Although the data Cannon collected were at best impressionistic, he nevertheless became convinced of their ultimate usefulness and began to exhort physicians to chart such abdominal sounds as a technique in diagnosing the various disorders of the digestive tract.[44]

Cannon's interest in clinical problems not only allowed him to make friends with the leaders of the medical community but also helped provide him with audiences whose admiring as well as critical commentary encouraged him to carry his research forward.[45] From time to time he used his addresses to clinical societies to advance new ideas or theories. Early in 1905, while relating the results of his latest studies on the movements of the alimentary canal to a meeting of the American Gastro-Enterological Association, Cannon advanced the theory that chemical control of the pylorus could be central to the process of regulating the discharge of foods from the stomach.[46] It was the first public hint of the future direction of his research. This particular idea was not solely the result of Cannon's speculations about the implications of his research on the rate of discharge of foodstuffs from the stomach; it was also related to his recent utilization of surgical procedures in his research. Although physiologists had long used a variety of surgical techniques in their investigations, Cannon's use of such methods had its origin more directly in the development of experimental surgery at Harvard.

Surgical research in the United States during the early years of the twentieth century was not the exclusive property or idea of

President Charles W. Eliot

Dean William L. Richardson

Professor Henry P. Bowditch

Associate Professor
William T. Porter

Four turn-of-the-century figures at Harvard Medical School.

Albert Moser

Ernest A. Codman

Walter B. Cannon

Fred T.
Murphy

Francis H.
Williams

John B. Blake

Cannon and his collaborators, 1896–1906.

any one surgeon or institution. In 1902 a group of young surgeons led by Harvey Cushing, George Crile, Charles Frazier, and George Brewer began to lay the foundation for a Society of Clinical Surgery to foster the examination of problems in physiological pathology. That same year plans were made to organize experimental surgical laboratories at Harvard, Western Reserve, Pennsylvania, and Johns Hopkins.[47] At Harvard such an interest had been demonstrated several years earlier when an instructor was appointed in surgical pathology and given a place to work within the Sears Laboratory of Pathology and Bacteriology.[48] Although this modest laboratory was initially devoted to dissection and morphology, within a year of its organization its purpose expanded to include an experimental investigation of cancer.

Early in 1902 J. C. Warren, with the help of Edward H. Nichols, Herbert L. Burrell, and Robert B. Greenough, established a special Committee of the Surgical Department for Research Work for the purpose of encouraging students and young surgeons to engage in surgical research.[49] In order to attract applicants, research was defined broadly to include clinical and statistical studies as well as experimental laboratory work. Recognizing that sufficient space was not available within the Surgery Department or the Laboratory of Surgical Pathology, the committee arranged makeshift laboratory quarters in the locker room of the Boylston Street building and acquired additional facilities at the nearby Lyman Animal Hospital for applicants who wished to engage in studies using larger or more numerous animals.[50] Within months of publishing its purpose, the committee received a variety of interesting applications ranging from proposals to study the suture of arteries in dogs and the physiology of shock to several dealing with problems in abdominal surgery. In the latter group was an application from John Bapst Blake and Walter B. Cannon to study the relative merits of gastroenterostomy and pyloroplasty in treating nonmalignant pyloric stenosis.

The proposal, one of the first interdepartmental collaborative research projects in the Medical School, in part stemmed from the high regard that Blake and others in the surgery department had for Cannon. Blake, for example, with H. L. Burrell, then chairman of the Committee on Surgical Research, had earlier introduced Cannon's case method in their course on operative surgery. More important, he had closely followed Cannon's investigations with x-ray and was interested in applying his physiological techniques to compare the efficacy and validity of the two abdominal operations. Cannon, for his part, eagerly joined Blake in this work. The study Blake proposed was not only a chance to expand his perspective of the process of digestion, but also another opportunity to demonstrate to surgeons the usefulness of physiology in coping with long-standing clinical problems.[51]

In 1881 surgeons in Europe and America led by Anton Wölfler and Theodor Billroth began to treat problems of pyloric stenosis, cancer of the stomach, and gastric ulcer by gastroenterostomy—a surgical procedure that formed a permanent connection between the stomach and a portion of the small intestine in order to bypass the pylorus. Although the operation was deemed beneficial, it also resulted in a significant number of undesirable after-effects (including regurgitation of food from the intestine into the stomach, persistent vomiting and hiccough, hemorrhage, new ulcers, and intestinal obstruction) that caused a number of physicians to question its usefulness. Some surgeons seeking solutions to these new problems began to modify their procedures by connecting first the anterior and then the posterior portions of the stomach to one or another part of the jejunum or ileum of the small intestine. Others adopted new methods of suturing, and still others devised different operations.[52] One of the more successful of the latter, developed by Johann von Mikulicz and Walther Heinecke and later modified by J. M. T. Finney, called pyloroplasty, involved making a surgical enlargement of the lumen of the pylorus. Although a low-risk procedure in appropriate circumstances, pyloroplasty too had drawbacks, and many surgeons were not convinced of its value.[53] Most surgeons, however, came to judgment about the validity of these procedures empirically by counting the number of successful operations, untoward results, and mortality. Cannon and Blake's investigation was the first American effort that sought to examine either operation experimentally.[54]

Many surgeons who performed gastroenterostomies for pyloric stenosis believed that if an opening, or stoma, was made midway in the stomach and connected to the small intestine, it could act as a drainage outlet for gastric contents and thus serve to relieve the pylorus from irritation by food and gastric juices. The belief was grounded on an assumption that the stomach was a passive reservoir whose contents were drained by gravity. Cannon and Blake were quick to challenge this as well as other surgical assumptions about the operation. "No one," they cautioned the readers of the *Annals of Surgery* upon completion of their research, "should deceive himself by supposing that there is relief from the pressure of motor activity or acid secretions near the pylorus after a gastroenterostomy."[55]

There was good physiological evidence for such a warning. Most surgeons, Cannon and Blake pointed out, did not understand the mechanics of digestion and did not comprehend that intra-abdominal pressure relations made gravity discharge "impossible"; in fact, they claimed that the only force that could bring food forward from the stomach to the intestine was the intragastric pressure found in the pyloric antrum. Their experimental operations showed that if the food brought forward by this pressure was presented with two ways to pass out of the stomach—the artificial stoma of the gastroenterostomy or the pylorus—it almost invariably left by way of the pylorus. In short, it made little physiological sense to perform a gastroenterostomy if the pylorus was open. They further made clear that in their judgment pyloroplasty was a more reasonable operation for pyloric stenosis because it was not burdened by many of the difficulties that accompanied gastroenterostomies and allowed food to go out through its usual passage while preserving some of the important mechanisms of the duodenum.[56]

A number of distinguished surgeons such as William Mayo and Sir Berkeley Moynihan praised and accepted the results and implications of the research of Cannon and Blake. Perhaps the aspect that most attracted their attention was its obvious practical nature and range—especially its efforts to find the cause and solution to some of the more troublesome after-effects of gastroenterostomies.[57] Others, however, were less forthcoming, and some who had previously begun efforts to modify the operation continued their investigations in the hope of amending or confirming these latest findings. One of these was a young surgeon at Harvard, Alfred H. Gould, who aroused Cannon's anger. A year after Cannon and Blake began their research, Gould, who was one of the assistants working in the surgery department, received a modest grant from the Surgical Research Committee to modify some of the existing surgical techniques of gastroenterostomy. Gould was well known to the committee; indeed, they had received and supported an earlier application from him for a research project.[58] Gould was privy to the observations and findings obtained by Cannon and Blake, and in January 1905 he rushed into print with conclusions identical to those reached by the cooperating investigators.

Cannon and Blake, about to go to press with their own paper, were stunned. Blake subsequently did or said little. Cannon, however, promptly filed a protest with the Committee on Surgical Research. Gould's conclusions, he charged, were the same as those he and Blake had arrived at and were not supported by any evidence except the results of the experiments that he and Blake had conducted. Cannon's complaint troubled the committee. They realized that if the controversy erupted into a public debate, it might put at risk the other collaborative research between the physiology and surgery departments[59] or, worse, have a negative effect on the fund-raising campaign that Bowditch and Warren were still conducting in behalf of the new Medical School buildings. Early in February the committee brought Gould and Cannon together and, after a careful examination of the charges, decided that Gould must issue a published apology.[60] On February 13, 1905, an apology addressed to the editor appeared in the *Boston Medical and Surgical Journal*. It was precise and succinct:

Dear Sir,:

In my paper on "A New Method of Performing Gastro-Enterostomy" published in the Boston Medical and Surgical Journal, Vol. CLII, No. 3, January 19, 1905, I omitted to give credit to Drs. Cannon and Blake for their experimental work upon the movements of the stomach after gastro-enterostomy, one conclusion of which was published in my paper as a reason for the adoption of the technique of my operation.

The experimental work and the conclusions of Drs. Cannon and Blake are to be published shortly and I regret the premature publication of their results in my paper.

Although the apology was signed by Gould, the letter was not actually his. It had been composed by Burrell for the Committee on Surgical Research in order to avoid any appearance of controversy.[61]

The incident annoyed Cannon, but it in no way blemished his relations with the surgeons. Soon after he completed his work

with Blake, in addition to instructing young surgeons in physio-
logical techniques,[62] Cannon began a new cooperative research
project, this time with Fred T. Murphy, a former collaborator of
Gould. Cannon's interest in clinical problems had served him well.
It gave him new friends and enhanced his research capabilities.
Within a short time it would also enlarge his prospects.

7   The Longwood Avenue Medical School

A S THE SUCCESS of Cannon's research began to bring him recognition both at the Medical School and in the scientific community, his relationship with Porter almost imperceptibly began to change. Toward the end of 1905 hints of differences between the two men started to surface. "I think that from things Dr. Porter will cut out from the course this year," Cannon confided to his wife, "the administration of teaching during the second half-year will be easier than it was last year. But Dr. P. may say one thing one day and go serenely on in an opposite course the next."[1]

Several weeks later new differences emerged. When Porter and Cannon were asked for their opinions about the relations of the physiology and biochemistry departments, they expressed opposing views. Moreover, when new editions of Porter's book *Introduction to Physiology* and his pamphlet *Physiology at Harvard* were published, Cannon was disappointed to find that Porter had paid scarcely any attention to his suggestions and corrections.[2] Behavioral differences, which at another time might have been overlooked, were now perceived as unforgivable slights, and Cannon began to complain more frequently that his ideas for administering the department were not receiving the consideration he believed they merited. When Porter increasingly stayed away from the Medical School in the winter of 1905–06 because of illness, Cannon once again found himself burdened with both the teaching and administration of the physiology department. As the term progressed, the troubles between the two men began to be aired openly.

Late in February 1906, following a guest lectureship, Cannon received an offer of a professorship in the Medical School of Cornell University from its president, Jacob Gould Schurman. The offer in hand, Cannon presented Eliot and Bowditch with the differences he had with Porter and indicated that unless they were resolved he would seriously consider leaving Harvard.[3] Cannon's stance brought the crisis that had been brewing to a head. When the news became common knowledge, the Medical School found itself in a dilemma and, moreover, sharply divided. Although both men were excellent physiologists, Porter suddenly found himself under siege—charged with spending too much time on the production of physiological apparatus and editing the *American Journal of Physiology* and thereby neglecting not only his duties at the School but more especially his research. Eliot, Bowditch, and many members of the medical faculty were determined not to lose Cannon. In addition, an overwhelming proportion of the students who had come to have great affection for Cannon signed a petition supporting him.[4] There was, to be sure, some endorsement of Porter as well. A number of senior members of the faculty led by Charles S. Minot along with a group of students (including, ironically, some of those who had petitioned in Cannon's behalf) rose to Porter's defense.[5] Porter, for his part, defended his research record, his teaching, and his administration staunchly—and then tendered his resignation, reminding Eliot that its acceptance would reflect ill on Harvard in light of his substantive service to the Medical School.[6]

Eliot received no respite. No sooner did he open Porter's letter than Cannon presented him with a series of conditions that had to be met if he were to stay at Harvard. As the barrage of claims and counter-claims continued, it became increasingly clear that Cannon was too valuable an asset to lose. Bowditch, who was then taking treatment for paralysis agitans (Parkinsonism) at a sanitarium in Battle Creek, Michigan, telegraphed the president on March 30, "Don't let Cannon go, I shall resign in the summer."[7] Two days later Henry Lee Higginson, long a principal benefactor of Harvard and one of the most influential members of the Corporation, threw his support behind Cannon as well. "Today," he wrote Eliot, "I asked a surgeon of much merit and judgment about Porter and Cannon. He said, 'Porter is a fair man, such as one can easily find—Cannon is the best man in our school, a man of very unusual merit and tact as well, who values even the slightest good work of others.—If we lose Cannon we've made a real loss.' All of which you no doubt know, yet a confirmation may be welcome."[8]

As the pressure increased, Eliot appointed a committee of senior medical professors to help him come to a decision. After approximately a week of special consultations with both Porter and Cannon, the committee arrived at a Solomonic judgment: Cannon was to succeed to Bowditch's chair as George Higginson Professor of Physiology and a new professorship of comparative physiology was to be established for Porter.[9]

News of the decision, however, was not officially announced until the fall. Eliot wanted nothing to detract from the dedication ceremonies of the new Longwood Avenue buildings or from the honors that were to be bestowed on Bowditch for his long and often arduous efforts in behalf of the School. In May of 1906 notice was given of Bowditch's impending retirement. Upon the recommendation of the medical faculty the Harvard Corporation voted him a retirement allowance of $2,916.66 per annum, and a room in the new buildings was assigned "for his use for as long as he may find it convenient."[10] In June an acknowledgment of Bowditch's thirty-five years of service was spread upon the record by the medical faculty. When the American Medical Association held its annual meeting in Boston that month and previewed the as yet unopened Medical School buildings, the new structures were the focus of attention. Eliot took a moment to write Bowditch a note of appreciation: "There was a unanimous chorus of admiration and praise all round the terraces," he rejoiced. "You and Dr. Warren have a right to feel the heartiest satisfaction in the great result of your faith and work."[11] Only the task of formally celebrating the opening of the new buildings remained.

During the summer of 1906 Eliot's secretary, Jerome D. Greene,[12] wrote Henry P. Walcott, a member of the Harvard Corporation, that Eliot did not like the plans the medical faculty had drawn up for commemorating the opening of the new Medical School buildings later that fall. "The President," Greene told Walcott, "wanted the first day of the ceremonies to be dedicatory, and not marred by the projected presentation of lengthy medical monographs." He also asked, Greene continued, "that a larger group of clinicians be added to the honors list, and for medical alumni to be included in the ceremonies."[13] For Eliot the dedication of the Longwood

Avenue School was to be more than a celebration; it was to mark the coming of age of the Harvard Medical School as a scientific institution, and he reserved for himself and guest speaker William H. Welch of Johns Hopkins the privilege of enunciating some of the demands that would be made on medicine in future.[14]

Although Eliot on more than one occasion had previously spoken of his vision of the future of medicine, his task at the dedication was by no means an easy one. This time he would not only have to articulate publicly new standards of medical education and practice that he knew were not acceptable to a large portion of the Boston medical community; he would also have to persuade that same group to support Harvard in its efforts to achieve such goals. The thrust of Eliot's speech was to expand on a theme he had developed only recently. At the opening of the Rockefeller Institute for Medical Research on May 11, 1906, Eliot as one of the keynote speakers had devoted the bulk of his remarks to extolling the virtues of the scientific investigator who, he claimed, more than any other man was responsible for many of the contemporary advances leading to the cure and prevention of disease. At the Longwood Avenue dedication, however, he was more politic and began his speech with a bow in the direction of the medical practitioner: "Whatever else the regular education of the physician provides in the future, it must provide all the elements of the best training for the practicing physician who is to treat diseased or crippled human bodies, and give advice about the sudden and the chronic ills which afflict humanity. So much will continue to be demanded of all good medical schools; but much more they must do."[15]

For Eliot these new demands were clear; they arose from his perception that both disease and health were social products. "The medicine of the future," he told his audience, "has therefore to deal much more extensively than in the past with preventive medicine, or in other words, with the causes of disease as it attacks society, the community, or the state, rather than the individual." Preventive medicine and medical science were no more abstractions for Eliot.[16] He saw them as elements of a new environment that would in future provide a fulcrum for advancing medical knowledge.

With the new physical plant in place and the prospect of scientific medicine so alluring, hardly anyone at the ceremonies appeared to notice that the Medical School still had not organized itself to cope with many of the requirements and demands of the new medicine or indeed with any of the School's immediate needs. When Frederick Cheever Shattuck announced at the dedication that much more endowment was needed to make the new buildings properly productive, his Cassandra-like warning was lost among the guests' expressions of admiration for the extraordinary power house that was to furnish the new medical buildings and the projected surrounding hospitals with heat, light, power, and refrigeration. The cost of maintaining the power house was to become one of the financial burdens of the Medical School in the years that followed.[17]

ಆ§   ಆ§   ಆ§

Paradoxically, one of the most pressing problems the School faced was the utilization of the generous space that was suddenly available. When Bowditch originally presented the plans of the new buildings to Eliot, the president was so astonished at their projected size that he told Bowditch he thought the medical faculty would "rattle around in this great plant of ours for years to come."[18] Bowditch, however, was not deterred. He vowed on behalf of the entire medical faculty that the School was moving to its ultimate home, one that would never be outgrown. It is clear that the inadequacy of the Boylston Street building after such a short habitation had impelled him to set his space goals higher than many thought were actually necessary or even attainable. For Bowditch the great size of the buildings was needed and, in fact, determined by the expansion of research and the laboratory method of instruction. Eliot, nevertheless, was prescient. When the new buildings opened their doors in the autumn of 1906, one of the impelling issues facing the administration was the need for a population to inhabit the School and use its facilities. There were a number of reasons for this state of affairs, perhaps the most important being the persistent decline in student enrollment from the turn of the century. Although the student body began to increase again in the 1906-07 term, the figures did not nearly add up to the number of matriculants that had been anticipated once the new buildings became available.

In an effort to utilize the new School more effectively, Eliot with the assistance of several members of the preclinical faculty proposed various schemes not only to attract new students but also to advance his plans for preventive and comparative medicine. Some proved very successful, especially the free weekly public lectures designed to instruct the Boston community on issues of public health and preventive medicine. The lectures given during the first year by Charles Harrington on sanitation, by Harold Ernst on contagion, and by Cannon on x-ray and digestion were so popular that on more than one occasion overflow crowds had to be turned away. In another direction, Cannon as head of the Committee on Advertising and Catalogue mounted a successful public relations campaign to persuade medical practitioners to enroll in summer courses to learn about recent developments in their specialties as well as in the medical sciences.[19] Not all of Eliot's schemes were successful. One of his plans to revive a proposal originally suggested by C. S. Minot in 1899 to foster graduate instruction in comparative medicine for students who wished primarily to pursue careers in teaching or research in one of the basic medical sciences[20] succeeded only in increasing wrangling among the medical faculty as well as in the Faculty of Arts and Sciences.

Although Minot's original proposal found few supporters, several years later a new demand for graduate instruction in the basic medical sciences emerged, this time sparked by two different plans. One of these urged that a special Division of Medical Sciences be established in the Faculty of Arts and Sciences to grant higher degrees in the laboratory sciences; the other suggested the creation of a Graduate School of Medicine allied to the Medical School but administered by a separate dean and administrative board dealing with all phases of graduate work including higher degrees. Neither plan proved attractive to the medical faculty. In fact, they caused so much bickering that by the time they came to the Corporation and the Faculty of Arts and Sciences for decision, they were promptly put aside.[21]

Early in the summer of 1906 Eliot, believing that the availability of space in the Longwood Avenue buildings made the time propitious to reopen the matter of graduate instruction, appointed a committee composed of some of the most active investigators in the Medical School (Minot, Cannon, Ernst, Carl Alsberg, and Theobald Smith) to examine once more the possibility of developing a program in the medical sciences. The committee after several months of debate recommended as the best way of accomplishing the task "that the administration of the new degrees in the medical sciences be entrusted to the Faculty of Medicine."[22] This time the medical faculty put their differences aside and accepted it, but the Faculty of Arts and Sciences vehemently objected. The requirements for the higher degree in medicine, they informed the president, were not as rigorous as those demanded by the Graduate Faculty of Arts and Sciences. Further, they balked at the notion of the medical faculty's granting such advanced degrees as doctor of philosophy or doctor of science; those degrees, they maintained, were traditionally their privilege.[23]

An ordinary administrator, given the years of wrangling, might have thrown up his hands at this point. But not Eliot. Perceiving that there was basic agreement about the need for a graduate program in the medical sciences, he arranged a compromise that tried to meet the demands of both faculties. Following in part the proposal of the Medical School committee, he suggested that a separate Division of Medical Sciences be established in the School but urged that it be administered by a joint committee composed of members of both faculties (the majority from the medical faculty) with the responsibility of organizing the instruction and examinations for all higher degrees in the medical sciences. He reserved for the Faculty of Arts and Sciences, however, the right to grant all higher degrees.[24] Although the Division of Medical Sciences did not, as some had hoped, bring in large numbers of additional students to inhabit the new buildings, in subsequent years it more than made up for this deficiency by providing a fulcrum for the dreams Eliot had of fostering research in the basic medical sciences.

Despite the problem of maintaining and utilizing the new buildings, the most common perception many Bostonians had of them was as a symbol of the future they appeared to promise. "The architectural success of these monumental buildings cannot be questioned," the *Boston Medical and Surgical Journal* editorialized shortly after the dedication ceremonies. "It remains for the Faculty of Medicine to justify the time and thought represented in their construction by a renewed sense of its responsibility toward the medical education of the future . . . What the School will need in the immediate future as never before is a group of men devoted on the one hand to teaching and others equally devoted to that essential element of medical advance—investigation of new problems."[25] For Thomas F. Harrington, the historian of the Medical

School, the buildings carried a similar message. They were, he wrote, "witness that a new era had come in the methods of teaching and learning medicine."[26]

Characteristically, even in the euphoria of celebrating the new, Eliot saw the necessity of maintaining continuity with the past. When, for instance, Warren informed the president in 1905 that he intended to resign from his chair of surgery, Eliot recognizing that Warren's presence gave a certain stability to the medical faculty asked him to stay on for a few years—or at least until the School was well established in its new buildings.[27] Such was the anticipation of the future, however, that few bothered to examine the strength of the faculty's habits of thinking or the vitality of their quarrels and differences. Once inside the Longwood Avenue School, the medical faculty soon discovered that the past had not really disappeared. This was nowhere more apparent than in the physiology department and the problems that beset Cannon in his new position.

As head of the department Cannon almost immediately faced the necessity of dealing with a problem that had arisen about the financial relationships between the physiology department and the Harvard Apparatus Company while Porter had administered the department. In September 1906 Walter S. Burke, one of the administrative officers of the University, wrote Porter and asked for an explanation about what appeared to be a tangle in the arrangements between the Harvard Apparatus Company and the physiology department. Although Porter in reply gave a detailed explication of the financial arrangements that existed between the company and the department, the explanation apparently did not satisfy Burke.[28] Early in October Jerome Greene at the direction of Eliot asked Cannon to define the attitude of the physiology department toward the Harvard Apparatus Company—in essence, a call for an accounting of the previous economic relationship between the department and the company. Cannon was blunt in his evaluation and told Greene that while the Harvard Apparatus Company surely benefited teaching and research in physiology throughout the country, he doubted that overall it was economically beneficial to the Medical School.[29] Cannon's report to Greene reopened old wounds. When Porter learned about Cannon's evaluation, he immediately defended his administration of both the department and the apparatus company in a letter to Eliot. He even offered to give a sum proportionate to his means to the Medical School, an offer Eliot firmly rejected. "I . . . inform you explicitly," the president replied, "that the Corporation accept as satisfactory your acts and accounts concerning the manufacture and sale of apparatus for physiological laboratories during the whole period of your administration of the Physiological Department of the Medical School, and they regard that series of transactions as satisfactorily closed."[30]

As the days passed Porter faced new problems—problems that in large part were created by the maneuver that had made him professor of comparative physiology and Cannon the Higginson Professor of Physiology. The difference between the two appointments was not merely one of status; Cannon received a far larger allocation of funds than did Porter, and in addition, he controlled departmental expenditures and appointments. The difficulties this created for Porter are revealed by the outcome of a request he made to the president for a small supplementary appropriation to sustain the research that he was then conducting. Richardson refused to support Porter's request. "I do not know of any students who are working in Porter's laboratory," he told the president. "The regular students of the School do not work there, as they take their courses with Dr. Cannon. As no graduates have registered for work in his laboratory, I do not see why his request for an additional appopriation should not be brought before the faculty just as all requests for appropriations are."[31] The dean was less than candid. Although it was true that Cannon taught physiology to undergraduate medical students and that no new graduate students had registered for work with Porter, Richardson was well aware that a number of very capable advanced students were still hard at work on a variety of research projects in Porter's laboratory.[32]

Porter, recognizing the insecurity of his new position, began a campaign to justify his various research programs. Writing to Eliot in the fall of 1907, he described the important research his advanced students were doing and once again emphasized the central role of his laboratory in setting an élan for workmanship and standards in the Medical School.[33] Porter's continuing difficulties with the administration and the strained relations that resulted upset Bowditch. In an effort to present a united appearance for physiology at the School, Bowditch urged Cannon on several occasions "to fix things up" with Porter. Cannon, although reluctant to deny Bowditch's request, wondered in his diary, "How can I?"[34]

Although both men subsequently kept the differences between them from exploding into a public issue again, the hurt and anger smoldered on both sides. In the months and years that followed they harassed one another whenever opportunity arose. Thus, when Porter guided visiting British physiologists Ernest Starling and Edward A. Schäfer on a tour of the Medical School, he carefully kept them away from Cannon's laboratory, leaving Cannon to fume in private at the slight.[35] On another occasion, when Porter's diener lied to Cannon about some matter, Cannon faced Porter with the lie—in effect holding him responsible for his assistant's behavior.[36] Amidst this struggle Cannon received an unexpected blow from the medical students: after he had suggested to them that they inaugurate a class-day celebration as a new tradition, they turned around and invited Porter to be their first faculty speaker.[37] Every incident, no matter how petty or trivial, served to widen the rift between the two men. Although each might have helped and sustained the other in the work of the department, they went their separate ways. In the end the division had an immediate as well as far-reaching effect on the development of physiology at the Medical School.

Although Cannon as Higginson professor held the keys to the kingdom of physiology at Harvard, that kingdom was very small indeed. With Porter's departure to his own laboratory, the future of only two of the members of the department—Cannon himself and Frank Foley, the laboratory boy—was assured. One of Cannon's earliest acts as departmental chairman was to replace the talented Ralph S. Lillie, an instructor selected by Porter, with two candidates of his own choice—Ernest G. Martin, a young physiologist from Purdue University, and John Auer, a Hopkins M.D. who was then working with Samuel Meltzer at the Rockefeller Institute.[38]

In addition, Cannon laid plans to remodel the physiology course and gradually made sufficient changes to warrant replacing Porter's laboratory manual. When Porter first introduced the laboratory approach to the teaching of physiology, he prepared a manual to guide students through fifteen different exercises on a single pithed frog, putting his greatest emphasis on nerve and muscle physiology.[39] In following years he added a series of new experiments in various other fields, including optics, the central nervous system, skin, and the cardiovascular system, and also put increasing stress on the detail of laboratory technique. Porter's laboratory manual of 1896 was a slim 52-page pamphlet; a decade later it had become a textbook of 587 pages.[40] The changes that Cannon initially introduced were not extensive. His early guides— mere pamphlets entitled *Directions for Students of Physiology*—contained brief descriptions of the rearranged experiments and demonstrations to be performed and referred students to fuller instructions in Porter's *Introduction to Physiology*. Porter's manual of 1906 and Cannon's first published full-length manual of 1910[41] do not differ markedly in either philosophy or methodology; even the content seems to be much the same save for two striking exceptions—the language in Cannon's manual is simpler and less esoteric and there is an addition of a section on digestion. In fact, the changes Cannon made were minor, such as the introduction of a blank page opposite each of the experiments so that students could write in their own observations or paste in a graphic record of their investigations. In part, such remodeling was an effort to incorporate and make use of his previous teaching experience as well as newer methods and results of his physiological research. In part, it was also an attempt to put his own mark on the course.

?§ ?§ ?§

The privileges that came to Cannon as chairman of the department of physiology were not without cost. In the years following his appointment as Higginson professor he continually complained in his diary of being tired and nervous and not feeling well. There were good reasons for his apparent fatigue, not the least of which was the enormous increase in his responsibilities. From the time of his appointment as assistant professor of physiology in 1902, Eliot had placed him on a number of important Medical School committees, including the Administrative Board, the Committee on Scholarships and Student Aid, and committees on Advertising and Catalogue and on the Library. After his promotion to the Higginson chair, Eliot asked him to take on additional work with appointments to committees on New Instruction, Public Lectures, the Medical Sciences, and Relations with the Dental School. Although some of the questions and issues Cannon faced in his various committee assignments were often removed from his immediate interests, he nevertheless dealt with them with the same kind of effort and diligence he gave to his departmental affairs and research. It was precisely this quality that Eliot cherished.

Very often his added responsibilities bore heavily on Cannon, and although he rarely complained in public, he candidly expressed his frustrations in private about the amount of time he had to devote to them. Over and over he lamented in his diary that they were a waste and took precious time away from his research. Still, for all of his complaints and frustration, Cannon understood, like Bowditch before him, that among his more important obligations as Higginson professor was a commitment to keep the School running on an even keel and to extend its capabilities. Toward this end he made a number of special efforts in behalf of the School, even enlisting in the plans of others because he felt that their objectives would help Harvard to develop as a great center of medical research. One such plan involved bringing the newly organized nutrition laboratory of the Carnegie Institution of Washington to Boston.[42]

Early in November of 1906 Francis G. Benedict, who had recently been appointed head of the projected Carnegie Nutrition Laboratory, visited Boston to speak with Cannon about his plans for the new research facility. Benedict, who wished to establish the laboratory in the vicinity of the Harvard Medical School, was concerned that some of the Carnegie board members might prefer another of the sites under consideration, especially the one in New York. Convinced, for some obscure reason, that if he showed his preference for the Boston location he would be overruled by his board, Benedict officially took a neutral position but privately asked Cannon to make his case for him.[43] Cannon, excited by the prospect of adding a new research facility near the Medical School, agreed and with great care began to lay the groundwork for bringing the Carnegie Nutrition Laboratory into the Harvard circle. During the annual meeting of the National Academy of Sciences held at the Medical School later that month, Cannon used his influence to enlist the help of Councilman and Minot—already on intimate terms with Carnegie president Robert S. Woodward and one of the board members, John Shaw Billings.[44] Schooled by Cannon, Councilman took particular pains to show Woodward and Billings around the laboratories in the Longwood Avenue buildings, and at dinner Minot described the projected research and hospital plans of the Medical School. Anxious for an independent confirmation of Harvard's attitude to the Carnegie laboratory, Billings spoke privately with his ailing friend Bowditch. The meeting erased many of the doubts that Billings previously had concerning the Boston site. Bowditch was so enthusiastic about the prospect of bringing the nutrition laboratory to Boston that he later asked Cannon to draft a letter to Billings listing the various advantages Harvard could offer over any other site.[45]

In February 1907 the Carnegie Institution approved the Boston location for its nutrition laboratory. Benedict could not have hoped for a better outcome to his schemes. In the weeks that followed he again sought Cannon's help, this time to gather data on the availability of land near the School and on costs of construction and maintenance of the laboratories and building. Cannon once more extended himself on Benedict's behalf, literally spending days facilitating the construction of the new laboratory.[46] In the end, however, while the nutrition laboratory did vital and important research, the early vision that Cannon and Benedict both had of establishing a cooperative research enterprise remained unfulfilled. Although the Carnegie laboratory was physically located within the Longwood Avenue complex, it never became an integral part of the Harvard Medical School, much to Cannon's disappointment and Benedict's bitter regret.[47]

Cannon's efforts in behalf of biological chemistry, however, had a profound effect not only on the subsequent development of the department but on the direction of the careers of its investigators as well. Up to this time the teaching of chemistry and chemical research at the Medical School had been largely traditional. The chemistry department in effect mirrored the interests of its chairman, Edward Stickney Wood, whose research focused on problems of toxicology, purity of water supply, and analysis of urine.[48] Late in 1904, several months before Wood's death, Cannon, impressed with the growing importance of physiological chemistry as a discipline and at the request of Bowditch, wrote Eliot urging the formation of such a department. "There is no doubt," he told the president, "that the most promising field for the future development of medical science is the field of chemical physiology. Problem after problem in the dynamics of growth and of function and of that response to abnormal conditions which constitutes disease have been driven into this camp for solution." Noting that other medical schools already had such departments with outstanding investigators, Cannon urged the president to appoint a leader in this new discipline to succeed Wood lest Harvard lose an important competitive edge in the development of medical science.[49]

Although Eliot found merit in Cannon's arguments, he did not move to implement his suggestion, deterred in large part by the School's increasing financial deficit. "If we cannot carry on our present School in the present building without a large annual deficit," he replied, "what will be our pecuniary condition when we move into five enormous buildings?"[50] Cannon was not discouraged. Eighteen months later when Frank B. Mallory was put in charge of a faculty committee to revise the medical curriculum, Cannon, seeing an opportunity to raise the question again, wrote Mallory urging him to give as much time to biological chemistry in the new curriculum as that given to other medical sciences.[51] He also set in motion a plan to bring Otto Folin, a research chemist then studying the metabolism of insane persons at the McLean Hospital, to the Medical School as head of biological chemistry.[52]

After Wood's death in 1905 two young instructors were left to run the chemistry department, Carl L. Alsberg and Lawrence J. Henderson. Both were exceptionally promising. Alsberg, a Columbia graduate who had trained with Oswald Schmiedeberg at Strassburg and Emil Fischer in Berlin, taught biological chemistry. Henderson, a Harvard man who had trained with Franz Hofmeister in Strassburg, also taught biological chemistry but was more interested in physical chemistry.[53] Spurred by his success in helping to bring the Carnegie Nutrition Laboratory to Boston, Cannon throughout the winter of 1907 discreetly probed various faculty members for their views of a possible appointment for Folin. Most of those asked proved enthusiastic. Alsberg, who had previously published a paper with Folin on protein metabolism in cystinuria, told Cannon he welcomed the prospect of Folin as a colleague. Councilman was even more eager—a very important acquiescence because the new department was to be affiliated with pathology as well as physiology. One of the few people apparently not sounded out for his opinion was Henderson, the junior member of the department, who was then engrossed in preparing a report for presentation to an international congress in chemistry.[54]

Cannon continued to campaign in behalf of Folin well into the spring, and by early May the full professors of the Medical School formally voiced their approval. Only Eliot appeared to hold back. With deliberate caution, he cast about for separate and perhaps more objective appraisals of Folin's abilities. When Cannon told him of a letter just received in which Francis Benedict said that Folin was regarded in Europe as a genius, Eliot relented and offered Folin an assistant professorship.[55] It was not a generous offer and Folin declined. Several days later Folin received an offer of a post at the Rockefeller Institute at the then handsome salary of $4,500 per annum. When Cannon learned of the Rockefeller offer, he went to Folin and asked what kind of an offer would induce him to come to Harvard. Folin did not mince words and indicated that he would not take a subordinate position in which his freedom might be compromised. In essence, he wanted a professorship at a salary of at least $4,000, with the services of an assistant and permission to continue his association with the McLean Hospital, where he also had an assistant and received funding. Cannon relayed this counter-offer to the president, stressing again Folin's expertise in nutrition, the chemistry of metabolism and urine, and especially his mastery of analytical methods useful in clinical work. Late in May the Corporation authorized Eliot to make Folin another offer as associate professor of biological chemistry and head of the department. This time Folin promptly accepted the offer.[56]

The new appointment caused difficulties for others in the department. Almost at once Alsberg told Cannon that although he had previously supported Folin, he wanted the province of the new chairman defined more rigorously.[57] More than a year later, when Alsberg received an offer of a post in the Bureau of Plant Industry in Washington, D.C., he wrote Eliot asking about his opportunities for advancement at Harvard, especially about the prospect of developing his particular interest in pharmacology. The president in turn wrote to Folin, and when he learned that Folin wished to keep Alsberg, Eliot told the young instructor that his prospects for promotion in future were good and that he did not see why Alsberg could not ultimately get possession of the field of pharmacology at the Medical School if he so desired. In closing, however, Eliot sharply reminded Alsberg that "the Corporation does not desire to retain any man who does not distinctly prefer service at Harvard to any other which is open to him." Alsberg, who had a good appreciation of his own talents and was neither shy nor diffident, requested an immediate promotion to assistant professor with an increase in salary. When Eliot again replied that he could depend on a promotion sometime in the future, Alsberg abruptly resigned.[58]

Henderson's experience, following Folin's appointment as chairman, was no less traumatic. When he returned from Europe in the fall of 1907, the young instructor found that his prospects for advancement in the department had become dimmer. An inquiry to Eliot about his future at the Medical School confirmed his fears. "You are justified in fearing," the president candidly replied, "that if the department of biological chemistry is ultimately to consist of two men, that you will not be one of them." "If I were you," he continued, "I should look out sharply for a better position in some other institution, not because I was discontented with my work here, but because my interests here and elsewhere would be promoted by the offer of a good place somewhere else."[59]

In the year that followed, Henderson devoted himself to a heavy program of teaching and research, instructing students at the Medical School and undergraduates at both Harvard College and Radcliffe. His research output was little short of amazing— that same year he published ten papers describing his applications of physical chemistry to explain the maintenance of acid-base balance of body fluids. This work, although unusually significant, ironically served to exacerbate the differences that existed between Henderson and Folin. As chairman of the department, Folin was upset about Henderson's lack of enthusiasm for teaching first-year medical students and the amount of time he spent in Cambridge; he was also eager for Henderson to develop rapid analytic methods using a colorimeter for the solution of physiological problems. In essence, Folin saw the major function of the department as increasing the use of chemistry in clinical diagnosis. Henderson, however, was not interested in clinical medicine and viewed physical chemistry as a key in shaping the future of biochemistry.[60]

Following Alsberg's resignation early in September 1908, Henderson received an offer of a post at Tufts, and the question of his future in the department became a matter of immediate concern to Eliot. An inquiry from the president to Folin brought a forthright reply. "Perhaps I should make a statement regarding Henderson," Folin wrote Eliot, "in order that you may know clearly what the situation is in the department. I had a conversation with Dr. Henderson yesterday in the course of which I suggested that he leave Cambridge and devote all his time to the work in the Medical School. He does not desire to do this, and I do not dare to push him into it . . . If Dr. Henderson had been willing to identify himself more completely with the Medical School I should have liked to secure his appointment as indicated without his asking for it, but since that seems not to be the case I drop the matter for the present."[61]

Others at the Medical School, however, had a more positive view of Henderson. Councilman, who had few reservations about expressing his opinions on the Medical School or his colleagues, wrote Eliot, "I am so convinced that the future direction of pathology is in the way of chemistry, especially physical chemistry, that I would be glad to have him as assistant professor of pathological chemistry . . . There is some criticism of Henderson on the ground that he is inclined to theory but that lies in the nature of a subject that is founded on hypothesis."[62] In the end, Eliot was persuaded to keep Henderson and reappointed him as an instructor in biological chemistry for three years. The basic issues that divided Folin and Henderson, however, were not addressed, and the differences between them were to bedevil their relations for years to come.

᠊ᢒᢃ   ᠊ᢒᢃ   ᠊ᢒᢃ

On April 27, 1907, Richardson wrote Eliot a letter tendering his resignation as professor of obstetrics and as dean of the Harvard Medical School.[63] Although the letter came as a surprise, the resignation was not unexpected. For months a number of Richardson's close friends on the faculty had voiced the opinion that he might resign because of illness. Some gossip even regarded his retirement as imminent. Councilman in a note to Eliot went so far as to suggest that if Richardson retired, faculty sentiment for a new dean centered on "Mallory, Cannon or Joslin."[64] It is clear that although Eliot had not anticipated the timing of Richardson's resignation, he nevertheless regarded it as an opportunity to fill the deanship with a person who would guide the School along the lines of medical research and preventive medicine. Still, neither

Eliot nor the medical faculty had considered the precise qualities they wished the new dean to have—whether he should be young or experienced, trained in the Harvard tradition or someone from outside the School, a clinician devoted to developing medical care or an investigator committed to extending scientific research. Eliot, however, understood that the sine qua non for the new dean was that he be acceptable to his colleagues. The medical faculty did not take long to make their feelings known.

Some of the older members enthusiastically promoted Harold C. Ernst, the professor of bacteriology, as heir apparent "Dr. Bowditch and I always regarded him as the one on whom the promoter's mantle would eventually fall," J. C. Warren wrote Eliot. "He is very loyal to and enthusiastic over the interests of the School, more public-spirited in that way than any member of the Faculty."[65] Others, like H. P. Walcott and A. T. Cabot, both members of the Corporation, suggested for the post Charles Montraville Green, who had long served as secretary of the medical faculty. But the president found neither man suitable—the former on the grounds of age (he had already passed his fiftieth birthday) and the fact that he had a number of outspoken enemies on the faculty, the latter because of lack of confidence in both his administrative skill and his understanding of medical research. Eliot was sure of one thing; he did not want a temporary or stop-gap dean.[66]

Early in May Cannon heard a rumor that Eliot was considering some of the younger men on the faculty and that he was one of those mentioned for the deanship. The rumor was true; the president was indeed reviewing the qualifications of those younger men whom he knew and admired. At first he hoped to fill the post with a member of one of Boston's medical dynasties and approached the anatomist John Warren (the son of John Collins Warren). Warren, who felt out of touch with the clinical activities of the school, declined.[67] Disappointed, Eliot turned to Theobald Smith for advice, particularly about several other of the younger candidates he was considering. Smith, after examining Eliot's requirements and candidates, bluntly replied: "Looking over the list of the faculty, I do not see however where this ideal dean is to come from. I think both Dr. Cannon and Dr. Christian would make good deans, although I should, on the whole, prefer Dr. Cannon."[68]

Reinforced by Smith's opinion, Eliot approached Bowditch

about the advisability of appointing Cannon dean. Bowditch was appalled by the prospect. Remembering how his own appointment as dean in 1883 had deflected him from his successful career as an investigator, he at once tried to dissuade Eliot. "I should . . . regard it as a misfortune to the School," he frankly wrote the president,

> were he to be appointed Dean. Dr. Cannon has, in an uncommon degree, the qualities which fit a man for the position of director of a laboratory of experimental science and, in that capacity, is now engaged, heart and soul, in a line of research which promises valuable results. Were he to be asked to assume the additional responsibilities of the Dean's office he would, undoubtedly, do the work well, but it would mean that he would have just so much less energy to give to his researches. It seems to me a mistake to withdraw a man from work for which he is peculiarly well fitted by nature and education for the sake of employing him in work which does not require so much special training. I am certainly not one of those who "have rather a low estimate of the value and influence of the Dean's position" but I do think it is easier to find a good Dean than a good director of a laboratory of research.

Bowditch felt so strongly that Cannon's appointment as dean would end his career in physiology that subsequently he personally visited him to persuade him to reject Eliot's proposal. Cannon did not need the advice; he was wed to his research. When the offer of the deanship did in fact come, he politely but firmly refused it.[69]

Following Cannon's refusal, Eliot focused his attention almost exclusively on candidates who were clinicians, including among others Henry Christian and Elliott Joslin, young teachers in medicine at Harvard, and J. M. T. Finney, a Harvard Medical School graduate and associate professor of surgery at Johns Hopkins. One of the new candidates aroused the ire of a certain member of the medical faculty. When Councilman, who had originally come from Hopkins, learned that Finney was being actively considered for the deanship, he erupted. "I should much regret to see him made professor of surgery or dean," he wrote Eliot. "We must have a much greater man than Dr. Finney. The future of the School depends on our having men in the clinical positions who not only appreciate the fact that modern medicine is becoming a science but who are contributing to it."[70] Councilman's rejection of Finney underscored for Eliot the difficulty of appointing an acceptable dean who could take office for the fall semester of 1907. Haste in filling the position would only add to the already manifold burdens of the School. Instead, Eliot did what he vowed in the beginning he would not do: he appointed Charles M. Green temporary dean. The stop-gap solution gave him some time to examine the suitability of Henry Asbury Christian for the post.

Christian was an attractive candidate. A graduate of the Johns Hopkins Medical School in 1900, he had interned at the Hopkins Hospital and spent a term working in pathology with Councilman and Frank Mallory at the Boston City Hospital. Subsequently he joined the Harvard medical faculty, initially as an instructor in pathology and later in the department of the theory and practice of physic. His work, particularly the skill with which he joined the pathology laboratory and clinic, won the admiration of both Councilman and Reginald Heber Fitz, then chief of medicine, and in the spring of 1907, Christian was appointed assistant professor of medicine.[71] It was Councilman and Fitz who brought the young Virginian to the attention of Eliot. Despite Christian's credentials and the recommendations in his behalf, the president moved slowly; not until the winter of 1908, after he had received an enthusiastic report of Christian's administration of continuous service in the medical department at Carney Hospital, did Eliot decide to offer the deanship to him. Although the offer included an immediate promotion to a professorship, Christian did not accept immediately; he had his own requirements. He accepted the deanship only when Eliot agreed that he would succeed Fitz as Hersey Professor of the Theory and Practice of Physic and receive an appointment as chief of medicine when the Peter Bent Brigham Hospital opened its doors.[72]

When the medical faculty learned of the appointment, there was an almost collective sigh of relief—and a particularly heartfelt one from Cannon. "I wish to express to you my deep satisfaction with the appointment of Henry Christian as Dean of the Medical School," he wrote Eliot.

> It is certain to be judged everywhere as an indication of a new spirit in the Institution. Dr. Christian is well known to the best medical men both in the East and in the West—I wish you could have heard Ravenel and Bardeen and Bierring, among the younger leaders in

the West, expressing to me their pleasure at Dr. Christian's election to Dr. Fitz's chair. Such men and the many alumni throughout the country who feel that the School has been too narrowly Bostonian in character will welcome the new Dean with rejoicing. And the younger men in the School also will have a new enthusiasm. The future of the School belongs to them and they will help Dr. Christian to make it great.[73]

The selection of Christian at the age of thirty-two made him the youngest dean ever appointed at Harvard. Even more, it marked another step in the Medical School's break with the past: the "boy dean" was not New England born nor was he academically or medically Harvard bred. A graduate of Randolph-Macon College, he was part of the stream of southern students who at the turn of the century absorbed the new doctrines and standards of medical science at Johns Hopkins. Although a clinician, he was firmly fixed on the unity of laboratory research and medical practice.[74] That outlook immediately became a factor in the direction of the School's policies, especially in the continuing debates on standards of admission and curriculum reform. Before long, however, Christian's youth, inexperience, and lack of insight into the complex relationships at the Medical School were to cause him serious problems in the deanship.

8   At Home in Cambridge

W HEN THE FRANCIS estate on Longwood Avenue was chosen as the new site for the Medical School, a number of faculty members opposed the selection because they believed that it would widen the gulf that already separated the School from the rest of Harvard University. For them, the choice meant that an opportunity to bridge long-standing differences was lost. From that time forward the Medical School was irrevocably set in Boston.[1] Unlike many of his colleagues who lived in Boston and Brookline, Cannon chose to make his home in Cambridge. The decision was not made out of economic necessity or on the grounds of convenience but because it allowed him and Cornelia to continue their lives in familiar surroundings and to take advantage of the ample opportunities for intellectual growth that the university community in Cambridge provided.[2]

By 1905 the Cambridge that Cannon first saw little more than a decade earlier had changed markedly in its physical appearance, perhaps most noticeably in its facilities for public transportation. In 1896, for example, the horse-drawn cars of the street railway that leisurely verged off in several directions out of Harvard Square to Boston and nearby suburbs were supplanted by electrified trolley cars. The new system was swifter and more efficient than the old and reflected growing changes in the uses of time. Conductors under instruction to keep to more precise schedules no longer stopped in the middle of a block to accommodate a familiar passenger. Indeed, as the population of Cambridge increased, familiar passengers lost their visibility. The habits of many of the riding public, however, did not change as quickly. Years later, Louise

Crothers, Cannon's longtime confidante, vividly remembered an altercation that occurred between a conductor on the new electrified trolley system and a passenger who had stopped to speak to a friend. When the conductor asked her "to step lively," her sister who was standing nearby exploded. "Things have come to a pretty pass," she harangued the passengers, "when Miss Kitty Parsons is not allowed to finish a conversation."[3]

There were other Cantabrigians who, like Miss Parsons, continued to live by the values and standards of the Cambridge mercantile and intellectual aristocracy of the preceding generations. When Mrs. Charles Eliot one summer day told her neighbor Miss Sarah Palfrey that she hoped Miss Palfrey would get away from the heat of Cambridge, Sarah replied, "Mother feels that the habit of leaving home in the summer just for a change is unsettling and does not conduce to an orderly mode of living." Some time later after Sarah's mother died, she and two other elderly sisters, Anna and Mary, took courage and decided to try two weeks in Gloucester. From there Sarah wrote a friend, "It has been a great surprise to me to find [here] so many well-conditioned people, quite unknown to ourselves or to our friends."[4] Despite new modes of thought that were sweeping through Harvard and Cambridge, the orderly living Miss Palfrey adhered to remained, dictating in part the pace and much of the manner of life in the community. Although Cannon and Cornelia were committed to a future many older Cantabrigians would reject, they nevertheless cherished the Cambridge past—not out of nostalgia but for the stability and continuity it gave to the present.

Many of the friendships Cannon maintained in Cambridge began during his undergraduate years. Some were with former teachers like George H. Parker and William James, others with longtime friends and intimates like Samuel and Louise Crothers and Rev. Francis Tiffany of the Unitarian Church, and still others with schoolmates from St. Paul like Earl Bond or relations in West Newton like the Jaynes family. The core of his social life, however, was made up of large numbers of young academics on the Harvard faculty and Cambridge neighbors—a long list that included George and Florence Pierce, Ralph Barton and Rachel Perry, Gilbert Lewis, Harry and Ella Morse, Ernest and Mabel Southard, Robert and Ada Yerkes, Edwin Holt, as well as Frank and Mabel Hammond, Charles and Isabel Whiting, and Allen and Louise Jackson. Save for Southard, a neuropathologist, most of Cannon's Harvard friends had little to do with medical research. Pierce and Morse were physicists, Holt and Yerkes were psychologists, Perry was a philosopher, and Lewis a chemist. They were all united, however, by their common interest in scholarly inquiry and scientific ideas. In 1903 they began meeting regularly to hear and criticize each other's research and formed themselves into a club called the Wicht. The club received its curious name when George Pierce and Harry Morse returned from a trip to Germany carrying with them a picture from the German comic magazine *Simpliccimus* of a little gnome-like figure in a red dress peering out from the niche of a huge tree, labeled *"Das Wicht."* The inquiring and mystified look in the gnome's eyes suggested to them that Wicht might well serve as the name for a club of young scientists and philosophers who were also frequently perplexed in their efforts to unravel nature's secrets.[5]

The Wicht Club was quite informal and met monthly in a once elegant hotel for dinner and to listen to a club member talk about his research. By rule, the talk was never allowed to be definitive or continuous. Indeed, speakers were kept to the mark by frequent interruptions and witty remarks. Ernest Southard, who had a penchant for employing unusual words or usual words in unusual ways, was prized by the club for his remarks. His talent was such, Cannon later recalled, that when a special edition of Webster's dictionary appeared with a line separating usual from unusual words, club members accused him of hitting the dictionary below the belt. Cannon, who loved to tell stories, used to make his points at meetings by telling Irish and Swedish dialect stories in the manner of Mr. Dooley. Presentations at meetings were never recorded, but each year the Wichts collected the papers they had published and bound them into an annual volume which they titled "Was Wichtiges" ("what is important"). The pun was more than justified: the nine volumes that were so produced are a treasure trove of the work produced by young Harvard scientists and philosophers at the beginning of the twentieth century. The originality of club members was especially prized by Cannon, and in later life he spoke feelingly of the enrichment of his values and scientific understanding through his association with them.

Cannon, in fact, took pride in the achievements of many of his colleagues at the University and often made special efforts to get to know them better. When they, in turn, invited him to meet others who worked in their fields, he accepted such invitations eagerly. Thus, when Thomas N. Carver, the economist, invited him to meet his colleague, W. Z. Ripley, who was one of the leading experts on railroad organization and regulation, Cannon, who was brought up on Ignatius Donnelly's populist ideas of regulation of railroad rates, accepted and later noted that he had spent a memorable evening. Sometimes, however, the promise of meeting leaders in the academic world did not turn out as expected. When Otto Folin, then at the McLean Hospital, arranged a special dinner so that Cannon could meet and talk to his visiting friend Thorstein Veblen, one of the most original economists in the United States, Cannon later observed in his diary that he had spent a very dull evening.[6] Still, more often than not his friends gladdened him. When George Parker was made a full professor of zoology in May 1906, Cannon celebrated the event in his diary as if it were his own: "Dr. Parker came in at supper time with Mrs. Parker and showed a letter from President Eliot stating that the Corporation had voted him a full professorship and $4000. Glory hallelujah!" Then, in deference to the politics he had recently learned were necessary for academic promotion, he added, "This the result of his call at Yale."[7]

His concern for his friends was often reciprocated; however, on one occasion it led to a brief but painful blow-up. In mid-February of 1908 Ralph Barton Perry had an attack of appendicitis. At his operation it was discovered that the appendix was not only gangrenous but had perforated as well. Although Reginald Heber Fitz had long since set out the diagnosis and methods of treatment for an inflamed appendix, such operations were still regarded as no small matter. A perforated appendix with the inherent peritoneal infection increased the uncertainty of the outcome. Dr. Scudder, Perry's surgeon, thought his prognosis grave. After several stormy postoperative days, however, Perry began to recover steadily. Later, with all danger apparently past, Cannon matter-of-factly told Rachel Perry how he had feared for her husband's life. The news came as a shock: throughout Perry's illness the gravity of his conditon had been kept from Rachel, and to learn of the danger after the fact horrified her.[8] The history of the event proved to be so much more painful than the event itself that it took Rachel some time to forgive Cannon for the distress he had inadvertently caused her. Cannon, who was sensitive, felt the rebuff keenly.

Of all his friends, George Washington Pierce was the one who best served Cannon as a kindred spirit.[9] Pierce, who pioneered in the field of wireless telegraphy, not only shared with Cannon the excitement of breaking through the boundaries of science but also had a knack of looking at the humorous side of life. When the occasion demanded, he would not hesitate to bring back to earth friends who exhibited unwonted stuffiness or an overwrought sense of propriety. In the spring of 1906 when Pierce felt that Cannon was making too much of his offer of a professorship from Cornell, he teasingly informed Cannon that he had probably received the offer because he took in Cornell's President Schurman with a variety of William Jennings Bryan's "cross of gold and crown of thorns" speech. Later, when Cannon drafted an eleven-point statement outlining what it would take to keep him at Harvard, Pierce tried to add perspective to the situation by dubbing Cannon's statement "the ultomato."[10] It was a light touch that Cannon appreciated. In general, both liked to outdo each other as punsters and took particular pleasure in topping one another's stories. At other times, however, particularly when Cannon was tired or discouraged with the progress of his research, he would become moody or depressed for days. On such occasions Cornelia always slyly managed to "drop in" on George and Florence Pierce. Pierce's ebullient Texas wit never failed to lift Cannon's spirits.[11]

At all times Cornelia kept the social calendar full by arranging dinners and parties. Although such affairs were frequent, they were never lavish; indeed, sometimes the menus proved sparse. After one clambake that Cornelia organized, Cannon wryly noted in his diary that there was "more crockery than clambake." On another occasion, at a dinner party to celebrate George Pierce's birthday, Cannon, to his distress, found "one small squab for six of us."[12] Parties were not given to demonstrate the amount of food one could put on the table but were rather occasions that furnished guests with opportunities for self-entertainment. Stunts and charades were often the high points of an evening out. At one party at the Jackson's house George Pierce appeared as a Texas tough, Cornelia and Rachel Perry as shopgirls, Cannon as a floorwalker, and Allen Jackson as Daniel Webster. Jackson's performance by all accounts was later judged to be the best of the evening.[13] At another party that the Cannons gave soon after moving to Ware Street in 1907, a stage was constructed in the barn adjoining the house upon which Perry appeared costumed as Sandow the Strongman and Cannon, with the help of his sisters, Ida and Bernice, and a garden hose, posed as Laocoon. Mrs. Hugo Münsterberg, who was present at the party, could not believe her eyes. It was difficult, given her German academic experience, to accept *Geheimrath* professors acting in such an undignified manner, even in their own homes and in the company of friends. One can hardly imagine what her reaction might have been when George Pierce at another party some years later attempted to portray "a nude skunk eating strawberry shortcake."[14]

ࣷ   ࣷ   ࣷ

Friends were not the only ones to help sustain Cannon's spirit or to stretch his mind. Cambridge and Boston offered more formal opportunities that worked in that direction as well. Each week, for example, the University brought in well-known lecturers to speak at the Twentieth Century Club on a variety of social and political issues ranging from King Leopold's rule in the Congo to juvenile delinquency, the Chinese peasantry, and municipal administration. Although not all of the lectures were to Cannon's taste, some completely engaged him. When Judge Lindsay and F. C. Howe lectured on the influence of corporate wealth on municipal administration for public ownership, Cannon noted in his diary that the meeting was inspired. On other occasions he wrote with equal approval of lectures by Louis Brandeis on industrial insurance and Lincoln Steffens on graft in cities.[15] The theater had a similar impact; although he approved of such plays as *Rip Van Winkle* and *Peter Pan*, other plays in several instances distressed him. During the season of 1906 and 1907 Minnie Maddern Fiske introduced Henrik Ibsen to Boston audiences, and it is clear that the themes of Ibsen's plays challenged some of Cannon's deeply held social convictions. After seeing *Hedda Gabler*, he noted in his diary "particularly good acting in a particularly unpleasant and unrealistic play. Whoever knew such monstrosities!" *Rosmersholm* fared little better. On another occasion Cannon reacted in a similar manner to a playwright whose work he generally admired. Although he enjoyed reading George Bernard Shaw's *Captain Brassbound's Conversion* with Cornelia, when he went to see *Man and*

Superman (then perhaps Shaw's most brilliant comedy), Cannon complained that it made him feel "ugly and unkind."[16] Whether palatable or not, the new ideas to which he was exposed increasingly began to work on him, and some of his previous attitudes began to be cast aside. In May 1907, while attending an exhibit of photographs depicting the nobility of Indian life at the Twentieth Century Club, he praised "the wonderful Indian pictures" taken by Edward Curtis—a far cry from his judgments about Indians when he had been a student.

At no time did Cannon cut himself off from his family or old friends. On Avon Street and later on Ware Street he welcomed visits not only from relatives but from old St. Paul friends as well. When May Newson sent other promising students to Harvard, their first haven in Cambridge was often Cannon's home. Cannon had a fondness for such students because they reminded him of his own trials and tribulations, and one, Lariz Voldt, made a particular impression on him. Voldt, the son of a Swedish immigrant in North Dakota, came to the St. Paul High School in 1902. When he entered the school, he was clothed in homemade sheepskins and spoke a mixture of English and Swedish. With incredible effort, he worked his way through the St. Paul High School, and under Miss Newson's tutelage he determined, like Cannon before him, to go to Harvard. Cannon took pride in Voldt's drive. Later, to his satisfaction, Voldt graduated from both Harvard College and the Harvard Law School with high honors and became a professor at the University of Nebraska Law School.[17]

Although Cannon maintained strong ties to his family, there was a growing separation from his father, not so much because of Cannon's new status as a professor but because of Colbert Cannon's pursuit of an old dream. Colbert had always wanted to be a doctor, and in 1904 at the age of fifty-eight he left a well-paid position as a superintendent on the Rock Island Railroad and entered the homeopathic Hering Medical School in Chicago to prepare for a new career.[18] The move immediately caused economic difficulties: "I am very anxious to talk over the financial situation of the family with you for I feel there is something wrong with it," Cornelia wrote Cannon while on a visit to St. Paul in 1905. "Ida and Bernice each give your father $15 a month and he is constantly asking them for more . . . There is a wrong attitude there and I think you and I are the only ones who can straighten it out. The girls are so unselfish and self-sacrificing that they will give their last cent but I think they ought to be protected from themselves."[19] Nor was this the only problem. Colbert had often voiced the hope that one day his son would join him in medical practice. The idea was now abhorrent to Cannon; he had no longer any desire to be a practicing physician and looked upon homeopathy as a species of medical practice akin to quackery.

In 1905 while attending a physiology meeting Cannon saw Colbert in Chicago. His father, he wryly confided to Cornelia, "has been hammering homeopathy into me with sledgehammer doses. Nothing infinitessimal about his treatment of my skepticism, I can assure you. But one moment he agrees with me that nature does the curing after all, and the next he says his drugs do it all. One moment it is foolish to treat any local trouble—the general bodily condition is all, and the next he is applying massage, electricity and light to do the local job. It is a great game!"[20] Two days later Cannon continued his complaints. "This afternoon," he wrote Cornelia, "I have tramped and ridden from one end of Chicago to the other—hobnobbing with homeopaths and being as agreeable as I could. I feel that they are either charlatans or transcendentalists and I have met representatives of both classes this afternoon. How I hate the whole scheme of it in its arrogant assumption that *drugs* cure people!"[21]

Others in the family understood Cannon and his research little better. On one occasion when Mrs. James tried to persuade Cornelia to come to Minnesota for a vacation, she wrote, "Child, do come out this summer . . . Walter *can* work here if he only can think so." Several days later Helen James querulously added, "If Walter could get an x-ray machine here, why couldn't he work happily for a month or two?"[22] Cannon himself knew how little the family understood his work or his relations to physicians. In December of 1905, when Cornelia wrote him from St. Paul that she and his sister Ida were planning to invite some local physicians to meet him when he joined her in Minnesota, Cannon hastily replied in an effort to deflect them: "If the doctors want to see me they will get together and have a dinner, and ask me to be present. For the family to ask *them* to come and see *me* is putting me on a pedestal where I couldn't bear to stand . . . It was very sweet of you and Ida to think of it, but you are putting into the attitude of some doctors in St. Paul your own feelings toward me. They don't know me and don't want to come to see me. Just this once, *please* don't."[23]

The following year, this time with Cornelia's strong support, Cannon expressed his sense of self in even sharper terms, rejecting outright the behavior of one of St. Paul's elite physicians as well as that of Miss May Newson. For many years May Newson spent her vacations in Blue Hill, Maine, often with her medical adviser C. Eugene Riggs, and his family. Miss Newson thought so highly of Riggs that at one point while Cannon was still a medical student, she tried to persuade him to spend a summer as Riggs's assistant.[24] In August of 1906, when Riggs and his wife invited Cannon and Cornelia to stay with them and May Newson at their summer home, they promptly accepted. From the start, however, the visit was a disaster. Mrs. Riggs, in her grandest lady-of-the-manor pose, complained and carped incessantly. Riggs was no better, and even Miss Newson acted in an autocratic and overbearing manner. After little more than a week Cannon and Cornelia were so miserable that they abruptly terminated their visit and returned home.[25] In effect, their leave-taking was a declaration of independence from the mores of St. Paul and, especially, from the counsels of May Newson.

One more trauma signaled Cannon's increasing separation from the world that had once nurtured him. In mid-September of 1906 Cannon's stepmother, Carrie Mower Cannon, discovered a lump in her breast. For Cannon the news was especially ominous. Some weeks earlier Jessie Sewall, May Newson's sister, had made a similar discovery. Initially Mrs. Sewall's condition was passed off as being "glandular." However, after an operation by Charles Mayo at the Mayo Clinic, the diagnosis was changed to cancer. Late in September Mrs. Cannon, who was then living in Chicago, was operated on by one of Colbert Cannon's acquaintances. Following the operation, her condition was also confirmed to be cancer. Carrie Cannon bore her illness stoically. Although there was some hope in the weeks after her operation that the cancer had been fully extirpated,[26] before the year was out the first signs of metastasis appeared.

In the spring of 1908 when another operation became necessary, Cannon took charge of his stepmother's care and asked Albert Ochsner at the University of Illinois to perform the surgery.[27] This time Mrs. Cannon's recovery was difficult, and she increasingly complained of pain. When Cannon discussed the pain with Ochsner some weeks after the operation, Ochsner ascribed it to a postoperative neuralgia that often appeared in cases subsequent to radical mastectomy. The explanation did little to relieve Cannon's anxieties. Before long, the pain eased and the family once more was encouraged by her steady progress. Little more than a year later, however, it became clear that Carrie Cannon was dying. Carrie's illness further exacerbated Cannon's growing estrangement from his father.

Colbert Cannon, after graduating from the Hering Medical School in 1906, left his wife in the care of his daughter, Jennie Williams, and went to Eugene, Oregon. His purpose ostensibly was to start a medical practice there and later send for Carrie. In truth, however, he abandoned her. In the years that followed, Colbert's contact with his family became more and more desultory. In the fall of 1909, when Cannon and his sisters realized that their stepmother was dying, they sent for their father, but time and again he delayed coming to her side. When the end came, he barely arrived in time to see and speak with his wife. Jennie later remembered how pleased Carrie was when she saw Colbert: "It paid to wait," she told her. Shortly thereafter, while Colbert was out of the sickroom visiting with some of his friends, Carrie died.[28] For Cannon, this sorry final episode closed yet another door to the past.

& & &

Cornelia was the bedrock of the Cannon household. The force of her person was not restricted to Cambridge but was felt equally in St. Paul. Whenever an opportunity presented itself, she extended a helping hand to strengthen family ties. For example, during the summer of 1905 Cornelia felt that it would be more profitable for her younger sister Frances to spend a year at Radcliffe rather than at the University of Minnesota, and she conspired with her mother to bring Frances to Cambridge. When Mrs. James later learned that Cornelia also planned to give Frances an allowance of $10 a month, she strongly objected, "I don't want you, Cornelia dear, to give that monthly allowance to Frances. It isn't right. We will try to keep her in funds in some way if you will only care for her and give what is impossible for us: the Culture with a big C of the East."[29] Cannon, who trusted Cornelia's instincts implicitly, agreed with her plans, and early that fall when Frances arrived in Cambridge he made his young sister-in-law especially welcome. Some weeks later when Cornelia had to go to St. Paul to care for her mother who had become ill, Cannon continued to look after Frances much as an older brother might have. The year Frances spent in Cambridge proved to be an enjoyable and productive time for her.[30] Not the least of that experience was the happy environment her thoughtful brother-in-law had provided.

Cornelia proved equally caring and generous with Cannon's unmarried sisters, Ida and Bernice. She had a special empathy for Ida Cannon and came to play an important role in her life. When Ida graduated from St. Paul High School in 1896, she decided to become a nurse and enrolled in the St. Paul City and County Hospital Training School for Nursing.[31] Following her graduation two years later, she took a position in Minnesota at the Faribault State School for the Feeble-Minded, where she organized a hospital unit. Her exposure to the unfortunate children at the school widened her interests in social service, and in 1900 she left her position to enter the University of Minnesota to study sociology. Ida later remembered that a guest lecture by Jane Addams helped change the course of her life: "I was deeply moved by the force of her passion for reform in the conditions of tenement-house life, in sweat-shops, and in factories, with their prevalent hazards to life and health. These appeals for public attention, and the pictures she drew of the lot of little children in slums and crowded dirty streets, suddenly enlivening my classroom studies in 'Social Pathology,' made me see the gap between social theory and reality in the lives of men. They started me on my way toward social work as a life interest."[32] To augment her growing interest in social work, she later took a post as a visiting nurse with the St. Paul Associated Charities.

Ida's talents were outstanding, yet despite her achievements as a nurse and the growing definition of her life goals, she was deeply unhappy. In part she was depressed by the hopelessness of the dreary world of poverty she was exposed to by her work, and in part she was made miserable by an unfortunate love affair. Colbert Cannon had brought up his children in a very puritanical manner. The strictness of this upbringing left its mark on Ida, and she subsequently found it difficult to express her innermost feelings to men. During her stay at the Faribault School she had fallen in love with the superintendent, a married man with five children. It is not clear whether she ever told the man that she loved him. In any case it was a painful experience.[33] Cornelia, who did not suffer impossible situations without making some effort to correct or mitigate them, invited Ida to come to Cambridge, holding out the prospect that she could get the professional training she was seeking at a new school for social workers that Jeffrey R. Brackett with the assistance of Harvard and Simmons College had established in Boston two years before.[34]

Early in October of 1906 Ida arrived in Cambridge to take up the schooling that Cornelia had suggested. From the moment of her arrival Ida became a valued part of the Cannon household and of their circle of friends as well. Shortly thereafter, while attending a gathering at Josiah Royce's house, she caught a glimpse of Richard Clarke Cabot, one of the heroes of the volunteer and professional social workers in Boston. A year earlier, concerned that he frequently did not know enough about the social background of his patients to understand their medical conditions and to institute adequate treatment, Cabot had moved to mitigate that deficiency by establishing a separate division in the Massachusetts General Hospital that would act as a link between medicine and charity. In sum, he saw that effective medical service needed social casework within its own sphere of responsibility.[35]

In January 1907, while attending a State Conference of Social Work in Worcester, Ida again saw Cabot. This time she heard him speak about the operation of social services within the hospital. For Ida, his ideas appeared to be the answer to the problems in patient care that she had encountered as a visiting nurse in St. Paul. She was so stirred by his account that after the meeting she approached Cabot to tell him how much she appreciated what he had said. Ida later remembered that Cabot, in response to her praise, impetuously asked her to join his department at the Massachusetts General Hospital. It is not known whether Cornelia or Cannon, who knew Cabot well, had spoken to him in Ida's behalf. It is clear, however, that Cabot needed help. His first assistant, Garnet Isabel Pelton, a Wellesley graduate who had done settlement work in the South End of Boston, was forced by illness to leave Cabot's department before the first year was out. Save for Gertrude Farmer, another volunteer who took Miss Pelton's position as head worker, Cabot initially had no other help. Whatever the impelling reason for Cabot's invitation, it marked the beginning of an extraordinary change for Ida.

Upon her return from Worcester, Ida asked her school to allow her to take her practical courses with Cabot at the Massachusetts General. When she was refused on the grounds that the work at the hospital was not yet suitable for student training, she joined Cabot as a volunteer instead. Although Ida had originally intended to return to her job in Minnesota after her year at the School for Social Workers was over, she changed her plans and took a more permanent post that was offered her by Cabot. In September of 1907, after a summer abroad with her sister Bernice examining the work of almoners in London and Parisian hospitals, Ida began her new career as Head Worker in the MGH Outpatient Department and moved into an apartment next door to her brother.[36]

◦ঃ   ◦ঃ   ◦ঃ

Nothing stood still in Cornelia Cannon's world. Her independent mind[37] and her abiding interest in the human condition inexorably drew her attention to the problems of the poor and their children in Boston and Cambridge. Long before she persuaded Ida Cannon to continue her training in social work, Cornelia was actively engaged in volunteer charity work as a "friendly visitor" with both the First Parish Church (Unitarian) in Cambridge and the Associated Charities in Boston.[38] In time she helped draw her husband into volunteer social work as well through her activities on the Milk Committee in Boston.

One of the most difficult problems that pediatricians in the United States faced during the late nineteenth and early twentieth centuries was the diarrheal diseases that afflicted babies during the summer months. The mortality was devastating. Although many physicians recognized that breastfed babies suffered less than artificially fed babies, most attributed the difficulties to the composition of cows' milk and devised elaborate formulas to approximate its quality with mother's milk. In addition, a handful of medical reformers led by Henry Coit in New Jersey, Nathan Straus, a philanthropist in New York, and Thomas Rotch, chairman of the department of pediatrics at Harvard, began to focus their attention on the necessity of providing clean milk. In 1891 Rotch helped organize the Walker-Gordon Farms and Laboratory to provide clean modified milk for babies in Massachusetts. The following year Coit succeeded in establishing a standard for clean milk and also helped to organize a special milk commission to oversee the production of such milk in New Jersey. A year later Straus established special milk stations in New York City to dispense clean milk to the poor.[39] Despite Rotch's effort, however, little was done in Massachusetts to increase either the production or the distribution of clean milk.

In 1905 Charles and Isabel Whiting, friends of the Cannons who were concerned that many poor babies were not receiving Walker-Gordon milk, formed a volunteer committee to get pure milk at cost for the babies of poor Boston families.[40] Cannon, who found it difficult to deny his young wife anything, soon found himself at Cornelia's insistence a member of the executive board of the Milk Committee. When he had courted Cornelia, he often implored her not to let him lead the life of a laboratory hermit. "Sometimes in this grind of work, without the control of social life," he once wrote her, "I wonder that I do not become queer. That the 'queerness' of the 'professor,' as commonly pictured, is due to his separation from ordinary human interests, I have no doubt. Think of working hard all day for weeks, then returning from dinner at night to sit dumb and alone in a solitary room."[41] Cornelia needed no further encouragement, and Cannon soon discovered that his wife was determined to bring the world to him. Beginning in 1906 he found himself enmeshed in the work of the Milk Committee—organizing milk stations, visiting nearby farms and milk companies, studying problems in pasteurization, adjudicating personality clashes between various members of the committee, and planning a merger of the committee with the Baby Hygiene Association.[42] In December of 1911, after five years of service on the Milk Committee, Cannon tendered his resignation. A year later he learned that no action had been taken; Cornelia had neglected to give him the secret of how to resign successfully.

Cornelia was so integral a part of Cannon's life that whenever they were apart for even a brief period of time he found the separation difficult to bear. "I have been trying, darling, to live just every moment by itself," he wrote her on one occasion when she was visiting her family in St. Paul, "not looking forward or back, but it is rather hard. The trouble is that as each *now, now, now* comes, you are not with me."[43] *Now* not only referred to home but to the laboratory as well. Although Cornelia had no training

Carl L. Alsberg   Lawrence J. Henderson   Otto Folin

William N. Bullard   Thomas Dwight   Charles S. Minot

Harold C. Ernst   Harvey Cushing   David L. Edsall

Some of Cannon's colleagues in Boston.

Samuel M. Crothers   Charles B. Davenport   George H. Parker

George W. Pierce   Ralph B. Perry   Ernest E. Southard

William James   Robert M. Yerkes   Hugo Münsterberg

Some of Cannon's friends in Cambridge.

in the biological sciences except for some undergraduate courses in zoology, she willingly assisted Cannon by typing his papers, listening to and discussing his ideas, and, from time to time, helping him with his laboratory housekeeping. Cornelia, who attacked such chores with verve rather than style, paid little attention to the precision and care required of some of the tasks her husband gave her. Cannon, who was meticulous in his work, often found Cornelia's slap-dash manner intolerable: "Mistakes found in the final proof all made by Cornelia," he lamented over one of his papers, "very blue—inaccurate, irresponsible, careless wife I have."[44] Such storms, although intense, passed quickly. Other differences, however, took longer to resolve.

After a faculty meeting at the Medical School in the evening Almost from the beginning of their marriage Cornelia found it difficult to cope with one of Cannon's characteristics. Whenever he found himself dissatisfied with his research or discouraged about the activities of his department, he became moody and depressed. Once during one of these blue spells, Cornelia reminisced, "He hardly spoke and made only the most necessary and perfunctory remarks. Finally, I burst into tears and asked him as I wept whether he had stopped loving me. He was much agitated and protested passionately that he was unworthy of me, unfit to tie my shoestrings, etc., etc., and that was why he had not spoken. I cheered up at this and told him that I could not help his thinking himself a mere worm encumbering the earth, if he wanted to, but I did ask that, when the mood came upon him, he would chat with me about it."[45] The depressions continued to come and go. As they recurred, Cornelia, who was now warned, moved right past them as if to deny their existence. There was, however, one survival—a haunting, unspoken fear. The extent of that fear was revealed during the early morning hours of January 6, 1907.[46]

After a faculty meeting at the Medical School in the evening of January 5, Cannon returned to his home in Cambridge only to discover that he had inadvertently given the latchkey of his house to a colleague. Unable to get anyone to open the door, he decided to spend some time with the Perrys, who lived down the street. When a subsequent attempt to reach his wife by telephone failed, Cannon assumed that she was asleep and decided to spend the night with the Perrys. Unknown to Cannon, Cornelia and his sister Ida had gone out for the evening and arrived home some time after his various efforts to rouse them. They, in turn, began to await his return from the faculty meeting. As midnight passed, Cornelia grew more agitated, recalling that her husband's work was going badly and that he had made a point of telling her earlier that week that his insurance was paid up. The usually intrepid Cornelia, now in a panic, called on his friends at the Medical School and his fellow Wichts to help her organize a search party. All reconstruction of Cannon's movements that evening led ominously to the Cottage Farm Bridge. By two o'clock in the morning the unspoken fear that he might have committed suicide could no longer be denied, and Robert Yerkes and Frank Mallory went out on the Charles River to look for Cannon's body. Nothing was found, and after some hours the search party, tired and discouraged, returned to the Cannon home to await daybreak and the help of the police.

The next morning, when hope was almost gone, a refreshed, well-rested Cannon appeared, wondering at the sight of his distraught wife and tearful congregation of friends. For Cannon, the incident represented a hugely amusing series of improbabilities in a comedy of errors. Cornelia, never one to dwell on painful matters, resolutely tried to put the episode out of her mind. Perhaps the person most pained by the incident was Mallory, who suffered a broken arm during the search.[47]

9   *At Work in Boston*

I N THE FALL of 1905, a year before Cannon became chairman of the physiology department, he gave an address on the ideals of science to the National Conference of Unitarian and Other Christian Churches.[1] The problem of the duties and obligations of the scientific investigator had long absorbed him, and although his talk was in line with these interests, it was not merely an effort to popularize science. It was also an attempt to persuade his audience to support medical investigators who were then under sharp attack by antivivisectionists. The scientist, Cannon told his audience, was a being uniquely endowed with a skeptical and discriminating intelligence who used his abilities to explore and advance the frontiers of knowledge. To succeed in these tasks, Cannon argued, the scientist had to be given a triad of special freedoms and rights—the freedom to denounce what was false and the right to seek and to declare what was true. But the scientist also had obligations, perhaps the most important of which was teaching and inspiring his students to become likewise lovers of truth and disseminators of knowledge. Although Cannon understood that the extension of knowledge was of economic importance, he maintained that the scientist had to be indifferent to motives of acquisition and wealth and indeed to the world's praise.

At first glance the ideals Cannon expressed appear to be pieties of the sort that one would expect to be voiced at a church meeting. They were in fact much more. Nowhere was their meaning for Cannon more manifest than in his response to his teaching and research responsibilities after taking up his post in the Higginson professorship. When at the end of 1906 Eliot reported to

the Harvard Corporation on the continuing decline in enrollment
at the Medical School, he concluded that the decline was of particular benefit to the preclinical professors because they were required to devote less time to teaching and therefore had more for
investigation.[2] Cannon made no such distinctions; for him teaching
and research were part of the same process of extending knowledge. In a report earlier that year on the prospective financial
condition of the physiology department, Cannon elucidated his
convictions and once again revealed his views of the functions of
the teacher as an investigator and his special obligation to his
students. "Every man active in investigation has more problems
in mind that he can work at himself," he wrote. "A part of his
service to the world consists in training others by giving to others
these problems to work at under his direction. These 'others' are
ordinarily his students,—young men who have been stimulated
by his example. They are not yet established in life, they require
remuneration until they have done enough work to warrant their
being taken into independent positions. They should receive during these years of training (which are very likely to be productive
of good results in research) sufficient compensation to afford comfortable support."[3]

Throughout the summer of 1906 Cannon, although teaching
summer school, continued his research and guided some of his
students in their various investigations. From the end of July he
spent a good deal of his time moving equipment from his quarters
in the Boylston Street School to the new building. Moving to the
Longwood Avenue quadrangle was not easy, and some faculty
members grumbled that the School had not prepared adequately
for the new semester's work. Frank Mallory of the pathology department was particularly indignant about the lack of equipment
and supplies, except what was brought from Boylston Street. "We
entered the new buildings just before school opened with nothing
provided but empty rooms, and stools for the students," he complained to Eliot. "Other departments must be in much the same
condition as we are . . . To add to our troubles we are compelled
this year for the first time to feed our animals at our own expense."[4]

If Cannon had such difficulties, he did not let them bother
him. In fact by mid-September he began his first animal experiments in the new buildings, and in the months that followed he
continued his various digestive studies. He did, however, have

some trepidation about teaching the first-year course in physiology later that winter and spring, in part because he was afraid that he might face some of the difficulties that Porter had with students in the introductory course. Early in January Cannon began to detail his plans for the course, preparing meticulous lectures and demonstrations and devising experiments that reflected his own research experience. In February when the course began, he appeared to be especially pleased with the quality of the students. "They are a fine lot of fellows," he noted in his diary. "They seem less overwhelmed by the beginnings of the work than hitherto." A few days later he continued in the same vein. "Students seem to be settling down like veterans, but," he added, "they are not so direct with me as before."[5]

Initially the work in the course went well, not the least because Cornelia performed a great deal of the routine, preparing bibliographies and thesis references for the students. By the end of the month, however, Cannon began to register a variety of complaints, some about the progress of the students' work, others about the quality of his demonstrations and lectures. "Demonstration action current of heart—poor," he fretted in his diary. Several days later, there were new laments: "Demonstration on paramecium—poor. First lecture on nervous conduction—poor."[6] It was the delivery of his lectures that bothered him most. As the term progressed, his self-criticism increased. On March 6 he noted, "At home in evening preparing lectures on nervous system. I am a very poor lecturer—a *very poor lecturer*."

To cope with the difficulty, Cannon invited his wife to visit his class and pinpoint his faults. Cornelia, ever a truth speaker, did not spare him. The next day he recorded the results of her visit: "Cornelia hears me lecture—objects to 'ugh' and general cold-fish attitude as I speak." Although Cornelia subsequently lightened his burden by undertaking to make diagrams to illustrate his lectures on the sympathetic nervous system, the quality of lecturing did not improve, and Cannon's gloom deepened. "Gave a miserable lecture this morning," he despaired in his diary toward the end of March, "—miserable, and I felt miserable because of it."[7] In April he invited Porter to lecture to the class on the cardiovascular system, not as an effort to mend his differences with him but rather as a way of gaining a respite for himself from lectures he believed were not going well.

Although Cannon's concern might have been warranted by his inability to improve his lectures, it was also an example of the standards and requirements he had set for himself as a teacher. The following semester his complaints and lamentations continued, perhaps even growing in intensity. Still, when fourth-year students in the fall of 1907 elected to take advanced work with him rather than with Porter, he willingly made room for them, although it interfered with his program of keeping the autumn months free for research.[8]

Good teaching has a variety of dimensions; perhaps a better measure of Cannon's ability in the classroom can be found in the way he prepared and inspired students to do research. Like Bowditch, Cannon suggested research topics to incoming as well as advanced students, and on occasion invited some of them to assist him in his own investigations. He worked beside them, instructing them in various investigative techniques including x-ray and surgery and in the discipline of research—not only in critically evaluating results but also in working within a modest budget. Throughout, his instruction was guided by his ideals of advancing knowledge and developing a new generation of medical scientists. Both goals were particularly important to him and can be seen in his relations with three of his advanced students at that time— Boris Sidis, Alexander Forbes, and Roy Hoskins.

➥ ➥ ➥

In the fall of 1906 a fourth-year student, Boris Sidis, asked Cannon if he could work under his direction on an experimental study of sleep. Sidis was unusual. Older than most of the students in the Medical School, he had a strong professional background, including a Ph.D. in psychology from Harvard, a variety of important hospital posts as a practicing psychotherapist, and an impressive list of publications. Two of his works, *The Psychology of Suggestion* and *Multiple Personality*, had earned the praise of his teacher, William James.[9] Still, for all his achievements, Sidis had difficulties with the medical faculty, in some measure because he had an abrasive personality and in part because he peppered them from time to time with petitions that he be allowed to go through the medical course on his own terms.[10] Despite Sidis's reputation, Cannon agreed to let him work in the laboratory. In the ensuing months Sidis, using conditions favorable for bringing about "sub-waking hypnoidal states," succeeded in establishing many of the requirements for inducing sleep in experimental animals. Ultimately, he came to the conclusion that sleep was a protective rather than a recuperative device, in effect verifying the sleep theories of the Swiss pioneer psychologist, Edouard Claparède.[11]

Cannon, who had carefully supervised Sidis's investigation, thought his work excellent. When in the spring of 1907 Sidis petitioned the medical faculty to award him the M.D. degree although he had not fulfilled a number of his clinical requirements, Cannon assured him that he would vote for him. The faculty, however, then in the midst of a sharp debate about standards and requirements leading to the medical degree, took a different position on the ground that in pursuing his particular interests Sidis had neglected to take the full four-year course. James Jackson Putnam, working in Sidis's behalf, tried to persuade Eliot and certain members of the faculty—E. H. Bradford, W. T. Councilman, and R. H. Fitz among them—to vote in favor of the petition. The faculty nevertheless remained adamant and voted against Sidis.[12] A year later, after he made up his deficiencies, he was granted the M.D. degree. In 1909 Sidis published his dissertation on sleep. Although the book was dedicated to Morton Prince, Sidis in a special note acknowledged the advice and consideration Cannon had given him when he worked in his laboratory.[13]

Cannon, like Bowditch, maintained an open laboratory in the sense that he accepted advanced students solely on the basis of their desire to engage in research. His laboratory as a result often had a diverse population of students. For example, Alexander Forbes, another advanced student who worked under Cannon's direction, was a descendant of an old and wealthy Brahmin family and was markedly different from Sidis, a Russian-Jewish immigrant, in his social outlook as well as in his special interests.[14] Yet the two men had a number of things in common. Both had the benefit of an undergraduate and graduate education from Harvard before entering Medical School, and both had well-defined research interests before they began to work with Cannon—in Forbes's case, a wish to study the organization of the nervous system.

Much of Forbes's interest derived from his work with George H. Parker at Harvard, who was then studying the reflexes of lower animals as part of a larger investigation of the origin and evolution of the nervous system.[15] When Forbes, as a fourth-year medical student, inquired about work in physiology in the summer and fall of 1909, Cannon in typical fashion gave him a list of eleven topics from which to choose for a research project. Two of these involved problems that stemmed from Charles Sherrington's studies on the spinal reflex—the first, a suggested examination of the effect of inhibition on the rate of discharge along a motor nerve; the second, a study of whether different rates of stimulation affected inhibition in the central nervous system.[16] In the months that followed Forbes began an investigation of both problems and in the process succeeded in developing new electrical techniques to record nerve impulses. Cannon was so pleased by the quality and progress of his research that upon Forbes's graduation he offered him a position as instructor in the physiology department. A year later Forbes, eager to continue his training abroad, with Cannon's strong support applied for and received a post as a visiting investigator in Sherrington's laboratory at Liverpool. The experience proved to be all that Forbes had hoped for and more. In the time spent with Sherrington, he not only completed the research he began in Cannon's laboratory[17] but also met and established friendships with a number of young English physiologists, including Keith Lucas and Edgar D. Adrian at Cambridge University. When Forbes returned to Boston in 1912, he came armed with new skills and equipment that enabled him to measure with increasing accuracy the various reflex activities in the central nervous system—in effect, adding another dimension to the nature of physiological investigation and instruction at Harvard.[18]

Roy Hoskins, in turn, was very different in his origins, training, and interests from either Sidis or Forbes. The son of a Nebraska farmer, Hoskins received his undergraduate and graduate training in the biological sciences at the University of Kansas.[19] When he came to Harvard in 1908, he did not enter as a medical student but rather as a doctoral candidate in physiology in the newly established medical sciences program. Just why he chose to work with Cannon is not clear.[20] Up to that time, the major thrust of Cannon's research had been directed to an examination of the functions of the digestive system. Hoskins, for his part, was interested in the emerging discipline of endocrinology. In fact, when he first met Cannon, he told him he had already mapped out a research program in which he would attempt to determine whether removing the endocrine glands of pregnant guinea pigs or feeding gland extracts to them would affect glandular development in the offspring, a purely morphometric study. Initially Cannon was at a loss about how to deal with Hoskins. The doctorate in medical sciences was a new program at the Medical School, and Cannon had never had the experience of preparing a candidate for the Ph.D. degree. Worse, as he later confessed, he only had "a literary acquaintance" with the glands of internal secretion.[21] Instead of giving Hoskins carte blanche, Cannon tried to persuade him to join in one of his ongoing investigations on digestion. Hoskins politely but firmly refused. The more Cannon pushed his program, the more adamant Hoskins became. At last, Cannon relented and allowed him to work on the interrelations between the thyroid and other endosecretory organs.[22]

Hoskins, as a teaching fellow, had his own ideas about the instructional program as well. As time passed, relations between the two men became increasingly strained. Late in January 1910 a blow-up occurred about a suggestion Hoskins had made to distribute the laboratory teaching more equitably. Some of the substance of the ensuing argument and its impact on Cannon is contained in one of Cannon's terse diary notes: "Jan. 31: Busy all morning getting ready for course and talking to Mr. Hoskins who tells me I am autocratic. Department of Physiology = Dr. Cannon, only academic freedom is in *my* office. Told Dr. Martin who assures me this is all nonsense."

The storm, for all its intensity, soon blew over. Two days later Cannon invited Hoskins to his home and spent the better part of the evening quizzing him on the nervous system in preparation for his final doctoral examinations. Hoskins came back to Cannon again and again for help in revising his dissertation. When the dissertation was submitted for evaluation to the other members of the doctoral committee—the ever-meticulous C. S. Minot and W. T. Porter—it passed without criticism or emendation. Hoskins's final doctoral examination was equally triumphant.[23]

Thirty-three years later, Cannon reminisced about Hoskins and underlined the importance of his relations with him for his own subsequent development as teacher and investigator: "When [Hoskins] received the doctorate in 1910, I had learned something about developing a disciple, and also had become so much interested in endocrine physiology that de la Paz and I undertook a research on the effects of emotional excitement on secretion from the adrenal medulla—an enterprise lying in the intermediate zone between gastroenterology and endocrinology."[24] Actually, what Cannon wrote about learning from his experience with Hoskins could have been said with equal justice about Sidis and Forbes. All three helped him realize his ideals of advancing knowledge and inspiring his students to become, like him, a lover of truth and disseminator of knowledge.[25] Further, his direction of their research not only stimulated his curiosity but also broadened and enhanced his understanding of the importance of the effect of emotions on bodily change. It was by no means the only circumstance that contributed to such understanding. Other factors led in the same direction—perhaps the most important was the process of his own work on the functions of digestion.

* * *

One of the striking aspects of Cannon's continuing research on the digestive system was his increasing use of surgery in his investigations. It allowed him, as he later explained, to produce in animals conditions of the stomach and intestines that permitted x-ray observations of the processes occurring in these organs after complete recovery from operation. Equally important, it extended his perspective of the functioning of the digestive system as a whole, and he began to see more clearly the interrelations of the different parts of the alimentary canal.[26]

Although Cannon's research with John Bapst Blake introduced him to some of the techniques and literature of surgery, the process of refining his surgical skills was directly related to his friendship and subsequent collaboration with Fred T. Murphy. Murphy, a young surgeon who had recently completed his residency at the Massachusetts General Hospital, was one of a small group of surgeons in Boston who had become convinced of the necessity of a laboratory experience in surgical training. From the time the surgery department began to actively foster surgical research, Murphy submitted a variety of research proposals ranging from studies of new procedures of gastroenterostomy and intestinal drainage to investigations of the problem of surgical shock. As soon as Cannon and Murphy met, their mutual interests and enthusiasm drew them together, and in a relatively brief period of time they became good friends.[27] Cannon's regard for Murphy, after working with him for several months in the fall of 1905, is whimsically revealed in a letter to his wife, then visiting her family in St. Paul. "I had a fine dream last night, about Dr. Murphy rising to speak at a smoker held by a great scientific meeting," he wrote her:

> All the Yale men rose to do him honor—he blushed and said modestly, "Oh, fellows, don't do that." Then he sat down, and thereupon all the Yale men who were standing sat down. Then Murphy rose again, and his college mates rose too. Murphy in desperation cried out, "Well, fellows, come along" and started to march around the room. One fellow, a perfect giant, stepped in front of Murphy. Murphy seized him by the collar and with one hand lifted the huge fellow into the air. But the effort was too great—Murphy fell in a heap on the floor, suffering as the man next to me at the smoker remarked from "Auswasserung" of the heart . . . I told the dream to Murphy. Murphy liked it, too.[28]

The bond between the two men was strengthened by an almost continuous exchange of ideas and information on a wide variety of physiological and surgical problems. Murphy, who was trying to perfect a new positive pressure apparatus to use in thoracic operations, came to Cannon for instruction on the physiological aspects of artificial respiration. Cannon's tutoring as well as his suggestions for modifying the apparatus proved enormously helpful and ultimately led to a series of successful animal experiments. "If the apparatus works equally well in operations upon human beings," Murphy reported in the *Boston Medical and Surgical Journal*, "it possesses the advantage of cheapness, portability, ease of manipulation and simplicity."[29] A number of months later Cannon described a chance meeting with Murphy after he had used the apparatus on a patient at the Massachusetts General Hospital: "He had just come from an operation with Dr. Scudder in which they had applied the principles which Dr. Murphy and I worked out. Instead of having flutterings of the heart and disturbed breathing and trouble with the etherization, as is usual, there was not the slightest sign of shock from the operation, although it lasted nearly an hour and a half. That made me feel very happy."[30]

Cannon in turn was equally well served by Murphy's tutoring in surgical techniques. After the completion of his research with Blake early in 1905, Cannon joined Murphy in an investigation of

the physiological behavior of the gastrointestinal tract after abdominal surgery. Throughout the rest of that year surgery became
a regular feature of Cannon's laboratory procedure, and both men
fell into a daily routine of operating together and then observing
by means of x-ray the rate of discharge of various foods from the
stomach and intestines of their experimental cats. Often whole
days were spent in making repeated observations of their animals,
and in the process both Cannon and Murphy were unwittingly
exposed to large doses of radiation.

Throughout the investigation Cannon spent many hours reading and gathering ideas from the surgical literature. In particular,
he became intrigued by accounts of Alexis Carrel's new vascular
surgical techniques because of their relevance to one of the problems of intestinal suturing that he and Murphy were examining.[31]
Learning about these new techniques absorbed and excited Cannon. "Dr. Murphy and I did a most difficult and interesting operation today," he wrote Cornelia early in December 1905, "sewing
together a severed blood vessel, just like the intestine, end to end.
It may make it possible to put in pieces of vessels where vessels
have been injured or where there is disease of the vessel."[32] Some
time later, anticipating that Carrel's techniques would be useful
in his future work, he sent Murphy and Charles Scudder to Carrel
so that they could learn his surgical procedures first-hand.[33] Cannon's fastidious care in organizing and conducting his research
extended to preparing the results of his investigations for publication as well. Although a report of his research with Murphy was
presented to the Boston Society for Medical Sciences in November
1905, he subsequently revised and polished the paper time and
again before it was finally published in the *Annals of Surgery*.[34]

Cannon's work with Murphy yielded a rich harvest of useful
as well as thought-provoking conclusions. Some of their findings
were unexpected. In their investigation of the effects of certain
surgical procedures on peristaltic activity of the gastrointestinal
tract—such as ether anesthesia, exposure to air, and cooling—
they discovered that these interventions had a minimal effect on
delaying the passage of food from the stomach through the small
intestine. On the other hand, they determined that handling the
stomach, depending on the degree of gentleness or roughness of
manipulation, could retard for a considerable period of time gastric

peristalsis.[35] They also found that other surgical conditions could lead to postoperative paralytic ileus (cessation of motor activity) of the intestine. Thus, if the small intestine was resected and then rejoined by a lateral or side-to-side anastomosis, food invariably stagnated in the region of the junction. However, if the resection was followed by an end-to-end anastomosis, food passed normally along that sutured part of the intestine as it had along other parts. One of their most provocative findings was the discovery that gastric peristalsis was not significantly affected by surgery but continued regularly. Nevertheless, despite its continued regularity, the pylorus remained closed and did not allow any food to enter the injured portion of the intestine until a certain degree of recovery had taken place.[36]

These findings generated additional physiological problems. The most obvious question was the nature of the mechanism that caused the pylorus to remain closed until the injured intestine effected some repair: was it a reflex effect, Cannon asked, that was mediated by the central nervous system, or was the activity controlled by a local mechanism in the wall of the intestine? Did manipulation of the intestine, which caused postoperative stasis in the bowel, act locally on the neuromusculature of the alimentary canal or indirectly through reflex inhibition from the central nervous system?

There is no denying the importance of the questions Cannon pondered.[37] Besides stirring him to undertake a new series of investigations, they encouraged him to attempt a synthesis of his findings with those of other physiologists, such as Pavlov, who had demonstrated the importance of the psychic phase of secretion, and Bayliss and Starling, who maintained that peristaltic contraction was a coordinated local reflex carried out by the neural network in the wall of the gut.[38] Cannon's effort to coordinate his findings with those of other physiologists led him to look at the digestive system teleologically—seeking to understand how the interrelations of the different parts of the alimentary canal united the digestive processes in an orderly series of successively dependent events. To determine the contributing factors, he began to focus his attention on the relations of the autonomic nervous system to the alimentary canal—in particular, those elements that determine the reflex control of peristalsis in the esophagus, stomach, and intestines and those that control the flow of pancreatic juice and bile.

୶ଽ   ୶ଽ   ୶ଽ

Even before he confirmed the results of his early surgical research, Cannon, with the aid of student assistants as well as with Murphy, began the first of his new studies on the physiology of the autonomic nervous system. His major purpose at this time was to learn whether by sectioning various nerve pathways he could demonstrate their role not only in gastric peristalsis but also in the rate of discharge of various foods from the stomach. Using sterile surgical technique, he cut the splanchnic nerves (the major sympathetic innervation of the stomach and intestines) bilaterally in a group of experimental cats, the vagus nerves (the parasympathetic supply of the esophagus, stomach, and small bowel) in a second group of animals, and both the splanchnic and vagus nerves in a third group.

When the animals were fully recovered from surgery and conscious, Cannon fed them by stomach tubes a meal of carbohydrates and proteins mixed with bismuth subnitrate and then examined them by x-ray. Using the semiquantitative method he had previously devised of measuring the length of shadows of the small intestine filled with radio-opaque material, Cannon found a persistence of peristalsis and the characteristic differential rates of discharge of carbohydrates and proteins in all of the experimental groups—with one notable exception. After the vagi of a number of animals were severed, he discovered that there is an initial depression of the movement of the alimentary canal followed several hours later by a recovery of peristalsis. He thus confirmed that peristalsis and the differential discharge of various foods are controlled by a local or hormonal mechanism and are not mediated through the central nervous system.[39]

Although Cannon was disappointed with his negative results on the role of the autonomic nervous system on the rate of gastric emptying, he immediately began a further series of experiments to determine the special effect of bilateral vagotomy on esophageal peristalsis.[40] Cannon was skeptical of the conventional physiological wisdom (as eminent as it was) which maintained that once the vagi were severed, esophageal peristalsis ceased. His skepticism derived in part from the results of his previous investigation of the effects of splanchnic and vagus section and in part from his critical reading of the physiological literature. Many of the early reports of a cessation of esophageal peristalsis after vagus section cited the experiments of John Reid, an early nineteenth-century Scottish anatomist and physiologist, as a prime authority for their postulations.[41]

Studying Reid's papers Cannon discovered that some of his peers had read Reid's work too rapidly. It was true that Reid had observed an arrest of food in the esophagus after the vagi in rabbits had been sectioned, but he also had found that in dogs the disturbance is temporary and is followed by what appears to be a free movement to the stomach. Reid's complete observations became central to the experiments that Cannon planned. "If it is possible for the stomach to recover from a primary paralysis [after vagus section]," he reasoned, "may not the oesophagus, at least that part of it similar in all essential respects to the stomach structure, be able to recover likewise from a primary paralysis?"[42] From that point on, Cannon focused his attention on the anatomical structure of the esophagus, and he sought the assistance of J. L. Bremer in the anatomy department and S. B. Wolbach in the pathology department in making histological analyses of sections of the esophagus in his experimental animals, which now, in addition to cats, included rabbits, dogs, and monkeys.

Cannon's first experiments with rabbits and dogs confirmed Reid's early observations, and Bremer's subsequent examination of the structure of the esophagus of both animals offered an anatomical explanation for his results. Bremer found that rabbits have striated muscle throughout the esophagus whereas only the upper half of the esophagus of the dog is composed of such muscle, the lower half being constituted wholly of smooth muscle. Some time later Cannon determined, with Wolbach's help, that vagus section in monkeys yielded the same results as the experiments with dogs because the esophagus of the monkey has a similar muscle structure. Cannon concluded that the part of the esophagus composed of striated muscle is controlled by the parasympathetic nervous system, whereas the portion composed of smooth muscle is like other similar parts of the alimentary canal and is capable of peristaltic activity without the aid of extrinsic nerves.[43]

At no time during this period did Cannon devote himself exclusively to working on any single problem. No sooner did he begin his research on the intrinsic and extrinsic innervation of the gastrointestinal tract than he turned almost simultaneously to a reexamination of a problem that had long absorbed him—the nature of the mechanism that controlled the emptying of the stomach.[44]

Twenty years earlier two German gastroenterologists, C. A. Ewald and I. Boas, had found by use of a stomach tube in man that free hydrochloric acid appeared before the volume of gastric contents began to diminish. Soon after, a number of European physiologists, notably Hirsch in Germany and Serdjukow in Russia, demonstrated that gastric evacuation was also inhibited by the introduction of acid into the duodenum.[45] Cannon focused his attention on the mechanisms controlling the action of the pyloric sphincter. His previous investigation of the different rates of discharge of various foodstuffs from the stomach had made him aware that gastric peristaltic waves do not show moment-to-moment variation, and from this he had surmised that a steady pressure was exerted on food contents in the prepyloric region of the stomach. Because his various feeding experiments had further shown that emptying of the stomach was intermittent, he reasoned that resistance in the pylorus varied with changes in gastric acidity.

When Cannon told a meeting of the Gastro-Enterological Society in April 1905 he believed there was a possibility that gastric acid controlled the functioning of the pyloric sphincter, he was merely voicing an idea.[46] He had not yet any convincing experimental proof to support such a theory.

~ ~ ~

Late in 1905 Cannon with Fred Murphy's help began a series of experiments to confirm his theories of gastric evacuation. Initially, they made a number of gastric fistulae in cats to determine the relationship between the first appearance of acid and the first exit of food from the stomach. These early experiments, however, proved to be negative, and Cannon began to despair. But then an unexpected success occurred. "Yesterday," he wrote Cornelia, "was another day of drudgery, relieved, however, by a very exciting observation. My gastric fistula method has at last worked. For 15 minutes I watched the waves passing over the stomach, with no change in the reaction of the food and no discharge from the stomach. At 11:29 nothing was out of the stomach; at 11:31 the first indication of a change of the reaction from alkaline or neutral to acid; at 11:33 looked and found food had left the stomach. I immediately sent Frank for a can of salmon and gave the cat a banquet!"[47]

Cannon did not immediately try to exploit these positive results but instead put the study aside. He did take time early in 1906, however, with little more than the hints from his gastric fistula experiments, to articulate in a detailed and comprehensive fashion his theory of acid control of the pylorus in the *American Journal of Medical Sciences:*

> It seems probable that the signal for the relaxation [of the pylorus] is the appearance of free hydrochloric acid in the stomach . . .
>
> If, then, free acid in the stomach is the signal for pyloric relaxation, the mechanism of the pylorus may be largely explained. Thus the first appearance of free acid in the stomach would open the pylorus, and initiate the chemical control of the sphincter. The opening of the pylorus permits the exit of the acid chyme. Acid in the duodenum keeps the pylorus closed. And acid in the duodenum also stimulates the flow of the alkaline pancreatic secretion. Since no inorganic acid is normally present beyond the first few inches of the small intestine, the acid must there be neutralized. As neutralizing proceeds, the stimulus closing the pylorus is weakened, until the acid in the stomach again relaxes the sphincter; again the acid food is discharged, and by its acidity closes the sphincter to further passage until the duodenal changes finish their slower course.[48]

In the autumn of 1906 Cannon began a study to obtain more experimental evidence for his theory of acid control of the pylorus. This time, in addition to his gastric fistula technique, he introduced a battery of surgical procedures to carry his research forward. He excised the stomach of one of his experimental cats and measured the intragastric pressure of the organ in a bath of continuously oxygenated Ringer's solution. He observed that although acidity in the pyloric antrum did not alter peristaltic activity, it did relax the pylorus and allow foodstuffs to be discharged from the stomach. In another experiment he created a duodenal fistula in a dog in order to sample the acidity of food entering the duodenum and later noted that the presence of acid led to closure of the pylorus.

To extend these findings, Cannon with Murphy's assistance next tied off the pancreatic and bile ducts to test the effect of the absence of normal alkaline secretions in the duodenum on gastric evacuation. The experiment proved Cannon's supposition to be correct—interference with the flow of pancreatic and gall bladder secretions did block the neutralization of acid in the duodenum and kept the pylorus closed, delaying the emptying of the stomach.[49] Not all of Cannon's experiments proved immediately successful. When he later tried to demonstrate that fats and fatty acids release secretin (a hormone that causes an increased flow of pancreatic juice), he failed time and again. It was not until Otto Folin suggested to him that he mix the fatty acid in a solution containing alcohol extract of intestinal mucosa that the experiment finally succeeded.[50]

The high point of Cannon's research occurred in mid-June of 1907 when a study he was conducting with one of his students on the functions of the cardia (or upper portion) of the stomach suggested that the presence of acidified food in the stomach kept the cardiac sphincter closed during digestion. The implications of the new finding excited him. A week later when he successfully repeated the experiment, he jubilantly recorded the results in his diary. "Worked with Smith on cardia . . . found acid in stomach kept cardia closed. Got conception that whole alimentary canal was one mechanism—stimulation causes contraction above, relaxation below."[51] For Cannon the finding appeared to be in line with Bayliss and Starling's general law of peristaltic movement of the intestine—that stimulation at any point on the intestine resulted in a contraction above that point and relaxation below.

Although the concept of acid control of the alimentary canal was supported by a growing amount of experimental evidence as well as the formidable framework of circumstantial data that Cannon had gathered, he was aware that some of his findings did not square with his theory. He knew, for example, that water, fluid egg albumin, and glucose did not stimulate the flow of acidic gastric juice and yet were rapidly discharged from the stomach through an apparently relaxed pylorus.[52] Such findings, however, appeared to be answerable, and he felt that they basically did not threaten the viability of the theory he had constructed.

When Cannon presented a brief account of the results of his latest experiments to the annual meeting of the American Gastro-Enterological Association in June 1908, his investigations of the pylorus were lauded. "It is just such experiments as those described by Dr. Cannon," Fenton B. Turk, a Chicago practitioner told the audience, "that add dignity to internal medicine."[53] Few disagreed with Turk's assessment. Cannon was a long-time favorite of the Association and had been commended several times before for the usefulness of his research in solving difficult clinical problems. There were, nevertheless, some present who openly challenged Cannon's theory. Max Einhorn, one of the leading gastroenterologists in the United States, told Cannon that he could not accept his theory because it did not adequately explain the relaxation of the pyloric sphincter in cases of achylia gastrica—a condition where there was no acid in the stomach and still food found its way into the intestine. Einhorn's objection was telling, and Cannon had no ready answer. "I cannot explain Dr. Einhorn's case of achylia gastrica, in which the findings seem to negative all physiological evidence that has been gathered during the past four or five years," he replied. "In that case there must have been some unexplained compensatory mechanism; otherwise, I cannot account for the flow of bile and pancreatic juice, which depends on the presence of acid in the duodenum. The case is a mystery to me at present." Later, Cannon dismissed the objection on the ground that Einhorn was dealing with a pathological condition whereas his experiments were concerned with the normal physiological aspects of pyloric control.

Cannon's research on acid control brought to a close the second phase of his work on the digestive system. He was now prepared to examine some other questions that had emerged during his latest investigations. The relationships between the activities of the alimentary canal and general bodily condition particularly absorbed him—especially the effects of depressive emotions on motor activities of the stomach and intestines. Despite his interest, Cannon was delayed in undertaking such a study by another problem that was directly related to his laboratory but ironically took him away from it—the ethics of using animals in research.

10   *The Antivivisectionist*
Agitation

D|URING THE COURSE of his investigations in 1906 and
the following years Cannon increasingly complained about
the lack of experimental animals to carry his research
forward.[1] The use of surgical procedures in his work had dramatically escalated his need for such animals, and he felt frustrated
by the relentless efforts of the Massachusetts Society for the Prevention of Cruelty to Animals and the New England Antivivisection Society to thwart the use of animals in research. Although
the question of using animals for experimental purposes appeared
to be primarily an ethical problem, it had been transformed into
a political issue as well. Cannon was a relative newcomer to this
controversy, which had initially erupted in America approximately
four years before his birth. It was only a matter of time, however,
before he would become involved in the struggle with the antivivisectionists.

In 1866 Henry Bergh, the son of a wealthy merchant, appalled
by the wanton cruelty displayed toward horses and other animals
in New York City streets, helped found the American Society for
the Prevention of Cruelty to Animals.[2] The new society, following
its charter, essentially devoted itself to apprehending and prosecuting cruel offenders; providing water places, rest farms, and
shelters for sick and abused animals; and developing educational
programs designed to instill traits of humane behavior in school
children. The following year Bergh went a step further and helped
introduce an anticruelty bill in the New York state legislature that
included a special proviso designed to restrict animal experimentation. It is not known what motivated Bergh in this particular

effort. There was actually little animal experimentation in New York at the time, and it may be, as some have suggested, that Bergh saw antivivisection as a logical extension of his general campaign against cruelty.[3] Although the bill subsequently passed, Bergh was not completely successful. At a strategic moment in the legislative process the New York State Medical Society succeeded in amending this particular provision, thus preventing the bill from interfering with properly conducted experiments performed under the authority of incorporated medical colleges.[4]

Although defeated, Bergh was not deflected from his new course. In 1874, soon after joining with Elbridge Gerry and John D. Wright in organizing the New York Society for the Prevention of Cruelty to Children, he reopened his attacks on animal experimentation, this time as part of a vast continuing educational campaign. In 1880, convinced that he had laid the groundwork for an effective legislative effort, Bergh drafted a new antivivisection bill for introduction into the New York state legislature.[5] In addition to making vivisection a misdemeanor, this bill defined the term so broadly as to negate the use of animals in any medical investigation, experiment, or demonstration. The reaction of the medical community to Bergh's bill was prompt and forceful. The New York State Medical Society, for example, declared its opposition in a ringing resolution "against a persistent and unreasoning design to thwart the progress of medical science" and also established a special Committee on Experimental Medicine to lobby with the governor and legislature in the event that similar bills were introduced in the future.[6]

A short time later the State Medical Society empowered its special committee, then headed by John Call Dalton, to join with members of other local and county medical societies in this struggle. Dalton, who had trained with Claude Bernard and was an experimental physiologist, saw the thrust of antivivisection legislation as a serious threat to medical science throughout the country and interpreted the resolutions of the State Medical Society in even broader terms. In January of 1881 he asked Henry Bowditch to become an associate member of his committee. "You see," he wrote Bowditch, "we are extending our ramifications, to be ready for future contests with antivivisection hysterics,—We ought to be organized so that Associate Members of the Committee in other States may be ready to give us notice of any movement in their neighborhood or transmit any information that may be useful for our common objects."[7]

Dalton was prescient. In 1883 the first antivivisection society, the American Anti-Vivisection Society of Philadelphia, was formed in the United States. It was followed by the organization of a number of regional and state societies, including among others the New York Anti-Vivisection Society, the Illinois Anti-Vivisection Society, and (some time later) the New England Anti-Vivisection Society.[8] The proliferation of these groups was not merely the result of organizational drives by those already involved in the work of animal protection societies; it was also due in part to the success of a sister group in England, the Victoria Street Society, in getting an antivivisection act passed in Great Britain in 1876.[9] In large measure that legislative success strengthened the thrust against animal experimentation in America. In the years that followed, the polemicists of the British movement increasingly informed antivivisection argument and strategy in the United States by means of vigorous lecture tours and through personal contact with American leaders. Indeed, Caroline Earle White, the founder of the American Anti-Vivisection Society in Philadelphia, had visited England several times to be schooled in the intricacies of antivivisection ideology and debate by Frances Power Cobbe, the doyenne of the British antivivisection movement.[10] Cobbe, a formidable woman described by a contemporary as having "inextinguishable eloquence especially in the direction of vituperation,"[11] soon instilled her valuable platform qualities in White and developed her into what one newspaper called "the phototype in America" of her inestimable self. For the next generation Mrs. White remained a dominating presence in the American antivivisection movement.

As the clamor for restrictive legislation in the United States began to grow, American medical scientists also turned to British counterparts for help. When Clifton Fremont Hodge, the professor of biology at Clark University, wrote Michael Foster late in 1890 for advice on how to deal with the problem in Massachusetts, the distinguished English physiologist, drawing on his personal experience with British antivivisectionists, warned of impending danger: "The effect of such an act with you would be, I imagine, much as with us. It would not stop physiological work,—it would worry it,—it would prevent many important researches being made complete—it would lead men to follow out, not the lines of research to which their ideas lead them, but those which they could pursue without the restraints of licenses and certificates,—it would, as with us, almost destroy the researches carried on by private individuals, working apart from established laboratories, and would certainly largely curtail the usefulness of Clark University." Continuing, he urged meeting such legislative tactics head on: "My advice to you is, accept no compromise whatever, refuse to admit for a moment the need of such a law, and fight against it everywhere, in the newspapers and on the platform, and if the situation demands it, even imitate your opponents and refuse a political vote to a candidate who will not pledge to vote against it."[12]

As experimental physiology, pathology, and bacteriology began to assume a more prominent and substantive role in the development of medicine in the United States, members of the animal protection movement became increasingly alarmed. In 1892, for example, the Massachusetts Society for the Prevention of Cruelty to Animals, under the leadership of its able founder and president, George Angell, and in alliance with antivivisection groups, called on the Massachusetts Medical Society to join them to persuade the state legislature to restrict animal experimentation. The reply of the Medical Society was blunt and firm: its members rejected the contentions of antivivisectionists that experiments on animals were immoral and cruel and reaffirmed the necessity of such research for the advancement of medicine.[13] The rebuff did not deter the antivivisectionists. Instead of persisting in their attempts to win the medical establishment to their cause, they changed their tactics and mounted a broader campaign to convince the general public of the inherent threat to public morality that lay in animal experimentation. Here they were more successful.

In 1894 the Massachusetts legislature approved an MSPCA-sponsored bill prohibiting "exhibitions of vivisection or dissection in public schools." The following year the society succeeded in convincing the legislature to consider even harsher legislation against animal experimentation.[14] These antivivisectionist victories finally persuaded medical scientists and educators in Massachusetts that they could no longer content themselves with writing polite letters to the editors of the *Boston Herald* or the *Evening Transcript* protesting the inaccuracies and distortions in the charges against them. They realized that they too would have to mobilize their forces in order to persuade the general public of both the necessity and value of their research.

⋘ ⋘ ⋘

The issue was joined in a series of public hearings held by the Judiciary Committee of the Massachusetts state legislature in 1896 on a proposed bill to restrict animal experimentation in medical schools. These hearings captured and held the attention of Bostonians in an extraordinary way. Not since the Parkman murder case almost fifty years earlier was so much public attention and concern exhibited by the general public about the activities of the scientific and medical establishment of Cambridge and Boston.[15] Throughout February, March, and April Bowditch, assisted by a number of medical scientists and practitioners including among others W. T. Porter, Theobald Smith, Harold C. Ernst, and James Jackson Putnam, countered the claims made by antivivisectionists and detailed the role of animal research in their own investigations, especially the victories achieved by that research in the struggle against disease.[16] They stressed that the antivivisectionist attacks were directed against medical science and endangered the freedom to acquire knowledge.

None of the testimony was more eloquent than that of President Eliot. For him the proposed legislation represented an attack on academic freedom and the entire educational process, and he brought to bear the power of his office in the hearings. Always forceful, he began with a blunt reply to the charges of George Angell: "The President of the Society for the Prevention of Cruelty to Animals said he was here to represent the dumb animals. I should like," he told the Judiciary Committee, "to be permitted to represent here some millions of dumb human beings."

There are thousands of them in this community who cannot appear at these hearings, but who deserve to be heard from. They are the people whose children die by the thousands in the warm weeks of summer. They are the people whose children are sent to the public diphtheria hospitals. They are the farmers and wage-earners all over New England who cannot send for the most skillful specialist in Massachusetts the instant any of their children are taken sick. These people, it seems to me, have some rights in this presence. It is for them that the scientific biologists are at work. It is to save them and their children from disease and death that the gentlemen who have testified before you are at work.[17]

It is not clear whether Eliot's presence and the reasoned presentations of Bowditch and his associates alone persuaded the Judiciary Committee to take the action it ultimately took, but following the hearings the bill was killed. The legislative battle in Massachusetts was won but the struggle between the medical establishment and the antivivisectionists had hardly begun.

As early as 1895, even as Bowditch was preparing his testimony for the Massachusetts legislature, he was already a leader of a special committee that had recently been organized to meet the threat of federal legislation against animal experiments. The threat was embodied in a bill that Senator Jacob H. Gallinger of New Hampshire, a former homeopathic physician, had announced he would support in the United States Senate "to prevent further cruelty to animals in the District of Columbia."[18] Mobilizing their forces as quickly as possible, Bowditch's committee, in conjunction with a committee of the Association of American Physicians headed by William Welch, sought to alert the members of professional organizations to the dangers posed to the development of medical science by this seemingly innocuous local bill.[19] Although a number of physicians and medical scientists were cautious about taking political action, the overwhelming majority pledged their immediate and whole-hearted support to oppose the bill. "Count me in for anything I can do to stop the crusade against vivisection," James Whittaker of Cincinnati wrote enthusiastically. "I believe that medicine would come to a dead block without it, for everything that can be done in the bedroom and the dead-room has been done, and all further progress lies through the field of experimentation." Russell Chittenden of Yale was even more warlike: "It will be a matter of conscience with me," he assured Bowditch, "to hurl all the anathemas possible against the antivivisectionists."[20]

Senator Gallinger's opponents, despite their enthusiasm, lacked two elements necessary for successful in-fighting in the U.S. Senate—patience and the political intelligence to know when a legislative battle was truly over and won. Despite sharp opposition, Gallinger, after some hurried hearings, almost succeeded in bringing the bill out of committee to a vote. Only a last-minute intervention by Welch and William Osler through two influential friends in the Senate—Arthur Gorham of Massachusetts and Edward Wolcott of Colorado—prevented the bill from reaching the Senate floor.[21] The experience, although salutary, was sobering. Welch and his colleagues learned what Bowditch already knew—namely, that a legislative battle with antivivisectionists could continue even after an apparent victory.

Faced with the gravity of the crisis that confronted medical science, Welch dropped all other activities and during the winter of 1897–98 devoted himself to political lobbying. As head of the physicians' committee, he urged congressmen to consider the views of the medical establishment and carefully watched the progress of the bills Gallinger introduced in the Senate. As president of the American Congress of Physicians and Surgeons, he also organized groups of physicians and patients in each of the then existing forty-five states to inundate the Senate with protests against such bills. In 1900 when Senator Gallinger decided that the time had come to hold public hearings on his latest bill, an impressive array of distinguished physicians, medical scientists, and laymen easily overwhelmed those who came to testify in behalf of the proposed measure.[22] Although the antivivisectionists were again defeated, their war with experimental medicine continued unabated at the state and local level.

In the years immediately following Bowditch's hard-fought legislative victory of 1896, the Massachusetts SPCA and the New England Anti-Vivisection Society with extraordinary persistence sought legislative approval of so-called milder bills against animal experimentation.[23] In 1900 antivivisectionists helped craft a bill that in addition to their usual demands for licensing and supervision of medical scientists also provided that no experiments be performed on unanesthetized animals. The suggestion in the new bill that medical scientists recklessly performed painful operations and generally did not anesthetize animals before experimenting on them outraged Bowditch and many of his colleagues. "Legislation of this sort," the Massachusetts Medical Society immediately retorted, "will of course seriously hamper and may even practically abolish biological and medical research throughout the state."[24]

Some weeks before public hearings on the bill were held, a series of letters arguing the merits of animal experimentation appeared in the pages of the *Boston Evening Transcript*.[25] Edward H. Clement, the editor-in-chief and an ardent antivivisectionist, concerned that the growing controversy in his newspaper might polarize public opinion and inadvertently prejudice the passage of the bill, editorially suggested that "the friends and foes of vivisection . . . meet on some middle ground, settle their differences, and thus put an end to an agitation that is hurtful to both sides of the controversy." Arguing that some regulation was necessary, Clement suggested that the governor appoint a nonpartisan committee composed of a scientist, a representative of a humane society, and a third member to represent the public to carry out supervision of research.[26]

Despite its seeming even-handedness, Clement's recommendation was pointedly ignored by both sides. The hearings, as he had anticipated, proved to be acrimonious and bitter. The antivivisectionists, represented largely by Herbert Ward, a writer, Joseph M. Greene, the treasurer of the New England Anti-Vivisection Society, and Arthur Westcott, a professional lecturer, heatedly argued three major points: first, that animal experimentation did not advance medical understanding or relieve human suffering; second, that it had a brutalizing effect on the scientific investigator as well as on those he taught; and third, that it ultimately led to human experimentation.[27] The petitioners, for all of their ardor, were not well prepared. Further, a number of their claims were ill conceived and poorly argued, and the bill, as others before it, was rejected in committee.

▝ ▝ ▝

The hearings, despite the outcome, nevertheless had a profound effect on both sides. The antivivisectionists, for example, in a subsequent review of their legislative effort saw themselves fighting not only against the cruelties involved in experiments on animals but, equally important, against a powerful intellectual elite as well. For them the fact that Eliot and other members of the Harvard community had once more spoken in favor of animal research was particularly galling. "Harvard College," J. M. Greene informed his fellow members in the New England Anti-Vivisection Society, "was most in evidence and presented its usual double attitude: first, of defense with exaggerated caution, refusing, except when obliged to do so, to acknowledge the most simple and apparent facts which might lead against itself; second, of arrogance, affecting to despise the opinion of anyone no matter how eminent who did not agree with Harvard Professors on the subject of vivisection."[28] Perhaps what Greene regretted most about the proceedings was the fact that although more than one hundred physicians in Boston had signed the antivivisection petition, not one of them came forward to speak before the public in support of the bill.[29]

Bowditch, although savoring another victory, also reflected on the issues raised at the hearings. He and others who spoke against the bill had easily met most of the claims advanced by the antivivisectionists, but one charge—that of experiments on animals leading to experiments on humans—struck a raw nerve. The example the antivivisectionists had used to illustrate their claim involved one of the Medical School's most promising young pediatric instructors, Arthur H. Wentworth, and his attempt to improve diagnosis of cerebrospinal meningitis. At the end of the nineteenth century cerebrospinal meningitis was one of the deadliest diseases; it has been estimated that approximately 80 percent of those who contracted the disease died.[30] In 1895, in an effort to make a diagnosis of a case of possible tuberculous meningitis at Children's Hospital, Wentworth used lumbar puncture to draw cerebrospinal fluid for bacteriological examination. The method at the time was new, and its value was not precisely understood.[31] In this instance the procedure was successful and allowed Wentworth to determine that the child was not suffering from tuberculous meningitis. Subsequently, when other suspected cases of meningitis were admitted to the hospital, Wentworth repeated the procedure and ultimately established it as a regular diagnostic test to differentiate cerebrospinal meningitis from other diseases of the spinal cord and brain. In all, Wentworth used lumbar puncture on twenty-seven patients. Of this group fourteen later died of the diseases that brought them into the hospital. Wentworth, eager to report the diagnostic value of lumbar puncture, published accounts of these cases in the *Boston Medical and Surgical Journal* in 1895 and 1896.[32]

When Wentworth presented an explication of his research at the annual meeting of the American Pediatric Society in the spring of 1896, commentators were emphatic in support of his investigation. A. D. Blackader at the Montreal General Hospital announced that in his view Wentworth's work on lumbar puncture could prove to be a successful guide to differential diagnosis of tubercular meningitis. Augustus Caillé, professor of pediatrics at the College of Physicians and Surgeons in New York and well known for his diagnostic ability, was even more positive: "I think

there can be no doubt as to the diagnostic value of the procedure,"
he told the audience. "There are very many cases on record now
in which the liquid [cerebrospinal fluid] has given positive results
and a positive diagnosis."[33] The only demurrers that were voiced
at the meeting were that practitioners had to understand that the
procedure was diagnostic and not a cure or relief for the disease.
Other medical commentators, however, were extremely critical.
The *Philadelphia Polyclinic* medical journal, for instance, castigated
Wentworth for conducting what were seen as experimental operations on children without obtaining prior consent from their
parents.[34]

Following the publication of the *Philadelphia Polyclinic*'s attack,
antivivisectionists mounted their own assault on Wentworth,
claiming that some of the children who had died while in his care
were victims of lumbar puncture. When antivivisectionists in
Massachusetts decided in 1900 to make Wentworth's work on
lumbar puncture one of the centerpieces of their efforts to restrict
animal experimentation, Bowditch and a number of other members
of the defense committee of the Boston Society of Medical Sciences
met to review Wentworth's papers and decide on a strategy to defend them. The majority of those present, including among others
Bowditch, Warren, Burrell, and Theobald Smith, decided that the
procedure despite its apparent value as a diagnostic tool would
be difficult to defend. Bowditch and Warren were particularly
troubled not only because they believed that lumbar punctures on
children were difficult and dangerous, but equally because they
felt that a vigorous public debate on the issue might interfere with
their efforts to raise funds for the new Medical School buildings.
Only Porter and Councilman rose to support Wentworth.[35]

In an effort to avoid controversy during the hearings, Bowditch prepared a public apologia to diffuse the issue. "Dr. Wentworth's experiments on lumbar puncture," it began,

have been universally and emphatically condemned by the medical
profession as violations of a fundamental principle of medical ethics
well expressed in the ancient Hippocratic oath: "Into whatever houses
I enter I will go for the advantage of the sick." Fortunately, no harm
was done to the patients by these experiments and the demonstration of the harmlessness of the operation which they afforded has
justified practitioners in resorting to it for diagnostic and therapeutic
purposes; but this gain to the practice of medicine by no means

excuses the performance of the experiments. Dr. Wentworth himself now entirely agrees with the opinion here expressed and regrets extremely that his enthusiasm for the advancement of medicine led him to forget his duty to his patients.[36]

It is clear that Bowditch hoped that Wentworth would sign the statement. There is no evidence, however, that Wentworth agreed. In fact the apology was never made public, and Wentworth, who had previously agreed to testify before the legislative committee, was never called. Some weeks after the hearings Wentworth quietly resigned from Harvard, although he retained his post at the Children's and Infants' Hospitals. Save for Porter and Councilman, no one at the Medical School spoke in defense of Wentworth's work on lumbar puncture—not even his chief, Thomas M. Rotch, who had co-authored Wentworth's first paper in the *Boston Medical and Surgical Journal.*[37] For Bowditch, the issue of human experimentation was a signal of the growing complexity of defending experimental research, and he was relieved that in this instance extended public debate was avoided.

In another direction, some members of the defense committee, recognizing that antivivisectionist agitation would undoubtedly recur, organized a statewide coalition of medical investigators, surgeons, physicians, and educators to fight future legislative battles.[38] Although Bowditch welcomed the new organization, he rejected the responsibility of its leadership, in part because his time and limited energy were increasingly taken up with planning and raising funds for the new Medical School buildings and in part because he had grown weary of meeting repetitive antivivisection claims and charges. "It is a fearful waste of time to have to do this sort of thing every year," he told his wife at the conclusion of the 1901 legislative hearings, "and I hope we shall be able to devise some plan for making the evidence given at one hearing serve for the *next* legislature also."[39] Once Bowditch's wishes became known, the responsibility of guiding the new coalition was given to Harold C. Ernst.

Ernst was a natural choice to succeed Bowditch.[40] He possessed impeccable credentials as bacteriologist, physician, and teacher; he also founded and ran the Boston Society for the Medical Sciences and edited its *Journal*, both of which served as forums for research and the exchange of information by laboratory investigators. Even more important, he had a personal interest in fighting antivivisectionists because his work with vaccines and antisera and his research on rabies were threatened by the attempts to abolish animal experiments.[41] Ernst's task was not an easy one; the legislature had to be monitored continually, and each year he had to rally practitioners, teachers, and medical scientists throughout the state for the inevitable hearings and testimony.

When Cannon joined the physiology department in 1900, he was well aware of antivivisectionist agitation. As a medical student he had already attended several of the legislative hearings at the State House and gained an appreciation for the issues that were debated there.[42] He did not at that time become involved in the controversy, however, and basically remained an observer. But once in the physiology department, he inherited the tradition that Bowditch had established and began to school himself in its responsibilities. For example, when the Massachusetts state legislature scheduled hearings to consider yet another bill in March of 1901, Cannon, although not asked, informed himself about a variety of antivivisection issues and attended the proceedings as a member of the department. There can be little doubt that the new attempt to restrict animal research had a special meaning for him. His identification with Bowditch and with the goals of scientific investigation, as well as his conviction of being on the side of righteousness, are revealed in a letter to Cornelia in which he analyzed the first day of the hearings. "On the one side," he wrote, "were all the prominent educators of the State, all the noted surgeons and the most prominent physicians. Their recognition of the beneficence of animal experimentation not only to man but to other animals was the most gratifying response to the senseless charges of the supporters of the bill. The leaders of the opposition were a Mr. Greene and Mrs. Elizabeth Stuart Phelps Ward. Mr. Greene it was who called Dr. Bowditch, a man beloved and honored in City, State and in the whole scientific world, 'a diabolical fiend.' The antis are the second of the two types Roosevelt described when he said, 'Common sense without conscience may lead to crime, but conscience without common sense may lead to folly which is the handmaiden of crime'."[43]

While the *ad hominem* attacks on Bowditch angered Cannon, it was the moralistic and sometimes absurd quality of Mrs. Herbert Ward's testimony that aroused his contempt. Mrs. Ward, a bestselling writer, in an effort to portray medical investigators as heart-less torturers of innocent animals, claimed at the hearings: "It is on record that a dog undergoing a shocking vivisection of the vertebral nerves twice escaped the knife, and, struggling up in his agony, put his arms around his vivisector's neck to plead for mercy; and that he prayed in vain."[44] "These well-intentioned women," Cannon told Cornelia, "are so short-sighted in cases, or so dis-criminating in their pity in other cases (they extend it to lower animals but refuse it to man), or so hysterical in maudlin senti-mentality (Mrs. Ward) in still other cases, that they refuse to listen to the facts, arguments or pleadings against them. You should see Mrs. Ward. Of all the affected, conceited-looking persons I have ever beheld she is most so. 'Lordosis and delusions of grandeur'— who can describe her!"[45]

As the hearings continued and apparently went well for the medical investigators and their allies, Cannon regaled Cornelia with a number of stories of the proceedings. "I heard a good story of the vivisectionist hearing today," he wrote in one letter. "The counsel for the petitioners is an extremely keen man, but he more than met his match in Dr. Porter. During a lull in the proceedings, a fair petitioner approached the counsel and whispered, 'Ask him to tell the *practical* value of his researches.' The attorney was heard to whisper back, 'Ask him! It's easy enough to ask him, but what in the name of Heaven will he answer!' " "I wish," Cannon con-tinued, "I could have gone to all the meetings, they are such a great intellectual treat."[46]

Shortly thereafter the legislative committee visited the Medical School to see for themselves the way students conducted animal experiments. The sight of more than a hundred students carefully examining the effects of fatigue in frog muscle and then studying the same process in their own muscles impressed the committee as being both painless and useful.[47] Upon their return to the State House they again killed the bill.

औष औष औष

The legislative hearings on animal research began to take their toll of both the petitioners and the remonstrants. Medical scientists in Boston, in particular, recognizing that their associates through-out the state were beginning to tire of answering Ernst's calls for help in preparing testimony for the now seemingly inevitable an-

Boris Sidis

Alexander Forbes

Roy G. Hoskins

Three of Cannon's early students.

Three cartoons in defense of medical research from *Puck*, 1911.

nual hearings, took steps to bring new members into their defense committee. By 1903 the coalition—now called the Committee on Experimental Biology—had in addition to antilegislative action a further goal of raising public awareness of the value of medical research. From that time forward, Cannon attended meetings more regularly and played an increasingly prominent role in the new committee's activities.[48]

The antivivisectionists, persuaded that the major reason for their lack of success was the ineptitude of the counsel who represented them in the legislative hearings, hired a new lawyer in 1906—an ex-congressman named Samuel Powers.[49] The new appointment particularly alarmed William Sedgwick of M.I.T., who immediately voiced his misgivings to Ernst. "Please make it perfectly clear to our private committee that with Sam Powers in charge," he told him, "we shall be very much more up against it than we have been for some years with French, for he is an extremely popular, persuasive and jolly fellow . . . and a politician of very wide influence and connections. We shall need, with him against us, to do our level best, and this makes it all the more evident that you *must* if you possibly can stick by us."[50] Although Ernst had for some time indicated that he was growing weary of the responsibility of countering the antivivisectionists, he nevertheless agreed to conduct the case for the remonstrants once more, in large part because of the enthusiastic support given him by some of the younger members of the committee, Cannon among them.

A year earlier, when Ernst had called on him to testify at the legislative hearings, Cannon had presented an account of his work with John B. Blake on gastroenterostomy and pyloroplasty.[51] It was a happy choice and impressed the legislature as another example of how research can aid clinicians to cope with everyday human complaints. Early in 1906, when Ernst again asked him to testify before the legislature, Cannon, now secretary of the Committee on Experimental Biology, promptly accepted. "I shall be at the State House," he assured Ernst, "ready to add my shot in the bombardment."[52] Despite Powers's aid, the antivivisectionists failed again to get their bill through the legislature. Their campaign, however, had one important unexpected result: this time the Medical School took steps to address some of the antivivisectionist complaints.

In the fall of 1907 the medical faculty approved the organization of a committee to supervise the procurement and care of laboratory animals for the entire School. Although the new committee was ostensibly organized to cope with faculty complaints that various teaching and research programs in the School were hampered by the lack of experimental animals, it had another purpose as well. A provision in the charter that gave the Committee on Animals the power to stop any experimental work that was considered improper or unnecessary signaled the faculty's determination to regulate and police its research laboratories. Recognizing the need for a strong committee, Eliot carefully screened the faculty for appointees and chose a committee composed almost entirely of the School's most active and respected experimentalists—Theobald Smith, Harold Ernst, Langdon Frothingham, Joshua Hubbard, and Cannon.[53]

Soon after taking up their duties, the members of the Animals Committee began to appreciate that their own laboratory experience would not suffice to establish rules and regulations to guide experimental research for the entire School and that they needed more information if they were to carry out their mandate successfully. To meet this need, Cannon asked medical scientists throughout the country how they dealt with the mundane tasks of acquiring, feeding, and housing their animals and especially whether they had undertaken any programs to educate the public about the process and purpose of experimental research. The replies he received were remarkably similar: most investigators informed him that they depended on boys and young men to supply them with vagrant cats or dogs for which they paid a modest fee of from 25¢ to 75¢ per animal.[54] Some intimated that it pained them "to encourage boys to evade the police in order to bring us dogs,"[55] but others claimed that they had no option because of the activities of animal protection societies. "The method that we use for obtaining dogs is necessarily a precarious method," Frederic Lee of Columbia wrote Cannon. "In this city the law allows the Society for the Prevention of Cruelty to Animals to catch and put to death all stray dogs. The society's work has been fairly thorough in this respect and it is probably largely due to them that our difficulty in obtaining dogs is increasing."[56]

The cost of caring for and feeding animals was not deemed to be an especially difficult problem. Although a small number of investigators bought commercial food, the majority depended on scraps from medical school dining rooms and hospitals.[57] Many of the investigators asserted that they took great care to prevent suffering of animals during experiments, but a few felt that there was room for improvement. Percy Dawson, one of Cannon's friends at Johns Hopkins, was particularly candid: "The present conditions existing in the physiological laboratories in this country are good," he wrote Cannon. "Physiologists are economical of life and careful to avoid the infliction of unnecessary pain." However, he warned, "it is probable that although animals are usually well treated in the operating room, their quarters are often very miserable and the care of the animals before they reach the operating table much worse than should be. These facts suggest to me that there should be instituted some form of control of mammalian vivisection."[58]

Although Cannon was taken aback by Dawson's criticism, he was even more perplexed by the attitudes expressed with regard to educating the public about the problems of experimental medicine and meeting antivivisectionist agitation. From 1900 Cannon had been impressed by the unity of medical scientists in Boston in fighting the antivivisectionists and of the special efforts they made to inform the public of the value of their research. The replies he received, however, indicated that few if any medical scientists outside of Massachusetts concerned themselves with raising the public consciousness about the process of medical research. "No attempt has been made to educate the public as to the care with which animals are treated during experimentation," Joseph Erlanger wrote from Wisconsin, "but when inquiries concerning this subject are received from interested parties they are invited to personally inspect our laboratory and methods."[59] A letter from Lafayette Mendel at Yale proved even more startling. "Personally," he told Cannon,

I think that the agitation which has arisen in certain quarters has been fostered by the unnecessarily outspoken and "public" attitude of our colleagues. My own policy—and that of most or all of us here—has been to permit no improper practices, to prevent undue experimentation, to educate those engaged in animal experimentation to have a proper appreciation of their responsibility and duty—and not to ventilate their views in any quarter where they are likely to be misunderstood. I cannot see that any advantage comes to our

science by catering to public expression. We feel morally certain of
our duties and privileges—but we don't enter into public expression
of the matter.[60]

Cannon was equally astonished by the attitudes of a number
of his colleagues at the Medical School. Maurice Howe Richardson
and Reginald Heber Fitz, two of the most respected senior clinical
professors at the School, for example, not only vetoed outright a
plan suggested by the Animals Committee to solicit and procure
needed experimental animals from the public but also vehemently
objected to the introduction of a course in experimental surgery.[61]
Although the opinions and information that Cannon gathered in
behalf of the committee alerted and educated him to aspects of
animal experimentation that he had not considered before, they
did not alter his own views. The often distorted and fabricated
claims and charges of the antivivisectionists demonstrated, in his
estimation, the immorality of those who opposed the advancement
of science. That sense of moral outrage never left Cannon. Indeed,
it was to sustain him in his future confrontations with the antivivisectionists.

11   *In Defense of*
Medical Research

I N 1908, following a series of sharp attacks by anti-vivisectionists against the Rockefeller Institute in New York, the American Medical Association, recognizing that such attacks were no longer a local but rather a national problem, organized a special defense committee in support of medical research.[1] The seriousness with which the AMA regarded the role of the new committee is demonstrated by the composition of its membership which included among others Joseph Capps, professor of medicine at the University of Chicago; Harvey Cushing, the neurosurgeon at Johns Hopkins; David L. Edsall, professor of therapeutics and pharmacology at the University of Pennsylvania; Simon Flexner, director of the Rockefeller Institute; Reid Hunt, pharmacologist at the U.S. Public Health Service; and Walter Cannon.[2] Cannon's inclusion was another sign of his growing status in the medical and scientific world.

Initially the defense committee had no chairman. However, a letter from William H. Welch to Cannon soon settled the matter: "As your name comes, I believe, first," Welch wrote, "perhaps you will take the initiative in communicating with other members. The choice of chairman is left to the members, but I hope you may be chosen."[3] Cannon needed no other suggestion. With Welch's hint to prime him, he took control of the committee and with his accustomed vigor began to develop plans for its operation. When the AMA Council on the Defense of Medical Research (as the new group was officially designated) held its first formal meeting in October of 1908, Cannon was unanimously elected chairman.[4]

Cannon was tutored in his work for the council by George H.

Simmons, the general secretary of AMA headquarters in Chicago. Simmons, who was wise in the ways of medical politics, not only furnished Cannon with the latest information on antivivisectionist tactics throughout the country, but more important, taught him how to utilize other AMA personnel and committees in his work. Thus, when Cannon was searching for a way to obtain information about laboratory procedures then in practice in medical schools, Simmons advised using a mechanism already in place. "As you know," he wrote Cannon, "Dr. Colwell, who is working here, acts as secretary of the Council on Medical Education, and during the year he visits practically every college in the country. It would be a very easy matter for him to make an investigation of this particular phase of the college work at the same time, without any added expense whatever." Other suggestions followed: "I hope you will not think that I am 'butting in'," Simmons apologetically concluded. "I am especially interested in the work—cannot help but be—and feel like excusing myself because I was responsible to some extent for the creation of the Council."[5] Although Cannon faithfully consulted with Simmons, he soon demonstrated that he was his own man.

To prepare himself and the council for the struggle he knew must come, Cannon assiduously began to gather information about antivivisectionists and advice on how to meet their tactics from physicians and medical scientists on both sides of the Atlantic. One of the first to whom he wrote was Stephen Paget, for many years the secretary of the British Association for the Advancement of Medicine by Research and founder of the Research Defense Society in London. Paget proved to be remarkably encouraging about prospects for successfully meeting the antivivisectionist threat, and he wrote enthusiastically to both Cannon and George Simmons in Chicago. His society had only just started, he told Simmons, but already had fourteen hundred members. "We have had a wonderful welcome. Leaders of science, Bishops, Deans, and Canons, Lords and Ladies, city men, poor country doctors, engineers, teachers—they have all come! . . . The plain fact is that public opinion is beginning to be *sick* of the Anti-vivisection societies."[6]

Paget emphasized the necessity of organizing a campaign for public education about medical research. To underscore the message, he sent Cannon the third edition of his book *Experiments on*

Animals and reports of testimony before the English Parliamentary Commission on Vivisection as grist for the AMA council's mill. Whenever an opportunity presented itself, Paget stressed the value of education and the necessity of organizing a lay auxiliary to help propagate the cause of animal experimentation. In recommending a plan of popular lectures, Paget continued, "I am sick of debates. Why not start a good popular lecture in every great city in the United States? That is the way to educate people. You would get large audiences of the right sort of people, and you would arrange to have the lecture reported at full length in the newspapers. People are longing to hear what we have to say for ourselves."[7]

The advice that Cannon received from American medical scientists, however, was largely in another direction. Sensitized in part by their previous experience in fighting the legislative battle of 1900 against Senator Gallinger and even more by the immediacy of combating proposed antivivisectionist legislation pending in New York, Pennsylvania, and the District of Columbia, a number of scientists and physicians led by Frederic S. Lee, Joseph Bryant, and John Curtis of New York stressed the necessity of organizing political action.[8] For Curtis, the problem posed by antivivisectionist bills in Washington, D.C., appeared so threatening that he advised focusing exclusively on developing a vast political campaign designed to persuade congressmen of the dangers of passing such legislation. "Nobody in the District of Columbia," he told Cannon, "has a vote, and the scientific people are government officials and afraid of the politicians . . . If Congress shall pass a bill for the District of Columbia, an identical one will probably be introduced immediately thereafter into the legislatures of New York and Massachusetts, with much prestige behind it." If a national campaign in opposition to antivivisectionist bills is not developed, he cautioned, "the profession in the U.S.A. will presently reach the degraded position which it holds, in this matter, in Great Britain only."[9]

Curtis's position was by no means held by all physicians. Most, however, agreed that the situation called for mounting an offensive against the antivivisectionists. Perhaps no one put it more cogently than an unnamed correspondent of George Simmons, who took exception to the name of the defense council. "It might be said," he wrote, "that no movement can be permanently successful that is always simply on the defensive. Unless the med-

ical profession takes steps—offensive steps—to silence the enemies of medical progress who resort to every form of vilification
and lying, we are going to have stringent laws against vivisection
in many states before long." "A defense always stands to lose,"
the physician angrily affirmed. "The final result is as inevitable as
that in the game of heads I win, tails you lose."[10]

Cannon needed no such exhortation. He had already made
explicit the tenets that were to guide him and the council in an
address he had given earlier in 1908 before the AMA Section on
Physiology and Pathology. That speech was hardly defensive; it
was in fact a rousing battle-cry. Cannon charged that antivivisectionists not only were ignorant of the complex relations of the
medical sciences to medical and surgical practice but also were
ignorant of the actual conditions of experimental research. Laying
down the gauntlet, he announced: "Investigators object to any
step tending to check the use of animals in medical research. They
maintain that such interference is not justified by the present treatment of the experimental animals. They declare that the imagined
horrors of medical research do not exist. The insane lust for blood,
the callousness to the infliction of pain, which are attributed to
the experimenters, they resent as most absurd and unjust accusations. Only the moral degenerate is capable of inflicting the
torments that the antivivisectionists imagine."[11]

ଏଏ ଏଏ ଏଏ

When Cannon's euphoria died down, he gradually realized
that many medical investigators also lacked information on the
conduct of research in laboratories other than their own. He therefore undertook two tasks that utilized techniques developed through
his service on the Committee on Animals at Harvard and paralleled
its efforts: first, he gathered information on the nature and quality
of animal experimentation throughout the country, and second,
he began to construct a model code of laboratory rules, which he
hoped would be adopted by medical schools and research institutions.

The code that emerged was by no means Cannon's work alone.
Using one set of laboratory rules originally developed at Harvard
by Bowditch as a working model, Cannon diligently sought the
advice and criticism of physicians and medical investigators across
the country.[12] Although most correspondents approved the code

submitted to them, some cautioned Cannon that the question of uniform rules should be carefully considered. Each comment was conscientiously examined by Cannon, and for good reason. For him the code was to be the keystone of the council's campaign and would serve a threefold purpose: first, to alert students and newcomers to medical experimentation of the standards expected of them; second, to answer the criticisms made by antivivisectionists; and third, to persuade other interested parties, particularly legislators and laymen, that medical scientists were not averse to self-policing and rational regulation.[13]

Wholesale adoption of the code was delayed, however, until Cannon personally circularized the deans of seventy-nine medical schools in its behalf. By March of 1910 he was able to point proudly to some impressive results: "Already these rules are adopted and enforced in the laboratories of thirty-seven medical schools and institutes, including the largest," he informed Governor Hughes of New York who was then considering antivivisectionist legislation. "Twenty-two other medical schools," he continued, "have asked for more copies of the rules and have expressed a willingness to cooperate with the Council. Before the year ends these regulations will probably be enforced in all the medical laboratories in the United States."[14]

Cannon had reason to be pleased with his success in the formulation and adoption of a uniform code of laboratory rules. He was, however, brought up short on more than one occasion by the difference of opinion he encountered on his plans for public education. From the beginning of his work for the defense council Cannon believed that in a democracy an informed public was crucial to the cause of medical research, and following Stephen Paget's advice, he tried to establish a large-scale auxiliary organization of laymen to support medical investigators and promote their programs. When he first broached the idea, he received some support from George Simmons at AMA headquarters and from Harvey Cushing at Johns Hopkins. However, he soon ran into a flood of objections. Some medical investigators, like Torald Sollmann of Western Reserve, felt that laymen would have to be educated gradually before they could understand the complexities of the issues involved. Others, like John Curtis of Columbia, went a step further and argued that a lay group might be persuaded to give approval to some innocent-seeming restriction "which we technical workers would understand and wish to oppose." Curtis announced that he would oppose giving laymen "any responsibility, authority, or voice in the management" of such a society.[15] No matter how hard Cannon tried to overcome these objections, he failed.

He was, however, more successful with another of his educational ideas—the publication of a series of authoritative pamphlets showing how animal experiments served to benefit mankind through the advancement of medical and surgical knowledge.[16] Cannon took the lead in outlining the topics to be presented and selected the authors to write the various papers. Although there was unanimous agreement as to the necessity of such publications, producing them was another matter. No one quarreled with Cannon's selection of Eliot to lend prestige to the projected series or with the content of the pamphlet that he produced,[17] but sharp criticism was voiced by some members of the council that other authors lacked the public stature and experience required and that several of the pamphlets were too technical and not popular enough. This last charge divided the chairman from many of his associates. In Cannon's opinion such objections were without merit because the purpose of the papers was to instruct physicians so that they, in turn, could inform the public. For Cannon, it was the instruction of the medical practitioner that was all important.[18]

The foregoing does not mean that Cannon was unaware of the importance of popularization. He understood very well the significance of public opinion and the role of newspapers and large circulation magazines in generating public support. Just as the antivivisectionists worked to gain a number of sympathizers among members of the press, so too did Cannon and his colleagues undertake sustained efforts to persuade editors and publishers to print articles and stories favorable to medical research.[19] William W. Keen, one of the leading surgeons of his day whose compendious system of surgery was used to educate generations of physicians and surgeons, had singular success in placing such articles with editors who were known to him or were his personal friends.[20] Simon Flexner had a similar relationship with editors in New York, especially Norman Hapgood of *Colliers' Weekly*, whose young daughter's life was saved through use of Flexner's antimeningitis serum. There were times, nevertheless, that the strategy failed, as on one occasion when the council found it difficult to persuade some New York editors to print articles in support of animal experimentation. When Keen discovered the source of the council's road block, he bristled with indignation: "I was told by a very well informed, intelligent woman yesterday that the New York Evening Post and the New York Nation have practically been muzzled in the defense of vivisection by reason of the fact that the mother of the owner of both these Journals is a rabid antivivisectionist. This is the more astonishing to me, because both of these Journals are such strenuous advocates of journalistic independence. I see myself no difference between the control of a mother and the control of an advertiser."[21] Such pressure, however, was not criticized when successfully applied by the council against a recalcitrant publisher.

✐ ✐ ✐

Among the major tasks for Cannon and the defense council were monitoring the public appearances of notable antivivisectionists and correcting fabrications and errors of fact in their lectures, literature, and traveling exhibitions. The speakers who aroused the most fear and anger of the council were Stephen Coleridge and Miss Lind-af-Hageby from England and Albert Leffingwell, a physician from Brooklyn, New York. Coleridge, a lawyer by profession, came to his hatred of animal experimentation through family tradition: his father, Chief Justice of the King's Bench, was one of the early leaders of the British antivivisectionist movement.[22] Emilie Augusta Louise ("Lizzie") Lind-af-Hageby, daughter of the Chief Justice of Sweden's highest court, was a well-educated and articulate woman who attained public notoriety through her book, *The Shambles of Science*.[23] Coleridge and Lind had a number of characteristics in common. Both abhorred cruelty to animals and believed there was no justification whatever for animal experimentation. Equally important, they shared the same philosophical convictions—they believed that knowledge and reason were a poor foundation on which to build character or base moral conduct. Their disregard for intellectual achievement made them formidable opponents in debates with medical scientists. Late in 1908, when Cannon learned that Coleridge and Lind were coming to America to give a series of lectures, he began to make inquiries about them in England and Canada and to gather ammunition to counteract their views. "If they do come," Paget warned Cannon,

"I fear that they will attract very large audiences, and will exercise a tremendous amount of influence. They are both of them excellent public speakers."[24]

If Cannon, schooled by Paget, was afraid of Coleridge and Miss Lind, others engaged in defending medical research feared Albert Leffingwell even more. Leffingwell, who had received the M.D. degree from the Long Island Medical Center Hospital, could speak with apparent knowledge about medicine; moreover, he was a skillful writer whose travel works as well as his two books on the antivivisection controversy had brought him renown. Like his English counterparts, Leffingwell detested cruel and reckless misuse of animals. Unlike them, however, he did not demand total abolition of animal experimentation but preached instead the reasonableness and necessity of some form of public regulation. Physicians in New York were especially alarmed by his activities. "He is the one individual," F. S. Lee told Cannon, "upon whom, more than anyone else, American antivivisectionists depend for their ideas and facts, and though he has only a very thin medical and scientific veneer, he is, in some respects, our most dangerous opponent."[25]

The anticipated dangers of this particular wave of antivivisectionist public lectures never materialized, however. In some instances the lectures attracted only true believers; in others Cannon successfully counteracted their appeal by funneling material favorable to animal experimentation to newspaper reporters and editors. A short time after Coleridge and Miss Lind completed their respective American tours, Cannon reported to the council that in his view the English agitators had hurt their cause more than they had helped it.[26]

The campaign against the lecturers was but one event in an almost daily effort by Cannon to correct misstatements and reply to accusations broadcast by the evangelists of the antivivisectionist cause.[27] In most of these exchanges he contented himself with presenting data in a dispassionate manner, for he was aware that an intemperate or patronizing response could generate support for the opposition's pronouncements. Privately, however, he did not hesitate to reveal the contempt he had for many of his opponents. When Miss A. E. Gazzam, a long-time supporter of antivivisectionist claims, published one of her many pamphlets attacking animal experimentation, Cannon wrote almost gleefully of the prospect of attacking it. "The pamphlet by Miss Gazzam," he informed Frederic Lee, "is one which someone should have a happy time in answering because it is so easy to do it, and do it in a trenchant and striking manner."[28]

Although Cannon ridiculed antivivisectionist views, at no time did he underrate the seriousness of their efforts to sway public opinion against animal experimentation. When W. W. Keen late in 1909 alerted him to the success of an antivivisectionist exhibit traveling from New Jersey to New York, Cannon immediately went to see it. "I went there and examined it carefully," he later reported to Keen. "Wherever the exhibit goes, we shall have a statement regarding it in the local medical journal; and after the exhibit has left the place, a description in the local papers of its seriously misleading character."[29] Cannon's defense of medical research did not solely depend on public relations campaigns. He devoted an even greater amount of time to political lobbying.

Antivivisectionist political debate was both shrill and fierce. In March of 1909 Keen, who had gone to Harrisburg with a number of medical friends to testify against a bill proposing to restrict animal experimentation, wrote Cannon of some of the conflicts he had with antivivisectionist supporters. "I had the pleasure of hearing myself," he noted, "with the other advocates of vivisection, designated by a very attractive, and I should think personally, charming woman as 'hyenas!' I have not, however, borne her any malice as a result of it!"[30] Cannon replied at once, describing the enormity of the political campaigns facing the council: "You have my heartiest congratulations on the success of your efforts at Harrisburg," he began. "This morning I learned from Erlanger at Madison, Wisconsin, that a widespread effort was being made to introduce legislation quietly in the various states, and that by chance the Wisconsin bill had been discovered. I have written a circular letter giving the main points against such legislation, and urging an active campaign against this hostile legislation."[31]

Neither Cannon nor any other member of the defense council needed instruction on how to conduct a political campaign. They understood the necessity of enlisting influential public figures in their cause, and one of Cannon's earliest acts as chairman was to draw up a plan to persuade President Theodore Roosevelt and other notables to join the fight against the antivivisectionists.[32] Harvey Cushing, who liked to work indirectly, suggested the use of prominent social figures to help coax politicians to support the cause. "I know one or two people in Washington who are I think more or less influential," he wrote Cannon, "and have Miss Mabel Boardman particularly in mind . . . She is a person of great influence, social and otherwise, in Washington, and I think it is possible that I might secure her interest and cooperation. If she did nothing more than make it a matter of dinner table talk from our side I doubt not that she would do a lot of good in repressing the possible activities of other well-meaning and misinformed Washingtonians." On another occasion, when Cushing learned from a friend that author Thomas Nelson Page, who headed the antivivisection movement in Washington, D.C., could with a little pressure be brought to support the cause of experimental research, he urged Cannon to endorse such a move. "It would be amusing," he concluded, "to thus invade the hostile camp and capture their chief officer."[33]

Keen, who was no less a schemer than Cushing, liked a more direct approach and did not hesitate to use his own status to persuade the politicians. Referring to an article he was then writing on animal experimentation for an issue of the *Ladies' Home Journal,* he wrote Cannon, "I told Gov. Hughes about it the other day and asked him whether I might use the case of his son by name, as an illustration of the use of Flexner's serum, as it would add greatly to the force of such an illustration if so prominent a man as his father was named. He not only gave his consent, but was most hearty in his expressions of sympathy with vivisection. You need not worry about any antivivisectionist law in New York as long as he presides at Albany."[34] Some time later Keen learned that President William Howard Taft at his wife's insistence had lent his name as sponsor to a meeting of the International Humane Society where several antivivisectionist resolutions were to be offered. Immediately sensing the import of the move, Keen called upon the president to withdraw. Such was Keen's influence with Taft (whom he had served as a surgical consultant) that the president, despite Mrs. Taft's opposition, agreed.[35]

Not everybody on the council approved of such political strategy. David Edsall, who was in charge of the defense council's campaign in Pennsylvania, was particularly outraged by a coterie of influential Philadelphia physicians who persistently called on political boss Boies Penrose to kill bills in the state legislature against medical experimentation. Edsall, who did not mince words, regarded such activities as "dirty politics." "I am always afraid," he wrote Cannon on one occasion, "they will so confidently expect political aid that some day they will get left and then find an uneducated and unreceptive public against them." Although Cannon agreed with Edsall that education was preferable to political pull in dealing with antivivisectionists, in this instance he succumbed to the temptation of deriving immediate victories from pressure politics and supported a continued alliance with Boies Penrose.[36] In time he would come to appreciate Edsall's warning that an unrestrained use of political influence could become a hazard to the cause of medical research.

⤳ ⤳ ⤳

Cannon's service on the defense council, while exacting a toll on his time and energies, brought a number of unanticipated benefits in its train. Not only did he learn new techniques for gathering and utilizing information to solve a variety of political, administrative, and educational problems, but he also gained entrée to the inner circle of the American Medical Association. In addition, his spirited leadership won for him the admiration and friendship of many of the foremost physicians and scientists in the country. Some, like Milton Rosenau and his fellow council members Harvey Cushing, David Edsall, and Reid Hunt, were soon to become close friends and colleagues at Harvard.[37] "You fully deserve the grateful acknowledgement of the entire profession," Cushing appreciatively wrote Cannon. "It scares me to think that someone else other than yourself might have been made chairman of our committee."[38] In short, Cannon's work on the defense council catapulted him to national medical prominence. The achievement, however, was not without cost. Some of the costs were to have long-term repercussions; an unpleasant and immediate price was exacted when he was forced to lock horns with an old friend and mentor—his former teacher, William James.[39]

The debate between James and Cannon began late in May of 1909, shortly after James allowed the Vivisection Reform Society of New York to publish a letter he had sent to them expressing his views on animal experimentation. James, then in failing health, was still one of the most powerful voices in the United States to speak on ethical and scientific issues. In his letter, which originally appeared in the *New York Post*, James essentially argued two major points: first, that medical and scientific men were members of a club and like other corporate beings could not be trusted to be either truthful or moral, especially when under attack; and second, that he regarded as preposterous the claim that every scientist had a right to experiment on animals without public accountability. "So long as the physiologists disclaim corporate responsibility," he concluded, "formulate no code of vivisectional ethics for laboratories to post up and enforce, appoint no censors, pass no votes of condemnation or exclusion, propose of themselves no law, so long must the anti-vivisection agitation, with all of its expensiveness, idiocy, bad temper, untruth and vexatiousness continue, as the only possible means of bringing home to the careless or callous individual experimenter the fact that the sufferings of his animals are somebody else's business as well as his own, and that there is 'a God in Israel' to whom he owes account."[40]

James's letter, which was subsequently reprinted in the *Boston Evening Transcript*, struck Cannon with particular force.[41] The ideas expressed in the letter, however, were not new to those who knew James. He had long expressed abhorrence of animal experimentation—an antipathy that had its genesis in his memories of the experiments he had viewed as a postgraduate student in Europe and the demonstrations he had conducted as an assistant in anatomy at the Medical School.[42] Nor was James's notion of physicians and scientists acting as a well-organized group against outsiders ("trade-unionism," as he termed it) particularly new; he had put forward such a view to the discomfort of physicians in 1894 and again in 1898 when he appeared at the State House in Boston to speak against a proposed medical licensing bill designed to prevent Christian Scientists, mental therapists, and faith healers from practicing medicine in Massachusetts.[43]

The day after the letter appeared in the *Transcript* Cannon wrote James and bluntly came to grips with the arguments that he had advanced. "There are some statements in the letter," Cannon began, "which I am sure your fair-mindedness would not have permitted you to make if you had not so long been unacquainted with the conditions of medical research." Many of the procedures James had asked for, he pointed out, were already in place, and most of the large laboratories operated under stated rules and regulations that were rigorously enforced. "You will be interested to know," he continued, "that the Medical School in which you were trained has a Committee on Animals, with plenary powers to control conditions of research and to discharge instantly any employee guilty of inhumanity to the laboratory animals."

The major thrust of Cannon's response, however, was reserved for answering James's call for special legislation to control medical investigations. "Have you not confused a protest by medical men against special legislation directed at them," he asked James, "and an assumption commonly made that they object to any control of their work?" Such legislation, he argued, was not needed because general laws against cruelty already existed and had been brought to bear very effectively in the year that had just passed to punish some cruel dissections of animals in a veterinary school. "We shall perhaps be unable to convince our opponents," Cannon concluded, "that we are not callous monsters rejoicing in pain, for they take the attitude which you take—that we 'cannot be trusted to be truthful or moral when under fire.' "[44]

Cannon's arguments did not move James. Although he candidly admitted that he did not know about the rules that had been adopted by laboratories to monitor and regulate animal experimentation, James still objected strenuously to the tack that Cannon and others had taken in defense of medical research. "I don't except Porter's manifesto of some years ago, or even yours, dear Cannon, of some months ago, which I turned to with expectations of something radical and vital on the whole question, only to be disappointed," he replied.

> You turned only a narrow edge of defense, to certain narrow attacks. But why not deal with the whole matter from the bottom, and constructively and radically, not as a class under fire, screening itself by a certain policy of retort? Why swell the public impression that it is a class-cause that is being defended, with all the lack of candor that in such cases prevails? I wouldn't guarantee our College faculty (individually extraordinarily conscientious men) not to *lie* thru thick and thin, to ward off attacks from without. I couldn't trust our philosophic department, myself included, not to lie when assaulted by the laity. Deny everything provisionally; and meanwhile get the house in order so as to reply more truly to the next attack! Don't you think that the anti viv. agitation has had much to do with the establishment of all those laboratory rules which your committee has collected?

For James, the struggle was strictly a moral and ethical issue, and it is clear that he wished Cannon to drop the campaigns he had organized against the antivivisectionists and to adopt a more philosophic approach in defending animal experimentation.

You are in a position to do more good, and to do *more to meet attack efficiently*, I am persuaded, if you will take the course I suggest, than in any other way. What individual physiologists are more in need of, I am sure, is more moral courage in face of their own club opinion. Why can't you yourself become a more aggressive leader along that line? I think you will be surprised at the adhesion you will get from persons now mute and inert within the profession, if you become an energetic advocate of reform from within, and let outside attacks be answered *only in that way*. The really judicious public is, I believe, equally [sick] of the idiocy of the one side and of the *suppressio veri* of the other.[45]

This early exchange inaugurated a debate that continued with increasing fervor in the weeks that followed. Throughout the discussion the arguments remained the same; only the detail that shored up each position changed.[46] In essence, both men spoke past one another, and at best each only heard an echo of what the other said. A philosophic chasm separated Cannon and James on this issue. Cannon's optimism was expressed in his belief in the essential goodness of man and the usefulness of, indeed the crying need for, science in the effort to improve the human condition.[47] James, a good deal more experienced and cynical, looked at life and men through a darker glass. For him there was an everlasting presence of vice and evil in the world. He was especially skeptical of groups of men who claimed exemption from the rules of behavior. Ethical codes, he argued, were not an encumbrance but rather a necessary means to control the powerful in society.[48]

There was irony in the debate. As a teacher, James did not suffer gladly the student who parroted his ideas. Instead he took pride in his pupils who showed an ability to stretch their minds and think for themselves. At least, that is how James saw himself. Faced with a former student who had followed his own drummer, however, James was grieved that Cannon did not share his views on the nature of man or grasp the substance of the ethical problem he himself saw so clearly. The exchange of views provided no solutions. Although James admitted to Cannon that he had not foreseen the consequences of his remarks, he later allowed his original letter to the Vivisection Reform Society to be sent out unchanged as a small pamphlet.[49] "I have not yet had the opportunity to call his attention to the failure on his part to stick close to the facts," Cannon fumed to Keen some months later, "though it seems to me that after his strictures on the physiologists I can do so with some force."[50] Nevertheless, he did nothing.

Early in February 1910 the conflict erupted once more. This time James, misinterpreting what Cannon had told him of the defense council's work in preparing rules and regulations for laboratory experimentation, told a reporter from the *New York Herald* that the AMA was about to assume disciplinary control over experimental research. When James's statement appeared in the newspaper, a torrent of telegrams from members of the council descended upon Cannon, asking that he obtain a formal retraction. Cannon again wrote James pointing out the inaccuracies in his statement. "I get very much discouraged at times about this fight," he confided in ending his letter. "We are all so prone to misinterpretations that I wonder if mutual understanding will ever come. Surely I should turn quietly to my investigations if I did not feel that grave problems of human welfare were dependent for their solution on freedom of medical research." James admitted to Cannon that the statement he had made was not true, but again he did not correct or retract it publicly.[51]

Cannon made no further effort to press his old teacher and friend.[52] He was aware that James's health was failing, and he allowed the differences that separated them to simmer. There were others with whom he could fight in defense of research. Several months later, while summering in New Hampshire, Cannon learned that William James had died the previous day. "It is hard to believe possible," he grieved.[53] Another link with the past had been severed.

12　A Family and a Farm

D|URING THE WINTER of 1906 Cannon received a request from his college class secretary for a personal history for inclusion in the tenth anniversary report of the Class of '96. Although he did not often look backward to see how far he had come, it must have given him much satisfaction to prepare a record of his accomplishments because he was, by any measure, one of his class's spectacular successes.[1] His research had brought him national and international recognition, and he had become a force in the University as well. At class day in June, Cannon moved with ease through the various meetings and ceremonies, taking particular pleasure in mixing with Brahmin classmates he had once scorned and envied as an undergraduate. Best of all, he was able to share his sense of belonging to Harvard by guiding May Newson and a group of his old friends from St. Paul through the College and the new buildings of the Medical School and introducing them to President Eliot.[2]

If Cannon had changed, so had Harvard, especially its faculty. Many of his teachers were gravely ill or had retired. That spring and summer two of the professors he had long admired died—Nathaniel Shaler, who taught geology and had joined with him and others at the Medical School in fighting the antivivisectionists, and Christopher Langdell of the Law School, whose case method of instruction he had adapted to the teaching of medicine.[3] The ebb and flow of life among family and friends increasingly absorbed him, and he carefully recorded its movement in his diary, grieving when Fred Murphy called to tell him that his infant daughter had died suddenly and rejoicing when his sister Jenny announced the birth of a baby girl and when his friend Earl Bond proudly reported that he had delivered twelve babies during his tour as a fourth-year student on the out-patient service at the City Hospital.[4] This record of the beginnings of life as well as its fragility reflected Cannon's growing preoccupation with starting a family, a problem that had troubled him and Cornelia for a number of years.

Late in March 1907 Cornelia observed the first signs of pregnancy. Neither she nor Cannon immediately shared their expectations with anyone else, however. Similar signs in previous years had ended in disappointment, and they decided to say nothing until Cornelia's physician, Dr. Davenport, assured them that all was well.[5] In the weeks that followed they went about their daily lives much as before, camouflaging both their excitement and trepidation. Their close friends did note that the Cannons appeared to be suffering from house-hunting fever—a condition that was corroborated early in April when they rented a new house on Ware Street.[6]

Later that month, when Dr. Davenport confirmed that Cornelia was pregnant and that there did not appear to be any danger of a miscarriage, they shared their joy with family and friends. Some days later when Cornelia began to suffer from morning sickness and took to her bed, there was another sharing as well. "I stayed in with her," Cannon wrote in his diary, "and we read together Lee's chapter on Reproduction in the American Textbook of Physiology."[7] Cornelia did not mark time easily and as soon as the discomfort of her morning sickness diminished, she resumed her normal activities with her accustomed vigor—furnishing the new house and establishing milk stations in and around Boston, as well as preparing a directory of social welfare agencies in Cambridge.[8] During the evenings she and Cannon visited their friends, taking part in the charades and stunts that were a feature of Cambridge parties, or read aloud to one another from the novels and plays of H. G. Wells, G. K. Chesterton, and George Bernard Shaw.

Late in August the young couple went on vacation to Cape Cod and the Islands.[9] Cornelia, determined not to let her pregnancy interfere with life's normal pleasures, sailed, swam, and played tennis with her usual verve. When news of her activity filtered back to St. Paul, her mother immediately cautioned her: "It worries me to hear of your swimming and violent exercise," she wrote. "You have got to be careful or all that you have longed for so long will end in grief for you. The seventh and eighth months are critical times. A seven-month baby seldom, and an eight-month almost never, survives. And it doesn't take much to outrage Mother Nature. You must give your vitality to your baby and not to all kinds of things that a wise woman will postpone. Again, while it is well to take exercise, still very much of it hardens the abdominal muscles and when the time for relaxation comes, they refuse to yield and birth becomes very difficult."[10] Cannon shared his mother-in-law's concern, and although he said little to his wife about her energetic activities, he became increasingly apprehensive as the time of birth approached. When soon after returning to Cambridge Cornelia told him that she was going bargain hunting at Filene's Basement, Cannon, fearful that she might inadvertently be injured by the store's milling shoppers, tried to deflect her. She heard him out but did not abandon her plans.

During the fall, in an attempt to allay his apprehensions about the unknown biological hazards of radiation exposure, Cannon devoted himself to household chores—making a crib for the baby, dyeing couch covers, and even sewing nightgowns for Cornelia. Despite these efforts, his anxiety remained and began to affect his ability to concentrate on his research. "The day has gone in fritterings and trivialities and so have many days past," he complained fretfully in his diary late in October. "I try to read at the laboratory and am constantly interrupted. The same is true at home in the evening. October is nearly gone and nothing is done."[11] The baby was expected in November, and as the month passed with no sign of imminent birth, Cannon's nervousness increased, especially when Dr. Swain, Cornelia's obstetrician, confided to him that he was worried about the baby's position. In an effort to escape from his concerns Cannon decided at Cornelia's urging to attend the Harvard-Yale football game. The planned relaxation turned into disaster. Yale beat Harvard 12–0, and after the game Cannon discovered that his bicycle had been stolen. When he returned home he found Cornelia out in the yard vigorously raking leaves.[12]

Thanksgiving passed quietly. Cannon, now convinced that he could do little to influence the course of events, contented himself with taking Cornelia on walks to the homes of friends who lived nearby. On the way home from a visit to George and Florence

Pierce on December 1, Cornelia went into labor. When the pains continued through the evening, Cannon summoned Dr. Swain. Swain came promptly and after a brief examination went to sleep in the guest room. There was, however, no sleep for Cornelia and Cannon, and both sat up through the night. The next morning just before ten o'clock Cornelia gave birth to an eight-pound boy.[13] Cannon later described to his mother-in-law the wonder of the delivery of his first-born: "As the baby was in danger of being asphyxiated, I was put to the job of keeping the water in a pail in the bathroom at a temp. of 105° F. My efforts were interrupted by the inrush of the Doctor who dangled a queer blue thing before my eyes and then plunged it suddenly into the water and began manipulations to start breathing. The Doctor said 'his mouth'—'his head'—'he breathes!' "

Throughout the months of waiting, the Cannons confidently expected that their first-born would be a girl. When Cannon found that he had a son, he could hardly find words to convey his shock. "Of course, you can imagine my *dismay* when I learned it was a boy!" he told his mother-in-law:

> A boy! Lord! what could *I* do with a boy? My plans for meeting responsibilities had all been directed toward the life of a girl. To have this brand new set of problems and possibilities thrown at me was completely flabbergastering!—I kneeled before the bath tub with my arms outstretched over its side, supporting its wobbly head above the water, and as this marvelous new phenomenon gasped and rattled his breath in his throat, and changed the blue of his flesh to a delicate pink, I was speechless, thoughtless, senseless, with the wonder and amazement that I, too, was a new phenomenon.[14]

If Cornelia felt a momentary disappointment in the arrival of a boy, she did not reveal it. "The whole experience goes so much deeper than I ever dreamed it would," she wrote her mother several days later, "—too deep for happiness—I find myself in tears almost as often as in smiles. When they brought the precious child to me, I could hardly believe my eyes that the lovely thing was mine. He has a startling resemblance to Walter, even his hands and feet are miniature copies. He bears not the slightest trace of our family—anyone might be his mother—but his paternity is undoubted. If he will only have his father's beautiful character, too, I shall ask no more."[15]

ॐ   ॐ   ॐ

The baby was named Bradford, and as the days passed, it seemed as though all of Cambridge was as delighted with him as his parents were. The house was filled with flowers sent by well-wishers as well as a steady stream of visitors—relations from West Newton and close friends like the Crothers, Perrys, Jacksons, Pierces and Parkers. Mr. Francis Tiffany, former minister of the Unitarian Church, at age 82 braved severe winter weather to pronounce the baby beautiful. At a luncheon honoring the visiting English physiologist Ernest Starling, Eliot leaned across the table to ask the new father, "And how is Bradford, Dr. Cannon?" William James and his wife called. Professor Münsterberg came armed with advice— "You mustn't experiment on ze baby," he told Cannon—and Isabel and Charles Whiting suggested proper ways of feeding. In the midst of congratulations Cannon did not forget the physicians who had tended Cornelia: he carried a primrose with Bradford's greetings to Dr. Davenport and a box of cigars to Dr. Swain.[16]

The arrival of the baby transformed Cannon and he became, as he suspected, "a new phenomenon." Things that he had done before without a second thought, such as attending a scientific meeting in another city, now required careful planning. He had always regretted being separated from Cornelia for even a brief period of time; now there was the added urgency of wanting to discuss and plan the baby's future. "What shall we do?" he wrote Cornelia while en route to Chicago less than a month after Bradford's birth. "Shall we teach him the best we know of self-protection and then let him go? It seems to me that we must try some such scheme as that or we shall be forever preventing him from getting life's experiences."[17]

As befitted a physiologist, Cannon began to keep a detailed record of each ounce and quarter inch that Bradford gained. When enough data had been accumulated, he charted Bradford's average weight curve and then graphically compared it against the average weight curve of ten thousand other babies. Almost every day he recorded a new incident in the baby's development—his first efforts at sucking his thumb, his cries and smiles—notations that almost invariably concluded with "he is a perfectly beautiful baby."[18]

When Bradford suffered digestive upsets or infections, Cannon sought advice from his friend Arthur Wentworth, one of Boston's most respected pediatricians, as to proper care and treatment, a course that relieved Cornelia of many anxieties.

Although life in the house on Ware Street now revolved around the baby, it did not appear to have altered Cannon's relationship to Cornelia. Indeed, he was even more accommodating to her needs and wants than before. When Cornelia indicated that she wished to go to a lecture, do some shopping, or tend to her social welfare obligations, she never had any difficulty in persuading the doting father, despite a heavy teaching and research schedule, to stay home with the baby. Watching and playing with the baby gave Cannon special pleasure, and he looked forward to the summer when he and Cornelia could show Bradford off to family and friends in the midwest.

Early in June 1908 Cannon set off with Cornelia and Bradford to St. Paul. The trip proved to be more than a reunion with family and friends. Before he left Cambridge Eliot had drafted him to give the Harvard entrance exams to applicants from a number of Minneapolis and St. Paul high schools. Further, he was scheduled to make two trips outside of Minnesota—one to Chicago to address the AMA as the newly elected chairman of its Physiology and Pathology Section, the second to give a paper to a meeting of the Wisconsin State Medical Society on the clinical applications of his research.[19] The visit at first was all that Cannon had anticipated. His address to the AMA was well received, and the task of conducting the Harvard entrance exams gave him an opportunity to revisit the Central High School and talk with teachers who sixteen years earlier had prepared him for similar exams. Family and friends feted him, Cornelia, and the baby at every turn. He revisited the houses he had lived in as a boy and was pleased to find that the neighborhood and houses were just as he remembered them.[20] Only the obligation of speaking to the Wisconsin State Medical Society remained before returning to Cambridge.

When he began to plan the trip home, Cannon received a shock: Cornelia indicated that she had no intention of joining him and that she had her own plans for staying on in the Midwest with Bradford for another three weeks. Cornelia's decision bitterly disappointed Cannon. Despite his pleas she remained adamant, and he returned to Cambridge alone. "I expect to have a most hilarious time while you are away," Cannon wrote his wife soon after coming home. "Get well and strong and be happy—I'll do the best I can to get and be likewise."[21] Despite the efforts of his sister Ida and his friends to keep him occupied until Cornelia and Bradford returned, he became despondent. "I do not know what is the matter with your old man," he complained to his wife a few days later.

> He wanders about this silent soulless house, he has plenty of time, and an abundance of work to do. Instead of getting at it, he reads advertisements, sorts over the papers, runs upstairs and washes his hands, looks at his watch and winds its few turns let loose since last it was wound. Somehow it doesn't go right . . .
>
> Cornelia, dear, I know it is a dreadful thing to write, but the fact is that I simply cannot live my life and do my work without you. I have been here four days and what have I done? Not a single first-class thing . . . I am convinced that this dismal attempt to live at "home" when there is really no home to live at is to be perennially a failure. This is my last "go" at it.[22]

To cope with his loneliness, Cannon finally went to stay with the Crothers in the country and renew himself in the physical labor of chopping trees and sawing wood. When Cornelia returned in mid-July, life resumed its accustomed pace.[23] Good talks with her not only settled the differences that had arisen between them earlier in the summer but also established parameters for their future relations as well.

Early in September Cornelia revealed that she was again pregnant. On learning the news, Cannon behaved far differently than he had the year before. This time, confident that his wife could take care of herself and did not need or want his hovering attention, he set out for two weeks of hiking and mountain climbing through northern New England with three of his friends.[24] Upon his return he continued to behave in the same vein. Instead of coddling Cornelia, he took her to dinners, lectures, and football games, even standing together on the Common on a cold November day "with 20,000 others" to watch *Herald* reports of the Harvard-Yale game.[25] Throughout the fall and winter he devoted himself almost exclusively to administrative problems at the Medical School and planning campaigns against the antivivisectionists—and for his own pleasure, to recording Bradford's early efforts to walk and talk.

As the winter ended and the time of confinement approached, Cannon appeared to be less concerned about Cornelia than with a number of debilitating illnesses that had beset Bradford.[26] He suffered little from the nervousness and apprehension that had accompanied the end of Cornelia's first pregnancy. The birth of the new baby was an equally joyous event and far less complicated. On April 23, 1909, at the first signs of impending birth, Dr. Swain was again called. This time he arrived at the Cannon house at 7:45 in the morning and a half hour later delivered a girl weighing 7-1/4 pounds. The delighted parents made use of the name they had previously selected for their first-born: they called the baby Wilma after Cannon's mother.

The new baby worked an almost immediate change in family relations. Initially Bradford appeared loving and tender to his little sister, touching his lips to her soft hair or cooing to her. Before long, however, his behavior changed: "Bradford twice ran away today," Cannon recorded in his diary early in May, "once broke fence in backyard and was found fingers in mouth sitting on front steps, again through back fence in Jones's yard."[27] A few days later Bradford started to cry fiercely before going to bed and continued for hours during the night. Bradford's behavior began to affect Cannon at work as well. "Had charge of room 202 in practical exam," he complained at the end of May. "Had been kept awake 4 hours last night by Bradford's yelling and suffered from severe headache. Nap in afternoon, n.g., went to bed with icebags."[28] Bradford's nerve-shattering distress continued, and although Cannon was planning new experiments on the emotions and carefully observed Bradford's moods, apparently he made no effort to seek a cause for his behavior nor did he think of relating it to the presence of the new baby.

At the term's end in June Cannon settled Cornelia and the children in a cottage at North Truro on Cape Cod, and after a brief vacation with them began a routine of working at the Medical School and commuting to the Cape on weekends and whenever time allowed. His preparations for new research on the emotions went well, and he enjoyed relaxing with his family as well as with friends and students who visited the cottage. To add to his pleasure, his sister Bernice, whom he had seen but briefly in previous years, came to stay with them for an extended period.[29]

The summer confirmed the joy Cannon felt as a newly minted father of two. The children's development absorbed him, and he could not help comparing them. "Wilma is a model baby, *so* different from Bradford," he noted in mid-July, adding, "She does not cry more than 15 minutes a day."[30] Bradford, now a toddler, fared equally well. He was, Cannon observed on various occasions, fascinating, beautiful, intelligent, and a veritable imp for mischief. Later, with more than a touch of pride, he recorded that Cornelia had made a list of more than one hundred words that Bradford used spontaneously.[31] The summer's experience proved such a happy one that it convinced Cornelia and Cannon they ought, like many of their Cambridge friends, to acquire a permanent second home. That fall they searched the countryside within commuting distance of Boston and finally found an old farm in Franklin, New Hampshire, that appeared to meet their needs.[32] It had a splendid view of the surrounding mountains, was large enough to accommodate their growing family and visiting friends, and gave promise of numerous opportunities to renew themselves with physical labor.

&ampe; &ampe; &ampe;

Buying the farm proved an absorbing exercise for Cannon. The owner (a local land speculator) and the real estate agent,[33] with Yankee pride in sharp bargaining, soon found that the young professor was different from what they had expected. He paid extraordinary attention to detail, read the fine print, and did in fact look a gift horse in the mouth. The farm as offered was said to contain "50 acres more or less." Cannon carefully read the deed, measured the land, translated rods and feet into acres, and discovered that the farm contained only forty acres. When he told the real estate agent of his calculations, the agent replied, "Without doubt, you are the first man for possibly 100 years who has taken the trouble to figure out the exact acreage." "I am very sorry regarding this matter and yet," he added, "it is not serious . . . We all thought it looked like 50 acres. Regarding your friends, none of them will ever know whether your farm contains 50 or 40 acres unless you see fit to inform them. There will be no sin or discredit to you if you do not enlighten [them] and no virtue shown or nothing gained if you do."[34] When the agent subsequently offered to arrange a mortgage with the owner, Cannon politely refused, paid $100 down, and took a $1,400 mortgage with the Cambridge Trust Company.

As the spring semester of 1910 began at the Medical School, the euphoria accompanying the purchase of the new home quickly dissipated. Cannon, as he had from the beginning of his tenure as Higginson professor, had some difficulty with the introductory course in physiology. This time he became oppressed with administrative matters as well. A continual round of visitors, students, and faculty meetings appeared to be part of a conspiracy to keep him from his research. "Afternoon spent in letter writing, conversations, and meeting of Division of Medical Sciences," he complained early in February, "so the days seem to go now—in little fiddle-te-diddle doings leading to no results. And I am not happy unless I am moving forward."[35] For the rest of the winter, except for the pleasure of watching the children grow and develop, nothing seemed to go well. During the spring vacation, in an effort to escape the doldrums, Cannon journeyed to Franklin with Cornelia to explore their property and meet their neighbors.

The real estate agent had described Cannon's new neighbors as "good American people, moral, peaceable, and *all right*."[36] Cannon found them to be somewhat less than that. He discovered that one neighbor at an adjoining farm was in jail for drunkenness. Another admitted that he had "swapping propensities." A third, who had served as a cavalry man with Custer, candidly told Cannon that he had had a somewhat "shady past."[37] Cannon, who generally was the soul of rectitude, put his scruples aside and made friends with all. They in turn accepted "the professor" with equal friendliness into the community. Throughout the spring break, Cannon and Cornelia, with the help of their neighbors, began to shape the house to meet their needs—tearing down partitions and ceilings, ripping up floors, and laying the foundation for a new fireplace.[38] They almost hated to return to Cambridge.

It was clear that the farm needed much work. That prospect, however, was regarded as an opportunity rather than a chore. The house in Franklin, unlike the house in Cambridge, was their own, and when the semester ended, they set about putting their stamp on it with a will. That summer whenever friends or family visited, they were immediately put to work. Ida, who came for a stay in June, was entrusted with removing old paint from the wainscoting and windows and helping Cornelia put up burlap around the walls of the living room. Visiting friends and students were invited to help with other tasks. Cannon and Cornelia, however, reserved the bulk of the remodeling for themselves—repairing the kitchen, hanging new windows and doors, putting up plaster board, making additional furniture, and sawing wood. The days were made up largely of physical labor, punctuated from time to time with picnics in the fields and canoeing on a nearby river. In mid-July, while clearing the barn, Cornelia matter-of-factly told Cannon that she was again pregnant.[39]

At about the same time Cannon began to work on a book. Earlier that spring Leonard Hill, a well-known English physiologist, had asked Cannon to prepare a book on the mechanical factors of digestion as the first volume in a proposed series of international medical monographs he was then organizing for Edward Arnold, a London publisher.[40] Cannon promptly accepted; he regarded the invitation as a further recognition of his contributions to the understanding of the digestive process and also saw it as an honor to be included in such an important and distinguished project. Once begun, the writing proceeded at a rapid pace. At the end of September, approximately eight weeks after starting, Cannon completed a draft of the first eleven chapters. That fall, despite a heavy schedule of preparing new experiments on the adrenals and directing advanced students in their research, Cannon continued to work on the book, and by late November he had finished the first draft.[41]

At first glance, the speed at which the book was written suggests that it was a scissors-and-paste collection of his previous articles. It was, in fact, much more. Rather than a chronological account of his own research, it was a synthetic work that incorporated the investigations of other physiologists with his own in order to present an account, as Cannon later stressed, "of understanding the mechanical activities of the alimentary canal as they are now known and understood."[42] There is no gainsaying the pride that Cannon felt in completing the book. The next day he wrote a note to Bowditch:

Last night I finished the manuscript of the book which I told you about last spring, on "The Mechanical Factors of Digestion." It is a full account of the work I have been doing for the past ten years. When you set me the problem in deglutition I had little notion of where it was to lead me, but in all the complex development of my investigations I have remembered that the initial stimulus came from you. And now that I have arrived at a stage which permits a summarizing of the results, I ask if I may show my gratitude to you for your service to physiology, and my own personal affection for you, by dedicating the book in your name.[43]

The momentum that carried Cannon through the summer and fall continued into the new year. The experiments he had begun on the adrenals earlier that winter went particularly well. Also, his sister Bernice, who had been teaching school in the Midwest, came to Cambridge at Cornelia's suggestion to seek a new career. Having both sisters close by during the final months of Cornelia's third pregnancy proved a tremendous help to the Cannons in caring for the children, and ultimately it led to a decision that affected all of their lives.

Early in 1911, concerned that the house on Ware Street would not long serve his growing family, Cannon began to look for a new place to live. When he learned that Professor Whitney's house on Divinity Avenue, which the University had recently acquired, was being offered for rent, he hurried to inspect it. The house, a huge rambling structure with a large yard, was a convenient distance from growing automobile traffic and had many of the features he was looking for.[44] Only the rent gave him pause: at $100 per month, it was double what he was paying at Ware Street. Four years earlier in similar circumstances Cannon had declined to rent a house on Berkeley Street, although it was preferable to the one he finally took, because its rent was $200 more a year. This time, however, the problem was solved when Ida and Bernice, after consultations with Cannon and Cornelia, agreed to move in with the expanding family and share the rent.[45]

In the midst of his increasing sense of accomplishment in his work and the happiness in his family life, Cannon received two blows. His close friend and collaborator, Fred Murphy, finding that Harvard offered little chance for advancement, accepted a post at Washington University in St. Louis.[46] In mid-March Bowditch, Cannon's scientific father and the chief guide in his career, died. Although neither of these events was unexpected, Cannon was deeply touched by them. In ordinary circumstances Cannon's sadness might have deepened into depression. Events, however, tran-

spired to save him: three days after arranging Bowditch's funeral
his gloom was dispelled by the safe and uncomplicated arrival of
his second daughter, Linda.[47]

﴾﴿ ﴾﴿ ﴾﴿

As the spring began, Cannon was almost overwhelmed by
the number of demands made on him. At home Cornelia and the
children were afflicted by a round of illnesses that so harried him
that he sent Bradford to the Crothers and Wilma to relatives in
West Newton in order to have time to look after Cornelia and the
new baby.[48] Some time later, he supervised moving the household
from Ware Street to Divinity Avenue and then spent time putting
the house in order. At the Medical School things were little better.
In addition to his own heavy teaching schedule, first-year men,
advanced students, and visitors almost daily sought him out for
advice and help in their work. To add to these burdens he had to
prepare papers to deliver at meetings of the American Gastro-
Enterological Association and the Massachusetts Medical Society,
as well as for graduation exercises at Yale—commitments he had
made some months before.[49] At one point, in desperation he wrote
reminders to himself to do nothing during the second half year
except run the physiology course. Despite the crush, by the end
of spring Cannon had met all of his obligations and had also
succeeded (with the help of a number of unusually gifted students)
in advancing his investigations on the effects of emotion on adrenal
secretion.

After classes ended in early June Cannon took his family and
his sister Bernice to New Hampshire. From the moment he arrived
in Franklin, he settled down to a daily routine of physical labor
around the farm, shifting from time to time to correcting the galleys
of his new book and planning a trip to Los Angeles for a meeting
of the American Medical Association. In ordinary circumstances
it is doubtful that Cannon would have left Cornelia and the children to make a month-long trip in order to attend a professional
meeting. This trip, however, was different; financed by the AMA,
it not only gave him a chance to report on the results of the Defense
Council's campaigns against the antivivisectionists but also provided an opportunity to visit his father in Oregon, whom he had
not seen for several years. Although Cannon still harbored some
resentment about his father's behavior toward his stepmother in

the last year of her life, he nevertheless wished to see him again and was not a little curious to meet his new wife—a graduate of the College of Physicians and Surgeons in Chicago.[50]

As soon as Cannon left Franklin for the West Coast, Cornelia with her usual skill and spirit took over running the household—making changes in and around the farm and devoting herself to solving a number of family problems. One of her first projects was to help Bernice decide on a career. Bernice was considering leaving teaching for a fellowship in sociological research at Smith College[51] but was uncertain whether she wanted to change to a career in social service. Cornelia, sensing her indecision, suggested that Bernice apply her considerable talents to the world of business and urged her to undertake courses in salesmanship with Lucinda Prince, one of the pioneers in industrial education in Boston.[52] Cornelia was so enthusiastic and persuasive that Bernice promptly registered for Mrs. Prince's courses. It proved to be the first step in what later eventuated as a career that included both personnel training and merchandising at Filene's department store.

One of Cornelia's other imaginative solutions to a troubling problem involved Wilma, who at age two delighted in sucking her fingers. "I made a glove for the two fingers she sucks with two thumb tacks sticking out on the back," she wrote Cannon soon after he left. "They will not get in her eye or hurt unless she puts the fingers in her mouth. She has grown so fond of red pepper that it is useless. B[radford] is advising her to *suck the other hand!*"[53] Although Cornelia sought Cannon's advice about her projects, she frequently put her plans into effect before he had time to either approve or disapprove of them. "I had a letter from Ida with the exciting news about the chance of a horse from the Coop," she wrote from Franklin. "If there is no charge, you may find a horse installed here on your return. Of course, the expense will be fabulous with horse-shoeing, curry comb, brush, harness, oil, feed, manure fork, pitch fork, etc., etc., and possible disease and death at the end! Shall we risk it?" Before Cannon could answer, she wrote of the arrival of the horse. "She is a charming horse, very gentle, and does not mind endless ladies round, ministering to her. The total outlay for curry comb, etc., was only $60 so I do not feel that we are ruined."[54]

There were more surprises awaiting Cannon. When he originally planned to visit his father, he did not know what to expect.

In addition to family differences, other things did not bode well for an easy meeting. Cannon had a dim view of homeopathic medicine, which he regarded as being akin to quackery. Moreover, he had misgivings about the qualifications of Colbert (and his wife, whom he sometimes derisively called "The Doctor") to practice medicine. Upon his arrival in Oregon, however, he discovered that Colbert and his wife not only had a very successful medical practice but also were widely regarded locally as pillars of the community. Although Cannon's visit was relatively brief, he was pleased to see how well his father was doing and left Oregon in a far happier frame of mind than when he had arrived.[55]

Despite Cornelia's newsy letters, some of the sights that greeted Cannon on his return to Franklin were unexpected. While he was away, Cornelia had decided to convert a dilapidated chicken house that leaned precariously against the barn into a guest cottage. To bring the transformation about, she asked a local farmer to haul the house to a high mound under some apple trees in a nearby field where it was set up on some well-rounded boulders. Once in place, she proceeded to modify it. Because the structure had no windows, she sawed out large rectangular slabs from the walls, then hinged them on the top and placed them back on the walls as shutters. To protect the house from rain, she shingled the top and sides with Bernice's help and then, to befit its new position and function on the farm, grandly named it "the chalet."[56] When Cannon came home, she could hardly wait to show it to him.

Generally, Cannon fell in with most of Cornelia's projects, but when it came to her efforts at carpentry, he emphatically drew the line. Once Cornelia thought about making something, she set to it enthusiastically but with none of the planning and the care in measurement that carpentry demands. Cannon, who was meticulous in his work habits, could not abide her slapdash efforts and remonstrated with her to no avail. "With Cornelia," he wryly commented, "it's no sooner done than said."[57] Fixing up the chalet occupied Cannon the rest of the summer.

Some of Cornelia's other ventures that summer proved more successful, especially the acquisition of a horse and carriage. Cannon loved the freedom it gave to explore and roam the countryside and often took the family on long trips to picnic or visit friends in nearby villages. Sometimes such trips turned into small adventures. About one such outing in late July, he noted: "This one of our *crazy* days. Started at 9:30 on 'picnic.' C and I with all three children, Linda in lattice cage swing from top of carriage. Decided to try old stage road over Sanbornton Mt. to New Hampton and Bristol. First part o.k.—got thicker and thicker—2 huge trees blown across road—had to go thru forest over huge stones—covered carriage caught all low branches, wheels caught on big stones . . . B[radford] very nervy, sat on front seat with me and took the flying branches without flinching and no cry."[59] Cannon clearly took pride and delight in the children's behavior. Although he was not demonstrative in his affection, he expressed his love by making them toys with his own hands—building a railroad out of lathes for Bradford, constructing a hobby horse out of a nail keg and some sticks salvaged from wood shingle bundles for Wilma, and crafting a miniature chair for Linda.[59]

During the latter part of the summer Cannon undertook a task that proved extraordinarily troublesome—compiling an index to his book. "Worked all day on Index of Mechanical Factors," he complained early in August. "Would rather break rocks."[60] Once the chore was completed, he turned with relief to his research and began commuting to Cambridge to complete the experiments he had been working on all year. All went well, but early in September an incident occurred in Franklin that caused Cannon great concern.[61]

A local teenager publicly boasted that he had broken into the Cannon house and taken a compass and a knife. When Cannon learned that the boy had also stolen a watch from some people in a nearby village, he wrote the Boston Children's Aid Society for advice and then went to talk to the boy's mother and a local magistrate about the thefts. Cannon was fiercely upright and found it difficult to countenance lying, cheating, or larceny of any sort by any one—child or adult. For him, the robberies were a clear signal that some action had to be taken to rescue the boy from what appeared to be the first steps leading to a life of crime. Later, when the magistrate sentenced the boy to four years "under the discipline of an industrial school," Cannon, convinced that this was the best course to take, helped persuade the mother to agree to the sentence. It was a sorry affair and although Cannon was commended by the magistrate at the trial for his concern with the boy's welfare, he took little satisfaction in the praise or the ultimate outcome of the trial. His stern moral standards were not simply a measure for the world around him but applied with equal rigor to his own family. His wife later remembered that while he could take his children's physical ills with equanimity, their moral delinquencies upset him. "A small boy's absconding of the pennies taken at a juvenile theatrical performance," she recalled, "discovered through a face suspiciously smeared with chocolate candy, seemed to threaten state prison for the child once grown to manhood. And the lies of childhood were hard for him to bear. Those early years of the twentieth century were a difficult time for the conservative fathers brought up in a puritan era. However, in time wisdom as a parent came to him as it comes to us all."[62]

Despite the unpleasantness at the end the summer refreshed him, and when he returned to Cambridge in the fall of 1911, Cannon immersed himself in his work with a new vigor. Early in October he completed four papers based on the research he had begun earlier in the year and submitted them to Porter for publication in the *American Journal of Physiology*.[63] Several weeks later he received six author's copies of *The Mechanical Factors of Digestion*, his first book. In the midst of the glow of accomplishment, he had a moment's pause: a week earlier he had celebrated his fortieth birthday. "Do not feel 40 years old," he reflected in his diary, "but the years are beginning to seem short."[64]

13 *New Pathways in Medical Education*

A S CANNON established himself as Higginson Professor of Physiology he increasingly found himself faced with the necessity of dealing with problems that involved the relationship of science to medical education—particularly those concerned with the status and role of science at the Medical School. These problems, Cannon discovered, required him to enter a distressing political arena in which he was forced to adjudicate differences between his colleagues at the Medical School and to debate with friends and people he admired. Among the issues that initially occupied and troubled him were the requirements for admission to the Medical School.

The admissions problem at Harvard stemmed directly from Eliot's reform that required all medical students to have a bachelor's degree from a recognized college or scientific school for entrance after 1901. Eliot's requirement allowed only one exception: if applicants of suitable age had acquired an equivalent education or training, they could by special permission of the Administrative Board be admitted to the School. Despite this qualification, one immediate result of Eliot's reform was a precipitous decline in the number of matriculants and, to the treasurer's distress, a persistent loss of student revenues.[1] In the beginning no one in the administration regarded the decline as more than a temporary phenomenon. Some even welcomed the relief it brought to the overcrowded conditions that had plagued the Boylston Street School. Nevertheless, as the low enrollment continued, the entrance requirement of a bachelor's degree began to be modified through the admission of sizable numbers of students who had received special permission from the Administrative Board. Initially the medical faculty did not oppose such admissions, because most of those who entered under this scheme were well-trained upperclassmen from Harvard College or the Lawrence Scientific School who subsequently carried on their medical studies with distinction.[2]

Although in time the downward cycle in student enrollment eased, the surge of matriculants that everyone had anticipated would accompany the opening of the new buildings on Longwood Avenue did not materialize. Indeed, given the School's new spacious quarters, the lack of students became embarrassingly apparent. Under this pressure, the medical faculty began to make serious efforts to increase the student body by further modifying the admission requirements. When it became evident in the fall of 1907 that men without collegiate degrees formed an increasing and distinct group within the student body,[3] Charles Minot, concerned that such students be fit to cope with the burgeoning scientific requirements in the medical curriculum, suggested at a faculty meeting that it might be expedient to admit applicants after they had completed two years of college, provided they were well trained in the laboratory sciences and could read French and German. The faculty immediately divided: Cannon, Folin, Councilman, and a number of other preclinical instructors supported Minot's plan, but some of the clinical faculty brought forward other plans.[4]

One that captured the medical faculty's attention for a time urged that the Faculty of Arts and Sciences in Cambridge allow courses in the first year of medical training to count toward the B.A. or B.S. degree. It was not a new idea. It was in fact congruent with a practice that allowed Harvard undergraduates to enter the Law School for a so-called combined course whereby work done there was permitted to count toward the completion of the bachelor's degree, thus shortening the time of their training. It was a procedure that Eliot as well as some of the other deans of the professional schools in Cambridge approved.[5] William Richardson, the dean of the Medical School, accepted it as well and had on occasion extended such an opportunity to students from several small colleges. When the medical faculty subsequently learned of Richardson's arrangement (which had been made without their knowledge or approval), they voted to terminate it.[6]

The problem of admission requirements continued to bother the faculty throughout the 1907–08 academic year, including Cannon. In one sense, the problem was brought to him through his administrative duties; as a member of the Medical School's Administrative Board he frequently had to vote on the admission of special students. In another sense, he was concerned because his own experience had shown him that possession of the baccalaureate degree did not necessarily prepare one adequately for medical studies. Even at this early stage of his career, Cannon regretted that he had not taken more work in physics, chemistry, and mathematics.[7]

After one faculty debate in February 1908 Cannon informed Eliot that he wholeheartedly supported Minot's proposals. "It seems to me," he told the president, "very probable that the specification of laboratory courses in physics and biology, in addition to chemistry, as preliminary to entrance to the best medical schools of the country will do much to bring about a recognition of these studies and a bettering of the methods of teaching them in colleges where at present these subjects are slighted." Aware that many of his clinical colleagues did not regard very highly the judgment of laboratory men as to the value of such preparation and favored instead the requirements already in place, he tried to persuade Eliot that specifying the laboratory courses would not raise Harvard's entrance requirements higher than the standards demanded by other schools. "Forty or more medical schools," he continued, "including almost all the first-class institutions, either require these subjects as preliminary to the medical course, or will require them by 1910. Harvard, therefore, instead of raising its standard above the general level, would be bringing its standard up to the general level with respect to these specified preliminary college studies."[8]

Eliot, despite Cannon's bill of particulars, was not persuaded. Several days later he wrote Cannon that he would rather see advice given to prospective students regarding subjects for admission than establishing absolute requirements. "I believe our requirement for a preliminary degree to be more advantageous than the specific requirements made by other medical schools," he told him, "even if we imagine these specific requirements to be enforced— which is doubtful." At the next meeting of the medical faculty, following a heated debate on admissions, Cannon cut the umbilical cord that bound him to Eliot and voted his support of Minot's proposals. It did not matter—Minot's plan was roundly defeated.[9]

Cannon's show of independence did not affect his relations

with Eliot. In fact, the president subsequently demonstrated his continuing belief in Cannon in a variety of ways. Soon after, he appointed him as Harvard's delegate to an informal conference in Chicago of representatives from some of the university medical schools so that Cannon might have an opportunity to sample the opinions of medical educators from other institutions on admissions policies. In another display of confidence in his judgment, he placed him on a committee that passed on nominations for promotion in the surgery department and then made him chairman of a new committee charged with organizing an x-ray department at the Medical School. Still later he put him on the board of a project that was of particular interest to Eliot—that of establishing a medical school in China to train young men there in the methods of modern Western medicine. It became clear to many on the medical faculty that Eliot, by these and similar acts, was grooming Cannon to be his spokesman on medical matters.[10]

Although Cannon revered Eliot and appreciated his confidence, he did not budge from his position on admissions policies nor did the president and some of the clinical faculty members deviate from theirs. When Minot's proposals had been formally put before the faculty for a vote in March of 1908, Frederick C. Shattuck described them as a brand of snake-oil. And when supporters of Minot tried to show that students who were not well prepared in the sciences failed in anatomy, they were sharply challenged by James G. Mumford of the surgery department who asserted that men who did well in their scientific medical studies invariably failed in their clinical studies. The scientist and the clinician, Mumford contended, were as unlike as a country parson and a city politician.[11] Each attempt made to modify existing entrance regulations seemed only to exacerbate the divisions within the faculty. Early in 1909, through what appeared to be a minor miracle, the faculty reached a *modus vivendi:* they passed an omnibus bill that contained Minot's previously rejected admissions plan along with a provision that required students who wished to take the combined course to maintain a grade average of 75% for one year before becoming regular candidates for the medical degree.[12] At best, the compromise was cosmetic. Believing that this particular struggle with the medical faculty was over, Eliot confidently left Cambridge to give a previously arranged series of lectures in the South and West.

No sooner did the president leave town, however, than some members of the medical faculty began to interpret the revised admissions rules as eliminating the bachelor's degree requirement. Nor were they alone: the deans of the graduate schools in Cambridge began to complain to Jerome Greene, secretary to the Harvard Corporation, that the new admissions policy at the Medical School was a threat to the degree standards set at their own schools. The dean of Harvard College, in particular, forcefully told Greene that the new medical plan was nothing more or less than an invitation to premedical students to terminate their college work after two years, and, worse, to devote one of those years to courses in the natural sciences, thus reducing opportunities to study literature, philosophy, and the arts.[13] Greene shared their doubts because he was certain that some of the members of the medical faculty would continue to render meanings to the agreed-upon admission requirements that Eliot had not intended. The more Greene learned about the medical faculty's interpretation of the new rules, the more alarmed he became. "Please tell the President," he wrote one of his friends who was traveling with Eliot,

> that I met Dr. Councilman at dinner last night, and he told me that he was so delighted by the action of the Medical Faculty abolishing the requirement of a degree for admission (sic) that he could hardly believe his ears, and did not dare to open his mouth lest he might stir up some contrary argument . . . In other words, he thinks that a medical training imposed upon high school training plus a few introductory courses in Natural Science will produce a man who is no less cultivated and no less able to hold his own in the society of liberally educated men than a man who has a three or four year's college training under his medical course.[14]

Eliot, although appreciating Greene's concern, was not upset by the information he received and remained firm in his belief that the medical faculty's interpretation of the new rules was no threat to graduate school standards. The true importance of rules, he reminded Greene, was how they were administered. The president had good reason for such beliefs: he had been confronted with other differences between the medical faculty and the Cambridge faculties that at first appeared to be intractable but were later adjudicated amicably. To salve Greene's feelings as well as those of the Cambridge deans, Eliot promised that he would discuss the new rules again with the Faculty Council before they were printed in the University Catalogue.[15]

On his return to Cambridge Eliot proposed a modification of the new admission rules that he thought would quiet some of the deans' apprehensions. Instead of transferring special students to regular status after they had satisfactorily completed one year of course work, he suggested that such students be accepted for the M.D. degree only if they had attained a specific grade point average throughout all of their years in the Medical School.[16] No one on the medical faculty objected to the modification—even Councilman remained silent. All were aware that the president's retirement was imminent, and they did not wish to mar his leaving with rancor. There would be time enough to let the new administration deal with the divisions and problems that remained.

﴾ع﴿ ﴾ع﴿ ﴾ع﴿

When the news that Eliot intended to retire became generally known in the fall of 1908,[17] there was much speculation as to who would succeed him. Such speculation was not new. Eliot was an educator of national importance, and in the past any rumor that suggested that someone had been chosen to succeed him was immediately taken up and broadcast by newspapers throughout the country. Several years before, for example, President Theodore Roosevelt casually told a delegation of Harvard alumni that after he turned over the reins of government to the next president of the United States, he "hoped to be free to take an active part in Harvard affairs again." Some reporters, schooled in the euphemisms used by politicians in putting themselves forward for an office, construed Roosevelt's remarks to mean that he expected at some future time to be elected president of Harvard.[18]

Shortly thereafter when Henry P. Walcott, a member of the Corporation, was asked by the *Boston Advertiser* if the report had any substance, he angrily replied, "President Roosevelt will never become the head of Harvard University as long as Charles W. Eliot is alive . . . There is no possibility of his ever becoming President of the University." The *Boston Herald* reported that others shared Walcott's sentiments. "Of course the Harvard Corporation," it informed its readers, "calls the report that President Roosevelt is to be President of Harvard sheer nonsense. It is a good deal of chestnut besides." "We suppose," the *Herald* continued, "that if any of the authorities at Harvard were pressed to name the most likely man for that office in the event of President Eliot's retirement, in the near or distant future, they would mention A. Lawrence Lowell." Both Roosevelt and Eliot took the rumors less seriously. When Roosevelt was questioned about the response of the Harvard Corporation, he replied, "I have no more idea of succeeding President Eliot than I have of becoming Grand Llama of Tibet or a medicine man among the Apaches." Eliot, in evident good humor, added, "President Roosevelt is said to want my job when I get through. Let me say I don't want his when he gets through."[19]

The Roosevelt incident, despite the strong feelings it engendered, was less a judgment on Roosevelt's abilities than a reflection of a growing perception that the University had arrived at a turning point and that a decision had to be reached on whether or not it would continue to subscribe to Eliot's educational philosophy. Fifteen years earlier, on the occasion of Eliot's twenty-fifth anniversary as president of Harvard, the Corporation affirmed his reforms in the undergraduate curriculum and endorsed his long-range program for raising standards and enhancing the quality of graduate training in business, law, and medicine.[20] During the early years of the twentieth century, however, that support began to erode. Increasingly members of Harvard's governing boards as well as a number of faculty leaders began to voice their opposition to Eliot's policies. Many felt that he had gone too far with his schemes for promoting the role of graduate and professional education at the University; they preferred a policy that would again focus on the primacy of the undergraduate experience.[21]

It was not idle speculation that put Abbott Lawrence Lowell's name forward as a possible successor to Charles W. Eliot. He had all of the qualifications required for the presidency of Harvard. He was a scion of one of the oldest families in New England, thereby fit to be a keeper of the Brahmin flame, and he was also a distinguished scholar of government. More important, he had for some years campaigned actively with members of the Corporation, the Overseers, and the Harvard faculty for the presidency. Lowell made no secret that he wished to put the University on a different course from that which Eliot had mapped out and followed for almost forty years. It was Lowell's persistent and articulate advocacy of the need to strengthen undergraduate education that ultimately helped persuade the governing bodies to choose him as Eliot's successor.[22]

At Eliot's last meeting with the medical faculty in May 1909 Frederick Shattuck, in a graceful and thoughtful speech, summed up the highlights of Eliot's contributions to the development of medical education at Harvard. While on such occasions praise frequently puts a mythic gloss on the past, Shattuck in the midst of his kudos sharply reminded Eliot of the differences that had separated him from the medical faculty. "It would be flattery to say that we think you have always been right," Shattuck told Eliot, "and we are not minded even upon this occasion to indulge in flattery." In his reply Eliot chose to overlook the differences and instead, in characteristic fashion, attempted to chart the direction he hoped that the Medical School would take in the future. The purpose of the School, he reminded the faculty as he had time and again, was not only to educate practitioners but to prepare young men for medical and surgical research. "Medicine has long been, to my thinking," he continued, "the most altruistic of the professions, but the profession has developed in recent times a second method of serving the people greatly—the method of medical research."[23]

If Shattuck's and Eliot's speeches were in large part a serene glance at the Medical School's recent history, they were no less an effort to give continuity to policies already in place. Both men viewed with some trepidation the changes they anticipated would occur in both the organization and the policies of the Medical School. As early as a year before Eliot's retirement Shattuck had expressed his concern about the future administration of the School: "Not only is it quite possible," he told Eliot, "that your successor may not be as much interested in the Medical School, but it is also possible there might not be two such wise medical men on the Corporation as Walcott and A. T. Cabot."[24]

Eliot, for his part, was also disturbed but about a more immediate matter—namely, Councilman's suggestion to reorganize the medical faculty into nine separate divisions, each having one representative on a Faculty Council, which in turn would govern the School. Eliot saw such a plan as a step backward—in essence, an effort to put the School into the hands of a few senior professors. "That was the state of the Medical School when I first became president," he complained to Edward H. Bradford; "it would be hard to imagine a worse form of government for a medical school.

The senior members of any teaching faculty ought to have great influence; but it should be an influence not due to their official positions but to their personal qualities."[25]

Still, for all of their foreboding, neither Shattuck nor Eliot really grasped the dimensions of the crisis the Medical School faced. For more than a generation Eliot had set policy and guided the School almost singlehandedly. Although the School had a number of deans during his tenure, none, with the possible exception of Bowditch, could be said to have functioned independently; most had served essentially as hands to carry out the president's wishes. When problems arose in the School, it was Eliot who adjudicated them. Lowell, the new president, on the contrary, knew little about the Medical School or its problems; he had already given notice that his basic interest was in refurbishing undergraduate education.[26] The medical dean, Henry A. Christian, was hardly in a better position: in office barely a year and still showing his youth and inexperience, he differed with the faculty on a number of substantive issues. Moreover, he could no longer count on Eliot to help him cope with the daily problems that confronted his office. The faculty, and especially the preclinical men, who for more than a generation had looked to the president as a court of last resort on major problems, now had no one to whom they could appeal in Cambridge. Even the grand marble buildings in which they worked conspired to isolate and separate them from one another. In sum, Eliot's retirement left a power vacuum that was to have a profound effect on the administration of the School as well as on its vision of the changing tasks and needs of medicine.

It is doubtful whether the medical faculty at first gave much thought to the administrative changes that might follow Eliot's retirement. Despite the squabbling over admissions policy, most faculty members were convinced that the School was on a winning course; if it was not then the leading medical school in the country, it would shortly take possession of that position.[27] Cannon subscribed to such beliefs. When his friend Robert Yerkes wrote him for advice in helping his cousin choose the best medical school to attend, Cannon unequivocally recommended Harvard. "It comes, in my mind," he replied,

to a choice between J[ohns] H[opkins] and Harvard. Personally I think there is little to shift the balance one way or the other at present. By the time your cousin is ready to graduate I'm inclined to think that Harvard will distinctly lead, both in the laboratories and in clinical advantages. The J.H. *esprit de corps* leads to a rather disagreeable smugness and a better-than-thou attitude (along with a splendid loyalty)—and that is against the place. Harvard, on the other hand, has been given to self-criticism, to an unhealthy extent at times, but I hope that that will be tempered under the new regime. At present H[arvard] has good labs, good clinics, small classes, an improving spirit of good fellowship and sense for scientific medicine, and I am inclined to favor it.[28]

Although Lowell was not inaugurated until the fall, he began to perform the duties of the presidency as soon as Eliot's resignation became effective. William James, writing to Bowditch later that summer, painted a vivid portrait of the new president as he conducted the commencement festivities for the first time. "Lawrence Lowell looked like a Roman Emperor in the Sanders Theater," he rejoiced, "—solid as a rock, and . . . his epithets were in Eliot's line and, if anything, better than Eliot's. *We've got a President!*—evidently, and I'm glad." Bowditch was not surprised. "Lowell seems to have won golden opinions from all sorts of people," he replied. "Personally, I expect great things from him, though we must not look for such striking effects as those which attended Eliot's administrative labors, for he will not be likely to encounter the vigorous and persistent opposition which made Eliot's work seem like contests and his successes like victories."[29]

❧ ❧ ❧

October 6, 1909, was a memorable day in Cambridge: for the first time in forty years Harvard was inaugurating a new president. In the rush of events Cannon described the excitement only briefly in his line-a-day diary: "Gowned with Pres. McVey at 9:30 and went to Phillips Brooks House where delegates to Mr. Lowell's Inauguration assembled—a glorious autumn day. Marched, [in] a glorious array, to platform in front of University Hall where ceremonies [held]. Luncheon at Union. Alumni meeting in afternoon in Memorial Hall—spendid singing. Students celebrated in evening at stadium." The next day there was more celebration and Cannon continued, "Went with Cornelia to luncheon in Faculty Room [given] by Pres. and Mrs. Lowell. Terrible crush. Went then to Medical School—tea—beautiful sights. Dr. Bowditch in his room—

Presidents Lowell and Eliot call on him. Dinner at Union in evening. Good speaking."[30]

Despite the euphoria and expressions of unanimity of purpose made at the inauguration, the environment at the Medical School had already begun to change. At his first meeting with the medical faculty earlier that year, Lowell advanced his interest in undergraduate education by quietly shifting the focus of faculty debate from admissions policy to the related and more complicated problem of curriculum reform. He then appointed L. J. Henderson (who had recently been turned down for promotion by the Committee of Full Professors) to chair an ad hoc committee to examine the overlapping courses given in Harvard College and the Medical School. Lowell's appointment of Henderson was not a casual act; he was well-acquainted with him through family ties, and Henderson's ideas of enhancing the scientific offerings in the College coincided with Lowell's desire to strengthen undergraduate education.[31] The way business was conducted at the Medical School changed with equal swiftness under the new president: in the fall the reorganization of the governance of the School that Eliot had so emphatically opposed passed with little disagreement. "Faculty votes reorganization into divisions and adjourns by 9:30!" Cannon noted in his diary, "Mr. Lowell certainly works rapidly!"[32]

The organization of Henderson's exploratory committee marked the beginning of a new series of debates on the form and substance of medical education at Harvard. Although the committee at its inception was made up of members of both the medical faculty and the Faculty of Arts and Sciences, Henderson quickly made it his own personal instrument by co-opting Ernest Southard to work with him. The choice was an excellent one. Southard was well known in the Boston and Cambridge communities, had an abiding interest in the reform of medical education stemming from his participation as a student in the School's 1899 curriculum report, and, unlike Henderson, was held in high regard by a majority of the medical faculty. Trained in pathology and a brilliant clinical investigator in neurology, he had just been appointed the first Bullard Professor of Neuropathology.[33] The committee had one other asset—an unofficial adviser. Both Henderson and Southard were friends of Cannon and had good reason to value his judgment. Knowing of his interest in promoting the teaching of laboratory sciences to undergraduates, they began to call on him privately, using him as a sounding board for their ideas and drawing on his experience and expertise to shore up their arguments.[34]

Early in November 1909 Henderson and Southard presented their views on curriculum reform in an article in the *Harvard Bulletin* entitled "Education in Medicine: The Relations of the Medical School and the College." Briefly, they argued that the advent of scientific medicine burdened Harvard students with increased demands on both their premedical preparation and later training in clinical specialties and also considerably lengthened their course of study. To cope with these difficulties, the authors proposed that the Medical School in Boston and the College in Cambridge join forces and offer various medical science courses under the Faculty of Arts and Sciences. Such a policy, they explained, not only would allow properly qualified undergraduates to take science courses given in the Medical School as part of the baccalaureate degree but also would bring to the School a variety of other students—lawyers, engineers, and social workers—who would profit in their work from a knowledge of the fundamental principles of medicine. "The greatest of all needs of the Harvard Medical School," they concluded, "is free and as far as possible untrammeled intercourse with every other department of Harvard and with every other American university."[35]

In an effort to forestall the attacks on Henderson and Southard that he felt were sure to come, Cannon prepared a strong editorial for the *Boston Medical and Surgical Journal* urging adoption of their plan. He focused not only on their proposal to make laboratory subjects in the medical curriculum available for undergraduate credit but also on the opportunities that would be available for individualized pursuit of medical course work. "It might reasonably be expected," he concluded, "that the greater freedom which the proposed scheme offers to students, and the cultivation of individual interests which it encourages, would tend to develop leaders and productive scholars, as well as serviceable practitioners, in the various clinical branches."[36] Cannon's support, however, proved of little help. Within days of publication the *Harvard Bulletin* received scores of letters attacking the article.

George V. N. Dearborn, professor of physiology at Tufts Medical School, in particular, charged that Henderson's and Southard's proposals were little more than a veiled attack against the general practitioner. If they are adopted, he warned, it would mark the first step taken by "the Harvard Medical School to fit young men to be medical scientists in general, and successful medical specialists in practice rather than 'all-round' general practitioners."[37] These charges gave new currency to the qualms many Boston practitioners had but did not readily express about the development of the medical sciences at Harvard. Following the appearance of Dearborn's letter, the *Boston Medical and Surgical Journal* drew back from its original approval, implicit in Cannon's editorial, of Henderson and Southard's plan and took instead a new position. "It is well to recognize, as Dearborn points out," the *Journal* editorialized, "that practitioners of medicine whether special or general are what the public demands from medical schools and what the medical schools are in their turn bound to supply. The main issue should not be ignored or lost sight of in the wholly commendable effort to develop highly trained specialists and original investigators."[38]

Perhaps the most telling criticism of Henderson and Southard's proposals was that offered by Thomas Dwight. A distinguished anatomist and one of the senior members of the Harvard medical faculty, Dwight took sharp issue with their implication that laboratory courses were exclusively concerned with medical science whereas clinical courses were essentially devoted to the art of medicine. For Dwight the distinction was meaningless. Although he agreed that one of the functions of science was to advance knowledge, he just as firmly believed that the primary purpose of all courses in the Medical School was to fit students to practice medicine. Although Dwight felt very deeply about the issue, he refused to add his criticism to the ongoing public debate. Instead, he circulated his views in a privately printed letter to Eliot, Lowell, and the Faculty of Medicine.[39] In one sense, Dwight's action was a reflection of his rectitude; in another, it was a statement of his conviction that problems in medical education were strictly an internal affair to be discussed and resolved by the medical faculty.

Although Dwight's letter did not succeed in limiting the controversy, it nevertheless played a role in crystallizing faculty opinion about curriculum reform. During the winter and early spring of 1910 the matter continued to simmer, erupting from time to time in brief but sharp outbursts that disturbed the flow of business at monthly faculty meetings. At one meeting, when Henderson proposed putting Minot's first-year course in histology and em-

bryology on a list of courses to be offered by the Faculty of Arts
and Sciences, Minot became so incensed that he initiated a series
of parliamentary maneuvers to abolish Henderson's committee.
The acrimonious faculty debates that ensued persuaded Lowell
that most of Henderson and Southard's proposals had reached a
stone wall and that a new tack would have to be taken to bring
about curriculum reform. Some weeks later, in an effort to break
the stalemate, Lowell arranged the formation of another committee
to consider means for "lessening the rigidity of the medical curriculum." This time, instead of leaving the organization of the
committee to Henderson, Lowell appointed a well-balanced committee of medical scientists and clinicians that included, in addition
to himself, Christian, Henderson, Bradford, and Cannon.[40]

The committee had barely been formed when it was faced
with an order of business it had not anticipated—a student protest.
Such protests were not a new phenomenon at the Medical School.
This one, however, was clearly incited by the publication of the
Henderson and Southard proposals. The curriculum, the students
announced, was a burden and a bore. "It is an almost universal
feeling," one of their complaints began, "that laboratory days are
so intellectually exhausting that they fail to accomplish as much
real instruction as would result if the work were reduced in bulk."
Another charged that lectures in the clinical courses were largely
superfluous and that the information transmitted by such instruction could be acquired as well or even better by reading textbooks.
Still another complained that the examination system was so rigid
that it led at the end of the year "to a panic-stricken cramming"
of undigested facts. In short, the students claimed that the curriculum, the teaching, and the examination system needed a complete overhaul to meet their needs.[41]

Early in May Charles Ryder and Richard Miller, two of the
more articulate student leaders, met with the new faculty committee to discuss informally the various complaints of their classmates. Ryder and Miller added little that was new to the criticisms
already made; however, their verbal emphasis brought home to
the committee the substance of student difficulties far more vividly
than their previously written resolutions and articles. Cannon,
more than the other members of the committee, followed the students' litany sympathetically. Eleven years before, as a medical
student, he had made similar criticisms and asked for similar re-

forms. Now, listening to echoes of his own experience, he sat on the other side of the table. One element in the discussion had particular meaning for him: when the students were asked if there were any redeeming features in the teaching methods used at the Medical School, they gave enthusiastic praise to the case method. Neither the students nor the committee members remembered that it was Cannon who had introduced the case method to teaching in the Medical School. All believed that the method was developed by Richard Cabot, and Cannon said nothing to correct them.[42]

In the fall of 1910 Henderson, who had spent the summer studying the curricula of various European medical schools, submitted another report on curricular reform. For all of his brilliance, Henderson had learned little from faculty opposition to the proposals he and Southard had presented several months earlier. The new report, which again highlighted the virtues and superiority of university instruction of scientific subjects, immediately created rifts in the committee. When placed before the medical faculty early in 1911 it fared no better. Most faculty members regarded it as a mere variation of the original Henderson and Southard plan. "The opposition to the report," Christian later informed Lowell, "originated in a spirit of antagonism toward Henderson, who has certainly stirred things up."[43] The more the faculty analyzed the new report, the more they determined to focus on those parts that coincided with student concerns about the rigid examination system. Finally the wrangling became so intense that Minot, in an effort to bring the dispute to an end, suggested that the faculty appoint a special committee to search for a practical way to carry out those provisions of the report that had previously been agreed upon. Exhausted by the bickering and hairsplitting, the faculty then asked Christian and Cannon to join with Greenough, Warren, and Rosenau to find a path out of the morass.[44]

Already overwhelmed by a host of personal and professional concerns, Cannon did not relish the new assignment. Although he favored a revision of the examination system, he also saw that it was only one of the issues that had occupied the previous committees on the curriculum. Worse, the continual meetings Christian called to develop a strategy to make a report palatable to the faculty began to wear him down. After one such meeting in May 1911 Cannon complained in his diary that Christian had deputized him to write the final report.[45] The report Cannon ultimately prepared solved none of the curriculum difficulties. Instead, following the faculty's most recent mandate, it focused entirely on reforming the examination system, recommending that the Medical School discard the customary year-end examinations in each course and use in their place a two-tiered system of general and practical examinations to be given at the end of the second and fourth years.[46] The recommendations eventually adopted and established as Medical School policy were hardly the result the faculty had hoped for when they originally agreed to revise the curriculum. For Cannon the inconclusive results of curriculum reform after two years of struggle marked more than merely the end to a thankless assignment; they also appeared to reflect the general dissatisfaction that he saw developing at the Medical School and that had begun with Eliot's retirement.

14 Continuity and Change at the Medical School

T HERE WERE a number of other aspects to the power vacuum at the Medical School that Eliot left behind him. In the spring of 1909, only days before Eliot formally retired, Christian called upon Cannon to discuss some plans he had in mind for changing the direction of the School. Christian needed close and influential allies on the medical faculty for the task he had set himself, and Cannon was a splendid prospect. Cannon had for some years been involved in policy making and was a member of every important committee in the School from the Administrative Board to the Committee on Course of Study. Equally important, he had the respect and admiration of his colleagues.

Despite Christian's desire to set the Medical School on a different course, he actually shared many of Eliot's ideas about medical education.[1] Like Eliot, he was firmly committed to the idea of the medical school as an integral part of the university and the development of medical science as part of advanced university work. Like Eliot, he also believed that students should be admitted to medical school only after they had gained their B.A. or B.S. degrees. In the matter of priorities, however, a fundamental difference existed between the two men. Eliot, a former chemist, had devoted himself almost exclusively to building up the scientific side of medicine. Christian, set on a career course in clinical medicine, was committed to improving clinical instruction and promoting affiliations between the Medical School and various Boston hospitals. He made clear in his meeting with Cannon that he believed the time had come for a change of emphasis at the School.

Although Cannon sympathized to some extent with Christian's desire to enhance the status of the clinical departments, a terse diary note reveals that he felt the young medical dean was sure to have trouble carrying out his plans.[2]

Some weeks after his meeting with Cannon, Christian gave an oblique public notice of his future intentions in his first annual report to President Lowell. Although he praised Eliot's achievements in medical education, he emphasized, wherever possible, the growing importance of clinical instruction for both students and practicing physicians, noting that students overwhelmingly chose clinical courses in the fourth-year elective program and that an increasing number of practitioners had registered for summer courses to update their clinical skills.[3] Christian took particular pride in the summer program, because it was his support of the enlargement of the original course of instruction that contributed to its growing success. When reporters came to discuss the summer program with him, Christian seized the opportunity not merely to advance the importance of clinical teaching but also to emphasize the School's need for a hospital of its own. "As a matter of fact," he told them, "teaching by the medical staff of a hospital is the most effective means known for keeping the practical work of a hospital up to the best standard."[4]

Sensing a new climate of opinion in the administration, clinicians who had previously said little openly about their status in the Medical School began to complain about the disproportionate number of laboratory men who had been taken into the faculty under Eliot's leadership and to press for additional recognition of their ranks. Edward H. Bradford, professor of orthopedic surgery and a close friend of Lowell, led the attack. "There is certainly no objection to having all possible research work at the School," he wrote Lowell early in 1910, "but it is desirable that enough should be done to relieve the School of its present reputation as an institution devoted chiefly to medical research and not teaching the practice of medicine . . . Men who are 40 or 50 years of age, who have been teaching for ten and fifteen years in a grade much inferior to that given their contemporaries connected with other schools, find younger men in other departments, often of no great ability, receiving quickly professorial rank directly."[5] Later that year Bradford was joined in his criticism by Maurice Howe Richardson, the Moseley Professor of Surgery who was also a friend of Lowell, in demands for an increase in the surgical staff as well as in their status at the School. "They don't particularly care about salary," Richardson told the president, "but they do want an appropriate or dignified title which signifies their position in the School."[6]

Cannon, however, questioned the capability of some of the young surgeons whom Richardson and Bradford wished to advance. When it was proposed at a faculty meeting held that fall that John Bapst Blake, Robert Greenough, and Paul Thorndike of the Boston City Hospital be made assistant professors to fill a gap in the department, Cannon, along with Councilman, vehemently opposed the appointments. Cannon did not begrudge the surgery department greater status for some of its members, but he did look askance at their standards—measuring their desire to advance three surgeons whose abilities he regarded as inferior against their failure to promote Fred Murphy, perhaps the most talented young surgical investigator in the department.[7]

The increasing number of personal squabbles at the Medical School was a symptom of a growing university-wide crisis. In the months after Eliot's retirement, Christian to his surprise learned that Harvard was in a parlous financial condition. To add to his alarm, he also discovered that he did not understand how the president had conducted Medical School business.[8] Others reluctantly came to those conclusions as well. As a member of the Faculty Council, Cannon commented on the poverty of the School when he discovered that some of the plans drawn up for expansion at the Longwood Avenue complex would have to be postponed because the School did not have enough money for construction.[9] In some measure the fiscal crisis was created by the manner in which Eliot transacted business, often making unrecorded arrangements with individual faculty members on questions of salary and expenditures; in part, it was caused by his policy of allocating the lion's share of the Medical School budget to the laboratory departments.

Christian, who wished to spur the development of the clinical departments, believed that the division of Medical School income was unfair. Determined to put his new policy into operation, he gave notice that there would have to be a sizable increase for the support of clinical departments in the foreseeable future, and he tried to block the efforts of some preclinical departments for more funds during preliminary budget discussions in the spring of 1910. Initially he attacked the most vulnerable preclinical departments— comparative physiology, comparative pathology, and comparative anatomy—which had at times been under fire for not contributing directly to the training of practicing physicians. In the process he came into conflict with C. S. Minot. The differences between the two men illuminate some of the complexities that faced the dean in his administration of the Medical School.

ᴗᶘ ᴗᶘ ᴗᶘ

In 1910 Charles Sedgwick Minot was one of the oldest and most eminent members of the medical faculty. A proper Bostonian, he was, like his friend and mentor Henry Bowditch, trained in part abroad in the laboratories of Louis Ranvier and Carl Ludwig. Unlike Bowditch, however, Minot did not take a medical degree and instead focused his studies almost exclusively on natural history and general biology. In 1878 he received a doctorate in science from Harvard and two years later was appointed by Eliot to joint lectureships at the Medical and Dental Schools. It was an unusual appointment. Minot was the first holder of a nonmedical doctorate to join the Harvard medical faculty. In ordinary circumstances he might not have prospered as a faculty member. He was, however, a New England Brahmin; if his medical credentials were not totally acceptable to some of his Harvard colleagues, he was more than acceptable socially.[10]

From the beginning Minot justified the president's faith in him. Throughout his tenure he made outstanding contributions to histology and human embryology, ranging from the development of the microtome to his classic studies of growth, senescence, and death.[11] Eliot saw the importance of Minot's work not just in terms of the development of medical science but as justification for his scheme of introducing a wide range of comparative graduate studies in pathology, anatomy, and physiology into the medical curriculum, and he went to great lengths to support him. In 1905, for example, he arranged that Minot be named the Stillman Professor of Comparative Anatomy and then reached a private agreement with him with respect to his future needs for funding and personnel. Above all, Eliot had a special understanding and appreciation of Minot's character: "Minot's advance through the Medical School was not facilitated by a yielding or compromising disposition," Eliot later remembered. "On the contrary, he pursued his ends with clear-sighted intensity and indomitable persistence."[12]

In mid-March of 1910, while preparing his departmental budget for the following year, Minot wrote President Lowell detailing the private agreements he had previously reached with Eliot so that Lowell might understand the basis for some of his forthcoming budgetary requests.[13] There is no evidence that Minot by writing directly to the president meant to challenge Christian's authority as dean; it was simply a procedure he had followed from the time he first joined the medical faculty. There can be no doubt, however, that the letter upset Christian—first, because Minot suggested that his understanding with Eliot actually made him the chairman of two separate departments (a department of comparative anatomy and a department of histology and embryology) with an implied right to two separate appropriations; and second and perhaps more important, because Christian could find no written record as proof of Minot's agreement with Eliot.

To resolve the issue Christian consulted Jerome Greene, who was one of his close friends, and asked if he, as Eliot's former secretary, knew of any private arrangement with Minot. Early that April Greene confirmed the existence of such an understanding. Nevertheless, when Minot's request for additional personnel came before the medical faculty the following month, Christian rose to challenge it. In defense of his request, Minot cited as justification his private understanding with Eliot. Christian stubbornly maintained there was no evidence in the Medical School files of any such agreement. Although the faculty ultimately approved his request, Minot was outraged that Christian had publicly questioned his word and wrote a sharp letter accusing him of knowingly misrepresenting the facts.[14] Christian was shaken by Minot's letter; it was a reaction he had not anticipated. He thought that when Minot got what he wanted, the debate was over. Aware that he had a tiger by the tail, Christian—as did others in the Medical School when they were in trouble—sought out Cannon. He complained that Minot had called him a liar and then asked Cannon if he would intercede on his behalf with Minot. Cannon, anxious to bring the quarrel to a close, agreed. But when he approached Minot, the latter with a New Englander's appreciation for precise langauge, maintained that he had not called Christian a liar. Further, he told Cannon that he felt Christian owed him an apology.[15]

The matter would not die. Worse, it fed a growing dissension in the School, and those who looked up to Cannon came to him to register their own complaints against Christian. Joseph H. Pratt, who was dissatisfied with Christian's plans for reorganizing the relations between the Medical School and the Massachusetts General Hospital, accused Christian of being two-faced. When Pratt later came back to Cannon with complaints about Harvard as compared with Johns Hopkins, Cannon lost his patience. Throughout the quarrel between Christian and Minot he had remained non-judgmental—a characteristic that facilitated his listening to both men. Pratt's complaints, however, were of a different order and a sign to Cannon that faculty discord was getting out of hand and becoming a danger to the School.[16]

In the days that followed Cannon tried to stem the growing criticism of the dean and also continued to speak to Minot on Christian's behalf. Several weeks later his efforts bore fruit when Minot extended an olive branch to the dean in a letter to Lowell: "My dear President, As I told you yesterday, I shall be glad if an amicable adjustment of the matter concerning Dr. Christian can be brought about, because it is important that dissensions within the Medical Faculty should be avoided and more harmonious relations maintained. Our motto might be 'Let us fight but not quarrel.' I am ready to do my part but the next advance must come from the other side."[17]

Minot's peace proposal fell on deaf ears. A short time later when he wrote a description of his courses for the Medical School Catalogue that implied he presided over two departments, Christian once more returned to the fray.[18] At this point, several months after Minot first informed him of his private understanding with Eliot, Lowell finally wrote his predecessor to learn first-hand the nature of the agreement. Eliot's reply gave Lowell little comfort. He confirmed that he did have such an arrangement with Minot, and although it did not have the force of law that a contract might have, it had another quality equally precious—the strength that came from an understanding between friends engaged in a mutual endeavor and from abiding by one's word.[19] Despite Eliot's explanation, Lowell essentially did nothing to mend the differences between Christian and Minot. It is clear, however, that Christian interpreted Lowell's reluctance to intercede as approval for his policy initiatives.

At the end of 1910 Christian brought his plans before the Visiting Committee of the Medical School, arguing that it would be necessary to increase substantially the endowment of the School in order to enhance the status and efficiency of its clinical department.[20] While there was no outright objection to raising funds for such a purpose, some members of the preclinical faculty who had had disagreements with Christian began to examine the implications of such a policy for the future development of their own departments. In ordinary circumstances Christian's program might have eventuated in a direct confrontation between the administration and the preclinical departments. But two unrelated developments—the building of the Brigham Hospital and the organization of the Graduate School of Medicine—created new channels that allowed Christian to achieve his goals with less friction than he had originally anticipated.

⋅⋅§   ⋅⋅§   ⋅⋅§

In May 1910 the president of the Board of Trustees of the Peter Bent Brigham Hospital informed Christian that he had been confirmed as the hospital's physician-in-chief and Harvey Cushing as its surgeon-in-chief.[21] Elated, Christian immediately wrote Lowell that he intended to resign the deanship when he assumed his duties in the hospital. "I rather welcome this opportunity," he told the president, "to withdraw at a time when it seems to me clearly for the advantage of the Medical School that I should devote my energies to the hospital and to instruction in and development of a medical department. It will be at least two years, possibly three, before the hospital will open and if you so desire, I can continue to serve as dean until then."[22] When Lowell approved this scheme, Christian with Cushing's help began to draw up plans for the organization of the new hospital.

Whatever Eliot might have thought about Christian's maneuvers in the deanship, he viewed the developments at the Brigham as a dream come true. "Now that you and Dr. Cushing have been put at the head respectively of the two departments of the Brigham Hospital," he wrote Christian some days after his confirmation, "I feel as if the Medical School were entering on a happier future. Ever since I have been a member of the Medical Faculty, I have seen clearly what a handicap on the School it was that the University had no hold on hospital appointments. Hereafter the School will be able to search all over the country for the very best men to fill the vacancies."[23] Nor did Christian disappoint him: almost his first order of business was to negotiate a contract between the Brigham trustees and Harvard which gave the professors of medicine and surgery at the Medical School the right to choose their own staffs for the hospital as well as to detail their duties and set their salaries and tenure.[24]

Using his contract with the Brigham as a model, Christian began to make similar agreements with other hospitals, including among others the Children's and Infant's Hospitals, the Boston Dispensary, and the Free Hospital for Women. For Christian these arrangements were prologue to achieving a better balance between the clinical and preclinical faculty in the Medical School.[25] For Cannon the new arrangements furnished the lever that he and others had long sought to break the hold that hospitals had in controlling clinical appointments to the medical faculty. Cannon had another reason for approving Christian's contractual arrangements. As part of his staff arrangement at the Brigham Christian appointed Cannon a consultant to advise the hospital on advances in physiological research. The appointment carried no salary and only the vaguest description of duties.[26] To some it appeared as a device by Christian to gain support for his policies. Not given to Machiavellian analysis, Cannon took pride in the appointment as a recognition of his ability and looked upon it as another opportunity to continue applying his research to the solution of clinical problems. Indeed, he had willingly joined in supporting Christian in other initiatives relating to improving clinical departments and instruction.

One of these involved the organization of a Graduate School of Medicine as a special branch of the medical faculty with its own dean and administrative board. Initially, the project grew out of Christian's reorganization of a program of summer school and graduate courses that the medical faculty had originally established to improve the skills of practicing physicians.[27] At its inception this program was essentially aimed at physicians in Massachusetts. Christian, however, thought the student body too parochial and early in 1910 called upon Cannon as chairman of the Medical School's advertising committee to develop a campaign to attract medical students and graduates from schools and hospitals in other parts of the country as well. Cannon's subsequent campaign proved so successful in attracting applicants that the following year when it was proposed that a Graduate School of Medicine be established, the faculty, attracted by the promising financial aspects of such a school, unanimously approved the plan.[28]

Carrying out the plan, however, proved more difficult. No sooner had the school been approved than a controversy arose about the choice of a dean. Some of the senior faculty members, impressed by Harold Ernst's efforts over the years in behalf of graduate instruction, nominated him for the deanship. Other names—even Cannon's—were put forward. Christian with Cannon's strong support recommended Horace D. Arnold, formerly professor of clinical medicine at Tufts Medical School and one of the leading men at the Boston City Hospital. The appointment of a clinician, they argued, was necessary because more than 90 percent of the curriculum in the school would be devoted to improving the clinical skills of practicing physicians. Although Christian's and Cannon's reasons for choosing a clinician as dean were generally accepted, their choice of Arnold offended a number of vocal and powerful faculty members.[29]

Throughout the fall of 1911 the faculty debated the choice of a graduate dean without result. The prolonged arguments so distressed Arthur Cabot, a member of the Corporation, that he advised Lowell he had had enough in the way of opinions about Arnold and that further discussions would likely result in the selection of "some compromise candidate who might not be the first choice of the majority." Lowell, already thoroughly annoyed with another protracted medical faculty debate, took Cabot's hint and appointed Arnold without faculty approval.[30]

In so doing he precipitated a new debate on faculty rights. Minot at once instructed the president that faculty rules explicitly forbade the appointment of a dean who was not already a member of the Harvard medical faculty and further that all nominations for dean were by tradition a faculty right. "Only increased cooperation, increased mutual confidence and loyal frankness," he catechized Lowell, "can produce the effects at Harvard necessary for what the University still has to do."[31] Christian, worried about another conflict with the faculty, quietly warned Lowell that the medical faculty had strong feelings about their rights in recommending appointments to the deanship or to vacant chairs. Anticipating debate on the choice of a replacement when he retired as dean, he suggested to the president that an open discussion at a meeting of full professors would be welcome. It would have gone down much better, he advised Lowell, if such a procedure had been followed before Arnold's appointment.[32]

ح§   ح§   ح§

The administrative and financial turmoil that followed Eliot's retirement was not unique to the Medical School; it affected all of the schools in the University and became one of Lowell's major concerns. "An opinion appears to be prevalent in the country," he noted in his annual report a year after taking office, "that Harvard is a rich institution which has only to ask for money in order to obtain it in limitless amounts, but unfortunately the work she is doing today exceeds her resources even with the most rigid economy."[33] To keep matters from getting out of hand at the Medical School until he could raise increased endowments, he began to tighten the purse strings.

At first Lowell's actions did not directly affect the physiology department. Cannon, whose needs were modest, continued to receive what he wanted for his department in the way of budget and personnel.[34] Although Lowell's way of running the Medical School gave him pause from time to time, Cannon had little quarrel with Christian's attempts to achieve a balance between the preclinical and clinical departments or his efforts to improve the quality of clinical instruction and practice. Perhaps the trend that made him most unhappy was the increasing number of administrative duties that took up his time. By the end of 1911, however, some signs appeared that indicated his previously favored position with the administration was also changing. Throughout Eliot's tenure Cannon had never had to ask for promotion or a raise in salary. But when, at the end of his fifth year as Higginson professor, he did not receive the automatic salary increase that was due him, he was forced to remind Christian of the lapse. He subsequently received the raise, but although it was a seemingly trivial matter it was a portent of things to come. Only a few days later he learned that the appropriation to his department had been cut—a circumstance that led him to protest for the first time at a faculty meeting that he would have to ask for an increased appropriation in the future.[35]

Perhaps the administrative decision that troubled Cannon most involved a question of personnel. Early in 1912 he learned from Alexander Forbes, then working in Sherrington's laboratory in Liverpool, that it would be possible to bring A. V. Hill of Cambridge University to Harvard for a year if a post could be arranged in the physiology department.[36] For Cannon the prospect of bringing Hill to the Medical School was an unusual opportunity to imbue the physiology department with the spirit and methods of the Cambridge School founded by Michael Foster, and he immediately wrote to Lowell for approval. Although Lowell replied that he was in favor of such a proposal, he also made it clear that the Medical School would be unable to pay Hill's salary and that funds for his appointment would have to be secured from private sources. Securing such funds in this particular instance was not difficult.[37] The president's reply, however, stressing financial restraint, was a distinct signal to Cannon that it might become increasingly difficult to upgrade either the department or the School—a condition that almost immediately manifested itself following the loss of a number of senior members of the medical faculty through retirement or death.

During the summer of 1911 Thomas Dwight, Parkman Professor of Anatomy and the oldest member of the medical faculty in terms of service, died after a protracted illness with cancer. Some months later three of the School's leading clinical professors, Frederick Cheever Shattuck, James Jackson Putnam, and Edward Hickling Bradford, announced their forthcoming retirements. In mid-January of 1912, faced with the prospect of preparing for the opening of the Brigham Hospital, Christian gave notice that he was planning to resign from the deanship.[38] The loss of these particular faculty members and the resignation of Christian caused Lowell great distress. The Medical School and its problems were still a *terra incognita* for him, and he depended on the dean as well as those who were about to retire for counsel and help. The latter were especially important to him; all were personal friends of long standing, and he felt comfortable sharing his thoughts and ideas about the Medical School with them. When Putnam formally announced his retirement, Lowell was taken aback. "It would be to me," he wrote him, "like having one of the lights go out in the Medical School to have you leave." Several months later when Shattuck tendered his resignation, Lowell replied in a similar vein. "It will not be a pleasure to see my friends' faces fall out of the

Medical Faculty," he wrote, "and so I shall present your resignation to the meeting of the Corporation next Monday with a heavy heart."[39]

If death, retirement, and resignation heralded difficulties for Lowell, they presented an opportunity for Cannon and others in the medical faculty to make decisions that would have a bearing on the development of the School for the next generation. Following Dwight's death, for instance, Minot began to lay the groundwork to consolidate all anatomical teaching at the Medical School under one department and bring Franklin Mall from Johns Hopkins as professor of anatomy. Minot saw Mall as a kindred soul; both had trained with Ludwig and shared similar ideas about the value of embryological research and the desirability of establishing a research institute in embryology.[40] When Minot broached his plans about Mall to Christian, the dean despite his previous disagreements with Minot enthusiastically endorsed them. As a Hopkins graduate, Christian needed no instruction regarding Mall's value as an anatomist or the quality of his thinking about problems of medical education and research.[41]

Early in 1912, when Mall received word from Minot that he was to be invited to come to Harvard for the chair in anatomy, he indicated that he would be quite willing if the Medical School met three demands: first, to give him a large enough salary to cover the difference in cost of living between Baltimore and Boston; second, to provide for a research staff; and third, to establish an institute for his collection of embryological specimens.[42] Neither Minot nor Christian regarded Mall's demands as excessive. However, when Christian learned that the Corporation planned to offer Mall a salary of $5,000 on the ground that it was not reasonable to pay him considerably more than the other preclinical professors, he voiced his disappointment: "It seems to me," he wrote Lowell, "that this is the most discouraging action I have ever known the Corporation to take in regard to the Medical School. My feeling is that they are blocking progress in the Medical School by so doing."[43] Lowell, however, saw things in a different light: Mall's ideas, he informed Minot, "are so far in advance of any immediate possibilities, that it is perhaps just as well, in view of the need of clinical expenditure, not to incur the luxury of having him here."[44]

In a last-ditch effort to forestall the Corporation's offer, Christian employed a new strategem: mindful of Lowell's approval of

Cannon's plan to bring A. V. Hill to Harvard if funding could be raised from outside sources, Christian asked for and received a similar privilege in Mall's behalf. In little more than a month, by pressing alumni and interested faculty members, Christian raised enough money to make possible a more substantive offer to Mall until a proper endowment could be raised. Correspondingly, the Corporation informally voted to offer Mall a salary of $6,000, as well as $5,000 for laboratory expenses and $10,000 for his embryological collections, and invited him to visit the University.[45] Christian and Minot, eager to impress Mall with Harvard's virtues and to gain support from the preclinical faculty for his appointment, invited him to Boston and arranged for him to meet with Cannon. The meeting proved to be all they had hoped for. "Mall came today from Johns Hopkins to look around," Cannon noted in his diary. "Lunched with him at St. Botolph Club—Dr. Minot's invitation. Dr. Mall has very fresh and stimulating way of regarding education. We all hope he will come."[46]

In the end, however, Mall turned Harvard down. In May 1912, a month after Mall's visit, Minot informed Lowell that Hopkins had not only bettered Harvard's salary offer but through William Welch's efforts had persuaded the Carnegie Institution to establish and fund the embryological institute Mall had long wanted. The president was not displeased by the news. "What an amount of gratitude we now deserve by improving the position of professors at Johns Hopkins," he wryly commented. "Is there not something slightly humorous in Dr. Mall's being retained at Johns Hopkins as a part of Dr. Woodward's policy of founding a research institute wholly independent of a university?"[47]

The search for a successor for Shattuck ended more happily. From the outset there were many attractive candidates for the post. Shattuck himself hoped that George Sears of the Boston City Hospital or Richard Cabot, his assistant at the Massachusetts General, would succeed him.[48] When news of Shattuck's retirement became known in the fall of 1911, Reginald Heber Fitz wrote to Lowell recommending William Thayer at Johns Hopkins for the chair or, in the event he refused to come (as he had in 1901), that Warfield Longcope at Columbia and David Linn Edsall at Washington University in St. Louis be considered as alternates.[49] This was not the first time that Edsall had been thought of as a successor to Shattuck. Several years earlier Edwin A. Locke, a young instructor at the Medical School and a charter member of the prestigious Inter-urban Clinical Club, asked Richard Cabot in a moment of candor whether he would step aside if it became possible to bring Edsall to Harvard as a professor of medicine. Locke was not the only one at Harvard who thought well of Edsall. Christian, who was also a member of the Interurban Club, had equal regard for Edsall's ability as a clinical investigator and educator and, on assuming the deanship and in following years, had frequently called on him for advice.[50]

When the question of choosing Shattuck's successor became imperative early in 1912, Lowell appointed a search committee composed of Christian, Bradford, C. M. Green, Milton Rosenau, and Cannon to consider the candidates. Coming to judgment was no easy matter. Traditionally Shattuck's chair—the Jackson Professorship of Clinical Medicine, one of the most prestigious posts in the Medical School—went to a Bostonian and a graduate of the Harvard Medical School. Cabot and Sears, given their credentials, were the choices of the traditionalists on the medical faculty and in the Boston medical community. Thayer was next in line: although a professor at Johns Hopkins, he too was a member of an elite Boston family and a graduate of the Harvard Medical School. Edsall, a Philadelphian and a graduate of the University of Pennsylvania Medical School, was clearly an outsider.[51]

For Christian the appointment of Shattuck's successor was central to the progress of clinical medicine at the School, because in making such an appointment Harvard was gaining for the first time the privilege of naming the chief of medicine at the Massachusetts General Hospital. Although Christian favored Edsall, he needed the support of the search committee to make such an appointment acceptable to both the Medical School and the MGH.[52] It was Cannon who gave him the help he sought. Cannon had worked closely with Edsall on the AMA Council in Defense of Medical Research and had come to rely on his judgment as well as his administrative ability in fighting the antivivisectionists. Moreover, he especially appreciated Edsall's understanding of the role of laboratory research in advancing clinical medicine. Indeed, several years earlier Edsall had earned Cannon's gratitude when he published a detailed explication of Cannon's research on the digestive process for clinicians in *Progressive Medicine*.[53]

When Cannon joined the search committee, he actively began

to canvass the medical faculty on Edsall's behalf. Although some of those to whom Cannon spoke, notably Shattuck himself and John Lovett Morse, remained skeptical about appointing an outsider, others including members of the committee were more easily persuaded. Cannon's campaign was so effective that the committee in its initial report indicated that Edsall was their first choice; but they were not sure that they could persuade him to leave the post he had so recently taken up at Washington University in St. Louis. Because of Edsall's reluctance to commit himself, the search committee deferred making a final decision and invited other candidates to Boston for talks. Some weeks later, when Edsall indicated that he would accept the appointment, the committee again put forward his candidacy, and despite last-minute opposition by some members of the MGH committee, he was named Jackson Professor and chief of the medical service at the hospital.[54] In securing Edsall's appointment, Christian, with Cannon's help, not only added new impetus to the development of clinical investigation at the Medical School but also moved closer to achieving parity between the clinical and preclinical faculties.

✑ ✑ ✑

Perhaps the most pressing problem that Christian faced before leaving the deanship was helping to find his successor. The task of choosing a medical dean, a difficult enough matter in ordinary circumstances, had become even more complex by 1912. For Christian it was not just a question of selecting a candidate who would be acceptable to the medical faculty; it was also a matter of finding someone who would have the ability to carry his policies forward and cope with the Medical School's mounting financial problems. The latter were so critical that Christian informed Lowell that it was becoming essential for the dean to have the assistance of a business manager.[55] Christian was not alone in such a belief. When Walter S. Burke, one of the University's ranking administrators, was asked by the Board of Overseers for advice on the future management of the Medical School, he replied that the School required both the services of a full-time dean and those of a special assistant of good executive and business ability, "not necessarily though preferably an M.D."[56]

It is not surprising that the person who best articulated the requirements for the deanship was Jerome Greene, who as Eliot's former secretary and a member of the Board of Overseers was better informed about the problems that the new dean would face than most others in the University or Medical School. Greene felt there were two alternatives to consider in filling the deanship. One was to choose as dean a leader in either medical practice or research who would appoint as coadjutor a man who would devote himself exclusively to business matters and be wholly responsible to him. The second was to choose a physician who was thoroughly posted on the problems and aims of medical education and who would make the promotion of the School the main object of his life. "Such a man would," he warned, "have no more time for general practice, and probably not much time for teaching. For research he would be useless. He would require as his assistant a young man between 25 and 30 years of age who would act as his aide and right hand in the administration of the School." "Under this plan," he continued, "you would need for the proper financial adminstration only clerical services to supplement the functions of these two men."[57]

Although Greene acknowledged that it would be difficult to find a man who would precisely fit the requirements he had outlined, he made it clear that he had a particular candidate in mind for the post. "There is one man who would probably develop the position in either of the two directions I have named," he wrote one of his colleagues on the Board of Overseers, "but it would be at the partial or entire sacrifice of his research, and I do not think that he would consider it. I refer to Professor Walter B. Cannon. Dr. Cannon's executive ability is such that he is in constant demand as the chairman of important committees. When he was in college and in the medical school he showed that he had a genius for business management. He is now recognized as one of the very best physiologists in the country, and his going over into administration would be universally lamented by scientific men."[58]

Other recommendations quickly followed. Fred Shattuck, who had long admired John Warren's efficient administration of the Medical School's building committee, wrote Lowell a strong letter in Warren's behalf. Harvey Cushing, in turn, thought the School needed a new type of dean, one who was not necessarily a physician but was young and energetic with a good knowledge of medical problems—in short, a person like Jerome Greene. John Bapst Blake, a surgeon at the Boston City Hospital, nominated his colleague Edward Bradford, shrewdly reminding Lowell that Bradford was about to retire from his professorship and would be able to devote himself full time to the deanship.[59] Blake's nomination of Bradford upset a number of members of the preclinical faculty, Minot in particular.

Minot, who had objected to Lowell's heavy-handed appointment of Arnold as dean of the Graduate School of Medicine, again sharply reminded the president that appointing deans to the Medical School was a faculty privilege. He informed Lowell that Bradford lacked certain indispensable qualifications to be dean and voiced the opinion that Cannon was on the whole the best man available for the job—cautiously adding that the decision perhaps needed more deliberation.[60] Minot's qualification was important. Although many members of the faculty favored Cannon, those who supported him were reluctant to take him away from the laboratory. Some of Cannon's friends, afraid that he might be cajoled into taking the deanship by appeals to his well-known sense of loyalty to Harvard, tried to warn him of the dangers in such appeals. When Fred Murphy, for instance, learned that a number of the young Turks on the medical faculty were increasingly speaking of the virtues of Cannon's candidacy, he humorously advised him "not to spoil a mediocre physiologist to make a poor dean!"[61]

Cannon did not need such advice. Although flattered to be nominated for the deanship, he understood full well that acceptance of the post would mean the end of his scientific career. Some time later, when Otto Folin tried to persuade him to press his candidacy, he replied that he would be disposed to refuse the deanship if it were offered. His selection as dean, he continued, would be an infraction of the principle that productive scholars should not be pushed into administration.[62]

Late in March 1912, when it became apparent that Cannon was not a viable candidate and that Lowell and Christian both preferred a clinician for the deanship, the faculty selection committee unanimously voted for Bradford.[63] Only Jerome Greene, it appeared, had any remaining reservations about Bradford's appointment. "It seems to me unfortunate," he wrote Lowell, "that the Medical School is to be directly in charge of a man who is wholly out of touch with recent advances in clinical medicine. . . . It seemed natural to suppose that the leader of Harvard's forces in medicine should be a man who was either a leader in modern medicine or one in close sympathy with it. I understand that the group of practitioners in Boston who have distrusted efforts to establish the Medical School on a thoroughly scientific basis regard the appointment of Dr. Bradford as a return to the safe traditions of the past."[64]

Lowell was quick to defend the appointment. "To my mind," he replied, "the question of the Dean of the Medical School is really one of personality, and not of technical knowledge. What we want is a man of progressive ideas and effective force, and these Dr. Bradford seems to me to have more than any other man in the Medical School, and I feel that he will give the School the greatest impulse that can be given to it."[65] Greene acknowledged that Bradford might in the short run serve the School well, but his criticisms left their mark on Lowell. To quiet the doubts raised by Greene, Lowell wrote to several friends for their views on Bradford's appointment. When Paul Thorndike, one of Bradford's colleagues at the City Hospital, replied that he considered the new dean "one of the best assets the School has now or has ever had," the president was delighted. "I am very fond of Dr. Bradford," he wrote Thorndike, "and I did not want to be biased in helping to make him Dean by any personal motives; but he does seem to me a man of extraordinary fitness for the position."[66]

Relieved that he had escaped being saddled with the administrative duties and problems of the deanship, Cannon optimistically looked forward to an understanding relationship with the new dean. Within weeks, however, that hope was shattered. When Cannon asked Bradford a short time after he had taken office for an increase in the staff of the physiology department, the dean bluntly informed him the Medical School had no money for such purposes.[67] Cannon was well aware of the School's financial difficulties; however, previously his friend Christian had always made some effort to meet his needs or at least presented them in a favorable light to Lowell. Bradford made it clear that he would not extend himself on Cannon's behalf. It was a signal that Cannon could not ignore and caused him to wonder about his future position at the Medical School.

15   *Shifting Research Interests*

"TIME," Cannon ruefully commented toward the end of his life, "is an essential requirement for effective research. An investigator may be given a palace to live in, a perfect laboratory to work in, he may be surrounded by all the conveniences money can provide; but if his time is taken from him he will remain sterile."[1] It was an old complaint, a lingering memory of the period following his work on the acid control of the pylorus when a series of circumstances—his obligations as head of a growing family, the struggle against antivivisectionists, and the divisiveness in the Medical School after Eliot's retirement—combined to make demands on him that frequently interfered with his research.

While there was an ebb in the number of Cannon's scientific publications between 1908 and 1910, that diminution was not solely the result of demands made on his time from outside the laboratory. It also stemmed in some measure from the character of the research he had undertaken, especially his efforts to develop a strategy to advance an investigation of the influence of emotional states on functions of the alimentary canal. This problem had interested him from the beginning of his studies when he observed that movements in the stomachs of his experimental cats ceased entirely if those animals became nervous or enraged and then resumed once their stress disappeared. Throughout 1908 and 1909, whenever Cannon had an opportunity to address physicians about his recent investigations on digestion, he focused on the relationship between the emotions and the pathological problems doctors faced in their daily practice.[2] Such reviews were useful not only because they gave him an opportunity to marshall clinical and laboratory data on the effects of the emotions on digestion but also because they provided the impetus for new and more meticulous investigations of the physiological aspects of the problem.

Beginning in 1910, initially alone and later in collaboration with one of his medical students, Clarence Lieb, Cannon began an investigation of the importance of tonus (a state of partial contraction) for the movements of the alimentary canal. The results of the new study convinced him that the vagi and the splanchnics were the nerves that modulated the tonus of the gastric musculature and thereby affected peristalsis; they also held out the prospect of serving to synthesize some of the diverse observations he had previously made of the impact of the emotions on gastric motility.[3] Cannon was so intrigued by these latter possibilities that he highlighted the research with Lieb in his presidential address to the American Gastro-Enterological Association in 1911. His findings harmonized very well with his previous notions that worry, anxiety, and distress stopped intestinal movements. "Such states accompanied by splanchnic impulses," he told the assembled physicians, "abolish tonus." The results of his work also furnished him with additional insights as to the nature of hunger: "Indeed, I am inclined to believe," he concluded, "that the sensation of hunger results from the tonic contraction of the empty stomach."[4]

Although Cannon's investigations of tonus helped to identify the complexities of the problems involved in studying the effects of the emotions on the bodily economy, they did not by themselves provide a strategy for future research. The ideas that helped to carry that work forward came from another part of the laboratory, and from an unexpected source—the research of Roy Graham Hoskins, Cannon's first graduate student.

If Cannon had been asked at the beginning of 1910 whether Hoskins could in any way be helpful to him in his research, it is more than likely he would have replied in the negative. Hoskins, who had been trained at the University of Kansas by Clarence McClung, then in the midst of his classic studies on the evolution of grasshoppper testes, had little or no interest in working on the gastrointestinal tract. He had decided even before coming to work with Cannon that he wished to do his doctoral dissertation on a problem in endocrinology. Although Cannon would have liked him to work on problems of digestion, Hoskins persisted and chose as his thesis topic the interrelations of the organs of internal secretion. The choice initially disturbed Cannon; the study Hoskins wished to do was primarily endocrine morphometrics—a discipline in which Cannon had little expertise. Ultimately, however, Hoskins's dissertation served him well: in addition to introducing him to the literature of endocrinology, it stimulated his interest in the functions of the adrenal glands—so much so that when Hoskins, after graduation, asked him for advice on how to develop his research, Cannon suggested that he examine the role of emotional states in the production of adrenalin.[5]

Hoskins, who had developed an enormous respect and fondness for Cannon for his help in preparing his dissertation, took his advice. In October 1910, some months after leaving Harvard to take up a post as professor of physiology at the Starling Medical College in Ohio, Hoskins wrote Cannon that he had found adrenalin in the blood of one of his laboratory animals after it became enraged during the course of a recent experiment. The report so excited Cannon that he immediately proposed that Hoskins join him in an investigation of the emotional production of adrenalin and laid out a research strategy for the proposed cooperative venture. Hoskins, equally elated, agreed. However, when it became apparent that he would not be free until the summer vacation, Cannon, eager to get started, asked Daniel de la Paz, who had recently come to Harvard for a year of postgraduate study in the medical sciences, to assist him in the investigation.[6]

At the time Cannon made his proposals to Hoskins he knew little about the structure and functions of the adrenals. Although he was acquainted with certain seminal research, such as the demonstration by G. Oliver and E. A. Schäfer that an extract prepared from the adrenals could dramatically increase blood pressure and J. J. Abel's isolation of epinephrine,[7] he was unaware of other important adrenal research. He did not know, for instance, of A. Kohn's pioneer anatomical study showing that the adrenal medulla is morphologically an extension of the sympathetic nervous system and not (as Cannon believed) a separate endocrine gland, such as the thyroid, parathyroid, or pituitary.[8] He was far more knowledgeable about the autonomic nervous system which he had learned about through his work on digestion. But even in this area there were lacunae—in particular, a lack of information about some of the early suggestive research then in progress in England on the chemical aspects of nerve impulses.

He did not know, to take an example, of T. R. Elliott's daring hypothesis that whenever a sympathetic nerve impulse arrived at a smooth muscle cell, it might liberate adrenalin locally on the cell, thus serving as an intermediary between the impulse and the reacting mechanism in the cell.[9] Nor was he aware of J. N. Langley's equally novel proposal that organs or cells innervated by the sympathetic nervous system contain two sorts of receptive substances, one excitatory, the other inhibitory, and that when adrenalin reaches such an organ or cell its final action is determined, in Langley's words, "by the proportion of the two kinds of receptive substances which was affected by the impulse."[10] Moreover, he was apparently unacquainted with the chemical and physiological investigation conducted by G. Barger and H. H. Dale on the similarity between the actions caused by stimulation of the sympathetic nerves and those induced by a group of amine compounds which simulated the effects of sympathetic nerves.[11] Cannon's lack of knowledge at this time of these and other studies on the chemistry of the autonomic nervous system was to have a profound effect on his analysis of the results of some of his early experiments on emotional production of adrenalin.

᠄᠊   ᠄᠊   ᠄᠊

Cannon knew from his reading of some of the pioneer students of endocrinology that adrenal extracts had remarkable effects—that they, for example, mimicked in a quite extraordinary way the actions of the sympathetic nerves and, among other things, caused inhibition of digestive activities, dilated pupils of the eyes, contracted blood vessels, erected hairs, and increased heart rate—in sum, they elicited the kinds of changes that he had frequently observed in his experimental animals when they had been distressed or excited.[12] The problem he first set for himself was to see if he could determine experimentally that adrenal secretion was under nervous control and that it in fact increased during periods of emotional excitement. To create the emotional stress necessary for the investigation, he bound some cats in comfortable holders, which restrained them but did not cause them any pain, and placed them in the vicinity of a barking dog to excite them. He hoped that by taking blood samples from the cats both before and after they were excited and testing each sample for the presence of adrenalin, he would be able to demonstrate that adrenalin was secreted into the bloodstream when the animal was under stress.[13]

The work began slowly, in part hampered by a scarcity of experimental animals and in part because the site Cannon used for taking blood samples (cardiac puncture), as well as the techniques he employed for testing for the presence of adrenalin proved neither efficient nor trustworthy. Time and again during the first week of his investigation he recorded his frustration in his diary "Find emotional production of adrenalin—equivocal results," he complained on November 26, 1910. In the days that followed he repeated his litany of failure—"worked with de la Paz on adrenalin with no results."[14] Three weeks after beginning his research Cannon decided to modify both his technique for obtaining blood samples and his method of testing for the presence of adrenalin.

In the first instance, Cannon utilized his surgical skill and under local anesthesia dissected the femoral vein in the groin of a cat without disturbing the animal. He then inserted a fine, well-lubricated catheter and advanced the tip up the inferior vena cava toward the heart until it reached a position above the adrenals. After he made sure that the animal had remained calm, he took a sample of "quiet" blood, placed a tie on the catheter at an appropriate distance from the tip to mark the extent of the insertion, and removed the catheter. He then placed the cat in the vicinity of a barking dog for a period of time to generate stress, and using the tie as a guide, he reinserted the catheter exactly the same distance into the vein and took a sample of "excited" blood.[15]

To assay his blood samples, Cannon decided to use a method that Samuel Meltzer and his daughter Clara Meltzer Auer had developed at the Rockefeller Institute for testing for the presence of adrenalin. Meltzer and Auer had demonstrated that when they cut the cervical sympathetic nerves and extirpated the superior cervical ganglia in an experimental cat, they could, by subcutaneous administration of adrenalin, dilate the pupils of its eyes.[16] On December 16, several days after experimenting with the Meltzer-Auer test, Cannon jubilantly recorded in his diary the first seemingly positive results of his investigation: "Found eye enlarges when splanchnic nerve cut and peripheral end stimulated." The following day he noted similar results: "Worked with de la Paz in morning, repeated yesterday's observations with record of eye changes and with nerve connections cut."

The eye test, despite its early promise, did not provide Cannon with sufficiently consistent results to draw definitive conclusions and he continued to look for more positive findings. "Operated with de la Paz in the morning," he recorded in his diary on January 4, 1911, "still on the hunt for adrenalin as result of emotion." Several days later he turned to another biological test to detect the presence of adrenalin, again without positive results. Undeterred, he decided to examine a reaction that Rudolph von Magnus in Utrecht had previously reported. In 1905 Magnus had demonstrated that strips of longitudinal intestinal muscle taken from an experimental cat continued to contract rhythmically in a solution of blood but were usually inhibited when even a small amount of adrenalin (as little as one part in twenty million) was added to the blood.[17] Although the Magnus reaction had never been used as a quantitative test for the presence of adrenalin, Cannon immediately saw its advantages—particularly the ability of a small amount of adrenalin to relax smooth muscle—and decided to adapt it as a semiquantitative test. Characteristically, he devised a simple apparatus to carry the experiment forward: he suspended a portion of longitudinal intestinal muscle from a cat in a cylindrical chamber, immersed it in Ringer's solution fixing one end of the muscle to a small spring forceps and the other to a lever that moved up and down as the muscle contracted and relaxed, and recorded its movements on a kymograph.[18]

On January 10, 1911, he noted in his diary the first successful results of his new assay when he added samples of quiet blood to the cylinder in place of the Ringer's solution: "Tried long strips of smooth muscle and get sharp rise of tonus—may be due to CO_2—adrenalin causes drop." The next day there was another success: "De la Paz and I find relaxation of long muscle in excited blood." Other positive findings followed; he discovered, for instance, that when he added varying amounts of adrenalin to quiet blood, it evoked all the degrees of relaxation that he had observed in excited blood.

The next series of experiments, to Cannon's distress, initially gave equivocal results. However, on January 16, a few days after he began these new experiments, the breakthrough he sought occurred. "This is a hallelujah day!" he rejoiced. "De la Paz and I get clear evidence of emotional production of adrenalin in cat." The following day he repeated the work again with positive results. However, when he and de la Paz tried variations on their experiments to justify the conclusion that what they had observed was the result of increased adrenal secretion, their findings puzzled them. When they tied off the adrenals in one of their cats and stimulated the splanchnic nerves, they found that their blood sample also inhibited the muscle strip. "Found adrenal effect in cat with vessels tied," Cannon noted in his diary on January 19, and then added, "Conceivably breakdown of gland. Got idea that possibly vessels deprived of sympathetic supply more sensitive than other vessels—thus tonus kept." The following day he and de la Paz repeated the experiment in a rabbit with the same ambiguous results.

From today's vantage point it would appear from Cannon's diary description that the effects he saw with the adrenals tied off were the result of the release of catecholamines into the blood from the nerve endings in the splanchnic bed. In other words, he had observed chemical mediation of nerve impulse but had not recognized its significance. Nevertheless, he imaginatively saw in his findings other possibilities that promised an extension of his research. "Got idea," he wrote on January 20, "that adrenals in excitement serve to affect muscular power and mobilize sugar for muscular use—thus in wild state readiness for fight or run!"

The next series of experiments continued to give useful but equivocal results. In an experiment that Cannon and de la Paz conducted on January 21 they found that excited blood, which produced inhibition of smooth muscle, lost its power on standing or being agitated by bubbling oxygen for a period of three hours— an indication that adrenalin was oxidized. Two days later, however, they were brought up short again: "Adrenalin effect from animal with adrenals removed three hours before," Cannon noted, "a most surprising and puzzling effect." These results unsettled him, and he spent the next day with de la Paz sifting through the evidence, finally deciding that the effect he had observed was due to rough handling, partial removal of the adrenals, and failure to tie off all of the blood vessels before he had handled the organ.[19]

Beginning on January 25 and in the days that followed Cannon and de la Paz tried unavailingly to repeat their latest experiments. In one instance the animal died, and in another the result proved completely negative. After almost a week Cannon began to review the evidence from the experiments he had conducted with de la Paz throughout the month of January and determined that the positive results they had accumulated justified the conclusion that they had obtained an emotional production of adrenalin. Nonetheless, a slight doubt remained, and the next day he returned to the laboratory for one last try. Later that day he noted with satisfaction that the experiment had been successful.[20]

Cannon was greatly exhilarated by the possibilities his investigation had opened, and he discussed his new ideas with friends like George H. Parker, who was then studying the development of the nervous system, and E. B. Holt, a psychologist interested in the emotions and a fellow Wicht Club member. Further, he began to write a paper on the results of the investigation. When he learned from Porter that the *American Journal of Physiology* could not publish his report before April (a delay of two months!), he submitted an abbreviated account to the *Journal of the American Medical Association* for more immediate publication.[21] In part, he was eager to give public notice that he had entered a new field of investigation; in part, he wanted physicians to be aware of some of the possible clinical implications of his findings. The latter was particularly manifest in the conclusion of his brief note: "Injected epinephrin," he postulated, "is capable of inducing an atheromatous condition of the arterial wall in rabbits . . . and is also capable of evoking hyperglycemia with glycosuria. As Ascher has shown, by prolonged stimulation of the splanchnic nerves, prolonged secretion of epinephrin with maintained high blood-pressure can be produced. In the light of the results here reported the temptation is strong to suggest that some phases of these pathologic states are associated with the strenuous and exciting character of modern life acting through the adrenal glands. This suggestion, however, must be put to experimental test."[22] Nowhere, however, did Cannon mention in the paper the inconsistencies that had puzzled him. It is clear they were not in accord with the results he had anticipated when he began his research with de la Paz. Not knowing their import, he apparently dismissed them from his mind.

᪥ ᪥ ᪥

When the new semester at the Medical School began in February of 1911, Cannon reluctantly put his research aside in order to assume his share of the teaching responsibilities for the first-year course in physiology. If circumstances had permitted, he might have set de la Paz, whose abilities he had come to admire, to work on continuing some aspect of the studies while he fulfilled his teaching obligations. Unfortunately, de la Paz's services were no longer available to Cannon because under the terms of the fellowship that had brought him to Harvard, he was required to move on to one of the clinical departments. De la Paz, who was no less frustrated than Cannon about leaving the work, confessed that he, too, regretted the transfer because research had made other things uninteresting to him.[23]

Cannon did not remain frustrated for long. It had become his practice to introduce some of the first-year medical students to research. At this time he was so eager to put some of his new ideas to an experimental test that he extended a blanket invitation to the class to come to the laboratory to do research. The response was swift; within a day five students—Alfred Shohl, Wade Wright, Joseph Aub, Carl Binger, and Arthur Washburn—asked for permission to work on a research project. With nothing more to go on except that the candidates appeared to be bright and eager, Cannon took them into his laboratory and gave them research assignments.[24] Shohl and Wright were asked to explore the role of emotional excitement in the production of glycosuria (sugar in the urine), Aub and Binger were assigned the problem of the influence of nicotine on the secretion of adrenalin, and Cannon suggested that Washburn join him in an experimental study of the nature of hunger.

The volunteers began their research with a great deal of enthusiasm, much as Cannon and Moser had fifteen years earlier when Bowditch first suggested that they use x-rays to study deglutition. Two days after making his assignments Cannon noted in his diary with a touch of pride, "students eager in research work—are taking hold with a will."[25] Forty-five years later, when Joseph Aub was asked if Cannon had used any special techniques in introducing his students to research, he replied, "Cannon just gave us a room and some equipment and let us plow ahead. Occasionally if you asked him, he would come around; basically, however, he let us have our own way. Most important, he was chock full of ideas which were available for the asking."[26] The freedom that Aub recalled was part of a mutual relationship of give and take between Cannon and his young charges. The investigations were not only a search for new knowledge but part of a learning exercise as well. The students, to be sure, carried out the research; the design and the goal of the experiments were Cannon's.

The first of the student projects to yield positive results was that conducted by Shohl and Wright.[27] There were good reasons for Cannon to suspect when he gave them their assignment that emotional disturbance might induce a glycosuria. For instance, he already knew from his study of the clinical literature that grief, anxiety, and mental illness could in certain cases result in a glycosuria. Then, too, his research with de la Paz showed that when his experimental animals became enraged, there was an increase in adrenalin secretion and, further, that an injection of adrenalin could cause sugar to appear in the urine—a result strongly suggesting that glycosuria could be evoked by emotional stress.

Following a suggestion made by Cannon, Shohl and Wright decided to see if the simple act of binding cats in the special animal holders used by the physiology department would cause sufficient stress to produce glycosuria. They discovered that the outcome depended in part on the sex and age of the cats. Elderly females, who were not disturbed by being confined, gave no evidence of glycosuria; young males on being bound, however, became enraged and in their struggles to be free showed sugar in their urine. Subsequently when either female or male cats were stressed by a barking dog, all developed a glycosuria. To determine the extent to which the adrenals were involved in emotional glycosuria, Shohl and Wright (this time with Cannon's active assistance as a surgeon) took a number of cats that had previously manifested glycosuria on being confined, removed their adrenals, and then after recovery placed them in the vicinity of a barking dog. Although all of the animals thereafter manifested signs of fear and rage when stressed, none had glycosuria.[28]

The outcome of Shohl and Wright's investigation put Cannon into a state of euphoria. Their study demonstrated to him beyond cavil that glycosuria following emotional excitement was dependent on an abnormally high level of blood sugar—a state that appeared to be useful to the organism. These findings encouraged him to return to an idea that had surfaced during his experiments with de la Paz—namely, that adrenals in excitement serve to affect muscular power and mobilize sugar for muscular use, thus preparing animals in a wild state to either fight or run away.[29] When the implications of his thoughts began to keep him up nights, instead of complaining of insomnia as he sometimes did, he used the time to plan new adrenal researches.[30] He shared the news of his research with anyone who would listen, from Bowditch to the members of medical and other local societies until it seemed that all of Boston and Cambridge knew of his investigations. Indeed, when Cannon attended a meeting of the Tuesday Evening Club early in April Eliot made a special point of asking him about the progress of his work on adrenalin.[31] Later that month during a lecture to the American Philosophical Society on his research with de la Paz, he added as a postscript some of the implications of Shohl and Wright's as yet unpublished investigation. Cannon was coupled on the program with George Crile, the Cleveland surgeon, who also gave a paper on the emotions. The next day to his amusement Cannon discovered that one of the Philadelphia newspapers had published a unique interpretation of the two lectures: "Don't Get Scared," a front-page headline announced, "It's Too Dangerous!"[32]

Cannon was not the only one pleased with the research conducted in his laboratory that winter and spring. The student investigators were equally enthusiastic and gave of themselves unsparingly to their respective assignments—not the least Arthur Washburn, who served as both investigator and guinea pig. When Cannon learned that Washburn had the unusual ability to vomit at will, he persuaded him to swallow an uninflated balloon attached to a tube each morning before breakfast preparatory to correlating sensations of hunger and contractions of the stomach. Students in the freshman physiology class were fascinated by the sight of Washburn coming to lectures with a tube sticking out of his mouth and tied around one of his ears. After the lectures, Aub later remembered with some delight, Washburn

> would trot up to the lab, sit down with his back to a kymograph and have the balloon inflated. Every time thereafter when he felt a hunger contraction of his stomach he would press a button and the contraction would be recorded and labeled. One day the tube came out and the balloon didn't. Washburn tried vomiting but with no success. Several days went by and with each passing day Dr. Cannon became more and more agitated because the balloon just wouldn't leave Arthur Washburn from any exit. Finally to Dr. Cannon's great relief he vomited it up undigested. The next day to Washburn's

credit he appeared with another balloon down his stomach ready to begin the experiment anew.[33]

Later that spring, whenever time allowed, Cannon with Washburn's assistance continued to gather data on hunger contractions of the stomach. In addition, he taught Aub and Binger the operative techniques he had perfected with de la Paz as prologue to their investigation of the effects of nicotine on the secretion of adrenalin.

In essence, the research problem that Cannon assigned to Aub and Binger was a follow-up of observations made two decades earlier by J. N. Langley and W. S. Dickinson that nicotine had the ability to first stimulate and then paralyze the sympathetic ganglia[34]—an action that led Cannon to believe that a small dose of nicotine stimulating the sympathetic ganglia innervating the adrenals might increase the discharge of adrenalin into the blood. The experience left an indelible impression on Aub; almost a half century later he could still convey in detail both the process and outcome of the study he and Carl Binger had undertaken. "Once in the lab," Aub recalled,

we put a catheter up the femoral vein of the cat until it was opposite the adrenals. (More accurately stated, until we assumed it was opposite the adrenals, because although we did come close more often than not, it was very largely an approximation.) We then sucked out the blood as it came from the adrenals and tested it for the tonicity and contraction it caused in the smooth muscle. In that way we tested the amount of adrenalin the adrenals were putting out normally. When we gave our animals a little nicotine and tested the blood again, we found that the nicotine caused a very considerable flow of adrenalin. Our experiments demonstrated to our satisfaction that nicotine stimulated the sympathetic nervous system. As a matter of fact, that was a nice discovery for us; although researchers today have forgotten this paper, it has been repeatedly demonstrated that smoking does cause increased blood sugar, relieves fatigue, stops hunger and decreases the temperature in the periphery—effects which can wholly or in part be attributed to the flow of adrenalin.[35]

Contemporaries saw other virtues in the outcome of the investigation. "These experiments of Cannon and his co-workers," an editorial in the *Journal of the AMA* suggested, "are . . . of interest as another illustration of how drugs may affect the activities of some of the organs of internal secretion—organs which until recently were supposed to be rather independent of the action of both drugs and of the nervous system . . . The activities of the organs of internal secretion are thus becoming of increasing interest not only in physiology and pathology, but also in pharmacology and practical medicine."[36]

⋅ ⋅ ⋅

Although Cannon was harried throughout the spring of 1911 by a number of obligations, the success of the student research and especially the buoyant mood in the freshman physiology class kept him in good spirits. For the first time in years he did not berate himself about the poor quality of his lecturing. Indeed, he was so heartened by the prospects of extending his research that he was impatient for Hoskins to join him later that summer to work on the next major problem he had set for himself—how the artificial production of asphyxia, hyperpnea, and sensory stimulation (pain) affected the secretion of adrenalin.

When Hoskins arrived in mid-June, he did not come empty-handed. During his year at Ohio-Starling Medical College he had applied himself to modifying the Magnus test and discovered that rings of intestinal smooth muscle taken from a rabbit provided a much more sensitive indicator for the presence of adrenalin than the cat's longitudinal muscle that Cannon and de la Paz had used in their study.[37] It was a modification Cannon gladly accepted. In turn, he introduced Hoskins to the operative techniques that he and de la Paz had developed—but with one exception. The new experiments required an anesthetic, and, aware that some anesthetics then in use might stimulate the adrenal glands, Cannon decided to try urethane, an agent that Elliott had previously shown to produce a satisfactory general anesthesia without the concomitant excitement that could affect the adrenals.[38]

From the beginning the research went well. Operating daily, Cannon and Hoskins patiently took blood samples from both the inferior vena cava above the adrenal glands and the femoral vein of a cat before producing various degrees of asphyxia. They soon found that the blood samples taken before asphyxia did not cause any inhibition of the sensitive rabbit muscle. The results following asphyxia, however, were quite different. There was a clear indication of the release of an inhibitory substance in the blood sample taken from the inferior vena cava but not in the femoral blood— evidence that something was being secreted from the adrenal it-self.[39] During the early phase of the investigation Cannon and Hoskins performed a very interesting experiment which they later scarcely discussed. At one point they tied off the inferior vena cava and the aorta below the diaphragm as well as both carotid arteries going to the head and then produced severe asphyxia for a longer period of time. They noted that when they did this, blood taken from the heart would also inhibit the smooth muscle of the rabbit intestine. "Probably," they concluded, "the inhibitory action of blood taken from an animal when extremely asphyxiated cannot be due to epinephrin alone."[40] Again, from today's vantage point, it would appear that they had good evidence that noradrenaline from the cardiac sympathetic nerves could also inhibit the small intestine. Unfortunately neither Cannon nor Hoskins, given the state of biochemical knowledge at the time, was prepared to un-derstand the significance of what they had observed.

In planning the investigation Cannon also determined to study the effects on the adrenals of overventilating the lungs because he felt that this condition, like asphyxia, might stimulate adrenal se-cretion. Nevertheless, when he and Hoskins (through use of ar-tificial respiration) put the idea to the test, they could find no augmentation in adrenal secretion.[41] Only one series of experi-ments remained to be done before bringing the investigation to a close.

Cannon knew from earlier research that stimulation of sensory fibers, particularly the large nerve trunks such as the sciatic nerve, resulted in discharges along sympathetic paths which in turn could easily stimulate the adrenals to augment the secretion of adrenalin. Using cats that were anesthetized with urethane, Cannon and Hoskins withdrew a sample of so-called normal blood from the inferior vena cava above the adrenals and compared it with a blood sample from the same source after a strong tetanizing electrical stimulus had been applied to the central end of the sciatic nerve. They found that the normal blood had no effect on contraction of rings of rabbit intestinal muscle whereas the sample drawn after stimulation produced a marked inhibition—clear proof that stim-ulating the sensory nerve increased the secretion of adrenalin into the bloodstream.

Colbert and Walter Cannon in Eugene, Oregon,
July 1911.

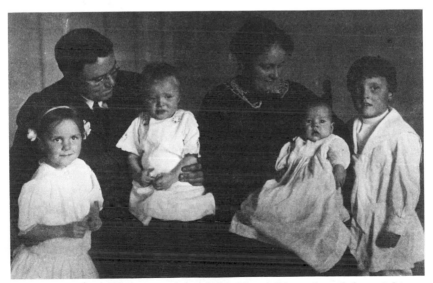

Cannon family portrait, Christmas 1912. The children, from left to right,
are Wilma, Linda, Marian, and Bradford.

Carl A. L. Binger

Daniel de la Paz

Leonard B. Nice

Walter B. Cannon

Henry Lyman

Alfred T. Shohl

Joseph C. Aub

Wade S. Wright

Cannon and his collaborators, 1911–1913.

The finding intrigued Cannon and in typical fashion he put it to use by postulating a relationship between surgical shock and injury to large nerve trunks. "The similarity between surgical shock and the condition of an animal after removal of the adrenal glands," he wrote, "suggests that possibly in surgical shock the injury to large nerve trunks may discharge the adrenal glands to such a degree that they are unable to continue their normal functioning. Hesitating to add another to the already numerous theories of surgical shock, we merely wish to point out that since sensory stimulation causes increased adrenal secretion, adrenal fatigue or exhaustion may reasonably be regarded as an element in the complex."[42]

Cannon's suggestion was certainly inventive, but again through no fault of his own, he was far from the mark. Medical scientists at the time did not have a complete understanding of the adrenal glands and did not yet differentiate adequately between the functions of the medulla and those of the cortex. Knowledge of the effects of steroids secreted by the adrenal cortex might have put a bridle on Cannon's imaginative suggestion.

The completion of Cannon's investigation with Hoskins brought to a close an exceptionally fruitful and productive year. He not only had successfully delineated some of the direct relationships of the autonomic nervous system and the adrenal glands in the functioning of the bodily economy under stress but also added new skills and techniques to his armamentarium as an investigator. That autumn instead of extending these investigations he began preparing for publication the results of the studies that he and his students had completed and, as time allowed, renewed the research he and Washburn had begun earlier in 1911 on the nature of hunger.[43]

Cannon's interest in the physiological aspects of hunger was a longstanding one and stemmed from a time when, using himself as a guinea pig, he had listened through the stethoscope to the rhythmic sounds produced by the movements of the stomach and intestines and tried to understand their significance for diagnosing certain pathological conditions of digestion. It was then that he noticed "the disappearance of a hunger pang as gas was heard gurgling upward through the cardia."[44] This phenomenon led him to a view of hunger as a sensation that had its source in the contractions of the stomach rather than (as conventional wisdom had it) as either a sensation arising from a general condition of the body or one having a peripheral source. Soon after, when W. N. Boldireff, one of Pavlov's assistants, demonstrated that the stomach contracted regularly while not digesting and further that the intensity of hunger sensations in cases of fasting gradually diminished from the day they first appeared, Cannon became convinced that the sensation of hunger was indeed related to the contractions of the stomach.[45]

At first glance the problem of hunger may not appear to be related to the research that Cannon was conducting on the adrenals but rather to his previous studies on digestion. Cannon, however, maintained that the sensations of hunger could evoke powerful emotions that were related to, if not the equal of, passions raised by fear and rage. In making the point, he went to some lengths to differentiate between hunger and appetite—terms that he claimed some investigators mistakenly used interchangeably. Hunger, he argued, was a primitive elemental sensation that drove men to eat; appetite, on the other hand, was not so urgent in its demands and merely increased the desire for food. In short, the conditions differed in sensory quality, their bodily references, and their effects on behavior.[46]

The experiments Cannon had designed for Washburn were essentially an effort to obtain data that he hoped would demonstrate that the appearance of hunger sensations was concomitant with the contractions of the stomach. During the fall he decided to measure the contractions of the lower esophagus as well—and once again Washburn's introspection of his hunger pangs agreed closely with the record he made of esophageal contractions.[47] "Hunger," Cannon concluded, "is normally the signal that the stomach is contracted for action; the unpleasantness of hunger leads to eating; eating starts gastric secretion, distends the contracted organ, initiates the movements of gastric digestion, and abolishes the sensation."[48]

In the weeks after the completion of his research Cannon explored the literature of hunger, gathering material from other physiological investigations to buttress his findings. Early that winter he presented a paper based on his work with Washburn in New York where it was warmly received. Today it is striking that the paper gives no clear idea of the number of observations Cannon actually made and contains no statistical analysis of the data he had gathered. It may well be that the results were so invariant that statistics were not required. Cannon himself was left with a puzzle and at the close admitted he had not discovered what caused the contractions to occur. In any event, he made no further effort to continue his research on hunger. A year later Anton J. Carlson at the University of Chicago, in a series of carefully conducted experiments using a human subject with complete closure of the esophagus and a permanant gastric fistula, substantiated most of Cannon and Washburn's earlier findings and extended their work.[49]

In December 1911 the *American Journal of Physiology* published five papers by Cannon and his coworkers. As a general practice Cannon asked all students who worked independently in the laboratory to prepare papers of their investigations and then required them to rewrite and edit them until they met with his approval for publication. When Aub and Binger submitted the final draft of their paper to Cannon, he surprised them. "When we finished our paper," Aub remembered, "Binger and I thought it fitting and proper to put Dr. Cannon's name on it, but this shy little man refused. It took a great deal of cajoling and pleading on our part to get him finally to agree." Cannon, like Bowditch before him (and Ludwig before him), encouraged medical students who had worked independently to publish their first papers under their own names as a way of supporting their interest in research. He did not miss with Aub, who later often spoke with great feeling of Cannon's faith in him. "It was my first publication," he said, "and it influenced my whole life in that it secured me in the belief that I wanted to do research." Aub was one of the first students in Cannon's laboratory who later became part of the cadre of a generation of superb clinical investigators.[50]

16   *Science versus Sentiment*

ANNON'S successful direction of the Council on Defense of Medical Research during the early years of its existence gratified the leadership of the American Medical Association, and in particular William H. Welch, who had been instrumental in arranging his chairmanship. In June of 1910, acting as president of the AMA, Welch rewarded Cannon for his successes by appointing him to another council—the newly organized Council on Health and Public Instruction. The purpose of this new council, George H. Simmons informed Cannon, was to prevent the duplication of tasks performed by the association's rapidly proliferating committees. "You are put on to represent the work you are now doing as Chairman of the Council on Defense of Medical Research," he told him.[1]

Cannon accepted his new post without protest. On its face, it appeared that the assignment would make few additional demands on him. Coping with the antivivisectionists had fallen into a routine. An efficient press clipping service daily brought to his attention the latest antivivisectionist news and pamphlets and allowed him to respond immediately to their various charges. Further, the mechanisms he had put in place to guide the efforts of the defense council had worked well and gave every prospect for future success. But despite his acceptance of these new responsibilities, there were signs that Cannon was beginning to tire of his battles with the antivivisectionists. Following his confrontation with William James, he increasingly worried about the prospects of ever coming to terms with them. If he could not come to an understanding with someone who was as knowledgeable as his former teacher, he reasoned, how could he hope to convince the self-declared rabid antivivisectionists of the necessity and importance of experimental research? To add to his doubts, the antivivisectionists continued to flourish. In addition to a growing membership, more than a score of British and American antivivisectionist and animal protection magazines, combined with a number of daily newspapers and journals ranging from the sensationalist Hearst newspaper chain and the *New York Herald* to such popular magazines as *Cosmopolitan, Life,* and *Vogue,* regularly published antivivisectionist philosophy, claims, and charges.[2] Indeed, in their struggle for the support of the public, the antivivisectionists seemingly did not allow for a prospect of defeat. No sooner did they lose a battle than they emerged phoenix-like to renew their attacks with even more vigor. In the spring of 1910, for example, after Cannon helped to defeat a bill that would have given antivivisectionists the right to inspect all medical laboratories in New York State, he found that they had introduced a bill in the next legislative session that was far more onerous than the one that had been defeated. In addition to inspection, the new bill included a provision to abolish animal experimentation entirely.[3]

If Cannon and the defense council faced the dilemma of an enemy that would not recognize defeat, the antivivisectionists faced an equally disturbing problem. Notwithstanding a decade-long struggle against animal experimentation, the number of vivisections in bacteriology, physiology, pathology, pharmacology, and surgery had during this period multiplied and continued to increase at what they considered an alarming rate.[4] That surge in experimental animal research had a marked effect on antivivisectionists and dictated a significant change in their tactics. From their beginnings in the latter part of the nineteenth century, antivivisectionist societies in the United States primarily focused their attention on the cruelties they believed accompanied animal experimentation. While some antivivisectionist theoreticians also attacked the emerging precepts of the bacterial etiology of infectious and contagious diseases, initially such charges remained secondary to the theme of the inherent cruelty and immorality of animal experimentation. During the first decade of the twentieth century, however, antivivisectionist attacks on the validity of medical science itself became more frequent.

One index of this tendency may be found in the speeches and

writings of Walter Hadwen, one of the physician-leaders of the British movement and a frequent lecturer on antivivisection in the United States.[5] Hadwen, the secretary of the British Union for the Abolition of Vivisection and a public advocate for the repeal of the Vaccination Act, did not believe in the germ theory of disease. "It is germs, germs, germs everywhere," he derisively claimed in one of his attacks on the theory. "There are germs above us, around us, within us, in everything we eat and almost everything we drink. It is a wonder that any of us are alive at all."[6] Not content with criticizing the validity of the bacterial etiology of disease, Hadwen mounted a blistering attack on the vaccines and serums recently developed as treatments for certain diseases, directing his greatest scorn toward the antitoxin treatment of diphtheria. There was no compelling proof, he maintained, to substantiate bacteriologists' claims that Loeffler's bacillus was the cause of diphtheria or that diphtheria antitoxin was effective or useful in coping with the disease. The whole notion of antitoxin therapy, he charged, was nothing less than a fraud.[7] Hadwen, whose credentials as a reformer were impeccable, found a ready public for his beliefs, and soon others following his lead went even further.

Some general practitioners, worried that scientific advances in medicine were helping to create a new competitive body of medical specialists, claimed that scientific and commercial conspiracies were involved in the development of vaccines and serums. "The truth of the matter," one correspondent wrote the editors of the *Journal of Zoophily*, "is that all of the 'serums' and 'anti-toxins' are kept alive by a powerful medico-commercial clique dominated by the leading experimenters, such as Koch, Behring, Haffkine, and Flexner. This clique holds the average doctor and his 'opinions' in the hollow of its hand."[8] Others hinted that the notion that bacteria cause specific diseases would in time turn medical scientists in their quest for knowledge from animal experimentation to human experimentation. One of the earliest of the charges of human experimentation to occupy Cannon concerned the "confessions" of a certain M. J. Rodermund, a physician in Milwaukee, Wisconsin.

In April 1906, in an article published in the *Medical Brief*, a semipopular Kansas medical journal, Rodermund claimed that while treating seventeen of his patients for various diseases, he had made experiments on them by spraying "the poisons" of diphtheria, smallpox, tuberculosis, and scarlet fever into their noses and throats. "Of course," he wrote, "I could not let the patients know what I was doing. I was supposed to be treating them for catarrh of the nose and throat." Given the obscurity of the *Medical Brief*, Rodermund's disclosure had little immediate public impact. Three years later, however, *Life* magazine, one of the long-term supporters of the antivivisectionist movement, discovered the article and published extensive excerpts from it.[9] The editors of *Life* portrayed Rodermund's confessions as another example of the atrocities committed in the name of medical progress and an index of the growing immorality of scientific investigation.

Realizing that much public sympathy could be aroused if the confessions were not promptly refuted, Cannon asked two of his friends in Wisconsin, Joseph Erlanger, professor of physiology at the University of Wisconsin, and J. L. Yates, a young medical practitioner in Milwaukee, for more information about Rodermund.[10] Cannon soon learned that Rodermund had little standing in the medical profession or in the community at large. An Eclectic, he had few patients and was largely distinguished by his persistent public opposition to the germ theory of disease and the practice of vaccination. Some physicians regarded him as an ignorant crank and advised that it was the better part of wisdom not to take public notice of his claims. "Please bear in mind," Yates warned Cannon, "that you can't stir up a skunk and escape a stink and what can be gained by stirring up this particular pole cat unless there is a certainty of getting his license? That part, I fear, must be left to the attorney of the State Board of Health."[11]

Although Cannon had no desire to interfere in local medical matters, Rodermund's claims provoked him. If Rodermund had actually performed the experiments he described and exposed his patients to disease without their knowledge and consent, Cannon felt that he should be punished and his license immediately forfeited. If Rodermund had lied, Cannon thought that he ought to know about it in order to refute an assumption on the part of the public that such experiments were commonly performed by doctors in treating their patients. In the end, however, neither Cannon nor the health authorities in Wisconsin took any action against Rodermund.[12] A year later Yates sent Cannon a news clipping from the *Milwaukee Journal* which noted that Rodermund had been arrested and charged with arson for setting fire to his office in

Chippewa Falls. Cannon received no more information as to Rod- ermund's subsequent fate. His account of human experimentation, however, continued to be cited in antivivisection pamphlets and journals as gospel, requiring almost constant refutation by Cannon and the defense council in the years that followed.[13]

Perhaps the most pervasive charges of human experimenta- tion by antivivisectionists were those mounted against the new tests physicians increasingly used to diagnose a variety of infec- tious and contagious diseases. In 1908 when Kenneth Blackfan and Samuel Hammill used the Calmette eye test and the von Pir- quet skin test to diagnose incipient cases of tuberculosis in an effort to cope with a rising mortality of babies in a foundling home in Philadelphia, they were charged by local antivivisectionists with "using infants as guinea pigs to satisfy their own sadistic tend- encies." A year later when L. Emmett Holt began to use these diagnostic tests at the Babies' Hospital in New York, he was also savaged by antivivisectionists.[14] All of these attacks angered Can- non. The one that perhaps most infuriated him, however, was the revival of the Wentworth case.

In 1910 Caroline Earle White, during the course of an anti- vivisectionist campaign against Alexis Carrel's animal experiments at the Rockefeller Institute, revived and embellished the Went- worth case in an editorial in the *Journal of Zoophily*, claiming that the lumbar punctures performed by Wentworth more than fifteen years earlier had caused the deaths of "40 or 50 little children" in the Children's Hospital in Boston. Cannon, who knew and ad- mired Wentworth and was a firm believer in correcting errors of fact, wrote the journal, pointing out Mrs. White's distortions, but he received no satisfaction.[15] A year later Mary F. Lovell, a contrib- uting editor of the journal, answered Cannon by publicly repeating Mrs. White's charges. "Dr. Cannon," she wrote, "is severe on the *Journal of Zoophily* for having referred last year to Dr. Wentworth's 45 experiments on children and for having mentioned the fact that the children died after the operation."[16] Mrs. Lovell's reply es- pecially irritated W. W. Keen, who a decade earlier was one of the few physicians in the United States who had publicly come to Wentworth's defense after he was attacked by antivivisectionists. Actually, following his vigorous defense of Wentworth in the *Jour- nal of the AMA*, the attacks on Wentworth subsided. "I urged W.[entworth] to prosecute Mrs. White for her *signed* (C.E.W.) Editorial in which she lied," Keen wrote Cannon several days after Mrs. Lovell's editorial appeared, "but I suppose his attorneys have probably advised against it. Naturally he shrinks from the disagreeable publicity. Is it true that it cost him his place at Harvard? I am told that Dr. Eliot advised or consented to his elimination because the University was about to ask for a large sum of money and W's further connection with the School would deter some from giving. That is so unlike Dr. E. that I expressed great doubt as to its being a correct statement."[17]

If Cannon knew anything of the circumstances under which Wentworth left Harvard, he made no mention of it in his response to Keen. "As you know," he wrote, venting his anger toward White and Lovell, "I pointed out a perfectly definite, clear cut falsehood which they had published regarding Wentworth and in their notice of my paper they slurred this matter over and did not even acknowledge that they had been mistaken. Until they can show some respect for the truth I am rather inclined to do nothing but insist that they tell it. There never was a better example of 'the antivivisecton agitation with all its untruthfulness' which Professor James called attention to."[18]

‑‑‑

From the beginning of his work with the defense council, Cannon made it a rule to answer all antivivisection claims and charges in a polite and civil manner because he believed that such an approach ultimately benefited the cause of medical science. The attacks that Hadwen and other physicians mounted against experimental research and especially the patently distorted charges Caroline Earle White and the *Journal of Zoophily* brought against Wentworth, however, so angered him that he determined to set his scruples aside and meet the antivivisectionists head on.

Late in the fall of 1910, in response to an invitation to address the New York Academy of Medicine, Cannon used the occasion to focus on the immorality of the charges and claims made in antivivisectionist literature.[19] He said little about antivivisectionist leaders except to cite them by name. Instead he directed his barbs at the distortions and slanders he found in the writings of the physicians who had joined the antivivisectionist cause. The antivivisectionists, Cannon told his audience, must "clear their literature of the anachronistic hostility of men long since dead, men who had no conception of the merciful procedures of modern experimentation, nor of its life-giving results. They must rid their publications of the testimony of spurious experts whose reputations were made in literature, art or theology, and not in the service of healing."[20] And then, in a passionate exhortation, he urged antivivisectionists to discard their beliefs and recognize the beneficence and humanity inherent in scientific investigation. It is doubtful that Cannon believed his exhortation would actually persuade antivivisectionists to change their views. The gauntlet he laid down did, however, have a personal salutary effect—it served as a catharsis for the frustrations and outrage that he had accumulated in his battles with those who opposed animal experimentation.

The problem of dealing with the antivivisectionists was never far from Cannon's mind. The rapid development of his research coupled with the lack of laboratory animals needed for his experiments almost daily reinforced his conviction that they were one of the prime roadblocks to the maturation of medical science in the United States. Although Cannon regretted the loss of time when he was asked to leave his laboratory to attend meetings of the AMA council or defend medical research before various public bodies, he went willingly, as when his friend Jerome Greene called on him for help early in 1911. Greene, who had left Harvard the year before to become business manager of the Rockefeller Institute,[21] had as part of his responsibilities the task of answering the charges and allegations brought by antivivisectionists and countering their efforts to introduce legislation to regulate medical research. In March, when the New York State legislature called hearings to consider two bills designed to restrict medical experimentation, Greene asked Cannon to testify against the proposed legislation. Although Cannon was then deeply involved in his research on the adrenals, he put his work aside to answer Greene's call. His straightforward testimony on the demands of medical research and especially the need for control of such research from within the profession, when joined with the persuasive testimony of other notable investigators, helped to defeat the bills.[22]

Greene and the Rockefeller Institute found it more difficult to counter other antivivisectionist actions. One of these was directed against a test that Hideyo Noguchi had developed for more accurate diagnosis of tertiary and congenital cases of syphilis. Antivivisectionist actions against animal and human experimentation at the Institute were not new; in the early years of the twentieth century Simon Flexner had been attacked for his experimental research on cerebrospinal meningitis and poliomyelitis, and Alexis Carrel was criticized for his animal experiments on the surgery of blood vessels.[23] Noguchi was an even more promising target. Syphilis was a disease that few discussed publicly; indeed, it carried a stigma similar to the one that branded leprosy. Further, Noguchi's experiments involved not only animals but humans as well. Briefly, in 1911, after demonstrating that paresis is the result of a long-term syphilitic infection of the brain, Noguchi discovered that when rabbits experimentally infected with syphilis were inoculated with killed emulsified *Treponema pallida* (which he called luetin), they had a specific cutaneous reaction. Eager to determine whether luetin could be used diagnostically to supplement the Wasserman test in chronic cases of syphilis where it frequently manifested itself by diverse and obscure symptoms, Noguchi with the encouragement of William Welch extended his tests to humans. Later that year, in cooperation with physicians in hospitals in and around New York City, he studied the effects of luetin in four hundred patients and found as he had hoped that luetin was indeed valuable as a supplementary diagnostic test.[24]

When Noguchi's patient studies became public knowledge—especially his use of nonsyphilitic patients as a control group—antivivisectonists charged that he had infected "146 persons of pure blood . . . many of them children with the virus of syphilis." The public furor created by these charges became so intense that the district attorney of New York County felt compelled to investigate them. Despite intensive efforts, however, he found nothing to substantiate antivivisectionist claims and after several weeks issued a report that completely exonerated Noguchi.[25] Convinced that the district attorney had whitewashed the case, the antivivisectionists continued their attacks on Noguchi, the Institute, and the physicians who had participated in the testing of luetin. The sensational implications of the case afforded antivivisectionists the widespread publicity they had long been seeking and soon involved Cannon as well.

By 1912 antivivisectionist claims that medical scientists were turning more and more to human experimentation led to reorganization of their societies. In some cities and states along the eastern seaboard new groups emerged that represented themselves as vivisection inspection societies. One of these new societies, the Vivisection Investigation League of New York, joined with five older antivivisection societies to form the Interstate Conference for the Investigation of Vivisection.[26] When the new confederation announced that it was going to develop a more militant program, it was joined by two more antivivisectionist societies. The auguries for the expansion of the new group were excellent, and many of its leaders looked forward to the International Antivivisection and Animal Protection Congress scheduled to be held in Washington early in December 1913 for the opportunity it promised as a national forum and recruiting ground. Cannon, however, took the projected congress less seriously and except for sending someone to take notes of the speeches made at the meetings decided for the time being not to make any effort to refute antivivisectionist charges.[27]

The international congress was all that its organizers had hoped for and more. Suffused with the spirit of the approaching Christmas holidays, it became the gala social event of the season in Washington. In addition to a full contingent of British and American antivivisection leaders, it also succeeded in attracting a large number of public officials and their wives, including such prominent figures as William Jennings Bryan, the Secretary of State, and Speaker of the House of Representatives Champ Clark. Two distinct themes dominated the meetings: first, the claim that cruelty was inherent in animal experimentation; second and perhaps more important, the charge that medical scientists were increasingly involved in human experimentation. Time and again, speakers regaled the congress with accounts of the Rodermund confessions, the tuberculin tests conducted by Blackfan, Hammill and Holt, and Noguchi's experiments with luetin. The sensational claims made compelling newspaper headlines. One story in the *Washington Post*, for example, captured readers' attention with a headline that began "Doctors of Death," followed by a series of blood-curdling subheadings: "Humans Murdered by Vivisection, Speakers Claim / Called Victims of Poison / English Physician Bitterly Assails Injections of Serums / Girls and Little Children Inoculated with Germs of Loathesome Diseases in the Name of Science, According to Mr. Stephens—'Practices Like Spanish Inquisition' Denounced by Dr. Albert Leffingwell—Legislation Urged."[28] Cannon, who daily reviewed the reports of the defense council's observer at the congress, was not moved by the speeches. Thoroughly familiar with their substance, he dismissed them. "The same old twaddle," he noted in his diary, "but great headlines in papers."[29]

Twaddle or not, by the close of the congress Cannon realized that he had erred by not providing for a response to the antivivisectionists during the meetings. Up to this time, with the exception of his fruitless defense of Arthur Wentworth, he had followed a policy laid down by Bowditch of refusing to engage in open debate with antivivisectionists on the ethics of human experimentation. In fact, the year before he had sidestepped the issue in one of his papers which reviewed the substance of all the pamphlets previously issued by the research defense council by simply stressing the positive gains made in medical care through experimental investigation.[30] Now, however, Cannon felt that immediate steps would have to be taken if medical scientists were to retain their credibility with the public. Recognizing that much of the antivivisectionist success rested on the charges they had broadcast against human experimentation, he decided to meet the issue squarely.

Late in December 1913 he addressed the matter in an editorial in the *Journal of the AMA:* "The public should definitely understand," he declared, "that the medical profession wholly repudiates and regards with abhorrence the employment of any procedure whatever which is in any way likely to injure rather than to benefit a patient who has entrusted himself or who has been entrusted to a physician's care. Such action would be absolutely at variance with the prime object of medical service—the welfare and the restoration of the sick."[31] Not content to stop there, he also undertook a campaign to expose the professional status and character of the "authorities" who had claimed at the congress that medical investigators had inoculated unsuspecting men, women, and children with disease germs solely for experimental purposes.

৺৯ ৺৯ ৺৯

Notwithstanding his moral indignation, by 1914 dealing with the antivivisectionists had become a burden for Cannon, and he began to hint that he was "losing interest somewhat" in the work of the defense council. Little more than a year earlier, when Abraham Jacobi had approached him with an offer of reappointment to the AMA Council on Health and Public Instruction, Cannon told him that he felt that the defense of research could be better served if it were taken up by someone with a fresh point of view and even suggested that Erlanger would be a good man to take his place.[32] Cannon did not ask the AMA to relieve him of his responsibilities of directing the defense council, however. In a sense, he had painted himself into a corner: few physicians or scientists in the country knew more than he did about the antivivisectionists and few had as much experience in defending medical research. Nor was there anyone on the defense council or elsewhere who appeared willing to shoulder the responsibility of countering the new militant campaigns the antivivisectionists had promised at their congress. Through circumstances beyond his control, Cannon had become indispensable.

One of the problems that contributed to Cannon's difficulties was that he had duplicate responsibilities locally and nationally. As head of the AMA defense council Cannon spoke and acted in behalf of a national professional organization. In Boston, however, he acted in behalf of the Committee on Animals at the Medical School[33] and thus was a spokesman for Harvard as well. Both posts required the defense of medical experimentation, but the pressures that were brought to bear on him locally were of a different nature.

From its inception in 1907 the Animals Committee was charged with the procurement and care of animals for all of the experimental research conducted at the Medical School. At first, the committee tried to meet these obligations by having animals supplied by breeders located outside of Boston. When this method of procurement failed, the committee turned to shopkeepers and children who lived in the market and slum areas of the city to round up stray dogs and cats for the School. The new system proved to be far more efficient. Children from the North End of the city, attracted by the prospect of earning easy money, became adept and zealous in supplying the Medical School with animals. When treasured pets as well as strays began to disappear from city streets, the Animal Rescue League[34] on behalf of angry pet owners complained to the University that the Medical School was conspiring with unscrupulous animal dealers. Complaints from the Animal Rescue League were not a small matter; the League was one of the favorite charities of Boston Brahmins, and its causes were supported by the social and economic elite of the city. One of the sharpest complaints that came to the Medical School on behalf of the Animal Rescue League was addressed to Lowell by Roger Ernst, a member of Ropes, Gray and Gorham, the distinguished law firm that acted as University counsel. Ernst was a member of the Board of the Animal Rescue League and an ardent anti-vivisectionist; further, he was on friendly terms with Lowell. When Ernst asked Lowell that a full investigation be made by Harvard into "the system now practiced for obtaining animals for vivisec-tion purposes," William Phillips, the Secretary of the Harvard Corporation, immediately wrote the Medical School for an expla-nation of the Animals Committee's procurement policy.[35]

Phillips's query indicated to Cannon that animal supply was no longer solely a Medical School problem but had been trans-formed into a University issue　one, moreover, that had the po-tential to threaten the entire program of animal experimentation at Harvard. Realizing the gravity of the situation, Cannon pro-ceeded to instruct Phillips (and through him Lowell) in the work and purpose of the Animals Committee and mounted a passionate defense of experimental research as well: "The authorities at the Medical School," he wrote them, "have no apologies to make for the use of animals in animal experimentation. They are fully con-vinced that this use of animals is in the highest degree humane, both from the point of view of the animals used and from the point of view of both animals and men who are benefited by the results of animal experimentation . . . we cannot make bricks without straw."[36]

Nevertheless, in an effort to mollify Phillips and Lowell Can-non began to seek an accommodation with the Animal Rescue League and the Massachusetts Society for the Prevention of Cru-elty to Animals. In the process he discovered that some of the leaders of both organizations were more understanding of the needs of medical investigators than he had previously suspected and that there appeared to be significant differences in outlook between humane societies and antivivisection societies on the question of animal experimentation. That perception changed many of Cannon's previously held attitudes about the usefulness of co-operating with humane societies.

In 1914, after Keen had suggested to Cannon that it might be a good policy to join the American Humane Society, he became a member. Later that year he agreed to send a speaker to debate with an antivivisectionist at a forum sponsored by the American Humane Society, although both he and the defense council had previously avoided sharing the same platform with antivivisectionists.[37] Cannon in due course developed such confidence in the judgment and ability of Francis H. Rowley, the director of the Massachusetts Society for the Prevention of Cruelty to Animals, that he agreed to allow an antivivisectionist to visit the laboratories at the Medical School accompanied by Mr. Rowley.[38]

This did not mean, however, that Cannon's changing attitude toward humane societies extended to antivivisectionists. Indeed, his attacks on antivivisectionists grew sharper and considerably more personal, especially his editorials and letters questioning the credentials of the physicians who had been presented at the international congress as "eminent medical authorities." Cannon's exposé of the actual status of "Dr. Richard Cowen, F.R.C.S. London" published in both the *Journal of the AMA* and the *Boston Herald* so angered Edward H. Clement, president of the New England Antivivisectionist Society, that he wrote a sharp letter to the *Herald* taking Cannon to task for impugning the reputation of "the renowned Dr. Cowen" and revived the charges that he and others had made at the international congress regarding human experimentation. No sooner did Cannon answer this letter than another appeared, the argument between the two men becoming more heated and more personal with each exchange.[39] By any standard Clement, a former editor of the *Boston Transcript*, was a formidable opponent, but Cannon did not give ground. There can be little doubt that the force behind his sharp attacks stemmed from both the inherent threat he saw in antivivisectionist charges to the future progress and development of medical science and the moral indignation he felt at antivivisectionist distortions. "We would do better," he counseled Keen in a letter at the outset of his fight, "to write to the papers and show, just as frequently as we can, the misleading and utterly false claims which they make. I do not believe that the ordinary American will stand for persistent falsehood and malicious slander, even if he were willing to support the claims of animals as against those of mankind. After a time we shall have antivivisectionists and liars as synonymous terms."[40]

Although at the beginning Cannon appeared to enjoy his confrontation with Clement, as it continued the personal attacks began to grate on him—especially when the debate was joined by Mrs.

Jessica Henderson, one of the leaders of the New England Anti-vivisection Society. Cannon was always ambivalent about how to meet the arguments advanced by women in the antivivisectionist movement because many of them in addition to their antivivisectionist activities were also engaged in social and political reform projects that he and Cornelia supported. What made things particularly difficult for Cannon was that he believed that at the international congress Mrs. Henderson had lied when she described George Crile's animal experiments on surgical shock.[41] Her distortions angered him, yet his code of moral behavior dictated that he be civil to her in public debate. His frustration at her statements as well as others made by Clement grew. But when Ernest Gruening, one of the editors at the *Boston Herald*, wrote him that the *Herald* found it difficult to use one of Clement's rejoinders "because it was really too insane to print,"[42] he realized that this particular battle with the antivivisectionists was over. To Keen he later boasted "if Clement breaks loose again, I still have some old scores to settle with him." Several days later he reported the outcome to the Council on Health and Public Instruction in more measured terms: "I think," he wrote, "that we have the Antis in a very weak situation now in this community."[43]

The problems that Cannon had with antivivisectionists in other cities and states were no less trying than those in Boston. In some instances they proved to be even more complex. To cope with these more efficiently he began to develop a network of younger men to advise and help him. In New York, for example, he turned to William James's son, Henry James, Jr., who in 1912 had succeeded Jerome Greene as business manager at the Rockefeller Institute. The irony of fighting the antivivisectionists and serving Cannon as a legal adviser in that struggle was not lost on young James: "Strange are the shifts of fortune," he wrote Cannon soon after taking up his post at the institute. "I am giving up my law practice . . . to take Jerry Greene's place . . . and I suppose that I shall have my father's words on vivisection quoted and misquoted at me fairly often."[44] There is no evidence that James's fears were ever realized, although he found himself almost continually enmeshed in debates with antivivisectionists while working at the institute. In Philadelphia Cannon recruited Richard M. Pearce, a young pathologist at the University of Pennsylvania Medical School, who had previously been trained in experimental pathology by

Frank Mallory and Simon Flexner.[45] James and Pearce became two of Cannon's most prized allies.

ᥫᦉ   ᥫᦉ   ᥫᦉ

Although Cannon's battles with antivivisectionists during the period from 1913 to 1915 were generally similar, each conflict had certain unique elements. The origin as well as the substance of antivivisectionist campaigns in Pennsylvania during this period, for instance, differed markedly from those that occurred in New York and Boston. In Pennsylvania problems with antivivisectionists were rooted in a number of specific local developments, including the changes in medical education at the University of Pennsylvania Medical School and the political strategies physicians in Philadelphia had followed in their campaigns against antivivisectionists from the beginning of the century.

In 1909 the University of Pennsylvania Medical School began to increase its commitment to medical research in two important ways: first, by expanding their existing research facilities through the acquisition of the Henry Phipps Institute for the Study, Treatment and Prevention of Tuberculosis; second, and perhaps more important, by recruiting a number of distinguished young investigators to the faculty in pathology, physiology, surgery, and pharmacology.[46] The increase in experimental research presaged by these developments soon posed a particular challenge to antivivisectionists in Philadelphia. Although they had previously engaged in a number of legislative battles with a medical research defense group in Philadelphia led by Keen, David Edsall, Silas Weir Mitchell, and Hobart Hare, now for the first time they had to fight a policy of experimental research adopted by one of the most prestigious medical institutions in the city.

While there was substantive agreement among physicians and medical scientists in Philadelphia of the necessity of fighting the antivivisectionists, significant differences were voiced by those involved about how to conduct the battle. From the inception of the AMA defense council a number of physicians and medical scientists in Philadelphia believed that the best way to counter antivivisectionists was through political activity. In 1909 when the Philadelphia Research Defense Society led by Hobart Hare succeeded in turning back a particularly fierce antivivisectionist legislative attack with the aid of Pennsylvania's long-time Republican political boss Boies Penrose, that belief hardened into conviction. Eventually, however, the medical scientists overreached themselves. Early in 1913 medical investigators at the University of Pennsylvania, faced with a growing need for a steady supply of experimental animals and persuaded that they could depend on their long-time political allies in the state legislature, decided to press for a bill that would ensure them a regular supply of experimental animals. The bill introduced on February 6, 1913, made it mandatory under threat of fine for local dog pounds to turn over unclaimed animal strays to medical schools and to commercial firms engaged in the manufacture of biological products.[47]

The proponents of the bill made a number of serious miscalculations, however. Despite their beliefs, they actually had no firm base of political power. Boies Penrose, their staunch ally who ruled the Republican party and the Pennsylvania legislature with an iron hand, had been dethroned a year earlier by a political reform movement that swept the state. In addition, the bill was poorly drawn; the mandatory nature of the bill with provisos of fines for noncompliance and especially the inclusion of biological firms as recipients of animals for research (raising the issue of animal experimentation for profit) drew active opposition from animal lovers throughout the state, including many supporters of medical research. When the bill came before the house, legislators overwhelmingly voted it down.

Sensing that the time had come for a counterattack, antivivisectionists proceeded to introduce a bill to abolish animal experimentation in Pennsylvania. When it, too, was defeated, they adopted a new strategy.[48] In June of 1913 the Philadelphia Anti-Cruelty Society secured warrants from a local magistrate against six of the leading investigators at the University of Pennsylvania Medical School (Joshua Sweet, Richard Pearce, Alonzo Taylor, Alfred Newton Richards, Edward Reichert, and Allen Smith) and had them arrested on four specific charges of cruelty against animals then held in the animal quarters of the school. Although the arrests created much public comment, those who were arrested dismissed the incident as of little importance. Henry James, Jr., then in the midst of another legislative battle with anitivivisectionists in New York, took a more serious view of the Philadelphia prosecutions, recognizing that they might serve as a model for attacks on the Rockefeller Institute, and he urged Cannon to personally monitor the case closely.[49] In spite of James's advice, Cannon did not involve himself in the proceedings. Instead, following his policy of letting local people fight their own battles, he assigned to Pearce the responsibility of dealing with the problem. In the months that followed Pearce mounted a successful public relations campaign to inform Philadelphians about the importance of animal experimentation in the development of medical practice and care.[50]

As the trial approached in the early spring of 1914 James again warned Cannon of the potentially grave consequences of the Philadelphia prosecutions and once more urged him to take a more active role in the case. James's second warning to Cannon was prompted by his recent experience in helping the Rockefeller Institute establish animal and plant pathology laboratories in Princeton. During the winter the institute had sponsored a bill in the New Jersey legislature that would allow it to organize such laboratories; eager to have the laboratories in Princeton, the legislature not only passed the proposed bill but also added a provision that granted the laboratories the right to conduct animal experiments. When the bill came to the governor's desk, he announced that he would not sign it until he knew the outcome of the Philadelphia trial.[51] James's account of the impact of the Philadelphia trial on the legislative process in New Jersey finally convinced Cannon of the gravity of the possible rippling effect of the prosecutions. Generally Cannon was parsimonious in utilizing the funds of the defense council; this time, however, alarmed by James's news, he hired an experienced journalist to conduct a public relations campaign to promote the interests of the indicted investigators with Philadelphia newspapers.[52]

The trial, which began on April 15, 1914 and lasted for three days, proved to be less of a threat than James or Cannon had anticipated. Two days before the trial opened, a special committee that the university had appointed to investigate the charges of cruelty brought against the investigators reported to the Board of Trustees that the accusations were without foundation and exonerated them of all charges. The Board thereupon not only approved the report but in a series of resolutions also publicly expressed its support of the principle of animal experimentation.[53] Equally important, at the outset of the trial the district attorney dropped three of the four original charges brought against the defendants and focused instead on one charge—not, as expected, that operations causing pain to animals to obtain scientific information were illegal, but simply that Joshua Sweet as superintendent of the animal house had been negligent in providing proper care and attention to the animals kept there.[54] Apparently the district attorney believed that he could best sustain his case on this issue. As the trial progressed, however, the evidence to support this charge when subjected to careful scrutiny in the courtroom proved less than convincing; to many observers it appeared that Sweet would be exonerated.

At the conclusion of the trial, however, to the consternation of the defense the judge instructed the jury that Pennsylvania law did "not allow pain and suffering to be inflicted upon dogs for any purpose except for the relief of the suffering of the dog itself." If the jury followed the judge's charge, Pearce gloomily reported to Cannon several days later, it meant that even if Sweet were acquitted, the original defendants as well as other investigators engaged in animal research in Pennsylvania could be tried on the basis that animal experimentation was presumed to involve suffering to animals.[55]

Despite Pearce's prognostications, the trial ended on a happier note for Sweet. The jury, confused by the judge's charges, could not reach agreement, making it necessary to have a new trial. Further, in the days after the trial some of the far-reaching implications of the judge's charges for the future development of medical research were increasingly perceived by opinion makers in the city. Newspaper editorials began to censure both the judge's conduct and the activities of antivivisectionists in attempting to interfere with the beneficent processes of experimental medicine. Many lawyers were also critical of the judge: Samuel Dickson, one of the leading members of the Philadelphia Bar, after a lengthy review of the case assured the Provost of the University of Pennsylvania there were so many errors at the trial that it could not reasonably be doubted the courts in Pennsylvania would ultimately hold that the activities of medical investigators were lawful as well as laudable.[56]

Cannon and the defense council savored the victory and made plans to capitalize on the favorable publicity that followed it. Within weeks a series of editorials and newsnotes appeared in the *Journal of the AMA* to inform the association's membership about the events that had taken place in Philadelphia. Locally, the County Medical Society passed a series of resolutions to affirm its confidence in the medical investigators who had been prosecuted and arranged to have a series of articles published in the *Philadelphia Ledger* to instruct the public of the value of animal experimentation in the diagnosis and treatment of disease.[57] Following a time-honored custom, the society asked Cannon if he would speak in one of the city's churches during the annual observance of Public Health Sunday. "I have promised to preach in Philadelphia on June 21," he wrote Pearce soon after, "and already I am beginning to quake at the thought of occupying the pulpit." When the congregation at the Girard Avenue Unitarian Church took their seats that Sunday morning, they were treated to a sermon by Dr. Walter B. Cannon on the subject of "Social Responsibilities Arising from Medical Progress."[58]

Encouraged by the manifest changes in public opinion, the Pennsylvania Society for the Protection of Scientific Research decided to approach the state legislature with a new version of the pound bill. "Our pound bill is in Committee," Pearce wrote Cannon some months after the trial, "and the anti's are paying a lobbyist $1000 to fight it. We will make them spend some money anyway."[59] Pearce's implied pessimism about the outcome of the proposed legislation proved to be justified: the bill was defeated. The idea behind the bill, however, began to take hold. The problems of acquiring animals from private dealers led medical investigators in other states to view passage of a pound bill as the only viable solution for the procurement of a steady supply of experimental animals. In the years that followed the Pennsylvania pound bill became a model for similar legislation elsewhere.

17   *The Emergency Function of the Adrenal Medulla*

T HROUGHOUT the autumn of 1911, while preparing for publication his preliminary studies on the adrenal glands, Cannon began to seek a unitary principle that might inform and guide his future research. The task was complicated; the observations he wished to synthesize were imbedded in a variety of disparate studies. Some resulted from his investigations of digestion when he first noted cessation of movements of the stomach during periods of emotional stress and later when he reported that stimulation of the splanchnic nerves was responsible for the inhibition of the smooth muscle activity he had previously observed. Other relevant observations stemmed from his preliminary studies with Daniel de la Paz on the emotional production of adrenalin.

During the course of the latter investigation Cannon had conceived the notion that adrenalin might serve to mobilize sugar from the liver for use by skeletal muscle—in effect, helping the body to mobilize its resources to improve muscular power during periods of stress and danger. The idea intrigued him, and in November he decided to put it to an experimental test. With the assistance of Leonard Nice, a new instructor in the physiology department, he began an examination of the effect of stimulating the splanchnic nerves on strength of skeletal muscle contraction.[1] Initially, Cannon isolated the splanchnic nerves of an anesthetized experimental cat, as well as the motor nerves of its *tibialis anticus* muscle, leaving the blood supply to the muscle intact. He then attached the tendon of the muscle by means of a ligature to a pulley leading to a weighted steel writing stylus. The nerve-muscle preparation in place, he stimulated the nerves to the muscle until fatigue was induced, recording the resulting muscular contractions on a kymograph and measuring at the same time the arterial pressure of the animal.[2] The results of these first experiments showed promise: "A great day," he noted in his diary on November 13. "Found augmentation of muscular contraction when splanchnics stimulated not related to blood pressure and disappeared when adrenal veins tied." The next day he was further encouraged when he came upon the work of two South American physiologists who had previously demonstrated that adrenalin augmented contraction of isolated skeletal muscle. With a characteristic intuitive leap he added in his diary, "Much excited by possibility of adrenalin activation explaining 'second wind'."[3]

Several days later Cannon began a series of experiments to see if he could determine more accurately the cause of the increased strength of muscular contraction when the splanchnics were stimulated. He found that when he stimulated the motor nerves to the *tibialis anticus* muscle at a high, uniform rate, fatigue soon ensued with a decrease in the force of contraction. He also discovered that if in this new steady state he stimulated the splanchnic nerve briefly, there was a sharp rise, then a fall in the strength of muscle contraction followed by a slow, prolonged rise of muscle performance that continued even after the blood pressure returned to its original level. These results perplexed him: Did adrenalin released by splanchnic stimulation, as his initial experiments suggested, specifically act of itself to improve muscular contraction? Or did such stimulation, as his later experiments seemed to indicate, generate better muscular performance as a result of an increased blood flow to muscle caused by a rise of blood pressure?[4]

Despite this uncertainty, the suggestiveness of Cannon's research so elated him that he decided to prepare a preliminary report of his work with Nice for the yearly Christmas meeting of the American Physiological Society. The report was not merely a recapitulation of the results of his experiments to date; it added a new speculation concerning the role of emotions on contraction of fatigued muscles. "Emotional increase of sugar and adrenalin in the blood, as already reported," Cannon told the society, "accompanies fear and rage. These major excitements are likely to be attended in wild life by the necessity of running or fighting. Sugar would supply energy, and adrenalin would tend to obviate fatigue in the laboring muscles." "The ability to continue during excitement prolonged efforts, ordinarily exhausting," he concluded, "can thus in part be explained."[5] It was the first of several reports that within a relatively brief period of time would eventuate in a theory of the emergency function of the adrenal medulla.

✑   ✑   ✑

The new year began uneventfully for Cannon except for one unanticipated piece of news: early in January Cornelia confided to him that she was again pregnant. Cannon now an experienced father was not fazed by the news. Indeed, the prospect of another child pleased him, and like the promise of the research he had just undertaken, it appeared to augur well for the future. Although he renewed his investigation of muscle fatigue in the following days, he made little progress and after several weeks decided to put the research aside—perhaps less out of a sense of frustration at the rate of its development than in deference to fulfilling an obligation he had earlier undertaken on behalf of the American Medical Association.

Late in 1911 the AMA, the National Electric Light Association, and the American Institute of Electrical Engineers organized a special commission to revise the rules of resuscitation used by laymen and physicians in giving first aid to victims of electric shock.[6] A number of physiologists had recently developed techniques of artificial respiration that appeared to be superior to those in use. In addition, they had begun to look at the problem of resuscitation from such accidents in a different way. For example, a French commission of physiologists had found that accidental electric shock received from live wires primarily affected the heart, inducing lethal ventricular fibrillation, rather than the respiratory center, as had been formerly assumed. Given these findings, it became clear that in addition to supplanting older methods of artificial respiration, it was also necessary to devise methods of restoring a fibrillating heart to its normal rhythm.

When the AMA asked Cannon to serve as chairman of the newly formed commission, he accepted despite the fact that he was immersed in a very promising program of research on the adrenals. Cannon believed that he had an obligation to use his expertise and knowledge for the public good. Moreover, he thought that his work for the commission would not be burdensome. Although he was not acquainted with those members of the commission appointed by the National Electric Light Association and the American Institute of Electric Engineers, he did know the medical members (George Crile, Samuel Meltzer, and Yandell Henderson), and he felt that with their help he could easily cope with any problems that might arise.[7]

As chairman, Cannon set the agenda for the commission, dividing its duties essentially into three classes of inquiry: first, to determine the best method of artificial respiration that could be applied by laymen and to provide a clear description of that method; second, to evaluate the claims made for commercially produced mechanical devices designed to maintain artificial respiration; and third, to investigate the problem of defibrillating the heart.[8] Some of the items on the agenda were settled with dispatch: at their first meeting the commission voted unanimously to recommend the "prone pressure" technique of artificial respiration that E. A. Schäfer of Edinburgh had recently developed in place of the older Silvester method then in use.[9] Other issues, however, needed more time and thought. Cannon assigned the task of dealing with claims made for commercially produced resuscitory mechanical devices to a subcommittee headed by Meltzer and reserved for himself the problem he believed central to the work of the commission—devising a method to defibrillate the heart.[10]

Cannon was by no means the first to undertake such an investigation. C. C. Guthrie, professor of physiology at the University of Pittsburgh, had earlier tried to defibrillate the heart in an experimental dog by a combination of techniques that included artificial respiration, cardiac massage, and an infusion of sodium chloride into the carotid artery. Others like George Crile, a Cleveland surgeon concerned with surgical shock, had tried to achieve the same ends as Guthrie by injecting adrenalin or potassium salts into the circulation of various experimental animals. Still others, like Nicolas Floresco, a Parisian physiologist, had attempted to defibrillate the heart of an experimental animal by direct electrical stimulation. Despite some early promising results, these experiments and others like them ultimately failed.[11]

Late in February 1912, Cannon, with the assistance of E. G. Martin, who had been working in his laboratory to improve methods of electrical stimulation, conducted the first of his experiments.

Like many of the investigators who had preceded him, Cannon found some of his early results promising: "Dr. Martin and I in afternoon," he noted in his diary on February 29, "produce fibrillation in heart of a dog and stop it by introducing K [potassium] salts." Although he and Martin repeated the experiment, they failed to duplicate the results, and after two months Cannon decided to discontinue the investigation.[12]

The investigation of Meltzer's subcommittee was no more successful. After several months of study it found there was no scientific evidence that the commercial machines designed to sustain artificial respiration were useful. When Cannon submitted the commission's preliminary report to the editor of *The Electrical World* in the spring of 1912, he noted with regret the failure of his efforts to defibrillate the heart. Although he realized that little could be done if the primary problem was circulatory failure, he recommended that for those with respiratory paralysis, artificial respiration might restore normal breathing. To underscore these conclusions, he prepared a booklet and chart with special instructions on how to conduct Schäfer's new method of artificial respiration. It was hardly the definitive report he had originally hoped to submit.[13]

Public perception of the commission's work, however, was quite different. When Cannon's preliminary report was published by *The Electrical World,* the chart and rules he had prepared were immediately perceived to be important and useful not only to victims of electric shock but to victims of asphyxia from illuminating gas and drowning as well. Newspapers reprinted the chart and rules in their Sunday supplements.[14] The Bureau of Mines wrote Cannon and asked if he and the medical committee would undertake to adapt the rules to help resuscitate miners overcome by carbon monoxide or methane gas.[15] Canada officially adopted the chart and rules, and a number of European and Asian nations asked for and received permission to translate the rules into their native tongues. These responses and others like them confirmed for Cannon the social usefulness of the work he had undertaken for the commission. The following year (1913) when the final report was published, there was additional praise: "The work of this commission is monumental and its effects will be wide-spread," the AMA reported. "It is an excellent illustration of the valuable results which can be secured through practical cooperation between the medical profession and enlightened business men for the saving of life and the prevention of accidents."[16] The National Electric Light Association reprinted and distributed five million copies of the chart and rules for artificial respiration that Cannon had prepared.

At no time did Cannon subsequently refer to the failure of his attempts to restore a fibrillating heart to its normal rhythm. That failure, however, touched the imagination of a young Harvard undergraduate who had witnessed one of the experiments. More than sixty years later Albert S. Hyman, a well-known cardiologist, spoke of the impact of Cannon's experiments with the fibrillating heart on his own work. "While I was a Freshman at Harvard College," he remembered,

> Dr. Cannon became my faculty adviser, and he took me in hand when I made my first visit to the medical school and to his laboratories. On that occasion I saw the pioneer experimental work then being carried out on the isolated turtle heart. I saw the complicated apparatus employed to register the various activities of the cardiac mechanisms, and I became deeply impressed with the physiologic processes involved in the simple beating of the animal heart.
>
> I recall that in one experiment the turtle heart preparation had failed to work, and that considerable discussion—much of it above my understanding—was taking place among the research personnel. The heart had stopped beating for no apparent reason, and all attempts to restore its activity had been unsuccessful. In the accepted language of the laboratory, someone said, "A stopped heart is a dead heart!" As we turned to leave the room, I timidly asked Dr. Cannon, "That heart looked exactly like all the other hearts which were working. What happened, and why can it not be started again?" Dr. Cannon looked at me with a wistful smile, just one of the many components of an unusually expressive face which was beloved by all of his students and associates. "Young man," he said, "that is indeed a very important question. All that I can say at this moment is that I am glad that you asked it; and if the seeds of inquiry have been properly implanted by this incident, perhaps some day you may be able to produce the answers."[17]

Hyman continued to think about the problem. When he entered the Medical School in 1914, he began to work in an experimental laboratory Cannon had set up to investigate electrical problems of the mammalian heart. Almost two decades later Hyman's research in New York led to the development of one of the early artificial pacemakers and a method for restarting a heart that had stopped beating.[18]

✑ ✑ ✑

Cannon's duties at the Medical School as well as his work on behalf of the commission on electric shock were no more onerous than similar obligations he had undertaken in previous years, but as the spring of 1912 progressed he gave increasing evidence of being drained of energy. He found it difficult to renew the research that he and Nice had begun on muscular fatigue earlier in the year; instead he immersed himself in school routine and caring for his family. Conversations with Harvard friends about their familial problems underscored for him how fortunate he was in his marriage. When Edwin Gay of the Harvard Business School confided that his wife had recently suffered a nervous breakdown, Cannon with some relief observed in his diary how different things were in his own home: "She [Mrs. Gay] is overconscientious and finicky about housekeeping—a slave to it. Thank goodness! C[ornelia] isn't!"[19] Gay's somber account, however, made a profound impression on Cannon, and as the spring semester drew to a close, he determined, given Cornelia's pregnancy, not to let the laboratory or the School interfere with his plans to vacation with her and the children at the family farm in Franklin during the summer.

From the time Cannon and the family arrived at the farm in mid-June, he occupied himself with homely matters. The opportunities that he and Cornelia had seen for physical labor when they purchased the farm had by a strange alchemy multiplied. Although they both had spent the better part of two summers restoring the farmhouse and barn, much remained to be done. In characteristic fashion, Cannon enthusiastically undertook a variety of physical tasks. He repaired the roof, shingled the barn, laid down a new porch, cleaned the well, put up new screens, and "wed" the garden. Such was his compulsion for physical labor that when tasks around the farm were completed, he traveled down the road to the home of his friend and neighbor, Robert Yerkes, who had bought a nearby farm on his recommendation a year earlier, to help him plant trees and get his house in order.

The relaxation provided by physical labor was more than offset by a concern that accompanied visits from family members, particularly that of his mother's sister (Aunt Em) who had taken care of him and his sisters during the first terrible months following his mother's death. Cannon, who adored his aunt, became aware during the visit that she had become perceptibly frail and appeared to be failing. Her condition depressed him, and the more he thought about her, the more he began to reflect on his own health, until he finally decided to apply for a new life insurance policy in order to better provide for Cornelia and the children. The decision instead of relieving his mind added to his concerns: during the course of a visit to Boston in mid-July to determine his eligibility for a new policy, a physician for the insurance company discovered that he had a trace of sugar in his urine. Upset by the report, Cannon hurried to his friend Otto Folin for an independent analysis of his urine, only to have the insurance company's findings confirmed. Cannon suspected that his glycosuria was the result of eating a good deal of sugar with his breakfast that morning, but he was concerned that it could be a sign of diabetes. The next morning, after avoiding sugar with his breakfast, he asked Folin to reexamine his urine. This time, to his great relief, Folin found it to be normal. Still, the incident worried him, and before returning to Franklin, he consulted Elliott Joslin, one of Boston's leading young specialists on diabetes, who reassured him that he was not suffering from the disease.

No sooner was this worry dispelled than Cannon faced another that proved even more alarming. On his return to the farm Cornelia began to complain of heart palpitations and almost constant nausea. Cannon decided that it would be wise to remain in Franklin for the impending birth in September rather than return to Boston. As an added precaution, he arranged with a local physician in whom he had great confidence for Cornelia to have the baby in his hospital in Franklin. Then to relieve her of everyday stress, he took over many of her household duties, including the daily care of the children. Actually, he looked forward to the latter task; from the beginning of the summer, the children had lifted and renewed his spirits.

As the August days passed, however, taking care of three small children in the midst of a steady stream of friends and visitors to the farm became trying, and on more than one occasion Cannon was overwhelmed by the requirements of being a surrogate mother. When Cornelia began to have labor pains, he faced the ordeal of taking her to the hospital by horse and carriage over rutted country roads in the middle of the night. The trip proved uneventful, but when they arrived at the hospital, Cornelia's pains ceased. The next morning, after several hours of waiting, they returned to the farm. In the days that followed everything seemed to unravel at once: Cornelia increasingly complained of heart palpitations; the children, generally well-mannered, started to misbehave; even Pegasus, the horse that Cannon had rented for the summer from the Harvard Coop, became ill. Finally, on September 13, after ten more days of waiting, Cornelia with little difficulty gave birth to a girl, who was named Marian.[20]

Cannon was overjoyed. "The family now consists of the same elements as my father's," Cannon elatedly telegraphed his in-laws in St. Paul, "one bad boy and three good girls. If they don't make him considerate of their feelings, no one can." And he continued, "Cornelia has taken Bradford for her own; Ida, Wilma; Bernice, Linda (though *I* like Linda myself!); it's my turn to take Marian."[21] He only regretted that at the beginning of the academic year he had to return to Cambridge with the other children before Cornelia and the baby were released from the hospital.

Cornelia's happiness was equally profound. "I have been reading over Martin's 'The Luxury of Children,' " she wrote Cannon several days after he returned to Cambridge. "It is only additional evidence that we have made no mistakes with our four little luxuries. Aren't they adorable? . . . It seems as if my heart was overflowing with love these days."[22] For Cannon, waiting for Cornelia's return proved difficult. Cornelia did not mind his impatience: "I love to have you miss me," she replied to one of his letters of complaint. "It does seem as if I were some use in the world, if there are people who would rather have me around than not—and when you consider who those people, or rather that person is, the dearest, lovingest, most interesting, wisest, and generally most wonderful person in the world!"[23] The summer could not have ended on a better note.

For a period of eight months Cannon had done little to extend his investigations of the adrenals, but when he returned to the Medical School in mid-September, he was ready to settle down and begin working in the laboratory. Although his work on the effect of adrenalin on muscle fatigue had raised intriguing questions, when he renewed his research that fall he put problems associated with muscle fatigue aside and began instead to work on other problems. Cannon's decision to change course was not the result of any new ideas that required modification of his plans for the investigation. The reason for delaying his studies on muscle fatigue stemmed rather from a change of heart on the part of his assistant, Dr. Nice.

When the fall semester began in 1912, Nice informed Cannon that he wanted to discontinue his physiological research and devote himself for the rest of the year to the study of pathology and bacteriology. The decision stung Cannon; he had expected that his assistant would continue to work with him, and he saw Nice's lack of interest in continuing the research on muscle fatigue as a personal criticism—a sign that he had failed to persuade him of the value of the research. Although he gave Nice permission to do pathology, he nevertheless required that he assist him in completing experiments they had begun.[24] Cannon then reorganized the research program in the laboratory and assigned Charles Gruber, a new graduate student enrolled in the medical sciences program, to work independently on one of the problems that had emerged from his studies with Nice, and he asked Howard Osgood, a first-year medical student, to join him in an investigation of the effect that adrenal secretion might have on bleeding.[25]

The study that Cannon undertook with Osgood differed in an important respect from those he had previously conducted on the adrenals: instead of using cats for his experiments, he chose to work with rabbits in the belief that measurement of the cessation of bleeding would be facilitated by using their ears, with their rich network of blood vessels. At first, the experiments Cannon devised using denervated rabbit ears appeared promising.[26] Later, however, the variability of his findings made it impossible to determine whether adrenalin actually shortened bleeding time in the denervated rabbit's ear after sensory stimulation. On November 20, after several weeks of intensive effort, he discontinued the investigation. "Osgood and I," he gloomily recorded in his diary, "found that sensory stim[ulation] (pain) stopt hem[orrhage] for a few moments, then started it up again—whether blood pressure high or low 'a tragedy of science'. Gave up the quest." It was the first major ackowledged setback he had encountered in his research on the adrenals.

Despite his disappointment with the results of the studies with Osgood, Cannon began a new investigation the next day—this time with Otto Folin on a problem that was peripheral, although important, to his basic research strategy, that of refining methods of assaying the amount of adrenalin in an unknown solution. Several months earlier Folin and his assistant, Willey Denis, had found that a phosphotungstic acid solution they had prepared was extraordinarily sensitive and gave a vivid blue color reaction when used as a reagent for uric acid and phenol derivatives, including adrenalin. They also discovered that adrenalin gave almost exactly three times as much color with phosphotungstic acid as an equal weight of uric acid, in effect providing them with a ratio that made it possible to determine the amount of adrenalin in an unknown solution without having on hand pure adrenalin solutions of known concentration.[27]

Folin and Denis's method for the determination of adrenalin appeared promising to Cannon, and he asked them to join him in double-blind experiments to see whether the method was as accurate as the more complicated bioassay methods then used by physiologists. While Folin and Denis determined the adrenalin content of the adrenal glands of a variety of animals colorimetrically, Cannon independently made similar determinations using physiological bioassay methods. The investigation proceeded smoothly, and after little more than two weeks the cooperating investigators found that the results of the determinations made by both methods were remarkably similar. The work with Folin and Denis, although brief, pleased Cannon not only because it appeared to add a reliable chemical assay test for the presence of adrenalin in the blood but also because it provided the first opportunity he had to collaborate with Folin, whom he greatly admired.[28]

◄§   ◄§   ◄§

As the year drew to a close, Cannon began to look for a new assistant. Although he was happy with the contributions his first-year students had previously made to his investigations, he realized that because of the increasing complexity of his work he needed an assistant with more experience and training who could devote himself full-time to research—one, moreover, who could work independently if he were not available to help. After searching for several weeks, he asked Henry Lyman, who had previously worked in his laboratory on an independent research project, to join him in his research. Lyman, a recent Medical School graduate with a strong interest in biological chemistry, agreed, and Cannon began preparations to induct him into one of the mysteries that had emerged from his previous investigations with Nice.[29]

From the inception of work on the adrenal glands by such pioneers as Oliver and Schäfer in England and Artur Biedl in Vienna, the idea had become firmly fixed that adrenalin raised blood pressure by vasoconstriction.[30] During some of his experiments with Nice, however, Cannon had noted a fall in blood pressure instead of the rise he had expected. He was by no means the first to make observations that suggested that adrenalin, under some conditions, might have a depressor effect on blood pressure. Benjamin Moore and C. O. Purinton at the Yale physiological laboratories more than a decade earlier had reported that when they gave "exceedingly minute doses" of an extract from the adrenal medulla of an ox, it caused a fall of blood pressure in a dog.[31] Other physiologists had contended that adrenalin might even have opposite effects on blood pressure, depending on both the dose and "purity" of adrenalin injected into an experimental animal. Samuel and Clara Meltzer at the Rockefeller Institute had claimed that when a small dose of adrenalin was injected subcutaneously in a rabbit, it induced dilatation of the blood vessels of its ears.[32] Henry Dale at the Wellcome Laboratories in England had demonstrated that after ergotoxine was administered to experimental animals, all doses of adrenalin, whether large or small, dramatically lowered blood pressure.[33]

Cannon found it difficult to accept the notion that sympathetic stimulation could lead to a fall in blood pressure. Was the decrease artifactual, he wondered, or was it a true physiological phenomenon? And what was the import of observations that adrenalin lowered blood pressure for the long-held assumptions that adrenalin would only raise blood pressure?[34] Such questions provided the main impetus for Cannon's research with Lyman; other factors helped to advance the pace of the research as well.

Late in December 1912 Samuel Meltzer told Cannon that he planned to give a paper on the depressor effects of splanchnic stimulation at the next meeting of the American Physiological Society. Meltzer's information upset Cannon: "My territory!" he complained in his diary.[35] Spurred by Meltzer's prospective competition, Cannon on his return from the Christmas meetings of the American Physiological Society began a study with Lyman of the conditions or circumstances that might contribute to the depressor effects of adrenalin. Initially they tried to solve the dilemma of the dual action of adrenalin (pressor and depressor) by producing fever in one of their experimental cats. The experiment failed, but they renewed their efforts: "Tried some experiments on blood pressure this morning," he noted in his diary on January 6, 1913. "Tried to lower it by warming animal to fever temperature, but *das geht leider nicht.*"

In an effort to advance the investigation Cannon put Lyman to work independently—again without positive results. Later when he and Lyman tried once more to determine the factors that led to a rise or to a fall in pressure (often doing only single experiments), they confirmed earlier observations that a depressor effect occurred with small doses of adrenalin and a pressor response with a larger amount. "Lyman and I work all day trying to untangle the puzzle of opposite action of adrenalin," he noted in his diary on January 13. The results, however, continued to be puzzling. Still later, in an effort to study the conditions that changed the depressor action of adrenalin to a pressor one, they pithed the brain and spinal cord of one of their experimental cats, producing a marked drop in blood pressure; when they then administered the same small dose of adrenalin to the animal, they noted a rise in blood pressure. Pithing, they concluded, by lowering blood pressure, transformed the vasodilator action of adrenalin to a vasoconstrictor action.[36] Still, the dilemma remained. "Worked in lab morning writing on adrenalin paper," Cannon noted in his diary on January 25. "Home in afternoon—wrote further on paper until midnight—a very puzzling problem. Do not know how it is coming out." The next day he continued his lament, "Worked til 1 o'clock Monday morning—chased problem into a corner and didn't know what to do with it."

Several days later, after injecting a minute amount of adrenalin into one of their cats, he and Lyman observed that the fall of blood pressure they recorded was accompanied by a swelling of the animal's hind leg.[37] The finding appeared to confirm an observation Henry Dale had previously made that after an injection of ergotoxine in an experimental cat the depressor effect of adrenalin was accompanied by an "increased volume of parts."[38] During the next few days Cannon and Lyman repeated some of Dale's work and found, as he had suggested, that following the administration of ergotoxine in an experimental cat, all doses of adrenalin, large or small, lowered blood pressure, whether or not the central nervous system was intact.[39] Strangely, the confirmation of Dale's observations disturbed Cannon; he found that he could not accept Dale's explanation of the phenomenon—namely, that ergotoxine paralyzed vasoconstrictor nerve endings in the muscle and that the administration of adrenalin revealed the action of the vasodilator endings that had formerly been overwhelmed and thus masked.

Dale's explanation was at variance with Cannon's understanding regarding the structure and functions of the sympathetic nervous system. Cannon thought there was "meagre evidence" that the sympathetic nervous system contained vasodilators; such nerve fibers, he averred, were in the parasympathetic nervous system rather than the sympathetic and did not "harmonize with the known organization of the autonomic system."[40] In place of Dale's explanation, Cannon fashioned a theory that appeared to answer the seemingly opposite effects of adrenalin. Influenced by his work on the gastrointestinal tract, he concluded that vasodilation and vasoconstriction by adrenalin could be attributed to the state of the vascular smooth muscle; that is, adrenalin had a vasoconstrictor effect if the muscle was relaxed and a vasodilator effect if it was constricted.[41]

When Cannon and Lyman published their findings, their paper provoked a sharp argument. Dale immediately undertook new experiments, as he later put it, "to remove any misconception which Cannon and Lyman's paper may have created as to the nature of the action of ergotoxine." In one series of experiments he demonstrated that after an adequate dose of ergotoxine, when the splanchnic nerves were stimulated (even after the adrenals were removed) there was a fall of blood pressure. Further, he was able to prove that ergotoxine did not reverse the motor effects of adrenalin merely by producing a high degree of tone of smooth muscle. In another series of experiments he showed that in the uterus of the virgin ferret sympathetic stimulation or adrenalin increased uterine contraction; and that after ergotoxine (which relaxed the muscle), adrenalin caused a further decrease in tone—a finding opposite to the notion proposed by Cannon.[42] In concluding, Dale sent off several barbs in Cannon's direction. "Instances for a nerve supply of mixed function from one source," he instructed Cannon, "are not wanting in this system, as, for example, the cranial autonomic innervation of the stomach through the vagus." "Nor . . . are we without an independent example of vasodilators of true sympathetic origin," he continued; "the sympathetic supply to the coronary arteries, the inhibitor effect of which is reproduced by adrenine, must, I imagine, be accepted as belonging to the true sympathetic system."[43]

Cannon found it difficult to respond to Dale's arguments and made no reply. Several months later, however, when Roy Gentry Pearce of Western Reserve published a paper on some of the vaso dilator effects of adrenalin in muscle, Cannon ruefully wrote him of his differences with Dale. "My papers previous to this one with Lyman were of the nature of rather sound investments, at least as sound as I could make them. In Lyman's paper I had a fling at speculation. In the short time that the paper has been in the literature, the speculation seems to have received more consideration than any facts I have ever published! I am rather inclined now to return to safe investments."[44] Although he appeared to make light of his disagreement with Dale, he did not abandon his so-called speculations. When Frank Hartman arrived as a teaching fellow in the department of physiology in 1914, Cannon promptly gave him the problem that he and Lyman had studied—that is, the depressor effect of adrenalin on arterial pressure.[45] Dale's criticism, for all its force, had not persuaded Cannon to discard the theory that he was carefully crafting to explain the changes that occurred in the bodily economy in response to fear, pain, and other major emotions.

Cannon received a lift later that spring when Gruber reported the results of the study he had independently undertaken to test the effects of increased arterial blood pressure on contraction of skeletal muscle. Gruber discovered in some of his experiments that the degree of improvement of contraction of fatigued muscle depended on the level of blood pressure at the outset of the experiment; that is, improvement was greater when blood pressure was raised even slightly from a low level than if it was raised markedly from a high level. Later, when he undertook to see if a decrease in blood pressure might have opposite effects on fatigued muscle, he found that such pressure had to decrease below a critical level (90–100 mm of mercury) before there would be a manifest lessening of the strength of muscular contraction.[46]

Gruber's experimental findings on the role of blood pressure and continued muscular contraction supplied some of the additional evidence Cannon was looking for to buttress his concept of how the adrenals served the functioning of skeletal muscle under stress. Seeking additional information, he encouraged Gruber in the fall of 1913 to undertake another study—this time to determine whether adrenal secretion itself, apart from its influence on blood pressure, directly promoted muscular efficiency as well. Again Gruber did not disappoint him. Using techniques that E. G. Martin had recently developed, Gruber measured the strength of electrical current necessary to stimulate the muscle. Such stimuli, he soon found, had to be increased several-fold when the muscle he was using was fatigued—that is, as the performance of the muscle diminished, the threshold stimulus (the least stimulus capable of causing the muscle to contract) increased. Moreover, the administration of adrenalin restored the threshold of fatigued muscle to normal.[47] In short, the results of Gruber's experiments were another demonstration of the remarkable effects of adrenalin on fatigued muscle and by extrapolation on muscular activities during pain and emotional stress.

One question remained to be answered before the theory Cannon was constructing could stand on its own—namely, the necessity of determining how the body dealt with a blood loss that might occur during a struggle for survival. In October 1913, this time with the assistance of Walter R. Mendenhall who had joined the department as a teaching fellow, Cannon began a reexamination of the problem that had given him and Howard Osgood such a difficult time the previous year.[48] In the interim months he had come to see that in order to solve the problem a different approach was required: rather than study the effect of adrenalin on bleeding time, as he and Osgood had done, he would have to examine the physiological process of blood clotting.[49]

Cannon, along with other physiologists, knew in general that blood began to change its character from a fluid to a jelly-like consistency within minutes after its escape from blood vessels. No one, however, had developed a way of accurately measuring the rate of clot formation. At the start the experiments did not go well, and as failure followed failure, Cannon became increasingly restive and was afflicted with insomnia. It was perhaps the most important thing that happened during the study: during periods of sleep-

T. R. Elliott

H. H. Dale

G. N. Stewart

J. N. Rogoff

Contenders in the scientific arena.

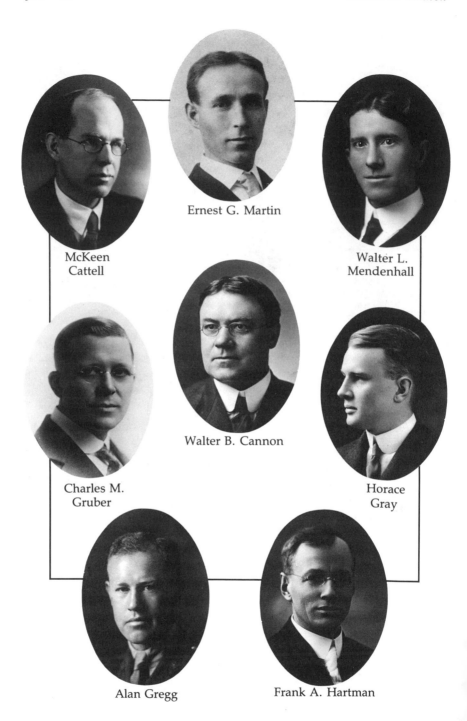

Ernest G. Martin

McKeen
Cattell

Walter L.
Mendenhall

Walter B. Cannon

Charles M.
Gruber

Horace
Gray

Alan Gregg

Frank A. Hartman

Cannon and his collaborators, 1914–1916.

lessness his ruminations provided new insights into the problem that led to the construction of an apparatus to register graphically the coagulation of blood.[50] The experience was not unique; such revelations had occurred before. Later Cannon wrote thoughtfully about the service of "unconscious processes" and "hunches" in his research. "In typical cases," he explained, "a hunch appears after long study and springs into consciousness at a time when the investigator is not working on his problem. It arises from a wide knowledge of facts, but it is essentially a leap of the imagination, for it reaches forth into the range of possibilities. It results from a spontaneous process of creative thought."[51] In this case Cannon's leap of the imagination opened a locked door.

Shortly thereafter, when he and Mendenhall began a series of experiments testing the effect of stimulating the splanchnic nerve in a cat anesthetized with urethane, they found that through use of the new device they could chart with some precision the clotting of the blood. "Thrilling day at the laboratory," Cannon noted in his diary after this first trial. "Mendenhall and I get pretty clear evidence that stimulation of splanchnic nerves hastens coagulation of the blood." The next day there was a half success: "Let cat be excited for three minutes before etherizing—first two samples [immediately after etherizing] coagulated so rapidly no possibility of recording them."[52] When the two investigators varied the conditions of the experiment and tried to measure the effect of stimulating the splanchnics with and without the adrenal glands, they were able to corroborate their early findings. In less than a month Cannon and Mendenhall had gathered enough data to substantiate the notion that rapid clotting of blood was due in part to discharges from the adrenal glands.[53] Cannon was so encouraged by these results that when Horace Gray, one of his fourth-year students, asked him for a research project, he invited Gray to join him in a study of whether injections of adrenalin accelerated or retarded coagulation of blood. At the same time he began another investigation with Mendenhall to see if pain or emotional stress also played a role in speeding up blood clotting.[54]

Working with Gray during the mornings and with Mendenhall in the afternoons, Cannon soon made a number of observations on the process of coagulation that clarified previously published discordant accounts regarding the accelerated clotting of blood by adrenalin. In one series of experiments conducted with Gray Cannon discovered that small doses of adrenalin injected' slowly into decerebrate cats produced a very rapid clotting of blood. Later, however, when he gave such cats a large dose of adrenalin, there was a contrary effect. Nor were these the only apparently contradictory results. In another experiment, when Cannon removed the liver and intestines of his decerebrate cats before injecting them with a small dose of adrenalin, he discovered that the previously potent small dose of adrenalin failed to shorten the clotting time. Also, when he added adrenalin directly to blood in a test tube, it did not hasten coagulation. The new phenomena, however, did not perplex him for long; he soon surmised that adrenalin did not produce its remarkable effects directly on the blood but rather accelerated the clotting process by stimulating the liver or intestines to discharge some unknown factors that were important to the process of coagulation.[55] The experiments that Cannon prepared with Mendenhall to test the impact of pain and emotional excitement on blood clotting proved equally fruitful. In short order they found that if splanchnic nerves or an afferent nerve like the sciatic or crural were stimulated in a decerebrate cat, or if the cat was roused to anger or fear, there was a marked hastening of coagulation.[56]

Generally, whenever Cannon finished an investigation he immediately prepared the results for publication. This time, however, he put the preparation of papers with Mendenhall and Gray temporarily aside and began instead to catalogue the important questions that he felt had animated and guided his research on the adrenals. In the process he once again demonstrated his belief that the body was organized for a particularly useful purpose. Why, he began, should a function as important to the body as digestion be stopped by emotional distress? Why should the blood under pain or other stress be shifted from the abdominal organs to the heart, brain, lungs, central nervous system, and skeletal muscles? What, he asked, was the reason for the liberation of sugar from the liver and into the blood? Was there any meaning in the action of adrenalin in refreshing tired muscles? Were there any circumstances in which more rapid clotting of the blood could be especially valuable to the organism? And perhaps most important, why were these effects of the nature of reflexes and not of voluntary action?

Although the theory that Cannon fashioned to answer these questions was first articulated during his research with de la Paz on the emotional production of adrenalin, it had its roots in his reading of biological and psychological literature relating to the emotions. Such reading had started during his undergraduate years at Harvard College when George H. Parker in zoology introduced him to Darwin's work on the expression of the emotions in animals and men. His interest from that time in the literature of the emotions never flagged; it continued to be stimulated by some of his psychologist friends like Robert Yerkes and E. B. Holt, who often brought new books on the subject to his attention. Of particular relevance was William McDougall's widely acclaimed work *An Introduction to Social Psychology.*[57]

It was McDougall who supplied the concept that Cannon adopted to answer the questions he had raised. McDougall maintained that a singular emotional excitement such as fear determined an instinct to flee, whereas an emotion of anger led to an instinct to fight or attack. Both reactions, he argued, were necessary for the survival of almost all species of animals.[58] McDougall's marriage of instincts and emotions was the unitary key Cannon had sought. Each of the papers that had come from his laboratory, he found, substantiated and clarified the effect of pain and emotional stress on increased adrenal secretion and the effect of such secretion on the bodily economy as well. Although the extent to which the slight constant secretion of the adrenals served the body was still not well understood, there was no doubt in Cannon's mind of the purpose and utility in bodily function of large amounts of adrenalin. "These changes in the body," he wrote in the review paper he sent to the *American Journal of Physiology* late in 1913,

are, each one of them, *directly serviceable in making the organism more efficient in the struggle which fear or rage or pain may involve;* for fear and rage are organic preparations for action, and pain is the most powerful known stimulus to supreme exertion. The organism which with the aid of increased adrenal secretion can best muster its energies, can best call forth sugar to supply the laboring muscles, can best lessen fatigue, and can best send blood to the parts essential in the run or the fight for life, is most likely to survive. Such, according to the view here propounded, is the function of the adrenal medulla at times of great emergency.[59]

When Cannon's research on gastrointestinal motility appeared, it was promptly introduced into physiology textbooks. The reception accorded the emergency theory, however, was markedly different: popular textbooks of physiology, both in the United States and abroad, with the notable exception of George N. Stewart's *Manual of Physiology*, included little or nothing about Cannon's theory. Stewart, who had also been engaged in research on the adrenals, found Cannon's theory provocative and attractive and summarized it for the revised seventh edition of his manual which appeared in August of 1914. "So far as our present data go," he wrote,

> the function of the adrenal bodies—at least that part of their function which is concerned with the liberation of adrenalin—is not to be considered a continuous, but an emergency function (Cannon), exerted at times of physical or emotional stress. It has been pointed out, and with much plausibility, that a rapid discharge of such large quantities of adrenalin as could really produce distinct physiological effects would be advantageous in such emergencies. The increased mobilization of sugar, for example, the increased action of the heart muscle, and the shortened clotting time of the blood occasioned by the outpouring of adrenalin in response to the accompanying excitement of fear or rage or pain might be helpful in a struggle associated with trauma. And as evolution has been so closely connected with physical struggle, an adaptive mechanism of this sort may have been developed.[60]

Stewart's appraisal contained no hint of disagreement with Cannon's theory, but two years later Stewart and his assistant, Julius M. Rogoff, in a complete turnabout mounted the first of several bitter attacks against the emergency function of the adrenal medulla.

18 Beyond the Boundaries of Physiological Inquiry

D URING THE WINTER of 1913–1914 Cannon, prompted by a confrontation with antivivisectionists in Boston, gave a series of lectures on the effect of the emotions on bodily changes in an effort to inform the public of the importance and utility of animal experimentation. Although it is difficult to gauge the impact of these lectures on public attitudes toward animal experimentation, they excited wide interest and discussion.

When the Harvard Medical School announced early in January that Cannon would deliver a free public lecture on the effect of fear and rage on the body, more than two hundred people braved a heavy rainstorm to hear him. The following day he was amused and startled to see that several newspapers carried not only accounts of the lecture but editorials as well. *The Boston Herald* in a light-hearted vein saw his findings as the answer to a grave economic problem: "Given the amount of tempers lost during a year," its editor declared, "if each man could distill and save at least one ounce of sugar, at such times enough sugar would be produced to bring the sugar trust to its knees."[1] In New York, in response to a newspaper report that Cannon's investigations suggested that "man was sweetest when he was angry," one reader, believing that such findings reversed the natural order of things, wrote Cannon an irate letter charging him with perverting the human soul. "I would not take millions," his correspondent wrote, "and hold the beliefs you do . . . Remember, you will be asked the question and have to answer it too, Which way did you help the soul to go? Upwards or downwards?"[2] Editors and reporters found that Cannon's lecture made good copy, and a spate of stories, editorials, and cartoons poking fun at Harvard savants and science continued to appear in newspapers and magazines throughout the country. Cannon took the jibes in good humor; indeed, he was pleased that his lecture had aroused such wide public interest in his work.

A lecture he gave to a professional group, however, got a reception that troubled him. When at the end of 1913 he addressed the American Psychological Association at their annual meeting, he focused his discussion almost exclusively on the physiological aspects of his research and said little about its import for psychology except to mention his indebtedness to McDougall.[3] Some members of the audience were disappointed with his brief treatment of psychology, especially with the lack of any discussion of William James's theory of the emotions. Several weeks later, when Cannon began to prepare an expanded version of his lecture for the *American Journal of Psychology*, he realized that he could no longer avoid discussing James's work. Once again his research put him directly at odds with his former teacher.

From its initial appearance in the magazine *Mind* in 1884, James's theory created a stir in psychological and physiological circles in both Europe and America.[4] James, who loved paradox and to stand things on their heads, sharply attacked the conception that emotional display was a consequence of emotional consciousness. In its place, he suggested that bodily manifestations of emotions had to be interposed between the perception of an exciting fact and the occurrence of the mental state of emotion. "We feel sorry," he explained, "because we cry, angry because we strike, afraid because we tremble, and not that we cry, strike or tremble because we are sorry, angry or fearful as the case may be." To cap his analysis, James maintained that the interposition of the bodily states he had described was caused by afferent nervous impulses that arose in the viscera. James's theory was purely speculative and introspective—a quality he did not try to hide. At the time he published his paper on the emotions he had little knowledge of the functioning of the autonomic nervous system, nor had he ever submitted his theory to an experimental test.[5]

Cannon was no stranger to James's theory or to the controversial literature that had grown up around it. As an undergraduate in James's course in philosophy, he had written a hundred-page essay on the emotions, but it was largely a description of the arguments advanced by both the critics and defenders of James's theory.[6] At no time had Cannon ventured a position of his own. Now he could no longer avoid taking a stand. The critique he published was brief and articulated in a moderate manner. "If various strong emotions," he wrote,

> can thus be expressed in the diffused activities of a single division of the autonomic . . . it would appear that the bodily conditions which have been assumed, by some psychologists, to distinguish emotions from one another must be sought for elsewhere than in the viscera. We do not "feel sorry because we cry," as James contended, but we cry because, when we are sorry or overjoyed or violently angry or full of tender affection—when any of these diverse emotional states is present—there are nervous discharges by sympathetic channels to various viscera, including the lachrymal glands. And in terror and rage and intense elation, for example, the responses in the viscera seem too uniform to offer a satisfactory means of distinguishing states which in man, at least, are subjectively very different. For this reason I am inclined to urge that the visceral changes merely contribute to an emotional complex more or less indefinite, but still pertinent, feelings of disturbance, in organs of which we are not usually conscious.[7]

In conclusion, Cannon argued that there were differences in emotional states, that these differences were central rather than peripheral in origin, and that their expression occurred instantly and spontaneously.

Although secure in the position he had taken, Cannon nevertheless felt uneasy dealing with psychological problems. While preparing his lecture for publication he spent a number of evenings with his friends in the psychology department discussing his projected opposition to James.[8] Later when his paper was published, he sent copies to them hoping for something more than a polite expression of interest in what he was doing. Little survives of this correspondence save the following reply from Hugo Münsterberg:

> Cambridge, Massachusetts
> June 2, 1914
>
> Dear Dr. Cannon:
> I must tell you how greatly interested I am in your recent researches and how much I appreciate especially your brilliant dash into psychology. I hope to include some of your results in a little textbook of psychology of which I am still reading the proofs.

To be sure, I have one objection to your statement in the American Journal: namely, it is too beautiful. That is, it looks too complete . . . Yet I am convinced that we are only at the beginning of this movement and that entirely different groups of chemical influences will be discovered in time. States like depression or enthusiasm and many others have so evidently chemical conditions of their own that we decidedly need some more ductless glands. But today I do not want to discuss: I only want to thank you for sending me your recent papers.

Although Cannon was gratified by Münsterberg's positive attitude, he continued to seek more substantive criticism from psychologists. Some time later, when he remembered that James McKeen Cattell at a meeting of the American Philosophical Society a few years earlier had raised pertinent questions about his research with de la Paz, he wrote Cattell to ask if he would be willing to discuss the psychological aspects of his work on the adrenals. "I have not been able to get much criticism from the Harvard psychologists that has led me to new points of view," he explained. "If you have published anything that bears upon our interpretation of the results we have been securing, I should be glad indeed to have it."[9]

In retrospect, Cannon's persistent solicitation of advice on the psychological aspects of his work on the adrenals seems less a search for criticism per se than a sign of his awareness that his investigations had brought him to the borderland of another experimental discipline in which he had little expertise. He saw that if he were to develop his research meaningfully, he would have to create bridges between physiology and endocrinology and forge ties with psychology as well. As a step in that direction, he began to plan both a book and an investigation of other endocrine glands. The book, he explained to Cattell, would be written for a popular audience and would contain an account of his experiments on the adrenals as well as an analysis of the psychological and philosophical implications of emotional excitement on human behavior.[10] To carry his literary plans forward, Cannon turned to James again—this time, ironically, for inspiration in helping him to synthesize and explain some of his physiological data.

In one of his later essays, "The Energies of Men," James had suggested that every person has a reservoir of physical and mental powers which could be called upon in times of stress.[11] Cannon found the idea provocative and at once took steps to exploit its similarities to some of his own experimental observations. "I am sending you some reprints which may amuse you," he wrote his friend Norman Hapgood early in May 1914. "You will find in the paper on 'The Emergency Function of the Adrenal Medulla' physiological support for the views Professor James expressed in his interesting essay on 'The Energies of Men.' I have wished so many times these past three years that I could have had a chance of talking over these matters with him."[12]

Cannon used James's essay as a model for one of his chapters. The psychological cases that James had gathered to illustrate his ideas fascinated him, and Cannon began a systematic search of historical, religious, and anthropological sources for additional examples of extraordinary feats of strength and greatly increased endurance of men under stress of emotional excitement. He was so avid in this hunt for psychological illustrations to supplement the materials he had gathered that he called on Frank Proctor, one of his neighbors in New Hampshire who had served for a time with General Custer, for a first-hand account of the psychological methods used by both the Army and Indians in preparation for combat on the Great Plains.[13]

✎ꜱ ✎ꜱ ✎ꜱ

Stimulated by the implications of his research, Cannon began to seek opportunities to present some of the psychological and philosophical material he had gathered to a public audience. Early in August, when he met L. J. Henderson by chance in Cambridge, he used the occasion to explore the possibility of giving lectures based on his research on the adrenals for the Lowell Institute. It was a fortuitous meeting; Henderson, who was a member of the Lowell family by marriage and greatly admired Cannon, promptly put his name forward as a prospective lecturer to the trustees of the Lowell Institute.[14] Cannon also received an invitation from the New York Academy of Medicine to give its prestigious Carpenter Lecture. Although the invitation did not allow much time for preparation, he promptly accepted it—less for the honor involved than for the opportunity it gave him to explore the applications of his research toward the solution of social problems, particularly in relation to the war that had erupted several weeks earlier in Europe.[15] From its inception the irrationality and destructiveness of the war horrified Cannon; as the carnage continued, he increasingly felt compelled to speak out against those who postulated a biological imperative that made war inevitable.

Once again, one of William James's essays helped to guide his thoughts. Shortly before he died, James had also wrestled with the problem of war. Unlike many of those who argued against it, James perceived that war despite its monstrosities possessed certain virtues that gave it enormous power; that war, in addition to disciplining and uniting society, energized it with extraordinary idealism and vitality. He contended that, in order to abolish war, it was necessary for man to invent an activity that had an equal power to evoke the discipline and ethos provided by war. James's solution was to conscript youth to fight against the inequalities in society fostered by nature as well as by man. Such a struggle, he maintained, would provide new outlets for heroic energy and endow society with healthier sympathies and ideals.[16] Cannon accepted and followed James's thesis in all particulars except his solution; in its place he provided a physiological alternative based on principles that were grounded in some of his recent research.

In 1913, following the annual Harvard-Yale game, Cannon found on examination that most of the Harvard football players who had participated in the contest had developed glycosuria. Such changes, he concluded, related to the powerful muscular efforts that the game demanded and were much like the changes required by animals in their struggle for existence. Somewhat surprisingly, he also discovered that a number of Harvard players who did not actually participate in the game had developed glycosuria as well. This increase in sugar he ascribed to the emotional excitement that stemmed from the singing and cheering that accompanied the game: in short, the setting of a sports contest itself created an environment for an acme of excitement.[17] This observation convinced Cannon that international athletic contests such as the Olympic Games could provide a physiological equivalent for war by diverting fighting instincts and emotions into channels where they could have a more satisfactory expression. It would "do for our young men," he later wrote in summary, "much that is now maintained as peculiar to the values of military discipline. They have further to commend them the high standards of honor and fairness of sports, its unfailing revelation of excellence without distinction of class, wealth, race, or color; the ease with which it becomes an expression of patriotism; the respect which victory and pluckily borne defeat inspire in competitors and spectators alike; the extension of acquaintance which follows from friendly and magnanimous rivalry among strong men."[18]

Still, no sooner did Cannon decide to address the members of the New York Academy on a physiological equivalent of war than he began to have doubts about the wisdom of his choice of topic. The more he thought about it, the more his misgivings grew. Even the arrival of a formal invitation to give the Lowell Lectures later that fall and winter instead of elating him served to increase his apprehension. Only his wife's insistence that the subject was too important to set aside kept him to the mark. "Finish 'Physiological Equivalent of War,' " he noted in his diary a few days before he was scheduled to give the Carpenter Lecture. "Badly rushed and now very doubtful whether it is good sense. At best a hazardous experiment."[19]

Notwithstanding Cannon's uncertainties and apprehensions, the lecture proved a success. The topic was so timely that not only did the daily press applaud the lecture but also the editors of the *Journal of the American Medical Association* printed excerpts from the lecture in a subsequent issue.[20] At least one member of the audience, however, responded to Cannon's argument with some skepticism. "I heard Professor Cannon lecture last night, going partly on your account," Cattell wrote his son McKeen, then beginning a doctoral program in physiology at Harvard. "His subject was a physiological substitute for war—which is international sports and I suppose motorcycle races—to encourage the secretion of the adrenal glands!"[21] Despite his wry remarks, Cattell had great respect for Cannon's research; several months earlier he had recommended that his son go to Harvard so that he might have an opportunity to work with Cannon.

Although Cannon was heartened by the reception given the Carpenter Lecture, he hardly had a chance to enjoy its success. Originally he had anticipated devoting most of his time during the fall to completing his book and preparing his Lowell Lectures. Instead heavy demands were made on his time by the unanticipated promising results of an investigation he had begun earlier in the spring. In the circumstances he rearranged his priorities and devised experiments to exploit the breakthrough. Fortunately, neither the book nor the Lowell Lectures suffered because of his focus on this research. Cannon completed the book in good time, and the Lowell Lectures elicited great interest not only at Harvard but in the Boston community as well. After their presentation the *Boston Transcript* printed detailed reviews and analyses of each of the lectures.[22] Perhaps the one that attracted the most favorable comment, to Cannon's surprise, was the lecture about which he continued to have the most doubts—that dealing with his proposed physiological equivalent of war. But as time passed he remembered little of the praise the lectures received. More than a decade later, when Theodore Lyman of the Jefferson Physical Laboratory invited him to give a talk to the Thursday Evening Club on the influence of strong emotions, Cannon reminisced: "I gave some Lowell Lectures on that years ago. They were attended by persons who were cold or who wanted a good chance to have a nap and I doubt whether there were any members of the Thursday Evening Club among them."[23]

When *Bodily Changes in Pain, Hunger, Fear and Rage* appeared during the spring of 1915, it received many favorable reviews, and friends and acquaintances sent congratulatory letters.[24] Walter Alvarez, a young San Francisco physician who two years earlier had worked in Cannon's laboratory on problems of digestion, was especially interested in the chapters on the psychological and philosophical aspects of the research, and he sent Cannon several additional literary and clinical examples of the effect of the emotions on the body.[25] Joseph Jastrow, a professor of psychology at the University of Wisconsin and an editor of *Dial* magazine, was unstinting in his praise: "I know of nothing in recent years," he wrote him, "that has more definitely illuminated one aspect of the emotional life than your admirable book."[26] Others, including many of the newspapers, focused their praise on his chapter on the use of international athletics as a substitute for war. Only his friend Robert Yerkes dissented from that view. Cannon was almost grateful when he received Yerkes's letter. "As I told you last fall," Cannon replied,

> I felt at times dubious about the last chapter, and at other times the pertinence of it seemed quite obvious. Cornelia rather insisted on

the latter view. So it's in, and perhaps in time it may strike some fanatic as it occasionally struck me, and he may do something with it. I thought I had saved myself from being laughed out of safe and sane society by insisting that what I was dealing with was the exercise of the physiological arrangement for struggle. Of course the problem confronting civilization is an immense one, with multitudes of aspects, but there is among them this inherited provision for delivering a punch with intense feeling, and certainly in the past that has underlain the fighting that has developed power in us. By restricting my vision to the physiological mechanism I felt safe, but I suppose I also did a foolish thing. At any rate I wish you would point out sometime your objections. You say merely that you were "disappointed" in the chapter.[27]

Commentary on the book was so extensive that within a relatively brief period of time the word *adrenalin* slipped into the mainstream of everyday speech as a metaphor for energy. Some reporters, seeking to elaborate on the implications of the power of adrenalin for their readers, claimed to Cannon's distress that adrenalin was a substitute for sleep.[28] Later that year, a mystery writer named Arthur Reeve bestowed a unique accolade on Cannon by arming his scientific detective, Craig Kennedy, with the techniques that Cannon and de la Paz had used in studying the emotional production of adrenalin in order to solve the disappearance of a madcap heiress:

That night, in the laboratory, Kennedy took the handkerchief, and with the blood on it made a most peculiar test before a strange-looking little instrument.

It seemed to consist of a little cylinder of glass immersed in water kept at the temperature of the body. Between two minute wire pincers, or serres, in the cylinder was a very small piece of some tissue. To the lower serre was attached a thread. The upper one was attached to a sort of lever ending in a pen that moved over a ruled card.

"Every emotion," remarked Kennedy, as he watched the movement of the pen in fine, zigzag lines over the card, "produces its physiological effect. I suppose you have heard of the recent studies of Doctor Walter Cannon, of Harvard, on the group of remarkable alterations in bodily economy under emotion? But one cannot see such evidences of emotion if he is not present at the time. How can we reconstruct them?" He paused a moment, then resumed: "There are organs hidden deep in the body which do not reveal so easily the emotions. But the effect often outlasts the actual emotion. There are special methods by which one can study the feelings. That is what I have been doing here."

"But how can you?" I queried.

"There is what is called the sympathetic nervous system," he explained. "Above the kidney there are also glands, called the suprarenal, which excrete a substance known as adrenin. In extraordinarily small amounts adrenin affects this sympathetic system. In emotions of various kinds, a reflex action is sent to the suprarenal glands which causes a pouring into the blood of adrenin.

"On the handkerchief of Gloria Brackett I obtained plenty of comparatively fresh blood. Here, in this machine, I have between these two pincers a minute segment of rabbit intestine."

He withdrew the solution from the cylinder with a pipette, then introduced some more of the dissolved blood from the handkerchief. The first effect was a strong contraction of the rabbit intestine, then, in a minute or so, the contractions became fairly even with the baseline on the card.

"Such tissue," he remarked, "is noticeably affected by even one part in over a million of adrenin. See—here, by the writing lever, the rhythmical contractions are recorded. Such a strip of tissue will live for hours, will contract and relax beautifully with a regular rhythm which, as you see, can be graphically recorded. This is my adrenin test."

Carefully he withdrew the ruled paper with its tracings.

"It's a very simple test after all," he said, laying beside this tracing another, which he had made previously. "There you see the difference between what I may call 'quiet blood' and 'excited blood'."

I looked at the two sets of tracings. They were markedly different.

"What do they show to an expert?" I asked, perplexed.

"Fear," he answered laconically. "Gloria did not elope. She was forced to go!"

Cannon was so amused by the imaginative rendering of his work in a detective story that he bound Reeve's story up in his scrapbook.[29]

The book and the Lowell Lectures capped a year of achievement for Cannon. They allowed him not only to continue instructing the public on the value and importance of animal experimentation but also to explain in lay terms the meaning of his research, thus enabling him to fulfill a responsibility he felt that as a scientist he had to the public. Best of all, there was the research itself: at the beginning of 1914 he had presented a suggestive theory of the functioning of the body under stress; by the year's end experiments he had devised to extend his research promised even more important results.

⋖§ ⋖§ ⋖§

One of the hallmarks of Cannon's research was that frequently during the course of an investigation he would look for ways of applying his experimental findings to the solution of clinical problems. In the spring of 1913, while still engaged in his investigation of the effect of the emotions on bodily changes, Cannon began to think of extending his research to the study of diseases that were often reported as having an emotional origin—in particular, diseases of the thyroid. It was not unreasonable for him to assume that the functions of the sympathetic nervous system and those of the thyroid gland might be closely related. In many ways the signs and symptoms of hyperthyroidism—high heart rate, cardiac palpitations, emotional hyperactivity, increased metabolism, and weight loss—are similar to those seen in heightened sympathetic activity. In fact, in the 1860s a number of distinguished physicians had claimed that exophthalmic goiter was due to disturbed action of sympathetic nerves.[30] Although this view was later supplanted by the tenet that hyperthyroidism was a primary disorder of the thyroid,[31] when some physiologists during the first decade of the twentieth century announced that they had found evidence suggesting the adrenal medulla exerted a stimulating influence on the thyroid, physicians once again began to regard the symptoms of hyperthyroidism as an expression of an increase of activity of the sympathetic nerves.[32]

Although Cannon was excited by the implications of these reports, he nonetheless felt he needed more direct proof before he could accept their conclusions and began to search for a method that might help him to assess and correlate the functions of both the sympathetic nerves and the thyroid. Later he would write that he was guided in this search by a conclusion he had come to during his experiments on the adrenals—namely, that repeated emotional experiences might lower a naturally high neurone threshold that would in time result in frequent stimulation of parts that were ordinarily only occasionally roused to special activity.[33] To achieve the frequent stimulation he felt was necessary to test the effect of the sympathetic nerves on the thyroid, he decided to suture the phrenic nerve to the cervical sympathetic ganglion. It was an ingenious idea: ordinarily, with each inspiration of breath there is a burst of activity from the phrenic nerve to the diaphragm causing diaphragmatic contraction. Cannon reasoned that, if he cut the phrenic nerve on one side and joined it to the sympathetic fibers to the thyroid gland, a stimulation of the gland would occur with each inspiration.

The idea left Cannon with a major problem, however: he had no experience in suturing nerves. But once again, he was served by good fortune. A year earlier Harvey Cushing, then perhaps the leading neurosurgeon in the United States, became chief of surgery at the Brigham Hospital. He and Cannon had long known and admired each other. Late in March, when Cannon suggested to Cushing that they cooperate in cross-suturing the phrenic nerve with nerves of glands of internal secretion, Cushing promptly agreed. During the course of an afternoon he taught Cannon how to unite the phrenic nerve with the vagus and splanchnic nerves.[34] Nonetheless, Cannon put his projected investigation of the thyroid on hold. A year later, when he completed his final experiments on the adrenals, Cannon, with the help of Carl Binger, one of his fourth-year students, began his long-deferred investigation of the thyroid gland.[35]

The investigation had hardly started when the routine of the Cannon household was interrupted by illness, first chickenpox and then measles. For the next two weeks Cannon spent most of his time with his wife and children. The delay in the investigation left him conscience-stricken because he felt he had let Binger down.[36] In May 1914, when he returned to the laboratory to make up what he believed were his delinquencies, he began a daily operating routine to teach Binger how to suture nerves. By the end of the month he and Binger had become so adept at operating on nerves that they were able to unite the phrenic nerve with the cervical sympathetic nerves in six cats.[37] They then waited to see whether the nerves would successfully regenerate and become functional.

The cats passed the summer quietly. However, one evening near the end of September Frank Foley, the laboratory diener, telephoned Cannon to inform him that one of the cats, although it ate ravenously, had lost a considerable amount of weight. Cannon confirmed Foley's observations and instructed Foley to watch the cat carefully until he returned from the lecture he was scheduled to give at the New York Academy of Medicine. Several days later when he returned from New York and reexamined the experimental cats, Cannon expressed his excitement. "Took wts. and heart rates on all cats operated last spring," he noted in his diary, "all *cerv. symp.* phrenic cats have high heart rates—[Cat] 37 has 240–288! Looks more like hyperthyroidism."[38]

Two days later on October 5 Cannon asked Reginald Fitz, another of his fellows, to investigate the basal metabolism of the cats, and simultaneously he began a survey of the literature on exophthalmic goiter. Promising signs continued to appear in his experimental cats. On October 14, for example, he found that the pupil in one cat enlarged rhythmically each time it took a breath, suggesting that it had hyperactive pupillary nerves. Several days later he noticed that hair fell from the sides of the neck of another cat—a sign that sometimes appeared in human cases of exophthalmic goiter.[39] Although still not completely sure, he hinted to Reid Hunt, who had previously studied the relation of iodine to the physiological activity of thyroid preparations, that there was every indication he had produced exophthalmic goiter experimentally.[40] At the end of October, when Fitz submitted the results of his investigation, Cannon's caution evaporated. In addition to finding a marked difference in the basal metabolism of the experimental cats compared with that of normal cats, Fitz reported a number of other unusual signs. In one animal the pupil protruded on its operated side, dilated with every breath taken, and contracted with every expiration. Also, at autopsy the adrenal glands of this cat were three times the average weight of those of a normal cat. Later when Cannon catalogued the various signs that Fitz had reported, he noted with great satisfaction that they were in the main characteristic of exophthalmic goiter as seen in man.[41]

Convinced that the techniques he had employed could be profitably used to study other endocrine diseases, Cannon began to plan an investigation to produce diabetes experimentally. He hoped that by joining the phrenic nerve to the splanchnic nerves innervating the pancreas, he might by continuous stimulation of the splanchnics exhaust the Isles of Langerhans of insulin, creating a deficiency that would in time lead to a diabetes. The promise of Cannon's idea was such that when he asked John Homans, one of Harvey Cushing's talented assistants, to join him in an investigation, Homans promptly accepted.[42]

Cannon began to tell friends about the progress and the implications of his investigation of the thyroid. "Somewhat to my surprise," he wrote William Keen early in November, "some experiments which I started last spring seem to be turning out in a very remarkable way and if present promises are fulfilled, I am confronted with 15 or 20 years of work of very great interest and I believe of very great importance. Certainly this new realm of investigation now suddenly opened seems likely to bring results of greater value than any I have ever accomplished hitherto."[43] Several days later, intrigued by Cannon's report that overaction of the thyroid was due to stimulation of the cervical sympathetic nerves, Cushing removed the right cervical sympathetic ganglia in one of his patients with exophthalmic goiter. Although nothing is known of the outcome of this operation,[44] Cushing continued to be enthusiastic about the implications of Cannon's research. Little more than a year later, when Cannon presented a review of his latest thyroid research at the Brigham Hospital, Cushing rose to praise him. "Dr. Cannon," he told the audience, "in this very clear and interesting exposition of a small part of his work, has opened up a new field which may serve to determine the interrelations of the whole system of internal glands. We now begin to understand through the study of the neurogenic supply of the thyroid gland that fright may really be an etiological factor in the development of exophthalmic goitre, as clinicians have often supposed."[45]

Despite the promise of the results of his experiments with Binger and Fitz, Cannon realized that he was far from understanding how the thyroid functioned or the nature of its relationship to other endocrine glands. He was in fact in much the same position as others who were then investigating the thyroid. Although physiologists had long been able to interpret the functions of such organs as the salivary glands and kidneys by direct examination of their external secretions (saliva and urine), understanding the secretory activities of ductless glands was much more difficult because no chemical means or bioassay tests had yet been devised to measure the secretions of such glands.

﴾﴿ ﴾﴿ ﴾﴿

Early in 1915, with the help of McKeen Cattell,[46] Cannon attempted to develop a technique for estimating the secretory activity of the thyroid. The first hint that such a method might be devised came from a paper Cannon read that had originally appeared in England a generation earlier. In 1885 William Bayliss and John Bradford, during an experimental investigation of the functioning of the salivary glands in dogs and cats, discovered that when they connected the surface of the gland to the hilum through a galvanometer a change in electrical activity occurred when secretory activity was enhanced. They also found that when they stimulated the sympathetic fibers to the gland, increased secretion was accompanied by alteration in the electrical current. They further discovered that when they cut off the blood supply to the gland, secretions as well as electrical changes continued. They inferred as a result that the electrical activity was not related to vasomotor changes but to metabolic changes in the gland relating to secretion.[47]

As a preliminary step in his own investigation, Cannon moved to reexamine Bayliss and Bradford's findings. It is clear that he had only modest hopes for such an exercise: "Obviously," he wrote, "an electrical change cannot yield information as to the nature of the materials elaborated in the several structures, it cannot determine the course which the products of secretion actually take in passing away from their region of origin, indeed it might leave somewhat uncertain whether secretion or preparation for secretion were the process occurring in a gland at any given period of disturbed potential. Nevertheless the method, by revealing the difference between relative quiet and activity, would indicate conditions which affect the functioning of glands and thus might suggest more definitive studies . . ."[48]

Although the electrical techniques were new to Cannon, they presented few experimental difficulties, and in a relatively brief period he and his assistant were able to confirm their predecessors' findings. Convinced that he had found a reliable technique for measuring the secretory activities of endocrine glands, Cannon began a new series of experiments to determine whether Bayliss and Bradford's method could help elucidate the secretory innervation of the thyroid gland. Although physiologists had long known that the thyroid was well supplied with nerves, no one had identified whether the nerves went to the secretory cells or to the blood vessels. By analogy with what he knew of the innervation of the adrenals, Cannon anticipated that the secretory cells of the thyroid would be supplied solely by fibers from the sympathetic nervous system.

From the outset of this new investigation, however, Cannon and Cattell encountered a variety of setbacks. First, they discovered that urethane, which Cannon had used as the anesthetic of choice in his previous experiments on the adrenals, reduced thyroid secretion. Deep ether anesthesia proved to be no better. In addition to the difficulties of etherization, for some inexplicable reason they encountered problems with the electrical equipment they employed. These difficulties became so burdensome that at one point Cannon felt compelled to reassess the techniques he was using. Although in time he was able to find answers to most of the problems, some defied solution. For those that remained, he wryly noted that he and Cattell "learned how to intelligently avoid the pitfalls."

As the experiments continued, Cannon found that when he stimulated the cervical sympathetic fibers of the experimental animals electrical changes in the thyroid occurred that were similar to those that he had previously observed in the salivary glands. In contrast, he found that stimulation of the vagus nerves had no such effect on the thyroid. On the basis of these as well as other confirmatory experiments, Cannon came to the conclusion that the nerves distributed to the secretory cell of the thyroid belonged to the sympathetic nervous system.[49] Although pleased with the outcome, Cannon was aware that some of his evidence was soft. In deference to the weakness of his data, he concluded the final report of these experiments with a warning: "A part of the evidence for secretory nerves," he alerted his readers,

> is . . . based on the assumption that the action current is a sign of secretory activity—and *that* might be doubted. To some degree the assumption is based on analogy with the submaxillary gland. An action current in that gland is the regular concomitant of secretion, and fails when secretion fails. The action current of the thyroid has a latent period characteristic of physiological processes, it may outlast the period of stimulation by many minutes, it appears after stimulation of sympathetic fibres—the filaments of which are known to be distributed to the gland cells—and all these evidences indicate that the action current is a true signal of physiological events taking place in the gland as a result of nerve stimulation.[50]

Despite his expressed caution, Cannon regarded the results of his latest experiments with Cattell much more positively, and he immediately launched a third investigation to see if adrenal secretions might be effective in stimulating the thyroid.[51] In addition to his suspicion that the sympathetic nerves controlled the thyroid, Cannon had other reasons to believe that such a study might be fruitful. He knew from his previous investigations that the adrenals as well as the thyroid reacted quickly to stimulation, and if the adrenals, as he suspected, excited thyroid secretion, such activity would be demonstrable by the changes charted by his electrical recording. He also knew from his reading on exophthalmic goiter that some experimental evidence suggested that the adrenals had a stimulating influence on the thyroid. Cannon and Cattell's new investigation in fact carefully followed one such experimental lead. Several years earlier three talented investigators in Vienna, Hans Eppinger, Wilhelm Falta, and Karl Rudinger, reported that when they injected adrenalin into a dog, they increased its basal metabolism and eventually created a condition similar to hyperthyroidism in man.[52]

During the course of one of his early experiments Cannon discovered that when he injected o.1 cc. of adrenalin intravenously into a cat, there was a striking electrical change in the thyroid. Subsequently when he stimulated the splanchnic nerve to the adrenals, he again observed a marked change in action current in the thyroid—a reaction, however, that did not occur if the adrenals were removed. The results of these experiments appeared to him to be proof that another bodily change could be added to those that he had previously indicated occurred during times of great emotional excitement. Later when Cannon gave an account of this research to the Johns Hopkins Medical Society, he imaginatively drew one more conclusion from these experiments: "The evidence previously presented shows that, besides any routine function, the adrenal gland has an emergency function brought out in times of great excitement. It is not unreasonable to suppose that the thyroid gland likewise has an emergency function evoked in critical times, which would serve to increase the speed of metabolism when the rapidity of bodily processes might be of the utmost importance, and, besides that, augmenting the efficiency of the adrenin which would be secreted simultaneously."[53]

Following the completion of his research on the thyroid, Cannon gave lectures to a number of medical societies on the application of his studies to the solution of clinical problems. At times the implications of his findings struck audiences with particular force. Following one lecture to the Vermont Medical Society, an elderly practitioner, after detailing the different interpretations of the etiology of diseases of the nervous system that he had encountered during his long practice, thanked Cannon for the new insights he had provided and then asked, "Is it not possible that in the future field of medical research that sociology—social environment—in other words, happiness and unhappiness may come to be a part of the function of the physician, and that pure psychology, psycho-physiology and psycho-pathology will come to have a particular place in the medical curriculum? And also become an important part of the physicians' work instead of it being left almost entirely, as it now is, to a certain cult who pretend to treat the human body."[54] The acuity of the question delighted Cannon; it fit in very well with his desire for cooperative investigations of clinical medicine and psychology.

Not all audiences, however, reacted in this fashion. At the conclusion of a lecture at the New York Academy of Medicine,[55] a number of noted physicians revealed doubts about both the value of Cannon's research and the general effect of scientific research on clinical practice. Charles Dana, one of the leading neurologists in New York, after politely commending Cannon, launched a fierce attack on medical scientists, complaining that they needed a more humanizing spirit and that they frequently led practitioners astray by issuing incomplete reports of their research. Joseph Collins, another prominent neurologist, took Cannon to task for suggesting that diseases of the nervous system might stem from disordered emotions. The theory that explained most functional nervous diseases, he instructed Cannon, was Freud's. Unfortunately, there is no indication how Cannon responded to these criticisms, but he was not without supporters. Near the conclusion of the meeting Samuel Meltzer of the Rockefeller Institute rose to Cannon's defense. Meltzer was not only a distinguished physiologist; as one of the founders of the Society for Clinical Investigation, he was also one of the most powerful voices in New York City on the importance of clinical research. "Dr. Cannon's laboratory," he informed the audience, "does possess a humanizing influence. It is dominated by the clinical spirit of no less a person than Dr. Cannon himself . . . He offers facts and when he offers theories, they fit in closely with the facts."[56]

Generally after Cannon's lectures there were few questions from the floor about the electrical techniques he had used during his investigations. In June of 1916, however, following an address by Cannon at the annual meeting of the American Medical Association, A. J. Carlson, chairman of the physiology department at the University of Chicago, carefully picked at the soft spots of the electrical method that Cannon had employed. "I should like to know," he bluntly asked Cannon, "if on continued stimulation of the cervical sympathetic for half an hour whether the secretion and the electrical response continued for that half hour or possibly longer . . . I am not certain that the electrical response is the true measure of the duration or the extent of secretory activity." It was a telling question. Was the electrical change that Cannon had observed really concomitant with the secretory activity of the thyroid or did the change in electrical potential only appear briefly at the beginning and then disappear although secretory activity continued? Cannon had no ready answer: "No exact studies have been made of that matter," he replied.[57]

Carlson's question was not new; Cannon had already asked it himself. In fact, he had carefully warned physiologists in a paper on the innervation of the thyroid that was soon to appear that the results of his research rested on analogy with his previous findings of the electrical changes in the secretion of the salivary gland.[58] Carlson's question only underscored the vast amount of research that was necessary before physiologists and endocrinologists unraveled the relationships of the glands of internal secretion. Cannon took great pride that his research despite some shortcomings had reached beyond the narrow limits of physiology. When late in 1916 Eliot asked him about the future study of physiology and psychology, Cannon shared with him his vision of the importance of developing an interdisciplinary approach in medical research. "I think that you are right in surmising that Physiology and Psychology should be more closely related," he wrote Eliot.

My own work, as you know, has made a bridge between the two subjects. The work of the Russian physiologist, Pawlow, in St. Petersburg, has done similar service to Psychology. It is interesting to see now that the psychologists are taking up the suggestions which physiological work has offered and are applying them to human conditions. A recent letter from Professor Watson of Johns Hopkins has informed me that he has been studying the effects of feeling on human subjects and getting results very similar to those I have described for laboratory animals. It is interesting to note that Professor Watson, who is a comparative psychologist, has thrown illumination on the character of mental diseases by interpreting to the psychiatrists the significance of Pawlow's experiments on the physiology of the brain. I feel sure that some of the most important advances in science, in coming years, will be made in the borderlands lying between related sciences and in the integration of related phenomena in different sciences whose relations have thus far failed to appear because of the limitation of attention and insight.[59]

19   *Hard Choices and Conflicts of Interest*

F ROM THE TIME of his appointment as Higginson Professor of Physiology and throughout the development of his research on the adrenals and his work for the committee in defense of medical research, Cannon gave unstintingly of himself to the Medical School. Indeed, the faculty almost reflexively came to rely on his presence to provide stability in times of trouble.[1] By 1913, despite the long-awaited opening of the nearby Brigham Hospital and success in recruiting several excellent new faculty members, the Medical School appeared to be in a state of perpetual administrative crisis.

For all of his ability (and it was considerable), Lowell found it difficult to deal with the persistent problems facing the Medical School. Unlike Eliot, who passionately wanted to establish at Harvard the premier scientific medical school in the United States, Lowell had few plans for developing the School. All too often he did not understand the differences between the preclinical and clinical faculties about appointments and plans to improve the School, especially their deep divisions with regard to modification of the curriculum and rules of admission. He did, however, understand the meaning of failure. Following the defeat of Henderson's proposals in 1910 and 1911 to change the medical curriculum, Lowell decided that he would take the lead in dealing with the question of admissions—a problem he had deliberately postponed soon after taking office.

This time, instead of seeking advice from faculty members, Lowell began by engaging in a debate with Abraham Flexner. A short time earlier Flexner had urged in a report on the state of

American medical education for the Carnegie Foundation that admission to a really modern medical school required at a minimum two years of collegiate work that featured study in the basic sciences.[2] Lowell, who firmly believed in a broad academic experience leading to the bachelor's degree, did not mince words in discussing the implications of Flexner's requirements. "Do you not start," he wrote him,

> by assuming your conclusion that scientific studies in college are the better preparation for the study of medicine and having made that assumption, all facts inconsistent with it become improbable? . . . Surely, the question which is agitating the world now that we have left behind the doctrine of formal discipline is how far the value of education depends on the training of processes of thought and how far its value depends on the accumulation of knowledge. The latter is a thing comparatively easy to determine but the training of processes of thought is a very subtle and difficult thing to measure.[3]

Flexner was unimpressed with Lowell's reasoning. Mental ability and conscientiousness had shown they could take care of themselves with or without deliberate educational adjustments, he replied. The reality the medical student had to face was of a different order. Such students, Flexner noted, for the most part entered medical school after only two years of collegiate training and immediately faced the task of learning about a score of medical specialties dependent on a background in the basic sciences. Since it was nearly impossible to cover even the basic rudiments of these specialties in the four-year medical curriculum, the burden of preparation in the basic sciences had to be anticipated during the undergraduate years. These facts, Flexner concluded, are the relevant ones for determining whether the undergraduate interested in a medical career should do classics or the sciences.[4]

Although Lowell was not persuaded by Flexner's argument, he nevertheless found it difficult to deny its thrust. When the Council on Medical Education of the American Medical Association increasingly urged that medical schools adopt the standards advocated by Flexner, Lowell without consulting the medical faculty attempted late in 1912 to reach an understanding on admissions with Arthur D. Bevan, chairman of the council. He would try, he wrote Bevan, to relax the rule of the Harvard Medical School that required a bachelor's degree for admission and put in its place the requirements asked for by the council if Bevan in turn would try to relax the council's rule and allow graduates of colleges of the highest standard the privilege of attending medical schools without the necessary preliminary work in science.[5] It is evident that Lowell hoped that such an exchange would give Harvard men who did not decide on a medical career until their collegiate work was done the option of attending medical school anywhere in the United States. Bevan agreed, and to bind the understanding, he invited Lowell to present his views before the council at its next regular meeting.[6]

To carry his plan forward, Lowell asked Cannon to act as floor manager to shepherd his proposal through the medical faculty. It was the first time he had called on Cannon for help. In a sense Cannon was almost a necessary choice; there were few men at the Medical School whom Lowell could call on to assist him. Several of his close friends on the medical faculty had recently retired. Christian, the former dean and a logical candidate for the job, had previously opposed a similar two-year admissions program,[7] and Bradford, the current dean, although in office but a short time, had already antagonized a number of faculty members. Not only was Cannon well regarded by the medical faculty; Lowell also knew that he had joined with Minot several years before in promoting a similar admissions policy. Cannon welcomed the administration's new initiative on admissions, and gave himself eagerly to his new responsibilities.

Early in 1913 when Cannon asked the medical faculty to adopt a minimum standard of admission as set forth by Flexner and endorsed by the Council on Medical Education, his proposal passed by a handsome majority.[8] Despite the victory, Cannon knew that if the new policy was to be adopted by the University others would have to be convinced—the University faculty council, the Board of Overseers, and not the least, Charles W. Eliot. Initially Eliot said little publicly or privately of the administration's proposals; but when he learned some time later that Bradford had publicly come out in favor of a two-year admissions policy, he erupted. "I have been very sorry to hear this week," he wrote J. Collins Warren, "that Dr. Bradford is in favor of abandoning the A.B. requirement for admission to the Harvard Medical School . . . To adopt the two years in college plan which he advocates would inflict serious injury on the prestige of the Harvard Medical School and would put the School in a position inferior to that of any other professional school which belongs to the University."[9]

Cannon's efforts to gain support for the new policy outside the Medical School met with little success. In mid-January, when he discussed the policy with his friends at the Tuesday Evening Club, he found to his surprise that they were adamantly opposed to it and unimpressed with his argument that the two-year program was necessary in order to meet the requirements set by other medical schools and universities. Several days later at a meeting of the Faculty of Arts and Sciences in Cambridge, he listened quietly while George L. Kittredge, the English department's great Shakespearean authority, speaking for most of those present roundly condemned the Medical School's admissions policy "as a backward step" for Harvard.[10] Discussions with members of the medical faculty were little better. Even his good friend Milton Rosenau, although theoretically agreeing with the advisability of a two-year science-oriented entrance requirement, voiced fears for the Medical School's reputation if the proposals were agreed to by the Overseers and Corporation.[11]

The mounting criticism, while disturbing, did not discourage Cannon. Certain in his own mind that the new policy was best for the future development of the Medical School, he redoubled his efforts to win friends in the University for the admissions proposal. In February, when he was called to explain the new requirements to the University Council, he carefully planned a presentation that he hoped would win approval.[12] He did not, however, anticipate the reception that Dean Ezra Thayer of the Law School had prepared. When the Medical School's new admissions policy was first presented to the University Council for consideration, Thayer asked his brother William, a professor of medicine at Johns Hopkins, for a critical evaluation of it that he could share with the council. William, a firm believer in the necessity of the bachelor's degree for admittance to medical school, proposed making the rules even more stringent. "It isn't a question of the average requirement which medical schools in the United States should demand," he wrote his brother Ezra, "it is a question of what the leading institution in America should give. If Harvard does not set the example, who shall? And as for students—Heavens! Go farther than we do—discriminate more carefully—demand, if you will, four years work everywhere for an A.B. degree, or that which equals an A.B. degree at Harvard. Do what you will; it makes little difference what, provided you aim high enough; and the students will come as many as you want. Nothing could be worse than for Harvard to try to put itself on a level with the average good school of the country. It must try to lead."[13] Thayer's letter had a decisive effect on the council: when Cannon came to the meeting, he found a determined hostile opposition. Every argument he presented was attacked. Later that night he noted in his diary with some bitterness Ezra Thayer's ridicule of medical faculty standards and Eugene Wambaugh's inelegant but trenchant remark, "kick them out," at the conclusion of his presentation. The next day he continued to complain: "Had only two hours sleep last night . . . Much depressed by Medical School showing at Council meeting."[14]

In the midst of this trial Cannon received a letter from President George E. Vincent of the University of Minnesota which presented him with another kind of problem. Vincent, then engaged in the task of upgrading his entire university,[15] offered Cannon a post as dean as well as a professorship in the medical school. In normal circumstances it is doubtful whether Cannon would have seriously considered the offer; he had already turned down opportunities to be dean of the Harvard Medical School. Vincent's offer, however, given Cannon's disappointment at his reception by the University Council, could not have arrived at a more propitious moment. It was an attractive proposition: in addition to holding out the prospect of organizing and directing what amounted to a new medical school, it promised Cannon minimal teaching duties with ample opportunity to continue his research at a starting salary of $6,000 a year—$1,500 more than he was receiving at Harvard.[16]

News of Cannon's Minnesota offer rocked the Medical School. Recognizing the danger of losing him, Henderson and Rosenau went to Lowell to point out the importance of keeping Cannon at Harvard. Medical students, as they had in 1906, petitioned the dean and faculty not to let Cannon go. Friends and colleagues made special efforts to impress on him the difficulties involved in trying to do research and administration simultaneously. Edsall felt so strongly that a move to Minnesota as dean would end Cannon's career as a physiologist that he spent several evenings trying to dissuade him from accepting the offer. Cannon patiently listened to all of this advice, methodically investigated his options, and after approximately three weeks of deliberation rejected the offer.[17] He had always maintained as a matter of principle that the medical scientist's first duty was to pursue his research. His decision, however, was not simply a reiteration of long-held principles; it was also an expression of the promise he saw in the future development of his research. "If I were not in my most productive period," he wrote Vincent, "if there were not many physiological problems waiting urgently for solution, if I could drop out of this exciting game of exploration and after a few years return as ever to go on with it—then I might be persuaded. But I am in the fruitful years, there are crowding problems, and the man who drops out does not come back."[18]

Despite the rejection, Vincent was not easily put off. A week later William Mayo in Vincent's behalf offered Cannon a post as professor of physiology at the salary previously offered him as dean. Cannon found the new offer especially welcome and tried to use it to obtain a budget increase for his department that Bradford had previously denied. When Bradford again refused, Cannon artfully showed Christian a list of demands he had drawn up if he were to stay at Harvard. Appalled at the prospect of losing Cannon, Christian added his voice to the appeals made to Lowell of the importance of retaining Cannon at Harvard. Cannon's wants for himself and his department were modest, he advised Lowell. "I believe they should be met in such a way that he would feel free to say to Minnesota I am satisfied at Harvard and unwilling to leave, thus ending their proposals to him." Given the pressure that had already been extended by others on Cannon's behalf, Lowell needed little further persuasion. Leaving nothing to chance, he sent a copy of Christian's letter to Bradford with a note to meet Cannon's demands.[19]

Invigorated by such reinforcement on the part of his colleagues, in the weeks that followed Cannon undertook a new campaign on admissions to see if he could gain additional support from the medical faculty before the Board of Overseers rendered their final decision. Ironically, Christian bore the brunt of Cannon's new offensive. Christian, who had led the opposition to the two-year plan from its inception, was so disconcerted by the apparent success of Cannon's efforts with the faculty that he informed the administration he would urge Eliot and Jerome Greene to block the vote in the Overseers meeting "to save the Faculty from the results of its own folly."[20] It was not an idle threat; Lowell was well aware of the power Eliot wielded on the Board of Overseers and once again called on Cannon for help. In response, Cannon spent the next morning explaining to Eliot why he favored the change. Instead of arguing as he had before about the importance of bringing the Harvard Medical School admissions requirements into congruence with those of other medical schools, this time he carefully stressed one of Eliot's arguments—namely, that the basic sciences in addition to their value in advancing medical thought and practice had an important cultural value of their own. "Eliot," Cannon later wrote in his diary, "listened very patiently and sympathetically."[21] Several weeks later Lowell obliquely hinted at the importance of Cannon's influence on the outcome of the medical admissions debate. "The question of admission after two years of college work came up for final action before the Overseers last week," he wrote an interested friend, "and curiously enough, President Eliot said he had been converted by some of the Professors at the School and the action of the faculty was ratified unanimously."[22]

❧ ❧ ❧

Although Cannon worked hard promoting the new admissions policy, he found himself out of sympathy with other administration initiatives, especially some of Bradford's schemes. Bradford, for example, had little liking for the emphasis Cushing as head of the surgery department placed on research. In an effort to address what he perceived to be a growing imbalance in the relative status of practicing surgeons versus surgical investigators in the School, he recommended that Cushing promote Edward Nichols, one of his friends at the Boston City Hospital, from assistant professor to professor of surgery. Cushing bluntly refused, whereupon Bradford established a special faculty committee to look into the question of Nichols's promotion as a way of forcing Cushing's hand. Cushing, who did not take lightly any invasion of his authority, brought the matter to the attention of Cannon and his other friends at the School. In the process what initially seemed to be a contest of will between the dean and Cushing soon involved the entire faculty. The matter dragged on, and as the faculty grew increasingly restive, Cannon attempted to mediate the problem. When neither man would budge, the full professors, following a suggestion made by Cannon, rejected Bradford's efforts to promote Nichols to professor but as a compromise advanced him to associate professor.[23] Cushing accepted the compromise; the solution, however, angered Bradford. The following year, when another opportunity arose, Bradford tried again to promote the interests of those engaged in the practice of surgery as against those involved in surgical research. Cannon saw his action as another sign of the lessening of the administration's regard for the value of scientific investigation in the development of the Medical School.

The new admissions policy was not the only administrative effort to set the Medical School on a new course. There were others as well, and each attempt made it clear that Harvard could no longer depend solely on local constituencies for monetary support. This became particularly apparent in 1913 when the administration mounted a special effort to upgrade the clinical departments. There was need for such improvement, but that need was hardly unique to Harvard. Other schools faced the same problem.

Almost from the turn of the century Franklin Mall, the distinguished anatomist, had sought to persuade his colleagues at Johns Hopkins of the necessity of reforming the medical school's clinical departments. Convinced that one of the major obstacles thwarting the scientific development of clinical medicine was the fact that professors of clinical subjects had to spend the bulk of their time conducting busy private practices to support themselves, Mall urged that such professors have the same status as professors of laboratory subjects with salaries that would allow them to devote all their effort to research, teaching, and caring for hospital patients. Initially Mall's proposal, which came to be known as "full time," divided the faculty. In time, however, it began to take hold, helped in part by William Welch's request in the winter of 1910–11 to Frederick Gates of the Rockefeller Foundation's General Education Board for support of a special endowment he had organized to improve clinical opportunities at Johns Hopkins.[24] Welch's request set in motion an extraordinary train of events.

Gates needed no introduction to Welch. Little more than a decade before, Welch had served as his chief adviser in organizing the Rockefeller Institute for Medical Research. Welch's new project appeared to Gates to complement the Rockefeller Foundation's previous efforts to advance scientific medicine so well that he promised Welch that the General Education Board would "try to work in the direction of helping him."[25] He also invited Abraham Flexner (on the strength of his recently completed study of medical schools in the United States) to advise him how best to utilize a substantial sum of money to reform medical education. Flexner, who had used Johns Hopkins as a standard by which to judge the status of all other medical schools, advised Gates to give the money to Welch. Gates promptly borrowed Flexner from the Carnegie Foundation and dispatched him to Johns Hopkins to make an independent survey of its clinical needs.[26]

Hopkins held no surprises for Flexner. During his survey for the Carnegie Foundation he had had numerous discussions on medical education with Welch as well as with other professors.[27] His mandate to examine the problem of improving clinical medicine, however, opened prospects he had not previously considered. After a month of hearing the arguments for full-time medicine in conversations with Mall, Welch, William Halsted, and Whitridge Williams, he enthusiastically made a number of recommendations to Gates. First, he suggested that funds be made available to Johns Hopkins through the General Education Board to establish full-time professorships in medicine, surgery, pediatrics, gynecology, and obstetrics; and second, he recommended that the Board make no appropriations until they had received a specific proposal from Johns Hopkins for a grant to establish such full-time clinical professorships.[28] When Flexner's recommendations became known at Hopkins, they quickly raised the debate on full time to a new level. Indeed, the opposition to the concept became so fierce that Welch delayed two years before submitting a formal proposal in behalf of full time to the General Education Board.[29] Flexner's future was equally affected: Gates thought so well of his report[30] that in 1912 he invited Flexner to join the Board to help carry out the Foundation's new interests in medical education. The developments both at Johns Hopkins and at the General Education Board were to have a profound effect on Harvard's efforts to improve its own clinical departments.

From the establishment of the General Education Board in 1902, Harvard had made a number of requests to the Board for aid that, with one exception, were rejected. In January 1913, when Eliot, in his capacity as a trustee of the Board, informed Lowell that the Foundation at its last meeting had adopted a new policy to improve the level of clinical instruction in medical schools, it appeared that a corner in the relations between Harvard and the Board might be turned.[31] Eliot was especially hopeful about the Medical School's prospects of receiving aid from the Foundation. Harvard had one other friend at court—Eliot's protégé Jerome Greene, who had recently been appointed Secretary to the Rockefeller Foundation and as such became a trustee of the General Education Board as well. Neither Eliot nor Greene, however, knew the background to the Board's new policy. The year before, Eliot had been on a world tour and knew nothing either of the private talks between Welch and Gates or of Flexner's confidential survey of Johns Hopkins and his subsequent recommendation to Gates. Greene, as a newcomer to the Foundation, was equally uninformed of these events.[32] If these friends at the Foundation were better informed, they might have instructed Harvard officials that the policy to aid clinical instruction did not allow for modification. They might also have tried to temper extravagant expectations of receiving aid from the Foundation. Eliot and Greene did neither; they believed so strongly that this time the Board could not deny Harvard financial support that they inadvertently helped create an environment of unrealistic hopes at the Medical School.

When Lowell received the news about the General Education Board's new program, he immediately asked Christian to develop the necessary request for aid. It was a logical choice: Christian had recently negotiated a contract with the trustees of the Brigham that gave the chiefs of medicine and surgery authority to establish new forms of clinical instruction and patient care at the hospital. Moreover, as a former dean, he had readily available all of the necessary information for the improvement of clinical departments at the School.[33] Within weeks he developed a proposal that he felt would be acceptable to the General Education Board.[34] Like Flexner, Christian wished to establish all clinical departments on a full-time basis; they differed, however, about the method to achieve this goal. Flexner wished primarily to establish full-time chairs in the major clinical departments; Christian proposed that young assistants in the various clinical departments be placed on a full-time basis with an adequate yearly salary and that the salaries of the professors of pediatrics, gynecology, obstetrics, and psychiatry be increased so that they too could afford to devote themselves full time to their academic and hospital duties. He said nothing specifically, however, about full time in the departments of medicine and surgery because he believed that he and Cushing were already working on such a basis at the Brigham. Although Christian's proposal forbade members of the clinical departments (professors as well as assistants) to engage in general private practice, it did insist that senior professors have the privilege of seeing a limited number of private patients in the hospital on a consultative basis.[35]

When Eliot, Lowell, the dean, and the chairmen of clinical departments examined Christian's proposal, they unanimously approved it. Eliot was particularly enthusiastic: "The enclosed statement seems to me clear, moderate and convincing," he wrote Christian. "It is entirely in the line of Chairman Gates's recent proposal to the General Education Board."[36] Yet not all who approved the proposal liked it. Lowell in fact had reservations: "I cannot help wondering," he wrote Bradford, "whether Dr. Christian is not a little bit too much affected by his own position in striving to put all clinical professors in the position that he happens to occupy. I should have supposed that while he wanted some professors like himself, Cushing and Edsall, we also wanted some like Shattuck and Maurice Richardson. Therefore I wonder whether his limitations upon the practice of professors are wholly wise." Nevertheless, when the medical faculty endorsed the plan, Lowell appointed Christian, Cushing, and Edsall as a committee to oversee the submission of the proposal to the General Education Board.[37]

As chairman of the committee, Christian was meticulous about fulfilling his new responsibilities. For weeks he worried about the protocol for submitting the proposal to the General Education Board and fretted about what appeared to him delays on the part of the Foundation in responding to his requests to meet with them. These anxieties, however, did not diminish his confidence that Harvard would be successful in its quest for aid. Eliot and Greene, equally certain of Harvard's prospects, encouraged him in such beliefs.[38] Late in May, when the Board informed Christian that Flexner would soon visit him to discuss Harvard's proposal, he was convinced that except for some bargaining the grant was in hand.[39]

Despite Christian's anticipations, Flexner did not come to Boston prepared to give a grant. Four years earlier Flexner had measured Harvard against the standards of medical education set by Johns Hopkins and found it wanting, particularly because it had no hospital of its own.[40] He was also disconcerted by certain elements of Christian's proposal, especially the provision allowing senior professors the privilege of a limited consultative practice in the hospital. That proviso, he thought, did not look toward the total elimination of the pecuniary motive in clinical teaching, which he believed was central to the system of full time. But when he met with Christian, except for speaking in broad terms about full time, Flexner made no specific criticism of the proposal nor did he speak of the Medical School's relation to the Brigham Hospital—another issue that concerned him. Instead he limited his comments to requests for further data about the medical faculty and student body and promised on leaving that he would discuss matters more fully in the fall.[41]

It is not known whether Flexner had decided to reject the Harvard proposals before his meeting with Christian in June 1913. His actions afterward, however, clearly show that he was determined that the General Education Board's first grant to reform clinical education should go to Johns Hopkins. Following his visit to Boston, he sent a number of suggestions to Welch, John Howland, and Whitridge Williams about what should be included in the proposals they were preparing for submission to the Board. Flexner's help was well known to the Hopkins medical faculty; indeed, they resented it and at one point protested his involvement in the project.[42] Early in October, when Flexner learned that the Foundation would take final action later that month on the applications it had received for aid, he alerted Welch to the necessity of submitting the Hopkins proposals before that meeting.[43] In contrast, at no time did Flexner, following his visit with Christian, make an effort to communicate either with him or with any of his colleagues about the Harvard proposals. It was not until Christian wrote Flexner in late September for an opportunity to discuss his proposal that he finally agreed to a meeting in mid-October. The meeting proved a shock: Flexner told Christian plainly that the Harvard proposals were not acceptable and would have to be totally revised if they were to be seriously considered by the Foundation. He did not, however, inform him that the Foundation would make its final decision on the applications before it the next week. Christian immediately began to revise his proposals and was still in the process when the General Education Board met.[44] The outcome was predictable.

In a formal minute the General Education Board noted that the Harvard application for aid was rejected because the improvements it had recommended in clinical teaching were not "sufficiently fundamental." More pointedly, it added that although a member of the Board conferred with the committee at the Harvard Medical School and indicated that the Board would be interested in a more comprehensive proposal for reorganization, no such proposition had been received.[45] The Hopkins application had no such difficulty; it met every criterion the Foundation had set up and was unanimously approved. Several days later, when Wallace Buttrick, the Secretary of the General Education Board, formally notified Welch of the Board's action, he appended a note to his letter: "Nothing that our Board has ever done has given me so great satisfaction as this appropriation to the Johns Hopkins Medical School . . . Rather would I say the resolution naming the fund in honor of you was the greatest satisfaction of all. It is rare in this world for any man to be loved as you are. On the part of all the members of our Board as they discussed your proposition, there was a note of affection, as well as of profound respect for you personally and for your services to the cause of medical education."[46]

Although the Board's naming the first grant for full-time medicine in honor of Welch appears unusual, it was not a last-minute idea. Two years earlier, when Gates had forwarded Flexner's survey of Johns Hopkins's clinical needs to John D. Rockefeller, he not only recommended that Hopkins be awarded one and a quarter million dollars to reform clinical education but also urged that such a grant be named in honor of Welch.[47] In retrospect it appears that the first competition sponsored by the General Education Board to advance clinical education, given the prior commitment to Johns Hopkins and Welch, was little more than a charade organized by Gates and deftly carried to fruition by Abraham Flexner.

✑   ✑   ✑

The General Education Board's grant to Johns Hopkins inaugurated a period of despair and soul searching at Harvard.[48] The anticipation of receiving the grant had been so high that most of the medical faculty shared the disappointment, and not a few began to look for a scapegoat. When Eliot asked Cannon about faculty reaction to the Board's decision, Cannon indicated that except for voting approval of Christian's proposal at a faculty meeting, none of the faculty knew anything about the negotiations with the Foundation. The way to get a full-time program at the Medical School, he advised Eliot, was by publicity: "The faculty should decide, not three men."[49] Councilman was even more critical of the procedures Christian and the administration had used: "Under present conditions," he wrote Flexner, "the matters affecting the School are getting more and more into the hands of the President of the University and certain committees appointed by him, many of which committees do not report to the faculty but to other committees. I do not know how the general government of the University goes on, but in our School the government is cameral."[50]

If Lowell was aware of the medical faculty's disaffection with the way negotiations had been conducted with the General Education Board, he took little notice of it. He made no effort to discuss the matter with the faculty nor did he initially take them into his confidence about any new plans to improve the clinical departments. Instead he privately informed Christian and Jerome Greene that he would take personal responsibility for drafting as well as negotiating a new full-time proposal. He was so confident that the task was a relatively simple one that he informed the Foundation he would have a revised proposal ready for their consideration by the New Year.[51]

In the weeks that followed, Lowell learned that the promise he had made to the Foundation was unrealistic. When he asked Edsall, Christian, and Cushing if they would accept full-time positions such as those established at Johns Hopkins,[52] the replies he received gave him pause. All said yes and no simultaneously. Edsall told Lowell that although he agreed with the full-time principle, his assent did not mean that he did not want a consulting practice. Further he indicated that a special understanding concerning his tenure and pension would be needed because of the Massachusetts General Hospital rules that mandated a relatively early retirement (at the age of 63).[53] Christian, who had serious reservations about the Johns Hopkins program, informed Lowell that he would accept such a full-time post only if Lowell in turn would accept certain modifications—including almost all of the original proposals he had made to the General Education Board.[54] From the time of the Board's rejection of Harvard's proposals,

Cushing took a variety of positions depending with whom he discussed the matter. When asked by Henry Lee Higginson about his attitude to the Foundation's full-time program, Cushing excoriated Abraham Flexner as a socialist who wanted everyone to live on $5,000 a year and indicated in no uncertain terms that he could not in view of his economic circumstances agree to such a program. When he spoke to Cannon, he announced that he agreed totally with and supported the principle of full time.[55] Faced with Lowell's request for a decision, he wrote a letter describing how the clinical departments at Harvard were in practice working out their own full-time programs with the Brigham Hospital and concluded with a graceful appreciation of the difficulties Lowell faced and his wish to help him. "You have had the assurance of my interest in and sympathy with the essential features of the proposal from the General Education Board," Cushing wrote Lowell. "You have had the assurance also of my complete readiness to withdraw from my interlocked university and hospital position in favor of anyone whom you may wish to appoint on the new basis if you are convinced not only that the step should be taken but that it would be taken at this time, lest the opportunity be lost; for I am unwilling that my tenure of office should block the movement if it is the consensus of opinion that our more rapid advancement as a medical institution lies urgently in this direction."[56]

When Dean Bradford saw the letter, he immediately seized the opportunity to suggest a plan to Lowell to bypass Cushing:

April 8, 1914

My dear Lawrence;

Would it be possible, now that Cushing has definitely declined to consider the General Education Board plan, to attempt to arrange it with Dr. Cheever, now one of the surgeons at the Brigham, leaving Cushing also at the Brigham but not paid by the General Education Board Fund.

As Cushing is on record favoring the General Education Board plan he should be unable to oppose such an arrangement and the Brigham Hospital Trustees would in all probability agree if Cushing favored it.

There is no question that Welch and Flexner are right that the practice of Professors of Medicine and Surgery in exploiting themselves through their hospital and school to the neglect of their teaching work is becoming too common . . .

Dr. Cheever would eventually be a greater addition to our surgical teaching force I think than Murphy and I doubt if Cushing will ever be the teacher of general surgery we need.

Although Bradford's plan appealed to Lowell, he initially put it aside and began instead to examine the prospects of establishing a full-time program at the Massachusetts General Hospital.[57]

Throughout the fall and winter of 1913–14 Cannon frequently discussed the General Education Board's full-time policy with Christian, Cushing, and Edsall. At times the discussions proved difficult because he could not accept what he came to regard as Christian and Cushing's intransigence toward the Foundation's policies. Still, they were close friends and rather than risk his friendships, Cannon did not press them to change their minds about the positions they had taken.[58] Besides, he had become involved in another problem that was of more immediate concern to him than full time—this one created by his old adversary, William T. Porter.

Following Cannon's appointment as Higginson Professor in 1906, the anger between Porter and Cannon was so great that if each had an opportunity to get back at the other, he did so—often with self-righteous indignation. As the years passed, however, tempers cooled. There were few new arguments between the two men and what differences did arise were settled civilly. Early in 1914, soon after Cannon became president of the American Physiological Society, Porter announced that he intended to give up publishing the *American Journal of Physiology*.[59] For a period of more than fifteen years Porter had edited and published the journal at his own expense. In the early years he had few problems; however, with the blossoming of physiology as a discipline during the first decade of the twentieth century, editing the journal became increasingly difficult—so difficult that at the annual meeting of the society in 1913 a special committee had been formed to discuss with Porter the growing delay in publication of papers.[60] Although the call for discussion of his editorial policies upset Porter, it was not the compelling reason for his decision to give up the journal; perhaps his most important concerns were the rising costs of publication and his need for funds to support his daughter who was then studying abroad.

Taking over publication of the journal was a complicated matter.[61] Porter had copyrighted the journal's title, and although he informed Cannon that he was willing to transfer the copyright to the society, he also made clear that he would do so only if the society would meet certain stipulations regarding editorial policy. Even more troubling to Cannon was Porter's announcement that he expected the society to take the responsibility for publishing the next issue of the journal—a condition that gave Cannon and the council of the society only a matter of weeks to come to a decision. At first, maintaining continuity in the publication of the journal appeared to be out of reach; as the newly elected president of the society Cannon did not know if he had the authority to assume in behalf of the society the responsibilities of publishing a journal (including assuming debts) without a vote of the membership at large. Moreover, neither he nor the council knew much about the details involved in publishing a learned journal. Despite these difficulties, Cannon's negotiations with Porter, which might have proved awkward because of the differences that had previously existed between them, were fruitful—in a measure because of the open way Cannon approached him. For the first time in years Porter felt at ease talking to Cannon and even confessed to him some of the hardships and strains of his personal life.[62] That the problems in editing and producing the journal were settled so expeditiously stands as testimony to the commitment with which Cannon and his colleagues approached their task. Each member of the council—A. J. Carlson, Joseph Erlanger, William Howell, and F. S. Lee, all men inclined in ordinary circumstances to have their own way—accepted many of the time-consuming chores Cannon assigned without complaint. The obligation of meeting debts that might occur in publishing the next yearly volume was assumed by Cannon and the council by personal subscription, and Joseph Erlanger gave up a summer's vacation to temporarily handle the journal's daily financial matters. In the end there was no break either in the regularity of appearance or in the editorial standards of the journal.[63]

During the spring of 1914, despite the progress in his research and his sense of accomplishment in dealing with Porter, Cannon found himself increasingly dispirited by the changes in the environment at the Medical School. At times it appeared to him that he was almost constantly at odds with the administration on matters of policy. In April when an occasion arose to appoint a new professor of hygiene, Cannon saw an opportunity to advance the research and teaching capabilities of the physiology department and suggested to Bradford that he hire Thomas Storey, a graduate of the Medical School who had initiated a unique program in hygiene and physiological research at the City College in New York. In addition, he proposed that Storey be allowed to give a course in general physiology to undergraduates at Harvard College. Neither the dean nor Lowell saw any virtue in Cannon's proposals. Instead, following the advice of Frederick Shattuck, they decided to make the post exclusively a clinical one and appointed Roger I. Lee, a visiting physician at the Massachusetts General Hospital, to the professorship.[64]

Following this disappointment, the administration made another appointment that not only frustrated Cannon but thwarted others who were anxious to advance clinical investigation at the hospitals associated with the Medical School. Upon the death of Thomas Rotch, professor of pediatrics, earlier that year, Cannon and many of his colleagues hoped that the administration would make an effort to obtain the services of John Howland, who had built a strong investigative pediatric unit at Johns Hopkins.[65] Instead, Lowell and Bradford, again following Shattuck's advice, promoted John Lovett Morse, Rotch's assistant, to the chair. Morse, like Roger Lee, was a capable clinician but had little interest in research. It appeared that he had previously been hand-picked by Rotch to be his successor.[66] The administration's continuing inclination toward this kind of appointment was a sign to Cannon and others both inside and outside the School—and in particular to the General Education Board—of the administration's lack of commitment to upgrading the faculty at the Medical School.[67]

At the end of April Cannon had new cause for concern when he learned that Theobald Smith, one of the most distinguished scientists at the School, was leaving Harvard to take up a post at the Rockefeller Institute. Smith's resignation, owing in large part to the administration's failure to meet even his simplest needs, so incensed Cannon that he began to consider himself an outlander at the Medical School and pointedly stayed away from faculty meetings to protest the way the dean conducted matters at the School.[68] Cannon was by no means the only one upset with the administration's attitude toward research. Jerome Greene, concerned that Lowell's negotiations with the General Education Board for a new grant might be imperiled by the administration's attitudes, confided his fears to Eliot: "The representatives of the Harvard Medical School seem to make an unfortunate impression on the officers of the General Education Board. Is there no prospect of securing a new dean to take command of the situation at this critical time?" Eliot could offer no encouragement: "I have done my utmost with regard to Bradford," he wrote, "but have made no impression."[69]

By the spring of 1914 Lowell was convinced that he could meet the Board's requirements for a full-time program by establishing it at the Massachusetts General Hospital. He had reasonable grounds for such hopes. Edsall, the chief of medicine at the MGH, agreed to cooperate with the Foundation and also developed an enthusiastic rationale for establishing a full-time program there based on their principles. The hospital, which was then searching for a new chief of surgery, even indicated that one of its requirements for the post was acceptance of the full-time principle.[70] Despite these positive developments, the General Education Board reacted negatively to Lowell's proposal. Abraham Flexner, who believed that the Brigham was the only suitable hospital for a full-time program at Harvard, was especially critical. The Massachusetts General Hospital, he wrote Lowell, was too distant from the Medical School to function effectively in a program that required professors to make the best use of their time in teaching, research, and care of hospital patients. Nor was Flexner impressed with Edsall's rationale; in his view, Edsall's plans were flawed because they were essentially based on the amicable relations that existed between himself and the hospital's trustees and could easily be abrogated by a new hospital board or a new professor of medicine. Throughout the negotiations Flexner voiced his opinions freely and made clear that Harvard's best chance for a grant from the General Education Board was to try once more to establish a full-time program at the Brigham.[71]

Spurred by Flexner's criticisms, Lowell again approached Cushing and Christian, hoping to change their minds. Utilizing the proposal previously made by Bradford, he suggested that Cushing retain the Moseley professorship of surgery with as many beds as he needed at the Brigham to carry on his work but relinquish both his position as surgeon-in-chief and control of the clinics at the Brigham to the holder of a new professorial chair on the full-time basis.[72] It is evident that Lowell had little sense of the importance Cushing set on his independence; nor did he have any appreciation of Cushing's view that the surgeon-in-chief set the standards for the conduct as well as the development of surgery, both at the Brigham Hospital and at the Medical School. Cushing, however, understood Lowell only too well and informed him, as he had once before, that he would willingly step aside once the School was prepared to replace him with an appointee who accepted full time.[73]

Christian again refused as well.[74] His refusal reopened an old wound with a close friend. From the outset the General Education Board's rejection of Harvard's application for aid put Jerome Greene on the horns of a dilemma. Completely loyal to the Rockefeller philanthropies and deeply devoted to Harvard at the same time, he was disappointed that his alma mater had lost a chance to claim the primacy in medical education he felt it deserved. Still, in assessing the responsibility for the loss of the grant Greene did not blame the Foundation but rather his friend Christian. It was his feeling, he had written Lowell not long after the Board announced its decision, that Cushing and Edsall would have gone along with full time if Christian had not held back and assumed a half-hesitating, half-obstructive attitude.[75]

When in the fall of 1914 Greene learned of the failure of Lowell's new initiatives at the Brigham, he vented his feelings to Christian more openly: "I gather there is no longer any prospect of establishing clinical medicine on the full time basis as between the Harvard Medical School and the Brigham Hospital. The chief obstacle seems to be that you and Cushing, being in spirit full-time men yourselves, are unwilling to lend yourselves to a plan which would offer the surest guarantees of enlisting for the long run in your professorships men who would be immune to the temptations and distractions of private practice. You have certainly taken a mighty heavy responsibility."[76] Christian, angered by Greene's accusation that he personally had blocked the full-time system at Harvard, answered in kind: "May it not be true," he replied, "that the General Education Board has taken a very heavy responsibility in saying that only on one plan are they willing to help develop clinical instruction, intimating that that plan is the best possible one? Perhaps it is the best method, but there are thoughtful men who honestly disagree with this view and believe that a plan that is best in one locality is not necessarily the best for the other and that a fixed plan is less desirable than an elastic one."[77]

✑ ✑ ✑

Throughout Harvard's negotiations with the General Education Board Eliot carefully avoided taking an active role in the negotiating process—partly because of his position at the Foundation and partly because it did not seem proper for him to interfere with Lowell's conduct of the negotiations. For Eliot, more than for most at Harvard, a grant from the General Education Board to improve clinical instruction was not simply a matter of School pride or honor; he was keenly aware that the needs of the Medical School had outdistanced the support of local philanthropy and that funds from large foundations were a necessity if the School was to develop and thrive as a scientific institution. That conviction in time would allow him to put his reservations aside and play a more active part in Harvard's negotiations with the General Education Board. For the most part, however, the conduct of negotiations throughout the winter and spring of 1915 remained in Lowell's hands.

Although Lowell worked hard, he made little progress. He did not fully understand the implications of a full-time system, why Flexner insisted on full time at the Brigham Hospital as a sine qua non for receiving a grant from the Board, or, for that matter, why Cushing and Christian were so adamant in preferring their own version of full time. Early in 1915 during a new round of negotiations with Cushing, Lowell again tried to press Cushing to resign his post as chief of surgery at the Brigham in favor of a surgeon more amenable to the General Education Board's concept of full time. Again Cushing offered to resign.[78] This time, however, following Lowell's suggestion, he sent a copy of his offer to the chairman of the Board of Trustees at the Brigham Hospital.

The possibility of losing Cushing's services so upset the Brigham trustees that several days later, when Lowell approached them about his plan to appoint a new surgeon-in-chief, they forcefully informed him that they thought it neither advisable nor wise to make changes in the staff in order to introduce full time into the hospital.[79] Eliot was equally appalled when he learned of Lowell's discussion with Cushing and tried to advise the president through

Bradford to take the entire faculty into his confidence about the problems involved in full time and, above all, to delegate the burden of the negotiations to a new committee. "If the officers of the General Education Board want to talk with any representative of the Harvard Medical School," he suggested to Bradford, "the best persons to negotiate on the part of the School would be Drs. Cannon and Edsall and Mr. Pierce."[80]

Little came of Eliot's advice. Not only did Lowell continue to carry on negotiations for full time on his own, but later that spring he took a new tack and submitted a request to the General Education Board for funding to establish a School of Tropical Medicine at Harvard.[81] The proposal was immediately turned aside, and some members of the Board, who had witnessed Lowell's preliminary discussions with their representatives in New York, reported to Eliot that the proposal was tabled because of the inept way it had been drawn up and presented.[82] Although Eliot was galled by this latest failure to obtain a grant for Harvard, it inadvertently gave him an opportunity to take advantage of a new policy initiative the Board had recently adopted.

Late in May the General Education Board had voted to support the organization of an institute of hygiene devoted to the study of public health and preventive medicine.[83] Eliot found the Board's latest initiative particularly attractive; he had long tried to nurture such a program at the Medical School and almost at once made up his mind to take a hand in the matter. Before proceeding, however, he decided to speak with Simon Flexner to see if he could determine the basis for the Foundation's objections to Harvard's proposals. Simon Flexner had an important place in the Rockefeller philanthropic hierarchy: not only was he director of the Rockefeller Institute for Medical Research and a member of the Foundation but he was also one of Frederick Gates's principal advisers on medical matters. The Harvard Medical School's basic problem, he told Eliot, did not rest with the staff but rather with the administration, which appeared to him to have neither a single persistent aim nor an effective leader. When Eliot asked in reply if it would improve the administration of the School from his point of view if a person like Walter Cannon were made dean, Flexner answered affirmatively—and then added skeptically, "Hasn't the President the final word?"

Eliot's idea to make Cannon dean in Bradford's place was not merely a response to Flexner's remarks. Henry P. Walcott, a member of the Harvard Corporation, also disturbed by Bradford's administration of the Medical School, had previously made a similar suggestion. Encouraged by Simon Flexner's views, Eliot began to plot to make Cannon dean. "Is it possible," he wrote Walcott,

> to practically assure the appointment of Cannon as Dean within a short time, so that the appointment can be made known to the officers of the Rockefeller Foundation and the General Education Board? . . .
>
> Cannon is a person for whom both Simon and Abraham Flexner have great respect and a strong liking. Jerome D. Greene has the same feelings toward him; and Gates and Starr Murphy are both capable of appreciating him and his record. To put him in charge of the School is, in my opinion, the best thing the Corporation can do to make possible—yes, probable—the planting of that Institute of Hygiene at Harvard . . .
>
> The chilling fact is that nothing will come Harvard's way from the Rockefeller Funds which is not recommended by the Brothers Flexner. To make Cannon Dean of the School will help towards getting their support. It will also be a good thing in itself.[84]

It is not known whether Walcott broached Bradford's resignation with Lowell. In other matters, however, it appears that Lowell did follow a good deal of Eliot's advice. He asked Milton J. Rosenau, professor of public health and preventive medicine, to prepare a preliminary proposal for an institute of hygiene and appointed Roger Pierce, a loyal Harvard alumnus, business manager of the Medical School. He gave the responsibility of conducting the actual negotiations with the General Education Board to a special committee composed of Rosenau, Cannon, Richard P. Strong, and George C. Whipple.[85]

Rosenau was well aware of the difficulties involved in dealing with the General Education Board. A year earlier the Board had rejected his petition to establish a ten-year development program in public health and preventive medicine at the Medical School. That disappointment, however, did not dampen his spirits. When Lowell asked him to prepare a new proposal for an institute of hygiene, he immediately agreed. Actually, the building blocks for such an institute were already in place. From his appointment at Harvard in 1909, Rosenau had organized a two-tiered teaching and research program in public health at the Medical School, one

designed to introduce medical students to problems in preventive
medicine, the other to prepare graduate physicians for doctorates
in public health.[86] Several years later, in an effort to foster careers
in health administration, he joined with William T. Sedgwick of
M.I.T. and George C. Whipple of the department of sanitary engineering at the Harvard School of Applied Sciences to organize
a School for Health Officers. Although the School offered only a
certificate in public health, its wide-ranging course of study in
communicable disease, industrial hygiene, and sanitary engineering marked it as one of the first schools of public health in the
United States.[87] Nor were these the only public health activities at
the Medical School. In 1913 when Richard Strong returned to
America after more than a decade studying tropical diseases in the
Far East, the Graduate School of Medicine appointed him professor
of tropical medicine. Within a year of taking up his post Strong
led a successful research expedition to study the diseases of Central
and South America and inaugurated a sweeping teaching program
in tropical disease at the School as well. Strong's achievements
were so impressive that when a typhus epidemic broke out in
Serbia early in 1915 the Rockefeller Foundation in cooperation with
the Red Cross Sanitary Commission sent him there to help contain
the epidemic.[88]

In addition to their programs in public health and preventive
medicine, the Medical School had one other important strength—
the newly appointed negotiating committee. All of the members
of the committee understood the necessity of careful preparation
for their meeting with the General Education Board, and none
more than Cannon. In November 1915, when the Foundation sent
Abraham Flexner, Jerome Greene, and Wickliffe Rose to Boston
to appraise Harvard's proposal for an institute of hygiene, they
discovered that Cannon had arranged testimony from a wide range
of persons in the Boston area interested in the subject of public
health and preventive medicine. The testimony, which lasted for
three days, revealed the all-encompassing interest in the Medical
School, University, and city in the project and demonstrated the
personnel and cooperation the School could draw on in developing
viable programs in public health and preventive medicine.[89]

Despite the quality of the presentation, the Rockefeller visiting
committee had misgivings about awarding a grant to Harvard.
Several days after the committee hearings in Boston, Jerome Greene

Three of Harvard's negotiators with the General Education Board: Dr. Henry A. Christian, President A. Lawrence Lowell, and Dean Edward H. Bradford.

The General Education Board at the Hotel Samoset, Rockland, Maine, July 1915. Among those in the front row are F. T. Gates (second from left), C. W. Eliot (third from left), and Wallace Buttrick (far right); behind them are Wickliffe Rose (far left), J. D. Rockefeller, Jr. (third from left), Jerome Greene (second from right), and Abraham Flexner (far right).

Group assembled during opening of Brigham Hospital, 1913: from left to right, J. L. Bremer, Theobald Smith, W. B. Cannon, H. C. Ernst, M. J. Rosenau, D. L. Edsall, C. S. Minot, William Osler, Harvey Cushing, W. T. Councilman, H. A. Christian, and S. B. Wolbach.

The Tuesday Evening Club, May 20, 1916. Among those seated in front are Jerome Greene (second from left) and President Eliot (center); among those standing in back are David Cheever (second from left), Henry Christian (fourth from right), Walter Cannon (second from right), and Joseph Warren (far right).

confidentially suggested as much to Eliot: "It ought not to be necessary to say this," he wrote him, "but the fact remains that the authorities of the University seem to be more interested in getting the money than in adopting a rational policy for the Medical School. As a Harvard man, I cannot help wishing that the authorities would adopt a wise policy under efficient leadership, and not give another thought to Rockefeller money."[90] Several months later in its final report the committee made definite its rejection of the Harvard proposal. Although it agreed that the Medical School could command resources for an institute of hygiene that were far superior to those of any other school it had visited, it nevertheless felt that the administration, which it regarded as essential to the project, was wanting. In the end, the committee awarded the grant to the Johns Hopkins Medical School. Hopkins, it stated, had an efficient administration and a full-time faculty interested in clinical and scientific investigation; it had a hospital of its own to carry out educational and scientific policies; and above all, it had the leadership of William H. Welch.[91]

The Foundation's decision stunned Eliot. He had been certain that Harvard's resources in public health as well as the care with which their proposal was crafted and presented would earn them the grant. The more he read the Foundation's conclusions for establishing the new institute of hygiene at Johns Hopkins, the more irate he became, and finally he vented his anger to Abraham Flexner. "Johns Hopkins is a small and weak university compared with either Harvard or Columbia," he protested,

and Baltimore is a provincial community compared with either Boston or New York. In comparison with either Boston or New York, it conspicuously lacks public spirit and beneficent community action. The personality and career of Dr. Welch are the sole argument for putting the Institute in Baltimore—and he is almost sixty-six years old and will have no similar successor. This is the first time that a proposed act of a Rockefeller Board has seemed to me to be without justification or reasonable explanation. My lifelong interest in the great problems of public health and sanitation will account in your mind for this frank statement.[92]

Flexner's reply that the Foundation's decision in the last analysis depended more on the organization and administration of the Johns Hopkins Medical School and Hospital than on Welch did little to conciliate Eliot.[93] Indeed, it only served to confirm his belief that from the time of the Foundation's announcement to support an institute of hygiene, Flexner and Welch had planned to establish the new school at Johns Hopkins. Some time later Eliot learned that his outrage was shared by others at Harvard when he received a letter from Roger Pierce, the business manager at the Medical School:

8 March 1916

My dear Grandfather,

   Dr. Walcott announced to the Corporation that the Institute of Hygiene was destined for Johns Hopkins . . . The reasons given for refusing Harvard were based upon the Foundation's disapproval of the recent appointments in the departments of anatomy and pediatrics.[94] The Corporation feels that these appointments being known many months ago, to base their rejection of an Institute of Hygiene upon them, made a farce of their supposedly open-minded inquiry in Boston. It was felt that the visit to Boston, therefore, was made only because it afforded an opportunity to rebuke Harvard for the conduct of its own affairs. The Corporation considered that it had been insulted. The facts were announced at a meeting of the faculty of the Medical School, and the members thereof were incensed, and believed that the University had been shabbily treated, not because we failed to get the Institute but because of the reasons advanced which set at naught the admittedly superior facilities offered by the University at large and the community in general.

   Dr. Walcott did not speak to any one, to the best of my belief, in regard to the condition upon which Harvard might hope to receive a gift from the Foundation. Namely, the removal of Dr. Bradford as Dean and the appointment of Dr. Cannon in his place. He talked with me about it and I think he agreed with me that absolutely no steps should be taken to that end either directly or indirectly . . . I feel certain that the Corporation will make no appeals in the immediate future for financial support from any of the Rockefeller ventures for any purpose; nor at any time until it is certain beyond doubt that there is no disposition to control or regulate the internal conduct of university affairs. For my part, Harvard would cease to be Harvard if any grateful servant of the University were to be sacrificed as the price of a gift from either individual or institution.[95]

Pierce's letter had little manifest effect on Eliot. The need to obtain support to improve the Medical School so dominated his thoughts that as his anger slackened, he began to plan yet another proposal to the Foundation. Despite Pierce's suggestion that plans to have Cannon replace Bradford as dean be set aside, Eliot was convinced that such plans were a key to obtaining any funds from the General Education Board, and he asked Cannon privately if he would consider accepting the deanship. Eliot's request created a dilemma for Cannon. He dearly loved Eliot. In contrast, his relations with the administration had continued to deteriorate. A year earlier, in an effort to extend his power at the Medical School, Bradford sought to centralize control of all research funds in the dean's office.[96] Previously such funds had been available simply by request to the committee supervising a particular fund or to the Corporation. The prospect of having to ask the dean, who had little appreciation for scientific investigation, for funds to engage in research so appalled Cannon that he turned to one of his friends outside the Medical School to help him devise a scheme to thwart the dean. Eventually, Bradford's efforts failed; the incident, however, served to reinforce Cannon's conviction of being an outlander in the Medical School.[97]

Whatever his feelings, Cannon found it difficult to refuse Eliot outright and put him off with a promise to consider his proposal. Later that spring, when he could no longer delay a decision, he wrote Eliot that his growing lack of confidence in the methods of the administration made him unwilling to attempt cooperation. "It is with sincere regret that I refuse to do anything that you have asked of me," he concluded. "Only the conviction that such service that you have suggested would involve me in continual exasperation and futilities and in the misspending of valuable time has led me to withdraw my promise."[98]

If Eliot was disappointed by Cannon's refusal, he said nothing nor did he allow it to deflect him from going ahead with his plans. Private conversations with some members of the General Education Board convinced him that the Foundation desired to make a gift to the Harvard Medical School. Feeling that Lowell would be an encumbrance, Eliot bluntly informed him that he was persona non grata with the Foundation and that it would be wise for him not to take part in the new negotiations.[99] That matter settled, Eliot chose a committee composed of Cannon, Edsall, Reid Hunt, and William Thayer of Johns Hopkins (then a member of the Board of Overseers) to help him draft a proposal for a full-time system at Harvard.[100]

Eliot's choice of a planning committee is one index of the care he used in preparing his proposal. Another shows his understanding of some of the wider implications of receiving or not receiving foundation support. Concerned that another rejection by the Board might have an adverse effect on the morale of the medical faculty as well as on the reputation of the School itself, Eliot reached an agreement with the Foundation that his new request be treated informally and that, if found wanting, there be no public record that such a proposal had ever been made.[101] For the next several months the planning committee, driven by Eliot, devoted itself to preparing the proposal. There were few disagreements within the committee; all of the members believed in the principle of full time and gave wholeheartedly of their support to Eliot. Still, when they completed the application, it proved no more attractive to the Board than any of Harvard's previous requests.

Despite the respect and admiration within the Foundation for Eliot, the new plan was rejected on much the same grounds as the others. Eliot accepted the decision quietly.[102] He saw that the rejection had little to do with the substance of the proposal but rather was based on the Foundation's belief that the Medical School administration was not prepared to nurture a full-time system.[103] It was clear that what was needed to secure Rockefeller support was the appointment of a new dean who was committed to research and who had the fire and persistence to persuade Lowell of the value of research in advancing the prospects of the Medical School.

20   *A World at Risk*

I N THE YEARS immediately following the outbreak of war in Europe, Harvard, despite its inner administrative turmoil, was one of the preeminent medical schools in America—in some measure because it was an integral part of the country's oldest and most famous university, but even more because of the contributions of its preclinical and clinical faculties to the development of medical science and practice. For many, both inside and outside the University, Cannon and the physiology department exemplified what was best at the Medical School.

Cannon was so esteemed that distinguished scientists such as J. McKeen Cattell at Columbia University and Jacques Loeb at the Rockefeller Institute urged their sons to go to the Harvard Medical School in order that they might have an opportunity to study or work with him.[1] Physicians who appreciated his work on both digestion and the adrenals frequently wrote to him for advice on clinical matters or, like Walter Alvarez, came to Harvard for brief periods of time to be guided by him on investigations of problems that had emerged in their practices.[2] Medical students, eager to be at the cutting edge of the latest scientific developments, gravitated to the physiology department for the opportunities Cannon offered them to engage in research. One of these students, Alan Gregg, later recalling his own experience at this time, believed that student interest in the physiology department was the direct result of Cannon's "quality as a human being" and especially the affection he had for students.[3] Gregg's contemporaries at Harvard made similar observations.

Cecil Drinker, who came as a medical resident to the Brigham

Hospital in 1914, noted this same quality when he asked Cannon, whom he had met casually at Brigham staff meetings, if he could give his wife Katherine a place in his laboratory. Intrigued that the Drinkers were planning a joint study of the problem of blood coagulation, Cannon promptly agreed. "He took her on sight," Drinker wrote his friend A. N. Richards at the University of Pennsylvania, "and has made everything very pleasant and easy, so different from the difficult approach to physiology to which I have been used, that I was quite ashamed . . . I am surely going along into physiology and before next winter is past want to have a talk with you about it. I know my training has not been good but I am not afraid of working and I am going to be able to concentrate on just learning for as long as I please."[4] It was the beginning for Drinker of a lifelong attachment to Cannon and physiological research.

Cannon in turn cherished the stimulating camaraderie his colleagues and students provided in the laboratory. The closer the war came to disrupting everyone's plans and projects, the more Cannon sought out the haven his laboratory provided. This is not to suggest that everything was always serene in the laboratory. If Cannon perceived that members of the staff were not attending to their work with the diligence he expected or that their behavior was such that it offended his moral sensibilities, he could be harsh in his criticism and on occasion unforgiving.[5] Such blow-ups were not merely a matter of personality; they reflected his convictions of what he thought necessary to advance physiology. Nowhere is this better seen than in the way he administered his department. From the time he became chairman, Cannon followed a policy established by Bowditch that allowed junior members of the department to pursue their own interests. As a result, by 1915 the physiology department contained two research teams—one headed by Alexander Forbes, the other by Ernest G. Martin—working on investigative techniques and problems outside of Cannon's immediate area of expertise.[6] No matter what their interests, each of the junior members of the department had the privilege of recruiting graduate as well as undergraduate students to work with them.

In 1914, for instance, Alex Forbes chose Alan Gregg, a first-year medical student, to work with him on mammalian reflexes. Previously such reflexes had been studied by C. S. Sherrington, who analyzed tracings made of contraction of muscle by means of a myograph. Forbes, on this occasion, decided to use electrical recording devices to study the action currents of motor nerves as an index of central nervous system activity. Despite the difficulty of working with an untutored student, in the following year Forbes produced two important papers.[7] Several years later John Fulton, one of the leading experts in the United States on the physiology of the central nervous system, commended this research as a path-breaking achievement: "It had been supposed by some physiologists," Fulton wrote, "that impulses arising within the brain and spinal cord differed in kind from those elicited faradically in isolated preparations, and Forbes and Gregg were the first to provide satisfactory evidence that, however elicited, nerve impulses were always of the same nature."[8] More than forty years after his work with Forbes, Gregg noted another aspect of the investigation that he felt was important: "When we were done," he reminisced, "Alex insisted on putting my name on the paper. In my opinion, then and not far from it now, I felt that it was a dishonest thing to do because I didn't understand the stuff I was signing and Alex hadn't the faintest idea of the depth of my ignorance. I know now why he did it; it was done to get me interested."[9]

Although Cannon knew very little about the techniques Forbes and Martin used in their work, he sometimes understood better than they that the results of their research, besides extending physiological thought, could also have important clinical applications. When such occasions occurred, he would bring the relevant clinical problems to their attention. For example, after reading Forbes and Gregg's initial paper on mammalian reflexes, he became convinced that the study of action currents of motor nerves in addition to serving as an index of central nervous system activity might also be used to examine the question of whether ether anesthesia protected the brain from an incoming stream of nerve impulses during an operation. Forbes promptly put Cannon's suggestion to the test and discovered after some time that ether did in fact protect the brain from such damage as might be done by afferent impulses. In the process he incidentally confirmed Sherrington's earlier view that the synapse was the point at which the effect of an anesthetic occurred.[10]

The utility and importance of applying the results of physiological research to the solution of clinical problems were not lost on Forbes or, for that matter, on other members of the medical faculty. Because of his broad view of the function of physiological research, Cannon was frequently approached by members of the faculty for help in solving their clinical problems. If Cannon himself could not help, he invariably sought the assistance of another member of the department with the necessary expertise.

In 1914 Robert Lovett, professor of orthopedic surgery, knowing of Cannon's work on the effect of fatigue on muscles, asked him to help solve a problem that he had encountered during a recent polio epidemic in Vermont. Briefly, Lovett had discovered that most of the patients who survived the epidemic did not suffer a complete paralysis but rather various states of weakening of some of their muscles. He also found that although such muscles could be strengthened by a combination of exercise, massage, and muscle training, over-exercise or excessive massage invariably had a deleterious effect on the recovery of function of the affected muscles. The problem, he explained to Cannon, was that existing methods of testing muscle strength were unsatisfactory and what he needed was a practical quantitative test that would allow him to apply therapeutic exercise or massage according to the actual strength of the muscle.[11] In this instance Cannon, who was in the midst of his research on adrenals, directed Lovett to Ernest Martin. It was a happy suggestion: Martin, who had developed a variety of electrical techniques for measuring the stimulus threshold of muscles, found the problem to his liking. In short order he developed a test that made it relatively simple not only to determine the initial weakness of the affected muscles of polio patients but to gauge the subsequent loss or gain in the power of muscles under therapy as well.[12] During the spring and summer of 1915 Lovett and Martin applied the method in a series of state-wide polio clinics in Vermont with great success. For Martin the experience underscored the importance of Cannon's dictum of applying the results of seemingly abstract research to the solution of clinical problems. For Lovett it reinforced the view that collaboration with the physiology department was a useful and worthwhile activity.[13]

Years later on the occasion of Cannon's twenty-fifth anniversary as George Higginson Professor of Physiology, Walter Alvarez asked some of Cannon's early colleagues for their impressions of him. Alex Forbes, like others who had been asked, focused on Cannon's enthusiasm and zeal for research. "He thinks about it

almost all the time," Forbes wrote Alvarez. "Somebody jokingly
said that he would have to be prevented from taking any more
vacations because he only came back from them full of new problems for research that he had been thinking up during his holiday.
Of course he is a clear and logical thinker or his enthusiasm would
avail him little in obtaining results. He is also very ingenious, and
I think his ingenuity is perhaps the most notable of his intellectual
propensities."[14] None of the respondents, however, thought to remark on the factor in Cannon's life that provided him with the
balance he needed to develop as a person as well as an investigator—his wife, Cornelia.

✧   ✧   ✧

Throughout their marriage Cornelia continued to bring the
outside world to Cannon and on more than one occasion involved
him in public issues that she believed to be important. As the
children grew older, she became concerned with their education
and by extension with the quality of the Cambridge public schools
they attended.[15] Early in 1913 when the Harvard Division of Education announced plans to build a model school at the University,
Cornelia, sensing that such a school could be used to upgrade local
public schools, persuaded Cannon to devise a plan that would
join the new University school with the Cambridge school system.
Cannon's plan, which called for the city to assume the operating
expenses of the school in return for staffing and use of the University buildings, received little support either from the community or from Harvard.[16] The reaction, however, did not discourage
Cornelia. Several months later, when it became necessary to find
space for children who were temporarily displaced by the construction of the new Agassiz School, she offered the use of the
front porch of the Cannon house as an outdoor school for kindergarten and first grade. When the offer was accepted, she enmeshed Cannon in a plan to build an outdoor gymnasium for her
new charges.[17]

In a relatively short time the porch school became a model for
teaching kindergartners and first graders in Cambridge. It also
persuaded public school authorities to support Cannon's collaborative plan. The Harvard Division of Education, however, was
less forthcoming and decided to maintain the independence of its
projected model school.[18] The decision infuriated Cornelia: "The

department of education cannot grasp the social value of such a move," she angrily wrote her mother. "I cannot help suspecting that they want a nice private school of their own for their children and fear the coarse admixture of Irish and Italians would destroy its educational significance. If education is not democratic, of what earthly use is it?"[19] Despite the cool reception from Harvard educators, the porch school continued to prosper and gain attention. In the early fall of 1913 when Lucy Wheelock, head of the largest school for training kindgergarten teachers in Massachusetts, visited the porch school, she was so impressed with the program Cornelia had arranged that she informed the Cambridge superintendent of schools it was the best kindgarten she had seen in America. Several weeks later, when inclement weather threatened classes, Cornelia, using Miss Wheelock's encomiums, persuaded the school superintendent that the time had come to reopen negotiations with Harvard for a collaborative model school.[20] Although such a school did not then or ever become a reality, Cornelia's persistence ultimately led Harvard to offer space for the porch school in the Forestry Building until more permanent quarters became available.[21]

The porch school transformed home life at No. 2 Divinity Avenue. Outside, the backyard became a haven for neighborhood children who continually came to romp and play; inside, it became the headquarters for a movement to upgrade the Cambridge school system. Almost daily Cornelia and her friend Isabel Whiting peppered the school superintendent and other civic authorities with a variety of plans to reform the public school system. If the superintendent was harried by these persistent calls for reform, the Cambridge community welcomed the efforts of its self-appointed champions: in the late fall of 1915 Cantabrigians after a vigorous political campaign elected both of them to the local school board.[22] The victory took its toll not only in the school superintendent's office but in the Cannon household as well. "The family is worn out over my school campaign," Cornelia wrote her mother in November. "Walter says 'I will never vote for Suffrage again—Woman's place is in the home.' He thinks I have ceased to love him in these higher interests of education. I see I have got to take a day off, and devote it to telling him what a precious creature he is— and he is, too!"[23]

Despite Cornelia's extensive outside interests, there can be little doubt that Cannon remained at the center of her world.

Whenever she thought of something that might broaden his outlook or bring him pleasure, she brought it to his attention. She
had, for example, long noticed the enjoyment he had when his
more affluent friends took him on automobile rides and decided
that the time had come for him to have a car of his own. At first
Cannon balked at the idea, arguing that it might lead to "moral
degeneration." But under Cornelia's constant encouragement and
the cajoling of a persistent salesman, he finally succumbed and
with a great deal of trepidation bought a Model T Ford.[24] The
purchase, to his surprise, did not lead to the degeneration he
expected; instead, he found great pleasure in taking Cornelia, who
was again pregnant, for drives in the countryside and in tinkering
with the motor when the car broke down or did not perform to
expectations. The purchase did, however, change his lifestyle—a
change that was quickly noted by some of his colleagues. "Dr.
Cannon now owns a Ford and announces himself as one of the
idle rich," F. T. Lewis of the anatomy department wrote his chief,
Dr. Minot: "He has taken the streetcar to the School only twice
this fall, and often conveys members of his department and children. Owners of Fords take in children instead of running them
down, he says. At all events, it is a sort of public conveyance, just
as his yard and large piazza were turned over to the city for a
kindergarten."[25]

The children continually gave Cannon great pleasure. All were
bright and active, and at the end of the day when he came home
from the laboratory, he often discovered that they added a new
dimension to his world by their sayings and antics.[26] Once Bradford confessed to him that his teacher had punished him and other
children for throwing snowballs at each other. "What do those
teachers think the snow is for anyway?" he indignantly complained. Cannon was so taken by Bradford's logic that he used
the story as an illustration for a talk he gave that evening at the
Royce Club on the value of the teleological viewpoint in physio
logical research. "It was a fine talk and provoked a hot discussion,"
Cornelia later reported to her mother. "Dr. Parker, who is a literal
soul, as you know, made no remarks, but as they were going away
said to Walter, 'You do not know what teleology means, what
adaptation means, and I don't believe a word you said!'—Isn't
that a refreshing criticism, so complete and unflinching. Walter
was charmed with it."[27]

Early in 1915 the even tenor of life in the Cannon household

was disrupted when Colbert Cannon, after a brief illness in mid-
February, died quietly in his sleep in Oregon. His death left Cannon despondent: "I have a strange sense of being alone," he noted
in his diary after his father was buried, "of being the head of the
line with no one in front—of its being my turn next. I look on
Bradford with a new feeling that he is to take my place."[28] A few
days later his depression evaporated when Cornelia gave birth to
a baby girl. To maintain the continuities that had become important
to him, the little girl was named Helen Hanchett Cannon in honor
of Colbert's mother.[29]

The family was delighted with the baby, none more than
Bradford, who invited anyone who passed by in the street to come
in to see his new sister. But soon after, while praising the baby to
neighbors who had come to visit, Bradford announced, "I'm about
sick of sisters." When his Aunt Bernice reproached him, he turned
to her and asked, "How would *you* like to have a thousand sisters?"[30] Girls or boys, Cannon never cared; he had "a thousand
sisters" and felt the better for it. He doted on his daughters, was
proud of their cleverness, and not a little astonished at their independence and the ease with which they seemed to adapt to the
world. They underscored for him his happiness with his marriage.
In June 1915, on the occasion of his fourteenth wedding anniversary, he came home laden with gifts. Cornelia voiced her pleasure
at this show of affection: "I can certainly hardly realize that I have
been married fourteen years," she wrote her mother some days
later.

> It was a good gamble I took fourteen years ago and the winnings
> are all mine. Walter still seems pleased, too, so as yet there is no
> complaint from the interested parties. Isn't marriage a discipline
> and an education of the most inflexible kind? However gently and
> lovingly it may be done, it knocks off the angles, tempers the self-
> ishness, and turns the point of view outward instead of inward. I
> think the worst of us are improved by it, and of course the things
> it does to the best of us, make you want to take off your hat to God,
> to think he invented so wonderful a method. And the children are
> such a lovely touch! Altogether, between what nature intends and
> man devises, it is an institution to make the originator proud.[31]

Cannon's marriage to Cornelia, in addition to knocking off the
angles and turning the point of view outward instead of inward,

gave his life the stability he needed to meet the cascade of problems that came with being a scientific investigator. One such problem was political and involved an extension of his efforts to defend experimental research.

ᴇᴥᶴ ᴇᴥᶴ ᴇᴥᶴ

By 1915 much of the crisis atmosphere generated by the earlier antivivisectionist agitation seemed to Cannon to have disappeared. "The impressive fact at the present time," he wrote Richard Pearce early in January, "is the absence of any effectiveness of the anti-vivisectionists. Apparently in the presence of the enormous catastrophe in Europe where nations are thinking that the sacrifice of human life for national welfare is fully justified, the 'Antis' find some difficulty in convincing people that it is wicked to use the liver of a relatively small number of lower animals for the welfare of all mankind as well as the animals themselves."[32]

Although the antivivisectionists were relatively quiet at this time, they had not given up. Several weeks after Cannon wrote to Pearce, they began a new series of legislative campaigns in Pennsylvania, Massachusetts, and California featuring charges that medical scientists illegally seized dogs and other household pets for cruel and useless experiments. The agitation in Pennsylvania and Massachusetts did not overly concern Cannon: he was confident that physicians in Pennsylvania, who had a long experience with antivivisectionists, could easily cope with this new outburst, and in Massachusetts he drafted Harvey Cushing, David Edsall, Reid Hunt, and Elliott Joslin to help him counter the antivivisectionists' foray in the state legislature. The testimony he helped to arrange in defense of experimental research was so masterfully presented that after he delivered his closing speech members of the legislative committee assured him that the antivivisectionist dog bill would never leave the committee.[33]

California, however, proved a different matter. Prior to 1914 there had been little antivivisectionist activity in that state. The campaign against animal experimentation that erupted in 1915 appeared particularly threatening to Cannon because it was directed against the only medical research institute in the state—the Hooper Foundation laboratories at the University of California which had been organized only a year earlier.[34] In large part the Foundation came under attack following the successful research of one of its principal investigators, Karl Meyer, on typhoid and paratyphoid fever. Meyer's success brought immediate public recognition of the Foundation and just as quickly claims by antivisectionists of cruel animal experiments conducted in its laboratories. These claims were exploited with such skill by San Francisco newspapers that in the spring of 1915 a bill was introduced in the state legislature that gave humane societies wide latitude to investigate and to restrict all animal experiments conducted in the state. At first George H. Whipple, the director of the Hooper Foundation laboratories, did not take the proposed legislation very seriously. When Cannon on behalf of the research defense council urged him to make every effort to fight the growing threat of legislative control of experimental research, Whipple reassured him that he was well prepared to meet the antivivisectionists.[35] Nevertheless Whipple, for all of his confidence, had two qualities that put him at a disadvantage with the antivivisectionists—he was a gentleman and he believed in the power of rational discourse. The public debates were characterized by little gentlemanly behavior and even less rational discourse. Despite his best efforts Whipple found himself outmaneuvered by the opposition at every turn. Within weeks of its introduction the antivivisectionist bill was passed by the state legislature with comparative ease.

The antivivisectionist triumph in the California legislature appalled Cannon. It appeared to him that if the governor signed the bill into law, a ripple effect would ensue that would encourage the passage of similar legislation throughout the country. Spurred by visions of a legislative debacle that could undo the results of more than a decade of his efforts in behalf of experimental research, Cannon launched a national drive against the California bill. It is a measure of his political acumen that within days of starting his campaign a flood of protesting phone calls and mail from prominent scientists, physicians, educators, and political figures inundated the governor's office in California. This response, combined with the state's attorney general's opinion that the bill as drawn was unconstitutional, persuaded the governor to veto the bill.[36] The outcome, despite the relief it brought to the research defense council, did not completely settle matters in California. Within weeks a division occurred between Cannon and Whipple on how best to deal with the antivivisectionists. Cannon believed that the Hooper Foundation had little to fear from antivivisectionists in the immediate future. Whipple, however, was of a different mind. Attacked almost daily by antivivisectionists and the press in San Francisco, he came to the conclusion that the best way to counter the charges brought against the Foundation's laboratories (especially the claim that it used stolen pets for experimental purposes) was to persuade the legislature to pass a pound bill similar to the one that had then recently been proposed in Pennsylvania.[37]

At first Cannon thought that Whipple's plan for a pound bill— especially one based on the Pennsylvania model—was a poor one. Its provisions giving commercial firms access to impounded animals, he wrote Whipple, were provocative and might alienate members of humane societies who were favorable to experimental research and drive them into cooperation with the antivivisectionists. When Whipple persisted, Cannon cautiously urged him to keep his plans under cover and use them only in the event the antivivisectionists again tried to secure hostile legislation.[38] Although Whipple had great regard for Cannon, he was not persuaded by his advice. The following year, after several months of lobbying for a pound bill with the legislature, Whipple reached a private understanding with the governor and several key legislators that his bill would be passed in the next session of the legislature if he agreed to a proviso that would give the State Board of Health the right to supervise animal experimentation throughout the state. Whipple thought the bargain was to his advantage because the Board of Health at that time was composed entirely of physicians.[39] Cannon, who later examined the proposed legislation, was more skeptical and thought that Whipple had given away more than he had gained. But he did nothing to deflect Whipple. In fact, some time later in a complete turnaround he endorsed Whipple's proposed bill, arguing that it could serve as a precedent that other states might be urged to follow.[40] In the end their judgments were never tested; Whipple's bill reached the legislature for a decision in April 1917 soon after President Wilson's call to Congress for a declaration of war against Germany, and in the ensuing political turmoil the legislature never considered it.[41]

Although Cannon was especially involved in the antivivisection struggle in California and Massachusetts, little the antivivisectionists did or said elsewhere escaped his notice. When he learned early in 1916 that Senator Gallinger planned to introduce a bill calling for an investigation of animal experimentation by the

Department of Agriculture, he organized and orchestrated a political campaign with such skill that the bill was rejected in committee. The calm with which he met this most recent congressional
threat contrasted dramatically with the frantic measures employed
by Welch and his colleagues against another Gallinger bill sixteen
years earlier.[42] "I believe," Cannon wrote Simon Flexner when he
sent him a copy of the bill, "that the conduct of animal experimentation in the laboratories of research institutes, medical schools
and hospitals, and possibly also in commercial houses, is now in
a thoroughly defensible state."[43] But if the conduct of animal experimentation was defensible, the same was not true of the conduct of human experimentation—a problem that was soon borne
out by the clinical investigations undertaken by Udo J. Wile, a
young professor of dermatology and syphilology at the Medical
School of the University of Michigan.[44]

Late in 1915, stimulated by Hideyo Noguchi's previous discovery of spirochetes in the brains of deceased paretic patients,
Wile decided to examine the possibility that such spirochetes represented a special type that was more virulent and active than
those found in primary and secondary cases of syphilis. Convinced
that spirochetes obtained from the brains of living paretic patients
were more likely to infect than those obtained at autopsy, he asked
for and received permission from Edmund Christian, the chief of
medicine at the Pontiac State Hospital, to trephine the skulls of
six patients with advanced paresis to obtain the necessary matter
for animal experiments. Later Wile infected a number of experimental rabbits with the material he had obtained by trephining
and came to the conclusion that such spirochetes were in fact more
infective and more virulent than other strains.

Early in February 1916 Wile published the results of his research in the *Journal of Experimental Medicine*.[45] The appearance of
the article immediately raised a controversy. The Vivisection Investigation League and antivivisectionist magazines not only protested that Wile had violated the rights of the six patients in the
Pontiac State Hospital, but also castigated the Rockefeller Institute
and Simon Flexner for publishing Wile's paper in the *Journal of
Experimental Medicine* without comment or censure. Their protests,
strong as they were, did not match those voiced by physicians
and medical scientists. A critical editorial in the *Philadelphia En-
quirer*, a newspaper that had previously been supportive of ex-

perimental research, so upset W. W. Keen, one of the most vociferous opponents of the antivivisectionists, that he sent it to Victor C. Vaughan, the dean of the University of Michigan Medical School, calling at the same time for a vigorous protest by the research defense committee of the AMA.[46] George H. Simmons at AMA headquarters in Chicago was no less disturbed, and he wrote directly to Cannon, asking what to do or say in behalf of the Association.

Cannon himself felt betrayed and angry that the *Journal of Experimental Medicine* had published Wile's report. Two years before, in the wake of antivivisectionist attacks on Noguchi's experiments with luetin, he had sent a circular letter to medical editors asking that particular scrutiny be directed to the question of pain in animal experiments and to the issue of consent in cases of clinical investigations involving humans.[47] Faced with Simmons's request for guidance, Cannon turned to Henry James at the Rockefeller Institute for legal advice. Certain in his own mind that Wile's experiments could not be justified on either ethical or scientific grounds, he asked James if a stand might be taken on the basis of extant law that would make it unnecessary to defend Wile's research.[48]

James did not mince words: Wile's operations, he informed Cannon, were an assault and punishable by law. He also offered Cannon some advice: "Nothing could be more fatal to the defense of research in the long run," he told him, "than an unvarying, thick and thin defense by you and others of all doctors attacked by the Press. I think many medical men are really in danger of supposing that any harmless operation on a patient is justifiable if performed with a scientific purpose, even though the patient doesn't consent . . . In fact this view assumes a different society from the one we live in. Leaders of the profession . . . cannot afford to countenance operations performed for the operator's, rather than for the patient's, good."[49]

Although Cannon did not condone Wile's experiments, he was not prepared to denounce him publicly, in part because he felt that such a denunciation would sustain the antivivisectionists but even more because he saw Wile's experiments as part of a rapidly developing form of research for which he had great regard—clinical investigation. Instead, he began to draft a statement on human experimentation that he hoped would help to establish guidelines for investigators engaged in clinical research. In the main he followed the principle laid down by Claude Bernard almost a half century earlier that it was right and moral to perform experiments on humans provided such experiments could save life, cure, or at the very least provide some benefits to the subject. Keeping James's advice in mind, he added another principle to Bernard's prohibition of all experiments harmful to man, namely that even if a human experiment was harmless and could advance knowledge, it was not justified unless the subject of the experiment gave his consent.[50] Cannon thought his statement would have a greater impact if it was published in the *Journal of the AMA* as an editorial. Indeed, he hoped that it would serve as a basis for a resolution to be presented to the House of Delegates of the AMA at their annual meeting and adopted for inclusion in the Association's code of ethics.[51] Nowhere in the editorial, however, was there any mention or condemnation of Wile's experiments.

Late in May 1916, after discussion with Simon Flexner, Frederic Lee, and Henry James, Cannon sent the editorial to Simmons at the AMA with a copy to Keen. The lack of discussion of Wile's investigation infuriated Keen, an anger he promptly communicated to Henry James. "If we remain silent as to these specific experiments," he wrote James, "we shall be accused, and I think rightly, of approving them. I cannot approve them and the more I look into the matter and the more I think over it, the more certain I am that they were unjustifiable." "You may be sure," he warned, "that if no dissent from these particular experiments is expressed we shall meet them in every Legislature, in the lay press as well as the A-V press, and we shall suffer *very* greatly indeed." Keen told James that he had drafted an article for publication in the *Journal of the AMA* that would publicly censure Wile for his research. "I am sending copies of this to Cannon, Lee, and Welch, and I should be very glad indeed if you would show it to Dr. Flexner," he continued. It is clear that Keen was determined to be heard whether the medical academy would join with him or not.[52]

Although James agreed with Keen that Wile should be condemned, he balked at the substance of the protest. The central issue for him as for Cannon was not Wile but rather the whole range of questions relating to human experimentation that he believed would emerge because of the growth of clinical research. The basic problem, he wrote Keen in an attempt to placate him, was how to draw the line between experiments on human patients that might be performed ethically and those that were unjustifiable. Criticism of Wile from within the medical profession, he cautioned, would have to be expressed in such a way that it would not jeopardize the legitimate use of human subjects in clinical research. James's rationale slaked Keen's anger and he revised his original public condemnation of Wile's experiments.[53] Some time later when Cannon heard from Lee that a deferment of a formal declaration on the ethics of human experimentation by the AMA was likely, he like Keen began to fear that there might be a tendency to drop the matter.[54] On November 4, 1916, six months after Cannon sent his editorial to Simmons, it appeared unchanged in the *Journal of the AMA* under a headline "The Right and Wrong of Making Experiments on Human Beings." As far as is known, the resolution that he hoped for was never presented to the House of Delegates.[55]

The Wile incident was thus more an internal struggle within the medical profession than a battle against antivivisectionists. In all of the soul-searching that went on, hardly anyone on the research defense council remarked that some of their strongest adversaries were passing from the scene. Late in 1916 Mrs. Caroline Earle White died, and Albert Tracy Leffingwell, who of all the antivivisectionists had been the one most active in opposing human experimentation, was critically ill.[56] The diminution of antivivisectionist activity, however, did not mean the end of controversy for Cannon. He soon found himself embroiled in a debate that was more personal than those he had with the antivivisectionists and more threatening to the pride he took in his work.

Throughout Cannon's early career most of his research was readily accepted by physiologists as well as clinicians, generally with a great deal of praise for its ingenuity. To be sure, he had debates from time to time with some of his peers like Max Einhorn, Henry Dale, and Anton Carlson about some of his findings, but such skirmishes were by and large fleeting.[57] During the summer of 1916, however, George N. Stewart at Western Reserve Medical School, with the aid of his assistant Julius M. Rogoff, published the results of research that seemed to contradict Cannon's theory of the emergency function of the adrenals. It was the first time the entire corpus of one of Cannon's scientific investigations was challenged.[58]

Stewart was a formidable opponent. A product of the University of Edinburgh and its medical school, he was extraordinarily well trained in physics and mathematics; from the outset of his career as a physiologist he devoted himself to investigating the physicochemical problems of electrolytes in plasma and red blood cells and the application of such information for the measurement of circulation time and blood flow. Stewart believed that if physiologists carefully evaluated their research methods and pursued their inquiries appropriately, they would always arrive at questions that could be settled only by knowledge of the physicochemical constitution of living matter. As a result of these concerns, Stewart's papers contained detailed protocols, figures, and a great deal of quantitative data as well as analyses of the investigative techniques used in his experiments.[59] At times when his research required it, he developed new techniques to carry it forward; during his investigation of the mammalian circulation, he devised an ingenious dilution method of measuring blood flow—the principle of which is in use to this day. It was this study on blood pressure and blood flow that led him to the field of adrenal research and ultimately to his confrontation with Cannon.[60]

In 1911, during an investigation of claims that an increased level of adrenalin in blood was responsible for the persistently high blood pressure seen in certain diseases such as nephritis, Stewart became convinced that a single bioassay test was not sufficient to measure the presence or the absence of adrenalin in a liquid as complex as blood. To cope with this problem, he urged that at a minimum two tests be made to diminish the chance of error: one in which adrenalin caused contraction of smooth muscle (such as the uterus), and another in which the opposite response, inhibition, was produced, as in the intestinal strip.[61] Stewart found that although existing bioassay methods sufficed to detect adrenalin in serum obtained directly from the adrenal glands when they were excited to activity, he could not find adrenalin in the blood when he used the catheter method for withdrawal of blood from the upper abdominal vena cava that Cannon had devised for his research with de la Paz. Concluding that adrenalin in such blood was diluted beyond detection by existing bioassays, he decided to adopt a method proposed by J. J. R. MacLeod, one of his colleagues at Western Reserve Medical School. Although the procedure was extremely traumatic—involving anesthetizing an experimental animal, opening its abdomen, clamping the vena cava above and below the entrance of the adrenal veins (forming a pocket as it were), and then ligating all the blood vessels entering the pocket other than the adrenal veins—in Stewart's view the method had distinct advantages over other techniques for obtaining blood for adrenal assays. He discovered, for example, that by ascertaining the rate of blood flow into the caval pocket, he could measure blood flow through the adrenals and estimate more precisely the quantity of adrenalin secreted into the blood. In addition, when he released the top clamp on the vena cava, blood circulated throughout the animal's body enabling him to use in vivo adrenalin assays, such as blood pressure readings or Meltzer's denervated eye test. Still further, by placing a cannula in the vena cava and then releasing the bottom clamp, he could easily remove blood from the pocket for adrenalin assays using the uterus or intestinal muscle strips.[62]

Despite the promise of MacLeod's method, Stewart's results were largely negative and for the next three years he put his research on the adrenals aside and devoted himself to problems of circulation time and blood flow. In 1915, when Julius Rogoff, a young endocrinologist, joined his laboratory, Stewart turned once again to an investigation of the adrenals[63]—this time to see if he could confirm the results of some experiments that T. R. Elliott had conducted several years earlier in England. In 1912 Elliott, who had played a key role in elucidating the relationship between the adrenal glands and the sympathetic nervous system, claimed that stimulation of the splanchnic nerves caused increased release of adrenalin without a decrease in medullary content. But he also noted that the administration of morphine to a cat induced what he called "a state of fright" that led to a decrease in adrenal medullary content. Elliott, however, had little experimental data of his own to support the claim of a state of fright and leaned heavily on the results of Cannon and de la Paz's experiments on the emotional production of adrenalin.[64] Stewart and Rogoff built their attack on this feature of Elliott's argument.

Using as a bioassay one of the battery of tests afforded to them by MacLeod's caval pocket method (in this instance the increased reactivity of the sympathectomized eye described by Meltzer), Stewart and Rogoff found, as Elliott had claimed, that stimulation of the splanchnic nerves caused a marked release of adrenalin without a decrease in medullary adrenalin content—suggesting that nerve stimulation caused an increase in adrenalin production that kept pace with secretion. They also confirmed, as Elliott had reported, that administration of morphine to a cat led to a state of agitation and a decrease of medullary adrenalin content. Despite these results, Stewart and Rogoff were not willing to accept Elliott's notion that "morphine fright" could be equated with emotional disturbance. In one of their experiments in which they had used a dog, they found that although morphine decreased medullary content, the animal was sedated rather than excited.[65]

Cannon knew nothing of these experiments until late May 1916 when he read in the *Proceedings of the Society of Experimental Biology and Medicine* that Stewart and Rogoff were to present two papers on the adrenals to the society at its next annual meeting. The titles of the papers, "The Alleged Exhaustion of the Epinephrin Store in the Adrenals by Emotional Disturbance" and "The Liberation of Epinephrin from the Adrenals," upset him. "The titles suggest," he wrote Stewart, "that you may have evidence of failure of the adrenals to respond to emotional disturbance, at least to such a degree as Elliott has suggested. I should be very glad indeed to know whether the results you have obtained indicate any error in the conclusion which I have drawn from the evidence I had regarding the discharge of adrenin as a result of emotional excitement. You can realize that this is an important matter in relation to work that I have been carrying on, and that if I have made a mistake, I should wish to know at once about it."[66]

Stewart replied that his papers with Rogoff were essentially criticisms of Elliott's report on the exhaustion of the adrenal medulla during "morphine fright" and had no reference to Cannon's demonstration of the emotional secretion of adrenalin into the circulation. "I do not myself see," Stewart continued, "that there is any necessary connection between exhaustion or diminution of the epinephrin store and the rate of liberation of epinephrin into the blood. A classical example of a discharge which for the time at least does not tell upon the store, is seen in the effect of artificial stimulation of the splanchnics. By properly choosing the duration of the periods of stimulation and of rest, a relatively large amount of epinephrin can be liberated into the blood in a few hours; but the diminution in the content may be very much less than the amount so discharged, or there may be no diminution at all." In effect, Stewart affirmed his conviction that the adrenal medullary production could keep pace with the adrenalin release so that adrenal content was not necessarily decreased.[67]

Little more than a month later, when Stewart and Rogoff published their papers, Cannon discovered that they not only had criticized Elliott but also had attacked his work with Hoskins on the effect of sensory stimulation and asphyxia on the liberation of adrenalin—one of the bulwarks of his emergency theory of the adrenals. The two Western Reserve investigators reported that, unlike Cannon and Hoskins, they had not been able to find any increase in the adrenalin liberated during asphyxia as compared with that liberated in control observations in which the anesthetized animal was breathing normally. This was true, they asserted, whether they used as bioassays the caval pocket technique for eliciting the pupillary response of Meltzer or the rise in systemic blood pressure to measure the rate of adrenal secretion. Throughout, they stressed the superiority of their research methods over those used by Cannon and Hoskins. "It is, of course, possible," they allowed in conclusion, "that with the more extensive operation in our observations the spontaneous discharge of epinephrin is already so much increased that there is no room for a detectable increase by asphyxia, etc."[68] This caveat did not appear to them to be important and they promptly forgot about it.

The attack stunned Cannon. Two years earlier Stewart had spoken warmly of the utility of the emergency theory in a new edition of his *Manual of Physiology*. Even more recently he had assured Cannon that his research with Rogoff contradicted Elliott's findings on "morphine fright," not the emergency theory. Yet it was not Stewart's turnaround or the challenge to his findings alone that upset Cannon; rather it was the continuing attacks on the quality of his investigative methods that he found increasingly distressing. During the spring of 1917 Stewart and Rogoff published a number of studies, again featuring a vast amount of quantitative data gathered through MacLeod's traumatic caval pocket method, that appeared to demonstrate that the output of adrenalin was constant and not elevated by emotional or sensory nerve stimulation, as Cannon and his coworkers had claimed.[69]

Although Cannon found the burgeoning controversy distasteful, he was not intimidated. From the outset he had suspected that the caval pocket technique was flawed and set out to contravene its results. During the winter of 1916–17, with the aid of H. F. Pierce, a graduate student,[70] he searched for a method that would incontrovertibly demonstrate the validity of his emergency theory. The method Cannon finally adopted was the denervated heart, a technique utilized to good effect several years earlier by Walter Meek and Herbert Gasser at the University of Wisconsin Medical School in a study of the nervous control of the heart rate during exercise.[71] Following Gasser and Meek's suggestive paper, Cannon found that when he and Pierce denervated the heart of an experimental cat by severing both vagi in the neck and removing the stellate ganglia, and allowed the animal to recover, the heart then became a very delicate indicator of adrenalin in the blood— one that under afferent stimulation increased its rate in proportion to the amount of adrenalin circulating in the blood, whereas in an adrenalectomized animal there was no detectable increase in its rate.

Although the method had the qualities Cannon had been searching for, he had little time to utilize it. Upon completion of his research with Pierce, he put his work with the denervated heart aside and began to study the problem of surgical shock in preparation for going overseas with the Harvard Medical Unit to serve in the war.[72] He did prepare an article on the research, however. Using his surgical experience, Cannon focused his remarks on the caveat Stewart and Rogoff had mentioned in their first paper and then ignored. "A great deal of care must be taken in operating on the abdominal cavity to avoid manipulation," he reminded them. "As was shown many years ago, such operations produce changes which can be best accounted for by continuous discharge of the nerve impulses along splanchnic courses. Thus the adrenal glands would be persistently stimulated. A potent source of error in previous work, in which the abdominal cavity has been opened, has doubtless been the failure to exercise extreme care to avoid rough manipulation."[73] Cannon's rejoinder appeared in *Science* on May 17, 1917. The controversy, originally over the validity of the emergency theory, had become one of method as well. Although Cannon had left for France, Rogoff prepared another attack on his techniques. Others joined the fray, some as adherents of Stewart and Rogoff, some as supporters of Cannon. The dissenting views warmed the pages of the new journal *Endocrinology* and served as prologue to a dispute that would engage physiologists with increasing ferocity for more than a decade before being resolved in Cannon's favor.[74]

21   *Prelude to the Great War*

W HEN THE EUROPEAN war erupted in August of 1914, President Wilson assumed a stance of neutrality. The mood of a number of congressmen and government officials was far more belligerent, however. Some even appeared to be in the grip of a war fever. A program of army recruitment and training, which had been defeated in Congress a year before, took on a new life—not the least because of the drive and support it received from a number of Harvard graduates who were eminent lawyers, businessmen, and government officials. While many of these men, including among others Grenville Clark, Robert Bacon, Hamilton Fish, and Franklin Roosevelt, perceived Germany as the future enemy, others at Harvard, both students and faculty, did not share their convictions—some because of their close intellectual ties to Germany and others because of their opposition to war in general.[1] Cannon, who belonged to the latter group, initially avoided taking any position on the war other than to propose a way of channeling hostile instincts and acts of aggression—a move that elicited favorable comment from many newspapers throughout the country.

As the war continued, however, attitudes in the Cannon household began to change. Cornelia, outraged by the German destruction of the library of the University of Louvain, increasingly began to view the war as a struggle for freedom and Germany as an enemy of the human spirit. Individual faults of Germans, which she had previously accepted for what they were and criticized as such, were now seen as national faults and not as easily forgiven, particularly if they reflected in some way on Cannon or his work. "German Kultur," she complained to her mother some months after the war began, "is the only hope of the world, and if you won't take it, it must be forced down your throat. They show it by their complete ignoring of any research done in science in this country. Walter received a paper the other day from a German professor, reporting a research he had just done, which Walter had done and *published* four years ago! If nothing worse, that is frightful inefficiency."[2] In time Cornelia's complaints about Germans and Germany became even sharper and more pointed. It is not known whether Cannon shared all of his wife's convictions or came to believe as she did that Germany had to be whipped like a child for the good of its soul. He said little publicly at the time about any of the combatants. What is known is that early in 1915, he resisted pressure from some of his friends at the Medical School to participate in the war.

The Medical School, despite some of its manifest ties to German medical science, was among the first in the University to go beyond rhetoric and take steps to actively help the British and French. Harvey Cushing organized a volunteer surgical unit to serve in a British hospital near Paris and tried on several occasions to persuade Cannon to join him. For all of Cushing's cajoling, Cannon refused, offering as excuse that he needed to exploit a new breakthrough in his investigation of the adrenals. Cornelia provided another explanation: "In some ways he is tempted," she wrote her mother, "but I think he fears the horror of the thing would so overcome him that he would be useless."[3] War was the antithesis of all that Cannon believed and held dear; however, resisting pressure to participate in it became increasingly difficult. In May 1915, after a German submarine sank the *Lusitania*, the mood at Harvard changed dramatically. Almost overnight, the spirit of neutrality that had previously seemed to exist on campus disappeared. Some of the passions that were let loose can be gauged by one of the letters Cornelia sent home soon after. "We are still staggering under this awful blow! Horror and grief are swallowed up in rage. I find myself full of the most primitive emotions . . . Mr. Crothers I have never seen so moved. Saturday he said was the worst day in his life. Must we go to war? It seems as if it might be the only way to wipe out this horrible blot on humanity. As if life itself were the least payment we could make for so tragic a thing. The awful thought is Where is our Christianity and our boasted civilization?"[4]

In the months that followed, Cannon, under pressure of events, found himself increasingly caught up in the war. When William Bayliss asked him in late September to ascertain if the American Physiological Society would join the British Physiological Society in publishing a journal of physiological abstracts in place of the German *Zentralblatt,* he readily agreed and helped the project through to fruition.[5] Some time later, the deaths of a number of young English physiologists whose work he knew so affected him that he began to feel guilty for not taking a more active part in the war. "I told Mrs. Cannon," he wrote Charles Sherrington early in 1916,

> that if I had not my family obligations, I should surely go over to do anything I could to help.The night after making this statement I dreamed that I was dwelling in a great house not far from a battle line. We heard the booming of the guns begin, and then the ambulances began to bring back the wounded who were temporarily laid on the ground outside. It was pitch dark. Instead of going out to succor them, I went upstairs to the roof and began looking about among the chairs and other things that were there, for a blanket which I could not find. My search was occasionally interrupted by a glance down at the flaring torches carried by the orderlies and by the hoarse cries of anguish that arose from the dark field. There was a Freudian symbolism about this vision, for it seems to me that as I stay here in the laboratory, I am quite truly "looking for a blanket in the dark" while there is great need for more direct and practical work elsewhere.[6]

In addition to serving as a catalyst for Cannon's changing stance on the war, the sinking of the *Lusitania* also touched off a conflict that was not easily resolved and affected Cannon and Cornelia for some time almost constantly in their daily lives. The problem involved Cannon's old teacher and long-time friend, Hugo Münsterberg.

From his arrival at Harvard in 1892 to direct the laboratory of experimental psychology, Münsterberg was widely regarded as an important addition to the University community.[7] Colleagues prized his research and teaching and extended their friendships. There can be little doubt that Münsterberg was pleased by this reception; indeed, it encouraged him to regard himself as Germany's cultural representative in America. In 1904, in an effort to help Germans and Americans better understand each other, he published a massive interpretive work of life and thought in America. Some years later, to help further such understanding, he organized a Transatlantic Institute in Berlin to facilitate study by Americans in Germany.[8]

When the war broke out, Münsterberg took it as his mission as a German patriot to interpret his country's aspirations and war aims for the American public. While the articles, essays, and books he subsequently wrote found an appreciative audience among Americans of German descent, many members of the Boston and Cambridge communities were incensed by his support of Germany. Some even believed that he was a German agent and that the pigeons he kept in his backyard were for the purpose of sending secret messages to other German agents in America. Others assumed that he was a paid German propagandist. A number of Harvard alumni were so angered by the lectures and interviews he gave on behalf of Germany that they threatened to rescind their bequests to the University if he were not fired.[9] Although the administration was unhappy with Münsterberg's activities, it was not prepared to dismiss him. Lowell had little sympathy with the position that Münsterberg had taken but nevertheless met all demands that he be dismissed with an ardent defense of his right to express his opinions freely. "This University," Lowell forcefully wrote one irate Harvard alumnus, "will certainly not abandon the principle of academic freedom, nor discharge any professor on account of his opinions . . . Moreover, it would destroy wholly the intellectual force of the University if the ruling bodies attempted to lay down what its professors might or might not say."[10]

Lowell's defense of Münsterberg became the core of a small but incisive essay in his next annual report to the Harvard Corporation on the necessity of maintaining academic freedom at the University.[11] Although Lowell's stance on academic freedom kept the public at bay, ironically it did little to control the growing hostility on campus toward Münsterberg. Following the sinking of the *Lusitania*, Josiah Royce, one of Münsterberg's closest friends in the philosophy department, broke with him, holding him almost personally responsible for the act. Ernest Hocking, another colleague and close friend, engaged in acrimonious public debate about the contents of a letter Münsterberg had sent the German chancellor that in Hocking's view was so clearly pro-German as to be anti-American. Edwin Holt, who had translated Münsterberg's massive volume, *Die Amerikaner*, circulated stories that the German psychologist had falsified the results of some of his experiments. In short order Münsterberg became a pariah on campus, shunned by most of the faculty.[12] The ostracism shattered him. When an acquaintance asked him early in 1916 to speak to the Dean of Harvard College in behalf of her son's application, Münsterberg replied that he was persona non grata at the University. "At present about one fourth of my Harvard colleagues," he complained bitterly,

no longer bow to me on the street. About one half bows, but everyone does it with a face either frozen or filled with disgust distinctly mixed with a feeling of fear that some one might see him in the reprehensible act of recognizing me . . . The social club which I enjoyed most in Boston, the Thursday Evening Club, of which I was a member for fifteen years, has expelled me this winter; leading people stoop to write most insulting letters to me; people who owe everything to me have cut their connections entirely; and the one man (Royce) who almost forced me to stay here, when a most attractive call tempted me home some years ago, and who at that time promised me his most intimate friendship and assured me of the loyalty of Harvard in every possible life situation, was first in line to treat me brutally.[13]

Despite the mounting pressure to drive Münsterberg from the University, a handful of people—including Cannon and Cornelia as well as Robert Yerkes and his wife, Ada, and George Foot Moore, Professor of the History of Religion—remained steadfast in their friendships with him. Cornelia, although very pro-Allied in her feelings, was particularly sensitive to the burdens Mrs. Münsterberg carried and did what she could to comfort her with frequent visits. In time, the enmity took its toll. On one visit early in December 1916, Cornelia noted that Mrs. Münsterberg's hair had turned completely white. "We did not mention the war," she wrote her mother, "but talked of the high cost of living—a safe topic."[14] Two weeks later, while lecturing to a class at Radcliffe, Münsterberg suddenly died. Typically Cornelia immediately rallied her friends to help Mrs. Münsterberg. Later when she paid a condolence call, Mrs. Münsterberg expressed her gratitude that she had come but remained unforgiving and bitter about the rest of the Harvard community. Her husband had died for his country like all the other Germans, she told Cornelia, but was killed by America and not by England or France.[15] When Harvard offered her Appleton Chapel for a University funeral, she refused and held the service at home. George Foot Moore's eloquent eulogy encapsulated with rare perception the difficulties that had made a misery of his friend's last years: "All in all," he told the assembled mourners, "his was a character so alien to our American, and perhaps especially to our New England, temper and habit that it was inevitably misunderstood and misjudged . . . Strangely, it may some day seem when passion has subsided, nothing that he wrote about war was taken so much amiss as that he should presume to speak of peace."[16]

ᔆ   ᔆ   ᔆ

Throughout 1916 there was a perceptible growth of a war spirit at Harvard. As the months passed, increasing numbers of undergraduate as well as graduate students entered the French ambulance service or joined the army or navy reserve officers' training programs that the University had then recently organized. All of Harvard eagerly followed news of the activities of the various volunteer surgical and medical teams that had gone abroad to serve in military hospitals in France. Few in Boston and Cambridge did not take pride in the reported achievements of such familiars as Harvey Cushing, David Cheever, and Hugh Cabot or marvel at the news of the extraordinary results of plastic surgery performed by the Medical School's little-known demonstrator of prosthetic dentistry, Varaztad Kazanjian.[17] Despite these developments Cannon steadfastly resisted another effort to persuade him to play a more active role in the war. Early in the year, when Henry James asked him on behalf of the Rockefeller Institute to help Alexis Carrel in France with problems of traumatic shock, he refused. The problem, he explained to James, was so overwhelming and complex that he simply had no strategy to deal intelligently with the issues involved. Disappointed, James thereupon made the same request of William T. Porter, who agreed to take on the assignment.[18]

Several months later, however, when the National Academy of Sciences established a National Research Council to address the problems incident to the growing threat of war, Cannon began to feel a pressure he found increasingly difficult to deny. In October when he was asked by the council to become chairman of a special physiological committee to develop research programs to maintain the life and safety of the armed forces as well as of the general population, he finally succumbed.[19] In the weeks and months that followed, Cannon, although still involved in research bearing on his controversy with Stewart and Rogoff, began to define the problems he thought would be important for carrying out the mandate of the Research Council. He drew up a list of topics he considered worthy of investigation including surgical shock, irritable heart of soldiers, and fatigue among munitions workers, and emphasized the need for more information to establish their priorities. "What we, as physiologists, can do in the present critical juncture is not yet clear," he confided to his fellow committee member, Joseph Erlanger, in March 1917. "I have written to Sherrington, Hill and Richet to learn from them what the physiologists of England and France have been able to do for their countries in the Great War. As soon as I receive answers, I shall distribute the information."[20]

Cannon also discovered that a number of investigators were not particularly pleased with the assignments he intended for them. When he suggested to Erlanger, for example, that he work on problems of the irritable heart, Erlanger politely rejected the assignment and indicated that he much preferred to work on surgical shock—a problem that Cannon had chosen for himself. At first, he was taken aback but later recognized that there were enough facets to the problem for Erlanger and others who had indicated an interest in the subject to choose those aspects in which they had the greatest expertise.[21] It was to prove a happy compromise.

At that time there were as many explanations for the cause of shock as the number of physiologists and surgeons who had investigated the subject.[22] George Crile, for example, who had spent years investigating surgical shock, believed that the cardiac, motor, and respiratory failure he had observed in his patients during shock were secondary to the failure of circulation—in fact, that the failure of arterial pressure was the primary cause of shock. Yandell Henderson at Yale argued that the reduction of cardiac output and arterial pressure so prominent in shock were primarily the result of a reduction of venous return through a loss of carbon dioxide. William T. Porter, recently returned from his work with Carrel in France, maintained that the shock he had observed in wounded soldiers was the result of fat embolism caused either by the escape of fat into the bloodstream from fractured bones or from lacerated subcutaneous adipose tissue.[23] While some of his collaborators devoted themselves to such problems as the experimental production of shock in animals or determining the role of the autonomic nervous system in the process, Cannon focused on clinical issues—a procedure that was to lead to yet another concept of the cause of shock.[24]

"The problem of dealing with the condition is, of course, an old one," he wrote Erlanger at the outset of his research.

> Are there not untried ways of treating it? May it not possibly be a vicious circle started initially by severe trauma which leads to vascular relaxation especially in the splanchnic region and then continued because the central nervous system is not sufficiently supplied with blood? May it not be that the important factor is improving the blood supply until the normal conditions of the nervous system have been restored? Might not the introduction of sterile salt solution in the abdominal cavity instead of into the blood vessel, in sufficient amount to produce increase of pressure there, be worth trying? Or the fluid introduced might be somewhat viscous and have within it adrenin which might continue to keep up the arterial pressure until the nervous apparatus again obtains control.[25]

The factor of the reduction of blood volume intrigued Cannon. Although he had no clear notion of what happened to the blood and assumed that it was lost from the circulation by accumulating in the splanchnic bed, the more he thought about the problem the more he began to focus on the acidosis that accompanied the diminished blood volume. For Cannon acidosis increasingly appeared to be an important secondary factor that led to the perpetuation of shock.[26] In late March 1917 following his correspondence with Erlanger, he began a series of animal experiments to see if he could, by increasing the alkali reserve in the blood by injection of sodium bicarbonate, control acidosis and through such control mitigate shock.

The need to quickly find a treatment for shock so gripped him that his experiments began to dominate his existence. The war he had once found so repugnant not only gave impetus to his research but also appeared right and just. When President Wilson on April 2, 1917, asked Congress for a declaration of war against Germany, Cannon and Cornelia organized a patriotic celebration at home in order that the children might remember the events of the day. "We sang the Star Spangled Banner and America and the Battle Hymn of the Republic," Cornelia later wrote home,"—then I read them things from the first and second Inaugurals of Lincoln and told them what the significance of the day was. We met at 12, as Congress assembled, each child had a flag and I had a big silk one across the book case—We ended with the salute to the flag and the pledge to allegiance they have in school. It was a cunning sight to see the little patriots . . ."[27]

Cornelia and Cannon's patriotic fervor was more than matched by others at Harvard, and not the least by their close friend Ralph Barton Perry. Perry, who had earnestly given himself to the preparedness movement from the organization of the Plattsburg training camp in 1915, was piqued that Cannon and George Pierce were considered to be more important to the war effort than himself. "He says he went to Plattsburg," Cornelia later recalled, "spent weeks learning the war manual etc. to serve his country, and is only good enough to go out into the fields and say 'hep hep,' while Walter and George, who have done nothing, are now found invaluable!"[28]

Cannon made no such comparisons. The sense that his research might one day help to treat the more than one thousand cases of shock that occurred weekly on the European battlefields was his sole measure of the importance of his work. He felt the pressure so keenly that some time later, in the midst of a meeting of the National Research Council in Washington, he abruptly announced that he had to return immediately to Boston to continue some important experiments he had under way.[29]

Cannon was so excited about the progress of his research that, according to Cornelia, he could hardly eat or sleep.[30] Late in April he decided that he could no longer delay putting the results of his research to the test and asked Harvey Cushing, who was then organizing a Harvard Medical Unit for the army, to find a place for him with the understanding that he be detailed as a special investigator and given the freedom to visit the advanced aid stations where cases of shock were first seen.[31] The next night Cannon told Cecil Drinker and L. J. Henderson who had joined him for dinner that he had some second thoughts about going abroad. "I don't know," he confessed, "whether I should have the nerve to experiment on humans." "Yes, you will," Drinker replied, "when you know that you are their only hope and without you they will die." Henderson was even more positive. "Cannon," he said, "if it turns out as you hope, it will be the biggest thing that comes out of the war."[32]

Although Cornelia took pride in the promise of Cannon's research and the enthusiasm it engendered among his friends, the fact that he had finally decided to join Cushing began to wear her down. At first she resisted giving in to her fears and put on a bold front: "I would not lift a finger to hold him back," she confided to her mother.[33] As the days passed, however, and Cannon's departure drew near, she could no longer contain her concern. On May 4 she wrote home again: "We only wait the telegram from Washington. It may not come until Monday. I seize each precious moment like a miser. I am calm and I know I can keep so until Walter goes. After that there will be plenty of time!" Cannon's actual departure five days later was almost an anticlimax. "Walter went this morning at 10 a.m.," Cornelia informed her family. "There was not a tear except those shed copiously by Dr. Cushing's chauffeur, who was inconsolable. We had the true Anglo-Saxon horror of showing emotion evidently—Isn't it curious? To onlookers I suppose it seems heartlessness to joke and be merry at such a time, but we carry ourselves over tremendous crises that way. Do we suffer more or less for it?—It enabled us to send dear Walter off with smiling faces, anyway, and saved him pangs of memory."[34]

When Cannon left for France in May of 1917, he was forty-five years old and the father of five. For him, going to war was a duty he owed to his country; one, moreover, that by a stroke of fortune offered him, unlike so many others, an opportunity to save rather than destroy lives. For Cornelia, Cannon's departure was a terrible detour that had to be taken in order to preserve the ideals that both of them lived by and cherished. Neither one, however, in the moment of parting, suspected that the war was a prelude to an extraordinary transformation of the world they knew and that life for them as for others would never be the same again.

ABBREVIATIONS
BIBLIOGRAPHICAL NOTE
NOTES
INDEX

෨

Abbreviations

AMA	American Medical Association
Am. J. Physiol.	*American Journal of Physiology*
Annual Reports	*Annual Reports of the President and Treasurer of Harvard University*, Harvard University Archives
BM&SJ	*Boston Medical and Surgical Journal*
Christian/GEB	"Correspondence between Henry A. Christian and Others and the General Education Board and Others in Regard to Improving Clinical Instruction in Harvard Medical School," Harvard Medical Archives
Diary	Entries in Cannon's personal diaries, in Cannon Papers
"Family Memory"	"Introduction to a Family Memory," as told by Ida Cannon, Bernice Cannon, and Jenny Williams to their niece, Linda Cannon Burgess, 1959, in Cannon Papers
GEB	General Education Board
HMA	Harvard Medical Archives, Countway Library
HMS	Harvard Medical School
HUA	Harvard University Archives, Pusey Library
JAMA	*Journal of the American Medical Association*
Life & Contributions	*The Life and Contributions of Walter Bradford Cannon, 1871–1945: His Influence on the Development of Physiology in the Twentieth Century*, ed. C. M. Brooks, K. Koizumi, and J. O. Pinkston (Brooklyn: State University of New York, Downstate Medical Center, 1975)
MGH	Massachusetts General Hospital
Minutes of Medical Faculty	Harvard University Faculty of Medicine, Minutes of meetings, Harvard Medical Archives
RAC	Rockefeller Archive Center
"Recollections"	"Recollections of Bernice, Ida, and Jane Cannon," as told to their niece, Linda Cannon Burgess, 1959, in Cannon Papers
"Servant of Science"	Cornelia J. Cannon, "A Service of Science: Walter Bradford Cannon," unpublished manuscript in Cannon Papers

"Snatched from Oblivion"	"Snatched from Oblivion," extracts from letters written to her mother by Cornelia James Cannon, photocopy of family scrapbook in Cannon Papers
Snatched from Oblivion	Marian Cannon Schlesinger, *Snatched from Oblivion: A Cambridge Memoir* (Boston: Little, Brown, 1979)
Way of an Investigator	W. B. Cannon, *The Way of an Investigator: A Scientist's Experiences in Medical Research* (New York: W. W. Norton, 1945)

Bibliographical Note

Manuscript and Archival Sources

The Walter Bradford Cannon Archive in the Francis A. Countway Library, Harvard Medical School, Boston, constitutes the major repository of Cannon's papers. The nucleus, drawn from the Harvard Medical Archives, has been supplemented since the establishment of the Cannon Research Project in 1973 with photoreproductions and additional materials from the Cannon family, from colleagues and former students, and from collections in other libraries. All of these materials have been organized and preserved in more than two hundred manuscript boxes; a detailed inventory of the collection may be found in the Countway Library.

This book could not have been written without access to a number of other archival and manuscript collections both at Harvard and elsewhere. An asterisk(*) in front of certain entries indicates that there are also files—often quite substantial ones—in the holdings at the Rockefeller Archive Center and in the Rockefeller University Archives.

John Jacob Abel Papers
Alan Mason Chesney Medical
  Archives
Johns Hopkins Medical Institutions
Baltimore, Md.

American Physiological Society
  Council Minutes
American Physiological Society
  Archives
Bethesda, Md.

Anti-Vivisection Papers
Rockefeller University Archives
New York, N.Y.

Baumgarten Family Papers
Washington University
School of Medicine Library
St. Louis, Mo.

Francis Gano Benedict Papers
Francis A. Countway Library
Harvard Medical School
Boston, Mass.

Henry Pickering Bowditch Papers
Francis A. Countway Library
Harvard Medical School
Boston, Mass.

Richard Clarke Cabot Papers
Harvard University Archives
Pusey Library
Cambridge, Mass.

Ida Cannon Papers
Social Service Department
Massachusetts General Hospital
Boston, Mass.

*Alexis Carrel Papers
Georgetown University Library
Washington, D.C.

James McKeen Cattell Papers
Divison of Manuscripts and
 Archives
Library of Congress
Washington, D.C.

Russell Henry Chittenden Papers
Sterling Memorial Library
Yale University
New Haven, Conn.

Henry Asbury Christian Papers
Francis A. Countway Library
Harvard Medical School
Boston, Mass.

Ernest Amory Codman Papers
Francis A. Countway Library
Harvard Medical School
Boston, Mass.

George Washington Crile Papers
Western Reserve Historical Society
Cleveland, Ohio

Harvey Cushing Papers
Sterling Memorial Library
Yale University
New Haven, Conn.

Henry Hallett Dale Papers
Royal Society
London, England

Charles Benedict Davenport Papers
American Philosophical Society
Philadelphia, Penn.

Charles William Eliot Papers
Harvard University Archives
Pusey Library
Cambridge, Mass.

Joseph Erlanger Papers
Washington University
School of Medicine Library
St. Louis, Mo.

Harold Clarence Ernst Papers
Francis A. Countway Library
Harvard Medical School
Boston, Mass.

*Abraham Flexner Papers
Division of Manuscripts and
 Archives
Library of Congress
Washington, D.C.

*Simon Flexner Papers
American Philosophical Society
 Library
Philadelphia, Penn.

Alexander Forbes Papers
Francis A. Countway Library
Harvard Medical School
Boston, Mass.

Frederick Taylor Gates Papers
Rockefeller Archives Center
North Tarrytown, N.Y.

General Education Board Papers
Rockefeller Archive Center
North Tarrytown, N.Y.

*Jerome Davis Greene Papers
Harvard University Archives
Pusey Library
Cambridge, Mass.

Ross Granville Harrison Papers
Sterling Memorial Library
Yale University
New Haven, Conn.

Harvard University Corporation
 Records
Harvard University Archives
Pusey Library
Cambridge, Mass.

Harvard University Faculty of
 Medicine, Minutes of meetings
 and official papers
Francis A. Countway Library
Harvard Medical School
Boston, Mass.

Harvard University Reports to the
  Overseers
Harvard University Archives
Pusey Library
Cambridge, Mass.

Lawrence Joseph Henderson Papers
Harvard University Archives
Pusey Library
Cambridge Mass.
  and in
Baker Library
Harvard Business School
Boston, Mass.

Henry Lee Higginson Papers
Baker Library
Harvard Business School
Boston, Mass.

*Henry James, Jr., Papers
Rockefeller University Archives
New York, N.Y.

William James Papers
Houghton Library
Harvard University
Cambridge, Mass.

William Williams Keen Papers
American Philosophical Society
  Library
Philadelphia, Penn.

Frederic Schiller Lee Papers
Butler Library
Columbia University
New York, N.Y.

Frederic Thomas Lewis Papers
Francis A. Countway Library
Harvard Medical School
Boston, Mass.

Jacques Loeb Papers
Division of Manuscripts and
  Archives
Library of Congress
Washington, D.C.

Abbott Lawrence Lowell Papers
Harvard University Archives
Pusey Library
Cambridge, Mass.

Lafayette Benedict Mendel Papers
Sterling Memorial Library
Yale University
New Haven, Conn.

Adolph Meyer Papers
Alan Mason Chesney Medical
  Archives
Johns Hopkins Medical Institutions
Baltimore, Md.

Charles Sedgwick Minot Papers
Francis A. Countway Library
Harvard Medical School
Boston, Mass.

Hugo Münsterberg Papers
Boston Public Library
Boston, Mass.

Ralph Barton Perry Papers
Harvard University Archives
Pusey Library
Cambridge, Mass.

William Townsend Porter Papers
Francis A. Countway Library
Harvard Medical School
Boston, Mass.

Frederick Haven Pratt Papers
Boston University Medical Library
Boston, Mass.

Henry Smith Pritchett Papers
Division of Manuscripts and
  Archives
Library of Congress
Washington, D.C.

James Jackson Putnam Papers
Francis A. Countway Library
Harvard Medical School
Boston, Mass.

Rockefeller Foundation Papers
Rockefeller Archive Center
North Tarrytown, N.Y.

Edward Albert Sharpey-Schafer
 Papers
Contemporary Medical Archives
 Centre
Wellcome Institute of the History of
 Medicine
London, England

George Neil Stewart and Julius
 Moses Rogoff Papers
Francis A. Countway Library
Harvard Medical School
Boston, Mass.

Victor Clarence Vaughan Papers
Michigan Historical Collections
Bentley Historical Library
University of Michigan
Ann Arbor, Mich.

Henry Pickering Walcott Papers
Harvard University Archives
Pusey Library
Cambridge, Mass.

William Henry Welch Papers
Alan Mason Chesney Medical
 Archives
Johns Hopkins Medical Institutions
Baltimore, Md.

*Robert Mearns Yerkes Papers
Sterling Memorial Library
Yale University
New Haven, Conn.

Major Published Sources

Chronological bibliographies of Cannon's publications may be found in *The Life and Contributions of Walter Bradford Cannon, 1871–1945: His Influence on the Development of Physiology in the Twentieth Century,* ed. C. M. Brooks, K. Koizumi, and J. O. Pinkston (Brooklyn, 1975), pp. 239–263, and in *Walter Bradford Cannon: Exercises Celebrating Twenty-five Years as George Higginson Professor of Physiology, October 15, 1931* (Cambridge, Mass. 1932), pp. 73–94. The former volume appends a list of obituaries and biographical articles about Cannon at the end of his bibliography. In addition to the above works and Cannon's autobiographical memoir, *The Way of an Investigator: A Scientist's Experiences in Medical Research* (New York, 1945), another published source of information about him is the volume of essays, *Walter Bradford Cannon, 1871–1945, A Memorial Exercise* (Boston, 1945). The two major short biographies to date are those by Saul Benison and A. Clifford Barger in the *Dictionary of Scientific Biography* (1978) and by Donald Fleming in the *Dictionary of American Biography* (1973). Bradford Cannon's article, "Walter Bradford Cannon, M.D.: Reflections of the Physician, the Man, and His Contributions," published in *Gastrointestinal Radiology* (vol. 7, 1982), and Marian Cannon Schlesinger's book, *Snatched from Oblivion: A Cambridge Memoir* (Boston, 1979), have contributed immeasurably to a more personal view of their father and his world.

Notes

Full information on the archival and manuscript collections cited below in short form appears in the Bibliographical Note.

1. A Family History

1. For a full program of the festivities held on Oct. 6 and 7, 1909, see "Inauguration of President Lowell," *Harvard Graduates' Magazine* 18 (1909–10):270–294. See also Cannon's 1909 Diary, Oct. 6 and 7, Cannon Papers.

2. See further C. B. Davenport, *Heredity in Relation to Eugenics* (New York: Henry Holt & Co., 1911), esp. pp. 26–27; Harry H. Laughlin, "The Eugenics Record Office at the End of 27 Months' Work," Eugenics Record Office Report no. 1 (Cold Spring Harbor, N.Y., 1913), esp. p. 7.

3. W. B. Cannon to Lucius H. Cannon, Feb. 7, 1921, Cannon Papers.

4. Mark Haller, *Eugenics: Hereditarian Attitudes in American Thought* (New Brunswick, N.J.: Rutgers University Press, 1963), esp. pp. 63–66. See also Kenneth M. Ludmerer, *Genetics and American Society* (Baltimore: Johns Hopkins University Press, 1968), pp. 7–43, 45–73.

5. There are two "Records of Family Traits" in the Cannon Papers. One, dated 1909 and revised in 1924, was filled out by Cannon; the other, dated April 1912, was filled out by his father, Colbert Cannon.

6. Almon B. Cannon, comp., *The Descendants of Samuel (Carnahan) Cannon of Ulster, Ireland, and Blandford, Massachusetts* (Wadsworth, Ohio: privately mimeographed and bound, 1932), p. 4.

7. Henry James Ford, *The Scotch-Irish in America* (Princeton: Princeton University Press, 1913), pp. 165–208.

8. A. B. Cannon, *Descendants*, pp. 5–6, 19–20; Ford, *Scotch-Irish*, pp. 221–248. See also S. G. Wood, *Ulster Scots and Blandford Scouts* (West Medway, Mass., 1933).

9. Lois K. Mathews, *Expansion of New England* (Boston: Houghton Mifflin, 1909), pp. 171–195, 221–247.

10. *Way of an Investigator*, p. 13. See also unidentified 1864 newspaper article by John Seward, written as part of a series on pioneer women, Cannon Papers.

11. A. B. Cannon, *Descendants*, p. 47.

12. Ibid., p. 50.

13. This account of Cannon's paternal grandfather is based primarily on

an undated reminiscence by his third son and namesake, Lucius H. Cannon; in Cannon Papers.

14. "Family Memory," pp. 11–12; "Servant of Science," p. 3. Both in Cannon Papers.

15. "C. H. Cannon's Record" and unidentified, undated biographical sketch, Cannon Papers.

16. Francis B. and Herbert W. Denio, comps., *A Geneology of Aaron Denio of Deerfield, Massachusetts, 1704–1925* (Montpelier, Vt.: Capital City Press, 1926). Abigail Stebbins (1684–1740) was the second child of John Stebbins, Jr., and Dorothy Alexander.

17. Ibid. For more on the early history of the Denio family, see esp. pp. 9–11, 29–30, 32–34, 40–53. See also *Way of an Investigator*, pp. 11–12.

18. See further "Family Memory," pp. 2–11, for descriptions of Wilma Denio's family and the farm at Elba, Minnesota.

19. The name "Walter" was apparently chosen without relevance to family genealogy or friends. The middle name, however, was selected in honor of a medical friend of Colbert Cannon's, a Dr. Bradford of Milwaukee; it may have had additional significance because of the senior Cannon's life-long ambition to become a physician. "Servant of Science," p. 2.

20. Cannon was quite taken by the coincidence that tied him to Beaumont and referred to the connection on several occasions. See, for example, *Way of an Investigator*, pp. 28–29; also "Some Modern Extensions of Beaumont's Studies on Alexis St. Martin: I. Thirst and Hunger," *Journal of the Michigan State Medical Society* 32 (March 1933):155–192.

21. "Family Memory," esp. pp. 2, 13.

22. *Way of an Investigator*, p. 15; "Family Memory," pp. 5–6. Wilma Denio Cannon died just before midnight on Dec. 31, 1881. Cannon was ten years old at the time, his sisters six, four, and two. The baby died at Elba, where she had been sent to be cared for by her mother's family.

23. "Recollections," esp. Ida's Memories, p. 2; also "Servant of Science," p. 4.

24. "Family Memory," pp. 18–19.

25. *Way of an Investigator*, p. 14.

26. "Family Memory," pp. 15–16.

27. "Recollections," Jane's Memories, p. 12.

28. "Family Memory," p. 14. The charcoal was added to control gas that may have developed after taking milk, and it is still used today for the same purpose.

29. "Recollections," esp. Jane's Memories, p. 12. In later years Cannon often remarked on his father's ingenuity and credited his father for his own skill in carpentry: see, for example, *Way of an Investigator*, p. 14.

30. "Family Memory," p. 14; "Recollections," Ida's Memories, p. 5.

31. "Servant of Science," p. 5.

32. "Family Memory," p. 15; "Servant of Science," p. 5.

33. *Way of an Investigator*, p. 15; see also "Servant of Science," p. 12.

2. St. Paul High School and Harvard College

1. "Recollections," esp. Memories of Walter Bradford Cannon, pp. 22–24.

2. W. B. Cannon to Cornelia J. Cannon, Oct. 23, 1918, Cannon Papers.

3. For more on the school, later known as the Central High School of St. Paul, see M. J. Newson file of newspaper clippings, St. Paul Public Library, esp. *St. Paul Pioneer Press* for May 29, 1925.

4. Cannon, who served for a year as editor of the school newspaper, *The High School World*, later remembered: "At that time Ignatius Donnelly, a local politician and a writer with fantastic imagination, brought out his Great Cryptogram designed to prove that Bacon wrote Shakespeare's plays. By use of methods similar to Donnelly's, I found in my Latin Virgil and published in the *World* pompous pronouncements, one of which was 'Alas, alas, fame is no fun!' " *Way of an Investigator*, p. 15.

5. Leonard Huxley, *Life and Letters of Thomas Henry Huxley* (New York: D. Appleton, 1901), pp. 235–242; William Irvine, *Apes, Angels, and Victorians* (New York: McGraw-Hill, 1955), pp. 320–330.

6. *Way of an Investigator*, p. 16.

7. "Servant of Science," p. 7.

8. Ibid., p. 7; *Way of an Investigator*, pp. 16–17. See also Charles H. Grandgent, "Samuel McChord Crothers, 1857–1927," in *The Saturday Club, A Century Completed, 1920–1956*, ed. E. W. Forbes and J. H. Finley, Jr. (Boston: Houghton Mifflin, 1958), pp. 143–150.

9. "Servant of Science," p. 13. "We are not living for those gone; we are living for those present, and those to come," Cannon told his fellow classmates. "We have our part in making our age. We have everything to do, and many things to learn, never was the outlook brighter." See also *Negatives of '91* and other St. Paul High School memorabilia in Cannon Papers.

10. See file of newspaper clippings about Miss Newson in the St. Paul Public Library; see also biographical file on Thomas McLean Newson in the Archives/Manuscript Division, Minnesota Historical Society.

11. May Newson took such criticism in stride and continued to send her best students to eastern schools. Her warm interest in her students, which was reflected in their devotion to her, is well illustrated in a letter she wrote to one of them—John F. Fulton—upon his graduation from Harvard College; see further M. J. Newson to Fulton, June 3, 1921, in J. F. Fulton Papers, Yale University School of Medicine.

12. Cf., for example, J. Gray, *The University of Minnesota, 1851–1951* (Minneapolis: University of Minnesota Press, 1951); S. E. Morison, *Three Centuries of Harvard, 1636–1936* (Cambridge Mass: Harvard University Press, 1936).

13. M. J. Newson to W. B. Cannon, undated, Cannon Papers. This is the first letter in a lengthy correspondence that continued throughout Cannon's student years at Harvard, although the frequency gradually diminished. Unfortunately, it has not been possible to locate Cannon's letters to Miss Newson.

14. Ibid. For a further description of the college recorder, see John Hays Gardiner, *Harvard* (New York: Oxford University Press, 1914), p. 117.

15. See further Hugh Hawkins, *Between Harvard and America: The Educational Leadership of Charles W. Eliot* (New York: Oxford University Press, 1972); Henry James, *Charles William Eliot: President of Harvard University, 1869–1909*, 2 vols. (Boston: Houghton Mifflin, 1930); Samuel Eliot Morison, ed., *The Development of Harvard University since the Inauguration of President Eliot, 1869–1929* (Cambridge, Mass.: Harvard University Press, 1936).

16. *Annual Reports*, p. 7.

17. W. E. B. Du Bois, "That Outer Whiter World of Harvard," in *The Harvard Book: Selections from Three Centuries*, ed. William Bentinck-Smith (Cambridge, Mass: Harvard University Press, 1953). Dù Bois, speaking of his own experience as a black undergraduate, added, "I was in Harvard but not of it and realized all the irony of 'Fair Harvard.' I sang it because I liked the music" (p. 228).

18. See further *Harvard University Catalogue, 1891–92*, p. 159.

19. F. W. Fiske to the President and Faculty of Harvard University, Dec. 23, 1891; in Cannon's student file, HUA.

20. For information on Price Greenleaf Aid, see *Harvard University Catalogue, 1892–93*, p. 215.

21. 1892 Diary, June 30, July 1, July 2.

22. 1892 Diary, July 27.

23. 1892 Diary, July 29.

24. A further donation of $80 from Colbert Cannon made his total contribution to his son's Harvard education $180. "Servant of Science," p. 15; *Way of an Investigator*, p. 17.

25. 1892 Diary, Sept. 12.

26. 1892 Diary, Sept. 15 and 16.

27. 1892 Diary, Sept. 23 and 24.

28. Cannon to Cornelia James, Sept. 24, 1900, in Cannon Papers.

29. See, for example, *Harvard University Catalogue, 1892–93*, p. 217. Expenditures for the academic year were estimated in four columns from the "Low" of $372, through "Moderate" at $472 and "Liberal" at $622, to "Very Liberal" at $1,010.

30. R. W. Greenleaf, "Student Diet at Harvard," *Harvard Graduates' Magazine* 2 (1893–94):176–177. See also 1892 Diary, Sept. 29; *Harvard University Catalogue, 1892–93*, p. 217.

31. 1892 Diary, Sept. 27; Harvard College transcript in Cannon's student file, HUA.

32. *Way of an Investigator*, pp. 17–18.

33. 1892 Diary, Sept. 28, Oct. 4. See further Montague Chamberlain biographical file, HUA.

34. 1892 Diary, Nov. 4.

35. 1892 Diary, Nov. 8 and 9.

36. M. J. Newson to Cannon, Nov. 23, 1892, Cannon Papers.

37. 1892 Diary, Nov. 24.

38. For example, Cannon's diary entry for Dec. 24, 1892, reads: "Went to Prof. Norton's reception this morning. Books, pictures, statuary everywhere. What an advantage a fellow has who is born to such surroundings." For a later memoir of the Sunday "Dante evenings" at the home of Charles Eliot Norton, see Van Wyck Brooks, *An Autobiography* (New York: E. P. Dutton, 1965), p. 120.

39. See, for example, "Pioneers of Now-a-days," Oct. 24, 1893, and "In Aid of a Snow-bound Train," Nov. 7, revised Nov. 28, 1893, among other undergraduate papers, in Cannon Papers.

40. "The Latest Fad," Nov. 27, 1892.

41. M. J. Newson to Cannon, Nov. 23, 1892, Cannon Papers. See further Miss Newson's childhood memories of the Sioux wars (in which her father served as a captain of Minnesota militia) in her "Memories of Fort Snelling in Civil War Days," *Proceedings of the Minnesota Historical Society*, Dec. 1934, pp. 395–404.

42. Theme 43, Feb. 16, 1894, in Cannon Papers. The "mucker" was part of the Cambridge scene around the turn of the century; see further caricature drawn by Elmer E. Hagler, Jr., in his picture gallery entitled *Harvard Inside-Out* (Boston, 1916).

43. Laurence Curtis, John C. Ropes, Gordon Abbott, for the Trustees of the Hasty Pudding Club, to the President and Fellows of Harvard College, Dec. 14, 1897, Eliot Papers.

44. College House still exists in Cambridge and is now an office building. Cannon's room was no. 32. *Harvard University Catalogue, 1893–94*, p. 164.

45. "Servant of Science," pp. 15–16.

46. Among others, Cannon's classmates included Sidney Bradshaw Fay, Roger B. Merriman, Jerome D. Greene, John Lord O'Brian, J. S. P. Tatlock, and Robert S. Woodworth.

47. See esp. section on "Lectures, Evening Readings, Concerts, Etc." in *Harvard University Catalogue, 1893–94*, pp. 126–136.

48. The essay on Holmes, written for English 22 in the spring of 1894, was a six-part paper that explored various aspects of the great man's life. In Part III, The Doctor and Scientist, Cannon particularly focused on two essays Holmes had written that roused the anger of the homeopaths and the "so-called allopaths." "The lecture on homeopathy," Cannon wrote, "is conceived and written in a vein of noble scorn and the thought is poured out along the pages with a lucidity, pungency of satire, and cogent understatement that give the performance the velocity of a cannon-shot"—a remark that in turn caused his instructor to comment with his red pencil, "Who is responsible for this absurd metaphor?"

49. See, for example, M. J. Newson to Cannon, Dec. 12 and 25, 1892, April 16, 1893, Cannon Papers.

50. M. J. Newson to Cannon, Sept. 27, 1893, Cannon Papers.

51. M. J. Newson to Cannon, April 5, 1894, Cannon Papers.

52. *Way of an Investigator*, p. 19.

53. Excerpt of letter from H. S. Jennings to Joseph Brennemann, enclosed with S. W. Geiser to Cannon, Jan. 14, 1934, Cannon Papers.

54. Cannon to Geiser, Jan. 18, 1934, Cannon Papers.

55. 1895 Diary, April 10 and June 27; see also programs for Phi Beta Kappa ceremonies in 1895 and 1896. All in Cannon Papers.

56. Harry Wolfson, who lived there in 1911, took a dim view of the quality of life and social opportunities in Divinity Hall, whereas Cannon found it a decided improvement over his previous college accommodations. Cf. Cannon's communication, "To Encourage Sociability," *Harvard Graduates' Magazine* (Sept. 1897), pp. 145–147, with Wolfson's account in Lee W. Schwarz's *Wolfson of Harvard: Portrait of a Scholar* (Philadelphia: Jewish Publication Society of America, 1978), pp. 30–31.

57. Cannon's work with Davenport resulted in the publication of his first research article; see C. B. Davenport and W. B. Cannon, "On the Determination of the Direction and Rate of Movement of Organisms by Light," *Journal of Physiology* 21 (Feb. 1897):22–32.

58. 1896 Diary, Jan. 9.

59. 1896 Diary, Feb. 8. Parker, Davenport, and William James were among Cannon's most influential teachers at Harvard College, and Parker later became one of his closest friends. See further *Way of an Investigator*, p. 19.

60. 1896 Diary, May 6. Cannon's continuing association with the Foxcroft Club, both as a member and as an employee, led to his writing a paper on "Cooperative Dining Associations in American Colleges" for his Philosophy 5 course, in Cannon Papers.

61. M. J. Newson to Cannon, May 10, 1896, Cannon Papers.

62. Cannon also asked Welch whether he could use his premedical preparation at Harvard as a means of shortening his medical studies by going into advanced work at Hopkins. The original letter in the Welch Papers shows a notation at the top "answered April 21/96," but no reply has ever been located. Bradford Cannon published his father's letter in a personal reminiscence in *Life & Contributions*, p. 152.

63. Harvard College transcript in Cannon's student file, HUA. Having taken more than the requisite number of advanced courses and passed them with distinction, Cannon was awarded the M.A. degree in 1897.

3. Reforming Medical Education

1. Officials of one state health department surveying the quality of medical education in the 1890s lamented that out of 150 schools, 46 were essentially diploma mills. See further U.S. Department of Interior, Bureau of Education, *Annual Report of the Committee on Education, 1892–93*, p. 1622; also L. F. Barker, "Medicine and the Universities" and "Some Tendencies in Medical Education in the United States" in *Medical Research and Education*, ed. J. McKeen Cattell (New York: Science Press, 1913), pp. 223–278.

2. See Alan M. Chesney, *The Johns Hopkins Hospital and the Johns Hopkins University School of Medicine: A Chronicle* (Baltimore: Johns Hopkins University Press, 1943), I:210–211.

3. The most valuable and reliable published source of information about the School until its move to Longwood Avenue is Thomas F. Harrington, *The Harvard Medical School: A History, Narrative, Documentary*, 3 vols. (New York, 1905), ed. James G. Mumford. For Eliot's reforms, see especially III:989–1016, 1019–40, 1043–51. For a contemporaneous account of the changes, see also the *Annual Reports* for the years in which they occurred.

4. See further Harrington, *Harvard Medical School*, II:495–505.

5. See remarks by Dr. Morrill Wyman in *BM&SJ* 142 (1900):569. The full text of Dr. Walker's offer is published in Harrington, *Harvard Medical School*, III:1347–50.

6. Mark D. Altschule, "Reactions to Educational Innovation at Harvard Medical School," unpublished manuscript, rev. ed., 1982, p. 20.

7. For more on his part in the reforms, see further J. C. White, *Sketches from My Life, 1833–1913* (Cambridge, Mass.: Riverside Press, 1914).

8. For a full discussion, see esp. Michael F. Nigro, Jr., "Reform at Harvard Medical School in 1871," undergraduate thesis submitted in partial fulfillment for the B.A. degree, Harvard College, 1966, HUA. Some published accounts of the reforms at HMS are W. B. Cannon, "President Eliot's Relations to Medicine," *New England Journal of Medicine* 210 (1934):730–738; F. C. Shattuck and J. L. Bremer, "The Medical School, 1869–1929," in *The Development of Harvard University, 1869–1929*, ed. S. E. Morison (Cambridge, Mass.: Harvard University Press, 1930); E. D. Churchill, ed., *To Work in the Vineyard of Surgery: The Reminiscences of J. Collins Warren, 1842–1927* (Cambridge, Mass.: Harvard University Press, 1958); Henry K. Beecher and Mark D. Altschule, *Medicine at Harvard: The First Three Hundred Years* (Hanover, N.H.: University Press of New England, 1977), esp. pp. 87–96; Kenneth M. Ludmerer, "Reform at Harvard Medical School, 1869–1909," *Bulletin of the History of Medicine* 55 (1981):343–370.

9. For Bigelow's views, not only on the conduct of HMS but also regarding the training of medical practitioners, see his *Medical Education in America* (Cambridge, Mass.:University Press, 1871); see also H. J. Bigelow to C. W. Eliot, April 15, 1871, Eliot Papers.

10. Oliver Wendell Holmes expressed the latter viewpoint a few years earlier when he addressed the student body at the school on Nov. 6, 1867: "A Medical School is not a scientific School, except just so far as medicine itself is a science. On the natural history side, medicine is a science; on the curative side, chiefly an art . . . The bedside is always the true center of medical teaching."

11. *Annual Reports*, 1870–71, esp. pp. 8–10, 18–22; Elin L. Wolfe, "Calvin Ellis, M.D.—Harvard's Forgotten Medical Dean," *Harvard Medical Alumni Bulletin* 56 (1982):27–31; Reginald Fitz, "President Eliot and Dr. Holmes Leap Forward," *Harvard Library Bulletin* 1 (1947):212–220. Matters, however, could not proceed until the governing boards of the University had passed the new plan. Eliot himself told the story, as he later remembered it, in more than one version: see further C. W. Eliot, *Harvard Memories* (Cambridge, Mass.: Harvard University Press, 1923); Eliot, *A Late Harvest: Miscellaneous Papers Written between Eighty and Ninety* (Boston: Atlantic Monthly Press, 1924).

12. The most authoritative biography of Bowditch to date is W. B. Cannon's "Biographical Memoir: Henry Pickering Bowditch, 1840–1911," *Memoirs of the National Academy of Sciences* 17 (1924):183–196. For other views of Bowditch by his contemporaries, see the obituary notice by C. S. Minot in *Science* n.s. 33 (1911):598–601, and the article by Fielding H. Garrison in *Dictionary of American Biography,* s.v.

13. Born in Boston in 1840, Bowditch was heir to considerable scientific interest and ability. His family on both sides represented the best of New England's inquiring spirit. In the Bowditch lineage were his grandfather Nathaniel, mathematician and author of *The Practical Navigator;* his uncle Henry Ingersoll, who was the second Jackson professor of clinical medicine at Harvard and was noted for his work in the fields of preventive medicine and public health; and his father Jonathan Ingersoll, a successful merchant with a scientific turn of mind. The heritage from his mother's side was equally outstanding, including among others the astronomers Edward and William Pickering and the mathematician Benjamin Mills Pierce.

14. For an appreciation of Brown-Séquard by Bowditch, see *Memoirs of the National Academy of Sciences* 4 (1897):95–97. For Jeffries Wyman's influence on Bowditch, see W. B. Cannon, "Biographical Memoir," p. 184.

15. See further *Memoir of James Jackson, Jr., M.D.,* with extracts from his letters to his father and medical cases collected by him (Boston, 1835). See also J. I. Bowditch to H. I. Bowditch, Feb. 27, 1869; H. P. Bowditch to H. I. Bowditch, Jan. 26 and Feb. 8, 1869; and H. P. Bowditch to Lucy Bowditch, March 21, 1869; all in Bowditch Papers.

16. For Ludwig's impact on Bowditch, see W. B. Cannon, "Biographical Memoir," p. 185; also George Rosen, "Carl Ludwig and His American Students," *Bulletin of the Institute of the History of Medicine* 4 (Oct. 1936):609–650. Bowditch described his early impressions of Ludwig's institute in "The School of Physiology at Leipzig," *BM&SJ* 82 (1870):205–207.

17. Bowditch's results were published in Ludwig's *Arbeiten,* 1871, but were never published in English. Cannon called attention to the fact that the first description of the "staircase" phenomenon appeared on p. 669 and on p. 687 the all-or-none law was described. "It is rare," he commented, "to find two fundamental observations reported within twenty pages of an investigator's first report." See further W. B. Cannon, "History of the Physiology Department of the Harvard Medical School," *Bulletin of the Harvard Medical School Alumni Association* 1 (Mar.1927):12–19.

18. See further H. P. Bowditch to J. I. Bowditch, Jan. 2, 1870, Bowditch Papers; and H. P. Bowditch to C. W. Eliot, April 21, 1871, Eliot Papers. Graham Lusk, the well-known physiologist at Cornell, contended that his father, William Thompson Lusk, who conducted the course at Harvard in 1870–71, left because there was some hesitancy on the part of authorities to appoint him or Bowditch as assistant professor in 1871; see note for "Physiology at the Harvard Medical School, 1870–1871," *BM&SJ* 167 (1912):921. For a contrary view, see C. W. Eliot to O. W. Holmes, June 13, 1870, in Eliot Papers, which leaves little doubt that the post was earmarked for Bowditch.

19. For new appointments in 1871 and 1872, see Harrington, *Harvard Medical School,* III:1048–1051. During this period the medical faculty was also

enlarged by appointments in four new clinical specialities—ophthalmology, hygiene, mental diseases, and dermatology. See also *Annual Reports, 1871–72*, p. 27.

20. J. C. Warren later described not only his friendship with Bowditch but also the changes that took place in 1871; see Churchill, *Vineyard of Surgery*, esp. pp. 122–123, 176–177. See also *Annual Reports, 1870–71*, pp. 38–39. For a description of Bowditch's attic domain, see his letter to J. J. Putnam, Feb. 4, 1872, in Putnam Papers.

21. Originally, Oliver Wendell Holmes served as professor of anatomy and physiology. When he became the Parkman professor of anatomy, there was no professor of physiology until Bowditch was promoted to the post in 1876. Some years earlier, according to Harrington, the University Council of Great Britain had refused to recognize Harvard's medical degree because "they recognized the degree of no college in which there was not a Professor of Physiology." Harrington, *Harvard Medical School*, III:1048n.

22. F. W. Ellis, "Henry Pickering Bowditch and the Development of the Harvard Laboratory of Physiology," *New England Journal of Medicine* 219 (1938):819–828.

23. A. B. Palmer to J. B. Angell, May 7, 1877; with special thanks to Horace W. Davenport for calling this letter in the Bentley Historical Library, University of Michigan, to our attention. William Osler, on the other hand, after visiting the North Grove Street School on two occasions, regarded it "as the most progressive medical institution on this continent." Touching on the changes taking place since Eliot's sweeping reforms, Dr. Osler found the class of students much improved. "Nothing that I saw at Harvard pleased me more than the teaching of clinical medicine," he noted; "it is scientific, thorough, and practical." W. Osler, "Communication: Harvard School of Medicine," *Canadian Journal of Medical Science* 2 (1877):274–276.

24. W. B. Cannon, "History of Physiology Department," p. 17. For prior claims to the establishment of physiology in America, see further Edward C. Atwater, "Squeezing Mother Nature—Experimental Physiology in the United States before 1870," *Bulletin of the History of Medicine* 52 (1978):313–335.

25. Garland's experiments on "intestinal digestion" as well as those by Charles H. Williams on the action of bile in promoting fat absorption were performed in Bowditch's laboratory and provided the basis for prize-winning essays of the Boylston Medical Society in 1874; see further *BM&SJ*, suppl. to vol. 90, 1874. For more on assistants and instructors who held appointments in physiology, see Harrington, *Harvard Medical School*, III:1368–69; also "The Department of Physiology," in *The Harvard Medical School, 1782–1906*, p. 91.

26. Bowditch's first results were published in 1877 as "Growth of Children," in the *Eighth Annual Report, State Board of Health, Massachusetts*. See further Thomas E. Cone, Jr., "Dr. Henry Pickering Bowditch on the Growth of Children: An Unappreciated Classic Study," *Transactions & Studies of the College of Physicians of Philadelphia* 42 (1974–75):67–76; James Allen Young, "Height, Weight, and Health: Anthropometric Study of Human Growth in Nineteenth-Century American Medicine," *Bulletin of the History of Medicine* 53 (Summer 1979):214–243; J. M. Tanner, *A History of the Study of Human Growth* (Cambridge: Cambridge University Press, 1981), pp. 185–196.

27. Physiological Laboratory, HMS, Boston, *Collected Papers, 1873–1879*. Bowditch's foreword appears on the verso of the title page.

28. For a description of the North Grove Street School, see Churchill, *Vineyard of Surgery*, pp. 62–71, 174–175; Harrington, *Harvard Medical School*, II:509–530. See also Thomas Dwight, *Frozen Sections of a Child* (New York: William Wood & Co., 1881); F. H. Lincoln, "Edward Stickney Wood," *Harvard Graduates' Magazine* 14 (1905–06):24–27.

29. See broadside, "The Harvard Medical College—Meeting to Promote the Erection of a New Building," HMA; reprinted in Harrington, *Harvard Medical School*, III:1102–11.

30. For a description of the difficulties the committee faced, see Shattuck and Bremer, "The Medical School," p. 563; Harrington, *Harvard Medical School*, III:1060.

31. In 1881, a second appeal for funds for the new building had been sent out, signed by C. W. Eliot, O. W. Holmes, and H. J. Bigelow, the latter now completely converted to the new education. See further *The New Century and the New Building of the Harvard Medical School, 1783–1883: Addresses and Exercises at the One Hundredth Anniversary of the Foundation of the Medical School of Harvard University, Oct. 17, 1883* (Cambridge, 1884).

32. [Joseph Weatherhead Warren], "The Harvard Physiological Laboratory," *Science* 4 (1884):128–135.

33. Under Bowditch's guidance Harvard was the first American medical school to give formal instruction in pathology and the new science of bacteriology, and the subject of histology was expanded to include embryology and placed under the charge of C. S. Minot. Bowditch was equally concerned with upgrading clinical instruction; for a summary of his accomplishments as dean, see Harrington, *Harvard Medical School*, III:1128; also Osler's obituary notice in *Lancet*, April 8, 1911, p. 975.

34. Hall collaborated with Bowditch for his work on "Optical Illusions of Motion"; both of his studies, as well as Lovett's examination of strychnine poisoning, were included in the collected papers of the physiology department. For more on Hall's relations with Bowditch, see "Eight Letters from G. Stanley Hall to H. P. Bowditch, with Introduction and Notes" by W. R. and C. C. Miles, *American Journal of Psychology* 41 (1929):326–336. As for Ernst, his work was first "unofficially begun by permission of Prof. H. P. Bowditch" in a small corner of the physiology laboratory on Boylston Street, until bacteriology was given official sanction at Harvard with his appointment as demonstrator in 1885.

35. Half a century later, Cannon, in a paper on "Experimental Neurology in the Harvard Medical School" (*New England Journal of Medicine* 216 [1937]:89–91), traced the course of development of neurological investigations at Harvard from the early interest shown in Bowditch's laboratory.

36. See W. H. Howell, "The American Physiological Society during Its First Twenty-Five Years," *History of the American Physiological Society Semicentennial, 1887–1937*, pp. 4–5; also K. F. Franklin, "A Short History of the International Congresses of Physiologists," *Annals of Science* 3 (1938):245.

37. In 1891 Bowditch lost his assistant of ten years, Joseph Weatherhead Warren, who left Harvard for a professorship in physiology at Bryn Mawr

College. A favorite collaborator of Bowditch, Warren had worked with him on plethysmographic experiments on the vasomotor nerves of the limbs and on studies of the knee jerk.

38. For details on the evolution of the four-year course of study, see further Harrington, *Harvard Medical School*, III:1063, 1098-1101.

39. When commenting on the new salaries, Eliot noted: "The professors and other teachers who practice medicine are not remunerated on that scale; first, because they do not give their whole time to the School, and secondly, because their connection witih the School ordinarily increases their private practice." *Annual Reports*, 1892–93, p. 33. For further comments on HMS salaries at this time, see also *Bulletin of the Harvard Medical Alumni Association*, no. 3 (1892):44–46.

40. See further J. S. Billings, "The Plans and Purposes of The Johns Hopkins Hospital," in *The Johns Hopkins Hospital: Addresses at the Opening of the Hospital* (Baltimore, 1889); reprinted in Chesney, *Chronicle*, I:252–253.

41. Originally, it was expected that H. N. Martin would teach physiology to the medical students; for more on what happened, see W. Bruce Fye, "H. Newell Martin—A Remarkable Career Destroyed by Neurasthenia and Alcoholism," *Journal of the History of Medicine and Allied Sciences* 40 (1985):133–166. For more on the preclinical faculty at Hopkins, see also Chesney, *Chronicle*, I:221–232.

42. Harvey W. Cushing, *The Life of Sir William Osler*, 2 vols. (New York: Oxford University Press, 1925), I:388; Simon Flexner and James T. Flexner, *William H. Welch and the Heroic Age of American Medicine* (New York: Viking Press, 1941), p. 220; "Report of the Dean of the Medical School," *Twenty-Third Annual Report of the President of the Johns Hopkins University, 1898*, p. 103; Chesney, *Chronicle*, II:176.

43. See file, "Committee on Improved Clinical Facilities," HMA. For discussions of Harvard's relations to its hospitals, see Morris J. Vogel, *The Invention of the Modern Hospital, Boston, 1870–1930* (Chicago: University of Chicago Press, 1980); also Churchill, *Vineyard of Surgery*, pp. 193–196.

44. The original candidates for the post were Frederic S. Lee, a physiologist at Columbia, and Benjamin K. Rachford, a Kentucky practitioner who had a degree from the Medical College of Ohio as well as advanced scientific training abroad. Although the position was offered to Rachford, he declined and suggested that Bowditch consider Porter. See further Bowditch to Eliot, June 30, 1893, Eliot Papers; Rachford to Porter, Aug. 11, 1893, Porter Papers.

45. In recent years Porter's contributions to the development of physiology have been reexamined by A. Clifford Barger; see, for example, his articles on Porter in the *Dictionary of American Biography*, supp. 4, and in *The Physiologist* 14 (1971):277–285. Barger's more recent article, "The Meteoric Rise and Fall of William Townsend Porter, One of Carl J. Wiggers' 'Old Guard'," *The Physiologist* 25 (1982):407–413, formed the basis for the above account. See also A. J. Carlson et al., "The Harvard Apparatus Company, the *American Journal of Physiology*, and Dr. W. T. Porter," *Science*, Dec. 8, 1944, pp. 518–519; *History of the American Physiological Society Semicentennial*, pp. 79–83, 171–173, 193–194; Mary L. Stocker, *Dr. Porter and the Harvard Apparatus Company* (Dover, Mass., 1963).

46. Barger, "Meteoric Rise and Fall," p. 408. "Researches on the Filling of the Heart," Porter's first major physiological study, was done in R. P. H. Heidenhain's physiological institute at Breslau under the tutelage of Karl Hürthle and appeared in 1892 in the English *Journal of Physiology*. See also W. T. Porter, "On the Results of Ligation of the Coronary Arteries," *Journal of Physiology* 15 (1893):121–138.

47. Porter's wide-ranging interests were to earn him the friendship and respect of diverse figures such as the physiologist C. S. Sherrington, the anatomist F. P. Mall, and the anthropologist Franz Boas. See, for example, letters to Porter from Boas (Nov. 27, 1892), W. S. Chaplin, (Sept. 13, 1892), and others, in Porter Papers.

48. "The Physical Basis of Precocity and Dullness," the first in a series of reports by Porter on physical measurements of school children, was read before the Academy of Science of St. Louis and published in their *Transactions* in 1893. This was followed the next year by "The Growth of St. Louis Children," also published in the *Transactions of the Academy of Science of St. Louis* 6 (1894):161–181. For an evaluation of Porter's anthropometric studies, see further Tanner, *History of the Study of Human Growth*, pp. 215–223.

49. W. T. Porter, Circular letter to American physiologists (Dover, Mass., privately printed, 1942), quoted in Barger, "Meteoric Rise and Fall," p. 412. A further description of what Porter encountered during his first year at Harvard may be found in his letter to Dr. Gustav Baumgarten, April 1, 1894, in Baumgarten Family Papers.

50. The early history of the Harvard Apparatus Company is given in Stocker, *Dr. Porter and the H.A.C.*, p. 3, and by Carlson et al., "H.A.C., *Am. J. Physiol.*, and Porter," pp. 518–519. See also A. J. Carlson's obituary notice of Porter in *Science* 110 (1949):111–112.

51. Porter's initial eleven-page instruction manual was titled *Harvard Medical School, Experiments Required of First-Year Students in the Department of Physiology*. Although supposedly required for every first-year student, not all of the men actually performed these experiments. His expanded version, *Experiments for First-Year Students in the Department of Physiology of the Harvard Medical School* (Boston: J. L. Fairbanks, 1896, 52 pp.), went through several revisions and was eventually incorporated into a larger volume entitled *An Introduction to Physiology*, first published in 1900. Porter's laboratory manuals describe not only the experiments but also the apparatus to be used in them.

52. Porter, "The Teaching of Physiology in Medical School," *BM&SJ* 139 (1898):652. A more detailed and expanded version of this article appeared two years later in a special number of the *Philadelphia Medical Journal* devoted to medical education (vol. 6, Sept. 1, 1900, pp. 379–384).

53. See further "The New Curriculum at Harvard Medical School," editorial in *BM&SJ* 140 (1899):560–561. For responses to the new system, see also letters to Porter from Mall (Jan. 26, 1899) and from Jacques Loeb (undated), in Porter Papers. For a later report on Porter's system, see Henry A. Christian, "The Concentration Plan of Teaching Medicine," *Bulletin of the American Academy of Medicine* 11 (Dec.1910):705–719.

54. When Porter arrived at Harvard in 1893, he found the production of

research publications from the physiology department in a moribund state. During the five-year period from 1894 to 1899, however, his name was on no less than fifteen of the thirty investigations that reached publication, and nine more papers were produced by students whose work he directed. See further tabulation of "Investigations Published by the Department of Physiology in the Harvard Medical School during the Past Ten Collegiate Years— 1889–1899," Porter Papers. An appreciation of Porter by one of his students may be found in a letter from F. H. Pratt to his mother, Nov. 23, 1897, HMA.

55. W. H. Welch to W. T. Porter, Dec. 11, 1895, Porter Papers. Porter's articles were "Further Researches on the Closure of the Coronary Arteries" and "A New Method for the Study of the Intracardiac Pressure Curve."

56. Welch to Porter, Jan. 27, 1897, Porter Papers.

57. See especially 1897 correspondence with R. H. Chittenden, then president of the society, and others, in Porter Papers. See also Howell in *History of the American Physiological Society Semicentennial*, pp. 79–83.

58. Another research journal emanating from Harvard at this time was edited by Harold C. Ernst of the Bacteriology Department. Begun in Jan. 1896 as the *Journal of the Boston Society of Medical Sciences*, its title changed in 1901 to the *Journal of Medical Research*. Encouraged by Porter's success, C. S. Minot joined forces with F. P. Mall to establish the *American Journal of Anatomy* in 1901; see further Florence Sabin, *Franklin Paine Mall: The Story of a Mind* (Baltimore: Johns Hopkins University Press, 1934), p. 235.

59. Ida Hyde wrote on the effect of distention of the ventricle on coronary blood flow, Pratt on the endocardial nutrition of the heart, and Bancroft on the venomotor nerves of the hind limb. Porter, following the tradition of Ludwig and Bowditch, was not in the habit of putting his name on the publications of his pupils, a practice he continued throughout his career. All, however, in their articles acknowledged their indebtedness to him for suggesting the research topic as well as directing, assisting, or encouraging the work. For a discussion of one such research article published in 1899 by Walter Baumgarten, son of Porter's former physiology teacher at the St. Louis Medical College, see W. H. Welch to Porter, Jan. 17, 1899, in Porter Papers.

4. Harvard Medical Student

1. Some of the material on which this chapter is based has previously been published in A. C. Barger's Sosman Lecture, "New Technology for a New Century: Walter B. Cannon and the Invisible Rays," *American Journal of Roentgenology* 136 (1981):187–195, and *The Physiologist* 24 (1981):6–14.

2. *Annual Reports,* 1895–96, p. 156; *Annual Reports,* 1896–97, pp. 26, 166–167; Thomas F. Harrington, *The Harvard Medical School: A History, Narrative, and Documentary,* 3 vols. (New York, 1905), III:1139.

3. *Annual Reports,* 1895–96, p. 24. See also *Annual Reports,* 1892–93, pp. 33, 145; *Annual Reports,* 1893–94, pp. 27, 124–128.

4. Although many of Cannon's fellow students have been described as

"immature high school graduates," of the 172 men who entered HMS in 1896, 130 graduated in 1900—more than one-third with honors.

5. Frank Spiller Locke (1866–1949), of Locke's solution fame, had been educated at Cambridge and the University of London (M.D., 1897). Some years later, Cannon reminisced: "We students used to sit at desks in a gallery (of very shaky construction) around the main laboratory. Dr. Locke, with his hands clasped behind his back as if plunged in profound thought, would walk about the gallery agitating everything and everybody every time he banged his heel on the floor. I still have in old records the heel marks of Dr. Locke's step. He was here from England for the period 1895–97, and returned there in 1897." "History of the Physiology Department of the Harvard Medical School," *Bulletin of the Harvard Medical School Alumni Association* 1 (March 1927):12–19.

6. Ibid. p. 12

7. This is the only entry Cannon made in the 1896 diary after he started medical school, in Cannon Papers. The Ether Day speakers were Charles McBurney, a surgeon from the College of Physicians and Surgeons; Louis McLane Tiffany of Maryland, credited with performing the first gastroenter-ostomy; Silas Weir Mitchell, the preeminent neurologist from Philadelphia; John Collins Warren, grandson of the first J. C. Warren who performed the initial operation with ether at MGH; Robert Thompson Davis, a Fall River physician who was a witness at the ether operation; and David Williams Cheever, successor to Henry Jacob Bigelow in the chair of surgery at Harvard.

8. After years without special notice of the anniversary of the intro-duction of ether anesthesia in surgery, J. C. Warren initiated the celebration to instruct the surgical staff at the MGH in the history of that singular in-novation and its significance for the development of surgery as well as the hospital. For more on the first use of ether and the celebrations of its anni-versary, see further F. A. Washburn, *The Massachusetts General Hospital: Its Development, 1900–1935* (Boston: Houghton Mifflin, 1939), pp. 167, 538–546; M. J. Vogel, *The Invention of the Modern Hospital, 1870–1930* (Chicago: University of Chicago Press, 1980), pp. 79–80.

9. Years later, Cannon told Simon Flexner that he did not recall having heard Welch's address. Cannon to Flexner, May 11, 1938, Cannon Papers. For a description of Walter Dodd's demonstration by one of Cannon's fellow students, see Percy Brown, *American Martyrs to Science through the Roentgen Rays* (Springfield, Ill.: C. C. Thomas, 1936), footnote on p. 146.

10. For more on the first-year course, see further W. T. Porter, "The Teaching of Physiology in Medical Schools," *BM&SJ* 149 (1898), esp. pp. 647.

11. "Servant of Science," p. 31. See also Percy Brown's introductory remarks to Cannon's Caldwell Lecture, "Some Reflections on the Digestive Process," *American Journal of Roentgenology and Radium Therapy* 32 (1934):576.

12. For more on Moser and his collaboration with Cannon, see further H. W. Davenport, *An Eagle-Feather: The Short Life of Albert Moser, M.D. A Footnote to the Life of Walter B. Cannon* (Boston: Countway Library of Medicine, 1974).

13. For an account of Codman's early use of x-ray in Boston, see his Autobiographic Preface to *The Shoulder* (Boston, 1934), pp. viii-xi.

14. Cannon to J. F. Fulton, April 14, 1942, Cannon Papers.

15. See further correspondence between Codman and Thomson in *BM&SJ* 135 (1896):610–611; Cannon, "Some Reflections on the Digestive Process," pp. 577–578. The long-term effects of Cannon's exposure to x-rays are discussed in Barger, "New Technology for a New Century," pp. 192–195.

16. This is the first entry in the manuscript notebook labeled "RECORD: Work in Physiology, W. B. Cannon," which contains observations in alimentation by x-ray from Dec. 9, 1896 to Dec. 21, 1897, as well as reading notes related to the investigation. Unless otherwise noted, subsequent observations as quoted above are taken from this notebook, which is hereafter cited as X-Ray Notebook and is in the Cannon Papers.

17. See, for example, Cannon to F. S. Lee, Sept. 11, 1936, and to W. H. Howell, Sept. 12, 1936, Cannon Papers. For an account of the demonstration, see Davenport, *An Eagle-Feather*, pp. 18–25. Cannon was elected to membership in the American Physiological Society at its thirteenth meeting held in Baltimore, Dec. 1900.

18. Communication from H. P. Bowditch, "Movements of the Alimentary Canal," *Science* 5 (1897):901.

19. "Early Use of the Roentgen Ray in the Study of the Alimentary Canal," *JAMA* 62 (1914):1–3. Although Cannon is generally credited with pioneering the use of radio-opaque materials, he noted that in 1897 Rumpel had published a report on the visualization of a pathologically dilated esophagus by pouring into it a suspension of bismuth subnitrate. In addition, Rieder in 1905 used bismuth subnitrate mixed with food as a means of rendering opaque the alimentary canal of man. "The mixing of heavy salts with the food to render gastro-intestinal movements visible was," Cannon concluded, "so far as I have been able to learn, first used in the Laboratory of Physiology in the Harvard Medical School; but the method contained, to my mind, no principle which has not been utilized before." (p. 3)

20. See further H.W. Davenport's analysis of Cannon's contributions to gastroenterology in *Life & Contributions*, pp. 3–25.

21. Porter also presented a more detailed report of the work Cannon was doing alone on gastric motility. The two reports were on "The Movement of Food in Deglutition," by A. Moser and W. B. Cannon, *Am. J. Physiol.* 1(1898):xii, and "The Movements of the Stomach, Studied by Means of the Roentgen Rays," by W. B. Cannon, *Am. J. Physiol.* 1(1898):xiii. Although Moser and Cannon started to work together in the fall of 1896, Moser apparently became preoccupied with his clinical studies; the collaboration, which had been irregular, tapered off in the fall of 1897. It should be noted that in the early reports of the work on deglutition, Moser's name was given precedence as the first author. It is clear, however, that Cannon took the responsibility for writing the final paper, which was published in the July 1898 *Am. J. Physiol* (pp. 435–444) with his name as first author. Moser, who died at an early age, only published one other paper on "Tuberculosis of the Heart," *Medical and Surgical Reports of the Boston City Hospital* (11th Series, 1900):194–203.

22. Porter described how a small cylinder, covered with lead foil and of the same specific gravity as blood, was fastened by a short thread to the end

of a probe and passed through the carotid artery and aorta to a position just above the semilunar valve. He noted that the movements of the cylinder are those of an equal mass of blood, and they may be watched with the Roentgen rays after removal of the ribs. See further *Am. J. Physiol.* 1(1898):xiv.

23. C. P. Worcester to Cannon, Jan. 5, 1897, Cannon Papers. The above entry appears under "Notes for 1897" in Cannon's 1896 Diary. There are no further diaries extant for the the 1890s in the Cannon Papers, although a few notes from 1899 have been saved.

24. See further "A Report from the Committee of Graduates and Undergraduates upon the Course of Study at the Harvard Medical School, 1899," unpublished manuscript in HMA.

25. Ibid., Report on the Second Year Course, pp. 11–19; see also pp. 50–57.

26. Ibid., pp. 16–17. There was obviously a problem in bridging the gap between the laboratory and clinical courses. While the Graduate Committee urged abandoning any attempt to teach the practice of medicine or surgery in the second year, they did ask that extended instruction in physical diagnosis be offered (p. 55).

27. Cannon to C. K. Drinker, Sept. 24, 1925, HMA.

28. See M. J. Newson to Cannon, Nov. 22, 1897, Dec. 12, 1897, Jan. 16, 1898, Cannon Papers.

29. Louise Crothers to Cannon, Dec. 10, 1898, Cannon Papers. For another view on immigrants, see reminiscences of Frederick C. Irving in *Safe Deliverance* (Boston: Houghton Mifflin, 1942), pp. 26–33.

30. Report on the Third Year Course, in "A Report from the Committee of Graduates and Undergraduates upon the Course of Study at the Harvard Medical School, 1899," pp. 20–37. Other members of the Committee were John M. Connolly and Sumner Coolidge. The Graduate Committee in their review of the third-year course (pp. 55–62) indicated complete accord with the views expressed in Cannon's report, which was by far the most thorough and carefully considered of the class reports.

31. Ibid., p. 35.

32. C. A. Ewald, *The Diseases of the Stomach,* trans. Morris Manges (New York: D. Appleton, 1893), p. 54. For various qualitative and quantitative methods used to test the motor function of the stomach at this time, see further John C. Hemmeter, *Diseases of the Stomach* (Philadelphia: Blakiston, 1900), pp. 65–78.

33. W. B. Cannon, "Some Reflections on the Digestive Process," p. 578.

34. J.-Ch. Roux and V. Balthazard, "Sur l'emploi des rayons de Röntgen pour l'étude de la motricité stomacale, *Comptes Rendus . . . des Séances et Mémoires de la Societé de Biologie* Paris, 49 (1897):567–569; "Note sur les fonctions motrices de l'estomac du chien," ibid., pp. 704–706; "Étude des contractions de l'estomac chez l'homme à l'aide des rayons de Röntgen," ibid., pp. 785–787; "Étude du fonctionnement moteur de l'estomac à l'aide des rayons de Röntgen, *Archives de Physiologie Normale et Pathologique* 5th series, 10 (1898):85–94.

35. "Beaumont's methods, however," Cannon commented, "may be

justly criticized on the ground that the thermometer-tube which he held in the stomach was wholly unlike food and very liable to bring about unwonted contractions in so sensitive an organ as the stomach." "Movements of the Stomach," *Am. J. Physiol.*, pp. 367–368.

36. Cannon, "The Movements of the Stomach Studied by Means of the Röntgen Rays," *Journal of the Boston Society of Medical Sciences*, 2 (1898):59–66.

37. "Movements of the Stomach," *Am.J. Physiol.*, p. 381.

38. See entries for Dec. 3 and 8, X-Ray Notebook.

39. "Francis Henry Williams, 1852–1936," obituary notice in *Radiography and Clinical Photography*, April 1937. Cannon later wrote John Fulton: "In answer to your letter of May 9 let me tell you that F. H. Williams was a fairly prominent internist in Boston, the son of a former Professor of Ophthalmology at the Harvard Medical School and the inventor of the so-called Williams valve—a device which he contrived while working, I think, with Schmiedeberg as a young man. When I knew him he seemed very elderly, though I suppose he was considerably younger than I am now!" Cannon to Fulton, May 10, 1940, Cannon Papers.

40. F. H. Williams, *The Roentgen Rays in Medicine and Surgery, as an Aid in Diagnosis and as a Therapeutic Agent* (New York: Macmillan, 1901), p. 372.

41. Ibid., pp. 398–401.

42. Cannon's unpublished manuscript detailing the experiments that took place in the fall of 1899, "An X-Ray Investigation of the Human Stomach," is enclosed in a letter from Williams to Cannon, Aug. 17, 1900, in the Cannon Papers.

43. Among the responses Cannon received were warm acknowledgments from Marian Walker, a medical student at Johns Hopkins (May 22, 1898); J. C. Hemmeter, director of the clinical laboratory, University of Maryland (May 5, 1898); and W. A. Bastedo, a gastroenterologist who was then curator at the New York Botanical Garden (July 1, 1898); all in Cannon Papers.

44. D. W. Cheever to Cannon, May 22, 1898, Cannon Papers.

45. *Way of An Investigator*, p. 85. The idea for applying the case system to medicine was in the back of Cannon's mind even before his participation in preparing the third-year report. "The unmentionable 'system' . . . was all planned a year ago in August," he wrote Cornelia James on Oct. 26, 1900, "and the reading for it all done at that time; it was not until Mr. Norton had urged me several times to put the idea into finished form that I finally completed the job." In Cannon Papers.

46. "First Case Presented According to the Case Method, by Dr. G. L. Walton, Dec. 1899," in Cannon Papers. Printed cases were subsequently given out in three other courses at the Medical School, as well as at the University of Pennsylvania and the University of Minnesota; see further Cannon's "The Case System in Medicine," *BM&SJ* 142 (1900):563, and Walton's comment, ibid., p. 571. For an interesting description of Walton, see also Cannon to Cornelia James, Oct. 2, 1900, Cannon Papers.

47. "The Case Method of Teaching Systematic Medicine," *BM&SJ* 142 (1900):31–36. Later Cannon read a paper on "The Use of Clinic Records in Teaching Medicine" before a meeting of the Association of American Medical

Colleges held in Atlantic City on June 4, 1900, which was published in the *Bulletin of the American Academy of Medicine* 5 (1900–02):203–213.

48. Osler to Cannon, Jan. 26, 1900; and Dock to Cannon, Feb. 26, 1900, Cannon Papers.

49. H. L. Burrell to Cannon, Feb. 7, 1900; see also "Cases Given Out by Dr. Putnam, Dec. 18, 1899, to Students in His Course in Neurology"; C. M. Green to Cannon, Jan. 15, 1900; all in Cannon Papers.

50. A report of the meeting was published in *BM&SJ* 142 (1900):567–571, with Cabot's comments on p. 569.

51. Ibid., pp. 569–570. Bowditch later developed this theme in his talk "The Study of Physiology," delivered in Philadelphia in the summer of 1904; *University of Pennsylvania Medical Bulletin* (1904):131–134. See also Bowditch to C. W. Eliot, Jan. 4, 1905, Eliot Papers.

52. Cannon, "The Case System in Medicine," p. 3. The first large collection of medical cases, entitled *Studies in Neurological Diagnosis*, was published by J. J. Putnam and G. A. Waterman in 1902. In 1904, H. L. Burrell and J. B. Blake brought out a small volume, *Case Teaching in Surgery*, which proved of such value for instruction in surgical diagnosis that E. H. Bradford and J. D. Adams followed with a *Casebook in Orthopedic Surgery* in 1905. Richard C. Cabot's *Case Teaching in Medicine* (Boston: D. C. Heath, 1906) was an outgrowth of an earlier casebook he had used for teaching general medicine; see further W. B. Cannon, "Dr. R. C. Cabot's 'Case Teaching in Medicine,' " *Harvard Graduates' Magazine* 14 (1906):609–610.

53. "Notes from Old Diaries," entries for Oct. 7 and 10, 1899, Cannon Papers. For an example of the responses to Eliot's inquiries about Cannon, see also W. N. Bullard to C. W. Eliot (addressed to "Dear Cousin Charles"), Oct. 1, 1899, Eliot Papers.

54. W. T. Porter to C. W. Eliot, Sept. 30, 1899, Eliot Papers.

55. Cornelia James to Cannon, Sept. 9, 1900, Cannon Papers.

56. See, for example, M. J. Newson to Cannon, Jan. 17, March 5, April 2, July 12, and esp. Nov. 22, 1897; all in Cannon Papers.

57. A year later Cannon recalled the occasion in a letter to Cornelia James, Sept. 9, 1900, in Cannon Papers.

58. Cannon to Cornelia James, Jan. 23, 1901. Cannon traced the course of the romance in several other letters to Cornelia, for example, Sept. 12, 1900 and Feb. 11, 1901. All in Cannon Papers.

59. H. S. Jennings to Cannon, Feb. 4, 1900: "I was greatly rejoiced to hear of your fine prospects, for next year and the future in general . . . It will be a great thing to take Dr. Porter's place for next year,—that's a pretty big step for the first year out of college even for *you!*" In Cannon Papers.

60. One of the Cannon children later wrote: "My mother, after much to-ing and fro-ing, is said to have written him a note of rejection on a piece of brown paper that had wrapped up the fish, a gesture of offhandedness that she often ruefully referred to in later years. But my father . . . seemed unperturbed; he offered an X-ray picture of his hand, presumably taken while it was pressed to his heart, as an avowal of his devotion and won the day." *Snatched from Oblivion*, p. 40.

61. Cannon to Cornelia James, May 12, 1900, Cannon Papers.

62. Cannon to Cornelia James, June 21, 1900, Cannon Papers. The transcript of Cannon's courses and grades throughout his four-year medical course has been provided through the kindness of Audrey Noreen Koller, Office of the Registrar, HMS.

5. Beginning of a Career

1. Cannon's daily letters to Cornelia James give a detailed account of his life during the year of their engagement and are preserved, along with her letters to him, in the Cannon Papers.

2. Cannon to Cornelia James, July 29, 1900; see also Cannon to Cornelia James, Aug. 10, 1900.

3. Cannon to Cornelia James, July 31, 1900.

4. Cannon to Cornelia James, July 30, 1900.

5. Cannon to Cornelia James, Sept. 9, 1900. Cannon was referring to the second edition, revised, of the *American Textbook of Physiology*, 2 vols., ed. W. H. Howell (Philadelphia: W. B. Saunders, 1900); see esp. I:375, 378–380. For other references to Cannon's work, see also E. A. Schäfer, *Text-Book of Physiology*, vol. 2 (Edinburgh & London: Young J. Pentland; New York: Macmillan, 1900), pp. 319–325.

6. Cannon to Cornelia James, July 7, 1900.

7. Cannon to Cornelia James, Sept. 19, 1900.

8. Cannon to Cornelia James, Aug. 31, 1900.

9. Cannon to Cornelia James, Sept. 16, 1900.

10. Cannon to Cornelia James, Oct. 2, 1900.

11. Cannon to Cornelia James, Oct. 3, 1900. For more on the large size of the entering class and Cannon's conference with Bowditch, see also Cannon to Cornelia James, Oct. 1 and 2, 1900.

12. At first, Cannon apparently was alone in the laboratory while the other staff members were on vacation. Serving under Bowditch and Porter in physiology this year were Cannon and A. P. Mathews, instructors; A. M. Cleghorn, S. I. Franz, W. H. Parker, and Waldemar Koch, assistants. See further *Harvard Medical School Catalogue for 1900-01*, pp. 21-22; W. T. Porter to C. W. Eliot, April 1, 1900, Eliot Papers.

13. Allen Cleghorn had already published research undertaken at the suggestion of W. T. Porter on "The Action of Animal Extracts, Bacterial Cultures, and Culture Filtrates on the Mammalian Heart Muscle," *Am. J. Physiol.* 2 (1899):273–290. Another article by Cleghorn in the same volume (pp. 471–482) on "The Physiological Action of Extracts of the Sympathetic Ganglia" contained work on the extracts of the medulla of the suprarenal bodies, which may have proved suggestive for Cannon's later research. Albert Mathews's previous work had included "The Physiology of Secretion" (*Annals of the New York Academy of Science* 11 [1898]:293–368) and "The Origin of Fibrinogen" (*Am. J. Physiol.* 3 [1899]:53–85). He collaborated with Cleghorn in the performance of perfusion experiments described in the latter paper.

14. Cannon to Cornelia James, Feb. 20, 1901.

15. Cannon to Cornelia James, Oct. 25, 1900. For Porter's change of plans, see also H. P. Bowditch to W. T. Porter, Oct. 28, 1900, Porter Papers; W. T. Porter to C. W. Eliot, Nov. 10, 1900, Walcott Papers.

16. Cannon to Cornelia James, Nov. 19, 1900.

17. Finsen received the Nobel Prize for this work in 1903. See also Edgar Mayer, *Clinical Application of Sunlight and Artificial Radiation* (Baltimore: Williams & Wilkins, 1926), pp. 39–40, 72–79, Sidney Licht, ed., *Therapeutic Electricity and Ultra-Violet Radiation* (New Haven: Elizabeth Licht, 1959), pp. 188–195.

18. Cannon to Cornelia James, Nov. 19, 1900; see also Cannon to Cornelia James, Nov. 2, 1900, and H. S. Jennings to Cannon, May 21, 1898. Cannon's interest in this work may further be traced in letters to Cornelia James of Dec. 8, 1900, Feb. 1 and 4, 1901, April 10, 1901.

19. W. N. Bullard, "Considerations of Some of the Indications for Operation in Head Injuries," *BM&SJ* 132 (1895):73–75; see also discussion on pp. 83–87. Other neurologists at the time, following Bullard's lead, were concerned with this phenomenon, although they were not able to adequately explain the cause of such increase in cerebral pressure; see, e.g., George L. Walton, "Subarachnoid Serous Exudation Productive of Pressure Symptoms after Head Injuries," *American Journal of Medical Sciences* 116 n.s. (1898):269–275.

20. For more on Bullard, see obituary notice by E. W. Taylor, "William Norton Bullard, M.D., 1853–1931," *Archives of Neurology and Psychiatry* 26 (1931):179–183.

21. For a description of the fourth-year elective course in neurology, see *Announcement of the Medical School . . . of Harvard University for 1899–1900*, p. 36. A brief account of von Leyden's life may be found in *Biographisches Lexikon der hervorragenden Ärzte der letzten fünfzig Jahre*, vol. 2 (Berlin: Urban & Schwarzenberg, 1933), ed. Isador Fischer, pp. 908–909.

22. "Physiologische untersuchungen über ionenwirkungen. Zweite mittheilung," v. Jacques Loeb, *Archiv für die gesammte Physiologie* 71 (1898):457–476. Cannon on two occasions was able to talk with Loeb about his work on frog muscle; see his letters to Cornelia James of Sept. 8, 1900 and June 10, 1901. On the latter occasion he wrote: "Professor Loeb was in the Laboratory for a while today and was much interested in the application I had made of his work on frog's muscle. How intricate the ways of discovery are! There is some enjoyment in talking with a person who understands; these clinicians cannot be made to understand—they have too many preconceptions that prevent clear vision."

23. Cannon, "Intracranial Pressure after Head Injuries," a paper read at the annual meeting of the Massachusetts Medical Society, June 12, 1901, pp. 11–12. A full version, "Cerebral Pressure Following Trauma," was published in the *Am. J. Physiol.* 6 (1901):91–121.

24. See, e.g., Cannon to Cornelia James, May 17, 1901; Charles H. Frazier in *Progressive Medicine: A Quarterly Digest of Advances, Discoveries, and Improvements in the Medical and Surgical Sciences*, March 1902, pp. 18–19. See also F.

H. Pratt to Adolf Meyer, April 29, 1903, and W. B. Cannon to Adolf Meyer, April 30, 1903, both in Meyer Papers. Today, one of the methods of treating increased intracranial pressure is the intravenous infusion of hyperosmotic solutions in an attempt to decrease the brain edema. Cannon was far ahead of his time.

25. Cannon to Cornelia James, Jan. 13, 1901.

26. Cannon to Cornelia James, March 11, 1901; see also Cannon to C. B. Davenport, March 16 and 27, 1901, Davenport Papers.

27. Cannon to Cornelia James, March 22, 1901.

28. Cannon to Cornelia James, Aug. 22, 1900. Stewart wrote several high-spirited letters to Cannon during this time; but by the end of 1903 he was dissatisfied with "the downward movement" of the Medical School at Pennsylvania and subsequently moved to Dartmouth, where he spent the remainder of his career.

29. Cannon to Cornelia James, Dec. 4, 1900.

30. Cannon to Cornelia James, April 4, 1901.

31. Cannon to Cornelia James, May 8, 1901.

32. Cannon to Cornelia James, May 3, 1901; see also letters of April 11 and 25, 1901.

33. Cannon to Cornelia James, May 6, 1901. "Dr. Porter informed me," he wrote, "that as I was appointed before Dr. Mathews I should stay, though that, I am sure, is no good excuse. It happens, however, that a good opening for a physiological chemist is being made in Chicago, and Dr. Mathews stands a good chance of getting that. If Dr. Mathews and one assistant go away, there may be a larger salary in store for me; on that, however, I am not counting. The medical training that I have had gives a very satisfactory sense of security, for, should anything happen in the School, I could enter practice with, I think, a fair certainty of making a success of it. (Dr. Mathews is a Ph.D., not M.D.)." For more on Mathews, see also Cannon to C. B. Davenport, April 18, 1901, Davenport Papers.

34. Cannon to Cornelia James, June 8, 1901.

35. For the negotiations with Bullard, see Cannon to Cornelia James, May 17, 19, 22, 23, and esp. 25, 1901. Cannon wrote that Bullard had asked him to present the paper on brain pressure before the American Neurological Association, whose June meetings would have delayed his planned departure for St. Paul. "I hoped he would do it," he explained in his letter of May 17, "but he declares he doesn't understand the reasoning well enough to defend it from criticism." For Cannon's doubts about the practitioner's ability to understand the substance of his work, see also his letter to Cornelia James, June 10, 1901.

36. Cannon to Cornelia James, May 31, 1901.

37. Cannon to Cornelia James, April 19, 1901.

38. Cannon to Cornelia James, May 20, 1901.

39. Frances Haynes James to Helen Haynes Jaynes, June 27, 1901, Cannon Papers.

40. "Diary of Wedding Journey, 1901, Remembered in 1903," Cannon Papers.

41. *Snatched from Oblivion*, p. 46.

42. Cannon to Cornelia James, June 4, 1901.

43. A detailed description of the climb may be found in W. B. Cannon to C. H. Cannon, July 21, 1901, which was later published in the *National Parks Magazine* 29 (Oct.–Dec. 1955):152–154. Cannon later described the climb again in *Way of an Investigator*, pp. 23–27. The note in the bottle that was left on top of Mt. Cannon, partially concealed by a rock cairn, was recently discovered by two modern-day climbers who made headlines in local newspapers; see, for example, *Bozeman* (Montana) *Daily Chronicle*, Sept. 9, 1985.

44. "A Servant of Science," pp. 58, 60.

45. The James family correspondence upon which the above account is based, consists mostly of letters to Cornelia from her mother and her sisters, 1901–1909, and has been deposited in the Cannon Papers.

46. For more on Mrs. Cannon's family background, see further *Snatched from Oblivion*, pp. 26–40.

47. See Francis H. James to Cornelia J. Cannon, Sept. 22 and Oct. 29, 1901.

48. Francès H. James to Cornelia J. Cannon, Sept. 14, 1901; Helen James to Cornelia J. Cannon, Sept. 24, 1901.

49. Frances H. James to Cornelia J. Cannon, Nov. 1, 1901.

50. Frances H. James to Cornelia J. Cannon, May 2, 1905.

51. Helen James to Cornelia J. Cannon, Oct. 17, 1901. See also Cannon to Cornelia James, March 4 and April 3, 1901.

52. Frances H. James to Cornelia J. Cannon, June 1, 1902.

53. Helen James to Cornelia J. Cannon, Jan. 26, 1902.

54. See, for example, C. H. Cannon to Mrs. W. B. Cannon, Dec. 24, 1902, Cannon Papers.

55. Frances H. James to Cornelia J. Cannon, Jan. 1, 1904.

56. Frances H. James to Cornelia J. Cannon, Dec. 16, 1903. In her letter Mrs. James also referred to Cornelia's sister Margaret (Mrs. Aaron Burt), who also was unable to bear children.

57. In 1904 Mrs. Cannon was admitted to the Boston City Hospital by her gynecologist, C. M. Green, for surgical treatment of a gynecological problem that she believed was related to her inability to have children. See excerpt of letter from C. J. Cannon to her family, May 8th, 1904; also private communication from Wilma Cannon Fairbank, Nov. 15, 1983. It is of interest, however, that Homer G. Fuller reported in 1907 that until recently unfruitful marriages were almost always ascribed to the wives (who in many cases were subjected to needless gynecological treatment and operations), whereas the subject of sterility in men was only beginning to be carefully considered. See further H. G. Fuller, "Sterility in the Male, Its Causes and Surgical Treatment," *Medical Record* 42 (1907):229–231.

58. F. T. Brown and A. T. Osgood, "X-Rays and Sterility," *American Journal of Surgery* 18 (1907):179–182.

59. Ibid., pp. 179, 182.

60. See, for example, "Untoward Effect of X-Rays," *BM&SJ* 152 (1905):173–174; Margaret A. Cleaves, "The Röntgen Ray and Sterility," *Medical Electrology*

and Radiology (London) 5 (1905):65–68. An editorial entitled "The Subtle X-Ray—A Two-Edged Tool" claimed that "aside from editorial comment upon [the report by Brown and Osgood] and a brief statement by its authors in the current number of the *Archives of the Röntgen Ray*, the first study of sterility among x-rayists is presented in this issue of the *American Journal of Surgery*" (p. 203).

61. The above account is based on a packet of materials marked "Data on the Effect of Exposure to X-Ray on Fertility, 1905" in the Codman Papers, which was called to our attention by Charles D. Wrege, Professor of Management, Rutgers University.

62. Cannon's report was entered on a 3 × 5 notecard and is No. 8 of a group of thirty collected by Codman. Another index of Cannon's concern is the aid he gave in the fall of 1906 to William C. Quinby, a Harvard surgeon who was working on the problem of male sterility. See, for example, Cannon's 1906 Diary, Nov. 6 and 28.

63. Cannon to Cornelia James, Oct. 28, 1900.

64. Cannon to Cornelia J. Cannon, March 20, 1903.

65. Cannon to Cornelia J. Cannon, April 3, 1903.

6. Divergent Pathways

1. Harvard's lack of a hospital of its own had long been a burning issue. James C. White, who was instrumental in enlisting the president's aid in bringing the scientific departments up to a "high and satisfactory standard of excellence," was among those who later urged Eliot to build up the clinical departments if Harvard were to have a truly great medical school. J.C. White, *Sketches from My Life, 1833–1913* (Cambridge, Mass: Riverside Press, 1914), pp. 163–165. Eliot elaborated on this theme in his *Annual Report* for 1888–89 (pp. 23–24). For more on Harvard's relations with its hospitals, see 1889–92 materials in HMA file; also Morris J. Vogel, *The Invention of the Modern Hospital, Boston, 1870–1930* (Chicago: University of Chicago Press, 1980,) esp. pp. 78–96.

2. C. W. Eliot to W. L. Richardson, Dec. 27, 1894, Eliot Papers.

3. *Annual Reports*, 1897–98, p. 37. Eliot had already set out his ideas for a School of Comparative Medicine in his *Annual Report* for 1894–95 (pp. 27–28).

4. For details concerning the comparative pathology professorship, see April 1896 correspondence with George A. Fabyan and Theobald Smith, in Eliot Papers; also further materials in HMA, esp. AA114.2 file and Box 4 of the dean's files.

5. The consolidated Faculty of Medicine was contrived as a means of providing funds for the impoverished Dental and Veterinary Schools as well. Although the Dental School eventually was put on a firmer footing, the Veterinary School, which had been established in 1882, closed at the end of the academic year in 1901. For more on the Veterinary School, see further "Suggestions for the Reorganization of the Harvard Veterinary School," four-

page broadside prepared for the Board of Overseers in 1896 by Theobald Smith, and correspondence with Charles P. Lyman, dean of the Veterinary School, both in Eliot Papers; *Annual Reports, 1900–01*, pp. 26–27. For more on the proposed comparative medicine program, see, for example, Eliot to C. S. Minot, March 13, 1899, and W. T. Porter to Eliot, March 9, 1899 and May 5, 1899; all in Eliot Papers.

6. Report from the Dean of the Medical School in *Annual Reports 1899–1900*, p. 195; see also *Dedication of the New Buildings of the Harvard Medical School* (Boston: published by the Faculty of Medicine, 1906), pp. 7–9.

7. Minutes of the first meeting of the newly constituted Faculty of Medicine, Dec. 2, 1899; T. F. Harrington, *The Harvard Medical School: A History, Narrative, and Documentary*, 3 vols. (New York, 1905), III:1167–69. See further "Committee on Use of Ellis and Pierce Funds, 1900" file and materials in Box 4 of the dean's files, HMA.

8. See H. P. Bowditch to H. L. Higginson, April 9, 1900, Higginson Papers. For further details regarding the acquisition of the 26-acre estate, see also Harrington, *Harvard Medical School*, III:1171–1172; E. D. Churchill, ed., *To Work in the Vineyard of Surgery: The Reminiscences of J. Collins Warren 1842–1927* (Cambridge, Mass: Harvard University Press, 1958), p. 207.

9. *Annual Reports*, 1901–02, esp. pp. 32–37, 336–345. For more on the roles played by Bowditch and Warren in the development of the Longwood Avenue project, see further *The Harvard Medical School, 1782–1906* (Boston, 1906), pp. 177–193; Churchill, *Vineyard of Surgery*, pp. 208–217; H. K. Beecher and M. D. Altschule, *Medicine at Harvard, The First Three Hundred Years* (Hanover, N.H.: University Press of New England, 1977), pp. 167–169.

10. C. W. Eliot to J. C. Warren, Nov. 27, 1901, Eliot Papers. Earlier that year Bowditch had written his wife, Selma, about a visit he and Warren made to New York: "We saw some of the richest men in New York (or in the world for that matter) and on the whole we felt that something rather nice would be likely to come our way. We are asking for $2,000,000. Modest! aren't we? But it is often easier to get a large sum than a small one from men whose only trouble is how to get rid of their wealth." March 3, 1901, Bowditch Papers.

11. For Porter's understanding of the terms under which he agreed to come to Harvard, see his letter to Bowditch enclosed with Porter to Eliot, both dated June 21, 1904, in Eliot Papers.

12. It would appear that Cannon's research was probably the sole exception; see one-page tabulation headed "Investigations Published by the Department of Physiology at Harvard Medical School during the Past Ten Collegiate Years—1889–1899," Porter Papers. For more on Porter's teaching, see also Porter to Eliot, April 1, 1900, Eliot Papers.

13. Porter to Eliot, March 19, 1900, and Bowditch to the President and Fellows of Harvard College [April 1900]; both in Eliot Papers.

14. Porter to Eliot, March 19, 1900, Eliot Papers.

15. Porter to Eliot, June 20, 1900, Eliot Papers. Earlier the president had attempted to co-opt a portion of the Ellis bequest for an endowed professorship of clinical medicine as part of his scheme to bring W. S. Thayer from

Johns Hopkins to head the medical service at Boston City Hosptial; see further Vogel, *Invention of the Modern Hospital,* pp. 81–82.

16. Porter to Eliot, June 28, 1901. Porter wrote two letters to Eliot on June 28; one was handwritten, and the other, a more formal statement of his relations with Bowditch in the physiology department, was typed. Both in Eliot Papers.

17. Funds for the establishment of the Higginson Professorship were received by the Harvard Corporation in April 1902, shortly after the medical faculty expressed a debt of gratitude to Bowditch and Warren for securing gifts amounting to more than $3,000,000 and voted to take the Francis Estate off the hands of the syndicate that was holding it for the new School (Trustees of Harvard Medical School to H. L. Higginson, April 25, 1902, Higginson Papers; Harvard Corporation Records, April 28, 1902, HUA). Under his new title Bowditch continued the special arrangement begun a few years earlier whereby he returned two-thirds of his salary to be used as appropriations for the department of physiology (Bowditch to Eliot, Dec. 18, 1902, Eliot Papers; J. D. Greene to Bowditch, Dec. 30, 1902, Bowditch Papers).

18. See, for example, advertisement for assistants in physiology at HMS in *Science,* n.s. 9 (April 28, 1899), p. 631; also Porter to Eliot, Nov. 12, 1902, Eliot Papers.

19. Bowditch to Eliot, Jan. 25, 1902. For more on the trip to Europe, see Cannon to Eliot, Jan. 25, 1902. Porter wrote Eliot in Cannon's behalf throughout 1902; see, e.g., his letters of Jan. 23, Oct. 25, and Nov. 12. On March 13, 1903, Porter wrote Eliot that Cannon had been invited to Western Reserve as a replacement for G. N. Stewart, who was succeeding Jacques Loeb in Chicago. All in Eliot Papers.

20. Cannon to Eliot, Jan. 15, 1903, Eliot Papers.

21. See, e.g., Cannon to Eliot, April 4, 1903, Jan. 5, 1904, Jan. 21, 1904, Oct. 28, 1904; also F. B. Mallory to Eliot, June 27, 1903; all in Eliot Papers. Cannon, as an assistant professor, began to attend meetings of the medical faculty on a regular basis; he often returned to Cambridge with Eliot and along the way continued in a more informal manner to discuss the affairs of the School.

22. See further Preface to *The Harvard Apparatus Company: Organized for the Advancement of Laboratory Teaching in Physiology and Allied Sciences,* a 58-page catalogue and price list issued in Boston, Mass., 1904; also W. T. Porter, Circular Letter to American Physiologists (Dover, Mass.: privately printed, Dec. 15, 1942), Porter Papers.

23. Bowditch and Porter to the President and Fellows of Harvard College, Dec. 14, 1903. See also exchange of letters between Eliot and W. L. Richardson, Dec. 26, 1903. All in Eliot Papers.

24. Eliot appeared to waver between two conflicting attitudes during the months of discussion about the manufacture of apparatus at Harvard—at times he was encouraging and supportive of the venture and at others hostile and disapproving. Cf., for example, Eliot to Bowditch, Dec. 11, 1903, and Eliot to Porter, March 15, 1904, both in Eliot Papers. For the early history of the company, see also Mary L. Stocker, *Dr. Porter and The Harvard Apparatus*

Company (Dover, Mass., 1963); A. C. Barger, "To Assist Young Men and Women in the Study of Physiology: The Porter Development Program," *The Physiologist* 14 (1971):280–281.

25. Petition to the Dean of the [Medical] Faculty from members of the second-, third-, and fourth-year classes, [Nov. 1904], Eliot Papers. The signers of the petition included among others, Francis Lowell Burnett, Francis Weld Peabody, Channing Frothingham, and James B. Ayer, Jr.—all members of Boston Brahmin families in good standing who, after completing their training, went on to have distinguished careers of their own.

26. Eliot to Porter, Nov. 7, 1904, and Porter to Eliot, Dec. 19, 1904, Eliot Papers.

27. Eliot to F. L. Burnett, Jan. 18, 1905, Eliot Papers. Eliot also told Burnett (the grandson of Judge Lowell) that Dean Richardson had declined to read the student petition and had never seen Porter's printed statement.

28. Bowditch to Eliot, Jan. 9, 1905, Eliot Papers. For an expression of Bowditch's pedagogic principles, see further "Address of Dr. Henry P. Bowditch to the Alumni of the Medical School," *Quarterly of the Harvard Medical Alumni Association* (Oct.1903):605–609.

29. See esp. I. P. Pavlov, *The Work of the Digestive Glands,* trans. W. H. Thompson (London & Philadelphia, 1902); E. H. Starling, *Mercer's Company Lectures on Recent Advances in the Physiology of Digestion* (Chicago, 1906); Lafayette Mendel, "Recent Advances in Our Knowledge of the Chemical Processes of Digestion," *The Medical News* 86 (1905):913–918.

30. The results of this investigation were reported by Cannon to the Boston Society of Medical Sciences, in Nov. 1901, and published as "The Movements of the Intestines Studied by Means of the Röntgen Rays," *Am. J. Physiol.* 6 (1902):251–277. It is of interest that at no time did Cannon consider working on cardiovascular problems, although this was then the leading research interest of the department. One might speculate that he recognized he did not have the expertise to pursue problems in cardiovascular research independently and would have had to subordinate himself to Porter's direction and help. Further, Cannon may also have felt that if he chose to work with Porter, he would be slighting Bowditch, who originally encouraged his research on digestion.

31. W. B. Cannon, "Movements of the Intestines," p. 276.

32. Ibid., pp. 272–274.

33. Ibid., pp. 275–276.

34. See Student notebooks of C. L. Overlander, HMS '05, HMA. There are three volumes of Notes on Physiology in this series, of which vol. I has the Chittenden lecture. See also reviews of Cannon's work in *Progressive Medicine: A Quarterly Digest of Advances, Discoveries, and Improvements in the Medical and Surgical Sciences,* esp. for 1899, 1902, 1904.

35. Little is known about the trip abroad in the summer of 1902. A letter Cornelia Cannon wrote to her family from Lucerne, Switzerland, on Sept. 12, is more descriptive of a honeymoon than a research trip; in Cannon Papers.

36. W. B. Cannon and H. F. Day, "The Salivary Digestion in the Stom-

ach," *Am. J. Physiol.* 9 (1903):396–416. This was the first research Cannon undertook with the assistance of a student.

37. Vol. 4, Dec. 1904, p. 4.

38. See further Horace Fletcher, *The A.B.-Z. of Our Own Nutrition* (New York, 1903), in which he reprinted all of Cannon's early published papers on digestion (pp. 284–388). Fletcher was a fascinating if unorthodox figure, who commanded the respect of many physiologists and medical scientists of the day, among them, Henry P. Bowditch. An especially vivid portrait of him is presented in James C. Whorton's " 'Physiologic Optimism': Horace Fletcher and Hygienic Ideology in Progressive America," *Bulletin of the History of Medicine* 55 (1981):59–87.

39. W. B. Cannon, "Movements of the Intestines," p. 263.

40. W. B. Cannon, "The Passage of Different Food-Stuffs from the Stomach and through the Small Intestine," *Am. J. Physiol.* 12 (1904):387–418. In his Annual Report for 1903–04, Harvard's medical dean noted (p. 186) that Cannon attended the meeting at Cambridge, England, of the British Association for the Advancement of Science, and delivered an address before the English Physiological Society on the passage of food-stuffs. Cannon then went on to Brussels for the International Congress of Physiology, where he gave a demonstration of the movements of the stomach and intestines, both by zoetrope and by x-rays.

41. W. B. Cannon, "The Passage of Different Foodstuffs from the Stomach," *JAMA* 44 (1905).15–19. Read at the fifty fifth annual meeting of the AMA before the Section of Pathology and Physiology.

42. W. B. Cannon, "Observations on the Mechanics of Digestion," *JAMA* 40 (1903):749. This paper was read at the fifty-third annual meeting of the AMA before the Section on Pathology and Physiology.

43. Jean-Charles Roux and Victor Balthazard of Paris, who simultaneously began with Cannon in 1898 to use x-rays in studying the movements of the stomach, had long left the field. By 1903 Roux had shifted his interests from physiology to gastroenterological surgery; Balthazard increasingly devoted himself to studies of bacteriology and legal medicine.

44. W. B. Cannon, "Auscultation of the Rhythmic Sounds Produced by the Stomach and Intestines," *Am. J. Physiol.* 14 (1905);339–353.

45. See, for example, discussions with clinicians, which followed his presentations to the Section on Pathology and Physiology in *JAMA* 40 (1903):73, and 44 (1905):18–19; also *Transactions of the American Gastro-Enterological Association* for 1905 for discussion following Cannon's presentation to the eighth annual meeting, variously paged. An appreciation of the importance of Cannon's contribution of the development of gastroenterology may be found in Henry Wald Bettman, "The Evolution of Gastroenterology: A Presidential Address," *Transactions of the American Gastro-Enterological Association* for 1907; see esp. his comments on pp. 4–6.

46. W. B. Cannon, "Recent Advances in the Knowledge of Movements and Innervation of the Alimentary Canal," presented at the eighth annual meeting of the American Gastro-Enterological Association, New York, April 1905, which appeared in *The Medical News*, May 29, 1905, pp. 923–929. It is

of interest that another paper read at the same meeting was Lafayette Mendel's "Recent Advances in Our Knowledge of the Chemical Processes of Digestion" (pp. 913–918).

47. Harvey Cushing, "The Society of Clinical Surgery in Retrospect," *Annals of Surgery* 169 (1969):1–9.

48. See Edward H. Nichols, "Letter to Dr. J. Collins Warren Relative to Space Allotment at the Harvard Medical School Adequate for the Teaching and Research in Surgical Pathology" [1901], HMA.

49. The above account is largely based on Department of Surgery materials in HMA, especially letters and minutes of meetings relating to the Committee on Surgical Research. See also Harrington, *Harvard Medical School*, III:1388–90.

50. The search for outside facilities in which to conduct experiments on dogs and larger animals may be followed in Committee on Surgical Research letters of Nov. 14, and Dec. 7, 16, and 18, 1902. Several years later, Dr. Warren pointed out that opportunities for research work under the auspices of the Division of Surgery had been provided in a number of laboratories, and more especially in the Department of Physiology. See further Warren's Introduction, in Division of Surgery, *Bulletin of Research Work* no. 5, Dec. 1908, HMA.

51. See further H. L. Burrell and J. B. Blake, *Case Teaching in Surgery;* also publisher's advertisement for "The Case History Series," put out by W. M. Leonard, Boston, which quotes Dr. Blake's summary of the early history of the case method as presented in Sept. 1911. At the same time that Cannon was collaborating with Blake, he joined for a brief time with Dr. Charles L. Scudder to work on stomach surgery; see further exchange of letters between R. B. Greenough and C. L. Scudder, Jan. 29, 1904 and Feb. 8, 190[4], HMA.

52. For a discussion of the historical development of gastroenterostomies and variations of this operation, see John B. Deaver and Astley P. C. Ashhurst, *Surgery of the Upper Abdomen* (Philadelphia, 1909), I:368–385. For a contemporaneous discussion of procedures of gastroenterostomies and their results, see further A. Ernest Maylard, *The Student's Handbook of the Surgery of the Alimentary Canal* (London, 1900), pp. 177–186, as well as I. Boas, *Diseases of the Stomach,* trans. Albert Bernheim (Philadelphia, 1907), pp. 528–531. Boas is particularly interesting for his understanding of the problems of the social conditions of the patient; see esp. pp. 524–525. For another excellent contemporaneous discussion, see Henry J. Paterson, *Gastric Surgery* (New York: William Wood & Co., 1906), pp. 1–33.

53. Maylard, *Student's Handbook,* pp. 190–192; Boas, *Diseases of the Stomach,* pp. 526–528. See also A. W. Mayo-Robson and B. G. A. Moynihan, *Diseases of the Stomach and Their Surgical Treatment* (New York, 1901), pp. 263–264; for a discussion of after-effects, see esp. pp. 274–278. For other discussion of drawbacks of pyloroplasty, see Deaver and Ashhurst, *Surgery of the Upper Abdomen,* pp. 113–116, and Paterson, *Gastric Surgery,* pp. 42–44.

54. Cannon and Blake were preceded in their experiments by the German experimental surgeon Johann Kelling and the Swiss surgeon Cesar Roux, as cited by Cannon in "The Physiological Aspects of Gastroenterostomy," *BM&SJ* 161 (1909):720–722.

55. W. B. Cannon and J. B. Blake, "Gastro-Enterostomy and Pyloro-plasty: An Experimental Study by Means of the Röntgen Rays," *Annals of Surgery* 41 (1905), p. 690.

56. Ibid., pp. 709–710.

57. See, e.g., Cannon and Blake's discussion of the so-called "vicious" circle of food, kinking, and the appearance of jejunal ulcers that sometimes followed operations that initially appeared to be successful (pp. 698–703). See also William J. Mayo, "A Review of 500 Cases of Gastro-Enterostomy," including Pyloroplasty, Gastroduodenostomy, and Gastrojejunostomy," *Annals of Surgery* 42 (1905):641–655; B. G. A. Moynihan, *Abdominal Operations* (Philadelphia & London: W. B. Saunders, 1905).

58. See application from F. T. Murphy and A. H. Gould to investigate the subject of relations between pancreatic secretions, liver secretions, and the coagulation of blood, Feb. 14, 1903, HMA.

59. For example, a progress report to Warren of Jan. 24, 1903 reported that "an experimental study of Surgical Shock along the lines of the work recently done by Dr. Crile is proposed under the cooperation of the Physiological Department with the Committee on Surgical Research." This investigation, undertaken by W. T. Porter of the Physiology Department and W. C. Quinby of the Surgery Department, was published as "The Condition of the Vasomotor Neurons in 'Shock'," *BM&SJ* 119 (1903):455.

60. See Minutes of meeting of Committee on Surgical Research, Feb. 7, 1905, HMA. Cannon and Gould were at the meeting by invitation of the committee (Burrell, Nichols, and Greenough); Blake was not present.

61. Minutes of meeting of Committee on Surgical Research, Feb. 13, 1905, HMA.

62. For instance, Cannon was invited by the Surgery Department in Nov. 1905 to demonstrate the use of x-ray in his researches on digestion before members of the Society of Clinical Surgery, which met at Harvard that year. See further Cushing's retrospective article on the Society of Clinical Surgery, p. 9. See also Samuel Robinson to R. B. Greenough, Feb. 27, 1907; and Robinson's acknowledgment to Cannon in "Experimental Surgery of the Lung," Division of Surgery, *Bulletin of Research Work* no. 5, Dec. 1908, p. 222; both in HMA.

7. The Longwood Avenue Medical School

1. Cannon to Cornelia J. Cannon, Dec. 12, 1905, Cannon Papers

2. See 1906 Diary, Jan. 3 and 30. A few days later, on Feb. 5, Cannon noted: "Dr. Porter spoke to me regarding need of sticking to the program he laid down. In afternoon Dr. Bowditch asked me about Dr. P.'s new book (many mistakes in it) and time Dr. P. spent on course (about ¼ mine) and his interests (farming)."

3. For the visit to Cornell, see 1906 Diary, Jan. 25, Feb. 24 and 25. Cannon was not able to tell Porter about the Cornell offer until he returned to the School from a further bout of illness on March 24: "Dr. Porter returns.

Says two things to consider—money and happiness in going to New York City. $4000 there—$3000 here. Recognizes I am not likely to be happy here unless independent. When he asks 'Money or independence?' I answer 'Independence'."

4. Student petition, March 31, 1906, accompanied by Cannon to George R. Minot, June 1, 1937, and subsequent Cannon letters to Minot and Anna Holt, June 11, 1937. All in HMA.

5. See, for example, R. H. Fitz to C. W. Eliot, March 29, 1906; William Sharp and George G. Smith for the second-year class to W. T. Porter, April 3, 1906; also C. S. Minot to C. W. Eliot, April 13, 24, and 26, 1906; all in Eliot Papers.

6. Porter to Eliot, March 31, 1906, Eliot Papers. Porter enclosed with his letter a memorandum of the work done by him during his connection with the University, including a detailed statement regarding the development of the Harvard Apparatus Company.

7. Bowditch, in failing health, spent the winter months of 1905 in California and then tried the Zander apparatus at the Massachusetts General Hospital, hoping the result might be beneficial to his shattered nervous system. H. P. Bowditch to H. C. Ernst, July 10, 1905, Ernst Papers. The following year he took a leave of absence from Harvard and, upon the advice of health faddist Horace Fletcher, underwent treatment with John Harvey Kellogg at Battle Creek. William James to Bowditch, Nov. 1, 1905, Bowditch Papers; Bowditch to James, Nov. 3, 1905, William James Papers.

8. H. L. Higginson to C. W. Eliot, April 1, 1906, Eliot Papers.

9. For the committee's decision, see W. L. Richardson to Eliot, April 6, 1906, Eliot Papers; also F. B. Mallory to Cannon, April 9, 1906, Cannon Papers. Before the Medical Faculty had voted the respective professorships, Cannon received another job offer—this time from the Mayo Clinic to take charge of their research laboratory in surgical problems.

10. Harvard University Medical Faculty, Minutes of meeting, May 5, 1906, HMA. For more on Bowditch's retirement, see also minutes for June 2 and 20, 1906.

11. Eliot to Bowditch, June 8, 1906; see also J. C. Warren to Eliot, June 6, 1906. Both in Eliot Papers. The fifty-seventh annual meeting of the AMA was held in Boston, June 5–8, 1906, and was considered a huge success; see further *JAMA* 46 (1906), esp. issue of May 5, "The Boston Session," pp. 1356–77.

12. Jerome Davis Greene, whose father and mother were among the first American missionaries sent to Japan, was, like Cannon, a member of the Harvard Class of '96. He went on to study at the University of Geneva and Harvard Law School and in 1898 became the founder and editor of the *Harvard Alumni Bulletin*. Three years later he was appointed secretary to Eliot, with whom he maintained a close personal relationship, and from 1905 to 1910 he served the first of two terms as secretary to the Corporation. After many years in New York and abroad he returned to Harvard in 1934 where he served again as secretary to the Corporation and directed the Harvard Tercentenary Celebration. For further details, see Greene's printed "Reminiscences" and his pamphlet, "Years with President Eliot," HUA.

13. J. D. Greene to H. P. Walcott, July 30, 1906, Eliot Papers. Eliot, in formulating his plans for the ceremonies, was well aware of the Harvard Medical Alumni Association's usefulness as a fund-raising agency; see further his *Annual Report* for 1905–06, p. 189.

14. See *Dedication of the New Buildings of the Harvard Medical School, September 25th and 26th, 1906;* see also Cannon's 1906 Diary, Sept. 25 and 26.

15. *Dedication of the New Buildings,* p. 21.

16. Eliot, although fortunate to enjoy good health throughout his life, perhaps came to his interest in preventive medicine and public health through the losses he suffered in his family. Henry James, in his 2-vol. biography, *Charles W. Eliot: President of Harvard University, 1869–1909* (Boston & New York: Houghton Mifflin, 1930), gives touching accounts of Eliot's trials with the severe illnesses of his parents in the winter of 1861–62 and with trying to find treatment for his first wife, Ellen Derby Peabody, who contracted tuberculosis in the autumn of 1866 and died three years later. But the cruelest instance, by Eliot's own account, came in 1897 when his eldest son Charles was stricken with cerebrospinal meningitis and died within a few days, leaving a young family behind. "No death which has occurred in my family or in the circle of my intimate friends," Eliot wrote President Gilman of Johns Hopkins, "since I was old enough to know what death is, has seemed to me such a heavy loss and calamity as this one." James, *Charles W. Eliot,* II:91.

17. Ibid., p. 13. For more on the power house, see "The New Harvard Medical School," *Harvard Graduates' Magazine* 14 (1906).616–651, "The Mechanical Plant of the New Harvard Medical School, Densmore & LeClear, Engineers, Boston, Mass.," reprinted from *Harvard Graduates' Magazine,* June 1906; Frederick W. Coburn, "The Mechanical Plant of the Harvard Medical School: The Heart and Lungs of an Architectural Group, Incessantly Supplying Hot Water, Fresh Air, and Other Necessities to the Buildings," *Indoors and Out* 3 (1906):62–67. All in HMA. See also "Report to the President and Fellows of Harvard College upon a Method of Dividing the Costs of Operation of the Power House of the Harvard Medical School among the Institutions Served," March 1915, Lowell Papers.

18. "Address of Dr. Henry P. Bowditch," *Quarterly of Harvard Medical Alumni Association,* No. 10 (Oct. 1903), p. 605.

19. For the free public lectures, see further *Annual Reports,* 1906–07, pp. 39, 157–158; also *Annual Reports,* 1907–08, pp. 30, 170. For the summer courses, see *Annual Reports,* 1905–06, pp. 186–189.

20. See "Proposition of C. S. Minot to the Faculty of Medicine, 1899" and C. W. Eliot to C. S. Minot, March 13, 1899, Minot Papers.

21. See further Reports of the Committee on University Education, the Special Committee on Higher Degrees, and the Committee on Graduate Courses, as printed in the Minutes of the meetings of the Faculty of Medicine, Jan. 9 and March 5, 1904, HMA.

22. Minutes of the meeting of the Faculty of Medicine, Feb. 2, 1907. Cannon was the only member of the committee who dissented from the recommendation. He offered a substitute proposal whereby the division would be located in the Medical School but degrees would be granted by the Faculty of Arts and Sciences. His motion, however, was defeated.

23. See further "Higher Degrees in the Medical Sciences," HMA.

24. The final step was taken on Nov. 17, 1908, when the Division of Medical Sciences was officially constituted; on Dec. 15, the president appointed Theobald Smith as the first chairman of the division. Detailed historical accounts may be found in the Division of Medical Sciences file, HMA. See also Eric G. Ball, "The Fiftieth Anniversary of the Founding of the Division of Medical Sciences," *Harvard Medical Alumni Bulletin*, May 1958.

25. "Opening of the New Harvard Medical School Buildings," editorial in *BM&SJ* 155 (1906):351.

26. Harrington, *Harvard Medical School*, III:1203.

27. C. W. Eliot to J. C. Warren, June 14, 1905, Eliot Papers.

28. See further exchange of letters between Burke and Porter, Sept. 18 and 21, 1906, enclosed with W. S. Burke to C. F. Adams, Sept. 29, 1906, all in Eliot Papers. Burke, the inspector of buildings and grounds, sent the letters to Adams, the Harvard treasurer, with the suggestion that the university comptroller might straighten out the tangle.

29. Cannon to J. D. Greene, Oct. 20, 1906. This lengthy handwritten report of Cannon's earlier telephone conversation with Greene (see Cannon's 1906 Diary, Oct. 5) gives a very different opinion of the relations between the department and the company from that given by Porter in his Sept. 21 letter to Burke. See also Greene's version of the complicated relations in his letter to C. F. Adams, Oct. 10, 1906, in which he referred to the "loose understanding" that had existed between Porter and Eliot with regard to the manufacture of Harvard apparatus. All in Eliot Papers.

30. Exchange of letters between Porter and Eliot, Nov. 9 and 30, 1906, Eliot Papers. Eliot ended his letter by repeating a statement he had made several times before—namely, that Porter's efforts to promote the laboratory method of teaching physiology through the manufacture and distribution of good, cheap apparatus was "a valuable contribution to medical science and medical teaching."

31. W. L. Richardson to C. W. Eliot, Feb. 7, 1907. The dean's continuing grudge played an important part in effecting Porter's decline in status at the School; see, e.g., Richardson to Eliot, Oct. 5, 1906. Both in Eliot Papers.

32. Porter to Eliot, Feb. 9, 1907, Eliot Papers. Among the advanced students working with Porter in 1907 were F. H. Pratt, a graduate of Harvard Medical School; W. I. Clarke, a surgeon in Worcester; H. K. Marks, a fourth-year medical student at HMS; and a Dr. Lothrop, who was working at the request of Burrell on the effect of surgical dressings on absorption. See further Porter to Eliot, Nov. 15, 1907, Eliot Papers.

33. Porter to Eliot, Nov. 15, 1907, Eliot Papers. "Men engaged in research in physiology have never been registered at the Dean's office," he told the president, "but their names and their work have appeared in the President's Report. They have always, both by Dr. Bowditch and myself, been received as guests." Porter went on to tell Eliot about the weekly physiological conferences he was then conducting, which attracted a large attendance of practicing physicians—among them Drs. Christian, Joslin, Joseph H. Pratt, and Horace D. Arnold, a professor of medicine at Tufts.

34. 1906 Diary, July 3. Soon after, at the insistence of Bowditch, Cannon made an effort to seek out Porter and talk over the arrangements for the coming year; see also entries for July 9–12.

35. This sort of slight happened more than once; see, for example, Cannon's 1908 Diary, Jan. 16–17 and May 15, and his 1909 Diary, Sept. 21.

36. 1907 Diary, Nov. 12.

37. 1908 Diary, May 29. Porter was introduced by William Sharpe, president of the class, as "a man who had great influence on our lives." Porter's Class Day address, "The Critical Periods in the Life of a Physician," was published in *JAMA* 52 (1909):1305–7.

38. In 1905–06 Lillie replaced S. S. Maxwell, who left the instructorship in physiology for the University of California. For Cannon's proposed personnel changes, see 1906 Diary, May 11, 17, 21, 24; also E. G. Martin to Cannon, May 9, 1906, in Cannon Papers.

39. Harvard Medical School, Experiments Required of First-Year Students in the Department of Physiology, 11 pp., HMA.

40. After the splendid beginning Porter had made in 1895 with the single day's experiment, he became so carried away by his devotion to the laboratory method that he eventually went overboard—emphasizing large amounts of its minutiae and going into far too much detail for students and faculty alike. By 1901, however, Porter had begun to introduce some human physiology into the laboratory work for medical students; see, for example, stimulation of human nerves (pp. 89–97) and heart sounds (pp. 269ff.) in the 1901 edition of *Introduction to Physiology* (Cambridge, Mass.: University Press). For a detailed description of the physiology course as it was conducted from 1902 to 1906—with hours, topics, lectures, theses titles, etc.—see also the various editions of Porter's companion volume, *Physiology at Harvard* (Cambridge, Mass.: University Press).

41. According to his diary notes, Cannon began work on a laboratory manual in July of 1906. As he continued making changes in the physiology course in 1907, 1908, and 1909, he kept revising and enlarging the guide for students to coincide with the rearranged lectures, demonstrations, and experiments. The much-expanded version prepared by Cannon for use in 1909 was published the next year as *A Laboratory Course in Physiology* by the Harvard University Press and was followed by revised editions in 1911 and 1913.

42. See further *Yearbooks of the Carnegie Institution of Washington;* also *The Carnegie Foundation for the Advancement of Teaching, Founded 1905,* (Concord, N.H.: Rumford Press, 1919). The above account is based largely on letters and documents in the Benedict Papers.

43. For a report of his visit to Boston, see F. G. Benedict to J. S. Billings, Nov. 12, 1906; for a proposal assessing the opportunities near the Longwood Avenue School, see also Benedict to Billings, Nov. 20, 1906. Both in Benedict Papers.

44. For a description of the three-day meetings of the National Academy of Sciences, see *BM&SJ* 155 (1906):657–658. For details of Cannon's extensive efforts in behalf of the nutrition laboratory, see his letter to Benedict, Nov. 23, 1906, in Benedict Papers.

45. See H. P. Bowditch to J. S. Billings, Nov. 26, 1906, Benedict Papers. Bowditch's interest in the subject of nutrition was not a new one. For example, in an undated draft written for the purpose of soliciting funds for the Medical School, Bowditch had maintained, "Our first need is endowed professorships to utilize our facilities for research and to my mind there is no biological problem so important for mankind as the one which our friend [Horace] Fletcher is attacking so vigorously, viz., the question of nutrition. The changes which food undergoes in the body under normal and pathological conditions, i.e., the problems of healthy and diseased nutrition, are of course to be studied by methods of physiological chemistry, and it might perhaps seem best simply to seek an endowment for a chair of physiological chemistry with special provision for research"; Notes in Bowditch Papers.

46. Benedict to Cannon, Nov. 25, 1906, Cannon to Benedict, Dec. 6, 1906, and Benedict to Cannon, Feb. 14, 1907; all in Benedict Papers. See also Cannon to Eliot, Nov. 15, 1907, Eliot Papers.

47. See exchange of letters between Benedict and Cannon, March 22 and 23, 1934; also Benedict to Cannon, Sept. 24, 1937. All in Cannon Papers.

48. See further obituary notice of E. W. Wood in *Harvard Graduates' Magazine* 14 (1905–06):24–27; "The Department of Chemistry," in *The Harvard Medical School, 1786–1906* (Boston, 1906), pp. 34–35; Harry C. Trimble, "Biological Chemistry at the Harvard Medical School: Historical Notes," pp. 7–8, unpublished manuscript in HMA.

49. See Cannon to Eliot, Oct. 28, 1904, Cannon Papers. See also Bowditch's follow-up letters to Eliot, Dec. 6, 1904, in Eliot Papers, and to A. T. Cabot, Feb. 7, 1905, Notes in Bowditch Papers.

50. Eliot to Cannon, Nov. 4, 1904. Despite Eliot's financial concerns, he found Cannon's judgments commendable. See also W. L. Richardson to Eliot, July 1, 1905. Both in Eliot Papers.

51. See Cannon to F. B. Mallory, [May 8, 1906], Cannon Papers. See also 1906 Diary, May 8.

52. See further P. A. Schaffer in *Biographical Memoirs of the National Academy of Sciences* 27 (1952):57–82; also Trimble's historical note, pp. 8–9. Otto Knut Olof Folin (1867–1934), who left his native Sweden at the age of fifteen to be raised by relatives in Minnesota, had been at McLean Hospital (the psychiatric branch of Massachusetts General Hospital) since 1900 and was well known to the physiologists at Harvard. Folin's name had been mentioned for a post at the Medical School by Bowditch in the letters he wrote in 1904–05 about biological chemistry to Eliot and Cabot.

53. See further Trimble, p. 8; Joseph Davis, ed., *Carl Alsberg: Scientist at Large* (Stanford University Press, 1948); W. B. Cannon's obituary notice of L. J. Henderson in *Biographical Memoirs of the National Academy of Sciences* 23 (1943):31–58. See also the various studies by John Parascandola as listed in his article on Henderson in the *Dictionary of Scientific Biography*, VI, pp. 260–262.

54. The final decision reached by the trustees of the Carnegie Institution spurred both Cannon and Bowditch into renewed action; see Cannon's 1907 Diary, Feb. 26–27. Alsberg's and Councilman's reactions are noted in Can-

non's 1907 Diary, March 13 and 18. See also C. Alsberg and O. Folin, "Protein Metabolism in Cystinuria," *Am. J. Physiol.* 14 (1905):54–72. Henderson had previously locked horns with Folin because they had differing views about the acidity of urine, as noted by Cannon in his 1906 Diary, Feb. 18 and 20.

55. See Cannon's 1907 Diary, May 3, 6, and 10; also Cannon to Eliot, May 6, 1907, Eliot Papers. Eliot proposed offering Folin a salary of $2,500 a year for five years for an assistant professorship to teach advanced students only and to give the main part of his time to research.

56. 1907 Diary, May 13, 15, 19, and 20. See also undated, unsigned note from Cannon in folder for Otto Folin, Eliot Papers.

57. 1907 Diary, May 21.

58. The letters concerning Alsberg's job offer in Washington, Aug. 20 to Sept. 15, 1908, are in the Eliot Papers; see esp. Alsberg to Eliot, Aug. 20, 1908, Folin to Eliot, Aug. 27, 1908, Eliot to Alsberg, Aug. 30, 1908, Alsberg to Eliot, Sept. 8, 1908, and Alsberg's letter of resignation, Sept. 12, 1908. See also Cannon's 1908 Diary, Sept. 29. After he left Boston, Alsberg missed the academic atmosphere and recalled his Harvard days nostalgically; see further Davis, *Carl Alsberg,* p. 68.

59. Eliot to Henderson, Dec. 28, 1907, Eliot Papers. See also Cannon's 1907 Diary, Sept. 26.

60. For Henderson's published research, see bibliography to Cannon's obituary notice, pp. 52–53. For his preference for teaching in the College, see J. D. Greene to Henderson, April 9, 1907, in Eliot Papers. For a description of his relations with Folin, see unpublished memoir [ca. 1938], esp. pp. 132, 163–166, in Henderson Papers, HUA.

61. Folin to Eliot, Sept. 23, 1908; see also Eliot to J. D. Greene, Sept. 25, 1908, and H. A. Christian to Eliot, Oct. 23, 1908. All in Eliot Papers. Cannon noted in his 1908 Diary on Oct. 24: "Saw Pres. Eliot in morning—told him story of Alsberg and testified regarding value of Henderson."

62. Councilman to Eliot, undated, in Eliot Papers. For an example of the criticism of Henderson reported by Councilman, see Charles Harrington to Eliot, Sept. 25, 1905 and June 8, 1906, Eliot Papers.

63. Richardson, who had reached the age of retirement, had been in the service of the University for twenty-five years. His letter and Eliot's reply of May 1, 1907 are in the Eliot Papers.

64. Councilman to Eliot, Feb. 14, 1907, Eliot Papers.

65. Having previously refused the deanship for himself, Warren wrote Eliot in support of Ernst on June 4, 1907. For Bowditch's support of Ernst, see also his letter to Eliot of July 24, 1907. Both in Eliot Papers.

66. Eliot to Jerome Greene, July 14, 1907, with copies of his letters to Theobald Smith and Henry Lee Higginson (both dated July 9, 1907) enclosed. See also Eliot to Bowditch, July 29, 1907, and Walcott to Eliot, Sept. 5, 1907. All in Eliot Papers.

67. See Cannon's 1907 Diary, May 8. See also John Warren to Eliot, June 10 and 29, 1907, Eliot Papers.

68. Smith's letter is mistakenly dated June 13, 1907 instead of July. In his reply of July 15, Eliot told Smith, "I believe with you that Dr. Cannon

would make a good Dean; and we know much more about Dr. Cannon than we do about Dr. Christian. Dr. Christian seems to me, however, to be very promising." Two days later, on July 17, the president asked Jerome Greene, "Can you . . . inquire carefully among your younger medical school friends whether Cannon would make an acceptable dean of the Medical School? Professor Theobald Smith thinks him the best available candidate." All in Eliot Papers.

69. Exchange of letters between Bowditch and Eliot, Aug. 13 and 16, 1907, Eliot Papers; Cannon's 1907 Diary, Aug. 2.

70. Undated letter in Councilman folder, Eliot Papers, probably in response to Eliot's inquiry of Sept. 19, 1907.

71. The details of Christian's early career are given in "The New Dean of the Harvard Medical School," *Harvard Graduates' Magazine* 17 (1908):250–253. See also Scrapbook of Clippings, Programmes, and Letters in Christian Papers (vol. 14).

72. Commendations of Christian may be found, for example, in H. P. Walcott to Eliot, Sept. 5, 1907, in Eliot Papers, and "Report of the Carney Hospital for 1906," *BM&SJ* 157 (1907):342. Christian's conditions are set forth in his letter to Eliot of late Jan. or early Feb. 1908, in vol. I of Miscellaneous Letters, Christian Papers. For Eliot's offer of the Hersey Professorship and his subsequent plans for Christian, see his letters to Christian and R. H. Fitz, both dated April 28, 1908, in Eliot Papers.

73. Cannon to Eliot, Oct. 15, 1908, Eliot Papers; see also Cannon's 1908 Diary, Oct. 13, 14, and 15.

74. For an expression of such views, see Christian's address at the dedication of the department of medicine at Stanford University entitled "A Career in Medicine and Present-Day Preparation for It," *Science* n.s. 30 (1909):537–548.

8. At Home in Cambridge

1. See further *To Work in the Vineyard of Surgery: The Reminiscences of J. Collins Warren, 1842–1927*, ed. E. D. Churchill (Cambridge, Mass.: Harvard University Press, 1958), pp. 204–205. The vicinity of Soldier's Field, now the site of the Harvard Business School, was carefully considered for relocation of the Medical School, but prior to the erection of the Charles River dam in 1908, the land was flooded every spring by thawing snow, heavy rains, and high tides. "The ever-increasing importance of the natural and biological sciences to medicine," Churchill commented in a footnote, "has made the geographical separation of the preclinical scientists on Longwood Avenue from their many colleagues in Cambridge a matter of real concern. If the decision of 1900 were to be considered today, it is not at all likely that the Faculty of Medicine would be willing to place its science laboratories so far from the University area in Cambridge, or indeed that the rest of the University would concur in such a move."

2. Those whose lives centered on Harvard University lived in the en-

virons of what was originally Old Cambridge. For most of them, the disparate sections at the edges of the city—North Cambridge, East Cambridge, and Cambridgeport (and the Irish and Italian immigrants who inhabited them)— "were as remote as Timbuctoo, passed through on the streetcar or on the subway, but seldom penetrated." *Snatched from Oblivion*, p. 67.

3. "Reminiscences of Cambridge," by Mrs. Samuel McChord Crothers, read by Katherine F. Crothers, April 24, 1945, *Cambridge Historical Society Publications* 31 (Proceedings for 1945), p. 7. Between 1909 and 1912 the linkage of Cambridge to Boston was facilitated when the present subway system from Harvard Square to Park Street was completed.

4. Ibid., p. 10.

5. *Way of an Investigator*, pp. 175–176; F. P. Gay, *The Open Mind: Elmer Ernest Southard, 1876–1920* (Chicago: Normandie House, 1938), pp. 75–77. See further Cannon to F. P. Gay, Nov. 17 and 20, 1934, Cannon Papers.

6. Cannon referred to the meetings with Ripley and Veblen in his 1906 Diary, Jan. 30 and April 11.

7. 1906 Diary, May 10.

8. Perry's precarious condition was reported by Cannon in his 1908 Diary, Feb. 18–20. By Feb. 24, the worst was over and he recorded, "Best of news of Tom Perry—Jouett thinks he is out of the woods." Rachel Perry, a brilliant, sensitive woman, was the sister of Bernard Berenson. Her complaints are detailed in Cannon's diary entries for March 4 and 8.

9. Cannon later described Perry and Pierce as his two dearest friends; see *Way of an Investigator*, p. 175.

10. 1906 Diary, March 1 and April 2.

11. Pierce, like Cannon, was an outlander and a self-made man, who early in life had developed traits of independence and ingenuity. Pierce was also rather like Mrs. Cannon in that, when either came up against New England stuffiness and propriety, they were "unduly stimulated" to resort to outrageous behavior. See further *Snatched from Oblivion*, pp. 69, 98–99.

12. See 1906 Diary, Jan. 11 and March 22.

13. 1907 Diary, Jan. 23.

14. 1913 Diary, May 17; see also 1907 Diary, June 8. The incident with Mrs. Münsterberg was described by Cornelia J. Cannon in her memoir, "A Servant of Science," pp. 64–65.

15. See for example, Cannon's 1906 Diary, Feb. 10, April 4, Oct. 13. A wide-ranging selection of "Lectures, Evening Readings, Concerts, Etc.," was listed in the annual Harvard College catalogs as well as an assortment of such events sponsored by other agencies in the Boston and Cambridge communities. Mrs. Schlesinger writes that the women in the family were passionate lecture-goers, from Cornelia's mother on down through her own sisters; they would even leave a sickbed to attend an event of special interest. One such occasion led her father to remark, somewhat philosophically, "It's three generations of lecture-goers, heart palpitations and nose bleeds, it makes no difference. To lectures they will go." *Snatched from Oblivion*, p. 73.

16. Cannon commented on "Hedda Gabler" in his 1906 Diary, Jan. 12, and on Shaw in his 1907 Diary, March 2 and April 17. Some of his other

comments on the theater were recorded in diary notes of Oct. 25, 1906, April 24, 1908, and March 29, 1909.

17. See further Cannon's 1906 Diary, Sept. 30, and his 1910 Diary, Jan. 16. Lariz Voldt, who later changed his name to Lawrence Vold, was a member of the Harvard College class of 1910 and the Harvard Law School class of 1913; see also Lawrence Vold correspondence in the Cannon Papers.

18. "Family Memory," p. 17. See also "C. H. Cannon's Record" and unidentified biographical sketch; unpublished manuscripts in the Cannon Papers.

19. Cornelia J. Cannon to Cannon, postmarked Dec. 8, 1905. This letter and all family letters cited hereafter are in the Cannon Papers.

20. Cannon to Cornelia J. Cannon, Dec. 24, 1905.

21. Cannon to Cornelia J. Cannon, Dec. 26, 1905.

22. Frances H. James to Cornelia J. Cannon, Feb. 12, 1905, and Helen James to Cornelia J. Cannon, Feb. 19, 1905.

23. Cannon to Cornelia J. Cannon, Dec. 8, 1905.

24. M. J. Newson to Cannon, Nov. 22, 1897, Dec. 12, 1897, Jan. 16, 1898, Cannon Papers.

25. 1906 Diary, see esp. Aug. 30. The Cannons spent the time from Aug. 18 to 31 in Maine.

26. Samuel L. Sewall to Cannon, July 15, 1906, Cannon Papers; 1906 Diary, July 6, 7, and 17, Sept. 13 and 24.

27. Albert John Ochsner (1858–1925) was then chief surgeon at the Augustana and St. Mary's hospitals in Chicago and professor of clinical surgery in the Medical Department of the University of Illinois.

28. "Family Memory," p. 19. Colbert Cannon was sixty years old when he completed his medical course, and "with the enthusiasm of a boy was ready to begin life again." Although Cannon noted in his diary on June 14 and 15, 1906, that his father had asked him for money to relocate, Colbert practiced medicine in Chicago until the spring of 1907, at which time he moved permanently to Oregon. "C. H. Cannon's Record" and unidentified biographical sketch, in Cannon Papers.

29. Frances H. James to Cornelia J. Cannon, Sept. 27, 1905. A few months earlier Cornelia had proposed a scheme for her brother Henry to attend the Lawrence Scientific School. He was not encouraging, however, and let it be known that he did not intend to allow the women in his family to manage him.

30. See Helen James to Cornelia J. Cannon, Sept. 5, 1906, Cannon Papers.

31. Harriet Bartlett, "Ida M. Cannon: Pioneer in Medical Social Work," *Social Service Review* 49 (1975):208–229; see also Ida M. Cannon, *On the Social Frontier of Medicine: Pioneering in Medical Social Service* (Cambridge, Mass.: Harvard University Press, 1952).

32. "Jane Addams awakened in me, as she did in many," Ida continued, "a realization of the gross inconsistencies in our so-called democracy," I. M. Cannon, *On the Social Frontier*, p. 39.

33. "Recollections," see esp. Ida's Memories, p. 7.

34. In 1916 Harvard withdrew from the informal affiliation, and the

school later became the Simmons College School of Social Work. See further I. M. Cannon, *On the Social Frontier*, p. 5 and n. 1; also Roy Lubove, *The Professional Altruist: The Emergence of Social Work as a Career, 1880–1930* (Cambridge, Mass.: Harvard University Press, 1965), p. 141.

35. I. M. Cannon, *On the Social Frontier*, pp. 4–6; also chap. 5, "A Physician Takes Action," which is devoted to early developments at the MGH. For more on Cabot's role as a clinician, see also T. A. Dodds, "Opening the Windows: Richard Cabot and the Care of the Patient during America's Progressive Era, 1890–1920," undergraduate thesis submitted in partial fulfillment for the B.A. degree, Harvard University, 1980; "Richard Clarke Cabot, 1868–1939," obituary notice by Paul Dudley White, *New England Journal of Medicine* 220 (1939):1049–52; T. F. Williams, "Cabot, Peabody, and the Care of the Patient," *Bulletin of the History of Medicine* 24 (1950):462–481.

36. I. M. Cannon, *On the Social Frontier*, pp. 6–7, 48, 65; see also biographical materials in Ida Cannon Papers. In 1914 the hospital trustees appointed Miss Cannon Chief of Social Service; however, it was not until 1919, after fourteen years of probation, that the Social Service Department finally became an integral part of the hospital. See further Lubove, *Professional Altruist*, pp. 23–35, 62–63; F. A. Washburn, *The Massachusetts General Hospital: Its Development, 1900–1935* (Boston: Houghton Mifflin, 1939), pp. 459–467.

37. Mrs. Schlesinger comments at length about how her mother fit into "a tradition of freewheeling, independent-minded ladies of Cambridge." She points out that these women, far more than their conservative and conventional male counterparts, were responsible for the tone and atmosphere that characterized the community. Having dealt with their husbands by placing them on pedestals, "the ladies went ahead with the serious business of their lives: their own self-improvement, whether it lay in intellectual pursuits, in social reform, in educational innovation or in the arts or literature." *Snatched from Oblivion*, pp. 69–79.

38. Cornelia Cannon's interest in social service led her to undertake, in collaboration with Louise W. Jackson, the compilation of a directory, *Social Welfare in Cambridge: A Handbook for Citizens*, published under the auspices of the Social Service Committee of the First Church in Cambridge (Unitarian), 1907.

39. See further the section on "Milk" in J. L. Morse, "The History of Pediatrics in Massachusetts," *New England Journal of Medicine* 205 (1931):172–173; also Thomas E. Cone, Jr., *History of American Pediatrics* (Boston: Little, Brown, 1979), pp. 141–144.

40. Although Rotch, Morse noted, remained for some time the only person locally who took active steps to get good milk for babies, the movement took hold on a national scale. Milk committees became so numerous in various cities and states across the country that an Association of American Milk Commissions was established in 1905. Massachusetts, however, held back, and it was not until 1906 that the first medical milk commission in the Commonwealth was established by the Suffolk District Medical Society.

41. Cannon to Cornelia James, March 30, 1901, Cannon Papers.

42. The work of the milk committee was taken over by the Baby Hygiene

Association in 1909, in connection with the Welfare Stations that were established at the time. In 1922 the Baby Hygiene Association merged with the District Nursing Association to form the Community Health Association.

43. Cannon to Cornelia J. Cannon, Dec. 4, 1905, Cannon Papers.

44. 1906 Diary, March 22. See also entries for Aug. 3, Aug. 13, Dec. 3, Dec. 20, Dec. 21.

45. "Servant of Science," pp. 68–69.

46. 1907 Diary, Jan. 5 and 6. Newspaper accounts of the incident are inserted with the entry for Jan. 7.

47. Cannon, in *Way of an Investigator*, devoted a chapter to this unusual series of incidents, calling it "A Display of Human Frailties." His version ends with a bow to the superior wisdom of the Irish bridge tender, who advised the searchers, "Why don't you give a man a chance to come home?" (p. 194).

9. At Work in Boston

1. Cannon's address on "The Ideals of the Man of Science" was published in the Annual Report of the Unitarian Church for 1905 as well as in *The Christian Register,* the official organ of the Unitarian Church, 84 (1905):1192–95. See also S. M. Crothers to Cannon, Jan. 20 [1905] , in Cannon Papers.

2. *Annual Reports,* 1905–06, p. 30.

3. Undated, unsigned statement in Cannon's handwriting; in folder marked "Endowments for Laboratories . . . ," HMA. In his 1906 Diary, Cannon noted on May 25: "Dr. Ernst told me in morning of possibility of getting large sum for research and asked for statement of needs. Drew up statement of special needs and general reasons why money given to Harvard well-placed. At meeting Dr. Ernst, Dr. Mallory, Dr. Warren, Dr. Tyzzer agreed to use my statement as letter to donor." In Cannon Papers.

4. F. B. Mallory to C. W. Eliot, Nov. 22, 1906, Eliot Papers. See also Cannon's 1906 Diary, for example, July 28 and 30, Aug. 1, and entries continuing throughout parts of Aug. and Sept.

5. 1907 Diary, Feb. 4 and 6: Among the first-year students mentioned by Cannon were Bronson Crothers, Paul Lamson, Bowditch's son Harold, and Fitz's son Reginald.

6. 1907 Diary, Feb. 23 and 27.

7. 1907 Diary, March 7 and 27.

8. 1907 Diary, Oct. 1, Oct. 4, Nov. 6.

9. See further H. Addington Bruce, "Boris Sidis—An Appreciation," *Journal of Abnormal Psychology and Social Psychology* 18 (1923–24):274–276.

10. For an exchange of letters about one such petition, see J. D. Greene and W. L. Richardson, Oct. 19 and 20, 1905, in Eliot Papers. On Oct. 30, 1905, the Administrative Board at the Medical School voted not to grant Sidis leave to be excused from his clinical work in obstetrics (Faculty Records, HMA).

11. For Claparède's thoughts about sleep, see Carl Murchison, ed., *A*

History of Psychology in Autobiography, vol. 1 (Worcester, Mass.: Clark University Press, 1930), p. 78.

12. Minutes of Medical Faculty, May 4, 1907; folder for J. J. Putnam containing 1907 letters concerning Sidis, in Eliot papers; 1907 letters concerning Sidis in Putnam Papers.

13. B. Sidis, "An Experimental Study of Sleep," first published in parts in the *Journal of Abnormal Psychology* 3 (1908–09):1–32, 63–96, 170–207. The acknowledgment of Cannon's assistance appears on p. 19.

14. See further Wallace O. Fenn's obituary notice of Forbes in *Biographical Memoirs of the National Academy of Sciences* 40 (1969):113–141. For a description of the Forbes Papers deposited in the Countway Library, see also Robert G. Frank, Jr., and Judith H. Goetzl, "The J. H. B. Archive Report, The Alexander Forbes Papers," *Journal of the History of Biology* 11 (1978):387–393.

15. G. H. Parker, "The Origin and Evolution of the Nervous System," *Harvey Lectures, 1913–14*, pp. 72–84.

16. In his 1909 Diary, July 22, Cannon noted that while vacationing at Truro on Cape Cod, "Harry and Alexander Forbes came from Woods Hole in automobile and lunched with us. I outlined several researches for Alex Forbes." See further "Problems Suggested by Dr. W. B. Cannon for 4th Year Work in Physiology," July 22, 1909; "Notes on Reflex Inhibition of Skeletal Muscle, 1909–10"; both in Forbes Papers.

17. See further 1911 letters and related materials concerning Forbes's application to work in Sherrington's laboratory, in Forbes Papers; also Forbes, "Reflex Rhythm Induced by Concurrent Excitation and Inhibition," *Proceedings of the Royal Society* 85B (1912):289–298.

18. Frank and Goetzl note that improvements in physiological recording techniques were among the most important advances attributable to Forbes. Upon his return from England he acquired one of the new Einthoven string galvanometers, the first to be installed in the Boston area. This instrument brought a new degree of accuracy into the timing of delays and interactions in the spinal reflex centers.

19. For more on Hoskins, see Cannon, "Roy Graham Hoskins: An Appreciation," *Endocrinology* 30 (1942):839–845; also Roy O. Greep's obituary notice in *Endocrinology* 76 (1965):1007–11.

20. In a personal communication Greep expressed the belief that Hoskins was directed to Harvard by Ida Hyde, who had been one of his teachers at Kansas, but there are no materials in the Cannon Papers about his application.

21. Cannon, "Appreciation of Hoskins," p. 840.

22. Hoskins made a preliminary report of his work at the twenty-second annual meeting of the American Physiological Society held in Boston, Dec. 1909, which was followed by a paper published the following September, both entitled "Congenital Thyroidism: An Experimental Study of the Thyroid in Relation to Other Organs of Internal Secretion." See *Am. J. Physiol.* 25 (1909–10):xii; 26 (1910):426–438.

23. Hoskins's thesis, "Interrelations of the Organs of Internal Secretion," was handed in on May 1, 1910. On June 15 Cannon noted in his diary that when Hoskins took his final doctoral examinations "he did well and was unanimously recommended for the degree of Ph.D."

24. Cannon, "Appreciation of Hoskins," p. 840.

25. Other acknowledgments of Cannon's guidance and encouragement in the laboratory at this time may be found in Samuel Robinson, "Experimental Surgery of the Lung," *Annals of Surgery* (Feb. 1908):185–222; F. H. Pike, "Studies in the Physiology of the Central Nervous System: I. The General Phenomena of Spinal Shock," *Am. J. Physiol.* 24 (1909):124–152; and Joseph H. Pratt, "On the Importance of Determining the Potency of Digitalis Preparations," *BM&SJ* 163 (1910):279–283.

26. W. B. Cannon, "Recent Advances in the Physiology of the Digestive Organs Bearing on Medicine and Surgery," *American Journal of Medical Sciences* 131 (1906):563–578.

27. For more on Murphy, see obituary notice by Barney Brooks in *Transactions of the 68th meeting of the American Surgical Association* 66 (1948):582–584. For Murphy's research proposals, see also vol. 1 of Letters and minutes of meetings relating to the Committee on Surgical Research, HMA.

28. Cannon to C. J. Cannon, Dec. 4, 1905, Cannon Papers.

29. See F. T. Murphy, "A Suggestion for a Practical Apparatus for Use in Intra-thoracic Operations," *BM&SJ* 152 (Apr. 13, 1905):428–431. Later, Cannon was to apply this knowledge to his study of resuscitation.

30. Cannon to C. J. Cannon, Dec. 4, 1905, Cannon Papers.

31. For a full-length biography of Carrel, see further Theodore I. Malinin, *Surgery and Life: The Extraordinary Career of Alexis Carrel* (New York & London: Harcourt, Brace, Jovanovich, 1979).

32. Cannon to C. J. Cannon, Dec. 7, 1905, Cannon Papers.

33. On April 1, 1906, Scudder wrote Carrel about learning his techniques, adding: "Dr. Cannon was much interested in the work you have been doing and wanted me to know your methods thoroughly that perhaps when both of us had more leisure (in the fall) we might do some of this work also on dogs." This was followed by letters in Jan. of 1907 concerning Murphy, as well as from W. E. Castle of the Harvard Zoological Laboratory. On Jan. 26 Castle asked for reprints of Carrel's transplantation papers, stating, "Dr. W. B. Cannon recently called my attention to your work . . . I have been trying for some time to master the technique of skin grafting to get light on some of the pigment inheritance problems." Cannon's letter arranging for Murphy's visit was written on Jan. 10, 1907. All in Carrel Papers.

34. W. B. Cannon and F. T. Murphy, "The Movements of the Stomach and Intestines in Some Surgical Conditions," *Annals of Surgery* 43 (1906):513–537.

35. Ibid., pp. 532–534, 536–537.

36. Ibid., pp. 517–518.

37. Ibid., p. 518. Cannon later went on to publish a second paper with Murphy, "Physiologic Observations on Experimentally Produced Ileus," *JAMA* 49 (1907):840–843.

38. See further I. P. Pavlov, *The Work of the Digestive Glands* (London & Philadelphia, 1902), p. 66; W. H. Bayliss and E. H. Starling, "The Movements and Innervation of the Small Intestine," *Journal of Physiology* 24 (1899):99–143.

39. W. B. Cannon, "The Motor Activities of the Stomach and Small

Intestine after Splanchnic and Vagus Section," *Am. J. Physiol.* 17 (1906):429–442.

40. W. B. Cannon, "Oesophageal Peristalsis after Bilateral Vagotomy," *Am. J. Physiol.* 19 (1907):436–444.

41. See further John Reid, "An Experimental Investigation into the Functions of the Eighth Pair of Nerves, or the Glosso-pharyngeal, Pneumogastric, and Spinal Accessory," *Edinburgh Medical and Surgical Journal* 51 (1839):269–330.

42. W. B. Cannon, "Oesophageal Peristalsis," p. 438.

43. Ibid., pp. 443–444.

44. W. B. Cannon, "The Acid Control of the Pylorus," *Am. J. Physiol.* 20 (1907):283–322.

45. Ibid., pp. 286–287.

46. W. B. Cannon, "Recent Advances in the Knowledge of the Movements and Innervation of the Alimentary Canal," *Medical News* 86 (1905):923–929; see esp. p. 925.

47. Cannon to C. J. Cannon, Dec. 15, 1905, Cannon Papers.

48. W. B. Cannon, "Recent Advances in the Physiology of the Digestive Organs Bearing on Medicine and Surgery," *American Journal of Medical Sciences* 131 (1906):563–578; see esp. p. 569.

49. W. B. Cannon, "Acid Control of the Pylorus," see esp. pp. 296–306.

50. 1907 Diary, July 29–30.

51. 1907 Diary, June 20. For a fuller description of this work, see further W. B. Cannon, "The Acid Closure of the Cardia," *Am. J. Physiol.* 23 (1908):105–114.

52. W. B. Cannon, "Acid Control of the Pylorus," see esp. pp. 311–314.

53. The remarks following Cannon's paper, "An Explanation of the Motor Activities of the Alimentary Canal in Terms of the Myenteric Reflex," in *Transactions* of the eleventh annual meeting of the American Gastro-Enterological Association, held in Chicago, Ill., June 1 and 2, 1908, are unpaginated.

10. The Antivivisectionist Agitation

1. See, for example, Cannon's 1906 Diary, Oct. 22; 1907 Diary, Oct. 16; 1908 Diary, Jan. 25.

2. The early history of the humane society movement in America is described in Roswell C. McCrea, *The Humane Movement* (New York: Columbia University Press, 1910), and William J. Schultz, *The Humane Movement in the United States, 1910–1922* (New York: Columbia University Press, 1924). For an account of the earliest humane societies, founded for the purpose of "promoting attempts to recover persons from apparent death, especially in cases of suffocation and drowning," see further M. A. DeWolfe Howe, *The Humane Society of the Commonwealth of Massachusetts, An Historical Review, 1785–1916* (Boston, 1918).

3. Saul Benison, "In Defense of Medical Research," *Harvard Medical Alumni Bulletin,* Jan./Feb. 1970, p. 16.

4. The response of the New York State Medical Society to Bergh's proposed legislation was largely directed by John Call Dalton, whose pamphlet, *Vivisection: What It Is, and What It Has Accomplished,* was published that same year. At the time two investigators were pioneering in experimental medicine in New York—Dalton at the College of Physicians and Surgeons and the younger Austin Flint at Bellevue Hospital. See further James C. Turner, "Kindness to Animals: The Animal Protection Movement in England and America during the Nineteenth Century" (unpublished Ph.D. dissertation, Harvard University, 1975), pp. 295–297, or the shorter version published as *Reckoning with the Beast: Animals, Pain and Humanity in the Victorian Mind* (Baltimore: Johns Hopkins University Press, 1980), p. 85.

5. Schultz, *Humane Movement in the United States,* p. 142.

6. J. C. Dalton to H. P. Bowditch, Feb. 1, 1881; this letter and the one cited in the following note form a two-part letter, in Cannon Papers. Cannon inherited a collection of correspondence and related materials on the subject of antivivisection from Bowditch and Ernst when he took over the direction of the battle. Many of the letters and documents cited in this account may be found in the Cannon Papers.

7. Dalton to Bowditch, Jan. 31, 1881, Cannon Papers. For Dalton's views as well as a selection of provivisection resolutions from state, local, and specialist medical societies, see further his monograph, *Experimentation on Animals as a Means of Knowledge in Physiology, Pathology, and Practical Medicine* (New York, 1875).

8. As early as 1867, Boston, one of the major centers of the developing humane and animal protection movement in America, had its own SPCA, which was soon followed by a state society. The Massachusetts Society for the Prevention of Cruelty to Animals (MSPCA) was formed under the capable and energetic guidance of George Angell, a self-made man and prosperous lawyer, who proceeded to make it his life's work. Despite efforts by Angell and others to organize a society for the specific purpose of opposing animal experimentation, it was not until 1895 that the New England Anti-Vivisection Society came into being. The New England society, one of the most extreme of its kind, won instant support and claimed two hundred members within a month of its founding. Turner, *Reckoning with the Beast,* esp. pp. 49–51, 91–94; see also G. T. Angell, *Autobiographical Sketches and Personal Recollections* (Boston, 1908).

9. For a history of the development of the antivivisection movement in England, see Richard D. French, *Antivivisection and Medical Science in Victorian Society* (Princeton, N.J.: Princeton University Press, 1975).

10. Mrs. White had been a leader of the Women's SPCA, an auxiliary of the Pennsylvania Society for the Prevention of Cruelty to Animals. See Sydney H. Coleman, *Humane Society Leaders in America* (Albany, N.Y.: The American Humane Association, 1924), p. 204; also pp. 178–186. White wrote a sketch of her life, which appeared in the journal *Four Footed Friends* 11, no. 12 (Oct. 1912): Cobbe is treated at length in French; see also her autobiography, *Life of Frances Power Cobbe, by Herself,* 2 vols. (Boston & New York, 1894).

11. C. Adams, "The Anti-Vivisection Movement and Miss Cobbe," *Verulam Review* 3 (1892–93): 201; quoted in French, p. 62.

12. Michael Foster to C. F. Hodge, Dec. 1, 1890. Gerald Geison, in his full-length study, *Michael Foster and the Cambridge School of Physiology* (Princeton, N.J.: Princeton University Press, 1978), maintains that the antivivisectionist legislation in 1876 was never a very serious obstacle to English physiologists— that after 1882 it was little more than a bureaucratic annoyance (p. 331). It is true that animal experimentation increased exponentially in Great Britain after that time, but Geison has overlooked the fact that the Vivisection Act prevented student demonstrations and later had a profound effect on the development of surgery there through its interdiction of experimental surgery.

13. For a history of early antivivisectionist agitation in Massachusetts, see further H. P. Bowditch, "The Advancement of Medicine by Research," annual discourse delivered to the Massachusetts Medical Society (MMS), in *Proceedings of the Massachusetts Medical Society*, 17 (1896):1–56. The entire text of the vote of the MMS Councilors appears in the Appendix, p. 45.

14. Commonwealth of Massachusetts, An Act relating to Vivisection in the Public Schools, House . . . No. 414, March 1894. Bowditch blamed George Angell for the shift in policy by the MSPCA, which he said had "until quite recently treated this question with moderation and good sense." See further "Advancement of Medicine by Research," esp. pp. 14–15, 52–53; also H. P. Bowditch to C. W. Eliot, Oct. 12, 1896, Eliot Papers.

15. See further Cannon, *Antivivisection Legislation: Its History, Aims and Menace*, Defense of Research Pamphlet XXV, Chicago: AMA, 1913; also in *JAMA* 60 (1913):1511–14. For the Parkman murder case, see further Robert Sullivan, *The Disappearance of Dr. Parkman* (Boston: Little, Brown, 1971).

16. Transcripts of the testimony of remonstrants given at hearings held on March 12 and April 2, 1896, may be found in the Cannon Papers. Among the practitioners who testified were James J. Putnam, David W. Cheever, and Grace Wolcott—all of Boston.

17. Ibid., pp. 55–59 of April 2 transcript.

18. See further Donald Fleming, *William H. Welch and the Rise of Modern Medicine* (Boston: Little, Brown, 1954), pp. 148–151.

19. Bowditch's committee was made up of representatives from the American Physiological Society, the American Anatomical Society, the American Society of Morphologists, and the American Society of Naturalists. In Feb. 1896 they joined with members of committees of the American Society of Physicians and the American Society of Surgeons to issue a statement in behalf of science, introduced by the presidents of Harvard, M.I.T., and the Massachusetts Medical Society and signed by virtually every significant medical scientist in the country. See further circular printed letter from S. W. Mitchell, J. G. Curtis, W. H. Howell and H. P. Bowditch, Boston, Nov. 22, 1895; "Vivisection: A Statement in Behalf of Science"; and various 1896 printed resolutions and memorials in defense of medical research; all in Cannon Papers.

20. J. T. Whittaker to Abraham Jacobi, Dec. 9, 1895; Russell Chittenden

to H. P. Bowditch, Dec. 11, 1895. Jacobi was then president of the Association of American Physicians, whose defense committee Welch headed.

21. Fleming, *William H. Welch,* p. 149.

22. Simon Flexner and J. T. Flexner, *William Henry Welch and the Heroic Age of American Medicine* (New York: Dover, 1941), pp. 257–259; Welch's role in the fight against the antivivisectionists is detailed on pp. 254–262. See also U.S. Senate, Committee on the District of Columbia: *Hearing on the Bill (S. 34) for the Further Prevention of Cruelty to Animals in the District of Columbia* (Washington, 1900).

23. W. B. Cannon, *Antivivisection Legislation,* p. 4.

24. See further Massachusetts House Bill No. 917, entitled "An Act for the Further Prevention of Cruelty to Animals," Feb. 1900; also Massachusetts Medical Society, circular letter addressed to physicians, Feb. 27, 1900. Both in Cannon Papers.

25. See, for example, "Letters to the Editor" from Frederick Law Olmsted, Jr., and others, *Boston Evening Transcript,* Feb. 16, 24, 27, and 28, 1900.

26. "Tomorrow's Hearing on Vivisection," editorial in *Boston Evening Transcript,* March 1, 1900.

27. The hearings, held before the Committee on Probate and Insolvency at the Boston State House in March 1900, were described at length in the *Transcript* and other Boston newspapers. Summaries and reports of some of the proceedings may also be found in the Cannon Papers.

28. J. M. Greene, "The Hearing on Vivisection," *New England Anti-Vivisection Society Monthly* 5 (April 1900):6–7.

29. Ibid., p. 7.

30. Thomas E. Cone, Jr., *History of American Pediatrics* (Boston: Little, Brown, 1979), p. 116.

31. In 1891 Heinrich Quincke in Germany, hoping to find a safe way of recovering cerebrospinal fluid in children with hydrocephalus, simplified a technique previously developed by James Corning and successfully removed spinal fluid from one of his patients by inserting a fine needle with stylet in the vertebral interspace in the patient's lumbar region. For a brief historical account of the development of this procedure, see Stanley Cobb, "One Hundred Years of Progress in Neurology, Psychiatry, and Neurosurgery," *Archives of Neurology and Psychiatry* 59 (1948):63–98; esp. 91–92.

32. T. M. Rotch and A. H. Wentworth, "Report on Diseases of Children," *BM&SJ* 133 (1895):589–592; A. H. Wentworth, "Some Experimental Work on Lumbar Puncture of the Subarachnoid Space," *BM&SJ* 135 (1896):132–136.

33. *Transactions* of the American Pediatric Society, Eighth Session, held in Montreal, Canada, May 25, 26, and 27, 1896, vol. VIII. Wentworth's presentation appears on pp. 85–108; the discussion of lumbar puncture that followed is on pp. 110–112. See also the paper Caillé presented at this meeting, "Tapping the Vertebral Canal; Local Treatment for Tubercular Meningitis," pp. 79–84.

34. [John B. Roberts], "Human Vivisection," *The Philadelphia Polyclinic* 5 (1896):357–358.

35. Minutes of meeting of the Boston Society of Medical Sciences, Committee for the opposition of legislation restricting experimentation on animals, held at the St. Botolph Club, Tuesday, March 6, 1900.

36. Undated, unsigned note in the handwriting of H. P. Bowditch, in Cannon Papers.

37. Wentworth's letter of resignation dated June 4, 1900, addressed to the Dean of the Medical Faculty, was forwarded by Richardson to the President and Fellows of Harvard University on June 6, 1900; in Eliot Papers. See further diary fragment, entry for March 19, 1900, in H. C. Ernst Papers; Fritz B. Talbot's biography of Rotch in B. F. Veeder, ed., *Pediatric Profiles* (St. Louis: Moseby, 1957), p. 31; Clement A. Smith, *The Children's Hospital of Boston* (Boston: Little, Brown, 1983), pp. 76–77.

38. After undergoing several changes of name, the coalition became known as the Committee on Experimental Biology. Minutes of the early meetings and membership lists may be found in HMA.

39. H. P. Bowditch to Selma Knauth Bowditch, March 21, 1901, Bowditch Papers. Statements by the remonstrants were edited for publication by Harold C. Ernst; see further *Animal Experimentation* (Boston: Little, Brown, 1902).

40. See further J. W. Farlow's biographical memoir, *Proceedings* of the Massachusetts Historical Society (Nov. 1922):162–166. Ernst had previously joined with Bowditch in preparing the case for the remonstrants in 1900, as may be followed in his diary fragment in the Ernst Papers.

41. Ernst's laboratory at Harvard provided much of the tuberculin and diphtheria antitoxin available in the city of Boston. The *Transcript* reported on March 3, 1900, that more than thirty thousand bottles of diphtheria preventive were used in Massachusetts in the preceding year, and the demand for antitoxin had been particularly heavy during the few weeks just passed.

42. The *Transcript* reported on March 15, 1900, that the audience, said to be better behaved than at some of the previous sessions, heard testimony from Sedgwick of M.I.T., Mary Willcox of Wellesley, J. S. Kingsley of Tufts, and Putnam, Warren, Theobald Smith, and W. T. Porter of Harvard. Porter's testimony gives a detailed account of the work done in the physiology laboratory each day.

43. Cannon to Cornelia James, March 18/19, 1901, Cannon Papers. In this letter Cannon also noted that Greene had charged Nathaniel Shaler with advertising for five hundred cats: "Professor Shaler wrote a letter saying that he wished he had the man Greene in old Kentucky, where a man can go out with a gun and return with a smile. It is well the letter was not made public, or the antis would surely have held up their hands in horror and pointed again to the murderous tendencies of science."

44. "Why," she continued, "should a doctor or a professor be allowed to torture a dog or a cat for five weeks, when we arrest, fine or imprison a teamster in the street for beating his horse for five minutes? We have laws for the protection of animals from cruelty. But gentlemen, they do not reach the professor or the doctor. Give us something that will!" Mrs. Ward's testimony was later published as a broadside by the New England Anti-Vivisection

Society. Near the end of her autobiography, *Chapters from a Life* (Boston & New York: Houghton Mifflin, 1897), Mrs. Ward set forth her views on vivisection as part of her creed (p. 251).

45. Cannon to Cornelia James, March 18/19, 1901, Cannon Papers.

46. Cannon to Cornelia James, March 20, 1901, Cannon Papers.

47. Cannon to Cornelia James, March 22, 1901, Cannon Papers.

48. See Committee on Experimental Biology materials, esp. minutes of meeting, Feb. 3, 1903, HMA.

49. See, for example, S. L. Powers to H. C. Ernst, Feb. 12, 1906, Cannon Papers.

50. W. T. Sedgwick to H. C. Ernst, Feb. 15, 1906, Cannon Papers. After the hearings Sedgwick again wrote Ernst in behalf of the committee: "Every mother's son of us feels under deep obligation to you for your able and unremitting services . . . Whether we say much about it or not, our hearts are in the right place and we really deeply appreciate the devotion, self-sacrificing spirit and splendid skill with which you have year after year put to rout the enemies of vivisection" May 5, 1906, Cannon Papers.

51. See Ernst's 1905 notes in the Cannon Papers. This was Cannon's first experience with explaining his research to laymen.

52. Cannon to Ernst, Feb. 22, 1906, Cannon Papers; see also Cannon's 1906 Diary, Feb. 16, Feb. 27, April 26, and May 3.

53. Langdon Frothingham, previously an instructor in the Veterinary School, had recently been appointed to the Bacteriology Department of the Medical School. Joshua Hubbard, who did surgical research, later became a clinical professor of surgery at HMS. See further Minutes of Medical Faculty meeting, Nov. 2, 1907. See also Report of the Building Committee accepted at the Faculty Meeting, Nov. 2, 1907; Action taken by the Faculty of Medicine at its meeting in Nov. 1907; C. M. Green to H. C. Ernst, Nov. 7, 1907—all in Committee on Animals materials, HMA.

54. For an earlier set of "Rules to be observed in performing experiments on animals in the Physiological Laboratory of the Harvard Medical School," as drafted by Bowditch, see Committee on Experimental Biology materials, HMA. Cannon's circular letter of Nov. 19, 1907, and the replies he received may be found in the Committee on Animals materials. See also his 1907 Diary, Nov. 2, 15, 18, 20, 25, and Dec. 23.

55. Percy M. Dawson to Cannon, Nov. 27, 1907, HMA. Dawson, who went on to become a pioneer in the physiology of physical education, lived a long and illustrious life; see further obituary notice by D. B. Dill in *Medicine and Science in Sports* 2 (1970):v–vi.

56. F. S. Lee to Cannon, Nov. 23, 1907, HMA.

57. For example, concerning the animals kept in the basement of the Hunterian Laboratory at Hopkins, Percy Dawson wrote in his letter: "The dog food consists of scraps from the hospital (it is said that the nurses get one half and the dogs the other. This seems probable but I cannot vouch for it)."

58. Ibid. Dawson's letter supplemented another from Hopkins written by Harvey Cushing: "I have put a great deal of thought upon the matter,"

Cushing told Cannon, "and feel the responsibilities of the work very deeply . . . I feel the responsibility the more because our particular methods have been copied in so many places, where no one individual has given sufficient time or taken sufficient responsibility about the work to keep it free from local criticism." Cushing to Cannon, Nov. 22, 1907, HMA.

59. Joseph Erlanger to Cannon, Nov. 23, 1907, HMA.

60. L. B. Mendel to Cannon, Nov. 21, 1907. Mendel's colleague at Yale, Yandell Henderson, wrote in a similar vein from New Haven on Dec. 1: "On the point of the relation of the public to animal experimentation my endeavor has been to inculcate a maximum of ignorance and a minimum of education . . . All is quiet here just now and I had rather let well enough alone." Both in HMA.

61. For Richardson's views, see M. H. Richardson to H. L. Burrell, July 24, 1907, in Department of Surgery files, and his letter to H. C. Ernst, March 6, 1908, in Committee on Animals materials; both in HMA. For Fitz's views, see Cannon's 1908 Diary, Feb. 21, in Cannon Papers, and R. H. Fitz to H. C. Ernst, Feb. 27, 1908, in Committee on Animals materials, HMA.

11. In Defense of Medical Research

1. See further George Corner, *A History of the Rockefeller Institute* (New York: Rockefeller Institute Press, 1964), pp. 83–87. The AMA, spurred by resolutions passed earlier that year, established the defense group at its national meeting held in June 1908.

2. Herbert L. Burrell, the John Homans Professor of Clinical Surgery at Harvard Medical School, was president of the AMA at the time and selected the original members of the committee. Details concerning the formation of the group may be found in the Cannon Papers.

3. W. H. Welch to Cannon, July 3, 1908, also contains further details about the new committee. In Cannon Papers.

4. See further Saul Benison, "In Defense of Medical Research," *Harvard Medical Alumni Bulletin* 44 (1970), p. 18. An account of the council under Cannon's direction through 1919 may be found in William Gary Roberts, "Man before Beast: The Response of Organized Medicine to the American Anti-Vivisection Movement," undergraduate thesis submitted in partial fulfillment for the B.A. degree, Harvard College, 1979, HUA.

5. G. H. Simmons to Cannon, Nov. 13, 1908. Cannon saw Colwell's position as offering a unique opportunity, as evidenced by his response to Simmons of Nov. 16, 1908. Both in Cannon Papers.

6. Paget to Simmons, Aug. 8, 1908, Cannon Papers. Early in 1908 Stephen Paget, the son of Sir James Paget, the distinguished Victorian surgeon, founded the Research Defense Society "to make known the facts as to experiments on animals in this country; the immense importance to the welfare of mankind of such experiments; and the great saving of human life and health directly attributable to them." See further *Publications of the Research Defense Society, March 1908 March 1909* (London: Macmillan, 1909).

7. Paget to Cannon, March 31, 1909, Cannon Papers.

8. Lee and Curtis were on the faculty of the College of Physicians and Surgeons, Columbia University, whereas Bryant was at New York University Bellevue Medical College. Although all were seasoned veterans in the campaigns against the antivivisectionists, Lee especially took up Cannon's initial request for advice (Oct. 7, 1908) and continued to correspond faithfully about a wide variety of both national and local events.

9. Curtis to Cannon, Oct. 27, 1908, Cannon Papers.

10. Simmons sent the unidentified excerpt to Cannon in his letter of Dec. 17, 1908. Cannon, responding on Dec. 21, felt that the name of the council, doubtless suggested by that of the English Research Defense Society, was immaterial as long as its activities produced the desired results. Both in Cannon Papers.

11. W. B. Cannon, "The Opposition to Medical Research," Chairman's address in the Section on Pathology and Physiology of the AMA, June 5–8, 1908, *JAMA* 51 (1908):635–640.

12. Cannon first circularized the members of the Defense Council about the code (among other matters) on July 28, 1908; other letters seeking a wider range of advice and criticism were mailed out from AMA headquarters in Chicago later that year. The rules as finally formulated were as follows:

I. Vagrant dogs and cats brought to the Laboratory and purchased there shall be held at least as long as at the city-pound, and shall be returned to their owners if claimed and identified.

II. Animals in the Laboratory shall receive every consideration for their bodily comfort; they shall be kindly treated, properly fed, and their surroundings kept in the best possible sanitary condition.

III. No operations upon animals shall be made except with the sanction of the Director of the Laboratory, who holds himself responsible for the importance of the problems studied, and for the propriety of the procedures used in the solution of these problems.

IV. In any operation likely to cause greater discomfort than that attending anaesthetization the animal shall first be rendered incapable of perceiving pain and shall be maintained in that condition until the operation is ended.

Exceptions to this rule will be made by the Director alone and then only when anaesthesia would defeat the object of the experiment. In such cases an anaesthetic shall be used so far as possible and may be discontinued only so long as is absolutely essential for the necessary observations.

V. At the conclusion of the experiment the animal shall be killed painlessly.

Exceptions to this rule will be made only when continuance of the animal's life is unattended by suffering, or is necessary to determine the result of the experiment. In the latter case the same aseptic precautions shall be observed during the operation and so far as possible the same care shall be taken to minimize discomforts during the convalescence as in a hospital for human beings.

13. See further Cannon's address to the Massachusetts Medical Society, "The Responsibility of the General Practitioner for Freedom of Medical Re-

search," *BM&SJ* 161 (1909):428–432; also Cannon to Nathan P. Colwell, Jan. 21, 1909, Cannon Papers.

14. Cannon to Charles Evans Hughes, March 19, 1910, Cannon Papers; quoted in Benison, "In Defense of Medical Research," p. 19.

15. Curtis to Cannon, Dec. 11, 1908. See also Simmons to Cannon, Aug. 26, 1908; exchange of letters between Cushing and Cannon, Nov. 12 and 16, 1908; T. Sollmann to Cannon, Oct. 27, 1908. All in Cannon Papers.

16. Cannon announced the series publicly in an editorial, "The Defense of Medical Research," *JAMA* 54 (1910): 53–54. Between 1909 and 1915 twenty-eight pamphlets were published in the AMA series, four of them written by Cannon himself. For a discussion of the Defense of Research pamphlets, see further Roberts, "Man before Beast," pp. 34–37.

17. See C. W. Eliot, *The Fruits of Medical Research with the Aid of Anesthesia and Asepticism*, Defense of Research Pamphlet IX (Chicago: AMA, 1910). Eliot incorporated material supplied by Cannon into his discussion and gave the paper initially as the Ether Day anniversary address on Oct. 16, 1909, at MGH; see further Cannon/Eliot correspondence in fd. 4, Cannon Papers.

18. "As you well know," Cannon wrote W. W. Keen on March 12, 1910, "the average physician is not well enough acquainted with the history of medicine to be aware of the source of the devices he uses almost daily in the treatment of the sick. We felt that it was first of all desirable that the physicians should be instructed. If our papers have been too technical for the physicians, I see no way of obviating the defect except by their further education. Certainly they should be able to read such literature as has been submitted in this series." In Cannon Papers.

19. Cannon wrote D. L. Edsall on February 3, 1909, about a connection of his own in the person of "the editor and proprietor of the Boston Herald, who happens to be a relative of Mrs. Cannon, and who not only sympathizes with our point of view, but is planning popular articles describing the benefits which have been derived from medical research." In Cannon Papers.

20. W. W. Keen, whose involvement in the fight against the antivivisectionists may be followed in the large file of his papers at the American Philosophical Society, Philadelphia, and in a collection of his published papers entitled *Animal Experimentation and Medical Progress,* (Boston & New York: Houghton Mifflin, 1914), had long been an active supporter of medical research. For more on Cannon's and Keen's efforts to persuade editors and publishers to print articles and stories favorable to animal experimentation, see, for example, Cannon to Keen, March 8 and April 4, 1910; Keen to Cannon, March 11 and Nov. 28, 1910; all in Keen Papers.

21. Keen to Cannon, March 7, 1910, Keen Papers.

22. See further Richard D. French, *Antivivisection and Medical Science in Victorian Society* (Princeton, N.J.: Princeton University Press, 1975). An expression of Stephen Coleridge's views may be found in his published *Memories* (London, 1913).

23. Lind's autobiographical account, *The Shambles of Science* (London: Ernest Bell, 1903), was coauthored by Leisa K. Schartau and had the subtitle, "Extracts from the Diary of Two Students of Physiology." See further T. G.

Brodie to Cannon, Jan. 27, 1909, and related materials about Miss Lind in the Cannon Papers.

24. Stephen Paget to Cannon, Dec. 21, 1908. For more on the visiting lecturers, see also Paget to Cannon, Jan. 30, 1909, and Cannon to Paget, Feb. 18, 1909. All in Cannon Papers.

25. F. S. Lee to Cannon, Nov. 30, 1908; see also exchange of letters between Cannon and Lee, Dec. 3 and 5, 1908. All in Cannon Papers. Leffingwell was also a leading opponent of human experimentation; for an expression of his views, see his book, *An Ethical Problem, or Sidelights upon Scientific Experimentation on Man and Animals* (London & New York, 1914).

26. For more on Stephen Coleridge, see further Cannon's editorial, "An Antivivisection Leader," in *JAMA* 54 (1910):540.

27. Cannon dealt at length with the inaccuracies and "grossly garbled descriptions" of the antivivisectionists in *Some Characteristics of Antivivisection Literature*, Defense of Research Pamphlet XIX (Chicago, 1911).

28. Cannon to F. S. Lee, Dec. 3, 1908, Cannon Papers. Gazzam's pamphlet was *The Problem of Vivisection: A Plea for Proper Regulation* (New York, 1908).

29. Cannon to W. W. Keen, Dec. 13, 1909, Keen Papers; see also Cannon's editorial, "An Antivivisection Exhibition," *JAMA* 53 (1909):2102–3. For more on antivivisection exhibits, see also William J. Shultz, *The Humane Movement in the United States, 1910–1922* (New York, 1924), p. 153.

30. Keen to Cannon, March 10, 1909, Keen Papers; quoted in Benison, "In Defense of Medical Research," pp. 20–21. In the same letter, Keen advised Cannon, "One topic which . . . you could treat with great advantage in a leaflet would be the 'Surgery of the Heart.' This is a matter practically of the last ten years, and is a very striking evidence of the value of experiment upon animals."

31. Cannon to Keen, March 11, 1909, Keen Papers; quoted in Benison, "In Defense of Medical Research," p. 21.

32. See, e.g., Cannon to Harvey Cushing, Nov. 16, 1908, Cannon to F. S. Lee, Dec. 10, 1908. Both in Cannon Papers.

33. Cushing to Cannon, Dec. 3 and 19, 1908, Cannon Papers.

34. Keen to Cannon, June 22, 1909, Keen Papers.

35. See, e.g., Keen to Cannon, Nov. 9 and 13, Dec. 10, 1909; exchange of letters between Keen and Cannon, June 28 and 30, 1910; Keen to Cannon, Nov. 3, 1910. All in Keen Papers.

36. Exchange of letters between Edsall and Cannon, Jan. 28 and 30, 1909, in Cannon Papers.

37. Rosenau, then director of the Hygienic Laboratory at the U.S. Public Health Service in Washington, D.C., had written *The Role of Animal Experimentation in the Diagnosis of Disease*, Defense of Research Pamphlet III (Chicago: AMA, 1909). He was the first of this group to come to Harvard when he assumed the newly created professorship of preventive medicine and hygiene in the fall of 1909.

38. Cushing to Cannon, Feb. 12, 1909; see also G. H. Simmons to Cannon, Dec. 23, 1908. Both in Cannon Papers.

39. For more on James, see *The Thought and Character of William James*, a 2-vol. biography prepared by Cannon's friend Ralph Barton Perry (Boston, 1935), and *The Letters of William James*, 2 vols., edited by James's son Henry (Boston, 1920).

40. William James to Sidney R. Taber, Secretary of the Vivisection Reform Society, May 5, 1909, reprinted in Roswell C. McCrea, *The Humane Movement* (New York, 1910), pp. 274–275.

41. James's letter was a bonanza for those with antivivisectionist sympathies and they arranged for it to be reprinted in a large number of publications, among them the *Boston Transcript* of May 24, 1909.

42. For an early expression of James's views, see his unsigned editorial, "Vivisection," in *The Nation* 20 (1875):128–129. On Jan. 11, 1913, Cannon wrote Henry James, Jr., concerning his father's 1875 statement: "It is interesting to note how consistent the views then expressed are with those which your father expressed 30 years later in writing to Mr. Taber . . . There is little doubt in my mind that the antivivisection agitation, pro and con, has served to establish a conscience certainly in some workers, that would not have been established otherwise." In Cannon Papers. For more on James's medical training and career, see further Robert Hayes, "William James and the Harvard Medical School," *Harvard Medical Alumni Bulletin*, Oct. 1959, pp. 17–21.

43. See especially *Letters of William James* II:66–72. There were times, however, when James expressed regret for holding views contrary to those of his friends at the Medical School, especially those of Putnam and Bowditch. Around the turn of the century he had written to Bowditch about an incorrect report of his position: "You may have seen the reports, or you may have heard the letter read. It is bad enough, old man, to cross in any way your convictions in this matter, and still worse to cross them in imaginary form." James to Bowditch, undated, Cannon Papers.

44. Cannon to James, May 25, 1909, Wm. James Papers.

45. James to Cannon, May 28, 1909, Cannon Papers.

46. For instance, in a letter to James of June 4, 1909, Cannon maintained, "You have written, as many of the older antivivisectionists properly wrote, as if the physiologists were sole offenders in animal experimentation. If you should visit medical laboratories today, however, you would find that this important method of medical progress was being used by bacteriologists, pathologists, pharmacologists, hygienists, biological chemists, by surgeons in surgical laboratories, and by physicians in laboratories of clinical research. We physiologists take our place among these active investigators, but we are not preeminent, except possibly in our service as scapegoats." In Wm. James Papers.

47. Cf. Cannon's speech, "The Ideals of the Man of Science" (*Christian Register* 84 [1905]:1192–95), delivered at the beginning of his career, and his autobiography, *Way of an Investigator*, written at the end of his career, both expressing a native optimism that remained undiminished throughout his life. Of Cannon's outlook, James wrote, "I must say that you have a much higher opinion of human nature (it could hardly be otherwise, considering that Mrs. Cannon is so constantly in your mental field!!) than I have, both

from the point of view of candor under attack, and of conscientiousness in the use of absolute power." James to Cannon, Feb. 12, 1910, Cannon Papers.

48. James to Cannon, June 7, 1909, Cannon Papers. With special thanks to Eugene Taylor for elaborating on James's views about character development in the physician.

49. See pamphlet, "Concerning Vivisection: A Letter to the Vivisection Reform Society by William James . . . June 1909," in Cannon Papers.

50. Cannon to Keen, Nov. 12, 1909, Keen Papers. In his response of Nov. 13 Keen was not as even-tempered as Cannon and accused James outright "in plain language, of lying"; quoted in Benison, "In Defense of Medical Research," p. 18.

51. See further exchange of letters between Cannon and James, Feb. 11 and 12, 1910; also Cannon's 1910 Diary, Feb. 10 and 11, in Cannon Papers.

52. Cannon did, however, use the James incident to illustrate a point in his article, "Medical Control of Vivisection," published in the *North American Review* of June 1910 and issued as Defense of Research Pamphlet XVI later that year.

53. 1910 Diary, Aug. 27.

12. A Family and a Farm

1. See further *Harvard Class of 1896—Third Report, June 1906*, pp. 25–26; Jerome Greene, *Years with President Eliot*, pp. 13–14, in J. D. Greene Papers; both in HUA.

2. 1906 Diary, June 26. Cannon described the Harvard commencement activities in entries for June 22–28.

3. *Annual Reports*, 1905–06, pp. 5–6.

4. 1906 Diary, Aug. 13, Dec. 2 and 30.

5. See, e.g., 1907 Diary, March 29 and 30, and April 4. Francis H. Davenport had performed a gynecological procedure on Cornelia in West Newton the previous autumn. 1906 Diary, Oct. 30.

6. 1907 Diary, April 4, 5, 7, 12. The Cannons moved from 14 Avon Place to 17 Ware Street on May 23 and held a housewarming party in the barn on June 8.

7. 1907 Diary, April 28. A few days earlier, on April 25, Cannon had noted, "Cornelia and I went to see Dr. Davenport at noon. He says no doubt Cornelia is pregnant. We inexpressively grateful. Went after lunch to Dr. Swain and made arrangements for November." Howard T. Swain was then a young assistant in obstetrics at the Medical School with whom Cannon had become acquainted.

8. See further Cornelia J. Cannon and Louise W. Jackson, *Social Welfare in Cambridge: A Handbook for Citizens* (Cambridge, Mass., 1907).

9. In addition to recreational activities, Cannon took time to work in the Marine Biological Laboratory at Woods Hole on the movements of the alimentary canal in the dog-fish, which was briefly described in *The American Naturalist* 42 (May 1908):326–327.

10. Frances H. James to Cornelia J. Cannon, Sept. 15, 1907, Cannon Papers.

11. 1907 Diary, Oct. 22; see also Sept. 28, Oct. 27, Nov. 3. Bradford Cannon attributes a good part of his father's apprehension before his birth to the fact that a hydrocephalic baby had recently been born to one of his colleagues who had engaged in x-ray investigation. "Personal Reminiscences," in *Life & Contributions*, p. 158.

12. 1907 Diary, Nov. 22–24.

13. 1907 Diary, entries for Dec. 1 and 2.

14. Excerpt of letter from Cannon to the James family headed "Bradford's Birth," Dec. 2, 1907, in "Snatched from Oblivion."

15. C. J. Cannon to her family, Dec. 10, 1907, in "Snatched from Oblivion."

16. 1907 Diary, e.g., Dec. 3, 5, 6, 24; 1908 Diary, e.g., Jan. 15 and 17.

17. Cannon to C. J. Cannon, Dec. 29, 1907, Cannon Papers.

18. 1908 Diary, e.g., Jan. 5, Feb. 13, March 11, April 2.

19. Cannon's papers were published as "The Opposition to Medical Research," *JAMA* 51 (1908):635–640; "Some Practical Applications of Recent Studies in the Physiology of the Digestive System," *Wisconsin Medical Journal* 7 (1908):223–242.

20. For the visit to the Midwest, see 1908 Diary, May 31 to June 28.

21. Cannon to C. J. Cannon, June 28, 1908; see also his letter of June 21, 1908. Both in Cannon Papers.

22. Cannon to C. J. Cannon, July 2, 1908, Cannon Papers.

23. For example, near the end of July Cannon noted in his diary that after he was put off a streetcar with a collapsible baby carriage, his wife lost no time in writing to both the Railroad Commission and the Elevated Company on the subject of go-carts. A few days later, on July 31, 1908, the *Boston Transcript* published a note, "The go-carts will not have to go," accompanied by an announcement from the Boston Elevated Railway that passengers with children in folding carriages would no longer be excluded from their streetcars.

24. 1908 Diary, Sept. 14–25; letters and postal cards in fd. 2242, Cannon Papers. Cannon's companions on this occasion were Ed Holt, "Tom" Perry, and Ben Oppenheimer.

25. 1908 Diary, Nov. 21.

26. 1909 Diary, e.g., Feb. 24–March 2, March 8–12, March 25–26.

27. 1909 Diary, April 25, May 2, May 6.

28. 1909 Diary, May 26.

29. 1909 Diary, April 21; see also entry for June 28.

30. 1909 Diary, July 17. See also C. J. Cannon to her family, June 21, 1909, in "Snatched from Oblivion."

31. 1909 Diary, Aug. 21; see also Aug. 7, 9, 17.

32. 1909 Diary, e.g., Oct. 23, 24, 31, Dec. 10–12.

33. Actually, Cannon dealt exclusively with Lowell Hanson, the agent who represented R. E. Bean, the owner, in behalf of the E. A. Strout Company, a real estate firm with branch offices in several eastern cities.

34. L. I. Hanson to Cannon, Jan. 22, 1910, Cannon Papers. In assuring Cannon there was no intent to defraud, Hanson told him, "Without any doubt in my mind, not one in 20 or maybe in 50 of our country farms has been measured by a surveyor to learn correctly the acreage except to estimate or guess at the same."

35. 1910 Diary, Feb. 8.

36. Hanson to Cannon, Dec. 29, 1909, Cannon Papers. In 1983 members of the Cannon family spoke about Lowell Hanson when they entertained a capacity audience at a meeting of the Sanbornton Historical Society with recollections of Franklin and Sanbornton in the early 1900s; see "Historical Society Hears Cannon Family Recollections," *Laconia, N.H., Evening Citizen,* Aug. 22, 1983, p. 12.

37. See 1910 Diary, e.g., April 17, May 14, May 30.

38. 1910 Diary, April 15–23.

39. 1910 Diary, July 16 and 25; see also June 8, 9, 11, 13, 17–19, July 2, 14, 15.

40. Leonard Hill and William Bulloch were the general editors of the International Medical Monographs; see their Preface to Cannon's *Mechanical Factors of Digestion* (London, 1911), p. [iii]. Among the other notable volumes in this series were C. C. Guthrie, *Blood Vessel Surgery and its Applications* (1912); J. C. G. Ledingham and J. A. Arkwright, *The Carrier Problem in Infectious Disease* (1912); T. M. Legge and K. W. Goadby, *Lead Poisoning and Lead Absorption* (1912); and Leonard Hill, *Caisson Sickness and the Physiology of Work in Compressed Air* (1912).

41. On July 18 Cannon noted in his diary that he had begun working on research material and had developed a plan for his book. After outlining the chapters and fitting up a study for himself in the attic of the farmhouse, he engaged in a regular schedule of work on the book, which may be followed in the 1910 Diary entries from Aug. 8 until Nov. 24.

42. Author's Preface, *Mechanical Factors of Digestion,* p. v.

43. Cannon to H. P. Bowditch, Nov. 25, 1910, Bowditch Papers.

44. See Cannon to Jerome Greene, Feb. 20, 1911; in J. D. Greene file, RAC. The Whitney house was in the Norton's Woods section of Cambridge, later described by Cannon's friend Charles Whiting in a talk on "Francis Avenue and the Norton Estate: The Development of a Community," for the Cambridge Historical Society (*Proceedings,* 41 [1967–69]:16–39).

45. Ida Cannon, who urged buying the Franklin farm the previous year, encouraged the move to Divinity Avenue. Cornelia objected to the Whitney house because of its size and expense, but Ida promised that she and Bernice would help with the payments. The $100 per month rent never was increased in the thirty years the Cannons lived there. "Recollections" Ida's Memories, pp. 7–8.

46. Cannon's earlier efforts to promote Murphy's career through recommendations to both Eliot (see, e.g., Cannon to Eliot, Oct. 26, 1908, Eliot Papers) and the surgery department had been futile, and although he was pleased to see Murphy called to a professorship, he felt St. Louis's gain was Harvard's loss. For another appreciation of Murphy's worth as a surgeon,

see also Harvey Cushing to Henry A. Christian, Feb. 2, 1911, Christian Papers.

47. For Bowditch's death, see Cannon's 1911 Diary, March 13 and 15; for Linda's birth, see entry for March 18.

48. 1911 Diary, e.g., March 19, 22, April 2, 7, 9, 10.

49. "The Importance of Tonus for the Movements of the Alimentary Canal," Cannon's presidential address to the gastroenterologists, was published in *Archives of Internal Medicine* 8 (1911):417–426; his speech to the Massachusetts Medical Society, "Factors Involved in the Production of Arterial Blood Pressure, Physiological and Pathological," appeared in the *BM&SJ* 165 (1911):672–675; and his address at Yale Medical School, "The Career of the Investigator," was published in *Science* 34 (1911):65–72.

50. In Dec. 1910, little more than a year after Carrie Cannon died, Cannon's father married Alma Anderson, a practicing physician, and bought land near Eugene. Alma, who was a year younger than her stepson, took good care of Colbert Cannon in his last years, which were evidently quite happy. See further "C. H. Cannon's Record" and unidentified biographical sketch in the Cannon Papers.

51. 1911 Diary, March 10. Bernice Cannon (known as Bird or B. C. to her family) taught school, first in St. Paul and then in upper Michigan, before moving to Cambridge. After working in personnel training at Filene's for many years, she opened Miss Cannon's Shop for Children on Brattle Street, which became a Cambridge institution and was one of the landmarks in Harvard Square.

52. Mrs. Prince had been directing the Union School of Salesmanship under the joint sponsorship of the Women's Educational and Industrial Union and Simmons College since 1906. *Who's Who in New England, 1916*, p. 877.

53. C. J. Cannon to Cannon, June 20, 1911; in "Snatched from Oblivion." Whether Wilma took Bradford's advice or not, the glove device apparently worked no better than the red pepper: on Sept. 12, Cannon noted in his diary that Wilma sucked her fingers incessantly.

54. C. J. Cannon to Cannon, June 26, 1911; see also June 20, 1911. Both in "Snatched from Oblivion."

55. Cannon attended the AMA meetings in Los Angeles, June 26–29, and then traveled north, arriving in Eugene on July 2. Two days later he wrote his wife: "The Doctor I like very well. She knows how to manage my father better than anybody I have ever seen with him. He is very happy, indeed, he has told me that he has never been so happy and carefree. People here seem to like him, and he has patients among the best of Eugene." Cannon to C. J. Cannon, July 4, 1911, Cannon Papers.

56. Linda Cannon Burgess dealt with the chalet incident in a reminiscence of her parents written in 1940, a copy of which has been deposited in the Cannon Papers. See also *Snatched from Oblivion*, p. 124.

57. Bradford Cannon, "Personal Reminiscences," p. 158; see also "Servant of Science," pp. 76–77.

58. 1911 Diary, July 23.

59. 1911 Diary, Aug. 7 and 25. Bradford Cannon later remembered a locomotive on which he could sit, as well as the railroad system in a pine

grove adjacent to the farmhouse; see further "Personal Reminiscences," p. 155.

60. 1911 Diary, Aug. 3.
61. Cannon described this incident in his 1911 Diary, Sept. 4–11.
62. "Servant of Science," pp. 70–71.
63. On Oct. 2, 1911, Cannon noted in his diary, "Learned that four papers which I had prepared could not appear in Journal until December. Also no increase in salary. A day of disappointments." He later added another paper, all five of which were published in the Dec. issue, *Am. J. Physiol.*
64. 1911 Diary, Oct. 19–20. Cornelia had written a poem for Cannon's birthday, and it is pasted over the entry for Oct. 19.

13. New Pathways in Medical Education

1. *Annual Reports,* 1902–03, p. 21; see also Treasurer's Statement for 1903 listing student receipts at the Medical School, p. 92.
2. Harvard University Medical Faculty, Administrative Board Records, HMA; see esp. minutes of meetings of Oct. 3, 1903, Sept. 20, 1904, and Oct. 2, 1905.
3. Although upperclassmen from Harvard still accounted in 1907 for the largest number of those entering by special vote of the Administrative Board, there was increasing representation from other colleges and universities, and some who even came from abroad.
4. Minutes of Medical Faculty; for Minot's proposal, see esp. minutes for Nov. 2, 1907. For a review of the various proposals concerning admissions policy that came under discussion at this time, see also *Annual Reports,* 1907–08, pp. 168–169.
5. This proposal was embodied in the Committee on Course of Study's report; see further Minutes of Medical Faculty meeting, Feb. 1, 1908. For a discussion of the three-year bachelor's degree and of the combined course, see also Eliot's *Annual Reports* for 1907–08, pp. 14–18, and for 1908–09, pp. 26–27.
6. Minutes of Medical Faculty, March 7, 1908. Dean Richardson's special arrangement had been made with Carleton College, the University of Rochester, and Trinity College.
7. For a measure of how Cannon had been influenced by his own experience, see his letter to W. H. Welch, April 13, 1896, Welch Papers; published in Bradford Cannon's "Personal Reminiscences," *Life & Contributions,* p. 152.
8. Cannon to Eliot, Feb. 14, 1908; see also C. S. Minot to C. W. Eliot, Feb. 8, 1908. Both in Eliot Papers. Cannon's views echo those set forth by Bowditch in his article, "The Medical School of the Future," reprinted in *Medical Research and Education,* ed. by J. M. Cattell (New York: Science Press, 1913), see esp. pp. 517–520.
9. Eliot to Cannon, Feb. 26, 1908, Eliot Papers; Minutes of Medical Faculty, March 7, 1908. See also Cannon's 1908 Diary, March 7, in which he

noted that the vote was ten in favor to twenty-seven opposed. In Cannon Papers. A few days later Minot, writing to one of his assistants, told him that he had never known any important improvement made at the Medical School "without its being first postponed by a solid and stupid opposition." Minot continued, "Though the vote about the admission requirements might seem disheartening, we must rest and fight again, but we will win in the end, because we are right." C. S. Minot to F. T. Lewis, March 12, 1908, Lewis Papers.

10. See, e.g., Minutes of Medical Faculty, June 6, 1908, Dec. 5, 1908, and April 29, 1909; also Eliot to Cannon, Nov. 10, 1908 and April 29, 1909; both in Eliot Papers.

11. Minutes of Medical Faculty, March 7, 1908; see also F. T. Lewis to C. S. Minot, incomplete, undated letters in Minot Papers.

12. Minutes of Medical Faculty, Feb. 5, 1909; see also Cannon's 1909 Diary, Feb. 5.

13. See especially J. D. Greene to C. W. Eliot, Feb. 18, 1909, and to Joseph Warren, Feb. 19, 1909, both in Eliot Papers. In his letter to Warren, Greene described changes in admissions policy at both the Medical and Law Schools. "It takes the wind out of the sails of the new professional Graduate Schools of Applied Science and Business," he told him, "to have the departments which have created the prestige of Harvard in professional instruction, and which have been constantly looked up to as models by the new schools, go back on the fundamental principle of supporting the A.B. degree."

14. Greene to Warren, March 6, 1909, in Eliot Papers. Young Warren, the son of J. Collins Warren, had a brilliant record as a member of Greene's class at Harvard Law School. He was at this time serving temporarily as assistant secretary to Eliot and later became a professor of law at Harvard.

15. Eliot to Greene, Feb. 25, 1909, and March 9, 1909, both in Eliot Papers. In the first of these letters Eliot was not especially concerned about the action of the medical faculty and expressed the feeling that the deans of the Cambridge faculties had overreacted. In his second letter, however, Eliot admitted that the subject had taken on a new importance in his mind, and continued, "if you look to the country at large, the requirement of a degree for admission is really prohibitory. What I have seen on this journey confirms me in that opinion. A suitable method of admitting competent Special Students for one or two years is, I think, essential to any enlarged influence of our School on the medical education of the country at large."

16. For a discussion of the new admission policies adopted at the Medical School, as well as the establishment of a Division of Medical Sciences to award higher degrees, see further *Annual Report*, 1908–09, pp. 26–27.

17. See further *Harvard Graduates' Magazine* 17 (1908–09):221. Shortly before noon on Nov. 4, 1908, the *Harvard Crimson* issued an extra with the news of Eliot's retirement. The resignation was to take effect on the anniversary of his election forty years before; at that time, May 19, 1909, he would be just past his seventy-fifth birthday.

18. Theodore Roosevelt, Harvard Class of 1880, had served a term on the Board of Overseers and was active in the Harvard Alumni Association.

For a description of Roosevelt on the occasion of his twenty-fifth class reunion, see excerpt of 1905 letter from Cornelia J. Cannon to her family, in "Snatched from Oblivion."

19. "President Roosevelt and Harvard," *Harvard Graduates' Magazine* 16 (1907–08):017. H. G. Wells, on the occasion of his visit to Cambridge in the spring of 1906, also commented on the rumor; see further *The Future in America: A Search after Realities* (New York & London: Harper & Brothers, 1906), p. 216.

20. For Eliot's impact on professional education, see "President Eliot's Administration, 1894–1909," *Harvard Graduates' Magazine* 17 (March 1909), esp. pp. 376–380; also Hugh Hawkins, *Between Harvard and America: The Educational Leadership of Charles W. Eliot* (New York: Oxford University Press, 1972), pp. 58–61, 220–222.

21. Some of the concern was tied to a reaction against Eliot's elective system and the resulting specialization it encouraged; Samuel Eliot Morison, *Three Centuries of Harvard, 1636–1936* (Cambridge, Mass.: Harvard University Press, 1936), pp. 384–390. For a detailed discussion of the resurgence of collegiate concerns at this time, see further Hawkins, *Between Harvard and America*, pp. 263–289.

22. For more on Lowell, see H. A. Yeomans, *Abbott Lawrence Lowell, 1856–1943* (Cambridge, Mass.: Harvard University Press, 1948); also Ferris Greenslet, *The Lowells and Their Seven Worlds* (Boston: Houghton Mifflin, 1946). Lowell's succession of Eliot in the presidency is dealt with in Morison, *Three Centuries*, pp. 439–481; for a comparison and contrast of Lowell with Eliot, see also Hawkins, pp. 269–272.

23. See further Minutes of Medical Faculty, May 1, 1909. On the suggestion of A. C. Barger, excerpts of Shattuck's and Eliot's remarks were published as "Eliot's Farewell Address, May 1, 1909," in the *Harvard Medical Alumni Bulletin* 56 (Spring 1982):14–16.

24. F. C. Shattuck to C. W. Eliot, May 11, 1908, in Eliot Papers. While Shattuck on this occasion acknowledged Eliot's benign leadership, he and the president had not always seen eye to eye. For instance, he and his brother George, leaders of the establishment at the MGH and the Boston City Hospital, had previously forestalled efforts to bring clinicians of national reputation to posts at the Medical School by blocking their hospital appointments. See further Morris J. Vogel, *The Invention of the Modern Hospital, Boston, 1870–1930* (Chicago: University of Chicago Press, 1980), pp. 80–82.

25. C. W. Eliot to E. H. Bradford, Dec. 19, 1908; see also Eliot to H. A. Christian, Jan. 21, 1909; both in Eliot Papers. The Committee on Faculty Reorganization was chaired by Bradford and had as members Drs. Shattuck, Ernst, Councilman, and Burrell. See further Minutes of Medical Faculty, Dec. 5, 1908; also Committee on Faculty Organization, 1909, file in HMA.

26. Lowell, serving as a member of the most important special faculty committees from 1902 to 1909, had emerged as a major spokesman on college policy. (Hawkins, *Between Harvard and America*, p. 269). For an expression of his educational philosophy, see further Lowell's Inaugural Address and other early essays in *At War with Academic Traditions in America* (Cambridge, Mass., 1934).

27. On Jan. 24, 1909, Eliot, as usual in the vanguard of faculty enthusiasm, wrote Jerome Greene, then making a tour of western state universities: "When our Medical School got its present superb buildings and laboratory equipment, it was impossible for the other medical schools not to admit that the Harvard School had a fine residence and equipment. As an offset to this advantage, the only thing that could be suggested was that the men did not match the buildings. You can safely inquire of any medical man who takes that tone with you if he knows any medical school in this country that has a better group of men . . . The real question is—Where is there a better group of medical teachers?" In Greene Papers.

28. Cannon to R. M. Yerkes, July 7, 1909, Yerkes Papers. Yerkes was then working with Harvey Cushing in Baltimore at the Hunterian Laboratory, where he spent several months in the spring and summer of 1909.

29. Exchange of letters between William James and H. P. Bowditch, July 1 and 9, 1909; from notes in Bowditch Papers.

30. 1909 Diary, Oct. 6 and 7. It was Lowell himself who wanted the exercises to be held in the open so that a larger number of spectators could be accommodated. "Inauguration of President Lowell," *Harvard Graduates' Magazine* 18 (1909–10):270.

31. Minutes of Medical Faculty, June 5, 1909. Lowell's selection of Henderson marked the beginning of a long and intimate relationship between the two men, which blossomed when they walked back and forth between Cambridge and the Medical School to attend faculty meetings. Henderson was at this time serving as adviser to premedical students and was soon to marry Edith Lawrence Thayer, a member of the Lowell family. See further L. J. Henderson, "Memories," unpublished autobiography in HUA; John Parascandola in *Dictionary of Scientific Biography*, Suppl. 1, pp. 260–262; D. B. Dill in *The Physiologist* 20 (1977):1–15.

32. 1909 Diary, Oct. 2. Councilman's plan for a Faculty Council, which Eliot had so strongly opposed, was thus approved and became effective in Dec. 1909.

33. For more on Southard, see F. P. Gay's biography, *The Open Mind: Elmer Ernest Southard, 1876–1920* (Boston: Normandie House, 1938). Harvey Cushing later recalled that soon after coming to Boston he met Henderson and Southard at a session of the Royce Club and thought them "the most brilliant minds of their time in Cambridge"; Gay, *The Open Mind*, p. 33.

34. See, e.g., 1909 Diary, Oct. 8. Some days later Cannon recorded that he had discussed the subject of medical education with Abraham Flexner and N. P. Colwell, who called on him at the Medical School; 1909 Diary, Oct. 18 and 19.

35. A portion of Henderson and Southard's article was also published in *Science*, n s 30 (1909):679–680. Describing conditions at Harvard, the authors noted a discrepancy between the requirements for entrance to the Medical School, where undergraduate medical science courses were not counted, and those of the Graduate School of Arts and Sciences or the newly constituted Division of the Medical Sciences, where they were. In contrast, they pointed to the practice in effect elsewhere—especially in the middle and far western colleges and universities under the "combined A.B." degree plan—

which permitted two years of college work, largely prescribed, and two years of specified work in the medical sciences. For Lowell's reaction to the report, see his letters to Henderson, Oct. 12 and Dec. 22, 1909; both in Lowell Letterbooks, 1909–10, HUA.

36. "The Relations of the Medical School and the College," *BM&SJ* 161 (1909):790–791. Although the editorial was unsigned, Cannon noted that he was writing it in his 1909 Diary, Nov. 10–12.

37. *Harvard Bulletin*, Dec. 1, 1909. Henderson and Southard answered Dearborn's objections in the pages of the *Harvard Bulletin*, Dec. 9, 1909.

38. "The Medical School and the College," *BM&SJ* 161 (1909):865–866. Once again, Southard and Henderson answered Dearborn's criticisms, this time in light of the editorial comments published by the *BM&SJ* on Nov. 23 and Dec. 9; see further Correspondence, "Education in Medicine," in the Dec. 23 issue, pp. 948–949.

39. Thomas Dwight, "The First Duty of a Medical School," Dec. 15, 1909, HMA.

40. See further Minutes of Medical Faculty, Jan. 15, Feb. 5, and April 2, 1910. Part of Minot's strategy involved the formation of a new joint committee composed of members from the Faculty of Medicine and the Faculty of Arts and Sciences, but Lowell had doubts that the Cambridge faculty would agree to participate in such a committee; see, e.g., A. L. Lowell to F. T. Lewis, Feb. 12, 1910, and to E. E. Southard, March 3, 1910, both in Lowell Papers.

41. The students' criticisms were published in "The Medical School— Suggestions in Regard to the Course for the Degree of M.D.," *Harvard Bulletin*, Jan. 5, 1910.

42. "May 12 Meeting of the Committee on Information," 1910 transcript in fd. 1163 of Lowell Papers.

43. H. A. Christian to A. L. Lowell, Feb. 21, 1911; in fd. 1091, Lowell Papers. See also Minutes of Medical Faculty, Feb. 4, 1911.

44. Minutes of Medical Faculty, March 4, 1911. After the meeting Cannon noted in his diary, "Scheme for requiring A.B. degree, Physics and Biology, and 2 general exams approved. Walked home with Pres. Lowell and Henderson."

45. 1911 Diary, May 19 and 20.

46. Minutes of Medical Faculty, June 3, 1911. The committee's report was printed and bound in with the faculty minutes for this meeting.

14. Continuity and Change at the Medical School

1. For Christian's conception of the unity of laboratory research and medical practice, see further his article "A Career in Medicine and Present-Day Preparation for It," *Science* n.s. 30 (1909):537–548.

2. 1909 Diary, April 24. See also C. W. Eliot to David Houston, Nov. 11, 1908, Eliot Papers. Eliot had advised Houston, the president of Washington University in St. Louis, on the conduct of a superior medical school and recommended that he consult Christian because of the latter's experience

on the continuous service at the Carney Hospital as well as his avowed intention to build up the clinical side of HMS.

3. In *Annual Reports*, 1908–09, pp. 171–172.

4. "Harvard Summer Medicos—Dean Christian's Plans for a Larger School," *Boston Transcript*, June 12, 1909, in scrapbook of Clippings, Programmes and Letters . . . 1907–1910, p. 287, Christian Papers.

5. E. H. Bradford to A. L. Lowell, March 19, 1910, Lowell Papers.

6. M. H. Richardson to A. L. Lowell, Sept. 2, 1910, Lowell Papers.

7. See further Cannon's 1910 Diary, Oct. 26; M. H. Richardson to Lowell, July 16, 1910, Lowell Papers. Everyone spoke well of Murphy, and even Lowell wondered why he had not been given an instructorship in the surgery department; see further his letter to E. H. Bradford, March 17, 1910, Lowell Papers.

8. Not only did Christian find Eliot's business system difficult to unravel but he also found that the system of accounting in use by the comptroller's office was hampered by poor communication between Cambridge and Boston. See further fd. 1098, Medical School finances, in Lowell Papers, esp. H. A. Christian to J. A. L. Blake, Oct. 14, 1910.

9. See, for example, 1910 Diary, April 28.

10. Major biographies and obituaries of Minot: F. T. Lewis in *BM&SJ* 171 (1914):911–914; W. T. Porter in *BM&SJ* 172 (1915):467–470; W. T. Councilman in *Proceedings of the American Academy of Arts and Sciences* 53 (1918):840–847; E. S. Morse in *National Academy of Sciences Biographical Memoirs* 9 (1920):263–285. Minot, as W. T. Porter remarked, was born "not merely a Bostonian, but a legendary Bostonian." The son of William Minot, a well-to-do Boston lawyer, and Katherine Maria Sedgwick, a descendant of Jonathan Edwards, he was a member of one of Boston's most distinguished medical dynasties. His older cousin, Francis Minot, had been the third Hersey Professor of the Theory and Practice of Physic at HMS, and later a younger cousin, George Richards Minot, a professor of medicine there, went on to share the Nobel prize in 1934 for his contributions to the understanding of pernicious anemia.

11. Minot had become associated with the developing department of histology and embryology in 1883 and was named professor and head of the department in 1892. See especially his monumental study, *Human Embryology*, published in 1892, and *The Problem of Age, Growth, and Death*, which was based on a course of Lowell Lectures he gave in 1907. A full bibliography may be found in Morse's 1920 biographical memoir.

12. Eliot, Address before the Boston Society of Natural History, March 17, 1915, in the Society's *Proceedings*, p. 911. For the Stillman professorship, see, for example, Minot to Eliot, Oct. 25, 1905, and the large file of other letters in the Eliot Papers.

13. Minot to Lowell, March 17, 1910, Lowell Papers. The above account is based largely on a file of correspondence with and regarding Minot in the Lowell Papers; see esp. fds. 1086 and 1131.

14. Minutes of Medical Faculty, May 7, 1910; J. D. Greene to H. A. Christian, April 2, 1910, Lowell Papers.

15. See Cannon's 1910 Diary, May 9 and 10.

16. 1910 Diary, May 10–12.

17. Minot to Lowell, [June 14, 1910], Lowell Papers. The date is supplied from another angry letter Minot had written Lowell just the day before (June 13, 1910).

18. Christian to Lowell, July 2, 1910; in fd. 1091, Lowell Papers.

19. There are four letters in this series: Lowell to Eliot, July 5 and 16, 1910, and Eliot to Lowell, July 11 and 18, 1910; all in Lowell Papers. In the first of his letters to Lowell Eliot wrote that he did not doubt the Corporation would "be disposed to fulfill completely the expectations of Dr. Minot with regard to the facilities to be furnished to the Department of Comparative Anatomy." At the same time, he also did not see how they could admit that Minot was "at the head of two independent Departments, one called Comparative Anatomy, and the other, Histology and Embryology."

20. Christian to George B. Shattuck, Chairman of the Visiting Committee, Dec. 20, 1910, Lowell Papers.

21. For the appointments of Christian and Cushing, see further Reginald Fitz, *At the Heart of a Great Medical Centre, 1913–1938* (Boston, 1938), pp. 9–11, published on the occasion of the Brigham's twenty-fifth anniversary. For more on the background and history of the hospital, see also another anniversary publication charmingly written by David McCord, *The Fabrick of Man: Fifty Years of the Peter Bent Brigham Hospital* (Boston, 1963).

22. Christian to Lowell, May 28, 1910, Lowell Papers. Christian also lost no time telling Eliot the good news, writing him a personal note of thanks for all the president had done to help him. Christian to Eliot, May 18, 1910, Eliot Papers.

23. Eliot to Christian, May 26, 1910, Eliot Papers; published as a footnote in McCord, *Fabrick of Man*, pp. 32–33. In addition to remaining in the deanship, Christian continued his service at the Carney Hospital and conducted an outpatient clinic in the basement of one of the Medical School buildings until such time as the new hospital would be ready for opening.

24. A definitive plan of organization for the Brigham Hospital, signed by both Christian and Harvey Cushing, was sent to Alexander Cochrane and the Board of Trustees on Dec. 7, 1911; in vol. 5 of Christian Papers.

25. See *Annual Reports,* 1910–11, pp. 16, 136–137; also fds. 1112–22 in Lowell Papers for correspondence concerning relations with hospitals. After his initial success Christian continued to apply his efforts toward effecting similar agreements with other hospitals—the Lying-In, the Boston City, the MGH, and the new Cancer Hospital then under construction on Huntington Avenue. For an assessment of Christian's great value in this capacity, see further A. T. Cabot, writing as a member of the Board of Trustees at the MGH, to Lowell, March 23, 1912; in fd. 1120, Lowell Papers.

26. For details, see Christian to Lowell, Nov. 6, 1911, Lowell Papers; Cannon to F. S. Lee, March 17, 1913, Cannon Papers; exchange of letters between Lee and Christian, March 18 and 29, 1913, Christian Papers. In his letter to Lowell Christian also recommended that Councilman and Folin be nominated to consulting positions at the Brigham.

27. Thomas F. Harrington, *The Harvard Medical School: A History, Narrative, and Documentary* (New York, 1905), III:1332–34; Report of the Dean of the Graduate School of Medicine, in *Annual Reports, 1912–13*, p. 152.

28. Harvard University Medical Faculty, Minutes of Faculty Council meetings held on Jan. 26, Feb. 23, March 23, and April 27, 1911, HMA; see also *Harvard Graduates' Magazine* 19 (1910–11):661, and 20 (1911–12):114–115.

29. See, e.g., Christian to Lowell, June 1 and 5, 1911, and other letters in fd. 1107, Graduate School of Medicine, Lowell Papers. For more on Arnold, see his obituary notices in the *New England Journal of Medicine* 212 (1935), pp. 532, 699.

30. On Feb. 26, 1912, Lowell informed Arnold that the Corporation had voted to elect him dean of the Graduate School of Medicine. See also exchange of letters between A. T. Cabot and Lowell, Dec. 13 and 14, 1911. All in fd. 1107, Lowell Papers.

31. C. S. Minot to Lowell, undated, in answer to Lowell letter of March 9, 1912; both in fd. 1092, HMS Deanship, Lowell Papers. See also Minot to Lowell, March 4, 1912, in fd. 1131, Lowell Papers.

32. Christian to Lowell, undated, in fd. 1092, Lowell Papers.

33. *Annual Reports,* 1909 10, p. 23.

34. In the spring of 1910, for instance, Cannon had the full cooperation of Christian, Dean Smith of the Dental School, and other administrative personnel when he requested an assistant professorship for E. G. Martin. 1910 Diary, March 15, 16, 18, 23, 24.

35. 1911 Diary, Oct. 3 and 6; see also memorandum of vote of Harvard Corporation to increase Cannon's salary to $4,500, Oct. 9, 1911, in fd. 1098, Lowell Papers.

36. Forbes to Cannon, Dec. 2, 1911, Cannon Papers.

37. Exchange of letters between Cannon and Lowell, Feb. 9 and 15, 1912, in fd. 1111, Lowell Papers. In the end, however, Hill decided he could not afford to interrupt his work then in progress with Keith Lucas in Cambridge.

38. For details concerning Christian's resignation from the deanship and the three retirements, see further *Harvard Graduates' Magazine* 20 (1911–12):490. For more on the illness and death of Dwight, see the letters in fd. 1093, Lowell Papers; also obituary notice in *Harvard Graduates' Magazine* 20 (1911–12):259.

39. Lowell to J. J. Putnam, Dec. 13, 1911, in fd. 1147, and Lowell to F. C. Shattuck, June 4, 1912, in fd. 1159, both in Lowell Papers.

40. Minot to Lowell, Sept. 22, 1911, in fd. 1131, Lowell Papers. For more on Minot's and Mall's common interests, see Florence R. Sabin, *Franklin Paine Mall: The Story of a Mind* (Baltimore: Johns Hopkins University Press, 1934), pp. 223–225; also George Rosen, "Carl Ludwig and His American Students," *Bulletin of the Institute of the History of Medicine* 4 (Oct. 1936), esp. pp. 626–630, 639–645.

41. See further Christian to Lowell, Feb. 9, 1912, in fd. 1091, Lowell Papers. A search committee appointed to consider filling the chair of anatomy voted on Jan. 15, 1912, to recommend Mall for the Parkman Professorship.

42. Exchange of letters between C. S. Minot and F. P. Mall, Feb. 2 and

5, 1912, enclosed with Minot to Lowell, Feb. 7, 1912; Mall to Minot, Feb. 16, 1912; all in fd. 1067, Lowell Papers.

43. See further exchange of letters between Lowell and Christian, Feb. 13 and 14, 1912, in fd. 1091, Lowell Papers.

44. Lowell to Minot, Feb. 19, 1912, in fd. 1067, Lowell Papers.

45. Lowell to Christian, April 8, 1912, in fd. 1091, Lowell Papers. A few days earlier Christian informed Lowell that funds had been raised for Mall in the amounts of $30,000 through Shattuck, $2,750 through Minot, and $600 through John Warren. Enough had been promised to add to Dwight's salary that Warren and Christian could guarantee the small amount lacking until full endowment was raised; April 3, 1912, in fd. 1130, Lowell Papers.

46. 1912 Diary, April 25, Cannon Papers.

47. Exchange of letters between Minot and Lowell, May 28 and 29, 1912, in fd. 1131, Lowell Papers. Thereafter, the Parkman Professorship of Anatomy remained vacant for twenty years, until in 1931 it was filled by George B. Wislocki.

48. Christian was also a supporter of Sears. He felt Sears was "one of our soundest, most effective clinical teachers" and considered him the strongest local candidate for Shattuck's position. Christian to Lowell, May 20, 1911, in fd. 1091, Lowell Papers.

49. R. H. Fitz to Lowell, Dec. 20, 1911, in fd. 1082, Lowell Papers.

50. For details regarding Locke's efforts in behalf of Edsall, see J. C. Aub and Ruth Hapgood, *Pioneer in Modern Medicine: David Linn Edsall of Harvard* (Boston: Harvard Medical Alumni Association, 1970), pp. 60–63. For more on Edsall's relations with Christian, see also pp. 41, 87.

51. For details about an earlier attempt to bring Thayer to Harvard, see further Morris J. Vogel, *The Invention of the Modern Hospital, Boston, 1870–1930* (Chicago: University of Chicago Press, 1980), pp. 81–82. This time Thayer decided to remain in Baltimore and did not wish to be considered as a candidate; Christian to Lowell, April 1, 1912, in fd. 1082, Lowell Papers. Edsall, although viewed as an outsider, was no stranger to the Harvard community. In 1911, for example, he spent a good part of the year preparing himself for the move to St. Louis with a period of study and research in Boston, especially at the Carnegie Nutrition Laboratory; Aub and Hapgood, p. 103.

52. Christian's tentative negotiations with Edsall are reported in a series of letters he wrote Lowell early in 1912; in fd. 1082, Lowell Papers.

53. Edsall's review of Cannon's work appeared in his article on "Diseases of the Digestive Tract and Allied Organs, the Liver and Pancreas," *Progressive Medicine: A Quarterly Digest of Advances, Discoveries, and Improvements in the Medical and Surgical Sciences* 4 (Dec. 1908):19–24, 72–74.

54. The course of Cannon's involvement in the negotiations for Edsall may be followed in his 1912 Diary notes—see, e.g., Jan. 18, 19, 21; Feb. 9, 12, 13, 19, 21; April 9, 11, 23. For an account of the reorganization of Washington University Medical School and Edsall's brief but stormy career there, see further Aub and Hapood, pp. 66–123. For details regarding Edsall's appointment, see further F. A. Washburn, *The Massachusetts General Hospital: Its Development, 1900–1935* (Boston, 1939), pp. 91–92.

55. See especially exchange of letters between Christian and Lowell, March 7 and 8, 1912, in fd. 1091, and A. L. Lowell to J. A. L. Blake, March 9, 1912, in fd. 1098, both in Lowell Papers. Christian resigned from the deanship on Jan. 17, 1912, and asked to be relieved of his duties by the end of April.

56. W. S. Burke to J. C. Warren, Feb. 9, 1912, in Overseers Committee to Visit the Medical School file (AA267), HMA. See also Burke to Lowell, Feb. 9 and 13, 1912, in fd. 1064, Lowell Papers.

57. J. D. Greene to C. H. Tweed, March 12, 1912, in AA267 file, HMA. After Eliot's retirement Greene had worked for a year in association with Lowell, then left Harvard to become business manager of the Rockefeller Institute for Medical Research. Shortly after writing this letter, he entered the office of John D. Rockefeller to take charge of his business and philanthropic interests, and Henry James, Jr., was appointed to succeed him as business manager at the Rockefeller Institute. For more on Greene's affiliation with the Rockefeller philanthropies, see his files in RAC.

58. Ibid. Charles Harrison Tweed, '65, a prominent New York lawyer and financier, was a member of the Committee to Visit the Medical and Dental Schools; see further *Harvard Graduates' Magazine* 21 (1912–13):795.

59. F. C. Shattuck to Lowell, Jan. 3, 1912; Harvey Cushing to Lowell, March 14, 1912; J. B. Blake to Lowell, Feb. 26, 1912; all in fd. 1092, Candidates for Deanship, in Lowell Papers. E. H. Bradford, a descendant of Governor William Bradford of Massachusetts, pioneered in the specialty of orthopedic surgery under the tutelage of Buckminster Brown at the House of the Good Samaritan in Boston. Early in his career Bradford was invited to join the surgical departments of the Boston City Hospital and the Boston Dispensary, but gradually he became more closely associated with the Children's Hospital, where he did outstanding work with patients afflicted with bone and joint diseases. In 1903 he became the first professor of orthopedic surgery at Harvard. See further George H. Monks's obituary notice, "Edward Hickling Bradford," in *Surgery, Gynecology, and Obstetrics*, Oct. 1927, pp. 564–566.

60. Minot wrote two letters to Lowell about the deanship at this time, one dated March 1, 1912, the other undated. Lowell responded by proposing a preliminary informal meeting between himself and some of the professors at the Medical School and diplomatically invited Minot to be one of them. In fd. 1092, Lowell Papers.

61. 1912 Diary, Feb. 27.

62. 1912 Diary, March 22.

63. 1912 Diary, March 25. "Dr. Christian tells me," Cannon noted, "that committee (Shattuck, Coolidge, Ernst, Minot, Christian, President Lowell and Walcott) met Saturday and voted unanimously for Dr. Bradford as Dean. I meet Sabine and Haskins who express regret, tho' congratulating me on escape!"

64. Greene to Lowell, April 13, 1912, in fd. 1092, Lowell Papers.

65. Lowell to Greene, April 16, 1912. Greene, writing again to Lowell on the same date, not only was glad to hear the news about Edsall but also told him it looked as though they would get Mall, too. "The unquestioned

primacy of the Medical School," he commented, "now seems to be in plain sight." Both in fd. 1092, Lowell Papers.

66. Exchange of letters between Paul Thorndike and Lowell, May 5 and 7, 1912, in fd. 1092, Lowell Papers.

67. 1912 Diary, April 8.

15. Shifting Research Interests

1. *Way of an Investigator,* p. 87; see also pp. 46–47.

2. See further Cannon's papers on "Some Practical Applications of Recent Studies in the Physiology of the Digestive System," the annual address in medicine delivered at the sixty-second annual meeting of the State Medical Society of Wisconsin, *Wisconsin Medical Journal* 7 (1908):223–242; and "The Influence of Emotional States on the Functions of the Alimentary Canal," *American Journal of Medical Sciences* 137 (1909):480–487.

3. See further W. B. Cannon, "The Nature of Gastric Peristalsis," *Am. J. Physiol.* 29 (1911):250–266; W. B. Cannon and C. W. Lieb, "The Receptive Relaxation of the Stomach," *Am. J. Physiol.* 29 (1911):267–273. Clarence W. Lieb, who had done his undergraduate work at Colorado College, began assisting Cannon as a first-year medical student in the winter of 1910 but performed most of the experiments in the fall when he was a second-year student.

4. W. B. Cannon, "The importance of Tonus for the Movements of the Alimentary Canal," *Archives of Internal Medicine* 8 (1911):417–426. Cannon served as president of the American Gastro-Enterological Society for a two-year term from 1910 to 1912.

5. At the time Cannon began working on the endocrine glands, the secretion from the adrenal medulla was called variously suprarenin(e), adrenin(e), epinephrin(e), or adrenalin(e). He himself was not consistent with regard to terminology when he wrote his early papers on the subject, although his preferred term was *adrenalin.* By 1915, however, when he collected his work into the volume *Bodily Changes in Pain, Hunger, Fear and Rage,* Cannon noted: "The name 'adrenalin' is proprietary. 'Epinephrin' and 'adrenin' have been suggested as terms free from commercial suggestions. As *adrenin* is shorter and more clearly related to the common adjectival form, *adrenal,* I have followed Schäfer in using *adrenin* to designate the substance produced physiologically by the adrenal glands." (p. 36) Nevertheless, the term *adrenalin* may be found in some of his papers published after 1915. For an extensive discussion see Horace W. Davenport, "Epinephrin(e)," in *The Physiologist* 25 (1982):76–82.

6. See Cannon's 1910 Diary, Oct. 31, Nov. 1, 7, 8. De la Paz, a Filipino, had been offered a graduate fellowship after he received his M.D. degree from the University of Illinois in 1910 and decided to spend a year at Harvard. He later returned to the Philippines, where he became professor of pharmacology; see further de la Paz correspondence in the Cannon Papers, esp. his letter of Aug. 7, 1941.

7. G. Oliver and E. A. Schäfer, "The Physiological Effects of Extracts of the Suprarenal Capsules," *Journal of Physiology* 18 (1895):230–276; J. J. Abel and A. C. Crawford, "On the Blood-Pressure-Raising Constituent of the Suprarenal Capsule," *Bulletin of the Johns Hopkins Hospital* 8 (1897):151–156; J. J. Abel, "Further Observations on the Chemical Nature of the Active Principle of the Suprarenal Capsule," *Bulletin of the Johns Hopkins Hospital* 9 (1898):215–218. The pure hormone was soon after obtained by J. Takamine. See "The Isolation of the Active Principle of the Suprarenal Gland," Proceedings of the Physiological Society in *Journal of Physiology* 27 (1901–02):xxix–xxx.

8. A. Kohn, "Die Paraganglien," *Archiv für Mikroscopische Anatomie* 62 (1903):263–365. See also A. Biedl, *The Internal Secretory Organs: Their Physiology and Pathology* (New York: William Wood, 1913), pp. 149–150; an excellent discussion of early anatomical and physiological research on the adrenals may be found on pp. 124–305.

9. T. R. Elliott, "On the Action of Adrenalin," *Journal of Physiology* 31:(1904):xx–xxi. Although Cannon knew Elliott's various articles, this 1904 abstract is not cited in his earliest papers on the adrenals. In 1913, while working on "The Emergency Function of the Adrenal Medulla in Pain and the Major Emotions," Cannon discovered and used the 1904 reference (see *Am. J. Physiol.* 33 [1914], p. 372, n. 1) and then apparently forgot it. Years later, one of his students, Z. M. Bacq, reminiscing about Cannon, wrote: "I can still recall how happy W. B. Cannon was when he brought me this note [Elliott, 1904] in December 1930; he was in process of preparing our paper on sympathin for the *American Journal of Physiology*. Cannon loved to pay homage to the work of his predecessors or contemporaries with a generosity inherent in his nature." Bacq, *Chemical Transmission of Nerve Impulses: A Historical Sketch* (New York: Pergamon Press, 1975), p. 12. Cannon had, in fact, rediscovered the paper; see also Bacq, p. 38. Elliott's short note caught the attention of some of his contemporaries, like W. E. Dixon, who tried to extend it; Dixon, "On the Mode of Action of Drugs," *Medical Magazine* (London) 16 (1907):454–467. Henry Dale, however, attacked it; G. Barger and H. H. Dale, "Chemical Structure and Sympathomimetic Action of Amines," *Journal of Physiology* (1910–11):19–59. Dale nevertheless always had the highest regard for Elliott's research, as evidenced by his later praise of Elliott's 1904 paper; see the unpublished autobiography in Dale Papers, Royal Society, London, pp. 36–38, and the *mea culpa* for his criticism on pp. 73–75; also *Adventures in Physiology: A Selection of Scientific Papers by H. H. Dale* (London: Pergamon Press, 1953), pp. 531–532.

10. J. N. Langley, "On the Reaction of Cells and of Nerve-Endings to Certain Poisons, Chiefly as Regards the Reaction of Striated Muscle to Nicotine and Curari," *Journal of Physiology* 33 (1905–06):374–413, see esp. p. 412.

11. G. Barger and H. H. Dale, "Chemical Structure and Sympathomimetic Action of Amines," *Journal of Physiology* 41 (1910–11):19–59.

12. See J. N. Langley, "The Sympathetic and Other Related Systems of Nerves," in *Textbook of Physiology*, vol. II (New York: Macmillan, 1900), ed. E. A. Schäfer, pp. 616–696; W. H. Gaskell, "On the Structure, Distribution, and Function of the Nerves Which Innervate the Visceral and Vascular Sys-

tems," *Journal of Physiology* 7 (1886):1–80. See also Gaskell's later history of the involuntary nervous system in his volume, *The Involuntary Nervous System* (London: Longmans, Green, 1920), pp. 1–30.

13. Cannon and de la Paz, "Emotional Stimulation of Adrenal Secretion," *Am. J. Physiol.* 28 (1911):64–70; see esp. pp. 64–65.

14. Ibid., p. 65. See also Cannon's 1910 Diary, Nov. 28, 29, Dec. 3, 6–9.

15. Ibid., p. 66. See also Cannon, *Bodily Changes in Pain, Hunger, Fear and Rage* (New York: Appleton, 1915), pp. 41–43.

16. Meltzer and his daughter wrote a number of articles on the effect of adrenalin on pupil dilatation. See further S. Meltzer and C. M. Auer, "Studies on the 'Paradoxical' Pupil-Dilatation Caused by Adrenalin: 1. The Effect of Subcutaneous Injections and Installations of Adrenalin upon the Pupils of Rabbits"; "2. On the Influence of Subcutaneous Injections of Adrenalin upon Eyes of Cats after Removal of the Superior Cervical Ganglion"; "3. A Discussion of the Nature of the Paradoxical Pupil Dilatation Caused by Adrenalin"; "The Effect of Suprarenal Extract upon the Pupils of Frogs"; all in *Am. J. Physiol.* 11 (1904)28–36, 37–39, 40–51, 449–454. For Cannon's use of the eye test, see his 1910 Diary, Dec. 13 and 14.

17. R. Magnus, "Versuche am überlebenden Dünndarm von Säugtieren," *Archiv für die Gesammte Physiologie* 108 (1905):1–71; see esp. pp. 1–10 for the development and method of Magnus's technique.

18. Cannon and de la Paz, "Emotional Stimulation," p. 66. For a more detailed explanation, see also Cannon, *Bodily Changes*, pp. 44–46.

19. 1911 Diary, Jan. 24.

20. 1911 Diary, Jan. 30 and 31.

21. 1911 Diary, Feb. 1.

22. Cannon and de la Paz, "The Stimulation of Adrenal Secretion by Emotional Excitement," *JAMA* 56 (1911):742. Toward the end of the year, on Dec. 2, 1911, Alexander Forbes, then working in Liverpool with C. S. Sherrington, wrote Cannon: "Sherrington told me something that would please you; I lent him my copy of the preliminary note of your work with de la Paz on adrenalin. He didn't know of it and read it with great interest. A few days later he was at a meeting in London where a man named Eliot [sic] was reporting some work on the production of adrenalin under chloroform. He said it was important to keep the cat calm when you chloroformed him as struggling impaired the subsequent yield of adrenalin. None of those present knew of your work, and Sherrington had some fun springing it on them." In Cannon Papers.

23. 1911 Diary, Feb. 3.

24. 1911 Diary, Feb. 14 and 15. Aub and Shohl, from Cincinnati, were cousins and had been Harvard undergraduates, as had Binger and Washburn, both from New York. All four went on to careers in academic medicine, with Aub and Binger maintaining lifelong associations with Cannon. Wade Wright had come to the Medical School from the University of Pittsburgh and does not appear to have continued his research interests.

25. 1911 Diary, Feb. 17.

26. Saul Benison, "Reminiscences of Dr. Joseph Aub," 1956, p. 27; man-

uscript on deposit in Oral History Research Office, Columbia University.

27. 1911 Diary, March 1 and 2. See further W. B. Cannon, A. T. Shohl, and W. S. Wright, "Emotional Glycosuria," *Am. J. Physiol.* 29 (1911):280–287.

28. Cannon, Shohl, and Wright, pp. 282–284; see also 1911 Diary, March 14.

29. Ibid., pp. 285–286; 1911 Diary, May 6.

30. 1911 Diary, March 3.

31. 1911 Diary, Feb. 21, March 6, April 3.

32. 1911 Diary, Apr. 22. For Crile's address, see "Phylogenetic Association in Relation to the Emotions," in G. W. Crile, *The Origin and Nature of the Emotions* (Philadelphia: W. B. Saunders, 1915), pp. 55–76.

33. Benison, "Aub Reminiscences," p. 28. For Cannon's reminiscence of the experiments with Washburn, see his *Digestion and Health* (New York: W. W. Norton, 1936), pp. 30–34.

34. J. N. Langley and W. S. Dickinson, "On the Local Paralysis of Peripheral Ganglia, and on the Connection of Different Classes of Nerve Fibres with Them," *Proceedings of the Royal Society* 46 (1889):423–431.

35. Benison, "Aub Reminiscences," p. 29.

36. Editorial, "Nicotin and the Adrenals," *JAMA* 58 (1912):1287–88. See also W. B. Cannon, J. C. Aub, and C. A. L. Binger, "A Note on the Effect of Nicotine Injection on Adrenal Secretion," *Journal of Pharmacology and Experimental Therapeutics* 3 (1912):379–385.

37. R. G. Hoskins, "A Consideration of Some Biologic Tests for Epinephrin," *Journal of Pharmacology and Experimental Therapeutics* 3 (1911):93–99.

38. Cannon and Hoskins, "The Effects of Asphyxia, Hyperpnoea, and Sensory Stimulation on Adrenal Secretion," *Am. J. Physiol.* 29 (1911):274–279.

39. Ibid., pp. 275–276. See also 1911 Diary, Aug. 16.

40. Ibid., p. 276.

41. Ibid., pp. 277–278.

42. Ibid., p. 278–279.

43. 1911 Diary, Sept. 30 and Oct. 2.

44. W. B. Cannon, "A Consideration of the Nature of Hunger," *The Harvey Lectures, 1911–1912* (Philadelphia: J. B. Lippincott, 1912), p. 144; see also W. B. Cannon, "Auscultation of the Rhythmic Sounds Produced by the Stomach and Intestines," *Am. J. Physiol.* 14 (1905):339–353, esp. p. 341.

45. W. N. Boldireff, "Le travail periodique de l'appareil digestiv en dehors de la digestion," *Archives Biologiques de St. Petersburg* 11 (1905):1–158. For the impact of Boldireff's investigations on Cannon's thinking, see Cannon's Harvey Lecture, esp. pp. 143–144, 146–147.

46. W. B. Cannon, "A Consideration of the Nature of Hunger," pp. 130–132; W. B. Cannon, *Digestion and Health,* pp. 20–23. For a current application of Cannon's thesis regarding hunger and proposed treatment for obesity, see S. L. Edell, J. S. Wills, L. R. Garren, and M. L. Garren, "Radiographic Evaluation of the Garren Gastric Bubble," *American Journal of Radiology* 145 (1985):49–50.

47. See further W. B. Cannon and A. L. Washburn, "An Explanation of Hunger," *Am. J. Physiol.* 19 (1912):441–454.

48. W. B. Cannon, "A Consideration of the Nature of Hunger," p. 151.

Cannon's explanation of hunger has been criticized as a simplistic approach to a complex problem; see H. W. Davenport, "Walter B. Cannon's Contribution to Gastroenterology," in *Life & Contributions*, p. 17; also Davenport, *Physiology of the Digestive Tract*, 5th ed. (Chicago: Yearbook Medical Publishers, 1982), pp. 54, 76–78. Although Cannon did not specifically differentiate between hunger and hunger pangs in much of his writing, it is of interest that he ends all three of his publications on the subject with the same sentence: "The periodic activity of the alimentary canal in fasting, therefore, is not solely the source of hunger *pangs* [our italics], but is at the same time an exhibition in the digestive organs of readiness for prompt attack of the food swallowed by the hungry animal." (*Harvey Lectures*, p. 151; Cannon and Washburn, "Explanation of Hunger," p. 454; *Bodily Changes*, p. 264.) We now know that patients in whom the motor nerves to the stomach (vagi) have been cut for treatment of peptic ulcers still experience generalized sensations of hunger when hypoglycemia (low blood sugar) is induced by insulin, but they do not have gastric contractions and do not describe hunger *pangs*, which they had emphasized prior to surgery. See further the 1948–49 paper by M. I. Grossman and I. F. Stein, Jr., "Vagotomy and the Hunger-Producing Action of Insulin in Man," *Journal of Applied Physiology* 1 (1948–49):263–269.

49. A. J. Carlson, *The Control of Hunger in Health and Disease* (Chicago: University of Chicago Press, 1916), pp. 28–29; see also historical introduction on pp. 16–29. For Cannon's complimentary comments on Carlson's extension of his research, see *Digestion and Health*, pp. 35–40; with a brief demurrer, pp. 41–42.

50. Benison, "Aub Reminiscences," p. 29. See further obituary notice, "Joseph Charles Aub, 1890–1973," *Transactions of the Association of American Physicians* 87 (1974):12–14; also Memorial Minute in *Harvard University Gazette*, vol. 70, Dec. 13, 1974.

16. Science versus Sentiment

1. G. H. Simmons to Cannon, June 15, 1910, Cannon Papers. Cannon's appointment and other materials relating to the formation of the AMA Council on Health and Public Instruction may be found in fd. 966 of the Cannon Papers. Thereafter, the Council on Defense of Medical Research became known as the Bureau (or Committee) for the Protection of Medical Research; but for purposes of clarity, we continue to use the term "defense council."

2. William J. Schultz, *The Humane Movement in the United States, 1910–1922* (New York, 1924), p. 154; William Gary Roberts, "Man before Beast: The Response of Organized Medicine to the American Anti-Vivisection Movement," undergraduate thesis submitted in partial fulfillment for the B.A. degree, Harvard College, 1979, HUA; see esp. pp. 21 and 33. Many of the publications that supported the antivivisectionists were women's magazines. Publications that supported medical research included the *New York Times*, the *Boston Herald*, and the *Philadelphia Ledger*, as well as the *Atlantic Monthly*, *Colliers' Weekly*, and the *North American Review*.

3. Schultz, *Humane Movement*, p. 152. See also Cannon's editorial, "The Antivivisection Agitation in New York," in *JAMA* 54 (1910): 1062–1063, and his 1910 Diary, March 19 and April 19.

4. See, e.g., statistics and graphs presented as evidence by Richard D. French in his Epilogue to *Antivivisection and Medical Science in Victorian Society* (Princeton, N.J.: Princeton University Press, 1975), pp. 393–405.

5. Walter R. Hadwen (1854–1932) took over the direction of the militant British Union for the Abolition of Vivisection after it had been founded by Frances Power Cobbe around the turn of the century. Cannon described Hadwen as engaged in reform movements relating to temperance, food, hygiene, sanitation, education, and burial laws—and then tartly commented, "He finds his recreation in changing his occupation." W. B. Cannon, *Some Characteristics of Antivivisection Literature*, Defense of Research Pamphlet XIX (Chicago: AMA, 1911), p. 7. For more on attacks on the validity of medical science, see also Schultz, *Humane Movement*, pp. 143–145.

6. W. R. Hadwen, *Vivisection: Its Follies and Cruelties, and the Way to Fight It* (British Union for the Abolition of Vivisection, 1905), p. 9.

7. W. R. Hadwen, *The Anti-Toxin Treatment of Diphtheria: In Theory and Practice*, 5th ed. (published by the British Union for the Abolition of Vivisection, 1906). Hadwen was a prolific pamphleteer, whose works included, among others, *The Blunders of a Bishop: A Reply to the Research Defence Society* and *A Vivisection Controversy . . . Carried on in the 'Chitenham Examiner' during December 1910 and January 1911, between Walter R. Hadwen and Stephen Paget.*

8. *Journal of Zoophily* 19 (July 1910), p. 81.

9. See further M. J. Rodermund, M.D., "Medical Wonders and Medical Blunders—A Story of Facts," *Medical Brief*, April 1906, p. 279; also "A Little Confession," *Life* ("Women's Rights Number," March 25, 1909), p. 393. Almost every issue of *Life* contained barbs against vivisection—so much so that one letter-writer accused the editors of "having it in for the medical profession" and suggested that perhaps they might be Christian Scientists.

10. Cannon wrote Erlanger and Yates on April 26, 1909, and enclosed extracts from Rodermund's article; see further materials in fd. 349, Cannon Papers.

11. J. J. Yates to Cannon, May 21, 1909, Cannon Papers. Rodermund was described in a letter from G. E. Seaman, president of the Wisconsin Medical Society, to Yates, May 10, 1909, which was forwarded to Cannon. For a further description, see also Martin Kaufman, "The American Anti-Vaccinationists and Their Arguments," *Bulletin of the History of Medicine* 41 (1967), p. 475.

12. For Cannon's views on how to deal with Rodermund, see his letters to Erlanger and Yates, both dated May 17, 1909, Cannon Papers. A year later (May 28, 1910), Alexander Forbes wrote a letter to the editor of *Life* about the Rodermund confessions in which he stated: "An effort was made by one of the leading advocates of vivisection in Boston to have this man's dangerous activities suppressed, but the doctors of Wisconsin assured him that his standing in the community was so low that he was no longer dangerous . . . and was therefore not worth prosecuting." In Forbes Papers.

13. See, e.g., Cannon to Frederick R. Green, Jan. 17, 1914, Cannon Papers; also Richard M. Pearce, *The Charge of "Human Vivisection" as Presented in Antivivisection Literature*, Defense of Research Pamphlet XXVI (Chicago: AMA, 1914), pp. 23–25.

14. A full account of the attacks against Hamill and his co-workers in Philadelphia and Holt in New York may be found in Pearce's *Human Vivisection* pamphlet, pp. 15–20. See also biographical sketch of Samuel Mc-Clintock Hamill in *Pediatric Profiles*, ed. B. F. Veeder (St. Louis: Moseby, 1957), esp. p. 96.

15. Cannon responded to an editorial captioned "Still More Barbarity" in the April 1910 issue of the *Journal of Zoophily*, p. 44. A measure of Cannon's regard for Wentworth may be found in his letter to W. H. Welch, Oct. 28, 1908, in which he told Welch that he had recently recommended Wentworth for the position in pediatrics at Johns Hopkins. In Cannon Papers.

16. *Journal of Zoophily* (July 1911), p. 219. For more on Mrs. Lovell, see further Sydney H. Coleman, *Humane Society Leaders in America* (Albany, N.Y.: The American Humane Association, 1924), p. 186.

17. W. W. Keen to Cannon, Aug. 19, 1911, Cannon Papers. Keen's earlier defense of Wentworth appeared in his letter to James M. Brown, President of the American Humane Association, Jan. 21, 1901; reprinted as "Misstatements of Antivivisectionists" in Keen's collection of essays, *Animal Experimentation and Medical Progress* (Boston: Houghton Mifflin, 1914), pp. 122–123; see also pp. 275–277.

18. Cannon to Keen, Aug. 15, 1911, Cannon Papers. An account of the Wentworth case was given by Keen in *The Influence of Antivivisection on Character*, Defense of Research Pamphlet XXIV (Chicago: AMA, 1912), pp. 35–37. See also Pearce's *Human Vivisection* pamphlet, p. 11, and Cannon's *Characteristics of Antivivisection Literature* pamphlet, pp. 10–11.

19. John A. Wyeth to [Cannon], June 3, 1910, in Cannon Papers; also 1910 Diary, esp. June 8 and Nov. 17.

20. Cannon, *Characteristics of Antivivisection Literature*, p. 13.

21. On May 22, 1910, Cannon noted in his diary that Greene told him of his proposed move to New York. See further George W. Corner's *History of the Rockefeller Institute, 1901–1953* (New York: Rockefeller Institute Press, 1964), p. 72.

22. 1911 Diary, March 6–8. See also E. Mark Houghton to Simon Flexner, March 28, 1911, and follow-up correspondence of J. D. Greene relating to the legislative hearings, May–June 1911, Anti-Vivisection Papers.

23. See esp. Corner, *Rockefeller Institute*, pp. 83–87.

24. H. Noguchi, "A Cutaneous Reaction in Syphilis," *Journal of Experimental Medicine* 14 (1911):557–568; see also "A Method for the Pure Cultivation of Pathogenic *Treponema pallidum*," *Journal of Experimental Medicine* 14 (1911):99–108, and "Experimental Research in Syphilis," *JAMA* 68 (1912):1163–72. Since the above account was written, a fuller version has been published by Susan Eyrich Lederer, "Hideyo Noguchi's Luetin Experiment and the Antivivisectionists," *Isis* 76 (March 1985):31–48.

25. Schultz, *Humane Movement*, p. 155; Pearce, *Human Vivisection* pam-

phlet, pp. 21, 29. See also correspondence in Anti-Vivisection Papers—e.g., Jerome Greene to Frederic S. Lee, Feb. 24, 1912; Greene to W. B. Jones, June 8, 1912; Simon Flexner to Sen. Griffin, Feb. 19, 1913.

26. Schultz, *Humane Movement*, p. 156.

27. George B. Roth, a technical assistant at the Hygienic Laboratory, Public Health Service, took notes at the Congress; see his report enclosed in J. F. Anderson to Cannon, Dec. 18, 1913, in Cannon Papers.

28. Dec. 11, 1913; in fd. 391, Cannon Papers (one of three folders of literature, clippings, and related materials on the Washington congress). See also *Proceedings of the International Anti-Vivisection and Animal Protection Congress* (New York: Tudor Press, 1913).

29. 1913 Diary, Dec. 10.

30. W. B. Cannon, *Animal Experimentation and Its Benefits to Mankind*, Defense of Research Pamphlet XXIII (Chicago: AMA, 1912).

31. "The Washington Antivivisection Congress," editorial in *JAMA* 61 (Dec. 20, 1913):2244–45.

32. Cannon to H. B. Favill, April 1, 1912, in fd. 967, Cannon Papers.

33. The above account is based on letters and related materials about the Committee on Animals (AA 204), HMA. President Lowell appointed Cannon chairman of the committee following the resignation of H. C. Ernst from that position in the spring of 1913.

34. For more on the Animal Rescue League and its directors, Mr. and Mrs. Huntington Smith, see Coleman, *Humane Society Leaders*, esp. pp. 193, 209. See also series of letters between Cannon and Mrs. Smith, April 1912, in Cannon Papers.

35. Roger Ernst to A. L. Lowell, Nov. 8, 1913, enclosing letter from Huntington Smith, managing director of the Animal Rescue League, Nov. 7, 1913, Lowell Papers. Phillips's letter to Francis W. Palfrey, secretary of the Medical School, was dated Nov. 10, 1913. George Alexander Otis Ernst (brother of the Harvard bacteriologist) had preceded Mrs. Smith as president of the Animal Rescue League. His son Roger received his law degree from Harvard in 1906 and joined the firm of Ropes, Gray et al. in 1911.

36. Cannon to William Phillips, Nov. 12, 1913, in Committee on Animals materials, HMA. See also Nov. 1913 letters concerning antivivisection in Cushing Papers.

37. See, e.g., exchange of letters between Keen and Cannon, Dec. 16 and 18, 1913, Sept. 23 and 25, 1914, Keen Papers. For more on relations of medical scientists with humane societies, see also Cannon to Harvey Cushing, Nov. 21, 1911, in Cannon Papers; exchange of letters between Keen and W. O. Stillman, April 12 and 19, 1911, Keen Papers; R. M. Pearce to Harvey Cushing, Nov. 25, 1913, and Keen to Cushing, Dec. 9, 1913, both in Cushing Papers.

38. For more on Rowley, see Cannon to H. C. Ernst, March 20, 1912, in Committee on Animals materials, HMA; also W. W. Keen to W. O. Stillman, March 22, 1912, and F. H. Rowley to W. W. Keen, March 23, 1912, both in Keen Papers.

39. For Cannon's exposé of Cowen and other "eminent medical au-

thorities," see his editorial, "Medical Support of the Antivivisectionists," in *JAMA* (Feb. 14, 1914), pp. 541–542, and his statement in the *Boston Herald* for Feb. 26, 1914, rebutting Clement's first communication. See also Henry James, Jr., to William [sic] B. Cannon, Feb. 26, 1914, Anti-Vivisection Papers. The subsequent series of letters to the editor of the *Boston Herald* between Cannon and Clement appeared in March 1914; see, for example, Cannon's 1914 Diary, March 11–13, 27, 30–31. For more on E. H. Clement, see also Coleman, *Humane Society Leaders*, p. 207.

40. Cannon to Keen, Jan. 29, 1914, Keen Papers.

41. Jessica L. C. Henderson was the secretary of the New England Anti-Vivisection Society; see her correspondence in fd. 362, Cannon Papers. For her attacks on Crile, see Keen to Cannon, March 17, 1914, Keen Papers, and Preface to Keen's *Animal Experimentation*, pp. vi–vii. For a later description of her, see also Cannon to Norman Hapgood, March 17, 1915, Cannon Papers.

42. Ernest H. Gruening to Cannon, March 24, 1914. On April 2, 1914, Cannon wrote Henry James: "You will be interested to know a fact which I have just learned, that the Managing Editor of the Herald under Mr. O'Brien is E. H. Gruening, a graduate of the Medical School, and a former student of mine. There is little wonder that he has been somewhat severe with antivivisectionists!" Both in Cannon Papers.

43. Cannon to Keen, March 25, 1914; Cannon to F. R. Green, April 2, 1914; both in Cannon Papers. See also exchange of letters between Keen and Cannon, March 17 and 18, 1914, Keen Papers; Henry James to Cannon, March 18, 1914, Anti-Vivisection Papers.

44. Henry James to Cannon, July 10, 1912, Cannon Papers. See also Cannon to Keen, Nov. 22, 1912, Cannon Papers; James to Norman Hapgood, March 23, 1914, Anti-Vivisection Papers; Corner, *Rockefeller Institute*, pp. 72–73.

45. With the relocation of David Edsall, Harvey Cushing, and Reid Hunt to Boston, Cannon sought new members for his AMA defense council and replaced them with Pearce of Philadelphia, George H. Whipple of Baltimore, and Major John F. Anderson of Washington, D.C. See further Cannon to Keen, Dec. 12, 1913; Cannon to F. R. Green, Jan. 1, 1914; both in Cannon Papers.

46. George W. Corner, *Two Centuries of Medicine: A History of the School of Medicine, University of Pennsylvania* (Philadelphia: Lippincott, 1965), pp. 219–220; see also pp. 242–244.

47. See exchange of letters between Henry James and R. M. Pearce, Feb. 24 and 25, 1913, Anti-Vivisection Papers.

48. For defeat of the pound bill, see exchange of letters between Henry James and R. M. Pearce, Feb. 26 and 27, 1913, Anti-Vivisection Papers; Cannon to F. S. Lee, March 7, 1913, Cannon Papers. For introduction of antivivisection counterbills, see Schultz, *Humane Movement*, p. 157.

49. Henry James to Cannon, June 20, 1913, Cannon Papers. See also exchange of letters between Pearce and James, June 18 and 20, 1913; William Pepper to James, June 23, 1913; all in Anti-Vivisection Papers.

50. For Cannon's response, see his letter to James, June 25, 1913, Cannon

Papers, and his editorial, "Recent Antivivisection Activity," *JAMA* 61 (July 26, 1913): 282–283. See also exchange of letters between J. A. E. Eyster and Cannon, July 8 and 14, 1913, Cannon Papers. For Pearce's efforts, see Cannon to Pearce, Nov. 8, Dec. 15 and 16, 1913, Keen Papers; also correspondence between Cannon and Pearce, fd. 358, Cannon Papers.

51. See further Henry James to Cannon, March 27, 1914. For the New Jersey bill, see also James to Cannon, April 1 and 13, 1914; Cannon to Pearce, April 14, 1914; Cannon to F. R. Green, April 15, 1914. All in Cannon Papers.

52. See further letters between James and Cannon, March 29 to April 14, 1914; also letters between F. R. Green and Cannon, April 9 and 13, June 8 and 11, 1914. All in Cannon Papers.

53. *Report of Special Committee of the Board and Resolutions of the Board of Trustees of the University of Pennsylvania Relative to Work in the Department of Medicine Involving Animal Experimentation*, April 13, 1914 (pamphlet, 9 pp). See also exchange of letters between H. S. Drinker and Henry James, April 20 and 22, 1914, in Anti-Vivisection Papers.

54. "Medical News," *JAMA* 62 (April 25, 1914):1341–42.

55. Pearce to Cannon, April 17, 1914, Cannon Papers. See also Pearce to Henry James enclosing report from *Philadelphia Press*, April 20, 1914, Anti-Vivisection Papers.

56. On April 22, 1914, Pearce reported to Cannon again and enclosed Dickson's letter to Edgar F. Smith, April 21, 1914, with related materials, Cannon Papers.

57. Besides the report of the Philadelphia trial on pp. 1341–42, the issue of *JAMA* for April 25, 1914, contains F. R. Green's editorial "Prosecution of Research Workers" on pp. 1331–32. See also Cannon to Green, April 28, 1914, Cannon Papers. Pearce later used some of the material in the *Philadelphia Ledger* articles as a basis for his *Animal Experimentation in the Diagnosis, Treatment and Prevention of Diseases of Children*, Defense of Research Pamphlet XXVII (Chicago: AMA, 1914); see, e.g., Cannon/Pearce correspondence, April and May 1914, in fd. 358, Cannon Papers.

58. Cannon to Pearce, June 3, 1914. For Public Health Sunday, see further Cannon to Pearce, May 4 and June 11, 1914; F. R. Green to Cannon, May 2, 1914. All in Cannon Papers.

59. Pearce to Cannon, April 17, [1915], Cannon Papers.

17. The Emergency Function of the Adrenal Medulla

1. 1911 Diary, Nov. 2–3, 6, Cannon Papers. L. B. Nice, who received his Ph.D. degree in physiology from Clark University that year, served as instructor in Cannon's department while Alexander Forbes was in England working with C. S. Sherrington in 1911–12.

2. See further W. B. Cannon and L. B. Nice, "The Effect of Adrenal Secretion on Muscular Fatigue," *Am. J. Physiol.* 32 (1913):44–60. For details concerning the plan and methods of the investigation, see esp. pp. 45–48.

3. 1911 Diary, Nov. 15. S. Dessy and V. Grandis, "Contribution à l'étude

de la fatigue. Action de l'adrenaline sur la fonction du muscle," *Archives Italiennes de Biologie* 41 (1904):225–233.

4. Cannon and Nice, "Adrenal Secretion," p. 51.

5. W. B. Cannon and L. B. Nice, "The Effect of Splanchnic Stimulation on Muscular Fatigue," *Am. J. Physiol.* 29 (1911–12):xxiv.

6. The above account is based on materials in a notebook containing 1912 Proceedings of the Commission on Electric Shock, in Cannon Papers.

7. Cannon noted this appointment, which came about through his service on the AMA Council on Health and Public Instruction, in his diary on Nov. 23, 1911.

8. "Preliminary Report of the Commission on Resuscitation from Electric Shock," pp. 20–22 of Proceedings notebook; see also circular letter from Chairman to members of the Commission, Feb. 3, 1912 on pp. 1–3.

9. The Silvester method, which was described in the old rules, directed that the victim be laid on his back and his chest expanded and compressed by drawing his arms forward and then pushing them back against his ribs. The Schäfer method consists of laying the victim on his stomach and applying pressure rhythmically on the loins and lowest ribs. For further comparison of the two methods, see *Report of the Commission on Resuscitation from Electric Shock* (New York: National Electric Light Association, 1913), esp. pp. 5–8.

10. Minutes of First Meeting of Commission, Feb. 24, 1912, pp. 5–6 of Proceedings notebook.

11. C. C. Guthrie described his work and that of George Crile on defibrillation in *Blood-Vessel Surgery and Its Applications* (London & New York: International Medical Monographs Series, 1912), p. 332; for the work on electrical stimulation by Floresco and others, see also p. 335.

12. 1912 Diary, see esp. March and April. Ernest Martin, who had been promoted to assistant professor of physiology the previous year, collected the papers he had produced on the subject of standardization of electrical stimulation and published them in book form under the title, *The Measurement of Induction Shocks: A Manual for the Quantitative Use of Faradic Stimuli* (New York: John Wiley & Sons, 1912).

13. See further "Preliminary Report of the Commission on Resuscitation from Electric Shock"; also editorial, "Preliminary Work of the Resuscitation Commission," in *Electrical World* for March 2, 1912, p. 443. Both in Proceedings notebook.

14. See, e.g., *Boston Sunday Post*, June 16, 1912, p. 28, in Proceedings notebook.

15. Subsequently the medical committee undertook a special investigation of the problem of resuscitation of miners. See 1912 Diary, Nov. 15–16, Dec. 28–29. For an account of this investigation and its findings, see Department of the Interior, Bureau of Mines, Technical Paper 77, *Report of the Committee on Resuscitation from Mine Gases* (Washington, D.C.: Government Printing Office, 1914).

16. "Work of the Commission on Electric Shock," editorial in *JAMA* (Nov. 1, 1913), p. 1637.

17. This remembrance was published in David C. Schechter, "Back-

ground of Clinical Cardiac Electrostimulation: V. Direct Electrostimulation of Heart without Thoracotomy," *New York State Journal of Medicine* 72 (March 1972), pp. 609–610. Hyman also acknowledged the influence of Cannon on his work in "The 1915 Boston Marathon Adventure," *American College of Sports Medicine Newsletter* (April 1969), pp. 6–8; *Life & Contributions*, pp. 236–237.

18. Schechter, "Direct Electrostimulation," pp. 611–614; personal communication from Paul Zoll to A. C. Barger.

19. 1912 Diary, April 12.

20. The above account is based on Cannon's diary entries for June through September 1912.

21. Telegram from Cannon to Cornelia's family headed "(Marian born 1:30 this morning)," Sept. 13, 1912, Franklin, in "Snatched from Oblivion."

22. Excerpt of letter dated Sept. 24, 1912, in "Snatched from Oblivion." The book referred to was Edward Sanford Martin, *The Luxury of Children and Some Other Luxuries* (New York & London: Harper & Bros., 1905).

23. Excerpt of letter dated Sept. 27, 1912, in "Snatched from Oblivion."

24. 1912 Diary, Sept. 24 and 26.

25. C. M. Gruber, who had received bachelor's and master's degrees from the University of Kansas, came to the physiology department in Sept. 1912 as an Austin teaching fellow. Howard Osgood, who had graduated from Harvard College in 1911, received his M.D. degree from HMS in 1916.

26. For their progress, see 1912 Diary, Oct. 22–Nov. 1; for subsequent developments, see also Nov. 5–20.

27. O. Folin and W. Denis, "On Phosphotungstic-Phosphomolybdic Compounds as Color Reagents," *Journal of Biological Chemistry* 12 (Aug. 1912):239–243. Denis, who was a frequent and favored collaborator of Folin during this period, held a rather tenuous position at the Medical School. For example, on June 20, 1911, Dean Christian wrote President Lowell: "I have discovered that the person nominated for research assistant in biological chemistry, Willey Denis, is a woman. If you will recall, there was considerable discussion occasioned a year ago in regard to the nomination of Dr. Mooers for a fellowship, and the feeling in the faculty was strongly against appointing a woman to be in a teaching position. I have just been talking to Dr. Folin about this and it seems satisfactory to him to change the title from research assistant to technical assistant and to omit the name from the roster of instructors and simply have her name appear upon the payroll as do other technical assistants, stenographers, etc." (in Lowell Papers). Later in life Denis became a professor of chemistry at Tulane; see further Joseph C. Aub and Ruth K. Hapgood, *Pioneer in Modern Medicine, David Linn Edsall of Harvard* (Harvard Medical Alumni Association, 1970), p. 166.

28. O. Folin, W. B. Cannon, and W. Denis, "A new colorimetric method for the determination of epinephrine," *Journal of Biological Chemistry* 13 (Jan. 1913):477–483. Cannon referred to this work in his diary notes; see esp. Nov. 21–26 and Dec. 3–6, 1912.

29. 1913 Diary, Jan. 6. Henry Lyman, who graduated from Harvard College in 1901 and from HMS in 1912, had completed a study several months before with Otto Folin on "Absorption from the Stomach." This study was

published as the fifth paper in a series, "Protein Metabolism from the Stand-point of Blood and Tissue Analysis"; see further *Journal of Biological Chemistry* 12 (1912):259–264 and 13 (1912):389–391.

30. G. Oliver and E. A. Schäfer, "The Physiological Effects of Extracts of the Suprarenal Capsules," *Journal of Physiology* 18 (1895):230–276; A. Biedl, "Action de l'extrait de capsules surrenales sur la pression sanguine," *Semaine Medicale*, 1896; Biedl, *The Internal Secretory Organs: Their Physiology and Pathology* (New York: William Wood, 1913), pp. 183–184.

31. Benjamin Moore and C. O. Purinton, "Über den Einfluss minimaler Mengen Nebennierenextracts auf den arteriellen Blutbruck," *Archiv für die Gesammte Physiologie* 81 (1900):483–490.

32. S. J. Meltzer and Clara Meltzer, "On the Effects of Subcutaneous Injection of the Extract of the Suprarenal Capsule upon the Blood-Vessels of the Rabbit's Ear," *Am. J. Physiol.* 9 (1903):252–261.

33. H. H. Dale, "The Physiological Action of Chrysotoxin," *Proceedings of the Physiological Society* 32 (1905):lvii; "On Some Physiological Actions of Ergot," *Journal of Physiology* 34 (1906):163–206.

34. W. B. Cannon and Henry Lyman, "The Depressor Effect of Adrenalin on Arterial Pressure," *Am. J. Physiol.* 31 (1913):376–398.

35. 1912 Diary, Dec. 21.

36. Cannon and Lyman, "Depressor Effect of Adrenalin," pp. 385–386.

37. 1913 Diary, Feb. 6.

38. Cannon and Lyman, "Depressor Effect of Adrenalin," p. 384; Dale, "On Some Physiological Actions of Ergot," p. 174. See also 1913 Diary, Feb. 6, 8, 10, and 14.

39. Cannon and Lyman, "Depressor Effect of Adrenalin," p. 385.

40. Ibid., p. 395.

41. Ibid., p. 398.

42. H. H. Dale, "On the Action of Ergotoxine; with Special Reference to the Existence of Sympathetic Vasodilators," *Journal of Physiology* 46 (1913):291–300.

43. Ibid., p. 300. Many years later in preparing comments for a volume reprinting his papers, Dale noted of this particular paper: "I hope that I did not often indulge in anything so near to a merely controversial paper as this one. I still think that the answer which it gives, to my friend Cannon's explanation of the reversal of adrenalin actions by ergotoxine, is complete; and he did not, in fact, attempt a reply." *Adventures in Physiology: A Selection of Scientific Papers by H. H. Dale* (London: Pergamon Press, 1953), p. 10.

44. Cannon to R. G. Pearce, Nov. 8, 1913, Cannon Papers.

45. Frank A. Hartman, who received his Ph.D. in physiology in 1914 from the University of Washington, came to Harvard as an Austin teaching fellow for 1914–15. Hartman's investigation in Cannon's laboratory eventuated in the publication of "The Differential Effects of Adrenin on Splanchnic and Peripheral Arteries," *Am. J. Physiol.* 38 (Oct. 1915):438–455, and marked the beginning of a distinguished body of research on adrenal function.

46. C. M. Gruber, "Studies in Fatigue: I. Fatigue as Affected by Changes in Arterial Pressure," *Am. J. Physiol.* 32 (1913):221–229.

47. C. M. Gruber, "Studies in Fatigue: II. The Threshold Stimulus as Affected by Fatigue and Subsequent Rest," *Am. J. Physiol.* 32 (1913):438–449.

48. 1913 Diary, Oct. 3. Walter Mendenhall, who had received his M.D. degree from Drake University and served in the physiology department there, was appointed Austin teaching fellow in Cannon's department for 1913–14.

49. For a general introduction to problems of coagulation at this time, see W. H. Howell, *A Text-Book of Physiology for Medical Students and Physicians*, 5th edition (Philadelphia & London: W. B. Saunders, 1914), pp. 444–458.

50. The device was a very simple one. Cannon described its construction and projected operation in the following terms: "It consisted of a very light lever with the long arm ending in a writing point. The long arm was not quite counterweighted by a fixed load on the short arm, but when in addition a small wire was hung on the end of the short arm it slightly overbalanced the other side. The wire was so arranged that it dipped into a small glass tube containing a few drops of blood freshly taken from the running stream in an artery. A check on the long arm prevented the heavier short arm from falling. When the check was lifted, however, the short arm fell and the wire descended into the blood as the writing point rose and wrote a record [on a revolving kymograph]. This showed that the blood had not clotted. The check was then restored; a minute later it was again lifted and again a record was written. The process was repeated thus at regular intervals. As soon as the blood clotted it supported the light wire and, now, when the check was raised, the heavier long arm did not rise and the fact that the blood had turned to a jelly was registered on the recording surface." *Way of an Investigator*, p. 59.

51. *Way of an Investigator*, p. 58. Cannon devoted an entire chapter to "The Role of Hunches" in his memoir, giving further instances of sudden revelations in his own work as well as in that of other scientists. See also 1913 Diary, Oct. 15.

52. 1913 Diary, Oct. 20–21.

53. W. B. Cannon and W. L. Mendenhall, "Factors Affecting the Coagulation Time of Blood. I. The Graphic Method of Recording Coagulation Used in These Experiments," *Am. J. Physiol.* 34 (1914):225–231.

54. 1913 Diary, Nov. 19.

55. W. B. Cannon and Horace Gray, "Factors Affecting the Coagulation Time of Blood. II. The Hastening or Retarding of Coagulation by Adrenalin Injections," *Am. J. Physiol.* 34 (1914):232–242. Cannon also put Gray to work on another study in the coagulation series with a fellow fourth-year student, Lawrence K. Lunt; this study resulted in "V. The Effects of Hemorrhage before and after Exclusion of Abdominal Circulation, Adrenals, or Intestines," *Am. J. Physiol.* 34 (1914):331–351.

56. The work with Mendenhall resulted in two further parts of the coagulation studies: "III. The Hastening of Coagulation by Splanchnic Nerves" and "IV. The Hastening of Coagulation in Pain and Emotional Excitement," *Am. J. Physiol.* 34 (1914):243–250 and 251–261.

57. W. McDougall, *An Introduction to Social Psychology* (London: Methuen, 1908). A great popular success, this work went through a number of editions

over the next several years. In the preface to his second edition, the author named William James as an inspiration for many of his ideas, including the nature of instinct and conation and their role in mental life. For more on McDougall, see further *A History of Psychology in Autobiography*, vol. I, ed. Carl Murchison (Worcester, Mass.: Clark University Press, 1930), pp. 191–223.

58. McDougall, *Introduction to Social Psychology*, pp. 49, 59.

59. W. B. Cannon, "The Emergency Function of the Adrenal Medulla in Pain and the Major Emotions," *Am. J. Physiol.* 33 (1914):356–372; see esp. p. 372.

60. G. N. Stewart, *A Manual of Physiology, with Practical Exercises*, 7th ed. (New York: William Wood, 1914), p. 643.

18. Beyond the Boundaries of Physiological Inquiry

1. *Boston Herald*, Jan. 5, 1914. See also Cannon's 1914 Diary, Jan. 4–5.

2. Letter signed with initials "A. M. B." addressed to Prof. W. B. Cannon, Jan. 6, 1914; see also Cannon to Ralph Barton ("Tom") Perry, Jan. 8, 1914. Both in Scrapbook in Cannon Papers; see esp. pp. 5–9.

3. A summary of Cannon's address to the American Psychological Association, New Haven, Dec. 31, 1913, was published as "Recent Studies of Bodily Effects of Fear, Rage, and Pain," *Journal of Philosophy, Psychology, and Scientific Methods* 11 (1914):162–165; for his remarks on McDougall, see esp. p. 164. A few months later an almost identical summary of Cannon's work, "The Utility of Bodily Changes in Fear, Rage, and Pain," appeared in the *Harvard Graduates' Magazine* 22 (1914):570–573.

4. James published his ideas first in an article, "What Is an Emotion?" in *Mind* 9 (1884):188–205, and later in Chapter 25, The Emotions, in his *Principles of Psychology*, vol. II (New York: Henry Holt, 1890) pp. 442–485.

5. In 1885, one year after James's original article in *Mind*, Carl Georg Lange, professor of pathological anatomy at the University of Copenhagen, presented independent evidence in support of his theory in a monograph published in Danish. A German translation, *Ueber Gemüthsbewegungen, uebersetzt von H. Kurella*, appeared in Leipzig in 1887, and from this George Dumas made in 1895 a French translation that ran through several editions. Several years later Knight Dunlap gathered together and reprinted the classic papers that formed the basis for what had become known as the James–Lange theory in the volume *The Emotions* (Baltimore: Williams & Wilkins, 1922). For a more comprehensive assessment of James's views by Cannon, see further his article, "The James–Lange Theory of Emotions: A Critical Examination and an Alternative Theory," *American Journal of Psychology* 39 (1927):106–124.

6. W. B. Cannon, "The Nature and Composition of Emotion," 102-page thesis written for Philosophy 5, May 15, 1895, Cannon Papers.

7. W. B. Cannon, "The Interrelations of Emotions as Suggested by

Recent Physiological Researches," *American Journal of Psychology* 25 (1914):252–282; see esp. p. 280.

8. 1914 Diary, Jan. 28. For more on Cannon's—as well as the English physiologist C. S. Sherrington's—differences with James, see further James R. Angell, "A Reconsideration of James's Theory of Emotion in the Light of Recent Criticisms," *Psychological Review* 23 (1916):251–261.

9. Cannon to J. McKeen Cattell, Oct. 2, 1914, Cattell Papers. Cattell's earlier criticism, raised at a meeting of the American Philosophical Society in April 1911, had emphasized the disabling and paralyzing effect of some emotions, especially that of fear, which did not appear to fit in with the "fight or flight" theory. Cannon concluded his letter, "If there are serious blunders in my suggestions from the point of view of the psychologists, I should be glad to know of them. I am not a psychologist, and really should tread more cautiously than I have hitherto in a realm that is foreign to me."

10. Ibid. See also Cannon to Cattell, May 29, 1914 and April 8, 1915, Cattell Papers; 1914 Diary, July 13.

11. William James, "The Energies of Men," *Memories and Studies* (New York: Longmans, Green and Co., 1912), pp. 229–264.

12. Cannon to Norman Hapgood, May 5, 1914, Cannon Papers.

13. 1914 Diary, July 5 and 8.

14. 1914 Diary, Aug. 4. Henderson had delivered the Lowell Lectures the previous year in connection with publication of his book *The Fitness of the Environment: An Inquiry into the Biological Significance of the Properties of Matter* (New York: Macmillan, 1913).

15. 1914 Diary, Sept. 17. For Cannon's comments on the war news, see diary notes for July 30, Aug. 4, 5, and 9.

16. William James, "The Moral Equivalent of War," *Memories and Studies*, pp. 267–296.

17. W. B. Cannon, "Wesley M. Carpenter Lecture: The Physiologic Equivalent of War," *JAMA* 63 (1914):1415–16. In his book *Bodily Changes in Pain, Hunger, Fear, and Rage* (New York & London: Appleton, 1915), Cannon supplied more detail for the examinations he and C. H. Fiske of the biological chemistry department had conducted of twenty-five Harvard football players after the final and most exciting game of the season (pp. 75–76); for more on his observations at athletic games, see also pp. 219–222.

18. W. B. Cannon, "Carpenter Lecture," p. 1416.

19. 1914 Diary, Sept. 27; see also Sept. 18, 23, and 25.

20. Cannon's "Carpenter Lecture" was published in excerpted form in the Oct. 17, 1914, issue of *JAMA* in a report on "Society Proceedings."

21. J. M. Cattell to McKeen Cattell, Oct. 2, 1914, Cattell Papers. "But," Cattell added, "they are doing good work on this subject in his laboratory."

22. Beginning on Nov. 23, 1914, Cannon gave a series of six lectures for the Lowell Institute; see further loose-leaf notes accompanied by printed program, "Lowell Institute, 1914–15, Lectures on Bodily Changes under Emotional Excitement by Walter B. Cannon, M.D.," Cannon Papers. See also clippings from the *Boston Transcript* on p. 8 of Scrapbook, Cannon Papers.

23. Cannon to Theodore Lyman, Dec. 24, 1928, Greene Papers. For a

lively account of another club in which Cannon enjoyed association with his Harvard colleagues, see further J. D. Greene, "The Tuesday Evening Club," *Harvard Alumni Bulletin* (Jan. 14, 1956).

24. A selection of reviews and press notices may be found in Cannon's Scrapbook, pp. 5–6, Cannon Papers. The popular appeal of the subject matter caused the book to receive wide coverage in newspaper and magazine reviews and articles. An especially lengthy review in *Science* (n.s. 42 [1915]: 696–700) by James R. Angell coupled Cannon's book with George W. Crile's *The Origin and Nature of the Emotions, Miscellaneous Papers*; another by Richard C. Cabot in *The Survey* (36 [1916]: 292–293) was a group review of Isador H. Coriat's *The Meaning of Dreams*, H. Addington Bruce's *Sleep and Sleeplessness*, James J. Putnam's *Human Motives*, and Cannon's *Bodily Changes in Pain, Hunger, Fear and Rage*. Shorter reviews by unidentified writers appeared in *JAMA, BM&SJ, The Nation, Independent Woman*, and other periodicals.

25. See, e.g., exchange of letters between W. C. Alvarez and Cannon, July 21 and Aug. 2, 1915, Cannon Papers. For more on Alvarez, see further his autobiography, *Incurable Physician* (Englewood Cliffs, N.J.: Prentice-Hall, 1963).

26. Joseph Jastrow to Cannon, May 8, 1915, Cannon Papers.

27. Cannon's handwritten reply of Aug. 20, 1915 is in the Yerkes Papers, but unfortunately Yerkes's letter to Cannon has not been located.

28. Cartoons and clippings in Cannon's Line-a-Day Diary, 1911–15; also p. 10 of Cannon's Scrapbook. Both in Cannon Papers.

29. Arthur B. Reeve, "The Social Gangster," *Cosmopolitan*, Nov. 1915, pp. 753–764; Reeve, *The Social Gangster* [and other stories] in the Craig Kennedy Series (New York & London: Harper & Bros., 1916), pp. 22–24.

30. Typical of this viewpoint are Francois Aran, "De la nature et du traitement de l'affection connue sous le nom de goître exophthalmique, cachexie exophthalmique, maladie de Basedow, etc.," *Archives générales de Médecine*, I (1861):106–108; Edmond Hiffelsheim, "Considerations sur la nature du goître exophthalmique," *Gazette Hebdomadaire de Médecine et de Chirurgie* 9 (1862):468; Albertus Eulenburg and Paul Guttmann, "Die Pathologie des Sympathicus," *Archiv für Psychiatrie und Nervenkrankheiten* 1 (1868–69):420–453. For a brief historical account of the evolution of the nervous hypothesis, see further H. D. Rolleston, *The Endocrine Organs in Health and Disease* (London: Oxford University Press, 1936), pp. 223–224.

31. See, e.g., P. J. Moebius, "Ueber das Wesen der Basedow'schen Krankheit," *Centralblatt für Nervenheilkunde, Psychiatrie und gerichtliche Psychopathologie* 10 (1887):225–229. For a brief historical note on the evolution of the thyroid hypothesis, see further Rolleston, *Endocrine Organs*, pp. 224–225.

32. H. Eppinger, W. Falta, and C. Rudinger, "Ueber die Wechselwirkungen der Drüsen mit innerer Sekretion," *Zeitschrift für Klinische Medizin* 66 (1908):1–52; A. Fraenkel, "Über den Gehalt des Blutes an Adrenalin bei chronischer Nephritis und Morbus Basedowii," *Archiv für Experimentelle Pathologie und Pharmakologie* 60 (1909):395–407.

33. W. B. Cannon, C. A. L. Binger, and R. Fitz, "Experimental Hyperthyroidism," *Am. J. Physiol.* 36 (1915):363–364; W. B. Cannon and R. Fitz,

"Results of Overactivity of the Cervical Sympathetic," *Transactions of the Association of American Physicians* 30 (1915):302–303. These two articles are virtually identical, but the one in *Transactions* is followed by a discussion between S. Solis-Cohen and Cannon on pp. 303–304. At the end of 1915 Cannon and Fitz reported on "Further Observations on Overactivity of the Cervical Sympathetic" at the twenty-eighth annual meeting of the American Physiological Society in Boston; see further *Am. J. Physiol.* 40 (1916):126.

34. 1913 Diary, March 26 and April 3. For more on Cushing, see further John F. Fulton, *Harvey Cushing, A Biography* (Springfield, Ill.: C. C. Thomas, 1946); Elizabeth H. Thomson, *Harvey Cushing: Surgeon, Author, Artist* (New York: Henry Schuman, 1950). For a history of surgery of the peripheral nerves, see further Kenneth M. Browne, "Surgery of the Peripheral Nerves," *A History of Neurological Surgery*, ed. A. Earl Walker (Baltimore: Williams & Wilkins, 1951), pp. 396–424.

35. 1914 Diary, see esp. April 10 and 15.

36. 1914 Diary, e.g., April 20, 22, 23, 24, 28, 30.

37. 1914 Diary, see esp. May 2 and 21.

38. 1914 Diary, Oct. 3; see also Sept. 29 and 30, and Oct. 2.

39. 1914 Diary, Oct. 20. Fitz, son of Reginald Herber Fitz, had received his M.D. degree from Harvard in 1909 and was affiliated with the Medical Clinic of the Brigham Hospital. In 1914–15 he also served as a fellow in the physiology department. See further R. Fitz, "Certain Aspects of the Medical History of Exophthalmic Goitre," *BM&SJ* 170 (1914):675–680.

40. 1914 Diary, Oct. 22. Reid Hunt, who had formerly been associated with Cannon as a member of the AMA Council in Defense of Medical Research when he was at the U.S. Public Health Service, came to Harvard as professor of pharmacology in the fall of 1913.

41. Cannon, Binger, and Fitz, "Experimental Hyperthyroidism," pp. 363–364; Cannon and Fitz, "Overactivity of the Cervical Sympathetic," pp. 302–303.

42. 1914 Diary, Oct. 27. John Homans and David Cheever (both sons of illustrious Boston clinicians) were the nucleus of Harvey Cushing's general surgical team at the Brigham Hospital. For an account of Homans's earlier experience as an assistant to Cushing in Baltimore doing experimental work on the pituitary, see his remembrance in Fulton's *Harvey Cushing*, pp. 280–282.

43. Cannon to Keen, Nov. 2, 1914. Later that month, on Nov. 20, Cannon reported to Keen again: "I am quite convinced now that the experimental work which I mentioned in my last letter has thrown exophthalmic goiter into the experimental field. And if all goes well, we shall have diabetes there, too, but this last statement, as you recognize, is only a prophecy. Do you wonder that I have been rather excited by the way things are going?" Both letters in Keen Papers.

44. 1914 Diary, Nov. 6.

45. "Medical Meeting in the Amphitheatre of the Peter Bent Brigham Hospital," *BM&SJ* 174 (1916):138–139.

46. See 1914 Diary, March 31.

47. W. M. Bayliss and J. R. Bradford, "On the Electrical Changes Accompanying Secretion," Proceedings of the Physiological Society, March 21, 1885, in *Journal of Physiology* 6 (1885):xiii–xiv.

48. W. B. Cannon and McK. Cattell, "Studies on the Conditions of Activity in Endocrine Glands: I. The Electrical Response as an Index of Glandular Action," *Am. J. Physiol.* 41 (1916):39–57.

49. W. B. Cannon and McK. Cattell, "Studies on the Conditions of Activity in Endocrine Glands: II. The Secretory Innervation of the Thyroid Gland," *Am. J. Physiol.* 41 (1916):58–73.

50. Ibid., p. 71.

51. W. B. Cannon and McK. Cattell, "Studies on the Conditions of Activity in Endocrine Glands: III. The Influence of the Adrenal Secretion on the Thyroid," *Am. J. Physiol.* 41 (1916):74–78.

52. Eppinger et al., "Ueber die Wechselwirkungen der Drüsen mit innerer Sekretion."

53. An abstract of Cannon's presentation, "Some Recent Investigations on Ductless Glands," was published in the *Johns Hopkins Hospital Bulletin* 27 (1916):247–248.

54. Cannon's lecture, "A New Concept of Diseases Having Emotional Elements," and the discussion that followed were published in *Vermont Medicine* I (1916):61–66; see esp. p. 65.

55. Cannon's lecture, "Some Disorders Supposed to Have an Emotional Origin," and the discussion that followed were published in *New York Medical Journal* 104 (1916):870–873.

56. Ibid., p. 873.

57. Cannon's address, "Results of Recent Studies on Ductless Glands," and an abstract of the discussion that followed were published in *JAMA* 67 (1916):1483–84.

58. Cannon and Cattell, "II. The Secretory Innervation of the Thyroid Gland," p. 71.

59. Cannon to C. W. Eliot, Nov. 21, 1916, Cannon Papers. For a later evaluation of the importance of Cannon's contributions to an understanding of the physiology of the emotions, see Philip Bard's outstanding overview, "The Neuro-humoral Basis of Emotional Reactions," in *A Handbook of General Experimental Psychology*, ed. Carl Murchison (Worcester, Mass.: Clark University Press, 1934), pp. 264–311.

19. Hard Choices and Conflicts of Interest

1. Several years later in a letter to Cannon, Robert W. Lovett, professor of orthopedic surgery at Harvard, compared these turbulent times to another critical moment in Medical School history when he told him, "the one thing the School needs most is men like you." And he continued, "I wonder if you realize what an influence you have been there, and how often you are quoted and referred to in matters connected with the School policy and the School's future." Lovett to Cannon, Sept. 30, 1920, Cannon Papers.

2. Abraham Flexner, *Medical Education in the United States and Canada: A Report to the Carnegie Foundation for the Advancement of Teaching* (New York: Carnegie Foundation Bulletin No. 4, 1910), pp. 22–38; see esp. pp. 25–26. For more on Flexner's Bulletin No. 4, see further *Abraham Flexner, An Autobiography* (New York: Simon & Schuster, 1960), pp. 73–88; Carleton B. Chapman, "The Flexner Report by Abraham Flexner," *Daedalus* (Winter 1974):105–117; Howard S. Berliner, "New Light on the Flexner Report: Notes on the AMA-Carnegie Foundation Background," *Bulletin of the History of Medicine* 51 (1977):603–609; Daniel M. Fox, "Abraham Flexner's Unpublished Report: Foundations and Medical Education, 1909–28," *Bulletin of the History of Medicine* 54 (1980):475–496.

3. A. L. Lowell to A. Flexner, Oct. 17, 1911, in fd. 434, Lowell Papers.

4. Flexner to Lowell, Oct. 18, 1911, in fd. 434, Lowell Papers.

5. For Lowell's understanding with Bevan, see further A. D. Bevan to E. H. Bradford, Dec. 17, 1912, and Lowell to Bevan, Oct. 31, 1913, both in fd. 1066, Lowell Papers.

6. Bevan to Lowell, Nov. 10, 1913, and Lowell to Bevan, Nov. 13, 1913, both in fd. 1066, Lowell Papers. See also A. L. Lowell, "The Danger to the Maintenance of High Standards from Excessive Formalism," read before the tenth annual Conference of the Council on Medical Education, Feb. 24, 1914, *JAMA* 62 (1914):823–826; March 1914 correspondence with E. H. Gruening and Hugh Cabot, in fd. 1063, Lowell Papers.

7. Christian reiterated his opposition to the two-year admissions plan in a letter to Lowell, Jan. 12, 191[3], in fd. 1066, Lowell Papers.

8. Harvard University Medical Faculty, Minutes of meeting for Feb. 3, 1913, HMA. Despite the opposition of H. C. Ernst, Cannon's motion carried by a vote of 25 to 13. See also editorial "Higher Preliminary Qualifications Assured," in *JAMA* 60 (1913):756.

9. Eliot to J. C. Warren, Jan. 21, 1913, Eliot Papers.

10. 1913 Diary, Jan. 21. Only a short time earlier Cannon had been chosen to serve with Kittredge and others on the first Board of Syndics for the newly established Harvard University Press. See further "The Harvard University Press," *Harvard Alumni Bulletin* for Jan. 29, 1913; also Cannon's diary entries for Jan. 15 and 23, 1913.

11. Cannon's discussions of the admissions policy may be followed in his 1913 Diary entries, for example, Jan. 20–22, 29–30, Feb. 4, 7, 9–10. One of the friends with whom he discussed the new policy was Robert Yerkes, as evidenced by an exchange of letters between Yerkes and A. Flexner, Jan. 24 and 25, 1913, in the Yerkes file, GEB Papers.

12. 1913 Diary, Feb. 15 and 17.

13. Upon receipt of his brother's letter, Dean Thayer promptly sent copies to Lowell and other members of the council. See further W. S. Thayer to E. Thayer, undated, enclosed in E. Thayer to Lowell, March 14, 1913, and other letters from William and Ezra Thayer in fd. 1066, Lowell Papers.

14. 1913 Diary, Feb. 18 and 19.

15. Vincent had assumed the presidency of Minnesota in 1911 but waited two years before he took any action with regard to medical education. He

then asked each member of the medical faculty, including the dean, to submit a resignation. See further M. B. Visscher, "A Medical School Dean Ahead of His Time," *Elias Potter Lyon: Minnesota's Leader in Medical Education*, ed. Owen H. Wangensteen (St. Louis: Warren H. Green, 1981), esp. pp. 15–17, 22–23.

16. Vincent's original offer of the deanship apparently proposed that Cannon take charge of the anatomy department, but this error was soon corrected. See, for example, Cannon to G. E. Vincent, Feb. 17, 1913, and Vincent to Cannon, March 6, 1913, both in Cannon Papers; also 1913 Diary, Feb. 20.

17. See further scattered entries in Cannon's 1913 Diary, Feb. 23 to March 26; Petition to the Dean of the Harvard Medical School from members of the Third, Second, and First Year Classes, undated, Cannon Papers; exchange of letters between Cannon and Lowell, March 11 and 14, 1913, Lowell Papers.

18. Cannon to Vincent, March 12, 1913, Cannon Papers. Cannon made clear in his letter that he was convinced the two tasks of laboratory investigation and administration were incompatible, that inevitably it was the research that would have to be abandoned. This, in fact, was what happened to E. P. Lyon, who accepted the post that Cannon declined; see further Visscher, "A Medical School Dean Ahead of His Time," pp. 22, 26.

19. Christian to Lowell, March 20, 1913; Lowell to Christian, March 21, 1913; Lowell to Bradford, March 21, 1913; all in fd. 1079, Lowell Papers. See also Vincent to Cannon, March 17, 1913, Cannon Papers; 1913 Diary, March 18, 20, 21.

20. 1913 Diary, April 5.

21. 1913 Diary, April 6. Bowditch, too, had referred to the study of the medical sciences as "a means of general culture and mental discipline," in his article, "The Medical School of the Future" (reprinted in *Medical Research and Education*, ed. J. M. Cattell, New York, 1913); see esp. p. 516.

22. Lowell to R. P. Strong, June 5, 1913, fd. 1168, Lowell Papers. For more on passage of the new policy, see further Medical Faculty, Minutes of meetings for May 2 and June 13, 1913; also *Annual Reports*, 1912–13, pp. 16–20.

23. This story may be followed in Cannon's 1913 Diary, March 13, May 21, 22, and 23.

24. For more on the invention of full time, as originally proposed by Mall and promoted by Welch for the improvement of clinical opportunities at Hopkins, see further Florence R. Sabin, *Franklin Paine Mall: The Story of a Mind* (Baltimore: Johns Hopkins University Press, 1934), pp. 254ff; Alan M. Chesney, *The Johns Hopkins Hospital and The Johns Hopkins University School of Medicine: A Chronicle*, vol. III (Baltimore: Johns Hopkins University Press, 1963), pp. 123–134. Further discussions of the establishment of full time at Hopkins may be found in Simon Flexner and James T. Flexner, *William Henry Welch and the Heroic Age of American Medicine* (New York: Viking Press, 1941), pp. 297–328; Donald Fleming, *William H. Welch and the Rise of Modern Medicine* (Boston: Little, Brown, 1954), pp. 161–180.

25. Exchange of letters between F. T. Gates and W. H. Welch, Jan. 1911, published in Chesney's *Chronicle*, III:131–134.

26. Chesney, *Chronicle*, III:134–136. For a further description of this event and subsequent developments, see also Abraham Flexner's *Autobiography*, pp. 109–115.

27. Flexner, *Autobiography*, p. 74.

28. Ibid., pp. 112–113; Chesney, *Chronicle*, III:136–137. Flexner's report on the Johns Hopkins Medical School is reproduced in full as Appendix B in Chesney's *Chronicle*, III:287–309.

29. Flexner, *Autobiography*, pp. 114–115; Chesney, *Chronicle*, III:138–140. A letter in opposition to the plan from William Osler to Ira Remsen, President of Johns Hopkins, Sept. 1, 1911, is reproduced in Chesney's *Chronicle*, III:176–183.

30. See further memorandum from F. T. Gates to J. D. Rockefeller, Aug. 1911, enclosed with JDR, Jr., to his father, Aug. 2, 1911, Gates Papers.

31. Eliot to Lowell, Jan. 27, 1913, Eliot Papers. The single exception to the rejections had been a grant in aid of establishing the Business School in 1907–08. For more on Harvard's requests for aid from the Board, see further materials in GEB Papers, series 1107a; exchange of letters between Eliot and Lowell, May 1911, Eliot Papers.

32. For more on Eliot's trip around the world in 1912, see Henry James, *Charles W. Eliot: President of Harvard University, 1869–1909* (Boston: Houghton Mifflin, 1930), II:214–228. Greene revealed the extent of his ignorance when he set forth his ideas for the improvement of clinical instruction in a letter to Wallace Buttrick, March 31, 1913; in fd. 6486, GEB Papers.

33. For Christian's previous efforts to upgrade clinical education at the Medical School, see copy of his letter to George Shattuck, chairman of the Visiting Committee, Dec. 20, 1910, regarding the need to establish an endowment for the clinical departments at HMS, and other materials in fd. 1091, Lowell Papers; "Overseers Committee to Visit Medical School, 1912–13," AA267 file, HMA.

34. Christian's proposal was contained in a statement sent to Eliot, Feb. 17, 1913; see further Christian/GEB.

35. Christian specifically asked for funding to pay the salaries of fifteen young assistants in the various clinical departments, at the rate of $2,000–$2,500 per year for five years, so that they would be able to put all of their efforts into research, teaching, and the care of hospital patients. "Without such men," he wrote, "Harvard University cannot develop the clinical branches of medicine as university subjects." As for permitting clinical professors to have consultative practices, there was precedent for Christian's argument. In 1904 a medical faculty committee had recommended that the heads of some of the clinical branches, notably the professors of medicine and of surgery, be required to give their entire time to teaching, research, and care of hospital patients, with the following exception: "Because direct contact with other than hospital patients is undoubtedly beneficial, such consultation practice should be accepted as would not interfere with the efficacy of teaching and research of the individual." See "Further Report of the Committee on University Education in Medicine" (p. 7) and discussion in the Minutes of Medical Faculty, Jan. 9, 1904.

36. Eliot to Christian, March 2, 1913; Christian/GEB.

37. Lowell to Bradford, March 5, 1913, fd. 1090, Lowell Papers; Christian to Eliot, March 8, 1913, Christian/GEB; exchange of letters between Christian and Lowell, March 26 and 27, 1913, Christian Papers.

38. See, for example, Eliot to Christian, March 6 and 10, 1913; Greene to Christian, March 24, 1913; Christian to Buttrick, and revised proposal, both March 28, 1913; Greene to Christian, May 16 and 23, 1913; all in Christian/GEB.

39. Buttrick to Christian, May 24, 1913, and Christian to Edsall, May 29, 1913; both in Christian/GEB. See also Christian to Bradford, May 29, 1913, Christian Papers.

40. A. Flexner, *Medical Education,* p. 240. In his assessment of the Medical School of Harvard University, Flexner had noted that the laboratory facilities were "unexcelled in equipment and organization, in respect to both teaching and research," but expressed serious reservations about the clinical facilities and especially the relations of the various hospitals with the University.

41. Exchange of letters between Flexner and Christian, June 26 and 27, 1913; see also Christian to Bradford, June 30, 1913, and another exchange of letters between Christian and Flexner, July 8 and 9, 1913; all in Christian/GEB.

42. See further heavy flow of correspondence between Flexner and Welch, Williams, and Howland throughout the summer of 1913, fd. 6262, GEB Papers.

43. Flexner to Welch, Oct. 6, 1913: "The Board meets on the 23rd and will, I believe, be ready to take prompt and final action if the proposition is in shape." See also telegram from Welch to Flexner, Oct. 19, 1913, and Flexner's undated night-letter reply. All in fd. 6262, GEB Papers.

44. See further Flexner to Christian, Sept. 25, 1913; Christian to Flexner, Sept. 30 and Oct. 2, 1913; and esp. Christian to Eliot, Nov. 1, 1913, which recapitulates the course of negotiations with the Rockefeller officers; all in Christian/GEB.

45. "Report of the Committee Appointed to Consider the Subject of Medical Education, Oct. 23, 1913," fd. 6486, GEB Papers.

46. Buttrick to Welch, Oct. 29, 1913, fd. 6262, GEB Papers. For more on the Hopkins application, see further Chesney, *Chronicle,* III:244–251.

47. Memorandum from Gates to Rockefeller, Aug. 1911, Gates Papers.

48. See esp. exchange of letters between Lowell and Jerome Greene, Oct. 31 and Nov. 1, 1913; Green to Christian, Oct. 31 and Nov. 3, 1913; Christian to Eliot (copies sent to Lowell and Greene), Nov. 1, 1913; Lowell to Christian, Nov. 3, 1913; all in Christian/GEB. Further correspondence between Christian and Lowell may be found in fd. 1102, Lowell Papers. See also series of letters between Greene and Lowell, Oct. 25–30, 1913, fd. 1103, Lowell Papers.

49. 1913 Diary, Oct. 26; see also entries for Oct. 27 and 28; Eliot to Christian, Oct. 31, 1913, Christian/GEB.

50. W. T. Councilman to A. Flexner, Oct. 28, 1913. Councilman could be depended on to provide Flexner with an inside view of Harvard's educational policies. Indeed, he had served such a function during Flexner's

educational survey for the Carnegie Foundation. On June 14, 1913, Councilman wrote a scathing criticism of the administration of the Medical School, referring to Christian as a dean who had "used the entire influence of his office to effect his personal advancement" and to Bradford as well-meaning but "incapable of either recognizing or correcting an evil." "I have no apologies for what I write though my actions would be condemned by most," he ended his letter to Flexner. "We can have the best there is . . . and we gain it best by a frank outside criticism of conditions." Both letters in fd. 6486, GEB Papers.

51. Lowell to Jerome Greene, Nov. 1, Nov. 15, Dec. 1, 1913; all in fd. 1103, Lowell Papers. See also Cannon's 1913 Diary, Dec. 5; Minutes of Medical Faculty, Dec. 5, 1913.

52. See, e.g., Lowell to Christian, Nov. 3, 1913, Christian/GEB; Lowell to Flexner, Jan. 19, 1914, fd. 1103, Lowell Papers.

53. For Edsall's views, see his letters in fd. 1105, Lowell Papers, for example, Dec. 11, 1913, Jan. 19 and April 15, 1914. At the same time, Edsall was concerned lest Flexner misunderstand his position and think he was against full time; see further Edsall/Flexner correspondence, Jan. 22–31, 1914, fd. 6486, GEB Papers.

54. Christian to Lowell, Jan. 6, 1914; see also Christian to Lowell, Jan. 8 and 9, 1914; all in Christian/GEB.

55. See Cannon's 1913 Diary, Dec. 17. Higginson reported his conversation with Cushing in a letter to H. P. Walcott, Oct. 31, 1913, Walcott Papers.

56. Harvey Cushing to Lowell, April 1, 1914, fd. 1105, Lowell Papers.

57. See, e.g., exchange of letters between Lowell and Flexner, April 14 and 15, 1914, fd. 6486, GEB Papers. Bradford's letter to Lowell is in fd. 1105, Lowell Papers.

58. The course of these discussions may be followed in Cannon's diary notes: entires for Nov. 18, Dec. 5, 11, and 17, 1913, and for Jan. 17 and 30, 1914. Cannon also noted that he talked about the full-time scheme with L. J. Henderson (Dec. 7, 1913) and with Councilman, who blamed Christian for Harvard's failure to get funds from the GEB (Dec. 11–12, 1913). For a statement reflecting Cannon's views on full time, see the report he prepared with F. S. Lee and R. M. Pearce, "Medical Research in Its Relation to Medical Schools," in *Proceedings* of the Twenty-Seventh Annual Meeting of the Association of American Medical Colleges, 1917, pp. 19–31; see esp. p. 25.

59. 1914 Diary, Jan. 18. Cannon became president of the American Physiological Society at its twenty-sixth annual meeting in Philadelphia, Dec. 28–30, 1913. This meeting marked the beginning of the second quarter century of the society; see further C. W. Greene's account in *History of the American Physiological Society Semicentennial, 1887–1937* (Baltimore, 1938), pp. 90–96.

60. Ibid., pp. 80–81. For an earlier report on the *Am. J. Physiol.*, see also Minutes of the Council of the American Physiological Society meeting for Dec. 27, 1912.

61. For details concerning the transfer of the journal to the society, see further 1914 correspondence between Joseph Erlanger, Cannon, and other council members in the Erlanger Papers.

62. 1914 Diary, Jan. 20.

63. For Cannon's role in this cooperative effort, see his 1914 Diary, Jan. 26, Feb. 2, 5, 6, 15, 23, 24, March 14 and 31. For an appreciation of Porter's service as founder and editor of the journal, see also frontispiece to vol. 37 (1915) of the *Am. J. Physiol.*

64. 1914 Diary, April 16 and 17. Bradford to Lowell, April 17, 1914, fd. 1090, Lowell Papers. For more on the appointment of Lee, see also *Annual Reports*, 1913–14, p. 12; *Harvard Graduates' Magazine* 23 (1914–15):359–361.

65. See esp. Christian to Lowell, April 24, 1912, enclosing and supporting a statement from Edsall about the desirability of bringing Howland to Harvard, in fd. 1139, Lowell Papers.

66. T. M. Rotch to A. L. Lowell, Nov. 15, 1913, fd. 1105, Lowell Papers. Shattuck's recommendation and other letters concerning the appointment of Morse, which did not become official until the following year, may be found in fd. 1132, Lowell Papers.

67. Abraham Flexner, for one, was highly critical of Morse's appointment; see, for example, his *Autobiography*, pp. 200–201. The determining consideration in Morse's appointment, Eliot later wrote Flexner, was that the pediatrics department "had no endowment or income whatever, and no resources except a valuable clinic in the adjoining Children's Hospital. Dr. Morse was in possession of that clinic." Eliot to Flexner, Nov. 1, 1916, fd. 6487, GEB Papers.

68. 1914 Diary, April 29. A few weeks later Eliot wrote Jerome Greene: "Rosenau told me yesterday that the situation at the Medical School seemed to him hopeless and that Cannon was profoundly discouraged—so much so that he stayed away from faculty meetings." Eliot to Greene, May 15, 1914, box 261, GEB Papers. For more on the events leading to Theobald Smith's departure from Harvard, see further exchange of letters between George Fabyan and Lowell, June 17 and July 1, 1915, fd. 381, 2nd series, Lowell Papers; also letters in fd. 1160, Lowell Papers.

69. Exchange of letters between Greene and Eliot, May 14 and 15, 1914, box 261, GEB Papers.

70. See Edsall to Lowell, Jan. 19 and April 15, 1914; also undated, untitled Edsall memorandum enclosed with Lowell to Edsall, April 23, 1914; all in fd. 1105, Lowell Papers. For more on Edsall's views on full time and his plan for the MGH, see further J. C. Aub and Ruth Hapgood, *Pioneer in Modern Medicine: David Linn Edsall of Harvard* (Boston: Harvard Medical Alumni Association, 1970), pp. 170–176.

71. Edsall's memorandum was enclosed with Lowell to Abraham Flexner, April 23, 1914, to which Flexner replied on May 1, 1914. For more on the MGH proposal, see also Simon Flexner to Abraham Flexner, May 2, 1914; A. Flexner to Starr Murphy, May 11, 1914; Lowell to A. Flexner, May 26, 1914; all in fd. 6486, GEB Papers.

72. Lowell to Cushing, July 10, 1914, published in John Fulton, *Harvey Cushing: A Biography* (Springfield, Ill.: C. C. Thomas, 1946), pp. 380–381; Lowell to A. Flexner, June 30, 1914, fd. 6486, GEB Papers.

73. For Cushing's reply, see Fulton, *Harvey Cushing*, p. 381; for an earlier exchange between Cushing and Lowell, see also letters of April 1 and 4, 1914, fd. 1105, Lowell Papers.

74. Christian to Lowell, July 18, 1914; see also Lowell to Christian, July 24, 1914; both in Christian/GEB.

75. Greene to Lowell, Oct. 25 and 27, 1913, both in fd. 1103, Lowell Papers. To Christian, Greene offered an apologia for the Board's action and held out hope for another chance in the future; see further Greene to Christian, Oct. 31, Nov. 3, and Nov. 22, 1913, all in Christian/GEB.

76. Greene to Christian, Nov. 24, 1914, Christian/GEB.

77. Christian to Greene, Nov. 24, 1914; see also Greene to Christian, Nov. 30, 1914; both in Christian/GEB. Edsall came to Christian's defense, as may be seen in his exchange of letters with Greene, Nov. 24 and 25, 1914, fd. 6486, GEB Papers. For an account of the Harvard negotiations up to this time from another viewpoint, see also letter from Abraham Flexner to Harry Pratt Judson, Dec. 29, 1914, endorsed by Wallace Buttrick, fd. 6486, GEB Papers.

78. See Lowell to Cushing, March 6, 1915, fd. 60, 2nd series, Lowell Papers; Cushing to Flexner, March 6, 1915, and Cushing to Lowell, March 7, 1915, both in fd. 6487, GEB Papers.

79. Alexander Cochran to Lowell, April 15, 1915, fd. 60, Lowell Papers. This episode may be followed in Fulton's biography of Cushing, pp. 381–382; for Cushing's retrospective view some years later, see also pp. 382–384.

80. Eliot to Bradford, March 11, 1915; see also letters between Bradford and Eliot, March 12–27, 1915; all in Eliot Papers.

81. On May 12, 1915, a committee composed of Edsall, Rosenau, Reid Hunt, and Lowell filed formal application with the GEB for support of the establishment of a School of Tropical Medicine at Harvard; see further materials, in fd. 181, 2nd series, Lowell Papers. See also Jean Curran, *Founders of the Harvard School of Public Health . . . 1909–1946* (New York: Josiah Macy, Jr. Foundation, 1970), pp. 12–13.

82. Eliot to H. P. Walcott, July 17, 1915, Eliot Papers. Eliot told Walcott, who had accompanied Lowell to the New York meeting, "You were said to have made an instructive and attractive statement of the needs and desires of the Harvard School . . . President Lowell was said to have made a statement which was by no means attractive, and, indeed, repelled several—perhaps all—of the Rockefeller group who were present."

83. Report on an Institute of Hygiene from W. H. Welch and Wickliffe Rose, [May 1915], in series 200L, Rockefeller Foundation Papers. See also Eliot to Jerome Greene, May 29, 1915, and Eliot to H. P. Walcott, June 3, 1915; both in Eliot Papers.

84. Eliot, after attending meetings of two of the Rockefeller Boards in Maine, reported his conversation with Simon Flexner and other board members in his letter to Walcott of July 17, 1915. "Lowell's personal relations with Bradford," Walcott responded on July 24, "are so close that it would probably be very difficult to effect any changes without Bradford's hearty assent. Hav-

ing no question in my own mind as to Cannon's fitness for the place of dean, indeed thinking him the best man in sight I shall gladly do what I can to bring his appointment to pass." Both in Eliot Papers.

85. The above account is based on materials in fd. 844, 2nd series, Lowell Papers, and in series 200L, Rockefeller Foundation Papers.

86. See "Announcement of New Department of Preventive Medicine and Hygiene," *Harvard Graduates' Magazine* 18 (1909–10):36–38. For more on Rosenau and preventive medicine at Harvard, see further Curran's *Founders of the HSPH*, pp. xvii–xviii; H. K. Beecher and M. D. Altschule, *Medicine at Harvard: The First 300 Years* (Hanover, N.H.: University Press of New England, 1977), pp. 357–359.

87. For more on the establishment of the Harvard–M.I.T. School for Health Officers, see *Annual Reports*, 1912–13, pp. 20–21; *Harvard Graduates' Magazine* 22 (1913–14):55–58; Curran's *Founders of the HSPH*, pp. 1–8. See also Jerome Greene to Wickliffe Rose, Sept. 19, 1913, in series 200L, Rockefeller Foundation Papers.

88. For Strong's expeditions to South America and his Red Cross work in Serbia, see *Report of the First Expedition to South America, 1913* (Cambridge, Mass.: Harvard University Press, 1915), and *Typhus Fever with Particular Reference to the Serbian Epidemic* (Cambridge, Mass.: American Red Cross, 1920). For fuller discussion of Strong and the Department of Tropical Medicine, see also Curran, *Founders of the HSPH*, pp. 236–247.

89. See further "Minutes of Conference on Public Health, Harvard University, Nov. 3–5, 1915," 123-page transcript accompanied by schedule, in series 200L, Rockefeller Foundation Papers; "Exhibits" in support of the Harvard proposal transmitted to the GEB, Dec. 16, 1915, and other materials in fd. 844, 2nd series, Lowell Papers.

90. Greene to Eliot, Nov. 11, 1915; see also Eliot to Greene, Nov. 12, 1915, and Greene to Eliot, Nov. 16, 1915; all in series 200L, Rockefeller Foundation Papers.

91. "Institute of Public Health, Final Report of the General Education Board," Jan. 26, 1916, 10 pp., in series 200L, Rockefeller Foundation Papers. See also Flexner and Flexner's biography of Welch, pp. 353–364; Fleming's *Welch*, pp. 180–184; Curran, *Founders of the HSPH*, pp. 14–16. "Although the first attempt to secure funds for an endowed school of public health in Boston was unsuccessful," Curran notes, "the existing Harvard–M.I.T. School for Health Officers continued on its course." Among those admitted to the school in 1915 was the first woman student, Miss Linda James—the youngest sister of Cornelia James Cannon (p. 16).

92. Eliot to Flexner, Feb. 1, 1916, in series 200L, Rockefeller Foundation Papers.

93. Flexner to Eliot, 11 Feb 1916, in series 200L, Rockefeller Foundation Papers. For more on the Foundation's role in establishing the first endowed schools of public health, see further Greer Williams, "Schools of Public Health—Their Doing and Undoing," *Milbank Memorial Fund Quarterly* 54 (Fall 1976):489–525; and Elizabeth Fee, "Competition for the First School of Hygiene and Public Health," *Bulletin of the History of Medicine* 57 (Fall 1983):339–363.

94. Morse's appointment to the chair of pediatrics had become official early in 1916. In addition, after the death of C. S. Minot late in 1915, the administration elected to leave the Stillman professorship vacant and instead promoted three junior staff members, John Warren, J. L. Bremer, and F. T. Lewis, to associate professorships. In 1931 Bremer became the Hersey Professor of Anatomy at the Medical School, and Lewis was named Stillman Professor of Comparative Anatomy.

95. Roger Pierce, a 1904 graduate of Harvard College, had accompanied Eliot on his trip around the world, serving as his secretary. At that time a romance developed between Pierce and the president's granddaughter, Ruth Eliot, who was also a member of the entourage, and they were married soon after their return to Boston in 1912. Besides his appointment as business director at the Medical School, Pierce also served as secretary to the Harvard Alumni Association and, from 1914 to 1919, as Secretary to the Harvard Corporation. For an earlier report on the status of the Harvard proposal, see also Pierce to Eliot, Jan. 20, 1915, Eliot Papers. For more on the charge that the GEB was guilty of dictating policy to academic institutions, see further H. P. Judson to Wallace Buttrick, Dec. 22, 1914, fd. 6486, GEB Papers; "The Influence of the Rockefeller Millions on Medical Education," undated, unsigned four-page memorandum in HMS Dean's files, HMA.

96. See esp. Bradford to Lowell, April 2, 1915, in which the dean wrote that he had consulted Cannon, a newly elected trustee of the independent Elizabeth Thompson Science Fund, about his plans for control of research funds; in fd. 224, 2nd series, Lowell Papers.

97. On July 22, 1915, Cannon had written Henry James, Jr., to ask whether James could meet with a group of "Outlanders of the Medical Faculty"—Rosenau, Hunt, Folin, Cushing, Edsall, Christian, and himself—who believed there might be a lesson for them in hearing about the management of the Rockefeller Institute; in RAC.

98. Cannon to Eliot, May 30, 1916, Eliot Papers. For another view of Cannon's sense of alienation (as well as that of other faculty members) at this time, see further exchange of letters between Councilman and Lowell, May 4 and 15, 1916, fd. 1110, 2nd series, Lowell Papers.

99. Lowell to W. S. Thayer, June 2, 1916, fd. 1135, 2nd series, Lowell Papers.

100. Eliot to Jerome Greene, June 9, 1916; announcement from Lowell, June 13, 1916; both in fd. 6487, GEB Papers. For more on the Eliot committee, see also 1916–17 materials in fd. 7, Cannon Papers. At the committee's first meeting (Thayer later reminded Eliot), it was recommended that the Board "be apprised of the serious needs of a department so valuable as that of Dr. Cannon—that the services done by this department should be enumerated and that an attempt should be made to interest the General Education Board in rendering assistance to a department which, though not clinical, is one of the most valuable assets of Harvard and of the whole country." W. S. Thayer to C. W. Eliot, Oct. 3, 1916, Cannon Papers.

101. See, for example, Eliot to Buttrick, Dec. 15 and 28, 1916, May 17, 1917; all in Cannon Papers.

102. "Provisional Memorandum about Aid for the Harvard Medical School from the General Education Board," Dec. 12, 1916, enclosed with Eliot to Buttrick, Dec. 16, 1916; Eliot to Buttrick, April 23 and 24, 1917; exchange of letters between Buttrick and Eliot, May 15 and 17, 1917; all in Cannon Papers. At the time of this final rejection for Harvard, Jerome Greene was no longer in the employment of the Rockefeller philanthropies, and by the end of the year both Eliot and Gates had resigned as members of the GEB.

103. In 1919 the GEB modified its policy of giving aid for medical education insofar as it concerned the installation of a full-time clinical program. For a later assessment of the program under Flexner's direction, see Raymond Fosdick, *Adventure in Giving: The Story of the General Education Board* (New York: Harper & Row, 1962), pp. 162–173.

20. A World at Risk

1. 1914 Diary, March 31 ("Prof. Cattell wishes his son to be a member of my department"). Jacques Loeb to Cannon, Feb. 27, 1915, Loeb Papers. Robert F. Loeb received his M.D. degree from Harvard in 1919 and McKeen Cattell's studies eventuated in Ph.D. and M.D. degrees in 1920 and 1924.

2. See, e.g., James J. Putnam to Cannon, Feb. 28, 1916, and Cannon's replies of March 2 and 3, 1916; 1914–15 correspondence between Cannon and Alvarez; all in Cannon Papers. Alvarez later remembered the few months he spent at Harvard at exercises held in 1931 commemorating Cannon's twenty-fifth anniversary as George Higginson Professor of Physiology.

3. Saul Benison, "The Reminiscences of Dr. Alan Gregg," 1958; manuscript on deposit in Oral History Research Office, Columbia University; see esp. pp. 41–42.

4. C. K. Drinker to A. N. Richards, July 11, 1914, HMA. Katherine Rotan Drinker was educated at Bryn Mawr and received her M.D. degree from the Women's Medical College of Pennsylvania in 1914. See further C. K. and K. R. Drinker, "Factors Affecting the Coagulation Time of Blood: VI. The Effect of Rapid Progressive Hemorrhage upon the Factors of Coagulation," *Am. J. Physiol.* 36 (1915):305–324.

5. Among others working harmoniously with Cannon or in his laboratory at this time were Richard H. Miller, Robert L. Levy, Neuton S. Stern, and L. N. Fleming; also B. R. Lutz, David L. Rapport, G. Philip Grabfield, and Dr. and Mrs. A. C. Redfield. In contrast, an unpleasant incident that caused Cannon a good deal of anguish in the fall of 1916 involved Frank Foley, the diener who under Bowditch had greeted him when he entered the physiology laboratory as a first-year medical student, but who had become an alcoholic. For details, see further Cannon to Cornelia J. Cannon, Oct. 2 and 3, 1916, Cannon Papers.

6. For more on the work in physiology, see Cannon's descriptions in *Annual Reports*, 1914–15, pp. 168–169, and *Annual Reports*, 1915–16, pp. 177–178.

7. Alexander Forbes and Alan Gregg, "Electrical Studies in Mammalian Reflexes: I. The Flexion Reflex," *Am. J. Physiol.* 37 (1915):118–176, and ". . . II. The Correlation between Strength of Stimuli and the Direct and Reflex Nerve Response," *Am. J. Physiol.* 39 (1915):172–235. See also A. Forbes and C. S. Sherrington, "Acoustic Reflexes in the Decerebrate Cat," *Am. J. Physiol.* 35 (1914):367–376.

8. J. F. Fulton, comp., *Selected Readings in the History of Physiology*, completed by L. G. Wilson, 2nd ed. (Springfield, Ill.: C. C. Thomas, 1966), pp. 235–236.

9. Benison, "Gregg Reminiscences," pp. 41–42. After Gregg moved on to his sophomore year, Forbes chose Stanley Cobb and Willard C. Rappleye to work on other aspects of the mammalian reflex. Gregg received his M.D. degree in 1916 and later went to the Rockefeller Foundation where, from 1931 to 1951, he was director of the division of medical sciences.

10. A. Forbes, R. McIntosh, and W. Sefton, "The Effect of Ether Anaesthesia on the Electrical Activity of Nerve," *Am. J. Physiol.* 40 (1916):503–513. The authors acknowledge Cannon's advice on p. 503; see also summary on p. 513.

11. R. W. Lovett, "The Treatment of Infantile Paralysis: Preliminary Report Based on a Study of the Vermont Epidemic of 1914," *JAMA* 64 (1915):2118–23; also *Annual Reports, 1914–15*, pp. 166, 168–169.

12. See further the three-part series of articles by Martin and his collaborators (Grabfield and Martin, Martin, Bigelow, and Wilbur; Martin, Withington, and Putnam) on "Variations in the Sensory Threshold for Faradic Stimulation in Normal Human Subjects," *Am. J. Physiol.* 31 (1913):300–308; 33 (1914):415–422; and 34 (1914):97–105; also E. G. Martin, *The Measurement of Induction Shocks: A Manual for the Quantitative Use of Faradic Stimuli* (John Wiley & Sons, 1912).

13. The collaboration eventuated in three papers: E. G. Martin and R. W. Lovett, "A Method of Testing Muscular Strength in Infantile Paralysis," *JAMA* 65 (1915):1512–13; Lovett and Martin, "Infantile Paralysis in Vermont: A Report of the Progress of Cases between January, 1915, and July, 1915," *Vermont State Medical Journal*, Feb. 1916; and Lovett and Martin, "Certain Aspects of Infantile Paralysis, with a Description of a Method of Muscle Testing," *JAMA* 66 (1916):729–733. These reports and other papers by Dr. Lovett may also be found in *Infantile Paralysis in Vermont, 1894–1922* (Vermont State Department of Public Health, 1924).

14. A. Forbes to W. C. Alvarez, Sept. 21, 1931. For further comments, see other 1931 letters in Alvarez file in Cannon Papers; also Alvarez's remarks in *Walter Bradford Cannon: Exercises Celebrating Twenty-Five Years as George Higginson Professor of Physiology, October 15, 1931* (Cambridge, Mass.: Harvard University Press, 1932), esp. pp. 16–22.

15. For more on Mrs. Cannon's involvement in Cambridge school and civic activities, see also *Snatched from Oblivion*, esp. pp. 80–86.

16. 1913 Diary, April 28 and May 15; see also Feb. 13, 16, April 21, May 3, 12. See further excerpts from C. J. Cannon to her family, Jan. 28, 1913, in "Snatched from Oblivion."

17. 1913 Diary, April 1, 8, 11, 27. The porch school (in vogue with the penchant at this time for outdoor or open-air schools) was in session that spring with Bradford and Wilma in attendance; see further Cannon's diary entries for May 8 and 21.

18. Paul H. Hanus, "A Proposed University School," *Harvard Graduates' Magazine* 22 (1913–14):45–47.

19. Excerpts from letter of Sept. 28, 1913, in "Snatched from Oblivion." Many years later, in a letter to a Harvard classmate who had become an educational adviser and publisher, Cannon voiced similar sentiments about the democratic value of a public school experience; Cannon to Porter Sargent, May 29, 1939, Cannon Papers.

20. Excerpts from letter of Nov. 1913, in "Snatched from Oblivion."

21. Although enough subscriptions were obtained to open the Harvard model school, lack of more substantial financial backing caused an indefinite postponement of the scheme; Hanus, "A Proposed University School," p. 47. For more on efforts to move the porch school indoors, see Cannon's 1913 Diary, Oct. 9, 13, 14, 21; excerpts from letters of Sept. 28 and Nov. 1913, in "Snatched from Oblivion"; C. J. Cannon to A. L. Lowell, Oct. 17, 1913, Lowell Papers. For a later description of the porch school and other classes held in temporary quarters during the building of the Agassiz School, see also Bradford Cannon's unpublished letter to the editor of *Harvard Magazine*; copy in Cannon Papers.

22. Excerpts from letter of Dec. 24, 1915, in "Snatched from Oblivion."

23. Excerpts from letter of Nov. 23, 1915, in "Snatched from Oblivion." As a school committeewoman, Cornelia continued her efforts toward effecting a cooperation between Harvard and the Cambridge school system; see, e.g., exchange of letters between C. J. Cannon and A. L. Lowell, Aug. 17 and Sept. 1, 1916, Lowell Papers. See also C. J. Cannon, "The Responsibility of University Women in Public Education," *Journal of the American Association of University Women* 18 (1924):16–18.

24. 1914 Diary, see esp. May 15 and 21. In June both Cannon and Cornelia qualified for their drivers' licenses. On Aug. 8, Cannon noted in his diary that he had logged more than 1600 miles on the Model T; cost in gas and oil came to about $18.50.

25. F. T. Lewis to C. S. Minot, Nov. 10, 1914, Lewis Papers.

26. Descriptions of the children occur frequently in Cannon's diary notes. Bradford was companionable and shared carpentering and railroading interests with his father; he alternated between taking tender care of his younger sisters and tormenting them. Wilma was described as imaginative, quick-witted, and artistic, but at the same time temperamental and hard to discipline. Linda was the vigorous one who entered the conversation with a handspring and hardly ever complained or shed a tear, whereas Marian was "a midget" who, her father noted, had "dancing dark eyes, red cheeks and an insistent nature, besides the misfortune to look like me." 1914 Diary, May 12.

27. Excerpts from letter of Jan. 18, 1915, in "Snatched from Oblivion."

28. 1915 Diary, Feb. 21; see also Feb. 5, 6, and 19; and excerpts from letters of Feb. 8 and 22, 1915, in "Snatched from Oblivion."

29. 1915 Diary, Feb. 24. The entries for the death of his father and the birth of his youngest daughter mark an end to Cannon's diary-keeping at this time in his life.

30. Excerpts from letters of Feb. 27 and March 9, 1915, in "Snatched from Oblivion."

31. Excerpts from letter of June 25, 1915, in "Snatched from Oblivion."

32. Cannon to R. M. Pearce, Jan. 9, 1915, Cannon Papers.

33. 1915 Diary, Feb. 19; Cannon to W. W. Keen, March 5 and 27, 1915, Cannon Papers. See also editorials, "Anti-Vivisection Legislation" and "Defense of Animal Experimentation in Boston," in *BM&SJ* 172 (1915), pp. 310 and 651. For the Pennsylvania dog bill, see R. M. Pearce to Cannon, March 10, 1915, Cannon Papers.

34. The above account of the campaign against animal experimentation in California is largely based on 1915 correspondence in the Anti-Vivisection Papers and 1916–17 correspondence in fd. 360, Cannon Papers. See also G. W. Corner, *George Hoyt Whipple and His Friends: The Life-Story of a Nobel Prize Pathologist* (Philadelphia & Montreal: Lippincott, 1963), esp. pp. 86–91.

35. Cannon to F. S. Lee, May 8, 1915; copy of letter in Simon Flexner Papers, in which Cannon detailed the background of his involvement in the California campaign.

36. Ibid.; Cannon to Simon Flexner, June 23, 1915, in Anti-Vivisection Papers. Among those whose protests prompted the governor's veto were President Eliot and Drs. Welch, Gorgas, and Flexner. "There is no other place in the country, outside the eastern states," Cannon warned Flexner in his letter, "where trouble was so likely to arise as in California, chiefly because of residence in the State of all sorts of queer idle people from the East. Los Angeles in that respect is, I think, a second Boston, and the theosophist colony at Point Loma is the acme of muddleheadedness."

37. Cannon to Simon Flexner, June 24, 1915, in Anti-Vivisection Papers.

38. Ibid. See also Henry James to Cannon, June 25, 1915; Cannon to James, June 29, 1915; and James to Cannon, June 30, 1915; all in Anti-Vivisection Papers.

39. G. H. Whipple to Cannon, July 7, 1916, Cannon Papers.

40. Cannon to W. T. Sedgwick, Nov. 20, 1916 [also sent to Eliot, Cushing, Rosenau, Edsall, and Hunt]; see also Cannon to Whipple, July 13 and Nov. 21, 1916. All in Cannon Papers.

41. Corner, *George Hoyt Whipple*, pp. 89–90; exchange of letters between Cannon and Whipple, March 30 and April 4, 1917, Cannon Papers.

42. For more on the latest Gallinger bill, see Cannon to Simon Flexner, with copy of Cannon to W. H. Welch, both Feb. 2, 1916, and Flexner to Cannon, Feb. 21, 1916; all in Simon Flexner Papers. For a recent review of Welch's earlier efforts, see Patricia Peck Gossel, "William Henry Welch and the Antivivisection Legislation in the District of Columbia, 1896–1900," *Journal of the History of Medicine and Allied Sciences* 40 (1985):397–419.

43. Cannon to Flexner, Feb. 2, 1916, Simon Flexner Papers.

44. For a full account of Wile's investigation and the issues that were debated in its aftermath, see Susan Eyrich Lederer's article, " 'The Right and Wrong of Making Experiments on Human Beings': Udo J. Wile and Syphilis," *Bulletin of the History of Medicine* 58 (1984):380–397.

45. See further U. J. Wile, "Experimental Syphilis in the Rabbit Produced by the Brain Substance of the Living Paretic," *Journal of Experimental Medicine* 23 (1916):199–202.

46. W. W. Keen to V. C. Vaughan, April 19, 1916, in Vaughan Papers. Wile's experiments were first condemned in a pamphlet, *Human Beings Vivisected*, issued by the Vivisection Investigation League in March 1916, with editorials appearing the following month in such antivivisectionist magazines as *Living Tissue*, *The Open Door*, and *Our Dumb Animals*. The *Philadelphia Inquirer* (April 14, 1916) was only one of many newspapers that picked up the story and published editorials in protest.

47. "Report of Committee on the Protection of Medical Research," *JAMA* 63 (1914):94; see also Cannon to Henry James, Oct. 19, 1914, Cannon Papers. The Vivisection Investigation League, which closely monitored activities at the Rockefeller Institute, had also been responsible for calling attention to Noguchi's luetin experiments; see, e.g., Susan Lederer's article, "Hideyo Noguchi's Luetin Experiment and the Antivivisectionists," *Isis* 76 (1985): 31–48.

48. Cannon to James, April 22, 1916, Anti-Vivisection Papers. The whole issue of consent to therapeutic measures and the status of patients' rights had been undergoing revision during this period; see further Lederer on Noguchi, pp. 40–41; Jay Katz, *Experimentation with Human Beings* (New York: Russell Sage Foundation, 1972), esp. pp. 523–529.

49. James to Cannon, April 24, 1916, Anti-Vivisection Papers. The series of letters continued along the same lines with another exchange between Cannon and James, April 25 and 26, 1916; both in Anti-Vivisection Papers. James, recognizing that the Rockefeller Institute was in an embarrassing position for having published the Wile article, was only too glad to let Cannon take the lead and provided him with the general principles that he needed to prepare a public statement: namely, that civilized society was based on the recognition of the fundamental right of every individual to control the uses to which his or her body might be put, and that the law, as an expression of public conscience, declared that deliberate injury done to the body of another was an assault and provided severe punishment for it. Cannon, in reply, told James that in his view such a declaration of principles could only lead to strengthening the public view of truth-telling in defense of animal experimentation.

50. The typescript draft of Cannon's statement, "The Ethics of Experimentation on Human Beings," may be found in the Anti-Vivisection Papers. For Claude Bernard's views of human experimentation, see his *Introduction to the Study of Experimental Medicine* (New York: Macmillan, 1927), pp. 101–102.

51. Cannon to James, April 27, 1916, enclosing a copy of his statement,

Anti-Vivisection Papers. At the same time, Cannon also wrote Udo Wile to privately express his disapproval of work that he felt had placed the freedom of research in great jeopardy and sent a copy of his letter to Victor Vaughan. Both letters, dated April 27, 1916, are in the Vaughan Papers.

52. Keen to James, April 29, 1916, enclosing typescript draft of statement, "Human Vivisection—A Protest," Anti-Vivisection Papers.

53. James to Keen, May 4, 5, and 11, 1916; Keen to James, May 6 and 16, 1916. All in Anti-Vivisection Papers.

54. Copy of letter from Cannon to F. S. Lee, June 5, 1916, Simon Flexner Papers. See also exchange of letters between Flexner and Cannon, June 6 and 7, 1916; both in Simon Flexner Papers.

55. W. B. Cannon, "The Right and Wrong of Making Experiments on Human Beings," editorial in *JAMA* 67 (1916):1372. Keen's article, retitled "The Inveracities of Antivivisection," appeared on pp. 1390–91 of the same issue.

56. The *Journal of Zoophily* for Sept. 1916 was a memorial number in commemoration of Mrs. White, its founder and editor-in-chief, who died on Sept. 6. Dr. Leffingwell succumbed on Sept. 1, 1917, and a year later, on Aug. 17, 1918, Senator Jacob Gallinger died.

57. For the debates with Einhorn, Dale, and Carlson, see Chapters 9, 17, and 18.

58. Laurie Rae Green has written about Stewart and Rogoff's attacks on Cannon in her undergraduate thesis, "A Study of Scientific Controversy: Walter Bradford Cannon and the Emergency Theory of Adrenin Secretion," submitted to Harvard University in 1972, HUA, and in her Richard C. Cabot prize paper, "A Study of Controversy in 20th-Century Endocrinology: Walter B. Cannon and the Emergency Theory of Adrenin Secretion," submitted to Harvard Medical School in 1976, HMA.

59. See esp. Green, "A Study of Scientific Controversy," pp. 18–20. Biographical material on Stewart may be found in Torald Sollmann's obituary notice, "George Neil Stewart, Physiologist," *Science* 72 (1930):158, and in his personal tribute, "George Neil Stewart: An Appreciation," *Bulletin of the Academy of Medicine of Cleveland* 14 (1930):7–8, 19, as well as in brief notices published in *JAMA, Lancet,* and the *British Medical Journal* after his death in 1930.

60. Green, "A Study of Scientific Controversy," pp. 21–22. Among Stewart's prolific published output, see, e.g., his paper, "Researches on the Circulation Time and on the Influences which Affect It: IV. The Output of the Heart," *Journal of Physiology* (London) 22 (1897):159–183, and his note, "Measurement of the Blood-Flow in Man," *Am. J. Physiol.* 27 (1910–11):xx–xxi. For a complete bibliography, see also printed "List of Published Papers, 1886–1930, by G. N. Stewart," in Stewart and Rogoff Papers.

61. See further G. N. Stewart, "So-Called Biological Tests for Adrenalin in Blood, with Some Observations in Arterial Hypertonus," *Journal of Experimental Medicine* 14 (1911):377–400.

62. G. N. Stewart, "The Alleged Existence of Adrenalin (Epinephrin) in Pathological Sera," *Journal of Experimental Medicine* 15 (1912):547–569. For MacLeod's method, see esp. pp. 555, 559, 564; for Cannon and de la Paz, see pp. 562, 569.

63. See esp. Stewart's "Studies on the Circulation in Man," parts V–XVI, published for the most part in the *Journal of Experimental Medicine* between 1912 and 1915. Julius Moses Rogoff received his M.D. degree from Ohio Wesleyan University in 1908 and worked for two years as an assistant in physiology there (during which time the medical department merged with Western Reserve). He then moved to Vanderbilt University where he served as demonstrator, instructor, and assistant professor in physiology, pharmacology, and materia medica. After returning to Cleveland he not only worked with Stewart on the adrenals but also conducted a series of studies with David Marine on the thyroid as well. For a summary of his initial investigations with Stewart, see J. M. Rogoff, "On the Liberation of Epinephrin from the Adrenal Glands," *Journal of Laboratory and Clinical Medicine* 3 (1918):209–219.

64. T. R. Elliott, "The Control of the Suprarenal Glands by the Splanchnic Nerves," *Journal of Physiology* 44 (1912):374–409; see esp. p. 385. See also Elliott's note "On the Action of Adrenalin," in *Proceedings of the Physiological Society*, May 21, 1904, pp. xx–xxi, and his longer paper, "The Action of Adrenalin," *Journal of Physiology* 32 (1904):401–466.

65. G. N. Stewart, J. M. Rogoff, and F. S. Gibson, "The Liberation of Epinephrin from the Adrenal Glands by Stimulation of the Splanchnic Nerves and by Massage," *Journal of Pharmacology and Experimental Therapeutics* 8 (1916):205–245. For Meltzer's eye test, see S. J. Meltzer and C. M. Auer, "Studies on the 'Paradoxical' Pupil-Dilatation caused by Adrenalin," *Am. J. Physiol.* 11 (1904):28–51, and "The Effect of Suprarenal Extract upon the Pupils of Frogs," *Am. J. Physiol.* 11 (1904):449–454.

66. Cannon to Stewart, May 20, 1916, Stewart and Rogoff Papers. A number of Stewart's and Rogoff's letters and papers, presented to the Countway Library of Medicine by the Rogoff Foundation and the G. N. Stewart Memorial Fund, were catalogued as a manuscript collection in 1977. In addition to the 1916 letters cited here, later exchanges between Cannon and Stewart occurred in 1921 and 1923. There are no letters between Cannon and Rogoff in this collection.

67. Stewart to Cannon, May 24, 1916; see also Cannon to Stewart, May 29, 1916, and Stewart to Cannon, June 6, 1916. All in Stewart and Rogoff Papers. This brief correspondence between Cannon and Stewart ended amicably, with a friendly exchange of information on the advantages and drawbacks of using Meltzer's denervated eye as an assay for the presence of secreted adrenalin under emotional excitement.

68. G. N. Stewart and J. M. Rogoff, "The Spontaneous Liberation of Epinephrin from the Adrenals," *Journal of Pharmacology and Experimental Therapeutics* 8 (1916):479–524; see esp. pp. 520–521.

69. See esp. G. N. Stewart and J. M. Rogoff, "The Relation of the Spinal Cord to the Spontaneous Liberation of Epinephrin from the Adrenals" and "Effect of Stimulation of Sensory Nerves upon the Rate of Liberation of Epinephrin from the Adrenals," both published in the *Journal of Experimental Medicine* 26:613–636, 637–656. During the remainder of 1917 Stewart and Rogoff published six more articles on the liberation of epinephrin from the adrenals; see bibliography in Stewart and Rogoff Papers for details.

70. Harold Fisher Pierce, who had an electrical engineering degree from Clark University, came to Harvard as a teaching fellow in physiology in 1915 and remained until 1917. He was enrolled in the Medical Sciences program, but his studies were interrupted by the war. Pierce later earned a Ph.D. degree from Columbia and an M.D. from Johns Hopkins.

71. See further H. S. Gasser and W. J. Meek, "A Study of the Mechanisms by which Muscular Exercise Produces Acceleration of the Heart," *Am. J. Physiol.* 34 (1914):48–71. See also Walter Meek's informal remembrance of 1952, "An Appreciation of Walter B. Cannon," *Medico-Historical Papers* (Madison, Wisconsin, 1954), esp. pp. 38–39 for the debate with Stewart and Rogoff.

72. See report for physiology department in *Annual Reports*, 1916–17, p. 176.

73. W. B. Cannon, "A Note on the Effect of Asphyxia and Afferent Stimulation on Adrenal Secretion," *Science* n.s. 45 (1917):463–464. A full account of this work was later reported by Cannon in "Studies on the Conditions of Activity in Endocrine Glands: V. The Isolated Heart as an Indicator of Adrenal Secretion Induced by Pain, Asphyxia, and Excitement," *Am. J. Physiol.* 50 (1919):399–432.

74. See esp. *Endocrinology*, vol. 1 (1917) for Swale Vincent article, "Recent Views as to the Function of the Adrenal Bodies," followed by comments of G. N. Stewart and R. G. Hoskins on pp. 150–152 and Hoskins article, "The Relation of the Adrenal Glands to the Circulation of the Blood," followed by comments of W. J. Meek on pp. 302–305. For references to the "fireworks" that subsequently took place at annual meetings of the American Physiological Society, see comments of Bradford Cannon and others in *Life & Contributions* pp. 165, 173; Laurie Green, "A Study of Scientific Controversy," p. 42. Cannon devoted a chapter to the subject of scientific controversy in *Way of an Investigator*; see esp. pp. 100–101 for the debate with the Cleveland investigators.

21. Prelude to the Great War

1. For more on the effect of World War I on Harvard, see Samuel Eliot Morison, *Three Centuries of Harvard, 1636–1936* (Cambridge, Mass.: Harvard University Press, 1936), pp. 450–460; for the military preparedness movement, see John Garry Clifford, *The Citizen Soldiers: The Plattsburg Training Camp Movement, 1913–1920* (Lexington: University Press of Kentucky, 1972).

2. Cornelia J. Cannon to the James family, Dec. 28, 1914, in "Snatched from Oblivion."

3. Excerpt from letter of Jan. 14, 1915, in "Snatched from Oblivion." Cushing's was the first of several Harvard units to go abroad as part of a larger effort by volunteers from American university medical schools to serve three-month rotations; see further *Annual Reports*, 1914–15, pp. 20, 156; John F. Fulton, *Harvey Cushing: A Biography* (Springfield, Ill.: C. C. Thomas, 1946), pp. 387–404.

4. Excerpts from letter of May 10, 1915, in "Snatched from Oblivion."

5. American Physiological Society, Minutes of Annual Meeting, Dec.

26–29, 1915, in Archives of the APS; W. M. Bayliss to Cannon, Sept. 16, 1915, March 24 and April 27, 1916, Cannon Papers; Cannon to Joseph Erlanger, Feb. 21 and March 10, 1916, Erlanger Papers.

6. Cannon to C. S. Sherrington, Feb. 14, 1916, Cannon Papers.

7. For more on Münsterberg, see Matthew Hale, Jr., *Human Science and Social Order: Hugo Münsterberg and the Origins of Applied Psychology*, (Philadelphia: Temple University Press, 1980); Phyllis Keller, *States of Belonging: German-American Intellectuals and the First World War* (Cambridge, Mass.: Harvard University Press, 1979), esp. "Hugo Münsterberg . . . On Being German in America," pp. 7–119.

8. George Foot Moore, "Professor Hugo Münsterberg," *Harvard Graduates' Magazine* 25 (1916–17):335–338; Hamilton Cravens, *The Triumph of Evolution: American Scientists and the Heredity-Environment Controversy, 1900–1941* (Philadelphia: University of Pennsylvania Press, 1978), pp. 62–63.

9. The pressure to dismiss Münsterberg made newspaper headlines when Clarence Wiener of the Class of 1900 threatened to cut out of his will a bequest of $10,000,000 to Harvard; see rebuttal in *Harvard Alumni Bulletin* for Oct. 21, 1914, p. 53. See also Morrison, *Three Centuries*, p. 453, and the large file of 1914–16 correspondence with and about Münsterberg in fd. 231, 2nd series of Lowell Papers. Münsterberg's activities on behalf of Germany even before World War I had brought him into conflict with many at Harvard, including both Eliot and Lowell; for details, see Keller, "Hugo Münsterberg," in *States of Belonging*.

10. A. L. Lowell to A. Maynard Butler, Feb. 4, 1916, Lowell Papers.

11. *Annual Reports*, 1916–17, pp. 18–21; reprinted by Morison in *Three Centuries*, pp. 454–456.

12. For Royce's defection, see Hale, *Human Science and Social Order*, p. 175; for the attacks on Münsterberg by Holt and Hocking, see also pp. 180–181. For a contemporaneous comment on the Münsterberg/Hocking debate, see "University Notes," in *Harvard Graduates' Magazine* for Dec. 1916, pp. 286–287; also in this issue is G. H. Palmer's obituary notice of Josiah Royce, who died on Sept. 14.

13. Copy of letter from Hugo Münsterberg to Mrs. _____, Feb. 14, 1916, Lowell Papers.

14. Excerpt from letter of Dec. 3, 1916, in "Snatched from Oblivion."

15. Excerpt from letter of Dec. 17, 1916, in "Snatched from Oblivion." Münsterberg, in failing health, feared the possibility of sudden death or disablement from stroke. He died at the age of 53 of a cerebral hemorrhage (Hale, p. 182).

16. G. F. Moore, "Prof. Hugo Münsterberg," pp. 337–338.

17. *Annual Reports*, 1915–16, pp. 23–24, 156; see also *Annual Reports*, 1914–15, p. 21.

18. For more on the verbal offer to Cannon, see Henry James to Alexis Carrel, March 16 and 29, 1916, Carrel Papers; also Cannon's rejection in his letter to James of March 21, 1916. For the offer to Porter, see James to Carrel, June 13, 1916. All in RAC. Porter made two trips to Europe to work on shock with Carrel, one in the summer of 1916 and the other a year later. Further

reports and correspondence concerning this work may be found in the Porter file at the RAC and in the Carrel Papers at Georgetown University; see also W. T. Porter, *Shock at the Front* (Boston: Atlantic Monthly Press, 1918).

19. See, e.g., circular letters and other materials regarding formation of the National Research Council and appointment of its research committees, in Erlanger Papers; the Physiology Committee was formally appointed on March 3, 1917. See also reports of the Organizing Committee and of meetings in New York and Cambridge in the *Proceedings of the National Academy of Sciences* 2 (1916):507–510, 602–608, 738–746.

20. Cannon to Joseph Erlanger, March 8, 1917, Erlanger Papers.

21. Cannon to Erlanger, March 26, 1917; Erlanger to Cannon, March 30, 1917; and Cannon to Erlanger, April 2, 1917; all in Erlanger Papers. See also Cannon to Henry James, March 26, 1917, in Anti-Vivisection Papers.

22. Cannon reviewed the previous literature in his Shattuck Lecture, "The Physiological Factors Concerned in Surgical Shock," *BM&SJ* 176 (1917):859–867. For a general summary of the problem of shock, with references, see also Carl J. Wiggers, *Physiology of Shock* (New York: Commonwealth Fund, 1950), pp. 1–25.

23. For Crile, see his book, *An Experimental Research into Surgical Shock* (Philadelphia: Lippincott, 1899); also Peter C. English, *Shock, Physiological Surgery, and George Washington Crile: Medical Innovation in the Progressive Era* (Westport, Conn.: Greenwood Press, 1980). For Yandell Henderson, see his series of articles on "Acapnia and Shock," esp. *Am. J. Physiol.* 21 (1908):126–156, and *Am. J. Physiol.* 27 (1910):152–176. For Porter, see "Shock at the Front," *BM&SJ* 175 (1916):854–858, and "Fat Embolism a Cause of Shock," *BM&SJ* 176 (1917):248. For yet another treatment of the subject, see further W. M. Bayliss, *Intravenous Injection in Wound Shock* (London: Longmans, Green, & Co., 1918).

24. Shock was not a completely new problem for Cannon. For his previous efforts, see *Report of the Commission on Resuscitation from Electric Shock* (New York: National Electric Light Association, 1913); W. B. Cannon and R. G. Hoskins, "The Effects of Asphyxia, Hyperpnoea, and Sensory Stimulation on Adrenal Secretion," *Am. J. Physiol.* 29 (1911):274–279, esp. pp. 278–279.

25. Cannon to Erlanger, March 8, 1917, Erlanger Papers.

26. See Cannon's Shattuck Lecture, p. 862. Cannon found particularly suggestive David L. Edsall's previous Shattuck Lecture, "The Clinical Study of Respiration," *BM&SJ* 167 (1912):639–651. For a later discussion of the theory of acidosis as a shock factor, see also W. B. Cannon, *Traumatic Shock* (New York & London: Appleton, 1923), pp. 127–128.

27. Excerpt from letter of April 2, 1917, in "Snatched from Oblivion."

28. Excerpt from another letter of April 2, 1917, in "Snatched from Oblivion."

29. See further Cannon to W. W. Keen, April 23, 1917, Cannon Papers.

30. Excerpts from letter of April 25, 1917, in "Snatched from Oblivion."

31. See further Cannon to Cushing, April 29, 1917, draft letter in Cushing Papers; Cannon to Lowell, May 1, 1917, Lowell Papers; Cannon to Eliot, May

2, 1917, Eliot Papers. For more on the final organization of Base Hospital No. 5, the unit Cannon joined, see also Fulton, *Harvey Cushing*, pp. 419–420.

    32. Excerpts from C. J. Cannon to her family, April 30, 1917, in "Snatched from Oblivion."

    33. Ibid.

    34. Excerpt from letter of May 9, 1917, in "Snatched from Oblivion."

Index